The MIT Encyclopedia of
the Japanese Economy

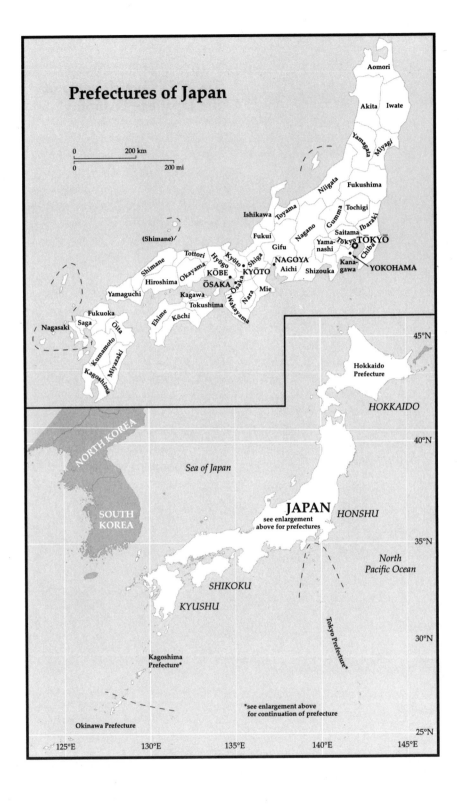

The MIT Encyclopedia of the Japanese Economy

second edition

Robert C. Hsu

The MIT Press
Cambridge, Massachusetts
London, England

This book was set in Palatino by Asco Typesetters, Hong Kong, and was printed and bound in the United States of America.

Library of Congress Cataloging-in-Publication Data

Hsu, Robert C.
  The MIT encyclopedia of the Japanese economy / Robert C. Hsu. — 2nd ed.
    p.   cm.
  Includes bibliographical references and index.
  ISBN 0-262-08280-2 (alk. paper)
  1. Japan—Economic conditions—1945– —Dictionaries. 2. Japan—
Economic policy—1945– —Dictionaries. I. Title.
  HC462.9.H73   1999
  330.952'003—dc21   99-19441
                                                                              CIP

to Sharon, Steven, and the memory of Nancy

Preface

The purpose of this book is to explain concisely the essentials of a large number of important topics on the contemporary Japanese economy, from A to Z, thereby filling a gap in the literature. The book contains 180 topical essays and 145 short definitional entries, all listed alphabetically. All **bold-lettered** terms in the text are the topics of separate essays. Definitional entries have cross references to indicate that they are also discussed in one or more essays in a larger context.

The essays vary greatly in length, depending on the importance and complexity of the topic. Each essay contains the definition and descriptions of the topic, discussions of important issues, some statistical information or tables, cross-references, addresses of relevant organizations where appropriate, and references in English for further reading.

Japanese government fiscal year (FY) begins on April 1 of each year and ends on March 31 of the following year. A lot of government and business publications and statistics are published on fiscal-year basis. However, some are published on both fiscal-year and calendar-year bases or just on calendar-year basis. Where statistics are based on the fiscal year, it is so indicated in the book.

With the exception of international trade and investment, economic figures such as income, production, sales, profits, and wages are given in yen (¥). This is because the yen–dollar exchange rate has fluctuated so much over the years, due to various factors, that it is not always meaningful to use it to translate yen figures into dollar equivalents. In particular, because of Japan's chronic trade surplus, the yen–dollar exchange rates do not reflect the real purchasing power of the two currencies in their respective countries. Readers interested in converting the yen figures into dollars can use the exchange rates of the relevant years given in the essay on **yen–dollar exchange rates** (table Y.1).

The book has been thoroughly updated and significantly expanded in this second edition to include developments in the Japanese economy since the early 1990s. Because of the wide range of topics discussed in the book, errors are no doubt inevitable. I would be grateful if knowledgeable readers would inform me of the errors so that they can be corrected in the next edition.

Acknowledgments

This book is an outgrowth of a course on the Japanese and Chinese economies that I have been teaching at Clark University for many years. My first intellectual debt therefore goes to my students in the course whose interests have stimulated my teaching and research.

In writing the two editions of the book, I had the privilege of visiting the following private organizations and companies in Japan: American Chamber of Commerce in Japan, Anelva Corp., Central Union of Agricultural Cooperatives (Zenchu), Federation of Economic Organizations (Keidanren), General Summit Enterprise Co., IBM Japan, Japan Economic Research Center, Japan Federation of Employers' Association (Nikkeiren), Japan Iron and Steel Federation, Japan Patent Information Organization, Japan Trade Union Confederation (JTUC-Rengo), Kansai Economic Federation, Matsumi Sangyo Co., Matsushita Electric Industrial, Mitsubishi Heavy Industries, NEC Corp., Nihon Unisys, Nihon Keizai Shimbun, Inc., Nissan Motor, Nomura Research Institute, Sony Corp., Toyo Keizai, Tokyo Stock Exchange, and Toyota Motor. To the organizations, companies, and the many individuals who hosted my visits and spent much time with me, I am deeply grateful.

I also had the honor of visiting the following ministries and agencies of the Japanese government: Bank of Japan, Economic Planning Agency, Export-Import Bank of Japan, Fair Trade Commission, Food Agency, Institute of Developing Economies, Land Agency, Ministry of Agriculture, Forestry, and Fisheries, Ministry of Finance, Ministry of International Trade and Industry (MITI), Osaka Municipal Government, Overseas Economic Cooperation Fund, Patent Office, Science and Technology Agency, Tokyo Metropolitan Government, and Yokohama Municipal Government. All these government organizations arranged for me to interview their senior officials and provided me with their latest publications and statistics. I want to thank, in particular, the Bank of Japan, Economic Planning Agency, and MITI, which I visited repeatedly over the years; I have benefited greatly from lengthy discussions with their senior economists in their research/statistics departments.

The following companies and private organizations provided me with timely materials: Federation of Bankers Association of Japan, Itochu Corp., Japan Automobile Manufacturers Association, Japan Economic Institute (in Washington, DC), Japan Economic Research Institute, Japan Iron and Steel Federation, Japan Securities Dealers Association, Japan Shipbuilders Association, Keizai Koho Center, Mitsubishi Corp., Mitsubishi Economic Research Institute, Mitsui and Co., NEC Corp., Sharp Corp., and Sumitomo Corp.

The following Japanese government ministries and agencies responded generously to my requests for materials: Ministry of Home Affairs, the Japan Institute of Labor, Management and Coordination Agency, Ministry of Health and Welfare, Ministry of Labor, Ministry of Posts and Telecommunications, Nagoya Municipal Government, National Tax Administration Agency, Osaka Municipal Government, the Prime Minister's Office, the Small and Medium Enterprise Agency, Tokyo Metropolitan Government, and Yokohama municipal government. The American Embassy in Tokyo also provided useful materials.

I am indebted to the following professors, professionals, and government officials who gave generously their time and expert advice:

James Abegglen, Sophia University and chairman of Gemini Consulting (Japan)

Kouki Arai, Fair Trade Commission

Robert Ballon, Sophia University

Elaine Crepeau, formerly Sophia University Library

Kiyomu Ennokoshi, Matsushita Electric Industrial Co., Ltd.

Akira Fueki, Hiroshima Prefectural University

Yasuyuki Fuchita, Nomura Research Institute

Yoshinobu Fukasawa, Land Agency

Yujiro Hayami, Aoyama Gakuin University

Naoki Higuchi, Central Union of Agricultural Cooperatives

Nobumi Hiramatsu, Mitsubishi Heavy Industries

Takamasa Hisada, Bank of Japan

Akinari Horii, Bank of Japan

Charles Horioka, Osaka University

Mitsuhide Hoshino, Ministry of International Trade and Industry

Hiroyuki Hotta, Ministry of International Trade and Industry

Mitsuhiro Ikehara, Science and Technology Agency

Ken-ichi Imai, Stanford Japan Center

Isao Inoue, Toyota Motor Corporation

Toru Inouye, formerly Anelva Corporation and NEC Corp.

Toyokazu Ishida, Nissan Motor Co.

Kanji Ishizumi, Chiyoda Kokusai Law Office

Yoshio Izumi, NEC Corporation

Naotaka Kaibara, Japanese Trade Union Confederation

Akio Kamio, Tokyo Keizai Inc.

Hisao Kanamori, Japan Center for Economic Research

Hiroshi Kasa, Japan Patent Information Organization

Michio Katsumata, Nihon Keizai Shimbun, Inc.

Naoya Kitamura, Japan Development Bank

Naohiro Kitano, Overseas Economic Cooperation Fund

Yoshihiko Kobayashi, Kansai Economic Federation

Nobuo Kodama, formerly Meisei University

Ryutaro Komiya, Aoyama Gakuin University and the Research Institute of MITI

Colin McKenzie, Osaka University

Ryuhei Matsumoto, Ministry of Agriculture, Forestry, and Fisheries

Noriaki Matsumura, Matsumi Sangyo Co.

Koich Motegi, Sony Corporation

Kenji Nagaoka, Nihon Unisys, Ltd.

Hiromu Nakamura, National Chamber of Agriculture

Takeo Naruse, Japan Federation of Employers' Associations (Nikkeiren)

Fumihira Nishizaki, Economic Planning Agency

Kazuo Ogawa, Institute for Russian and East European Economic Studies

Hajime Ohta, Japan Federation of Economic Organizations (Keidanredn)

Soji Okamura, Daito Bunka University

Tatsuo Sato, Patent Office

Yoshihiko Senoo, Economic Planning Agency and Fair Trade Commission

Kenichiro Seto, Export-Import Bank of Japan

Yoshinori Takasuka, NEC Corporation

Hoare Takenaka, LBS Co. and IBM Japan

Masaru Tanaka, Bank of Japan

Yoichi Tazawa, Nomura Research Institute

Tamao Tokuhisa, Aoyama Gakuin University

Kazuyoshi Tsurumi, Food Agency, Ministry of Agriculture, Forestry, and
Fisheries

Kazuyuki Tsurumi, Ministry of Agriculture, Forestry, and Fisheries

Masu Uekusa, Tokyo University

Fujio Uryu, Ministry of International Trade and Industry

Kenzo Yamamoto, Bank of Japan

Naohiro Yashiro, Japan Center for Economic Research

This book could not be written without the cooperation and assistance of
these individuals. I am particularly grateful to Masu Uekusa for his expert
advice, to Ryuhei Matsumoto and Fumihira Nishizaki for their meticulous
preparation of research materials and their professional assistance, and to
Elaine Crepeau and Nobuo Kodama for generous help in many ways over
the years.

I have utilized several libraries and received much help from many
librarians. Gail Skamarack of Goddard Library, Clark University, was extremely helpful in making available some essential serials on the Japanese
economy. The staff at the following libraries was also very helpful to me:
Harvard-Yenching Library of Harvard University, the library of the International House of Japan, and the library of the Ministry of International
Trade and Industry. I also received competent research assistance from
Steffanie Fewerestein at Clark University and Tsunemasa Hinoki in Tokyo
for the first edition and from Nadia Baryshinikova at Clark University for
the second edition. To all these individuals go my sincere thanks. Naturally all remaining errors are my responsibility alone.

Research for this book was supported by grants from Clark University's faculty development fund, Takahashi grants administered by Clark
University, sabbatical leaves from Clark University during the fall semester of 1991, and spring semester of 1998, and a Fulbright research grant
under the *Japan Today* program during the summer of 1992. The Japan—

United States Educational Commission (Fulbright Program) assisted me in arranging for some interviews in the summer of 1992.

I am grateful to Nihon Keizai Shimbun Inc., the publisher of Japan's leading business daily (see **Economic/Business Research and Publications**) for giving me permission to adapt some tables published in *The Nikkei Weekly* for use in the book.

Finally, my family—my wife Sharon, my son Steven, and my late daughter Nancy—was always supportive and understanding despite the countless hours during which I had to be away. I deeply appreciate such support and understanding.

Worcester, Massachusetts
September 1998

Contents

Tables

The MIT Encyclopedia of
the Japanese Economy

A

administrative guidance Administrative guidance (*gyosei shido*) refers to the suggestions or "unwritten orders" given by Japanese bureaucrats to firms in order to implement official policies. This practice is based on the broad discretionary power of bureaucracy rather than on specific laws. Administrative guidance is important in Japan because it gives the bureaucrats much flexibility in implementing policies. Hence it is frequently used in lieu of government regulations by bureaucrats to steer the private sector.

Compliance with the guidance is not mandatory. However, to maintain good working relationships with the bureaucrats, business managers usually find it advantageous to follow this practice, for fear that the latter may frustrate them in business operations. The high respect that the Japanese public traditionally accords elite bureaucrats and the close working relationship between bureaucrats and business managers are other factors that induce compliance with administrative guidance.

All government ministries and agencies practice administrative guidance in their interactions with the private sector. The **Ministry of International Trade and Industry** (MITI) and the **Ministry of Finance** are particularly active in its use because of their wide scope of jurisdiction. MITI has depended on administrative guidance primarily to coordinate investment as a tool of its industrial policy, that is, to encourage or discourage investment in certain industries. Since the mid-1980s it has also used it as part of its trade policy to deflect Washington's criticisms of Japanese trade practices. Over the years administrative guidance has been applied to a wide range of business activities. For example, in the early 1960s MITI advised firms in the steel and auto industries to merge into fewer firms in order to compete with foreign producers. In 1985 it urged the Japan Automobile Manufacturers Association to send an auto-parts buying mission to the United States to help reduce Japan's trade surplus and alleviate the U.S. protectionist sentiment. In 1991 it called on Japanese automakers to sell American-made cars in Japan through their sales networks.

The Bank of Japan's **window guidance**, practiced until mid-1991, was also a form of administrative guidance.

Administrative guidance, however, is rarely a one-sided top-down government measure imposed on unwilling business managers. Prior consultations with business managers usually take place before a guidance is given in order to ensure maximum cooperation. Oftentimes administrative guidance is given in response to industry's requests for government's guidelines (Eads and Yamamura 1987: 433). Since compliance with administrative guidance is voluntary, it is not always assured. This is because government bureaucrats can and have made errors of judgment and because their suggestions may contradict the interests of those to be guided. For example, the automobile industry did not follow MITI's suggestions of merger in the early 1960s, and it managed to become internationally competitive despite its relatively large number of firms.

In the wake of the securities industry's scandals revealed in 1991, and in light of the failure of the Ministry of Finance to prevent them, Japanese mass media has severely criticized administrative guidance as having protected big businesses at the expense of market competition. In addition, because administrative guidance is often vague and secretive, it is also criticized as having left the public uninformed while fostering an environment of collusion between the Ministry of Finance and big businesses. It is said to have caused businesses to cultivate smooth relations with authorities as the top priority.

As a result of these criticisms, the Administrative Procedure Law, a long proposed law, was enacted and went into effect in October 1994. It aims at curbing bureaucratic power by replacing administrative guidance with clear written directives. However, evidence to date suggests that most corporations remain extremely reluctant to disobey bureaucrats' verbal guidance. One reason is the lack of penalty provisions in the Law; companies would have to sue to penalize bureaucrats who violate the Law, which is an extremely time-consuming process in Japan. In addition companies fear retribution from bureaucrats in the future if they do not comply with administrative guidance. One final reason is that the Law does not apply to local governments, which accounts for two-thirds of all government directives (*Nikkei Weekly*, April 8, 1996: 1).

See also **industrial policy, window guidance**.

References

Bureaucratic "guidance" is unwanted, unwarranted. *Nikkei Weekly* editorial, August 24, 1991: 6.

Eads, George C., and Kozo Yamamura. 1987. The future of industrial policy. In *The Political Economy of Japan*, vol. 1: *The Domestic Transformation*, ed. by Kozo Yamamura and Yasukichi Yasuba. Stanford: Stanford University Press.

Gyosei shido: Inside Japanese bureaucracy. *Tokyo Business Today*, January 1986: 34–37.

Johnson, Chalmers. 1982. *MITI and the Japanese Miracle*. Stanford: Stanford University Press. Ch. 7.

Koh, B. C. 1989. *Japan's Administrative Elite*. Berkeley: University of California Press.

Okimoto, Daniel I. 1989. *MITI and the Market*. Stanford: Stanford University Press. Ch. 2.

Tsuru, Shigeto. 1993. *Japan's Capitalism: Creative Defeat and Beyond*. Cambridge: Cambridge University Press. Ch. 4.

administrative reform   Japan's central government has a vast and well-entrenched administrative structure. Currently it has 21 ministries and agencies along with the Prime Minister's Office. In the forthcoming administrative reform scheduled to begin in 2001, these will be reorganized into 12 ministries and agencies along with a cabinet office that will coordinate policies.

The current administrative structure evolved in the early postwar period to serve the needs of the economy and society. Because the economy was then underdeveloped—with a severe capital shortage, a low level of technology, and an underdeveloped market system—the administrative bureaucracy responded by adopting policies to guide, nurture, and regulate the economy. As a result the bureaucracy proliferated and gained much power. By the 1980s the economy was well developed and increasingly integrated into the global economy. However, the new economy could not function well in the straitjacket of the past. Deregulations such as interest rate deregulation were gradually introduced in the late 1970s, though only at the slow pace which bureaucrats deemed acceptable.

The speculative **bubble economy** of the late 1980s which led to the long stagnation of the 1990s, and the incessant financial abuses uncovered since the early 1990s, suggest that the slow pace of reforms to date is not enough. In the protracted process of deregulation and reform, it became clear that the government bureaucracy had become too vast and entrenched. Often bureaucrats were more interested in maintaining their own power than in implementing needed changes. As a result some agencies and ministries have overlapping functions, and it has become both a matter of inefficiency and interagency rivalry. Thus in 1996 the then Prime Minister Ryutaro Hashimoto struck a responsive cord when he proposed the streamlining of the central government as an election promise. After being elected into office, he appointed and headed an Administrative Reform Council to deliberate the issues. Oppositions to drastic reforms from the bureaucracy were encountered and some compromises were made before the Council came up with a plan in December 1997. On the basis of the plan, a key administrative reform bill was drafted; it has already passed both houses of the Diet. Additional implementing legislation is expected.

The following chart highlights the proposed changes for 2001:

Now	Proposed for 2001[a]
Prime Minister's Office Economic Planning Agency Okinawa Development Agency	Cabinet Office
National Public Safety Commission Defense Agency	National Public Safety Commission Defense Agency
Ministry of Home Affairs Ministry of Posts and Telecommunications Management and Coordination Agency	Ministry of General Affairs Postal Services Agency[b]
Ministry of Justice	Ministry of Justice
Ministry of Foreign Affairs	Ministry of Foreign Affairs
Ministry of Finance	Ministry of Treasury
Ministry of International Trade and Industry	Ministry of Economy and Industry
Ministry of Construction Ministry of Transport National Land Agency Hokkaido Development Agency	Ministry of National Land and Transport
Ministry of Agriculture, Forestry and Fisheries	Ministry of Agriculture, Forestry and Fisheries
Environment Agency	Ministry of Environment
Ministry of Health and Welfare Ministry of Labor	Ministry of Labor and Welfare
Ministry of Education, Science, Sports and Culture Science and Technology Agency	Ministry of Education, Science and Technology

Source: *Nikkei Weekly*, June 15, 1998: 2.

a. Some names are tentative

b. To become Postal Public Corp. after two years

The Prime Minister's Office will be expanded into a Cabinet Office. The prime minister will have more control over policy making and will coordinate overall administrative reforms. The office's incorporation of the **Economic Planning Agency** is expected to enhance its decisions on the economy. The postal system with its **postal savings** and postal life insurance will become a Postal Public Corporation after two years under the Ministry of General Affairs. This will not only reduce the size of the government but will also eliminate what banks and insurance companies have long complained to be unfair competition. The **Ministry of Finance** will retain its power to set fiscal policy and supervise the financial sector.

The reform proposal, supported by the **Liberal Democratic Party** and its allies, has been welcomed by the business community. Whether a streamlined government will mean an efficient and responsive government, however, remains to be seen.

See also **Liberal Democratic Party**.

References

Administrative reform. *Japan Economic Almanac, 1998.* Tokyo: Nihon Keizai Shimbun, Inc.

Choy, Jon. 1997. Blueprint developed for administrative reform. *JEI Report* 33B, August 29: 1–6.

Upper house action clears way for government streamlining. *Nikkei Weekly,* June 15, 1998: 2.

Agricultural Basic Law, 1961   A law enacted to support agriculture and to reduce the disparity in productivity and standard of living between the agricultural and nonagricultural sectors.

See **agricultural policy**.

agricultural cooperatives   Japan has an extensive and well-organized system of agricultural cooperatives (*nokyo,* or JA for Japan agricultural cooperatives). It promotes farming and farmers' interests in Japan under the political leadership of JA-Zenchu (Central Union of Agricultural Cooperatives), the nation's most powerful farm lobby group. JA-Zenchu has a politically active membership of more than 8 million people, of which 5.5 million are farmers. Agricultural cooperatives are politically powerful and are closely involved in various facets of rural lives.

Agricultural cooperatives are organized into three tiers:

1. *Primary agricultural cooperatives.* These are organized at the city, town, and village levels. They are classified into two types: (a) Multipurpose agricultural cooperatives (*sogo nokyo,* 1,937 as of March 1, 1998; author's

interview, March 26, 1998, JA-Zenchu) are engaged in processing and marketing members' agricultural products and in providing them with agricultural inputs, banking, credit, insurance, welfare, and educational services, and so forth. They serve as grass roots credit institutions in rural areas. They accept deposits from members and lend funds to members and the farming community. At the end of March 1997, agricultural cooperatives had ¥67.7 trillion in deposits and ¥20.6 trillion in loans. Virtually all farm households are members. (b) Single-purpose agricultural cooperatives (*senmonren nokyo*, 3,738 in 1995) are organized in specific market sectors—for example, fruits and vegetables, sericulture, and livestock raising. Almost all of their members are concurrently members of multipurpose cooperatives.

2. *Prefectural federations and unions.* At the prefectural level two types of federations are organized. (a) Federations that are composed of multipurpose agricultural cooperatives as members such as prefectural economic federations (*keizairen*), prefectural credit federations (*kenshinren*), prefectural mutual-insurance federations (*kyosairen*), and prefectural welfare federations (*koreiren*). These federations provide the cooperatives with services in their respective areas. For example, the prefectural credit federations accept deposits from, and make loans to, agricultural cooperatives, assist them in their credit operations, and smooth regional surpluses and deficits among the cooperatives. They are also involved in various investment activities. (b) Federations that are composed of single-purpose agricultural cooperatives as members such as dairy cooperative federations, sericultural cooperative federations, and horticultural cooperative federations.

Each of the 47 prefectures used to have a prefectural union of agricultural cooperatives. Their members are primary cooperatives and prefectural federations. They are engaged in guidance, coordination, and research, and they represent the interests of the cooperatives in each prefecture. In recent years some prefectural unions have been eliminated because of the decline in the number of primary agricultural cooperatives.

3. *National level organizations.* All prefectural federations have their counterparts organized at the national level such as the National Federation of Agricultural Cooperative Associations (Zennoh), Central Cooperative Bank for Agriculture and Forestry (Norinchukin Bank), National Mutual-Insurance Federation of Agricultural Cooperatives, National Federation of Dairy Cooperatives, and National Federation of Livestock Cooperatives. The Central Cooperative Bank for Agriculture and Forestry is one of

Japan's largest banks. As of March 31, 1997, it had ¥31.8 trillion in deposits and ¥16.9 trillion in loans. Finally there is the Central Union of Agricultural Cooperatives (JA-Zenchu), the political leadership of the agricultural cooperatives movement. Its members are primary agricultural cooperatives, prefectural federations, prefectural unions, and various national federations.

Zenchu is not only involved in services such as guidance, coordination, education, and information, but it also conducts political campaigns to promote farmers' interests. Its president is the spokesperson for agricultural cooperatives and the farming community's top negotiator with the government bureaucracy and business organizations. Zenchu is also involved in the following business activities: developing and improving farm land, entrusted farm operations, overseeing farmland trust holdings, marketing, storage and transport of agricultural products, insurance, hospitals and clinics, extending credit for agricultural production, and processing agricultural products.

Until 1997 the JA-Zenchu also served as a government agent in the agricultural sector. It assisted farmers in performing a number of semi-official duties under various agriculture-related laws—the Food Control Law, the Livestock Price Stabilization Law, the Feed Demand and Supply Stabilization Law, the Dairy Farming Promotion Law. For example, it was in charge of the collection and shipment of rice that was not sold to the government ("independent distribution rice") and charged commissions as rice passed through Japan. As a government agent it received commissions and subsidies from the government, and its activities were monitored by government administrators.

Structural changes are in store for the agricultural cooperatives. Because of financial deregulation, the Zenchu plans to reduce the number of the credit federations of agricultural cooperatives to make them more competitive with other financial institutions. The number of agricultural cooperatives will also continue to decline. The number had already been reduced from 8,273 at the end of 1965 to 3,223 at the end of 1992, and 1,937 on March 1, 1998. The purpose is to have fewer but stronger cooperatives, with more members in each of them. The prefectural organization may be eliminated altogether so that the current three-tier system may become a two-tier one (author's interview, March 26, 1998, JA-Zenchu).

See also **agricultural policy, banking system, rice production and distribution**.

Addresses

Central Union of Agricultural Cooperatives
8-3, Otemachi 1-chome, Chiyoda-ku, Tokyo 100
Tel: (3) 3245-7500   Fax: (3) 5255-7356

National Federation of Agricultural Cooperative Associations
8-3, Otemachi 1-chome, Chiyoda-ku, Tokyo 100
Tel: (3) 3245-7111   Fax: (3) 3245-7442

Norinchukin Bank
8-3, Ohtemachi 1-chome, Chiyoda-ku, Tokyo 100
Tel: (3) 3279-0111

References

Central Union of Agricultural Cooperatives. Undated. *JA-Zenchu*. Tokyo.

Cheng, Peter P. 1990. Japanese interest group politics. *Asian Survey* 30, 3: 251–265.

Domon, Takeshi. 1996. The inside story of the troubled farm co-ops. *Japan Echo* 23 (Summer): 21–7.

JA-Zenchu. Undated. *Sowing the Seeds of the Future: Japan's Agricultural Cooperatives*. Tokyo: Central Union of Agricultural Cooperatives.

Moore, Richard M. 1990. *Japanese Agriculture: Patterns of Rural Development*. Boulder, CO: Westview. Ch. 8.

Rothacher, Albrecht. 1989. *Japan's Agro-Food Sector: The Politics and Economics of Excess Protection*. London: Macmillan Press.

The power politics of rice. *Tokyo Business Today*, October 1990: 26–35.

Saeki, Naomi. 1996. Loan crisis clouds future of farm co-ops. *Nikkei Weekly*, February 19: 7.

Shida, Tomio 1989. Farm co-ops seek spot to sow huge cash harvest. *Japan Economic Journal*, April 1: 2.

Taro, Yayama. 1987. Cooperatives, the curse of Japanese agriculture. *Japan Echo* 14, 1: 7–8.

agricultural policy   In the postwar period the Japanese government had to deal with various agriculture-related issues: to increase food supply in the immediate postwar period, to support farmers' income as the agricultural sector declined in the economy, and to protect the domestic agricultural market from foreign producers who clamored to enter the Japanese market. The relative importance of these issues changes over time and helps to shape the focus of Japan's agricultural policy in any particular time period.

In the immediate postwar period the main objectives of the agricultural policy were to ensure adequate food supplies and to implement the agricultural land reform program as mandated by the U.S. occupation in its effort to democratize the society (see **postwar reforms and reconstruction**). These objectives were achieved as planned.

By the mid-1950s the Japanese economy had recovered from the devastation of war and its industry developed very rapidly thereafter, causing an outflow of labor from agriculture to industry. In addition productivity in industry rose much more rapidly than in agriculture, causing a growing disparity between industrial wages and farm income. To deal with these problems of structural changes in the economy, the Agricultural Basic Law was enacted in 1961. It authorized the government to protect and support agriculture and farmers' income. This became the focus of Japan's agricultural policy from early 1960s to the late 1980s. Various instruments were used to attain the objective. Through government purchase of rice at high prices—sometimes as high as four times the world price level —the government supports the income of farm households. The government purchase price is set annually on the basis of production costs including the imputed cost of farmers' own labor, which is calculated on the basis of industrial wages (see **pricing practices**). The import of rice was banned until 1993.

The production of selective agricultural products is promoted and protected. With rising income, Japanese households are changing their diets; they are consuming more meat, dairy products, fruits, and so on, and less rice. The government therefore has taken measures to promote the production of livestock, fruits, and vegetables. Import restrictions in the form of quotas are imposed on beef, fruits (particularly oranges), dairy products, flour, beans, fish, shellfish, and processed foods.

The general strategy of agricultural import protection is to give high protection (i.e., low quotas) to final consumer agricultural goods to encourage their domestic production or processing and to permit the imports of needed raw materials or products by giving them low protection. Examples of the latter are feed grains for livestock, wheat for flour and flour products, and soybeans for soy products. As a result of this strategy, Japan's self-sufficiency rate for agricultural products used as food decreased from 90% in 1960 to 72% in 1980 and about 64% in 1995. The rate for rice was 103% in 1995, and that for dairy products was 85% in 1985 but declined to 72% in 1995. There was rice surplus at times as high government purchase prices encouraged excessive production; the self-sufficiency rate of rice was 110% in 1975 and 107% in 1985.

Subsidies over and above the subsidy on rice prices are also given to agriculture. They amounted to 49% of total agricultural budget in 1960,

61% in 1980, and 66% in 1991. They are paid to growers of a large number of agricultural items. Thus a large number of small farmers benefit
from these payments; this is politically important to the ruling **Liberal
Democratic Party**. With the subsidy on rice prices (which appear in the
agricultural budget as a transfer from the general account to the food
control special account) the ratio of subsidy to total agricultural budget
can be as high as 80% (Hayami 1988: 57).

The protection program outlined above has expanded rapidly since the
mid-1960s for two reasons: the increased demand for protection coming
from the politically powerful farm block organized under the **agricultural
cooperatives** and the decline in domestic countervailing power against
agricultural protection. Since the Japanese have become more affluent and
the share of food in their total consumption expenditures has declined,
they have become more tolerant of high food prices. Consumers, trade
unions, and business leaders have seldom protested government protection policies (Hayami 1988; author's interview, July 2, 1992).

There are constraints, however, on the government's protection policies that come from both domestic and external sources. Domestically,
high rice prices have stimulated overproduction and strained the government's budget. Externally, foreign food-exporting countries, particularly the United States, have protested Japan's import quotas. Much of the
agricultural imports come from the United States. Japan has in fact become
the largest importer of agricultural products from the United States,
and the United States has become the largest food supplier to Japan.
However, as Japan–U.S. trade imbalance grew in the 1980s and as Japan
enjoys open markets for its manufactured goods in the United States,
Japan's remaining restrictions on food imports has become a major source
of Japan–U.S. trade frictions. Washington has demanded greater access to
Japan's agricultural market.

The products of particular interests to Washington have been beef,
oranges, and rice. Beef and oranges were protected in Japan by quotas. In
1978 Washington negotiated with Tokyo to increase quotas gradually
without disrupting Japanese domestic production. In 1988, after several
years of hard bargaining, the **Beef-Citrus Agreement** was reached.
Quotas were increased for 1988–90 and replaced by tariffs in 1991.

Washington's demand for the liberalization of rice imports encountered
very strong domestic opposition to it in Japan. It became one of the agricultural issues at the Uruguay Round of GATT negotiations because
Europe and other countries also protect their agriculture. The negotia-

tions were concluded in December 1993. Included in the agreements are "minimum access" terms for Japan's rice market; that is, Tokyo agreed to import specific minimum amounts of rice annually through FY 2000.

Another aspect of agricultural policy is to raise agricultural productivity by promoting farmland consolidation. In the land reform of 1945–49, Japan's farmland became fragmented, and many farms became too small to be efficient. Furthermore, by law, land transfers were restricted to prevent the reconsolidation of land (see **land uses and policies**). As Japan completed postwar reconstruction and entered the era of rapid economic growth in the 1950s and 1960s, many farmers found factory employment. The government expected them to leave farming altogether and sell their farms, which would permit the consolidation of small farms into larger ones for economies of scale. Unfortunately, this did not happen. Because of the high prices of agricultural products, particularly rice, due to government support, farmers kept and worked their land in their free time in order to raise their income.

Again, government effort to create larger farms appeared in 1970 to 1975, when restrictions on land transfers were relaxed. Small farmers were encouraged to sell their land to farmers with higher productivity, but the effort was not successful. In 1993, with the **Uruguay Round** of negotiation reaching an agreement on Japan's rice import, adverse impact on Japanese rice farmers was expected and an agricultural land consolidation program was legislated to speed up the transfer of land to efficient farms. Since 1995 various measures have been adopted for that purpose: (1) subsidized loans for eligible buyers, including special farming corporations; (2) land promoters ("special organization for agricultural landholding rationalization") which help facilitate transfers of titles to agricultural land, including leasing before sale; and (3) encouragement of the consignment of farmwork to more efficient farmers if the small farmer is not willing to sell (Matsumoto, 1998; also author's interview with Matsumoto, March 26, 1998).

The implementation of the program to date has been slow. One reason is the expectation of higher agricultural land prices in the future. As a result small farmers prefer consignment of work to sale of land. The growing share of aged farmers in the agricultural labor force has impeded the rise of agricultural productivity overall. If this trend continues, further decline of the Japanese agriculture will be inevitable.

See also **agricultural cooperatives, land uses and policies, postwar reforms, pricing practices, rice production and distribution**.

References

Hayami, Yujiro. 1988. *Japanese Agriculture under Siege: The Political Economy of Agricultural Policies*. London: Macmillan.

Hayami, Yujiro, and Saburo Yamada. 1991. *The Agricultural Development of Japan: A Century's Perspective*. Tokyo: University of Tokyo Press.

Matsumoto, Ryuhei. 1998. Assessment of current agricultural land policy for improving its land holding structure as well as for facilitating consignment of agricultural work to more efficient farmers or bodies. Ministry of Agriculture, Forestry, and Fisheries.

Moore, Richard M. 1990. *Japanese Agriculture: Patterns of Rural Development*. Boulder, CO: Westview.

Niimi, Kazumasa., 1997. Japanese agriculture: current situation and outlook: an international approach to the "agricultural problem." *Japan Research Quarterly* 6, 3: 50–99.

O'Rourke, A. Desmond, ed. 1994. *Understanding the Japanese Food and Agrimarket: A Multifaceted Opportunity*. New York: Food Products Press.

Ohsawa, Shinichi. 1997. Agri-business and agricultural reform in Japan. *Japan Research Quarterly* 6, 3: 100–130.

Reich, Michael, Yasuo Endo, and C. Peter Timmer. 1986. Agriculture: The political economy of structural change. In *American versus Japan*, ed. by Thomas K. McCraw. Boston: Harvard Business School Press.

airline industry   Japan has three major airlines, all privately owned—Japan Airlines Co. (JAL), All Nippon Airways Co. (ANA), and Japan Air System Co. (JAS). JAL and ANA are by far the largest two. JAS is a member of the Tokyu Group, a large family-controlled conglomerate. There are also some other smaller regional airlines.

Japan Airlines, the national flag carrier and one of the world's largest, is engaged in both domestic and international operations. In FY 1997 it derived 52% of its revenues from international passenger service, 24% from domestic passengers, and 13% from cargo operations. It has the largest number of Japan's international routes but is expanding its domestic services. Because it was only privatized in November 1987, it is still in the process of restructuring. It is known for quality service but is reportedly still suffering from the heritage of high operating costs, particularly personnel costs, and inefficient management. In FY 1990 and 1991 it had operating revenues of ¥1,119 billion and ¥1,115 billion, respectively, but its pretax profit was only ¥27.3 billion in FY 1990, which declined to a loss of ¥13 billion in FY 1991. Some cost-cutting measures have been adopted since the early 1990s, including the controversial hiring of contract stewardesses. Nevertheless, operating revenues stagnated at ¥1,195 billion with a loss of ¥17 billion in FY 1996.

All Nippon Airways is Japan's second largest airline. The bulk of its operations is in domestic passenger service (66% of revenues in FY 1997). It started international flights in 1986 when industry liberalization encouraged open competition among airlines and has been actively expanding its international routes ever since. It also operates hotels. In FY 1990 and 1996 it had sales of ¥733 billion and ¥887 billion, respectively, and pretax profits of ¥25.3 billion and ¥17.3 billion.

Japan Air System, the third largest airline, is currently limited to domestic routes but is attempting to break into international passenger service. It derived 92% of its revenues in FY 1997 from domestic passengers and 4% from air cargoes. As of September 1997, 30% of its shares were held by Tokyu Corp. because of its membership in the Tokyu Group. In FY 1996 it had operating revenues of ¥318.7 billion and pretax profits of ¥276 million.

Japan's airline industry enjoyed rapid growth in the 1980s. The Gulf War of 1991 and Japan's recession in 1991–92 adversely affected international air travel and industry profits. There was rapid growth in passengers in FY 1993, but the growth slowed for all big three airlines in FY 1994 and 1995, with Japan Airlines suffering the sharpest decline. In 1996 growth increased to 10.7% for Japan Airlines but continued to decline for All Nippon Airways and Japan Air System. Thus the prolonged stagnation of the economy has taken its tolls. The Asian financial problems since late 1997 have also reduced Japanese airlines' Asian business.

The industry has a severe and unique problem—namely the major airports have reached their capacity limits. Tokyo Narita Airport, the nation's major international airport, has only one runway; it handles more than 122,000 flights annually, 10% more than initially planned. Tokyo Haneda Airport, the main airport for domestic flights, handles more than 180,000 flights annually, and more than 42 million passengers use it annually, about double that of Narita. As a result it is extremely difficult to increase the number of flights or to open new routes out of these two largest airports. Osaka Atami Airport is limited to day flights because of its proximity to residential areas and hence unsuitable for some international flights. In recent years the airlines have expanded the use of regional airports for international flights. The major regional airports are located in Sapporo and Nagoya. Also JAL and ANA each set up a subsidiary in 1990 that specializes in charter flights out of regional airports.

This airport constraint eased somewhat since September 1994 with the opening of the new Kansai International Airport, constructed on an artificial island in Osaka Bay. It is part of a program by **Osaka and Kansai** to attract overseas business and investment. It began round-the-clock operations in July 1997. A new second terminal was opened at Narita Airport in late 1992 and a new runway is scheduled to be completed in the year 2001. Central Japan will have a new Chubu International Airport, being built offshore on an artificial island 30 kilometers south of Nagoya, to be completed in 2005 for the World Export 2005 (see **Nagoya and Central Japan**).

Internationally Japan's airlines are considered to be less competitive than those of the United States. The long period of regulation has contributed to management inefficiency and high personnel costs. Another factor is high airport costs and taxes. In January 1997, the cost of landing a Boeing 747 at Narita Airport was ¥948,000, three times as much as at John F. Kennedy International Airport in New York and more than double that of landing at Charles De Gaulle Airport in Paris (*Japan Economic Almanac, 1998:* 128).

The aviation relations between Japan and the United States was until recently governed by a 1952 bilateral agreement. Under that agreement that Japan–U.S. route was dominated by four "incumbent" airlines—three were American (Northwest Airlines Inc., United Airlines Co., and freight carrier Federal Express Corp.) and one Japanese (Japan Airlines Co.). Each country was allocated up to three "nonincumbent" airlines, each with fewer rights in subsequent memoranda of understanding.

Since 1952 much has changed in both countries, and the transpacific route has become most lucrative because of large Asian–U.S. trade and the booming Asian economies. Both Japan and the U.S. wanted changes in the bilateral aviation relations, and negotiations were started in April 1996. To Tokyo, the 1952 accord was inequitable because it gave Japan only one incumbent airline, which reflected the weak Japanese airline industry in 1952. Washington wanted changes to achieve the following goals:

1. Deregulated international "open skies" was and remains the primary U.S. policy goal, since domestic airline deregulation to enable U.S. carriers to fly into and beyond Japan as they would within the United States. Tokyo has resisted this to protect its own airlines.

2. "Beyond rights" for U.S. airlines would allow them to pick up passengers/cargoes in Japan for other Asian destinations. All U.S. incumbent carriers want the right to expand from Japan to other Asian countries. The Federal Express Corp. in particular had already expanded its service in various Asian countries in recent years, including its new routes to China in 1998.

3. "Code-sharing" is the practice of joint route operation and ticketing arrangements whereby an international airline links its flights to those of a domestic carrier in a foreign country, thus broadening its flight network without making expensive new investment. All U.S. airlines serving the Pacific route would like to make such connections. Tokyo resisted the granting of code-sharing for fear that the American carriers would dominate the business (*JEI Reports* 37B, October 3, 1997: 9–10).

In September 1997 Washington dropped its open-skies demand. A new agreement was reached in January 1998. Its main provisions are:

1. Two additional Japanese "incumbents" are added—All Nippon Airways Co. and Nippon Cargo Airlines Co. Each country can have four other nonincumbent carriers with restricted rights instead of the current three.

2. The "beyond rights" are liberalized for incumbent passenger carriers and unrestricted for incumbent cargo carriers.

3. Code-sharing is liberalized, extended to bilateral and third-party code-sharing.

The agreement will be revised by the year 2005.

Although the new accord gives Japan the numerical parity in incumbents, analysts expect the U.S. airlines to gain more because of their greater competitiveness.

See also **railway companies**.

Addresses

All Nippon Airways
2-5, Kasumigaseki 3-chome, Chiyoda-ku, Tokyo 100
Tel: (3) 3592-3065   Fax: (3) 3592-3039

Japan Air System
5-1, Toranomon 3-chome, Minato-ku, Tokyo 105
Tel: (3) 5473-4100

Japan Airlines
7-3, Marunouchi 2-chome, Chiyoda-ku, Tokyo 100
Tel: (3) 3284-2511   Fax: (3) 3284-2529

References

Airlines. In *Japan Economic Almanac*. Various years. Tokyo: Nihon Keizai Shimbun.

Alexander, Arthur J. 1998. Transpacific aviation pact yields extensive opportunities. *JEI Report* 7A, February 20.

Hasegawa, Mina. 1993. JAL restructuring: Will it fly? *Nikkei Weekly*, March 8: 1.

Is JAL losing its wing? *Tokyo Business Today*, September 1992: 56–58.

Japan Company Handbook. Quarterly. Tokyo: Toyo Keizai.

amakudari Literally "descent from heaven," *amakudari* refers to the time-honored practice of Japanese officials, upon early retirement, to move to high positions in an industry with which they had worked closely during their government service. This had its origin in the early Meiji period when the government set up industrial and commercial undertakings to provide jobs for functionless *samurai*.

On the basis of data from the National Personnel Authority, Usui and Colignon (1995) show that from 1963 to 1992 the **Ministry of Finance** headed the *amakudari* list, followed by the **Ministry of International Trade and Industry**, Ministry of Construction, Ministry of Transport, Ministry of Agriculture, Forestry and Fisheries, Ministry of Posts and Telecommunications, and the National Tax Administration Agency, although there were fluctuations in their relative rankings over the years. Various authors have used the number of *amakudari* of various ministries as a measure of their control over the economic sectors they regulate and as a measure of their relative power vis-à-vis other ministries.

Japanese companies reportedly like the practice of *amakudari* for various reasons. It provides them with fresh blood, expertise, and seasoned leaders, and it provides them with connections to government bureaucrats, thereby improving communication between the two groups. Caldor (1989) contends that this is particularly useful for medium-sized, less-established firms that normally cannot attract top college graduates. However, Aoki (1988: 266) maintains that ministries push to expand *amakudari* opportunities as rewards to retiring bureaucrats and as a means to extend their influence. Other critics charge that the practice leads to conflicts of interests and abuses of power. Government officials may curry favor with companies for possible postretirement jobs. Ministries may use *amakudari* bureaucrats in the companies to monitor company activities. Some companies do not like the pressure on them to hire retired government officials, nor do they think that former-bureaucrats have enough business sense. On the other hand, defenders of the practice such as Okimoto (1990) have argued that government ministries have been careful not to abuse their connections with *amakudari* officials lest the latter's careers be compromised.

In order to minimize possible abuses, Japan's National Public Service Law stipulates that government employees are not allowed to join private companies for two years after retirement if they had close relationships with the companies within five years before retirement; in these cases special approval from the National Personnel Authority is needed. The National Personnel Authority approved 232 such cases in 1988 and 246 cases in 1989.

In the wake of **securities companies** scandals in 1991, the Ministry of Finance has been criticized as having a collusive relationship with the securities industry. Consequently the ministry adopted a policy of voluntary restraint regarding the hiring of retired bureaucrats by securities companies. That policy, however, did not last long; nor was it effective. In early 1998, as part of its effort to improve its image with the public, the **Bank of Japan** adopted a new code of conduct for its officials which, among other things, requires them to wait two years after retirement before accepting a job with any financial institution that has a relationship with the bank.

In addition to private companies, **public corporations** and other government-related nonprofit institutions have been the recipients of *amakudari*. It is rare, however, for retiring officials to teach at universities. A notable exception are retired officials from the **Economic Planning Agency**, who by the nature of their work were engaged in economic research.

In the late 1990s with the prestige and power of government bureaucrats in decline due to various scandals and the prospect of **administrative reform**, the opportunities for *amakudari* are said to have diminished.

See also **corporate personnel practices**.

References

Aoki, Masahiko. 1988. *Information, Incentives, and Bargaining in the Japanese Economy*. Cambridge: Cambridge University Press. Ch. 7.

Blumenthal, Tuvia. 1985. The practice of *amakudari* within the Japanese employment system. *Asian Survey* 25: 310–21.

Caldor, Kent. 1989. Elites in an equalizing role: Ex-bureaucrats as coordinators and intermediaries in the Japanese government-business relationship. *Comparative Politics* 21: 379–403.

Johnson, Chalmers. 1995. *Japan: Who Governs?* New York: W.W. Norton Ch. 7.

Okimoto, Daniel I. 1990. *Between MITI and the Market*. Stanford: Stanford University Press. Pp. 161–165.

Schaede, Uirike. 1995. The "old boy" network and government-business relationships in Japan. *Journal of Japanese Studies* 21, 2: 293–317.

Tochigi, Makoto. 1997. "Decent from heaven" taking unexpected path. *Nikkei Weekly*, August 25: 23.

Usui, Chikako and Richard Colignon. 1995. Government elites and *amakudari* in Japan, 1963–1992. *Asian Survey* 35: 682–98.

Antimonopoly Law   The law was introduced in 1947 as part of the Allied Occupation's policy to decentralize the postwar economy and to promote competition. The Japanese economy during the war was highly concentrated under the leadership of the **zaibatsu**, the huge conglomerates, which were believed to have contributed to the war effort. Modeled on U.S. antitrust laws, the Antimonopoly Law bans trusts, **cartels**, as well as **holding companies**, which were an important part of the *zaibatsu* organization. It prohibits "private monopolization, unreasonable restraints of trade and unfair methods of competition" (Article 1). It restricts mergers and prohibits financial institutions from owning more than 5% of any single company's shares to prevent excessive concentration of business ownership. The law was subsequently revised several times.

The Fair Trade Commission (FTC) was created under the Prime Minister's Office to implement the law. However, it has remained a minor government agency and observers generally regard it as weak and understaffed, a "toothless watchdog" vis-á-vis big business and the Japanese bureaucracy, and too willing to make exceptions. These weaknesses reflect the low priority given by the Japanese government to the implementation of the Antimonopoly Law as compared with other policy areas, particularly the **industrial policy.** The law was sometimes contravened by the industrial policy of the **Ministry of International Trade and Industry** (MITI). In the 1950s the promotion of domestic industries was paramount for the government and the implementation of the Antimonopoly Law was ineffective. Consequently the law was revised in 1953 to ease the restrictions on cartels, trusts, mergers, and other competition-curbing measures. Recession cartels and rationalization cartels were permitted. The revision also exempted import-export businesses from the law. The ceiling on bank holding of company stock was raised to 10%.

In the 1960s, with trade liberalization, industries lobbied for further revision of the law to restrict competition, but their efforts were unsuccessful, in part because of the public's growing support for the law. In the early 1970s, after the oil crisis, there were a number of illegal cartels and other corporate activities that restricted market competition. In response the Diet passed bills in 1975 and 1977 to strengthen the law. Punitive measures such as surcharges and sale of part of operations were provided for the first time to curb violations of the law. As a sign of the growing importance of antimonopoly policy versus the industrial policy, oil company cartels formed in accordance with MITI's **administrative guidance** were found in 1980 to be in violation of the Antimonopoly Law. That was the only antimonopoly dispute ever to go to court in Japan.

Foreign analysts have often criticized the implementation of the law as weak and ineffective and have argued that this has aided Japanese firms' competitiveness in world trade. During the **Structural Impediments Initiative** talks between Washington and Tokyo in 1989–90, U.S. negotiators identified various business practices such as **cross-shareholding** in *keiretsu* groups, price cartels, and bid-rigging as violations of the Antimonopoly Law that restrict competition and exclude foreign firms from the Japanese market. Washington requested that Tokyo strengthen its antitrust enforcement in general and that tougher measures be taken against exclusionary business practices.

In response to Washington's pressure, and as part of the ongoing market-oriented reforms, Japan has begun to implement the Antimonopoly Law more seriously. In April 1991 the Law was revised to raise surcharges against illegal **cartels** (form 1.5% to 6% of a company's sales). In December 1992 revision was made to increase criminal fines against firms or trade associations for such violations as private monopoly and unreasonable restraint of trade. Subsequently the Fair Trade Commission has investigated a large number of companies that were suspected of violations of the Law. It investigated Nomura Securities Co. for allegedly controlling more than 5% of the subsidiary's shares through third-party manipulation. It also investigated cross-shareholding in automobiles, auto-parts, paper products, and glass industries, which Washington has accused of having exclusionary practices. In late 1991, in its first criminal antitrust complaint in 17 years, FTC accused eight plastic-wrap makers of price fixing. Subsequently it also reduced the scope for the establishment of cartels and retail price fixing (see **pricing practices**).

Some Japanese question whether all Japanese antimonopoly provisions, adopted in 1947 on the basis of the U.S. antitrust laws under pressure from the Occupation, are equally appropriate for Japan in the 1990s. For example, some Japanese argue that holding companies may not be inappropriate in some industries. After years of debate, an amendment to the Antimonopoly Law was made in December 1997 to lift the ban on holding companies, but with provisions against excessive concentration of economic power.

Foreign firms that have complaints to make about the possible violation of the Antimonopoly Law by Japanese firms should contact the International Affairs Division of the Fair Trade Commission. They can do so in person, by telephone or other forms of communication, and an investigation is promised (author's interview, Fair Trade Commission, April 9, 1998).

See also **cartels, holding companies, industrial policy, Ministry of International Trade and Industry**.

Address

International Affairs Division
Fair Trade Commission
1-1-1, Kasumigaseki, Chiyoda-ku, Tokyo 100
Tel: (3) 3581-5471
Internet: www.jftc.admix.go.jp/

References

Fair Trade Commission. *FTC/Japan Views*. Quarterly. (Ceased publication in March 1998).

Iyori, H. and A. Uesugi. 1994. *The Antimonopoly Laws and Policies of Japan*. New York: Federal Legal Publications.

Matsushita, Mitsuo. 1993. *International Trade and Competition Law in Japan*. Oxford: Oxford University Press. Chs. 1–2.

Matsushita, Mitsuo and John Davis. 1990. *Introduction to Japanese Antimonopoly Law*. Tokyo: Yuhikaku Publishing.

Oda, Hiroshi, ed. 1994. *Japanese Commercial Law in an Era of Internationalization*. London: Graham & Trotman/Martinus Nijhoff.

Uekusa, Masu. 1987. Industrial organization: The 1970s to the present. In *The Political Economy of Japan*, vol. 1: The *Domestic Transformation*, ed. by Kozo Yamamura and Yasukichi Yasuba. Stanford: Stanford University Press.

Uekusa, Masu. 1990. Government regulations in Japan: Toward their international harmonization and integration. In *Japan's Economic Structure: Should It Change?* ed. by Kozo Yamamura. Seattle: Society for Japanese Studies.

atogime Deferred price setting, a practice in paper and petrochemical industries of allowing sellers to renegotiate prices after delivery.
See **pricing practices**.

automobile exports and imports
See **automobile industry**.

automobile industry   The automobile industry became one of Japan's most important industries in the postwar period. Automobile production began in Japan in the 1920s when Henry Ford built a factory in Yokohama. In 1933 the Nissan Motor Co. was established to produce small vehicles. In 1937 the Toyota Motor Co. was established. In 1980, less than 50 years after Nissan's founding, Japan became the world's largest producing country of automobiles. It had remained the leader until 1994, and Toyota and Nissan have become two of the world's largest automobile manufacturers.

In their early years before World War II, both Nissan and Toyota produced mostly trucks for the military because of the lack of domestic demand for cars. The Ministry of Commerce and Industry, the predecessor of the **Ministry of International Trade and Industry** (MITI), protected the fledgling industry at the urging of the military by restricting imports and subsidizing domestic producers.

In the postwar period vehicle output increased rapidly, particularly between 1960 and 1970 (about elevenfold; see table A.1). Truck output continued to exceed that of cars throughout the 1950s and most of 1960s. By the early 1960s Japan became the world's second largest producer of trucks. Total vehicle production reached a peak of 13.5 million units in 1990. Thereafter, it gradually declined.

In the 1950s and 1960s MITI provided various assistance to the industry—low-interest loans, tax privileges, tariff exemption for imported machinery and tools, and import protection—over the objections of officials at the **Bank of Japan** and the Ministry of Transport, who would liberalize car imports and use Japan's limited resources to develop other industries. MITI argued that by promoting automobile industry, many other industries such as machinery and steel manufacturing would be promoted as well. However, MITI's 1955 plan to promote a mini "people's car" by 1958 failed because no company responded to it due to market considerations. In the mid-1960s MITI recommended mergers or tie-ups between automakers in order to prevent excess competition and promote economies of scale because there were too many auto companies (Nissan, Toyota, Isuzu, Hino, Mitsubishi, Prince, Toyo Kogyo, Daihatsu, Fuji Heavy Industries, Suzuki, and Honda). Only one merger took place between Nissan and Prince in 1966. Tie-ups made Toyota the largest shareholder in Hino and Daihatsu, and Nissan a major shareholder in Fuji

Table A.1
Automobile production, exports, and imports (in 1,000 vehicles)

Year	Production	Exports	Imports
1960	482	39	4.3
1965	1,876	194	13.4
1970	5,289	1,087	19.6
1975	6,942	2,678	46.1
1980	11,043	5,967	47.9
1985	12,271	6,730	53.2
1986	12,260	6,605	74.3
1987	12,249	6,305	110.8
1988	12,700	6,104	154.0
1989	13,026	5,884	196.7
1990	13,487	5,831	252.8
1991	13,245	5,753	197.4
1992	12,499	5,668	187.2
1993	11,228	5,018	213.8
1994	10,554	4,460	310.6
1995	10,196	3,791	404.7
1996	10,346	3,711	454.1

Source: Japan Automobile Manufacturers Association.
Note: Figures include cars, trucks, and buses.

Heavy Industries, but they did not reduce domestic competition or increase production scales because these companies specialized in product lines that Toyota and Nissan did not produce.

Nissan and Toyota have remained the two largest producers in the postwar period. Nissan had 54% of Japan's car output in 1950, with Toyota producing 29%. In 1953 Nissan's share dropped to 34.7%, whereas Toyota's share increased to 40.6% in the same year to become the largest producer. Since then Toyota has remained the leader. For both companies, peak production was reached in 1990 when 4.2 million and 2.4 million vehicles (including cars, trucks, and buses) were produced by Toyota and Nissan, respectively. In 1996, Toyota produced 3.4 million vehicles or 33% of Japan's total output; Nissan produced 1.6 million or 16% of the total (see table A.2), giving a combined share of 49%. Their share of total exports in 1996 was 34% and 16%, respectively.

In terms of profits, Toyota leads Nissan and other automakers by a wide margin, as shown in table A.3. In fact, for ten consecutive years through FY 1997, Toyota has ranked first in the economy in terms of corporate profits. In FY 1997, with ¥625 billion in pretax profits, it leads

Table A.2
Vehicle production and exports by manufacturer (in 1,000 vehicles)

	Production		Exports	
Make	1990	1996	1990	1996
Toyota	4,212	3,410	1,677	1,277
Nissan	2,417	1,611	956	582
Mitsubishi	1,333	1,200	609	455
Mazda	1,423	774	834	454
Honda	1,384	1,092	715	371
Suzuki	839	848	290	190
Daihatsu	636	536	146	63
Isuzu	563	331	366	186
Fuji	517	417	180	81
Hino	100	78	38	31
Nissan Diesel	62	49	22	21
Total	13,487	10,346	5,831	3,711

Source: Japan Automobile Manufacturers Association.
Note: Figures include minivehicles. Hino and Nissan Diesel type trucks and buses only.

Table A.3
Leading automakers (in ¥ billions)

	Sales		Pretax profits	
Company	FY 1991	1997	1991	1997
Toyota	8,564	7,769	574	625
Nissan	4,300	3,546	88	57
Honda	2,920	3,077	67	212
Mitsubishi	2,450	2,500	51	−22
Mazda	2,310	1,512	20	25

Source: *Nikkei Weekly*, June 13, 1992, and June 1, 1998.

by far the second-ranking Nippon Telegraph and Telephone Corp. (¥357 billion). The prolonged stagnation of the economy in the 1990s has depressed domestic sales of automobiles. Nissan in particular has had serious financial problems since the early 1990s, and this is clearly reflected in its low profit figures. It has tried to restructure and reduce costs in recent years.

Toyota's rise to preeminence in Japan's automobile industry has been aided by its innovations in production management. The most important and widely emulated production management method is the **just-in-time**

system, which utilizes the *kanban* **system** to keep parts inventory at a minimum. In connection with the operation of the just-in-time system, the company has developed an extensive **subcontracting system** to supply parts just before they are needed. In recent years an innovation has been made to link factory production directly to sales.

As Japan's automobile output increased and exceeded domestic requirements, manufacturers began to export. Exports started in the late 1950s at a low level but increased rapidly in the late 1960s, reaching 1.09 million units in 1970 (see table A.1). The greatest increase came after the 1973 oil crisis when the demand for small cars increased, particularly in the United States, Japan's major automobile export market. Between 1973 and 1980 automobile exports increased by 288% to reach 5.97 million units, surpassing domestic sales of 5.02 million units. In 1985 a record 6.73 million units were exported, accounting for a record 54.8% of total production. Since then the number of units exported has declined. The export ratio has also declined steadily to 43.4% in 1991 and 36% in 1996.

Alarmed at the rapid increase of auto import from Japan and its impact on the domestic auto industry, Washington requested Japan to institute the "voluntary export restraint" (VER) in order to slow down the increase without having to resort to more restrictive or protectionist measures. The Ministry of International Trade and Industry (MITI) has complied with the request in order to minimize trade frictions between the two countries, and the VER on Japan's passenger car exports to the United States was set at 1.68 million units in fiscal 1981. It was raised to 1.85 million units in fiscal 1984 and 2.3 million units in fiscal 1985. Nevertheless, exports of Japanese automobiles, especially passenger cars, remain heavily dependent on the U.S. market, although the share of total exports to the United States has been declining since the late 1980s. In 1991, of the 4.45 million passenger cars exported, 1.76 million or 39.6% went to the United States, down from 45.5% in 1989. Ironically that was below the VER limit of 2.3 million units that MITI allocated to Japanese automakers. Total vehicle exports (including trucks and buses) were 5.67 million units in 1992, of which 1.77 million units or 31.3% went to the United States, down from the peak of 49% in 1987. In 1996 total vehicle exports were 3.7 million units, of which 1.1 million units or 30% went to the U.S.

To soften the impact of the VER and to reduce trade frictions, Japanese automakers have increasingly produced and exported higher priced luxury models to the United States. More importantly, they have set up factories in North America and Europe for local production. Honda

Table A.4
Exports to and production in the United States by Japanese automakers (in 1,000 vehicles)

Year	Exports to the United States	Production in the United States
1986	3,434	426
1987	3,085	589
1988	2,696	628
1989	2,430	832
1990	2,237	1,307
1991	2,076	1,307
1992	1,773	1,490
1993	1,617	1,653
1994	1,643	1,934
1995	1,228	2,110
1996	1,098	2,194

Source: Japan Automobile Manufacturers Association.

pioneered in U.S. production in 1982, followed by Nissan (1983), Toyota (1984), Mazda (1987), Mitsubishi (1988), and Subaru-Isuzu (1989). As a result, local production in the U.S. by Japanese automakers rose rapidly from 0.4 million units in 1986 to 2.32 million units in 1996, which was double the 1.1 million vehicles exported from Japan to the U.S. in 1996 (see table A.4). Japanese automakers' **direct overseas investment** has attracted Japanese auto part producers to follow them in order to supply them overseas, touching off foreign criticisms of Japanese companies as extending their exclusionary group business relationships abroad.

In Europe, Toyota and Mitsubishi made capital investment in Portugal as early as 1968 and 1972, respectively. Nissan first produced passenger cars in Britain in 1986. Enticed by the prospect of a united Europe in 1992, Honda and Toyota have also set up plants in Britain to produce cars. In 1991 MITI also agreed with the European Community to limit Japanese auto exports to it to 1.23 million units a year until the end of 1999, but Japanese brand automobiles produced in the EC will not be included in the restrictions. In return the European Community will fully liberalize its auto market by the year 2000.

The automobile industry is the second largest industrial sector of the Japanese economy, after electrical machinery and equipment. Auto and auto parts constituted about 21% of Japan's total exports in 1991. The industry as a whole, including manufacturing, sales and repair services, and gasoline stations, employed over 5.6 million people, more than 10% of the total work force. Many industries, including auto parts, electrical machinery, general machinery, foodstuffs, chemical, iron, and steel, contribute to the production of automobiles.

Japanese automobiles are sold domestically through the manufacturers' sales networks that mostly sell the makers' particular models. According to its American critics, this has inhibited the sales of foreign cars; hence Japan's imports of foreign autos has remained limited—only 187,230 vehicles in 1992, of which 44,386 came from the United States and 140,759 from Western Europe. In 1996 total vehicle imports were 454,108 units, of which 143,920 came from the United States and 289,198 from the European Union. Japanese automakers attribute the small imports of American cars to U.S. automakers' insufficient effort to produce quality products and to adapt to local conditions (e.g., changing the driver's seat to the right). In January 1992, with continuing imbalance in Japan–U.S. trade and recession in the United States, President George Bush visited Japan in an effort to increase American access to the Japanese market. In response Japanese officials, as well auto executives, promised to step up their imports of American autos and auto parts. In late 1994 a Toyota dealer in the Tokyo metropolitan area started marketing Ford vehicles through a subsidiary, becoming the first Toyota-affiliated dealer to do so.

See also **just-in-time system, trade pattern, trade policy**.

Addresses

Honda Motor Co.
1-1, Minami Aoyama 2-chome, Minato-ku, Tokyo 107
Tel: (3) 3423-1111   Fax: (3) 3423-0511

Japan Automobile Manufacturers Association
6-1, Otemachi 1-chome, Chiyoda-ku, Tokyo 100
Tel: (3) 3216-5771   Fax: (3) 3287-2072

Japan Automobile Manufacturers Association, Washington Office
1050 17th Street, NW, Washington, DC 20036
Tel: (202) 296-8537   Fax: (202) 872-1212
Internet: http://www.japanauto.com

Mitsubishi Motor Co.
33-8, Shiba 5-chome, Minato-ku, Tokyo 108
Tel: (3) 3456-1111   Fax: (3) 3456-2649

Nissan Motor Co.
17-1, Ginza 6-chome, Chuo-ku, Tokyo 014
Tel: (3) 3543-5523   Fax: (3) 3543-5941

Toyota Motor Corp.
1, Toyota-cho, Toyota City, Aichi Prefecture
Tel: (565) 28-2121   Fax: (565)-23-5708

References

Clark, Kim B., and Takahiro Fujimoto. 1991. *Product Development Performance: Strategy, Organization, and Management in the World Auto Industry.* Boston: Harvard Business School Press.

Cusumano, Michael A. 1988. Manufacturing innovation: Lessons from the Japanese auto industry. *Sloan Management Review* 30: 29–39.

Cusumano, Michael A. 1989. *The Japanese Automobile Industry: Technology and Management at Nissan and Toyota.* Cambridge: Council on East Asian Studies, Harvard University.

Garrahan, Philip, and Paul Stewart. 1992. *The Nissan Enigma: Flexibility at Work in a Local Economy.* London: Mansell.

Japan Automobile Manufacturers Association. Annual. *Motor Vehicle Statistics of Japan.*

Japan Automobile Manufacturers Association. Annual. *The Motor Industry of Japan.*

Mutoh, Hiromichi. 1988. The automotive industry. In *Industrial Policy of Japan,* ed. by R. Komiya, M. Okuno, and K. Suzumura. Tokyo: Academic Press Japan.

Sako, Mari. 1996. Suppliers association in the Japanese automobile industry: Collective action for technology diffusion. *Cambridge Journal of Economics* 20, November.

Toyoda, Tatsuro. 1994. The strength of the Japanese auto industry. *Japan Echo* 21, 2: 19–22.

Yasuhiko, Shibata. 1995. Japan's changing automotive industry. *Journal of Japanese Trade and Industry,* no. 1: 19–21.

B

Bank of Japan The Bank of Japan was founded in 1882 as the nation's central bank. It was reorganized in 1942 when Japan's wartime military government enacted the Bank of Japan Law, giving the cabinet control over the central bank. In 1949 the Policy Board was established as the highest decision-making body of the Bank, but government influence over the Bank continued. In 1997 the Bank of Japan Law was revised for the first time to give BOJ more independence from the government.

As with any other central bank, the Bank of Japan's objectives are to regulate money and the **money markets**, and to ensure the stable development of the economy. Its functions include the following:

1. As the only bank of issue, it issues banknotes. The maximum issue limits for banknotes is determined by the minister of finance after consultation with the Cabinet Council, but excess issues may be made for a short period of time if the Bank deems it necessary. Issues of banknotes must be backed by assets (gold and silver bullion, government bonds, commercial bills, loans, etc.) of equivalent value.

2. The Bank of Japan is a bank for financial institutions. As such, it accept deposits from them, discounts commercial bills, makes loans on bills, buys and sells securities and bills, serves as the settlement institution for transactions among banks, and so on.

3. The Bank intermediates between the government and the private sector. All government receipts and payments are made through balances of government deposits at the Bank. The Bank can extend short-term (less than one year) loans to the government and underwrites or subscribes to government bills. The Bank is prohibited by the Finance Law of 1947 to extend long-term loans to the government or to underwrite government bonds with maturity of greater than one year. The Bank also acts as the government's agent in various types of businesses such as the issue,

redemption, interest payment of government bonds, and intervention in the foreign exchange market as agent for the Ministry of Finance.

An unconventional and unexpected operation was performed by the BOJ in 1997. In November 1997, Yamaichi Securities Co. and three other financial institutions collapsed due to mismanagement and mounting bad debt. That was unprecedented in Japan's postwar history and seriously eroded the public's confidence in the financial system. To prevent further erosion of confidence and because Japan's **deposit insurance system** was inadequate to cope with the unprecedented situation, the BOJ was authorized to make unsecured emergency loans to enable failing financial institutions to return assets to depositors. At the end of November 1997, the BOJ had ¥3.8 trillion in such loans outstanding (*Nikkei Weekly*, December 29, 1997: 15).

The Policy Board is the highest decision-making body of the Bank. Before April 1, 1998, it was composed of seven members: the governor of the Bank of Japan, four appointed representatives from the private sector (one each from city banks, regional banks, commerce and industry, and agriculture) and two representatives of the government (one each from the **Ministry of Finance** and the **Economic Planning Agency**). The governor was appointed by the prime minister with the consent of both houses of the Diet. The Board has broad jurisdiction over the official discount rate, open-market operations, reserve requirements, and regulation of main market interest rates. However, the Bank itself was not completely independent of the government. Where the Bank and the Ministry of Finance differed on monetary matters, more often than not the Ministry prevailed.

Effective April 1998, under the revised Bank of Japan Law, the BOJ is given more autonomy through various provisions. The Policy Board consists of nine members, six outside financial and economic specialists and three BOJ officials (the governor and the two deputy governors). The Ministry of Finance and the Economic Planning Agency each sends a representative to board meeting, but these officials have no voting power. The BOJ governor will continue to be appointed by the prime minister, subject to Diet approval. However, the government can no longer fire BOJ governor and vice governor due to policy differences; it can do so only if laws on banks statutes have been violated.

The Policy Board is the final authority on monetary policy. Where differences arise between BOJ and the government, government representatives can ask the Board to postpone its resolutions. The final decision, however, rests with the Board.

The main policy objective of the Bank is price stability, which is regarded as the prerequisite for the objectives of stable employment and growth. In addition equilibrium in the balance of payments is considered important. In terms of monetary policy, the call rate is considered the most important direct target of the Bank's policy (Ueda 1993; see **call money markets**). The policy instruments used by the Bank to pursue its objectives are similar to those of other central banks as outlined below:

1. *The official discount rate.* This is the interest rate on the Bank's discount and loans to client financial institutions. Changes in the discount rate influence the other interest rates in the short-term money market, thereby affecting the cost of raising funds by financial institutions through the lending by the Bank of Japan and in the money market. Changes in the discount rate also serve to signal the Bank's view of the economy and the changes deemed necessary, and are taken seriously by the business community.

2. *Open-market operations.* The Bank buys and sells securities and bills in the financial markets directly, thereby affecting liquidity in the financial system. Open-market operations are also conducted with a view to influencing market interest rates. In April 1996 a new **repo market** was established in Japan in which government bonds are lent for a fixed period for a fee and cash collaterial. In late 1997 the Bank of Japan started using this market as an important instrument to influence the market interest rates.

3. *Reserve deposit requirement.* Financial institutions have to deposit, with no interest, a certain percentage of their liabilities with the Bank of Japan. Changes in the required reserve ratio thus affect their ability to extend loans. The reserve ratio varies with the type of financial institution and the type of deposit.

4. *Window guidance (madoguchi shido).* Started in 1954 and abolished in July 1991, this is the guidance or "moral suasion" issued quarterly by the Bank to its client financial institutions, particularly **city banks**, to keep their lending within certain limits. The guidance varied with financial conditions but was usually more important when the Bank pursued a tight money policy. It is considered to have been effective before the late 1970s in supplementing the other monetary instruments. However, its role had since declined because the 1980 revision of the Foreign Exchange Control Law and the **financial liberalization** of the 1980s have given corporations alternative sources of funds. Hence the Bank of Japan decided to discontinue its use of window guidance.

See also **call money markets, interest rate structure, Ministry of Finance, money supply.**

Address

Bank of Japan
2-1, Nihonbashi Hongokucho 2-chome, Chuo-ku, Tokyo 103
Tel: (3) 3279-1111
Internet: www.boj.go.jp/

References

Cargill, Thomas F., and Michael M. Hutchinson. 1991. The Bank of Japan's response to elections. *Journal of the Japanese and International Economies* 5: 120–39.

Federation of Bankers Associations of Japan. 1994. *The Banking System in Japan*. Tokyo: Zenginkyo. Ch. 1.

Fukuda, Shinichi. 1995. The founding of the Bank of Japan and the changed behavior of interest rates and inflation rates. *Journal of the Japanese and International Economies* 9: 56–74.

Nakao, Masa'oki, and Akinari Horii. 1991. The process of decision-making and implementation of monetary policy in Japan. *Bank of Japan Special Paper*, no. 198.

Suzuki, Yoshio, ed. 1987. *The Japanese Financial System*. Oxford: Oxford University Press. Ch. 6.

Ueda, Kazuo. 1993. A comparative perspective on Japanese monetary policy: Short-run monetary control and the transmission mechanism. In *Japanese Monetary Policy*, ed. by Kenneth J. Singleton. Chicago: University of Chicago Press.

Tatewaki, Kazuo. 1991. *Banking and Finance in Japan*. London: Routledge. Ch. 12.

Werner, Richard. 1996. How the Bank of Japan won its battle for independence. *The Asian Wall Street Journal*, weekly edition, November 18: 12.

bankers' acceptance (BA) market The market in which yen-denominated bills of exchange, guaranteed by banks, are traded.
   See **money markets.**

Banking Act, 1982 The first comprehensive revision of banking legislation since 1927, this act permits banks to sell and deal in **government bonds**. Another major provision concerns disclosure requirements for banks.

   The provision for banks to deal in government bonds was a logical step and an important milestone in the evolution of Japan's postwar financial system. Since 1965 when the government was permitted by a special one-year law to engage in deficit financing, government deficits have increased steadily in Japan. Initially, when the amount of deficit was small, the **Ministry of Finance** raised the funds by issuing primarily long-term bonds at low-interest rates. The bonds were held by banks for one year, after which the **Bank of Japan** was willing to buy back 90% of the bonds from the banks. Only security firms were authorized to deal in government bonds. Banks were not interested in them because they felt that customers would merely shift funds from deposits into government bonds.

In the early 1970s government deficits and bonds increased rapidly due to the oil crisis. By the late 1970s the Bank of Japan was reluctant to buy back from banks large quantities of bonds for fear of inflationary increases in money supply. The banks, on the other hand, were not willing to hold large volumes of government bonds at low interest rates without being able to trade them. Consequently years of debate culminated in the new banking act, which has permitted banks to sell government bonds over the counter since April 1983 and to deal in government bonds in the securities market since June 1984.

See also **government bonds**.

Reference

Rosenblush, Frances M. 1989. *Financial Politics in Contemporary Japan*. Ithaca: Cornell University Press. Ch. 4.

banking regulation and deregulation   Japan's **banking system** in the postwar period has been closely regulated by the **Ministry of Finance** and the **Bank of Japan**, particularly before the mid-1970s, in various areas such as interest rates, types of services permitted, the types of financial instruments permitted, limit on loans to a single party, and capital adequacy requirement. The regulations were mainly enacted to attain stability in the system and to channel low-cost funds to different sectors of the economy.

Stability in the system is considered so important that no Japanese banks had been allowed to fail prior to November 1996; the typical solution for ailing banks was merger. Analysts have described commercial banking as a protective "convoy escort system" in which all banks move in tandem at the speed of the slowest members. It was not until the second half of the 1990s when the economy remained depressed after the bursting of the **bubble economy** in 1990 that the government decided that market forces should play the dominant role in the financial system and that weak banks should be allowed to fail.

An important area of banking regulation is the capital adequacy requirement. Because interest rates were regulated until recent years, banks had to depend on expansion in asset quantity to increase their earnings, and hence they competed with each other in asset expansion. In addition, since bank bankruptcy was nonexistent before 1996, they had little incentive to expand their equity capital. Between April 1, 1982, and May 23, 1986, although the Ministry of Finance required Japanese banks to maintain a capital ratio of 10% (the ratio being defined as that between capital and the balance of deposits plus CDs), the actual ratio maintained was much lower than that. On May 23, 1986, the required capital ratio was lowered to 4% (the ratio being defined as that between capital and total assets). For banks with overseas branches, 70% of their "latent" or "hidden" capital (i.e., the difference between market and book value of securities holdings) was added to their capital in the calculation, and the required capital ratio was 6% (Sasaki 1992: 185).

The situation changed after the Basle Agreement of 1988 (Basle Committee on Banking Regulations and Supervisory Practices) in which the rules of the Bank of International Settlement (BIS) required banks engaged in international finance to attain a capital/asset ratio of 8% by March 31, 1993. (However, BIS rules permit Japanese banks to include 45% of their latent capital in the capital). It was after the agreement that Japanese banks had to strive to raise their capital ratio. At first they relied on equity financing. After early 1990, falling share prices made equity financing virtually impossible; the latent capital of the banks was also greatly reduced. Many banks had to curtail risky loans and raise funds through subordinated loans, primarily from life insurance companies.

During the the **bubble economy** of the late 1980s, banks lent heavily to real estate business, which helped fuel the land-property speculation. For example, at the end of March 1987, outstanding bank loans extended to the real estate industry was as high as 32.7% of total loans outstanding. In the wake of the bursting of the bubble, a new regulation was belatedly introduced in 1990 to restrict banks' property-related lending. Partly as a result, outstanding real estate loan ratio declined from 15.3% of total loans outstanding at the end of March 1990 to 0.3% at the end of March 1991.

Regulation of the banking system is only one aspect of the broader regulation of the entire financial system by the Ministry of Finance. On the basis of the Securities and Exchange Act, the Ministry separates banking and securities services by prohibiting banks from offering securities services and securities firms from offering banking services. This began to change in the early 1990s as part of the broader **financial liberalization**.

Because of the failure of the Ministry of Finance to adequately oversee the banking system and prevent its mismanagement, a new Financial Supervision Agency was established in June 1998 under the Prime Minister's Office as part of the broader financial reform ("**Big Bang**") to supervise bank operations. The capital adequacy requirement remains at 8% of total assets for banks with international operations, as required by the Bank of International Settlement. For banks with only domestic operations, the minimum capital requirement is 4%.

As discussed in **financial liberalization**, various domestic and international changes in the 1970s and 1980s have led to the gradual deregulation of the financial system. Major deregulation of the banking system includes the following:

1. *Interest rate deregulation.* In the 1980s interest rates were gradually deregulated on many types of deposits, and the minimum amount of deposits required for market rates was lowered successively. In June 1993 interest rates on time deposits were deregulated. In October 1993 interest rates on nontime deposits were deregulated.

2. *Reduction in banking segmentation.* One result of regulation is that the banking system is highly segmented; different types of banking institutions are permitted to serve different sectors and different needs of the economy. Thus **city banks** specialize in short-term loans, **long-term credit banks** specialize in long-term development loans, and **trust banks** specialize in trust business, and so on. Changes in this respect include the following: (a) In 1989 the former *sogo* banks (mutual banks) were allowed to convert themselves into 66 second-tier regional banks. (b) Mergers took place within different categories of banking institutions such as city banks, *shinkin* **banks**, and **agricultural cooperatives**. (c) In October 1993 the Bank of Tokyo (now Bank of Tokyo-Mitsubishi), the only city bank that specialized in foreign exchange business, was permitted to enter trust-banking business through a new subsidiary. (d) In 1994 to 1996 several other city banks, one long-term credit bank (Industrial Bank of Japan), and the Norinchukin Bank were permitted to enter trust banking.

3. *Reduction in the barriers between banking and securities businesses.* On the basis of the Securities and Exchange Act, the Ministry of Finance separated banking and securities services by prohibiting banks from offering securities services and securities firms from offering banking services. Effective April 1993 banks and securities firms are allowed to establish subsidiaries for securities and banking business, respectively.

Foreign banks are traditionally subject to more stringent regulations in Japan. As part of the financial liberalization, more foreign banks and other financial institutions have been admitted into Japan as Japanese banks expanded their presence abroad.

See also **banking system, financial liberalization.**

Addresses

Bank of Japan
2-1, Nihonbashi Hongokucho 2-chome, Chuo-ku, Tokyo 103
Tel: (3) 3279-1111

Banking Bureau, Ministry of Finance
1-1, Kasumigaseki 3-chome, Chiyoda-ku, Tokyo 100
Tel: (3) 3581-4111

References

Crum, Colyer, and David Meerschwam. 1986. From relationship to price banking: The loss of regulatory control. In *America versus Japan*, ed. by Thomas McCraw. Boston: Harvard Business School Press.

Federation of Bankers Associations of Japan. 1994. *The Banking System in Japan*. Tokyo: Zenginkyo. Ch. 2.

Federation of Bankers Associations of Japan. Annual. *Japanese Banks*. Tokyo: Zenginkyo.

Marsh, Terry, and Jean-Michel Paul. 1996. BIS rules backfired in efforts to make banks safer. *Asian Wall Street Journal*, November 18: 13.

Oda, Hiroshi, ed. 1994. *Japanese Commercial Law in an Era of Internationalization*. London: Graham and Trotman/Martinus Nijhoff.

Sasaki, Toyonari. 1992. Bank Regulation. In *Capital Markets and Financial Serives in Japan*. Tokyo: Japan Securities Research Institute. Pp. 184–93.

banking system   Banks are financial institutions that accept deposits and extend loans. Japan's modern banking system, established after the Meiji restoration of 1868, is complex in its organizational structure. It is often described as segmented because it consists of many different categories of banks, each specializing by law in a different type of lending business. The system has been closely regulated by the **Ministry of Finance** and the **Bank of Japan**, especially before the mid-1970s when **financial liberalization** began to take place.

Excluding the Bank of Japan, which is the central bank, banks in the private sector are classified into two major categories: ordinary banks and specialized banks. Ordinary banks are the regular commercial banks,

Table B.1
Deposits and loans of banks and other deposit-taking financial institutions (in ¥ trillions)

	Deposits		Loans and discounts	
End of year	1992	1997	1992	1997
City banks	184.1	218.4	213.0	221.7
Regional banks	155.1	171.3	116.9	139.8
Regional banks II[a]	58.3	61.1	47.8	51.1
Foreign banks	1.6	9.3[b]	9.3	10.1[b]
Long-term credit banks	5.3	9.7	47.0	45.6
Trust banks	8.8	6.9	24.0	5.5
Credit cooperatives	22.9	21.8	18.3	17.0
Labor credit associations	8.2	2.6	4.3	0.2
Agriculture cooperatives	63.9	69.6	17.1	21.1
Norinchukin Bank	27.6	28.9	14.8	17.5

Source: Bank of Japan.
a. Members of the Second Association of Regional Banks.
b. 1996 figures.

which accept deposits, provide funds' transfer and short-term loans. They are further classified into three subcategories:

1. **City banks.** There are 10 city banks (13 before April 1990), which are the largest of Japanese commercial banks, and six of them are among the largest in the world in terms of assets. They have headquarters in the major cities, with over 3,200 branches all over the country. They receive a large share of all deposits, and have traditionally provided loans to big business, although consumer loans have increased in recent years. As shown in table B.1, at the end of 1997, city banks had outstanding loans of ¥221.7 trillion and deposits of ¥218.4 trillion, which are much larger than those of other banks. These figures do not include the activities of their branches in foreign countries. The largest city banks are Bank of Tokyo-Mitsubishi, Dai-ich Kangyo Bank, Sakura Bank, Sumitomo Bank, Fuji Bank, and Sanwa Bank.

2. *Regional banks.* There are 64 regional banks and 65 second-tier regional banks (i.e., former *sogo banks* that became members of the Second Association of Regional Banks in 1989). They are usually based in the principal city of a prefecture and conduct their operations mainly within that prefecture. Their clients tend to be local **small and medium enterprises**. As of December 1997 the 64 regional banks had a total of ¥171.3 trillion in deposits and ¥139.8 trillion in outstanding loans; the members of the

Second Association of Regional Banks had a total of ¥61.1 trillion in deposits and ¥51.1 trillion in outstanding loans.

3. *Foreign banks.* These are foreign bank branches in Japan with a license from the Ministry of Finance. At the end of 1996, there were 92 foreign banks with 145 offices in Japan; they had a total of ¥9.3 trillion in deposits, and ¥10.1 trillion in outstanding loans. All are heavily involved in foreign currency transactions.

Specialized banks and other deposit-taking institutions include the following:

1. **Long-term credit banks.** There are three banks in this category: the Industrial Bank of Japan, Long-Term Credit Bank of Japan, and Nippon Credit Bank. These banks specialize in long-term lending to promote industrial development. At the end of 1997, their deposits totaled ¥9.7 trillion, and outstanding loans were ¥45.6 trillion. In October 1998 the Long-Term Credit Bank of Japan was taken over by the government because of insolvency.

2. **Trust banks.** There are eight Japanese trust banks. They are engaged in pension and other trust fund management and administration, as well as in general banking activities. They provide loans to major corporations for long-term capital investment. The largest trust banks are Mitsubishi Trust & Banking, Mitsui Trust & Banking, Sumitomo Trust & Banking, and Yasuda Trust & Banking. At the end of 1997, their total deposits were ¥6.9 trillion, and total loans ¥5.5 trillion.

3. *Financial institutions for small and medium business.* These include *sogo* **banks** (mutual banks) until 1988, *shinkin* **banks** (credit associations), Zenshinren Bank (the national federation of *shinkin* banks), credit cooperatives, and labor credit associations. Credit cooperatives are financial institutions organized in the form of cooperatives to serve their members, who are owners and workers of **small and medium enterprises**. Their business consists primarily of taking deposits and installment savings from members and lending to members. At the end of 1997 credit cooperatives had a total of ¥21.8 trillion in savings and deposits and ¥17.0 trillion in loans and discounts. Labor credit associations accept deposits and make loans to promote the welfare activities of labor unions and consumer cooperatives. At the end of 1997, the labor credit associations had ¥2.6 trillion in deposits and ¥167 billion in loans and discounts.

4. *Financial institutions for agriculture, forestry, and fisheries.* Three levels of financial institutions exist to serve agriculture, forestry, and fisheries. At

the level of villages, towns, and cities, there are **agricultural coopera-tives**. They accept deposits from members and extend loans to members as well as nonmembers in the rural communities. They also market farm products and purchase farm equipment for their members. They belong to prefectural-level associations called *credit federations*. At the national level there is the Norinchukin Bank (*Norin chuo kinko*), the Central Cooperative Bank for Agriculture and Forestry. Its capital comes from subscription from private agricultural, forestry, and fishery organizations. Its funds are lent to subscribers and individuals engaged in agriculture, forestry, and fisheries and to corporations supplying equipment and facilities to agri-culture and forestry. It also invests its surplus funds in securities and in the interbank **money market** such as the **call money market**. As of end of 1997, Japan's 2,035 agricultural cooperatives had ¥69.6 trillion in deposits and ¥21.1 trillion in outstanding loans and discounts; the Norinchukin Bank had ¥28.9 trillion in deposits and ¥17.5 trillion in out-standing loans.

Government financial institutions are not deposit-taking institutions, but they supplement the activities of banks because they extend loans to the private sector. They include two government banks—the **Export-Import Bank** and the **Japan Development Bank**—which by law are engaged in export-importing finance and regional development, respec-tively. There are also nine public finance corporations that are established for specific purposes such as housing and small business finance. The **postal savings** system accepts deposits, which are channeled through the government **Fiscal Investment and Loan Program** to the two govern-ment banks and various **public corporations** as loans. Thus it is part of the government financial system.

The Federation of Bankers Associations of Japan (Zenginkyo) is the umbrella organization of 72 regionally based bankers' associations. It rep-resents the banking community vis-à-vis the government and the public; it operates interbank systems such as check clearing and domestic funds transfer, provides credit information at its Credit Information Center, and is engaged in research and publications.

The segmented nature of the banking system is the result of extensive government regulation; even bank deposits rates were regulated until 1994. During the rapid growth decades of the 1950s and 1960s, regula-tion served two pruposes: it ensured that the bulk of bank loans would go to growth industries at low cost and that other sectors of the economy (agriculture, small business, labor, etc.) would also have their modest shares of funds channeled from the savings of their own sectors. But with regulation also came protection—protection from competition and failures. Segmentation coupled with regulated interest rates means that banks would only face limited nonprice competition within their own segments. Until 1996 or 1997 the **Ministry of Finance** would also arrange rescue operations for failing banks. All of these impeded efficiency. In addition, given the importance of group ties and business relationships in the Japanese economy (as shown in the **main bank** system and **cross-shareholding**), the extension of loans is not always based on careful risk assessment. As a result Japanese banks generally have low profitability and low capital asset ratios.

Important structural changes have been taking place in the 1990s. As discussed in **banking regulation and deregulation** and **financial liberalization**, the segmentation of the banking system has been gradually reduced. In addition the barriers between banking and securities businesses have been reduced—banks and securities companies can establish subsidiaries to enter each other's business since 1993. Further deregulation of the banking system is planned by the government in its **Big Bang** financial reform. This will make the banking system more market oriented and competitive.

During the bubble years of the second half of the 1980s, many banks made too much real estate related loans when stock and land prices were excessively high due to speculative investment. The burst of the bubble economy in 1989 to 1990 led to great decline in stock and land prices, which in turn resulted in huge bad debts for many banks. A few banks have even gone bankrupt—the Hokkaido Takushoku Bank in November 1997 was the largest—which was unprecedented in Japan's postwar history. The financial conditions of the Japanese banking system in general has been greatly weakend. On the other hand, capital adequacy requirement has been increased by the Ministry of Finance.

In anticipation of the Big Bang and in light of their weakened financial status, most Japanese banks have been restructuring—to shed unprofitable operations, to reduce risky loans, to raise their capital-asset ratios, and in some cases to securitize their debts, to pursue mergers (as between the Bank of Tokyo and Mitsubishi Bank in 1996), or to form international alliances. The first case of international alliance is between the Long-Term Credit Bank of Japan and the Swiss Bank Corp in early 1998. They established three joint ventures, one each in investment banking, asset management, and private banking to provide integrated financial services.

This will combine the strengths of the two partners and will enable them to better compete in global financial markets. Analysts expect more cases of international alliances to follow.

See also **agricultural cooperatives, Bank of Japan, Banking Act of 1982, banking regulation and deregulation, city banks, financial liberalization, government financial institutions, long-term credit banks, Ministry of Finance, postal savings,** *shinkin* **banks,** *sogo* **banks, trust banks**.

Addresses

Federation of Bankers Associations of Japan
3-1, Marunouchi 1-chome, Chiyoda-ku, Tokyo 100
Tel: (3) 5252-3776   Fax: (3) 3214-3429

Regional Banks Association of Japan
1-2, Uchikanda 3-chome, Chiyoda-ku, Tokyo 100
Tel: (3) 3252-5171   Fax: (3) 3254-8664

The Second Association of Regional Banks
5, Sanbancho, Chiyoda-ku, Tokyo 101
Tel: (3) 3262-2181   Fax: (3) 3262-2339

References

Bank of Japan. Annual. *Economic Statistics Annual.*

Federation of Bankers Associations of Japan. 1994. *The Banking System in Japan.* Tokyo: Zenginkyo.

Federation of Bankers Association of Japan. Annual. *Japanese Banks, '97.* Tokyo: Zenginkyo.

Federation of Bankers Association of Japan. *Zenginkyo Financial Review.* Various issues.

Kitagawa, Hiroshi, and Yoshitaka Kurosawa. 1994. Japan: Development and structural change of the banking system. In *The Financial Development of Japan, Korea, and Taiwan*, ed. by Hugh Patrick and Yung Chul Park. New York: Oxford University Press.

Suzuki, Yoshio, ed. 1987. *Japanese Financial System.* Oxford: Oxford University Press. Ch. 5.

Tatewaki, Kazuo. 1991. *Banking and Finance in Japan.* London: Routledge. Ch. 7.

bankruptcies   In a market economy a certain number of business bankruptcies is inevitable. They can be regarded as a mechanism for the economy to reinvigorate itself, with efficient firms replacing inefficient ones. When the number of bankruptcies rises rapidly within a short period of time, however, there are likely to be other causes of bankruptcies in the economy, such as an oil crisis, sharp yen appreciation, tight business

Table B.2
Business bankruptcies

Year	Cases	Total liabilities (in ¥ billions)	Average liabilities (in ¥ millions)
1980	17,884	2,707	151.4
1984	20,841	3,626	174.0
1985	18,812	4,186	222.5
1986	17,476	3,752	214.7
1987	12,655	2,055	162.4
1988	10,123	2,059	203.4
1989	7,234	1,195	165.2
1990	6,468	1,944	300.6
1991	11,767	7,770	660.3
1992	14,167	7,563	533.8
1993	14,041	6,714	478.2
1994	13,963	6,500	465.5
1995	15,108	9,034	597.9
1996	14,544	7,994	549.6
1997	16,365	14,020	856.7

Sources: Teikoku Databank, Ltd. and Nikkei Economic Electronic Databank System.
Note: Figures include bankruptcies of corporations and unincorporated enterprises.

credit, a recession or depression. In these cases the number of bankruptcies can be regarded as an indicator of the economic difficulties in the overall economy or in some specific sectors.

There are different estimates of business bankruptcies in Japan, but they all show the same trend. Table B.2 shows some private estimates that are higher than official Bank of Japan figures. Bankruptcies during the 1980s reached a peak of more than 20,000 in 1984 but declined steadily afterward, reaching a low of 6,468 in 1990. In 1991 to 1992 the number rose rapidly and has been rising ever since. It reached a new peak of 16,365 in 1997, with record levels of total liabilities and average liabilities per bankruptcy (see table B.2).

Analysts commonly attribute the rising number of bankruptcies during the 1990s to the aftermath of the bursting of the **bubble economy** in 1990. During the bubble years in the second half of the 1980s, land and stock prices rose continuously due to speculative investments fueled by easy credit from banks and growing corporate funds. After the **stock market** crash in 1990, land and stock prices began to fall, and many banks found themselves saddled with large unrecoverable loans to construction and real estate firms that relied on land and stocks as collateral. As banks began to curtail loans to these sectors and to small businesses in order to reduce risks and restructure their operations, companies in these sectors became particularly vulnerable to failure. There are also other firms that failed because of their speculation in securities and land, not because of failures in their principal businesses.

References

Choy, Jon. 1998. Bankruptacies hi new record in 1997. *JEI Report* 4B, January 30: 6–8.

Isono, Naoyuki. 1991. Bankruptacies, liabilities hint at economic woe. *Japan Economic Journal*, February 23: 5.

Ostrom, Douglas. 1991. Bankruptcies continue rising in Japan. *JEI Report*, June 7, pt. B: 5–6.

Small-business bankruptcies mount as economic downturn takes toll. *Nikkei Weekly*, May 10, 1993: 1, 11.

Yokota, Hayato. 1992. Bankruptcy rise provoking lenders. *Nikkei Weekly*, February 8: 15.

Yokoyama, Kiho. 1998 Bankruptcies soar, showing wide shakeout. *Nikkei Weekly*, January 26: 1, 4.

Beef-Citrus Quotas Agreement, 1988   Until 1988 Japan's restrictive import quotas on beef and citrus had long been a source of trade dispute between the United States and Japan. In addition to quotas there were also regulations that constituted trade barriers. For example, only citrus products from California, but not from Florida, were permitted, and imported orange juice had to be blended with domestic tangerine juice. In April 1988, when a previous bilateral agreement on beef-citrus quotas expired and initial negotiations between Washington and Tokyo failed to reach an agreement, Washington filed charges with GATT that Japan violated GATT rules that prohibited agricultural quotas except under extraordinary circumstances such as the need to redress balance-of-payments deficits. At the same time Washington also urged Tokyo to negotiate further for an agreement that would dismantle the quotas, thereby obviating a lengthy GATT investigation.

The Japanese government, for domestic political reasons, initially preferred the dispute to be settled by GATT in order to avoid the appearance of giving in to the United States demand. However, an adverse GATT ruling could force Japan to compensate the United States for trade losses. Subsequently the Japanese government changed its position and resumed trade negotiations with the United States.

In June 1988 an agreement was reached between the two countries. It would permit U.S. beef producers to increase their exports to Japan annually by 60,000 metric tons over the next three years from the 1987 quotas of 214,000 metric tons and to replace the quotas in 1991 with tariffs. The tariff will start at 70% and gradually decline to 50% by 1993. The agreement would permit U.S. exports of citrus products to increase by 22,000 metric tons annually for three years; then the quotas would be abolished in 1991. During the three-year period exports from Florida would be allowed. The requirement that imported orange juice be blended with domestic tangerine juice would also be eliminated.

Evidence as of 1998 suggests that the lower-priced U.S. beef and citrus products have not inundated the Japanese market and hurt domestic producers in Japan.

Reference

MacKnight, Susan. 1988. Liberalization of Japan's beef and orange markets: Winners and losers. *JEI Report* 42A, November 4.

Big Bang   A term used since 1996 to refer to a program of wide-ranging financial reforms proposed by then Prime Minister Ryutaro Hashimoto on November 11, 1996, and to be implemented by 2001. The objective is to make Japan's financial markets "free, fair, and global" and to make Tokyo an international financial center on par with New York and London. The proposed reforms have been dubbed the "Japanese Big Bang."

The logic of the Big Bang is sound because a healthy and competitive financial system is the foundation of an efficient and competitive economy. The objective to make Tokyo a major international financial center will take time to achieve in view of the weakness of Japan's financial system in the late 1990s. The need for the Big Bang, however, is urgent, if only to revitalize the economy. After nearly two decades of slow-moving and piecemeal **financial liberalization**, Japan's financial sector in the late 1990s remains bureaucratically regulated, scandal-ridden, and heavily burdened with bad debts and losses that came from speculative investments in real estate and stocks during the **bubble economy** (1986–89). As a result the economy has suffered one of the longest recessions of the postwar era after the bubble burst in 1990.

The Diet has taken up Hashimoto's proposal, discussed extensively various areas of financial deregulation, and has passed some legislations. Furthermore, because deregulation will invariably reduce the need for regulators, and because some financial sector scandales have implicated high-level bureaucrats in the government, particularly the Ministry of Finance, the Diet has acted on another Hashimoto proposal, a broad **administrative reform** program. Various ministries, government agencies, and some public corporations are to be reorganized and streamlined by the year 2001.

The Big Bang formally began on April 1, 1998, and is to be completed by March 2001. The following shows some major changes that have already been introduced and others that are scheduled to take place:

December 1997	**Antimonopoly Law** revised to lift the ban on **holding companies**
March 1998	Financial institutions allowed to set up financial holding companies
April 1, 1998	Revised Foreign Exchange and Foreign Trade Control Law takes effect; free foreign exchange transactions permitted
June 1998	Financial Supervisory Agency established for rule-based financial supervision
In FY 1999	Banks to be allowed to issue straight bonds; securities companies free to set commissions; banks, trust banks, and securities companies free to enter one another's market
March 2000	Insurance companies free to enter banking sector
March 2001	Banks and securities companies free to enter insurance sector

If the whole program is implemented as scheduled, Japan's financial system should be greatly strengthened. There will be more market competition, including that from abroad, with the survivors becoming stronger and weak ones being weeded out. Ultimately it will be the consumers who will benefit. The Big Bang has been criticized for leaving out **postal savings** which constitutues a sizable part of domestic savings. However, the administrative reform is expected to deal with some of the related issues.

See also **banking regulation and deregulation, banking system, financial liberalization, foreign exchange control and decontrol, holding companies, postal savings.**

References

Big Bang special. *Japan Economic Almanac, 1998.* Pp. 6–57.

Choy, Jon. 1997. Financial market reform in Japan: Big Bang or just fizz? *JEI Report* 3A, January 24.

Choy, Jon. 1998a. Cabinet primes financial-market Big Bang. *JEI Report* 11B: 4–5.

Choy, Jon. 1998b. Japan's financial market Big Bang: The first shock waves. *JEI Report* 22A, June 12.

Ishibashi, Asako, Mosato Ishizawa and Makoto Sato. 1998. Big Bang marks start of survival race. *Nikkei Weekly*, March 30: 1, 3.

bill market   An interbank money market where bills are sold before maturity at a discount to obtain funds.

See **money markets**.

bond market   Bonds are debt instruments, that is, securities issued by government bodies and corporations to borrow money from investors. Japan's bond market developed only after the mid-1970s because of the rapid increase in government bond issues. It was then and still is dominated by government bonds. However, other types of bonds were issued and actively traded since the 1980s.

Bonds can be classified in different ways—in terms of the issuing body, collateral, linkage with equity, methods of redemption, maturity, methods of interest payment, and so forth. The following system is commonly used to classify the major types of bonds:

1. *Public bonds.* These include **government bonds** issued by the national government, local government bonds, and public corporation bonds. Local government bonds are issued by the prefectural or municipal governments. Public corporation bonds are issued for specific purposes; the bulk are government guaranteed and called *government-guaranteed bonds.* The issuance of government bonds (excluding a small amount of foreign currency bonds) increased rapidly after 1975 following the first oil crisis. The outstanding balance was ¥244.7 trillion at the end of FY 1996. Outstanding local government bonds totaled ¥38.8 trillion at the end of FY 1996 and public corporation bonds stood at ¥23.1 trillion at the end of FY 1996 (see table B.3).

2. *Bank or financial debentures.* These are bonds issued by long-term credit banks (the Industrial Bank of Japan, the Long-Term Credit Bank of Japan, and the Nippon Credit Bank), the Bank of Tokyo-Mitsubishi, the Norin-

Table B.3
Outstanding amounts of public and corporate bonds (end of FY; in ¥ trillions)

	1985	1991	1996
Government bonds	134.4	173.7	244.7
Local government bonds	20.8	19.6	38.8
Government guaranteed bonds	16.4	19.7	23.1
Bank debentures	43.5	74.4	74.4
Corporate straights bonds[a]	9.5	14.9	30.8
Convertible bonds[b]	4.6	17.0	19.5
Foreign bonds in yen	5.4	6.3	12.3

Source: Bank of Japan.
a. Domestic flotation only.
b. Includes the amount converted to stocks.

chukin Bank, the Shoko Chukin Bank, and the Zenshinren Bank. These financial institutions are authorized to issue bank debentures by specific laws because of the long-term nature of their lending or the specialized nature of their operations. There are two types of bank debentures: interest-bearing bank debentures and discount bank debentures. Their outstanding balance was ¥50 trillion and ¥24.4 trillion, respectively, at the end of FY 1996.

3. *Corporate straight bonds.* Corporate bonds are issued by private companies other than financial institutions. They are divided into corporate straight bonds, convertible bonds, and warrant bonds. Straight bonds are ordinary corporate debt instruments that do not have special provisions for bondholders to become shareholders, as convertible and warrant bonds do (see below). At the end of FY 1996, there was ¥30.8 trillion outstanding.

4. *Convertible bonds.* These bonds can be converted into stocks under certain conditions. Because of this advantage to investors, the bonds can be issued with lower cupon rates or at lower initial costs than straight corporate bonds. They are less risky to investors than stocks. At the end of FY 1996, there was ¥19.5 trillion outstanding.

5. *Warrant bonds.* These corporate bonds give bondholders the right to subscribe to new shares of the company at a predetermined price during a specified period. They differ from convertible bonds in that the warrant can be detached from the underlying bond and traded separately. Domestic issues of warrant bonds have not been significant. However, warrant bonds issued by Japanese corporations on the Euromarket have been

bought by Japanese investors and traded in the **over-the-counter markets** in Japan.

6. *Yen-denominated foreign bonds.* Popularly called *samurai* **bonds**, these are issued by nonresident institutions in Japan such as international agencies, foreign governments, and foreign private corporations. First introduced in 1970 when the Asian Development Bank issued such bonds in Japan, the outstanding balance was ¥12.3 trillion at the end of FY 1996. *Samurai* bonds should be distinguished from *shogun* bonds which are foreign-currency-denominated bonds issued by nonresident institutions such as the European Investment Bank and the World Bank. The amount issued has been small.

When a bond—public or corporate—is offered publicly for subscription by a large number of unspecified investors, underwriters normally organize a syndicate, consisting of various banks and **securities companies**, for the purpose of underwriting and publicly offering such issue on the open market. However, short-term treasury bills and medium-term notes that are distributed by means of competitive bids do not require underwriting. Financial debentures are issued through public sales and do not require an underwriting syndicate for their distribution. Corporate bonds that are privately placed are sold exclusively to specific institutions such as banks and life insurance companies and do not require underwriting.

Trading on the bond market was active throughout the 1980s, with government bonds dominating the trading volume. Bonds are traded on the securities exchanges and over-the-counter (OTC) markets. The latter accounted for the bulk of the trading volume (see table B.4). In the early 1990s the trading volume of bonds on the stock exchanges sharply declined following the bursting of the bubble economy. It has remained at low levels ever since, though the trading volume on the OTC markets has been relatively stable. Securities companies are the principal participants in the OTC markets as dealers, holding large inventories of bonds. Other major traders in the bond market are **trust banks, insurance companies, investment trusts**, and commercial banks. More than one-third of the OTC trade is in the form of *gensaki* transactions (i.e., repos, or transactions with repurchase agreement between a company seeking to invest its surplus funds in short-term investment and another in need of short-term funds).

In 1989 the over-the-counter markets started to offer cash-settlement bond options. The bond market was expanded further in May 1990 with

Table B.4
Total trading volume of bonds in Tokyo

	1987	1990	1996
Tokyo Stock Exchange (in ¥ billions)			
Government bonds	56,918	37,921	5,497
Convertible bonds	50,453	19,842	13,245
Warrant bonds	416	1	0
Foreign bonds in yen	88	12	8
Others	24	13	0.5
Total	107,899	57,787	18,881
OTC Markets (in ¥ trillions)			
Gensaki trade[a]	1,217	1,106	1,695
Total	5,544	3,360	3,183

Sources: Tokyo Stock Exchange; Securities Dealers Associations of Japan.
a. Transactions with repurchase agreements or "REPOS."

the introduction at **Tokyo Stock Exchange** of bond futures options. This helped to upgrade Tokyo's bond market with its diversity of bond instruments, including cash bonds, futures, cash-settlement options, and futures options.

Japan has three bond-rating organizations that carry out ranking (AAA, AA, etc.) of bonds and provide the information to investors. They are Japan Bond Research Institute (JBRI), Japan Credit Rating Agency Ltd., and Nippon Investors' Service. They were all established in 1985. JBRI is the largest. In addition to rating domestic bonds and yen-denominated external bonds, these organizations conduct research on both foreign and domestic financial, economic, and corporate information.

See also **government bonds, over-the-counter market, securities companies, Tokyo Stock Exchange, warrant bonds**.

Addresses

Bond Underwriters Association of Japan
5-8, Nihonbashi Kayabacko 1-chome, Chuo-ku, Tokyo 103
Tel: (3) 3667-2431

Japan Bond Research Institute
6-1, Nohonbashi Kayabacho 2-chome, Chuo-ku, Tokyo 103
Tel: (3) 3639-2840 Fax: (3) 3639-2848

Japan Securities Dealers Association
5-8, Nihonbashi Kayabacho 1-chome, Chuo-ku, Tokyo 103
Tel: (3) 3667-8451

References

Bank of Japan. Annual. *Economic Statistics Annual.*

Elton, Edwin, and Martin J. Gruber, eds. 1990. *Japanese Capital Markets.* New York: Harper and Row.

Fabozzi, Frank J. ed. 1990. *The Japanese Bond Markets: An Overview and Analysis.* Chicago: Probus.

Horiuchi, Akiyoshi. 1996. An evaluation of Japanese financial liberalization: a case study of corporate bond markets. In *Financial Deregulation and Integration in East Asia,* ed. by Takatoshi Ito and Anne O. Krueger. Chicago: University of Chicago Press.

Japan Securities Research Institute. 1998. *Securities Market in Japan, 1998.* Ch. 4.

Tokyo Stock Exchange. Annual. *Tokyo Stock Exchange Fact Book.*

Yamashita, Takeji. 1989. *Japan's Securities Markets: A Practioners' Guide.* Singapore: Butterworths. Chs. 6–7.

Ziemba, William T., and Sandra L. Schwartz. 1992. *Invest Japan.* Chicago: Probus. Ch. 1.

bond-futures options
See **bond market**.

bond-rating organizations
See **bond market**.

bonuses
See **wage structure**.

bubble economy   A term frequently used in the 1990s to refer to the asset inflation, or the speculative and inflated wealth in securities and land in 1986–89 that contributed to the apparent but unsustainable prosperity during those years. The bubble is said to have burst in 1990 when the stock and property markets fell. As a result financial instituions incurred huge bad debts and losses, and the economy subsequently suffered one of the longest recessions in the postwar era.

See **banking system, business cycles, land use and policies, securities companies, stock market, Tokyo Stock Exchange**.

burakumin   Literally "hamlet people," these are Japan's untouchable caste who are discriminated against economically and socially because they are the descendents of *eta* (literally the dirty), people who worked as tanners or butchers, jobs considered "unclean" by traditional Japanese standards.

See **employment discrimination**.

Table B.5
References dates of business cycles (year-month)

Number	Trough	Peak	Trough	Expansion	Contraction
1		1951–6	1951–10		4 months
2	1951–10	1954–1	1954–11	27 months	10
3	1954–11	1957–6	1958–6	31	12
4	1958–6	1961–11	1962–10	42	11
5	1962–10	1964–10	1965–10	24	12
6	1965–10	1970–7	1971–12	57	17
7	1971–12	1973–11	1975–3	23	16
8	1975–3	1977–1	1977–10	22	9
9	1977–10	1980–2	1983–2	28	36
10	1983–2	1985–6	1986–11	28	17
11	1986–11	1991–4	1993–10	51	32
12	1993–10	mid-1997[a]			

Source: Economic Planning Agency.
a. Preliminary; author's interview, April 10, 1998, Economic Planning Agency.

business cycles The **Economic Planning Agency** of the Japanese government has officially identified twelve business cycles in Japan in the postwar period (see table B.5). The identification is based on macro-economic indicators in nine broad categories. Thus the identification of peaks and troughs of business cycles can be controversial and is not as clearcut as the U.S. approach, in which a decline in real GNP for two consecutive quarters constitutes a recession. It is typically determined by a committee of experts long after the event.

As in other industrialized market economies, Japan's business cycles vary greatly in duration. In addition specific cyclical changes (inventory cycles, equipment cycles, construction cycles) have combined with autonomous changes and external shocks (technological progress, oil crisis, **yen shock**, Japan–U.S. trade frictions, etc.) to make all cycles multifaceted.

The salient characteristics of some of the cycles are as follows: (1) The expansion of November 1954–June 1957, named the *Jinmu Boom*, is attributed mainly to technological progress and world prosperity. The tight monetary policy adopted to deal with the resultant balance-of-payments deficit is considered to have triggered the subsequent recession. (2) The June 1958–December 1961 expansion, named the *Iwato Boom*, saw increases in equipment investment and personal consumption. Tight monetary policy to control the balance-of-payments deficit also caused the downturn. (3) The short-lived October 1962–October 1964 expansion, also called the *Olympics Boom*, is attributed to the easing of monetary policy and the construction boom for the 1964 Tokyo Olympics. (4) The October 1965–July 1970 expansion, named the *Izanagi Boom*, was the longest (57 months) in the postwar period. During the boom Japan became one of the world's leading exporters, and its balance of payments improved. Worldwide inflation and tight monetary policy brought an end to the boom. (5) The short expansion of December 1971–November 1973 was ended by the first oil crisis of fall 1973, which ushered in a long recession. (6) The economy recovered from the oil crisis during the March 1975–January 1977 expansion in response to appropriate fiscal and monetary adjustments. The rapid appreciation of the yen, however, brought about the downturn. (7) During the October 1977–February 1980 expansion, also called the *First Endaka* (high yen) *Boom*, the economy adjusted well to the higher yen and took advantage of the lower import cost of raw materials (in yen) and stable wages. However, the oil price increase and tighter monetary operation led to the longest postwar recession (36 months). (8) The expansion of February 1982–June 1985 benefited from the expansion of the U.S. economy, the increase in exports to the United States, low oil prices, and increases in domestic consumption and investment. (9) The expansion since November 1986, officially called the *Heisei Boom*, but commonly called the **bubble economy**, is one of the longest in the postwar period. It is based on a strong domestic demand due to increasing consumption, residential construction, and equipment investment and on the development of high value-added technologies and products. However, a large part of the domestic demand was made possible by easy credit and gains from speculation in land and stocks. When land and stock prices started to fall in 1990, a long and severe recession ensued. (10) Although the economy is officially dated to have entered the recovery/expansion phase in October 1993, the expansion was weak and the economy's growth rate low. This is due to the lingering aftermath of the bubble economy such as huge bad debts and losses suffered by financial institutions and other companies, and weak consumer demand. The peak of the anemic recovery is thought to have been reached in mid-1997 (author's interview, April 10, 1998, Economic Planning Agency), but the date has not yet been officially determined by the experts.

With the exception of the February 1980–February 1983 recession, all postwar recessions are much shorter than the expansionary phases of the business cycles. Thus, disregarding periodic fluctuations, the postwar Japanese economy is basically a dynamic and growth-oriented one.

To help forecast business cycles, the Economic Planning Agency has developed a series of business indicators for short-term forecasting and long-term analysis. The **Bank of Japan** also conducts business surveys and publishes indicators on business conditions.

See also **business-cycle indicators and forecasting**.

References

Boltho, Andrea. 1991. A century of Japanese business cycles: Did policy stabilize activity? *Journal of the Japanese and International Economies* 5, 3: 282–97.

Business Cycles in Japan and U.S.A. Monthly. Tokyo: Economic Planning Agency.

Chandler, Clay. 1991. Economy ties record length of expansion. *Asian Wall Street Journal Weekly*, September: 7.

Ito, T. 1990. The timing of elections and political business cycles in Japan. *Journal of Asian Economics* 1: 135–56.

Ito, Takatoshi. 1992. *The Japanese Economy*. Cambridge: MIT Press. Ch. 4.

Mizuno, Yuko. 1991. Executives less confident in economy. *Japan Economic Journal*, March 16: 1.

Shimizu, Yoshinori. 1997. Speculative bubbles, depression and the monetary policy in Japan. *Hitotsubashi Journal of Commerce and Management* 32: 23–58.

West, Kenneth D. 1992. Sources of cycles in Japan, 1975–1987. *Journal of the Japanese and International Economies* 6, 1: 71–98.

Yoshikawa, H., and F. Ohtake. 1987. Postwar business cycles in Japan: A quest for the right explanation. *Journal of the Japanese and International Economies* 1: 373–407.

business-cycle indicators and forecasting   There is a number of official business indicators that are developed to indicate business trends and help forecast business cycles. They include the following:

1. *Leading, coincident and lagging indicators.* The **Economic Planning Agency** (EPA) has selected 37 series of indicators that are sensitive to changes in business conditions and classified them into three categories: leading indicators (15), coincident indicators (14), and lagging indicators (8); this is based on the timing of changes in relation to overall changes in business cycles. The leading indicators tend to change before the overall changes in the economy. Hence they can help indicate economic conditions 6 to 9 months in advance. Coincident indicators tend to change as the overall economy changes and thus reflect the current state of the economy. Lagging indicators tend to lag behind in changes and thus reflect or confirm economic conditions 6 to 12 months earlier. It should be

pointed out, however, that the indicators are not foolproof for forecasting purposes. Some economists therefore do not have much confidence in them.

2. *Diffusion index.* This is an EPA index to indicate the overall direction of changes in the economy. To derive it, the current values of leading, coincident, and lagging indicators are compared with those three months earlier. The number of indicators that have increased is calculated as a percentage of the total number of indicators. That percentage number is the diffusion index. Thus when the diffusion index is over 50%, the economy is considered to be in an expansion. When it is less than 50%, the economy is considered to be in a contraction.

The **Bank of Japan** has a diffusion index or business-condition index to show the condition of the economy as seen by business managers. From its quarterly survey of a large number of enterprises in various sectors, the responses are sorted out into three groups: those who regard business conditions in their fields as "good," those who say "not so good," and those who say "bad." Discarding the second group, the business-condition index is obtained by subtracting the percentage of the "bad" replies from the percentage of the "good" replies. Thus, if the index is high and rising over time, a business expansion is indicated. If it declines, a contraction is indicated. The results are published in the Bank's *Tankan* (Short-Term Economic Outlook), a closely watched quarterly industrial survey.

The **Ministry of International Trade and Industry** also conducts a quarterly poll of companies in 19 industries, both manufactures and non-manufactures, to compile the diffusion index of business confidence. The index shows the percentage points of those companies seeing an improvement in business confidence minus those seeing a deterioration.

3. *Composite index.* This is an EPA index designed to measure the relative magnitude of cyclical changes. Using the average rate of change of the coincident indicators in the previous five years as the standard, the rates of change of the leading, coincident, and lagging indicators in each year are compared with that standard, and the differences are averaged and converted into index numbers.

The EPA, however, does not use any one single index to determine the duration of a business cycle, its trough and peak. A special committee is convened to examine a large number of indicators to determine such matters. It also utilizes macro and econometric models for forecasting purposes.

In the private sector there are various business and research institutes or "think tanks" such as Japan Economic Research Center and Nomura Research Institute that conduct their own analyses and make predictions about business trends in the economy. Nihon Keizai Shimpun, Inc., publisher of the leading business paper in Japan, publishes the results of its own survey as well as the forecasts made by some research institutes.

See also **business cycles; economic/business research and publications**.

Address

Economic Planning Agency
1-1, Kasumigaseki 3-chome, Chiyoda-Ku, Tokyo 100
Tel: (3) 3581-0261

References

Bank of Japan. Quarterly. *Short-Term Economic Outlook (Tankan)*.

Economic Planning Agency. Monthly. *Business Cycle in Japan and U.S.A.*

Economic Planning Agency. Quarterly. *Japanese Economic Indicators Quarterly*.

business ethics   Since the late 1980s and early 1990s, Japanese business ethics have come under attack, both at home and abroad. The criticisms stemmed from a number of sensational business scandals uncovered during the period. First, it was revealed in 1988–89 that the Recruit Company had bribed many **Liberal Democratic Party** officials for favors. In 1991 it was revealed that some large companies, banks, and securities houses had involvement with crime syndicates and that securities companies illegally compensated their big clients for investment losses. In 1997 several executives of Nomura Securities Co., Daiwa Securities Co., and Dai-Ichi Kangyo Bank were arrested for being involved in corporate payoffs to racketeers, which is a violation of the Commercial Code. These scandals caused an outrage in Japan and raised questions about Japanese business ethics. This was not the first time, however, that such questions were raised. Long before these incidents, business frictions between the Japanese and foreigners had led to recriminatory charges of "unethical" Japanese (and American) business behavior.

Objective observers would agree that no nation has a monopoly on ethics and high morality, and that scandals and unethical behavior are by no means unique to any society. Furthermore, because the ethical norms of a society are invariably rooted in its history and cultural background, what is ethical in one society may be unethical in another. Thus it is hazardous and often invalid to judge the ethical standards of a society with those of another. Nevertheless, scholars can legitimately compare the values and standards of different societies and attempt to understand the differences in terms of their different historical and cultural backgrounds. In addition they can legitimately assess the pros and cons of specific values in a given society, explore their appropriateness to changing circumstances and societal needs, and predict or suggest the direction of future changes.

Analysts who have studied frictions between Japanese and American companies in their business contacts have attempted to explain their behavioral differences in terms of several dichotomies or contrasts in social and business ethics. The first and most commonly mentioned dichotomy is between the Japanese "group orientation" and the American "self-orientation" or between groupism and individualism. The Japanese are said to place group interests above their self-interests, at least as an ideal. Consequently loyalty to the group, or its various forms (the family, the company, the corporate group, the bureaucratic elite, the nation, etc.), and reciprocal obligations and relationship between group members are considered paramount values. In business practices group loyalty and intragroup reciprocity are manifested in **lifetime employment**, corporate paternalism toward employees, a dedicated work force, union-management cooperation (see **labor-management relations**), **cross-shareholding** and reciprocal business ties, and a host of other arrangements to ensure that group members receive their "fair share" of benefits.

Unfortunately, group orientation also implies some extent of exclusivity, depending on the importance and cohesiveness of the particular group. Such exclusivity is manifested in subtle exclusion of, or blatant discrimination against, "outsiders," be they foreigners (*gaijin*, literally outside people), domestic rival groups, Korean residents who were born and raised in Japan, the handicapped Japanese, the Japanese outcast (*burakumin*), or Japanese women (in the context of corporate elite). This is the so-called *uchi*-versus-*soto* (inside-versus-outside) consciousness in which being an insider is crucial to almost any type of success. Seen in this light, it is not surprising that a corporate board of directors is typically made up of people who have worked their way up inside the company, not people appointed for their achievements in the outside world, as is the case in the United States. Nor is it paradoxical that Japanese businesses can be paternalistic toward their employees (or regular male

Japanese employees) and at the same time be indifferent toward philanthropy for society at large and rarely participate in local volunteer activities.

Another problematic aspect of group orientation is the pressure to conform. Yoshimura and Anderson (1997) have questioned or reinterpreted Japanese corporate loyalty, paternalism, and its family-like relations. They regard these as illusory, not being based on cultural values but merely the result of employees' conformity to group expectations. The Japanese people, they argue, conform to group expectations in order to avoid social embarrassment and ostracism. Consequently spontaneity is stifled and interpersonal or intergroup conflicts are hidden under surface harmony.

The group orientation of the Japanese is deeply rooted in Japan's historical experiences such as its long history of insular feudalism (late 1100s to the 1860s), the rise of militarism in the 1930s, and the hardships of the early postwar period. It is reinforced by its large homogeneous population and perhaps also by its compact area geographically separated from other countries. Furthermore it is consciously and continuously cultivated by companies through such activities/practices as entrance ceremonies, company songs and uniforms, company guest houses, and group recreation. Consequently the orientation has proved to be durable and may not change appreciably for a long time to come. On the other hand, some authors have suggested that it is already weakening among the young generation who have grown up in affluence and have not experienced the early postwar hardships. Miyanaga (1991) suggests that individualism is emerging in Japan, even among some entrepreneurs.

In any case some business practices that are group oriented have changed because of changing circumstances. For example, because of labor shortage midcareer job changes are no longer considered as evidence of disloyalty to the company. Exclusionary or collusive practices such as bid-rigging and price-fixing are increasingly regarded as unethical. These attitudinal changes are taking place since in the early 1990s because the Japanese society and economy have become more fluid and pluralistic, Japanese businesses have become global in scope, and foreign criticisms of exclusionary business practices have intensified. This does not mean, however, that the Japanese want to replace their traditional values wholesale with the Western values. The Japanese perceive America's social problems to be worsening and the Western culture itself as lacking in self-discipline (including work ethics and frugality) and in the sense of personal commitment. It is therefore not necessarily the model for the Japanese to emulate.

At the level of managerial rules for business operations and decision making, observers have pointed out that the Japanese tend to favor pragmatic "case-by-case" decision making on the basis of relationships and to follow bureaucratic **administrative guidance**, whereas the Americans tend to follow specific principles and laws and to resort to the legal framework. The Japanese rule gives decision makers flexibility but can degenerate into "situational ethics" that bend with the changing wind of financial interests and foreign pressures. Similarly, because administrative guidance is not based on specific laws or legal interpretations, it gives Japanese bureaucrats much discretion in steering the business community. However, it can be vague and arbitrary, so it is open to favoritism and other abuses. This does not mean that administrative guidance is necessarily rigid and control oriented. Some authors have pointed out that administrative guidance is rarely given in a uni-directional relationship based on bureaucratic power and control; suggestions from the business community are usually taken into account in the development and implementation of administrative guidance. Since Japanese bureaucrats themselves are not monolithic, they do not always agree on what guidance to give (see **administrative guidance**). Nevertheless, since the early 1990s a growing number of Japanese have come to agree with foreign critics that operational rules for Japanese businesses, including administrative guidance, should be made more "transparent." To what extent they should be reformed is not yet clear. The "principled" and legalistic approach of American corporate behavior has problems of its own and is not necessarily a model for the Japanese.

An important factor that affects management behavior is the nature of **corporate governance**. Many analysts have argued that, in the traditional Japanese style of corporate governance, there is inadequate internal corporate monitoring for several reasons: (1) Board directors are predominantly inside executives who tend to agree with the president. (2) Shareholders meetings are typically brief and perfunctory; shareholders are given little power and opportunity to check on corporate behavior. (3) **Cross-shareholding** and the **main bank** protect a firm from takeover and reduce the importance and "discipline" of the stock market and share prices to top management, and protect a firm from takeover. As a result management abuses of power may not be easily detected; managers often pay off extortionists who threaten to expose corporate scandals at shareholders meetings (see **underworld "businesses"**). Clearly corporate reform to strengthen internal monitoring is needed.

The best vehicle of change in business ethics in any society is invariably a well-informed general public. In the past some foreign critics have charged that the Japanese public is unduely influenced by the authorities to support government policies and big corporate interests. Whatever the validity of this charge, this does not seem to be the case in the 1990s. After the exposure of various cases of big business and government corruption, the Japanese public has become highly suspicious of any possible wrongdoing in high places, although arguably there is also a sense of resignation. The Federation of Economic Organizations (Keidanren), Japan's most important business organization, is aware of the public's changing mood and has initiated measures to restore the tarnished corporate image. For example, it drafted a "Keidanren Charter for Good Corporate Behavior" for corporate executives in 1991 to prevent the recurrence of financial scandals and corporate involvement with the underworld. Evidence to date suggests, however, that the new code of conduct has not been effective in influencing corporate behavior. Arguably it is the exposure and punishment of top executives who have violated the law that will be the most effective in deterring businessmen from wrongdoing. In this respect, arrests and prosecution of executives for corporate wrongdoing have increased in the 1990s.

In short, Japanese business ethics in terms of both operational rules and actual practices are not as diametrically opposed to their Western counterparts as they are often portrayed. Japanese business ethics are changing, just as some American business practices have been changing in response to changing circumstances. For these reasons Gundling (1991: 35) contends that Japanese and American business ethics should not be viewed as neat dichotomies; they are more accurately envisioned as "sets of contrasting cultural ideals embedded within a vast, interlocking web. We are different; we are the same; we overlap; they are our distant reflection." This author agrees with Gundling in this view.

See also **administrative guidance, corporate governance, employment discrimination, labor-management relations, management practices, Structural Impediments Initiative, underworld "businesses."**

References

Gundling, Ernest. 1991. Ethics and working with the Japanese: The entrepreneur and the "elite course." *California Management Review* 33, 3: 25–39.

London, Nancy R. 1990. *Japanese Corporate Philanthropy*. Oxford: Oxford University Press.

Miyanaga, Kuniko. 1991. The Creative Edge: *Emerging Individualism in Japan*. New Brunswick: Transaction Publishers. Chs. 1–2.

Morishita, Kaoru. 1997. Scandals put corporate culture on trial. *Nikkei Weekly*, June 23: 1, 4.

Ozaki, Robert. 1991. *Human Capitalism*. New York: Penguin. Ch. 5.

Prestowitz, Clyde V., Jr. 1988. *Trading Places*. New York: Basic Books. Ch. 3.

Sai, Yasutaka. 1995. *The Eight Core Values of the Japanese Businessman*. Binghamton, New York: International Business Press.

Sakai, Kuniyasu. 1990. The feudal world of Japanese manufacturing. *Harvard Business Review* 68, 6 (November–December): 38–49.

Schlosstein, Steven. 1991. Cracks in the Japanese monolith: A U.S. observer lists 12 political and social weaknesses. *Japan Times* (weekly international ed.), May 6–12: 8–9.

Seward, Jack, and Howard Van Zandt. 1985. *Japan: The Hungary Guest—Japanese Business Ethics vs. Those of the U.S.* Tokyo: Lotus Press.

Sheard, Paul. 1994. Interlocking shareholdings and corporate governance. In *The Japanese Firm: Sources of Competitive Strength*, ed. by Masakiko Aoki and Ronald Dore. Oxford: Oxford University Press.

Shimada, Haruo. 1991. The desperate need for new values in Japanese corporate behavior. *Journal of Japanese Studies* 17, 1 (Spring): 107–25.

Sullivan, Jeremiah J. 1992. Japanese management philosophies: From the vacuous to the brilliant. *California Management Review* 34, 2 (Winter): 66–87.

Yoshimura, Noboru, and Philip Anderson. 1997. *Inside the Kaisha: Demystifying Japanese Business Behavior*. Boston: Harvard Business School Press.

business groups
See *keiretsu* and **business groups**.

business organizations   Japan has four major business organizations, collectively known as *zaikai*. They represent the nation's businesses and top executives; they interact with politicians, bureaucrats, and labor groups and make policy recommendations on economic issues. They were particularly powerful between the 1950s and the mid-1970s when industrial development was the foremost goal of the nation. These four organizations are as follows.

1. *Federation of Economic Organization (Keidanren).* Founded in 1946, this is the largest and most influential business organization. Its members consist of 123 industrial associations and 1,012 companies as of July 1997. Its chairman is known unofficially as the "*zaikai* prime minister." It has 12 vice-chairmen and some 60 committees to focus on different aspects of the economy. Keidanren leaders are involved in economic policy dis-

cussions and make recommendations to the government and the ruling **Liberal Democratic Party**. Keidanren has long opposed the **Antimonopoly Law** and until September 1993 was responsible for channeling corporate contributions to the **Liberal Democratic Party**. For these reasons Uchihashi (1994) regards it as a "self-serving businessmen's mafia" that should be dissolved. Other critics have not gone that far but have often questioned the relevance of the organization.

2. *Japan Federation of Employers' Association (Nikkeiren)*. This is the second most important organization. Founded in 1948 by corporate leaders to deal with early postwar labor unrest, it has remained the organization that shapes Japan's corporate policy on organized labor and wage negotiations. It has some 30,000 enterprises as members; it advises them on labor-related issues.

3. *Japan Association of Corporate Executives (Keizai Doyukai)*. Founded in 1946, this is a forum for individual executives to express their personal views. Its membership consists of more than 1,500 executives.

4. *Japan Chamber of Commerce and Industry (Nissho)*. This organization represents small- and medium-sized enterprises. Founded in 1922, it comprises 515 local chambers of commerce and industry with a total of about 1.5 million members.

Although *zaikai* remains important in Japan, its influence is said to have declined since the mid-1970s partly because of the maturing and diversification of the economy. In recent years its image has also suffered because several of its leaders were tainted by financial scandals and had to resign from their corporate posts. Finally, critics have charged that *zaikai* elders, particularly Keidanren leaders, have failed to adapt to changing economic and social conditions of Japan.

In addition to the four major organizations mentioned above, Japan also has the following business organizations: Japan Junior Chamber, Inc.; Japan Overseas Enterprises Association; Japan Productivity Center; Small Business Corporation; Kansai Committee for Economic Development; Kansai Economic Federation (Kankeiren), and Japan External Trade Organization (JETRO). Kankeiren is western Japan's most powerful business organization. JETRO has more than ten overseas offices to promote trade with foreign countries. Initially set up by 1951 by business leaders in Osaka city, it was taken over in 1954 by the **Ministry of International Trade and Industry** (MITI). In 1958 it was transformed into a public corporation with funding from the central government. Initially it was to deal solely with promoting exports, but its role has expanded to include the furtherance of mutual understanding with trading partners, import promotion, and liaison between small businesses in Japan and their overseas counterparts. Finally, all major industries have organized their industry associations, and more than a dozen foreign countries have established their chambers of commerce in Japan.

Addresses

Federation of Economic Organizations
9-4, Otemachi 1-chome, Chiyoda-ku, Tokyo 100
Tel: (3) 3279-1411

Japan Association of Corporate Executives
4-6, Marunouchi 1-chome, Chiyoda-ku, Tokyo 100
Tel: (3) 3211-1271

Japan Chamber of Commerce and Industry
2-2, Marunouchi 3-chome, Chiyoda-ku, Japan 100
Tel: (3) 3283-7823

Japan External Trade Organization
2-5, Toranomon 2-chome, Minato-ku, Tokyo 105
Tel: (3) 3582-5511

Japan Federation of Employers' Association
8-1, Yuraku-cho 1-chome, Chiyoda-ku, Tokyo 100
Tel: (3) 3213-4474

Kansai Economic Federation
2-27 Nakanoshima 6-chome, Kita-ku, Osaka 530
Tel: (6) 441-0101

References

Fukuda, Takehiro. 1991. Weak leadership, scandal sap power of business old guard. *Nikkei Weekly*, November 2: 1.

Business Organizations. In *Japan Economic Almanac*. Various years. Tokyo: Nihon Keizai Shimbun.

Suzuki, Yumiko. 1996. Business groups cast about for new role. *Nikkei Weekly*, June 3: 2.

Uchihashi, Katsuto. 1994. Disband Keidanren. *Tokyo Business Today*, September: 30–34.

C

call loans Short-term loans made between financial institutions in the **call money market**.

See **call money market**.

call money market The call money market is at the center of Japan's interbank **money market**, which is a short-term financial market for lending and borrowing between financial institutions. Japan's three call markets are located in Tokyo, Osaka, and Nagoya.

City banks are the major borrowers of funds in the call market, accounting for 50% or more of total funds borrowed. Other major borrowers are regional banks and foreign banks. The major lenders are **trust banks**, which provided ¥15.7 trillion or about 41% of the average balance of ¥38.7 trillion of call loans in 1997. Other lenders are city banks, regional banks, the Norinchukin Bank, the Zenshinren Bank, and *shinkin banks*.

Call market transactions are intermediated by the **money market dealers**, the six *tanshi* companies. There have been a variety of call loans since 1955, classified on the basis of the loan period. Since 1985 uncollateralized loans have been added to the traditional collateralized loans. Currently there are overnight call loans (both collateralized and uncollateralized) and uncollateralized fixed-date loans with maturity of one week and one to three months.

Call rates, or the interest rates on call loans, have been free from government control since 1979. They reflect the supply and demand conditions of the short-term financial market. Call rates vary with type of call money as well as by season of the year as business activities, and hence the demand for money, vary seasonally. The rates on collateralized call money are slightly lower. The rate tends to be highest in December when year-end gift purchases and bonus payments are made.

According to Ueda (1993), the call rate is the most important direct target of the monetary policy of the **Bank of Japan**. The Bank uses its lending, open-market operations, and the discount rates to influence the call rate and, through it, other interest rates in the economy.

See also **Bank of Japan, interest rate structure, money markets**.

References

Bank of Japan. Annual. *Economic Statistics Annual.*

Hoshi, Takeo, David Scharfstein, and Kenneth J. Singleton. 1993. Japanese corporate investment and Bank of Japan guidance of commercial bank lending. In *Japanese Monetary Policy*, ed. by Kenneth J. Singleton. Chicago: University of Chicago Press.

Ueda, Kazuo. 1993. A comparative perspective on Japanese monetary policy: Short-term monetary control and the transmission mechanism. In *Japanese Monetary Policy*, ed. by Kenneth J. Singleton. Chicago: University of Chicago Press.

Yoshikawa, Hiroshi. 1993. Monetary policy and the real economy in Japan. In *Japanese Monetary Policy*, ed. by Kenneth J. Singleton. Chicago: University of Chicago Press.

cartels   A cartel is a formal arrangement or agreement among firms in an oligopolistic market to cooperate on price-fixing, maintaining market share, restricting output or imports, reducing industry capacity, and so forth. The purpose is to restrict competition and maintain profitability and market share. In postwar Japan there have been, for example, price cartels, import cartels, recession (or depression) cartels, rationalization cartels, and designated cartels.

A recession cartel is organized by firms of an industry facing reduced demand in a recession to reduce all firms' output by an agreed-upon percentage. The purpose is to avoid the bankruptcy of the weaker firms and the general debilitating effect on the industry if the firms had to compete for market share to survive. A rationalization cartel emphasizes the restructuring of a declining industry through industry capacity reduction, modernization, and/or reorganization. A designated cartel is formed in a designated declining industry to reduce industry capacity.

Although cartels are banned by Japan's **Antimonopoly Law** because they restrict competition, there are various exceptions provided for by numerous statutes. Cartels were first authorized by the 1953 Export and Import Trading Act, which allowed price cartels and import cartels. The 1953 revision of the Antimonopoly Law authorized recession cartels and rationalization cartels. The initiative in setting up a cartel is normally taken by the firms, but the consent of the Fair Trade Commission, which is responsible for implementing the Antimonopoly Law, is required. In implementing its industrial policy, the **Ministry of International Trade and Industry** (MITI) in the 1960s and 1970s sometimes permitted or even suggested the formation of cartels in order to restructure an industry or to reduce its capacity. In 1980, however, the oil company cartels established with its permission were found to be in violation of the Antimonopoly Law.

The revised Antimonopoly Law of 1953 permits a recession cartel (*hukyo karuteru*) in an industry when (1) a number of producers face bankruptcy because market prices are below the industry's average cost, and (2) the efforts of individual producers cannot resolve the crisis. Such a cartel can take joint actions to (1) restrict production, sales, and/or the utilization of existing capacity (e.g., by sealing machines), and (2) control product prices if production control is technically difficult (Sekiguchi 1994: 190–93).

Recession cartels were effective in raising prices in the 1950s and 1960s because the Japanese domestic markets were then protected from the external markets through import barriers. Consequently they were relatively common. Thereafter their number declined as Japan's import barriers were reduced. Also, because of increased enforcement of the Antimonopoly Law in the 1980s in response to international criticisms, the Fair Trade Commission allows them only under strict conditions and within a specific time limit. Since 1989 there has not been a recession cartel authorized, even during the prolonged recession of the 1990s (author's interview, Fair Trade Commission, April 9, 1998).

Designated cartels (*shiji karuteru*) for joint capacity reduction were authorized in the 1978 and 1983 laws for adjustment assistance to specified depressed industries (see **declining industries**). Of the 14 sectors specified under the 1978 law, 8 formed cartels (synthetic fiber, chemicals, worsted yarn spinning, cardboard industries); of the 22 sectors specified under the 1983 law, 7 formed cartels (petrochemicals. chemical fertilizer, paper, and cement). The shipbuilding industry was a unique case because a special law was enacted for that industry. Shipbuilders formed a "recession" cartel repeatedly in the 1970s and 1980s to reduce output and also to reduce capacity.

Some authors contend that cartels have not reduced competition among Japanese firms (Minami, 1994: 118). Washington believes that Japanese cartels invariably reduce competition and restrict imports, and has severely criticized them in its **Structural Impediments Initiative** talks with Tokyo in 1989–90. Washington wanted Japan's Fair Trade Commission to strengthen its implementation of the Antimonopoly Law and eliminate cartel practices. As a result, beginning in 1990, the commission has stepped up its investigation of illegal price fixings and other possible violation of the law, and has raised steeply the fines imposed on those found guilty of forming illegal cartels.

At the end of 1965, 1,079 cartels were exempted from the Antimonopoly Law. The number was reduced to 247 as of June 1991, to 67 in 1994 and 12 in 1997. The last recession cartel existed in 1989 and the last rationalization cartel in 1981 (author's interviews, Fair Trade Commission, July 28, 1992 and April 9, 1998). A 1997 legislation repealed or reduced the scope of various laws giving exemption to many types of cartels. Review of the remaining cartels will continue.

See also **Antimonopoly Law, industrial policy**.

References

Anderson, Douglas D. 1986. Managing retreat: Disinvestment policy. In *American versus Japan*, ed. by Thomas K. McCraw. Boston: Harvard Business School Press.

Cutts, Robert L. 1992. Capitalism in Japan: Cartels and *keiretsu*. *Harvard Business Review*, July–August: 48–55.

Fair Trade Commission. 1997. Outline of the Omnibus Act to repeal and reform cartels and other systems exempted from the application of the Antimonopoly Act under various laws. *FTC/Japan Views*, no. 29 (July): 7–13.

Minami, Ryoshin. 1994. *The Economic Development of Japan: A Quantitative Study*. New York: St. Martin's Press. Ch. 5.

Nakajima, Ai. 1991. Fair Trade Commission following tougher line. *Nikkei Weekly*, September 28: 3.

Nester, William R. 1990. *The Foundation of Japanese Power: Continuities, Changes, Challenges*. London: Macmillan. Ch. 11.

Sekiguchi, Sueo. 1994. Industrial adjustment and cartel actions in Japan. In *Troubled Industries in the United States and Japan*, ed. by Hong W. Tan and Haruo Shimada. New York: St. Martin's Press.

Toga, Mitsuo. 1991. Cement makers chip away at illegal cartel. *Nikkei Weekly*, December 28: 11.

certificate of deposit (CD) market   A money market where negotiable certificates of bank deposits are traded.

See **money markets**.

Chubu   Central Japan.
See **Nagoya and Central Japan**.

chugen   Midyear gift-giving season; the fifteenth day of the seventh month of the year according to the lunar calendar.
See **gift market**.

chu-sho kigyo   Small and medium enterprises.
See **small and medium enterprises**.

cities   Japan has 656 cities, of which the ten largest in terms of population as of March 31, 1997, are Tokyo (23 wards, 7.83 million), Yokohama (3.30 million), Osaka (2.48 million), Nagoya (2.09 million), Sapporo (1.77 million), Kobe (1.44 million), Kyoto (1.39 million), Fukuoka (1.25 million), Kawasaki (1.19 million), and Hiroshima (1.09 million). The largest four cities are also the centers of Japan's three major industrial areas.
See also **Osaka and Kansai**, **Nagoya and Central Japan**, **Tokyo and Kanto**, **Yokohama**.

city banks   City banks (*toshi ginko*) are the largest commercial banks in Japan. As of 1997 there are ten of them. They hold more than a third of all deposits of Japan's financial institutions and supply about 40% of the loans given to private corporations. At the end of 1997, city banks had a total of ¥221.7 trillion in outstanding loans and ¥218.1 trillion in deposits.

City banks are the major financial institutions that have lent heavily to industries at low cost to finance their reconstruction and growth in the postwar era. In particular, during the period of rapid growth and capital shortage before the first oil crisis in the early 1970s, large Japanese corporations had high demand for city bank loans, since Japan's capital market was underdeveloped. As a result the banks were often in a situation of "overloan" in which their loans exceeded their deposits, and the deficiency was covered by borrowing from the **Bank of Japan**, the central bank of Japan. Consequently the capital/asset ratio was traditionally very low. By providing funds to large corporations, city banks have contributed greatly to Japan's postwar economic development.

Each of the large city banks serves as the **main bank** to many Japanese corporations. In particular, the six largest of the city banks—Tokyo-Mitsubishi, Dai-Ichi Kangyo, Sakura, Sumitomo, Fuji, and Sanwa—are the main banks of Japan's six financial *keiretsu*, the giant corporate groups that are organized around the six city banks. The main bank relationship ensures that companies will have access to funds for investment even when company profits are too low for interest payments.

As part of their regular operation, but particularly in the **cross-shareholding** relationship in a *keiretsu*, city banks also hold shares of major client companies as their "stable shareholders" without the intention of selling them for profits. The value of these shares is understated at cost in their balance sheets, and thus they are said to have large "latent capital" or *fukumi* (unrealized profits of stock portfolio).

The decline in Japan's stock prices since early 1990 has strained this stable shareholder relationship. A ruling by the International Bank of Settlement that requires the banks to maintain a capital/asset ratio of 8% or more by April 1993 has further eroded the banks' ability to supply cheap credit. Although the rule allows the banks to count 45% of the unrealized profits of stock portfolio as capital, with the falling stock prices, some city banks have had difficulties in attaining the 8% capital/asset ratio.

During the bubble years of 1986–89, all city banks extended huge loans to construction and real estate companies with inflated land and stocks as collateral. By the mid-1990s, with continuous decline in land and stock prices, much of the loans had become bad debts. Their weak financial status led the Moody's Investors' Service to downgrade them. In November 1997 the former tenth largest city bank—Hokkaido Takushoku Bank—went bankrupt. In order to stave off further bank failures, the Diet approved in early 1998 a government rescue package that would inject ¥30 trillion (6% of Japan's GDP) into the banking system.

Table C.1 shows the deposits, core business profit, and pretax profit/loss of city banks. Although their deposits are large, their core-business profits from loans and investments have been declining. All banks had pretax losses in FY 1997 because some of the nonperforming loans were written off. In FY 1997 a total of ¥5.4 trillion was disposed of by the city banks. In FY 1996 the amount was ¥6.4 trillion.

The deposits of the city banks are given in table C.1. It can be seen that they declined between September 1990 and March 1996 due to the recession and slow growth of the economy.

Three of the largest city banks attained their large size through mergers. The first-ranked Bank of Tokyo-Mitsubishi resulted from a merger between Mitsubishi Bank and the Bank of Tokyo on April 1, 1996. Dai-Ichi Kangyo Bank came from the merger in 1971 of two well-established city banks, Dai-Ichi Bank and Nippon Kangyo Bank. Sakura Bank is the result

Table C.1
Deposits and profits of city banks

| Name of bank | Deposits (in ¥ trillions) | | Profits[a] (in ¥ billions) |
	9/30/1990	3/31/1996	FY 1997
Tokyo-Mitsubishi	64.29[b]	53.29[b]	342.8 (−917.5)
Dai-Ichi Kangyo	48.65	39.16	323.0 (−154.9)
Sanwa	42.47	39.84	351.9 (−413.3)
Sumitomo	44.07	39.08	308.0 (−617.3)
Fuji	41.45	36.97	320.3 (−576.3)
Sakura	45.85[c]	38.81	290.0 (−340.0)
Tokai	27.07	22.33	172.9 (−44.4)
Asahi	24.16[d]	23.11	156.4 (−189.8)
Daiwa	20.85	24.20	96.4 (−151.2)

Sources: Federation of Bankers Association of Japan for deposits; *The Nikkei Weekly*, May 25, 1998, for FY 1997 profit estimates.
a. The first column of profits are core-business profits. Figures in parentheses are pretax profits/losses.
b. Sum of Mitsubishi Bank and the Bank of Tokyo, which merged on April 1, 1996, and became the Bank of Tokyo-Mitsubishi.
c. Sum of Mitsui Bank and Taiyo Kobe Bank, which merged on April 1, 1990.
d. Sum of Kyowa Bank and Saitama Bank, which merged on April 1, 1991.

of a merger on April 1, 1990, of Mitsui Bank and Taiyo Kobe Bank. On April 1, 1991, Kyowa Bank and Saitama Bank, two of the smaller city banks, merged into Asahi Bank. The expected benefits of a merger are economies of scale in bank operations.

See also **banking system**.

Addresses

Bank of Tokyo-Mitsubishi
7-1, Marunouchi 2-chome, Chiyoda-ku, Tokyo 100
Tel: (3) 3240-1111

Dai-Ichi Kangyo Bank
1-5, Uchisaiwai-cho 1-chome, Chiyoda-ku, Tokyo 100
Tel: (3) 3596-1111

Federation of Bankers Association of Japan
3-1, Marunouchi 1-chome, Chiyoda-ku, Tokyo 100
Tel: (3) 5252-3752   Fax: (3) 5252-3755

Fuji Bank
5-5, Otemachi 1-chome, Chiyoda-ku, Tokyo 100
Tel: (3) 3216-2211   Fax: (3) 3201-0527

Sakura Bank
3-1, Kudan Minami 1-chome, Chiyoda-ku, Tokyo 102
Tel: (3) 3230-3111

Sanwa Bank
5-6, Fushimi-cho 3-chome, Chuo-ku, Osaka 541
Tel: (6) 206-8111

Sumitomo Bank
4-6-5, Kitahama, Chuo-ku, Osaka 541
Tel: (6) 227-2111

References

Aoki, Masahiko, and Hugh Patrick, ed. 1994. *The Japanese Main Bank System*. Oxford: Oxford University Press.

Bank of Japan. Annual. *Economic Statistics Annual*.

Federation of Bankers Association of Japan. 1994. *The Banking System in Japan*. Tokyo: Zenginkyo. Ch. 1.

Federation of Bankers Association of Japan. Annual. *Japanese Banks*. Tokyo: Zenginkyo.

Hoiuchi, Akiyoshi, Frank Packer, and Shin'ichi Fukuda. 1988. What role has the "main bank" played in Japan. *Journal of the Japanese and International Economies* 2: 159–80.

Ishizawa, Masato. 1998. Further drops in core profits seen for banks. *Nikkei Weekly*, May 4, 1998: 1, 8.

Mitsui-Taiyo Kobe merger creates a megabank. *Tokyo Business Today*, October 1989: 16–21.

Nakao, Shigeo. 1995. *The Political Economy of Japan Money*. Tokyo: University of Tokyo Press.

Outlook bleak for commercial banks. *Nikkei Weekly*, June 6, 1992: 1, 21.

Suzuki, Yoshio, ed. 1987. *The Japanese Financial System*. Oxford: Oxford University Press. Ch. 5.

Tatewaki, Kazuo. 1991. *Banking and Finance in Japan*. London: Routledge. Ch. 7.

commercial paper market   A commercial paper (CP) is an unsecured promissory note issued by corporations with high credit standing to raise short-term funds. Japan's CP market was first established in November 1987. At the end of 1988, the balance of CPs outstanding on the market was only ¥1.26 trillion. It increased to ¥15.76 trillion in 1990 but declined to ¥12.2 trillion in 1992 because of the recession. At the end of 1997, it was ¥12.0 trillion.

Commercial paper is issued with a face value of ¥100 million or more and with a maturity of between two weeks and nine months. It is a way to raise low-cost funds—the interest rate is calculated from the the discount at which it is sold—and some companies use the funds thus raised to invest in high-yield certificates of deposits. Only corporations with the highest (A-1) or the second highest (A-2) credit rating are eligible for issuing CPs. Prior to April 1, 1992, companies also had to have over ¥33 billion in net assets to be eligible. **Securities companies** were not permitted to issue CPs until February 1990. Since June 1993 **nonbank financial institutions** (nonbanks) with ratings of A-2 or better from at least two credit-rating agencies are permitted to issue CPs. Beginning in April 1994, **insurance companies** with ratings of A-2 or better are allowed to issue CPs.

Commercial papers can be issued and sold only through dealers, which include banks and security houses. Buyers are limited to institutional investors, usually large companies, especially the large **trading companies**.

See also **corporate finance, money market**.

References

Federation of Bankers Associations of Japan. Annual. *Japanese Banks*. Tokyo: Zenginkyo.

Ishibashi, Asako. 1994. Insurers turning to commercial paper. *Nikkei Weekly*, July 4: 16.

Securities Market in Japan, 1998. Tokyo: Japan Securities Research Institute. Ch. 4.

Tatewaki, Kazuo. 1991. *Banking and Finance in Japan*. London: Routledge. Ch. 4.

commodity markets   Japan's commodity markets are relatively small compared with the Chicago Mercantile Exchange, the Chicago Board of Trade, New York's Commodity Exchange, and the gold markets of London and Zurich. However, Japan had the world's first futures market for trading rice in Osaka in 1730. Currently it has the largest trading volumes in platinum in the world. Platinum is the most sought-after precious metal for jewelry in Japan, and Japan's platinum jewelry market is the largest in the world.

There are 12 commodity exchanges in Japan. The **Ministry of International Trade and Industry** (MITI) oversees the trading of metals and other industrial products while the Ministry of Agriculture, Forestry, and Fisheries controls that of agricultural products. The two largest exchanges are Tokyo Commodity Exchange for Industry (TOCOM) and Tokyo Grain Exchange. They account for about 70% of commodity trading in Japan. The other ten exchanges in the country—including the Osaka Textile Exchange, Osaka Sugar Exchange, and Kobe Grain Exchange—are small.

TOCOM is the world's leading platinum exchange mainly because of demand from local jewelers. Besides precious metals, it also trades rubber, cotton, and wool. In April 1997 it started trading aluminum also. The Tokyo Grain Exchange has the bulk of its business in trading soybeans imported from the United States and China. It also trades *azuki* beans. In 1993 it merged with the former Tokyo Sugar Exchange to become a comprehensive agricultural product futures exchange, the largest in Japan.

TOCOM has some 60 full members, all of which are Japanese firms. According to the Commodity Exchange Act, foreign firms are not permitted to become full members of Japanese exchanges. In April 1989, 30 foreign banks, commodity houses, and metal traders were accepted as associate members of TOCOM. However, they can only trade for their own accounts by placing orders through the Japanese members and pay the relatively high exchange commission fees.

The Nikkei Commodity Futures Index reflects the overall price level of all commodity futures traded. With the 1985 average as 100, the Nikkei Index was between 89 and 90 in early April 1989 and slightly under 63 in late September 1992. By early April 1998 it has declined to around 59.

Total turnover on the nation's commodity exchanges increased from 23.7 million contracts in FY 1986 to 44.6 million contracts in 1990, and 68.1 million contracts in 1995. The increase was most pronounced in three precious metals (gold, silver, and platinum) and in agricultural products. Trading volume in raw sugar, textiles, and the newly introduced aluminum has been sluggish.

To facilitate wider investment in commodity futures, a commodity fund market was opened in 1992 to subsidiaries of banks and brokerage houses. These companies could set up commodity futures funds, sell their shares to investors, and manage the funds in the commodity futures market. Investment in commodities funds is considered a safer alternative to investment in securities because most funds guarantee the capital. Commodity funds invest in commodities-futures markets worldwide, and most have maturity periods of five years. As of September 1997 outstanding investment in commodity funds was ¥284.9 billion.

See also **Tokyo Stock Exchange**.

Addresses

All Japan Grain Exchange Association
12-5, Nihonbashi Kakigaracho 1-chome, Chuo-ku, Tokyo 103
Tel: (3) 3666-6572

Japan Federation of Commodity Exchanges, Inc.
1-10, Nihonbashi Ningyocho 1-chome, Chuo-ku, Tokyo 103
Tel: (3) 3667-4381

Tokyo Commodity Exchange for Industry
36-2 Nihonbashi Hakozakicho, Chuo-ku, Tokyo 103
Tel: (3) 3661-9215   Fax: (3) 3664-0089

References

Commodities. In *Japan Economic Almanac*. Various years. Tokyo: Nihon Keizai Shimbun.

Inose, Hijiri. 1991. End users hinder commodities futures expansion. *Japan Economic Journal*, May 25: 48.

Inose, Hijiri. 1993. Commodity futures. In *Japan Economic Almanac, 1993*. Tokyo: Nihon Keizai Shimbun.

Inoue, Tatsuya. 1996. Local markets seek commodity niches. *Nikkei Weekly*, April 1, 1996: 12.

Inoue, Tatsuya. 1997. Desperate investors turn to commodities. *Nikkei Weekly*, November 3: 11.

Shida, Tomio. 1989. Japanese see bright future in futures. *Japan Economic Journal*, May 6: 1, 7.

Taking a shine to Japan's commodities markets. *The Economist*, August 5, 1989: 63–64.

Yamazaki, Akio. 1990. Commodity futures market. In *Japan Economic Almanac, 1990*. Tokyo: Nihon Keizai Shimbum.

commodity tax   A major indirect tax levied by the national government before 1989. Effective April 1, 1989, it was replaced by the **consumption tax**.
    See **consumption tax, taxation system**.

computer industry
See **electronics industry**.

computer-integrated manufacturing (CIM) system   A production control system that links and coordinates the design, development, planning, production, and marketing activities of a company through sophisticated computers and information networks. With the CIM system, changes in one area such as design or sales can be simultaneously conveyed to other areas in order to bring about needed adjustments immediately. Because the product life cycle is becoming ever shorter in many industries such as automobile and consumer electronics, such instantaneous communication and coordination is invaluable.

For the production of a highly complex product that requires the coordination of many production processes and suppliers, as well as branch offices and sales outlets, the CIM system offers the most cost-effective means of wedding computers to manufacturing. It has been increasingly adopted, since the late 1980s, by large manufacturing companies in Japan such as Toyota Motor Corp., Mitsubishi Heavy Industries, and Nippondenso (Japan's largest producer of electrical autoparts). An automobile, for example, has some 20,000 possible specifications. Changes in any of these, coming either from the designing engineer or a customer, can be integrated into the production system immediately. When a customer in Japan orders a Toyota car at a dealer with custom specifications, the order is sent on-line to Toyota plants and parts suppliers under the headquarters' management; many of the parts suppliers are integrated into the system. Within 11 or 12 days the custom-made car is delivered. The CIM system complements and improves on the **just-in-time system**.

A major limitation of the existing CIM systems is that they are limited to individual companies and their affiliates, and lack international compatibility. A problem of noncompatibility, for example, is that a computer-aided design system cannot send its design data electronically into an industrial robot, or a new machine developed by a new supplier cannot be connected to an existing system without developing a new interface. Another problem is the high cost of initial investment, making it beyond the reach of many companies, particularly in the developing countries.

See also **just-in-time system**.

References

Asian Productivity Organization. 1996. *CIM and Management Strategies: The Japanese Experience*. Tokyo: Asian Productivity Organization.

Beatty, Carol A., and John R. Gordon. 1988. Barriers to the implementation of CAD/CAM systems. *Sloan Management Review* 29, 4: 25–33.

Frank, Jeffrey. 1992. *The Teamwork Advantage: An Inside Look at Japanese Product and Technology Development*. Cambridge, MA: Productivity Press.

Mitsusada, Hisayuki. 1989. Japan seeks U.S., Europe cooperation in plan to create computer-linked factories. *Japan Economic Journal*, July 15: 1.

Mitsusada, Hisayuki. 1989. Toyota computer network speeds car orders. *Japan Economic Journal*, July 15: 4.

Oishi, Nobuyuki. 1989. Computer proves worth as production tool. *Japan Economic Journal*, July 15: 5.

Oishi, Nobuyuki. 1990. Suspicions slow implementation of IMS standard. *Japan Economic Journal*, July 21: 1.

Table C.2
Leading construction companies (in ¥ billions)

Company	FY 1991 sales	FY 1991 profits[a]	FY 1997 sales	FY 1997 profits[a]
Shimizu Corp.	2,130	124	1,474	23
Taisei Corp.	1,717	96	1,385	25
Kajima Corp.	1,951	124	1,513	20
Obayashi Corp.	1,509	53	1,465	24
Kumagai Gumi Co.	1,145	38	1,060*	29
Fujita Corp.	820	44	700	7
Toda Corp.	780	48	670	22
Hazama Corp.	697	33	528	18
Tokyu Construction Co.	591	22	530	0
Sato Kogyu Co.	543	18	520	7
Nishimatsu Construction Co.	622	27	708	18

Sources: *Japan Company Handbook* and *The Nikkei Weekly*, May 25, 1998.
Note: One of the big five, Takenaka, is unlisted.
a. Pretax profits.

construction industry   Japan's construction industry constitutes a large sector of the economy. It employs about 10% of total employees in the economy and construction investment by the government and the private sector typically amounts to more than 15% of Japan's GDP.

The industry has some 557,000 companies or contractors. Most of them are unincorporated or small to medium sized, and capitalized at less than ¥100 million. The industry is dominated by five general construction companies—Shimizu, Kajima, Taisei, Takenaka, Obayashi Corp.—each with sales over ¥1 trillion (see table C.2). Below the top five, there is a second tier of large companies, each with its own specialization such as civil engineering and development. For example, Kumagai Gumi Co., the sixth largest company, is Japan's largest contractor overseas. The small companies work for the large companies as subcontractors under some industry clubs affiliated with the big companies.

Japan's construction investment grew rapidly from about ¥50 trillion in FY 1985 to more than ¥80 trillion in both 1991 and 1992 but declined afterward. It recovered somewhat in 1995 and is estimated to be about ¥77 trillion in 1996. However, many construction companies overexpanded during the bubble years due to high demand and easy credit. Since the early 1990s many smaller firms could not repay the debts and have gone bankrupt.

About 34% of total construction orders in 1993–95 were government orders as compared with about 50% in the late 1970s. Many large public works projects such as the New Kansai International Airport have attracted the attention of some American construction companies. However, the latter have found the Japanese construction market extremely difficult to enter because of structural barriers such as the government's "designated competitive bidding system" and the industry's *dango* system.

In the designated competitive bidding system, only specific government-appointed contractors are permitted to bid for public works projects. Government offices rank the construction companies on the basis of their scale, performance, technology, and so forth. Depending on the size of a particular project, about ten appropriate companies are selected for bidding. *Dango* literally means "consultation," and the *dango* system is the prebidding collusion among the companies to determine the winning contractor and its bidding price for the project. It has been defended by industry people as work sharing, which ensures that smaller firms will have their share of profitable contracts. Government guidelines previously permitted such "information exchange" among contractors, thereby providing a loophole for the **Antimonopoly Law**. Critics have charged that the practice was permitted because local politicians depend heavily on the money and votes of local construction companies and that many government officials retire into the executive ranks of these companies. It has also been suggested that *dango* gives contractors incentives not to refuse unprofitable projects for fear of losing subsequent designations. Government purchasing agency has the power to eliminate any company from the designations and to refuse a contract unless the lowest bid is at or below the so-called "provisional value" (cost plus 3% profit margin) for the project as estimated by the purchasing agent (Matsushita 1993: 198).

Dango incidents have been well documented by the Japanese press. In several instances between 1983 and 1991, projects at U.S. military bases were involved. After the uncovering of such bid-rigging, the U.S. government demanded compensation and eventually did receive some. In 1988, for example, 99 Japanese companies paid ¥4.7 billion to the U.S. government for *dango* at Yokosuka U.S. military base.

Washington's efforts to open up Japanese construction market started in 1986 when it requested international bidding for jobs at the new Kansai International Airport. In the U.S.–Japan construction agreement of May 1988, Tokyo agreed to adopt preferential measures to help U.S. companies participate in 17 public works projects to acquaint them with

Japan's bidding system. During the U.S.–Japan **Structural Impediments Initiative** talks, Tokyo agreed in general to implement the Antimonopoly Law vigorously. Subsequently the Fair Trade Commission attempted to deter *dango* practice by raising the penalty for it from 1.5% of sales to 6%. However, industry analysts believe that it is impossible to abolish *dango* altogether and that it will be continued in new guises. In June 1991 another agreement was reached between Washington and Tokyo that will add 17 new public works projects for preferential foreign participation.

The construction industry employed 6.7 million workers in 1996, about 10.3% of total employees. The aging of the workforce in construction is said to be faster than in other industries because it is becoming relatively difficult to recruit young construction workers. Many smaller companies have hired workers from other Asian countries on a part-time basis.

See also **Structural Impediments Initiative**.

Addresses

Japan Federation of Construction Contractors, Inc.
5-1, Hatchobori 2 chome, Chuo-ku, Tokyo 104
Tel: (3) 3553-0701

Kamagai Gumi Co.
6-8, Chuo 2-chome, Fukui City 910
Tel: (3) 3260-2111   Fax: (3) 3235-5389

Ministry of Construction
1-3, Kasumigaseki 2-chome, Chiyoda-ku, Tokyo 100
Tel: (03) 3580-4311

Shimizu Corp.
2-3, Shibaura 1-chome, Minato-ku, Tokyo
Tel: (3) 5441-1111   Fax: (3) 5441-0349

Taisei Corp.
25-1, Nishi-Shinjuku 1-chome, Shinjuku-ku, Tokyo 163
Tel: (3) 3348-1111   Fax: (3) 3345-1386

References

Cash flow fosters web of corruption among politicians, contractors. *Nikkei Weekly*, August 23, 1993: 1–2.

Choy, Jon. 1998. Japan's construction industry: the economic engine that can't. *JEI Report* 34A, September 4.

Construction. In *Japan Economic Almanac*. Various years. Tokyo: Nihon Keizai Shimbun.

The crackdown on construction industry bid rigging. *Tokyo Business Today*, October 1991: 28–30.

Fukuda, Masako. 1997. Construction industry takes turn for the worse. *Nikkei Weekly*, August 4: 1, 19.

Japan Company Handbook. Quarterly. Tokyo: Toyo Keizai.

Krauss, Ellis S., and Isobel Coles. 1990. Built-in impediments: The political economy of the U.S.–Japan construction dispute. In *Japan's Economic Structure: Should It Change?* ed. by Kozo Yamanura. Seattle: Society for Japanese Studies.

Levy, Sidney. 1993. *Japan's Big Six: Inside Japan's Construction Industry.* New York: McGraw Hill.

Mamiya, Jun. 1995. Government and contractors prove: It takes two to *dango. Tokyo Business Today,* July: 28–31.

Matsushita, Mitsuo. 1993. *International Trade and Competition Law in Japan.* Oxford: Oxford University Press

U.S.–Japan construction talks reveal contraditions in American strategy. *Tokyo Business Today,* May 1991: 32–34.

consumer behavior
See **consumer groups, customer sovereignty**.

consumer cooperatives
See **consumer groups**.

consumer credit   Prior to the early 1980s financial institutions provided relatively little credit to consumers. This is considered to be one of the reasons for the high level of household **savings**. However, the situation started to change in the 1980s. The total amount of consumer credit balance grew from ¥7.1 trillion in 1975 to ¥27.4 trillion in 1985, and ¥53 trillion in 1989. These amounted to 6.5% of household disposable income in 1975, 12.4% in 1985, and 20.1% in 1989 (Economic Planning Agency 1991: 37).

Consumer credit (excluding mortgage loans) consists of two categories: *sales credit* for the payment of goods and services purchased, and *consumer finance*, which is granted directly to the consumer. Consumer finance is the larger of the two. It expanded rapidly during the **bubble economy**, from ¥19.6 trillion in 1986 to ¥47.8 trillion in 1990. In 1995, at ¥57.1 trillion, it constituted 76% of total consumer credit outstanding.

There are four major sources of consumer credit: banks, *shinpan* (sales finance companies or credit sales companies), retailers and their associated credit companies, and *sarakin* (consumer finance companies). Their relative importance has changed over time. Until 1981 retailers and their associated credit companies provided the bulk of consumer credit. *Shinpan* companies had the largest share in 1982–87, while banks became the dominant lenders since 1988.

Until the late 1970s Japanese corporations depended heavily on bank loans for investment. Consequently financial authorities have traditionally discouraged banks from extending credit to consumers through ceilings on consumer loan rates and by **administrative guidance**. Since 1986, however, Japan's **city banks** have become increasingly involved in consumer finance, including the credit card business (JCB Cards, VISA, MasterCard, etc.). At the end of 1991, city banks' outstanding consumer loans balance was ¥8.9 trillion, more than 12 times that of 1986. For all banks the outstanding consumer credit balance was ¥19.6 trillion at the end of 1992, compared with ¥1.5 trillion at the end of 1986. The amount declined in the early 1990s as the economy entered a recession. At the end of 1997, it was ¥6.3 trillion for city banks and ¥14.1 trillion for all banks (Bank of Japan, 1998). Banks provide about 25% of consumer credit.

Shinpan or sales finance companies are registered with the **Ministry of International Trade and Industries** as firms that intermediate in installment purchases in accordance with the Installment Sale Law of July 1961. They intermediate either in general installment purchases (credit card companies) or in installment purchases of specific goods (installment claims purchasing companies). In the mid-1980s they provided over 25% of outstanding consumer credit. The share has declined since then to less than 20%.

Sarakin or consumer finance companies (from the word "salaryman" and the Japanese word *kinyu*, "finance") used to be an important source of consumer finance. At their peak in the early 1980s, they numbered 220,000 and provided about 13% of consumer credit in 1982. These companies obtain funds from banks and life insurance companies and make small loans directly to individuals at high interest rates, which often exceeded 100% before 1983. In addition they have often resorted to threats and harassment in the collection of loans. In 1983 a law was passed to limit their interest rate to 73% per year in 1983, 54.75% in 1986, and 40% in 1991. Because of new competition from other lending institutions in the consumer credit market and tighter regulation by the **Ministry of Finance** of their lending limit and collection practices, these companies have declined since 1984 in importance, providing about 5% of the outstanding consumer credit.

For the purchase of houses, the principal sources of mortgage loans are the government Housing Loan Corporation and banks (see **housing finance**). Interest rates in such loans are generally fixed. For depositors of the **postal savings** service, small loans are available with their deposits as collateral.

See also **credit card industry, housing finance, savings**.

Addresses

Japan Consumer Credit Industry Association
7, Yotsuyo 4-chome, Shinjuku-ku, Tokyo 160
Tel: (3) 3359-0411

Nippon Shinpan
33-5, Hongo 3-chome, Bunkyo-ku, Tokyo
Tel: (3) 3811-3111

References

Alexander, Arthur. 1993. Thrifty Japan discovers consumer credit. *JEI Report* 26A, July 16.

Alexander, Arthur. 1997. Consumer credit in Japan since the bubble economy's end. *JEI Report* 23A, June 20.

Bank of Japan. Annual. *Economic Statistics Annual*. Tokyo.

Economic Planning Agency. Annual. *Economic Survey of Japan*.

Feldman, Robert A. 1986. *Japanese Financial Markets*. Cambridge: MIT Press.

Hamada, Koichi and Akiyoshi Horiuchi. 1987. The political economy of the financial market. In *The Political Economy of Japan*, vol. 1: *The Domestic Transformation*, ed. by Kozo Yamamura and Yasukichi Yasuba. Stanford: Stanford University Press.

Suzuki, Yoshio, ed. 1987. *The Japanese Financial System*. New York: Oxford University Press.

consumer electronics industry
See **electronics industry**.

consumer finance companies
See **consumer credit**.

consumer groups   There are thousands of consumer groups engaged in consumer-related activities. They can be classified into the following four categories:

1. *Consumer cooperatives (seikyo).* These groups are set up with funds from members. In 1988 there were 1,271 such cooperatives with 33.7 million members. Cooperatives purchase in bulk daily necessities, perishables, and processed foods directly from producers or wholesalers and sell them to members in their stores at relatively low prices. Some cooperatives do not

operate a store and their members purchase goods jointly. The cooperatives may also provide medical treatment, welfare, and housing and run mutual-aid insurance services. There are two types of consumer cooperatives: regional cooperatives, centered mainly on housewives, and employee cooperatives at workplaces and universities. Almost all consumer cooperatives belong to the Japanese Consumers' Cooperative Union.

Government policy toward consumer cooperatives has been more restrictive than toward **agricultural cooperatives**. It prohibits them from engaging in credit union activities, from crossing prefectural lines, and bars nonmembers from using their services (Nomura 1993: 31). This is consistent with many analysts' view that the Japanese government has been more supportive of producers than of consumers in the postwar era.

2. *Housewives organizations.* These groups are involved in various activities such as jointly purchasing products from farmers, price surveys, recycling, testing products, and attending cooking classes. They include the Japan Housewives Association (*shufuren*) and the National Federation of Regional Women's Organizations (*chifuren*). The former was established in 1948 and is the oldest of consumer groups.

3. *Advocacy groups.* These groups focus on problems of food safety, environmental protection, medical issues, and so on. The largest of these is the Consumer Union of Japan. It publicizes defective products, anticonsumer corporate behavior, and lobbys for consumer interest legislations.

4. *Experts groups.* These groups are made up of lawyers, consultants, and other experts. They attempt to broaden liability for product defects, to ban fraudulent contracts, and so forth.

Because there is no nationwide organization to integrate the consumer groups, the effectiveness of any one group or movement is inevitably limited. However, some analysts contend that the "effectiveness" of Japan's consumer groups, or more broadly the "rationality" of Japanese consumers, should not be viewed from the perspective of Western economic theories of consumer behavior. For example, high retail prices in Japan are accepted by consumers in part because of the Japanese emphasis on high product quality and after-sale service. In this regard Dore (1990: 371) views Japanese consumer behavior from the perspective of the "customer market" as opposed to the theoretical, minimum-price seeking "auction market" and argues that Japanese consumer behavior is rational in the context of a society that values relationships. Similarly the "inefficient" **distribution system** is accepted because consumers like its "personal touch" services.

Before Japan lifted its ban on rice imports in the 1990s, most consumer groups opposed opening the market to imports, even though the Japanese rice prices were about five times the U.S. average. They argued that keeping rice paddies in Japan is essential for the environment and national security, and hence more important than lower prices. An alternative explanation is that Japanese consumers are "more prone to simply follow rather than push the government" (Oishi 1993). In any case, for years Japanese consumer groups actively pushed for a product liability law, which was finally passed by the Diet in June 1994 and took effect on July 1, 1995.

See also **customer sovereignty**.

Addresses

Japan Consumers' Association
5-9, Hacchobori 4-chome, Chuo-ku, Tokyo 104
Tel: (3) 3553-8601

Japan Housewives Association
15, Rokuban-cho, Chiyoda-ku, Tokyo 102
Tel: (3) 3553-8601

References

Dore, Ronald. 1990. An outsider's view. In *Japan's Economic Structure: Should It Change?* ed. by Kozo Yamamura. Seattle: Society for Japanese Studies.

Ishizuka, Masahiko. 1989. Japanese consumers lack group identity, power. *Japan Economic Journal*, April 15: 11.

Japan Almanac. Annual. Tokyo: Asahi Shimbun Publishing Co.

Nishikawa, Kazuko. 1990. Why Japanese consumer groups oppose market opening measures. *Tokyo Business Today*, March: 40–43.

Nomura, Hidekazu, ed. 1993. *Seikyo: A Comprehensive Analysis of Consumer Cooperatives in Japan.* Tokyo: Otsuki Shoten Publishers.

Oishi, Nobuyuki. 1993. Consumer groups: advocates of what? *Nikkei Weekly*, August 23: 2.

Ostrom, Douglas. 1994. The Japanese consumer moves to center stage. *JEI Report 36A*, September 23.

Yamakoshi, Atsushi. 1995. Japanese consumer behavior and economic restructuring. *JEI Report 6A*, February 17.

consumption   Aggregate consumption (including general government consumption and private consumption) as a share of gross domestic

Table C.3
Consumption as a share of GDP (in %)

Year	Japan	United States	All industrial countries
1970	59.7	82.6	76.2
1975	67.2	82.4	78.4
1980	68.7	79.7	77.0
1985	68.5	83.3	79.4
1986	68.3	84.2	79.6
1987	68.3	84.8	79.8
1988	67.4	84.6	79.2
1989	67.3	84.0	78.7
1990	67.0	84.9	79.1
1991	66.2	85.5	80.1
1992	67.0	85.3	80.4
1993	68.0	84.7	80.5
1994	69.3	83.9	80.0
1995	70.0	83.8	79.7
1996	69.6	83.8	79.7

Source: IMF, *International Financial Statistics Yearbook*, 1997.

product (GDP) is relatively low in Japan as compared with that of other industrial nations. Between 1970 and 1996, the consumption/GDP ratio was typically between 66% and 70% in Japan, whereas in the United States it ranged from 80% to more than 85%, about 15% higher than that of Japan. The average of all industrial countries was 76% to 81%, about 10% higher than that of Japan (see table C.3). The share of government consumption is about 9–10% of GDP. Also government consumption has grown more slowly than private consumption.

According to surveys conducted by the Management and Coordination Agency, average household consumption as a ratio of household disposable income was 79.7% in 1970, 77.5% in 1985, and 72.0% in 1996. Dividing the sample households into five quintile groups by annual income, the average propensity to consume in 1996 ranged from 79.7% for the poorest group to 72.0% for the top income group, all relatively low by international standards.

Table C.4 compares the composition of household consumption expenditures in 1970 and 1996. The consumption of food as a share of the household budget declined substantially from 34% in 1970 to 23.4% in 1996. On the other hand, expenditures on services (housing, transportation and communication, education, recreation, etc.) have increased by

Table C.4
Composition of household consumption (in %)

	1970	1996
Food	34.1	23.4
Housing[a] and utilities	9.3	12.9
Furniture and utensils	5.0	3.7
Clothes and footwear	9.4	5.9
Medical care	2.6	3.1
Transportation and communication	5.2	10.6
Education	2.8	4.5
Recreation	9.1	9.7
Other living expenditures	22.6	26.1
(Social expenses)	7.8	9.9

Source: Management and Coordination Agency.
Note: Excludes households in agriculture, forestry and fishery, and one-person households.
a. Includes rental housing but not imputed rent of owner-occupied houses.

various extents. These changes are consistent with the experiences of other industrial countries. The final category, "other living expenditures," is a broad category of miscellaneous expenditures, of which "social expenses" are the largest item. Social expenses comprise mostly gifts and amount to nearly 10% of household expenditures, making the **gift market** an important segment of Japan's retail market. Between households in large cities and in small cities and towns, the former spend relatively more on food, **housing**, clothes, and education, whereas the latter spend relatively more on utilities, transportation and communication, and "other living expenditures."

Consumer spending on specific durable goods such as automobiles, color televisions, washing machines, and air conditioners fluctuates seasonally and over the **business cycles**. The Economic Planning Agency (1992: 136–47) has found that consumer spending on consumer durables is much more sensitive than spending on semidurables to changes in the following variables: (1) household disposable income, (2) interest rate on bank loans, and (3) financial asset balance. Spending on nondurables is also sensitive to changes in household disposable income. In addition households' consumption habits are important with nondurables. Spending on services is heavily influenced by consumption habits and prices.

Overall household consumption is affected by changes in household disposable income, but the consumers' expectation as to whether the changes are going to be temporary or permanent also affects their spending. In addition consumer spending can be reduced by job insecurity, as was the case in recent years (Economic Planning Agency 1997: 19–21). The increase in **consumption tax** in 1997 is also believed to have depressed consumption.

While the composition of Japanese household consumption changes as household disposable income increases, the average propensity to consume has remained relatively low and stable. This reflects Japanese households' desire to save a sizable portion of their disposable income for various personal reasons (see **savings**). The resultant high saving ratio of the economy has financed the economy's high rate of **investment**. While industries grew rapidly as a result, many consumer goods industries had to rely on the export market to sell their expanded output, thereby contributing to Japan's large and chronic trade surplus. The alternative to this export-driven growth is to rely more heavily on the domestic market for growth, as many countries have urged Japan to do. This would require an increased propensity to consume on the part of the Japanese households. This will not be easy to accomplish in a short period of time because the institutional and psychological factors that have underlied the high saving rate cannot be readily changed. In the longer run, however, many analysts expect Japan's saving ratio to go down as the population becomes older and as more people, not having lived through the hardships of the early postwar period, take an affluent way of life for granted.

See also **savings**.

References

Economic Planning Agency. Annual. *Economic White Paper* (in Japanese; English version is published as *Economic Survey of Japan*). Tokyo.

Ito, Takatoshi. 1992. *The Japanese Economy*. Cambridge: MIT Press. Ch. 9.

Management and Coordination Agency. Annual. *Japan Statistical Yearbook*.

Ostrom, Douglas. 1994. The Japanese consumer moves to center stage. *JEI Report* 36A, September 23.

Takenaka, Heizo. 1991. *Contemporary Japanese Economy and Economic Policy*. Ann Arbor: University of Michigan Press. Chs. 3–4.

Tsukada, Norifumi. 1993. Have consumers given up on the economy? *Tokyo Business Today*, March: 36–40.

Yamakoshi, Atsushi. 1995. Japanese consumer behavior and economic restructuring. *JEI Report* 6A, February 17.

consumption tax Japan's general consumption tax had been a controversial and divisive issue for more than a decade before it became effective on April 1, 1989. The government wanted to introduce the tax in order to broaden the tax base and reduce government debt, but strong opposition from the opposition parties and the general public aborted several prime ministers' attempts to introduce it since 1977. When it was finally enacted in late 1988, it was part of the **tax reform** package passed by the Diet or parliament under the leadership of then Prime Minister Noboru Takeshita. In the same tax reform, individual income tax, corporation tax, and inheritance tax were simplified and reduced, and a variety of excise taxes eliminated.

The main original provisions of the consumption tax are as follows:

1. A tax of 3% (6% for automobiles) is applied to all sales and service transactions (see exemptions below). Taxes are due twice a year.

2. The tax paid by a company to suppliers is credited against the tax on its sales in order to avoid tax cascading.

3. Small- and medium-sized businesses with sales up to ¥30 million per year are exempt. Companies with sales up to ¥500 million per year may use a fixed value-added rate of 10% for wholesalers and 20% for all others.

4. The following sales are exempt: export, land sales, securities transactions, foreign exchange deals, loan interest, parimutuel betting, postage stamps, medical expenses, education costs, and certain government administrative fees and social welfare payments. In a 1991 revision of the tax, residential rent, childbirth, funeral expenses, and school entry fees are also exempt.

The consumption tax broadens Japan's tax base because its tax system was previously based on wage-withholding income tax, which contained many exemptions for interest groups. The tax is welcomed by foreign exporters because it reduces the tax rate on luxury imports such as luxury cars and fine liquor, which were previously taxed at a higher rate. However, domestic consumers have been unhappy about it. Opposition to it by housewives contributed to the strong election victory of Japan's Socialist Party (renamed Social Democratic Party in January 1991) and the first loss of majority control by the **Liberal Democratic Party** in the Upper House of the Diet in 1989.

Effective April 1997, the consumption tax rate was raised from 3% to 5%. The increase was approved in September 1994 as part of a tax reform package by the coalition government of then Prime Minister Tomiichi Murayama who, as the leader of the Social Democratic Party of Japan, had long opposed it. Since the increase was long anticipated by consumers, it had the effect of temporarily raising consumer purchases before it went into effect, but seriously depressing consumer spending afterward. Because this took place when the economy was in a recession, it compounded the difficulties of economic recovery. The government of then Prime Minister Ryutaro Hashimoto was therefore widely criticized for policy rigidity. There were also widespread calls for the government to reduce income taxes, particularly the corporate income tax to offset the rise in consumption tax. Instead of a genuine tax reform, the government chose a onetime personal income tax cut of ¥2 trillion. Thus the consumption tax remains as controversial and divisive as ever.

See also **individual income taxes, tax reform, tax system**.

References

Choy, Jon. Tax reform passes lower house. *JEI Report*, December 2, 1988, pt. B: 1–8.

Gomi, Yuji. Annual. *Guide to Japanese Taxes*. Tokyo: Zaikeishoho sha.

Isono, Naoyuki. 1991. Some holes in consumption tax expected to be plugged. *Japan Economic Journal*, May 4: 5.

Ministry of Finance. Annual. *An Outline of Japanese Taxes*.

Odden, Lee. 1989. Tax reform 1989. *Tokyo Business Today*, March: 24–27.

Ostrom, Douglas. 1997. Japanese taxes in international perspective. *JEI Report* 24A, June 27.

Toshikawa, Takao. 1995. Taxation by puppet-masters. *Tokyo Business Today*, March: 22–25.

convertible bonds   A type of corporate bonds that can be converted into shares of the issuing company at some future date and under certain conditions.

See **bond market, corporate finance**.

cooperatives   A form of enterprise organization established by persons engaged in specific occupations or by consumers for the benefit of members in terms of consumption, credit, marketing, production, and so forth. Members provide the capital and participate in decision making. Cooperatives in Japan pay a lower income tax rate on their net income than ordinary corporations.

The following types of cooperatives exist in Japan: (1) **agricultural cooperatives** to assist members in purchasing farm inputs, marketing farm products, and in lobbying the government for agricultural support; (2) consumer cooperatives to help members obtain goods and services at lower prices; (3) **credit cooperatives** to accept deposits from, and to make loans to, owners and workers of **small and medium enterprises;** (4) life insurance companies; and (5) the Central Cooperative Bank for Agriculture and Forestry (*Norinchukin* Bank), one of Japan's largest banks, to serve agricultural cooperatives and individuals engaged in agriculture, forestry, and fisheries.

See also **agricultural cooperatives, banking system, consumer groups,** *kaisha.*

corporate finance Japanese companies generally have two broad sources of funds: internal sources and external sources. Internal funds consist of depreciation allowances and retained earnings. External funds include equity and debt offerings (i.e., stocks and bonds), bank borrowings, and so forth. Corporate finance in Japan is characterized by high depreciation charges and heavy reliance on bank borrowings.

In the postwar era Japanese companies have had a high rate of **investment** in plants and equipment as a means of growth; hence they have had large depreciation charges. However, their internal funds were not adequate for financing investment, and they had to reply on some external funds. Because the securities market was not well developed, at least prior to the 1980s, companies had to rely on bank loans as the main source of external funds. This was particularly true during Japan's high-growth period from the late 1950s to the early 1970s.

Because of the importance of bank loans, a main bank system developed in which a company's largest bank lender would maintain a close relationship with the company to ensure the latter's financial soundness and thus to minimize the risks for all its lenders. The **main bank** owns a certain percentage (currently up to 5%) of the company's shares, has access to its confidential information, and may advise it on its operations. Consequently studies of the main bank system suggest a positive effect on corporate investment. For example, Hoshi, Kashyap, and Sharfstein (1991) find that among Japanese firms, those with ties to a main bank as part of a *keiretsu* are not constrained in their investment by their own internal funds. In other words, loans from affiliated banks are as good as firms' own retained earnings in financing corporate investment. This gives Japanese firms an important competitive advantage over their U.S. counterparts who depend more heavily on their own retained earnings for investment. Koriuchi and Okazaki (1994) add that this main bank relationship can exist outside a *keiretsu;* some firms with strong main bank relationship do not belong to a *keiretsu.*

Minor sources of debt finance include borrowing from government financial institutions and the issuing of straight corporate bonds. Corporate bond issues have been relatively small in Japan because of the dominance of **government bonds** and the government's policy to keep bond interest rates low. There are also stringent regulations on the amount of bonds that companies can issue.

After the oil crisis of 1973, tighter monetary policy to control inflation led to a cash squeeze and higher interest costs of loans. Banks loans to companies began to decline in importance because equity financing became relatively cheaper. In addition **financial liberalization** since the late 1970s by the **Ministry of Finance** made it easier for companies to issue securities other than straight bonds and equities. Most important among these were equity-linked convertible bonds and **warrant bonds**.

Convertible bonds can be converted into shares under certain conditions. Warrant bonds are similar because the warrants attached permit holders to convert to shares at fixed prices; however, the warrants can be detached and traded separately. Most convertible bonds are issued in Japan, whereas most warrant bonds are issued in the Euromarkets but are purchased by Japanese investors and traded in the **over-the-counter markets**. Because of the advantages of flexibility and reduced risk to investors, these two types of equity-linked bonds became popular in the 1980s. At the same time share prices also rose rapidly in the 1980s, particularly in the late 1980s, making it ever more profitable for big corporations to increase their equity financing. The companies listed on the **Tokyo Stock Exchange** raised through the stock market ¥4 trillion in 1960–69, ¥11.6 trillion in the 1970s, and ¥70 trillion in the 1980s (Zielinski and Holloway 1991: 161).

Japanese companies typically pay their dividend at ¥5 per share, or 10% of the par value (¥50) of a share. As share prices rose in the late 1980s (see **stock market**), the dividend paid out as a percentage of net profits declined—it was 44% in 1977, 37.7% in 1982, and 27.6% in 1990 for all listed companies. In early 1992 the payout ratio remained below 30%, which is lower than that of U.S. and European companies. In order to stimulate the stock market in the midst of a recession, the Japan Securities Dealers Association revised, in March 1992, its guidelines for equity finance, requesting companies that issue new stocks, convertible and warrant bonds to pledge a payout ratio of more than 30%. The ratio has been above 60% since 1994.

Investors traditionally bought shares, not for the dividends, but for their growth potential. The number of shares available in the stock market, however, is limited by the system of **cross-shareholding** in which companies that have mutual business ties or are members of the same *keiretsu* group hold each other's shares. These companies are the so-called stable shareholders because they hold other companies' shares for long-term business purposes and are not likely to sell them for short-term gains. Hence the shares they hold are not available for trading in the stock market. When share prices rise, the unrealized capital gains are considered to be the "latent capital" of Japanese companies, which is considered to enhance their financial strength.

The rapid growth in equity financing in the 1980s has provided many companies with excess funds, which were utilized in various ways—for example, deposited in large-denomination deposits or invested in *tokkin funds*—in order to increase corporate profits. *Tokkin* funds are a type of investment trust fund with a tax advantage and high returns. In the 1980 many Japanese companies became heavily involved in *zaitech* (or *zaiteku*, literally financial technology) or the investment of surplus funds in the stock market for profits. Such profits sometimes exceeded the profits from the main lines of business for many companies. In the stock market boom of the late 1980s, even successful manufacturing firms such as Toyota Motor, Nissan Motor, and Matsushita Electric made 40% to 65% of their pretax profits through *zaitech* (*Economist*, June 25, 1988: 75). Ironically American companies' pursuit of such financial gains outside the firms' main manufacturing activities used to be criticized by the Japanese as a weakness of the American style of management.

The 1990s prove to be a period of financial stringency for Japanese companies. This can be seen in both equity and debt offerings and bank borrowings as discussed below:

1. *Equity and debt offerings.* After the collapse of share prices in 1990 and the revelation of scandals such as loss-compensation made by **securities companies** to their large clients, investors' confidence in general has remained low. From a peak of 2,800 in 1989, the Tokyo Stock Price Index (TOPIX) has remained depressed and has seldom exceeded 1,600 ever since. The total trading volume on the **Tokyo Stock Exchange** has never recovered to 50% of its heyday level in 1987–89. The new issue market for stocks has been inactive, and convertible bond and warrant bond offerings have greatly declined (see table C.5). Nor can the **stable share-**

Table C.5
Sources of corporate financing (in %)

FY	Internal sources			External sources			
	DC	RE	Total	EO	CB	BB	Total
1980	30.6	27.8	58.4	4.4	1.1	36.0	41.5
1985	38.8	14.9	53.7	4.5	3.5	38.3	46.3
1989	22.9	27.6	50.5	8.4	6.9	34.2	49.5
1992	56.4	11.4	67.8	1.7	0.0	30.6	32.3
1993	74.8	0.0	74.8	4.9	5.7	14.5	25.1
1994	80.5	5.6	86.1	4.3	−0.5	10.1	13.9
1995	69.8	23.8	93.6	3.1	−3.6	6.9	6.4

Source: Japan Securities Research Institute (1998: 2).
Notes: DC = depreciation charges; RE = retained earnings; EO = equity offering; CB = corporate bonds; BB = bank borrowings.

holders or the **main banks** be of much help because they are reluctant to hold more shares of their clients as share prices decline.

2. *Bank borrowings.* The ability of banks to extend low-cost loans has been curtailed by various factors:

a. Many banks have restricted lending to meet the new capital-asset ratio of 8% by the end of March 1993 imposed by the Bank of International Settlements.

b. Excessive loans to real estate business during the **bubble economy** of 1986–89, with inflated stock and land as collateral, saddled banks with huge bad debts after the stock market collapsed in 1990 and land prices declined continuously afterward. A few weak banks have gone bankrupt, which is unprecedented in Japan's postwar history. The **Ministry of Finance** did not rescue them, as it would have in the past, because it was realized that **financial liberalization** and bank restructuring are badly needed for market forces to revitalize the economy.

c. Because of the financial weakness of Japanese banks, as shown in their downgrading by Moody's Investors Service, it has become difficult for them to raise funds in overseas financial markets. There is a "Japan premium," the extra interest rate that Japanese banks must pay for raising funds in overseas financial markets.

As a result external corporate financing as a percentage of total corporate financing has declined from 49.5% in 1989 to 25.1% in 1993 and 6.4% in 1995 (see table C.5). Companies increasingly have to rely on internal funds—depreciation allowances and retained earnings—for corporate financing. This is not easy for many companies because corporate profits have generally declined in the 1990s. Not surprisingly, **bankruptcies** have increased, especially among **small and medium enterprises** and construction companies for lack of bank credit. In late 1997 and early 1998 some companies started issuing straight bonds. However, this option is not open to companies with less than an A rating because of the risk aversion of investors.

See also **banking system, Big Bang, bond market, bankruptcies, government bonds, shareownership, stock market, Tokyo Stock Exchange**.

References

Abegglen, James C., and George Stalk, Jr. 1985. *Kaisha: The Japanese Corporation*. New York: Basic Books. Ch. 7.

Ando, Albert, and Alan J. Auerbach. 1990. The cost of capital in Japan: Recent evidence and further results. *Journal of the Japanese and International Economies* 4: 323–50.

Aoki, Masahiko. 1988. *Information, Incentives, and Bargaining in the Japanese Economy*. Cambridge: Cambridge University Press. Ch. 4.

Ballon, Robert J., and Iwao Tomita. 1988. *The Financial Behavior of Japanese Corporations*. Tokyo: Kodansha International.

Bank of Japan. Monthly. *Monthly Report of Recent Economic and Financial Developments*. Tokyo.

Campbell, John Y., and Yasushi Hamao. 1994. Changing patterns of corporate financing and the main bank system in Japan. In *The Japanese Main Bank System*, ed. by Masahiko Aoki and Hugh Patrick. Oxford: Oxford University Press.

Horiuchi, Akiyoshi and Ryoko Okazaki. 1994. Capital market and the banking sector: Efficiency of Japanese banks in reducing agency costs. In *Japan, Europe, and International Financial Markets*, edited by Ryuzo Sato, Richard Levich and Rama Ramachandran. New York: Cambridge University Press.

Hodder, James E., and Adrian E. Tschoegl. 1990. Some aspects of Japanese corporate finance. In *Japanese Capital Markets*, ed. by Edwin J. Elton and Martin J. Gruber. New York: Harper and Row.

Hoshi, Takeo. 1994. The economic role of corporate grouping and the main bank system. In *The Japanese Firm: Sources of Competitive Strength*, ed. by Masahiko Aoki and Ronald Dore. Oxford: Oxford University Press.

Hoshi, Takeo, Anil Kashyap and David Sharfstein. 1990. The role of banks in reducing the costs of financial distress in Japan. *Journal of Financial Economics* 27: 67–88.

Hoshi, Takeo, Anil Kashyap and David Sharfstein. 1991. Corporate structure, liquidity, and investment: Evidence from Japanese industrial groups. *Quarterly Journal of Economics* 106: 33–60.

Japan Securities Research Institute. 1998. *Securities Market in Japan, 1998*.

Kester, W. Carl, and Timothy A. Luehrman. 1992. The myth of Japan's low-cost capital. *Harvard Business Review* 70, 3: 130–38.

Meerschwam, David M. 1991. The Japanese financial system and the cost of capital. In *Trade with Japan*, ed. by Paul Krugman. Chicago: University of Chicago Press.

Patrick, Hugh. 1994. The relevance of Japanese finance and its main bank system. In *The Japanese Main Bank System*, ed. by Masahiko Aoki and Hugh Patrick. Oxford: Oxford University Press.

Yamamoto, Yuri. 1998. Tight lending forces firms to issue bonds. *Nikkei Weekly*, January 26: 17.

Zielinski, Robert, and Nigel Holloway. 1991. *Unequal Equities: Power and Risk in Japan's Stock Market*. Tokyo: Kodansha International. Ch. 6.

corporate governance   Corporate governance is concerned about the balance of power shared by various groups of stakeholders—shareholders, top management, employees, creditors, and clients—over the direction and basic policy of a company, and the manner in which the power is exercised.

Analysts have no consensus on the nature of Japanese corporate governance. Their views differ so much that four different lines of thought exist in the literature; each of them emphasizes the importance or lack of importance of a particular group of stakeholders in corporate governance.

The first and most common strand of thought points out that Japanese shareholders do not have much power in corporate governance. For example, Abegglen and Stalk (1985: 184–91) consider the common stock shareholder of the Japanese company akin to a preferred shareholder in a Western company, entitled to a return on the investment but is "in no operational sense in control of the company."

The following Japanese corporate practices, discussed by various authors either in support, or in criticism, of the Japanese-style management, are all consistent with this line of thinking:

1. Unlike the American company where shareholders elect members of the board of directors from outside the company to set corporate policy and appoint the executives, the Japanese company appoints its directors largely from its own senior executives. Since inside directors are involved in company operations, the policy making and oversight functions of the board are not separated from the operational aspect of the company and are not properly emphasized. Japanese directors tend to be loyal to the chairman and president rather than to shareholders, and rarely oppose the president's management policies. In addition Japanese boards are rela-

tively large, consisting of 40 to 50 members, making it impractical to be a decision-making body (Wanner 1998: 4).

2. The annual shareholders meetings are typically perfunctory and brief, often over in 30 minutes. Moreover most companies hold their general shareholders meetings at about the same time, thereby preventing shareholders from attending more than one meeting. This practice is motivated by the desire to avoid the disruption of meetings by racketeers who threaten to disclose corporate scandals unless they are paid off (see **underworld businesses**). In 1997 more than 2,000 major companies throughout Japan held their annual shareholders meetings on June 27. They included 1,427 or 95% of the companies listed on the **Tokyo Stock Exchange** that end their fiscal year in March (*Nikkei Weekly*, June 30, 1997: 1). Thus shareholders meetings do not serve to check on corporate behavior or to initiate changes.

3. The stock prices, an important indicator of corporate profitability and watched over closely by investors and management alike in the United States, do not exert as much influence on Japanese companies. The reasons are that Japanese companies have traditionally relied more on bank loans than their American counterparts and that a smaller percentage of shares go through the stock market because of the dominance of institutional shareownership. Financial institutions and nonfinancial corporations own a much higher percentage of all shares of listed companies than individual investors (see **shareownership**). Many of these corporate shareholders are the so-called **stable shareholders** who practice **cross-shareholding**, not for investment returns, but to reinforce long-term business ties. Consequently fluctuations in short-term share prices do not affect a company's long-term prospects as much as they do in the United States, and managers presumably can concentrate on long-term corporate concerns (Dore 1987: 109–114).

4. For the same reason it is more difficult for a corporate raider to acquire a large percentage of shares and take over a company. The stable shareholders can help defend a company against hostile takeover, especially when the company is a member of a *keiretsu* or a business group. Hence **mergers and acquisitions** as an instrument of gaining corporate control are relatively rare in Japan. Supporters argue that this enables managers to concentrate on other important tasks.

5. As a claimant on corporate profits, shareholders' dividends are relatively low as a percentage of company earnings. Dividends are paid not

as a percent of earnings but as a percent of the par value of shares in the company (Abegglen and Stalk 1985: 184; Dore 1987: 115).

The second strand of thought, often given in a critical vein in recent years, argues that the Japanese corporate system is characterized by management autonomy; hence top managers are the most powerful stakeholders and virtual owners of the company. To supporters, this makes Japan "dynamic because its managers devote themselves to competing with other companies at home and abroad, without having to serve the parasitic interests of shareholders or the passive interests of workers who have no stake in the viability of the company" (cited in Johnson 1996: 63). Critics argue, however, that top Japanese executives nowadays tend to be motivated by their self-interests and that their decision making lacks transparency. Because of the inadequacy of management oversight by shareholders, corporate executives can abuse their power without accountability, and they "tend to regard their company as their belonging" (Inoue 1997).

There was evidence in the 1990s to support such criticism. There was a spate of corporate financial scandals and executive abuses. When the scandals broke, executives typically bowed, apologized, and resigned, seemingly taking responsibility for the scandals, but the corporate safety net often simply gave these executives different high positions in the same companies afterward (Inoue 1977).

A third line of thought stresses the importance of employees in the familylike Japanese companies. Because the company is traditionally regarded as managers and workers alike as a family or a community, regular employees are traditionally treated as important members of the company. They participate in **decision making**, enjoy **lifetime employment** in large companies, and receive pays, fringe benefits, and biannual bonuses that are not far below those received by managers. During a recession executives' pays are cut first before those of employees, and layoffs are avoided for as long as possible. For these reasons Abegglen and Stalk (1985: 198) contend that "to a considerable degree, the company belongs to its employees." In a more critical vein, Prestowitz (1988: 293) also concludes that it is the people who work for a company, not shareholders, who own the Japanese company.

Variations on this theme abound. For example, Ozaki (1991: 10–14) considers the Japanese firm to be a "humanistic firm" in which its own human resources, not outside shareholders, are of primary importance. Thus he characterizes the Japanese firm as having "joint management-worker sovereignty." And despite recent changes in corporate Japan, Ozaki does *not* believe that its "ethos of people-orientation will soon vanish as if it was but a midsummer-night dream." Furthermore he finds it inconceivable that in Japan top management would get millions of dollars while employees are paid the minimum wages (communications to the author, January 2, 1998).

Aoki (1988: 101) questions the idea that employees are the de facto owners of the company. He points out that employees lack explicit power over the firm in the event of bankruptcy; nor can they prevent their own layoffs. He regards the Japanese company as a coalition of shareholders and employees, integrated and mediated by management to balance the interests of both sides. In other words, the Japanese company is subject to "dual control" (Aoki 1990). As to the much touted corporate harmony and consensus, familylike closeness and "humanistic practices," Yoshimura and Anderson (1997: 47, 101) consider them illusory and superficial because they are simply the results of employees conforming to expectations; employees "feel pressure to adhere to group norms and to get along with others whose approval they need in order to maintain group membership."

Finally, some scholars emphasize the importance of the **main bank** to its client companies. Among the stable shareholders of a company, its main bank occupies a special role. The main bank is the bank that provides the largest share of loans to the company; this is a long-term business relationship. In return, the main bank has access to company information, and its representative sits on the company's board as a director or auditor. When a company is in financial distress, its main bank may come to its rescue by providing additional funds or take the leadership role in its restructuring. It may dispatch executives to the firm to participate in or take over top management (Sheard 1994b). Thus the main bank plays an important role in corporate governance, particularly in difficult times.

All these lines of thought have some grains of truth. However, the economy is ever changing, and since the mid-1980s the following changes have affected the nature of corporate governance:

1. The importance of the main bank to many companies has declined. There are three reasons for this: (a) During the second half of the 1980s, equity capital became more importance than bank loans to many large companies because it was easy for large companies to raise funds on the stock market. (b) In the 1990s many banks are saddled with huge bad debts due to the decline of stock and land prices; hence they have cur-

tailed risky loans and loans to **small and medium enterprises**. (c) Banks' capital adequacy requirements have been raised by the government, which have limited banks' ability to make loans.

2. In the 1990s the prolonged recession of the Japanese economy and reduced corporate profits have weakened many companies' commitment to employees' **lifetime employment** and benefits. Layoffs cannot be avoided when companies have to downsize or restructure. The hiring of contract or nonregular workers has increased. These workers do not enjoy job security and corporate benefits, nor do they participate in decision making.

3. Management attitude toward shareholders has changed favorably in recent years. For example, in a survey of 100 company presidents (with 85 responses) conducted by Nihon Keizai Shimbun Inc. in June 1997, 41 gave "shareholders" as most important to top management, 26 gave "customers," and only 8 chose "employees" (*Nikkei Weekly*, June 23, 1997: 4). At the same time shareholders have become more assertive in recent years and have filed more lawsuits against alleged abuses of management responsibilities.

4. An increasing number of executives have come to realize that outside directors with different background and outlook can energize their companies. For example, in January 1997 the Japan Association of Corporate Executives, in its Manifesto for a Market-Oriented Economy, called on corporate Japan to increase the number of outside directors to more than 10% of total board members (*Nikkei Weekly*, August 11, 1997: 14).

Thus the nature of corporate governance in Japan is in a state of flux. Given the need to reinvigorate the stock market and the economy, these changes are much needed and may portend the things to come.

In conclusion, currently no one single group of stakeholders has a dominant power in corporate governance in Japan, although the actual situation may vary from company to company. Currently the Japanese ideal for corporate governance, as stated succinctly by the Economic Planning Agency (1996: 348), is to "run the company in such a manner that the rights and interests of top-level management, stockholders, creditors, employees and clients are properly balanced." What exactly constitutes the proper balance is not clear. The trend of changes, however, points to a greater role for shareholders in the future.

See also **business ethics, corporate finance, decision making, labor-management relations, main bank, management practices, mergers and acquisitions, underworld "businesses."**

References

Abegglen, James C., and George Stalk, Jr. 1985. *Kaisha: The Japanese Corporation.* New York: Basic Books.

Aoki, Masahiko. 1988. *Information, Incentives, and Bargaining in the Japanese Economy.* Cambridge: Cambridge University Press.

Aoki, Masahiko. 1990. Toward an economic model of the Japanese firm. *Journal of Economic Literature* 28: 1–27.

Aoki, Masahiko, and Ronald Dore, ed. 1994. *The Japanese Firm: Sources of Competitive Strength.* Oxford: Oxford University Press.

Dore, Ronald. 1987. *Taking Japan Seriously.* Stanford: Stanford University Press.

Economic Planning Agency. 1996. *Economic Survey of Japan, 1995–1996.* Tokyo.

Inoue, Tatsuya. 1997. Critics chide safety net for scandal-tainted execs. *Nikkek Weekly,* February 24: 14.

Johnson, Chalmers. 1995. *Japan: Who Governs?* New York: W. W. Norton.

Ozaki, Robert. 1991. *Human Capitalism: the Japanese Enterprise System as World Model.* New York: Penguin Books.

Sheard, Paul. 1994a. Interlocking shareholdings and corporate governance. In *The Japanese Firm: Sources of Competitive Strength,* ed. by Masahiko Aoki and Ronald Dore. Oxford: Oxford University Press.

Sheard, Paul. 1994b. Main banks and the governance of financial distress. In *The Japanese Main Bank System,* ed. by Masahiko Aoki and Hugh Patrick. New York: Oxford University Press.

Sherman, Howard D. and Bruce A. Babcock. 1994. Redressing structural imbalances in Japanese corporate governance: An interantional perspective. In *Japanese Corporate Governance: A Comparative Study of Systems in Japan and the United States,* ed. by David Kaufman. New York: The Pacific Institute.

Tachibanaki, Toshiaki, ed. 1998. *Who Runs Japanese Business?* Northampton, MA: Edward Elgar Publishing.

Wanner, Barbara. 1998. *Sokaiya* scandals, economic woes spotlight Japanese corporate governance. *JEI Report* 3A, January 23.

Watanabe, Shigeru and Isao Yamamoto. 1992. Corporate governance in Japan: ways to improve low profitability. *NRI Quarterly* 3 (Winter): 28–45.

Yoshimura, Noboru, and Philip Anderson. 1997. *Inside the Kaisha: Demystifying Japanese Business Behavior.* Boston: Harvard Business School Press.

corporate personnel practices   Japanese corporate personnel practices constitute an important part of **management practices** or the Japanese-style management (*nihonteki keiei*). The "traditional" practices originated mainly in the early postwar period when large employers competed to attract and retain scarce skilled workers. The practices have remained through the 1980s mainly because of the continuing demand for skilled labor due to technology-oriented economic growth but also because the traditional practices are compatible with the Japanese cultural emphasis on human relationships. Naturally there have been exceptions and ongoing changes. As economic growth has slowed down in the 1990s, the pressure for change has increased. In the following, the traditional employment practices and some recent changes are highlighted:

1. **Lifetime employment** or commitment prevails in many large companies. Regular employees are recruited right after college graduation and are expected to stay with the same employer for the rest of their careers. For their part, employers do not lay off or fire their employees, even during recessions, except under extraordinary circumstances. Japan's **employment insurance** helps companies avoid laying off employees by subsidizing the wages of temporarily laid-off workers of industries hit by a recession. As part of the lifetime employment system, before the 1980s midcareer changes in jobs were discouraged.

2. Temporary workers are hired by large companies for tasks that are not expected to last long. These workers do not enjoy job security and receive less pay and benefits than permanent workers, and are therefore much less costly to hire. For this reason temporary workers may not, in fact, be temporary; they may be rehired year after year as a way of saving labor cost. For the same reason part-time workers are also increasingly employed. Part-time workers are nonagricultural workers who work less than 35 hours per week. In 1996, of the total number of 53.2 million employees, 4.5 million or 8.4% of them were temporary workers. Most of them (3.2 million) were female.

3. Changes in jobs are becoming increasingly frequent and socially acceptable. As some companies are thinning their ranks of middle management who were recruited before the 1973 oil crisis, this makes midcareer changes inevitable. Labor shortage in the 1980s and growing corporate restructuring in the 1990s due to recession and increased market competition have accelerated this trend. For their part, some large companies in recent years have actively sought experienced workers in midcareer instead of recruiting only new college graduates and investing in their training, as was the tradition.

4. A seniority-based wage system (*nenko*) reinforces the lifetime employment system and minimizes rivalry among colleagues. Promotion is virtually automatic on the basis of seniority in the early years of employment

but is increasingly based on individual merit afterward. This system has led to middle-management bulge in the 1980s. As many employees hired before 1973 reached that level, large corporations such as Toyota Motor have acted to eliminate some middle-management positions. In the 1990s a growing number of large companies are switching to some type of merit system for wage increases and promotion, although seniority may not have been completely discarded.

5. Companies routinely rotate and train their new employees in different divisions of the company. Traditionally they rely on in-house training rather than recruitment of outside experts for specialized skills. Middle-level managers may be sent out to subsidiaries or affiliates for training or for providing technical assistance to a subsidiary. The posting may be for a period of a few months or years. This practice of transferring employees to other related companies is called *shukko*.

6. Early retirement (traditionally at age 55, but increasingly near age 60) is mandatory except for the few who become senior executives or board members. However, employees upon or near retirement may be transferred to an affiliate or subsidiary to set up a new operation and/or to help strengthen the subsidiary and its ties with the parent company. This also helps to make room for their replacement or to trim off redundant personnel. This practice of long-term personnel transfer is called *tenzoku*, meaning literally changing one's affiliation. Alternatively, employees who are incompetent or near retirement may be moved to the windows, the symbolic periphery of the office. They are given minor assignments. Commonly referred to as *madogiwazoku* or window watchers, this status is a hint for retirement.

7. The majority of executives rise from the ranks on the basis of seniority and proven leadership ability rather than come from outside the company. Even board members will come from company senior executives, and the chairman is typically a former president. This reflects the importance of being an insider in the Japanese corporate culture and society (see **business ethics**). However, corporate directors reportedly do not have much power over corporate policies. They are executives and as such are subordinate to the chairmen and presidents who retain the ultimate authority over all personnel (Mori 1996).

Some large companies do employ outsiders—retired high government officials—as senior executives. The practice of retired officials seeking employment in private corporations is referred to as **amakudari**, literally "descent from heaven." Presumably companies hire them to benefit from their experiences in government and ties with government bureaucrats, but the practice is being increasingly criticized in recent years for possible abuses.

8. Small businesses do not offer lifetime employment. In addition they often hire part-time workers at low pay and with few benefits.

9. **Employment discrimination** exists in hiring and promotion. Female employees are paid less and have limited prospects for advancement. Minorities such as the outcast *burakumin*, who are ethnic Japanese whose ancestors worked in "unclean" vocations, as well as Japan-born descendents of Korean immigrants, tend to be shunned by employers except for lower-paying jobs. Other ethnic minorities also tend to be discriminated against in employment.

10. Foreigners are rarely hired as lifetime employees. They tend to be hired as short-term contract workers (*shokutaku*) on a full-time or part-time basis.

The practices of lifetime employment, seniority-based wages, routine job-rotation, and employee training by companies are the pillars of Japan's corporate personnel system. They are said to have created an internal or internalized labor market within a company. Workers are said to have much work incentives as well mobility in this internal labor market but to have little mobility in the external labor market between firms. Ozaki (1991: 26–30) contends that this type of system is superior to the Western capitalist system in which firms rely on the external labor market for different categories of specialized labor. He argues that the Japanese system is more conducive to higher labor productivity because the company is willing to invest in the continual training of workers without fear of losing them to competitors. On their part, the workers are said to have the incentives to cooperate with and teach other workers, knowing that they have job security and will benefit from the increased productivity of all workers and the higher profits of the firm.

However, Nakatani (1993) argues that this Japanese system is outdated in the 1990s. It was appropriate in the early postwar period when job security was most important to workers. Today the system has produced workers who are inept outside their company of origin. It inhibits external labor market mobility, which is increasingly important because of the need to exchange information with outsiders for a competitive edge. More broadly, Sugahara (1994) contends that Japan's corporate employment system along with its **business ethics** has created employees who are excessively dependent, both economically and emotionally, on the company. It has mass-produced "salaryman" clones whose imaginations never extend outside the framework of the company. To her, this is one of the major symptoms of what she calls the "Japanese disease."

Whatever the theoretical merits of the two sides of the debate, many Japanese companies are already modifying their personnel practices to meet their changing needs.

See also **business ethics, employment discrimination, employment pattern, labor force, women in the labor force.**

References

Ariga, Kenn, G. Brunello, Y. Okhkusa, and Y. Nishiyama. 1992. Corporate hierarchy, promotion, and firm growth: Japanese internal labor market in transition. *Journal of the Japanese and International Economics* 6: 440–71.

Clark, Rodney. 1979. *The Japanese Company*. New Haven: Yale University Press. Chs. 5–6.

Dore, Ronald, Jean Bounine-Cabale, and Kari Tapiola. 1989. *Japan at Work: Markets, Management and Flexibility*. Paris: OECD.

Hamada, Tomoko. 1991. *American Enterprise in Japan*. Albany: State University of New York Press. Ch. 4.

Hasegawa, Keitaro. 1990. The upheaval in personnel management. *Japan Echo* 17, special issue: 21–25.

Ministry of Labor. Monthly. *Monthly Labor Statistics and Research Bulletin*. Tokyo.

Mori, Kazuo. 1996. Corporate directors should lead, not be led. *Nikkei Weekly*, July: 7.

Nakatani, Iwao. 1993. Corporate paternalism losing symbiotic value. *Nikkei Weekly*, February 22: 6.

Noriaki, Kojima. 1997. Japanese employment and labor laws in transition. *Journal of Japanese Trade and Industry*, no. 4: 8–11.

Oshima, Izumi. 1998. Career-hopping gaining popularity. *Nikkei Weekly*, April 6: 17.

Ozaki, Robert. 1991. *Human Capitalism*. New York: Penguin.

Sugahara, Mariko. 1994. Five fatal symptoms of the Japanese disease. *Japan Echo* 21, 2: 68–74.

corporate taxes   Corporations in Japan pay the national corporate income tax (called "corporation tax" in Japan) levied by the national government, the local corporate "inhabitant tax" levied by the prefectural and the municipal governments, and the prefectural enterprise or business tax.

Table C.6
Corporate income tax rates, FY 1997 (in %)

	Income before taxes (¥ millions)			
	Under ¥3.5	¥3.5–¥7	¥7–¥8	¥8 & over
National tax				
Corporate income tax	28.0	28.0	28.0	37.5
Local taxes				
Prefectural inhabitant tax[a]	1.4	1.4	1.4	1.88
Municipal inhabitant tax[b]	3.44	3.44	3.44	4.61
Prefectural enterprise tax[c]	6.0	9.0	12.0	12.0
Effective tax rate[d]	36.65	38.39	40.04	49.98

Sources: Ministry of Finance. Effective tax rates are from Gomi (1998: 16).
a. Levied as 5% of national corporate income tax rate.
b. Levied as 12.3% of national corporate income tax rate.
c. Levied on taxable income.
d. Prefectural enterprise tax is deducted from taxable income in calculating this rate.

As shown in table C.6, the tax rates are high by international standard, although they are lower for small businesses with annual taxable income of less than ¥8 million. The prefectural and municipal inhabitant taxes are specified as 5% and 12.3%, respectively, of the national corporate income tax rate. However, the sums of these tax rates at both the national and the local levels (55.99% for companies with a taxable income of more than ¥8 million) would overstate the real tax burden imposed on the companies because the local enterprise tax can be deducted from taxable income for the other corporate taxes. Thus the Japanese often use the "effective tax rate," which takes this deduction into account, to measure the real tax burden. The effective tax rates for different taxable income levels are given in the table. The top effective tax rate is 49.98%, which is higher than that of any other industrial countries except Germany (Takahashi 1997: 7). The top corporate income tax rate was reduced in April 1998 from 37.5% to 34.5%. As a result the top effective tax rate was reduced from 49.98% to 46.36% (*Nikkei Weekly*, March 16, 1998: 4).

In the late 1950s and early 1960s, the corporation tax was the most important tax in Japan in terms of tax revenue. Since 1965 it has slipped behind the **individual income tax** as the second largest tax. In FY 1997 it yielded ¥13.4 trillion, or 24.3% of the total tax revenue collected by the national government.

Business organizations and analysts have long argued that Japan's effective corporate tax rate should be reduced to no more than 40% in order for Japanese corporations to regain their competitive edge. Theoretically this can be accomplished in several ways without reducing national government revenue, but none of them is politically easy, as detailed by Takahashi (1997). Essentially either the corporate income tax base has to be broadened or alternative taxes have to be raised to offset the income tax cut. To broaden the tax base of national corporate income tax, various tax-free reserves (retirement allowance reserve, bonus payment reserve, bad debt reserve, reserve for after-sale service, etc.) and special tax credits and allowances (for the purpose of **industrial policy**) have to be eliminated or reduced. Companies oppose any such change that would affect their interests.

Nor is it easy to raise other taxes such as **individual income tax** and **consumption tax** for obvious reasons. Theoretically from the point of view of tax revenue, it is better to raise consumption tax and cut corporate and individual income taxes because consumption tax revenue would not fluctuate as much as income tax revenues as incomes fluctuate over the **business cycles**. On the other hand, consumption tax is not as equitable as income taxes because the rich and the poor alike pay the same percentage rate, whereas income tax rates are progressive. In any case the government did implement a long-scheduled increase in consumption tax from 3% to 5% in 1997, with much adverse effect on consumer spending. The timing of the increase was simply inappropriate.

In its use of fiscal policy in the 1990s to stimulate the economy, the government has repeatedly chosen to increase its spending on public works instead of cutting taxes. Nakatani (1998) argues that such a policy is not appropriate. The reason is twofold. On the one hand, increased public-works spending is not based on careful cost-benefit analysis and it benefits mostly established firms that have become dependent on government spending; it won't encourage start-up companies in new industries. On the other hand, income taxes penalize individual and corporate efforts, and tax cuts, particularly corporate tax cuts, would "increase capital in the hands of producers, not the ones dispensing favors to special interests." Furthermore tax cuts can be designed to "inspire individuals and corporations to greater endeavors."

Nakatani echoes the sentiment of many analysts and business people. If his analysis is correct, Japan would need to restructure the whole **tax system** rather than giving special, one-time tax cut, as it did in 1998.

See also **consumption tax, individual income tax, tax reform, tax system**.

References

Gomi, Yuji. 1997. *Guide to Japanese Taxes, 1997–98*. Tokyo: Zaikei Shohosha.

Kaneko, Hiroshi. 1994. Problems of the Japanese corporate income tax system. In *Japanese Commercial Law in an Era of Internationalization*, ed. by Hiroshi Oda. London: Graham and Trotman/Martinus Nijhoff.

Ishi, Hiromitsu, 1993. *The Japanese Tax System*. 2nd ed. Oxford: Oxford University Press.

Ministry of Finance. Annual. *An Outline of Japanese Taxes*.

Nakatani, Iwao. 1998. Right remedy it tax cuts, not public works. *Nikkei Weekly*, April 13: 16.

Ogawa, Shinichiro. 1995/96. Corporate taxation and the globalization of the Japanese economy. *Japan Research Quarterly* 5, 1: 48–91.

credit associations   A special type of cooperative financial institutions or *shinkin* banks to serve **small and medium enterprises**. At the end of 1997 there were 405 of them.

See **banking system,** *shinkin banks*.

credit card market   As part of the **consumer credit** market, the credit card industry occupies a relatively small share. Although the increased affluence of the Japanese consumers since the early 1980s and the **bubble economy** of 1986–89 have stimulated the demand for consumer credit, the outstanding amount of credit card debt has not grown as rapidly as that of total consumer credit. More than 200 million credit cards have been issued in Japan, but the average credit card transaction amount is relatively small and the average payback period relatively short (less than three months). At the end of 1995, outstanding credit card debt was ¥2.5 trillion or 3.3% of total consumer credit outstanding.

There are two major types of credit cards, bank-affiliated cards and retailer-affiliated cards. Major bank-affiliated cards are JCB cards, VISA, and MasterCard, of which JCB cards are the most popular. They are issued by the subsidiaries and affiliates of banks (JCB Co., Sumitomo Credit Service Co., Union Credit Co., etc.) but not by the banks themselves because of a **Ministry of Finance** regulation. The JCB Co. is Japan's largest credit card company, holding 12.3% of the Japanese credit card market in 1996. It has established ties with banks abroad in an effort to make its cards international.

The share of bank-affiliated cards in the credit card market was relatively small in the 1970s and 1980s. It has grown rapidly and has provided more than 50% of total crdit card debt since 1991. At the end of 1995, outstanding bank credit card debt was ¥1.3 trillion.

Retailer-affiliated cards, such as the "Saison Card" and the "OMC (Orange Members Club) Card," are either issued by retailer-affiliated credit companies or by the retailers themselves. The major ones include the Credit Saison Co. and Daiei Finance Inc., which have tie-ups with VISA International and MasterCard International, and Marui Co. and Isetan Co., which offer their in-house department store cards. Some producers such as electrical manufacturers and oil companies also offer credit cards.

Some consumer credit companies issue credit cards. With the exception of Nippon Shinpan Co. (5.1% of the market in 1996), these companies have not done well in the credit card business. In March 1988 the International Credit Card Business Association was established by department stores, supermarkets, manufacturers, and Nippon Shinpan Co. It had issued more than 20 million credit cards for participating companies by November 1989. Thus the industry has become highly competitive.

Compared with its U.S. counterpart, Japan's credit card industry is not yet as well developed. It is still plagued with problems such as inadequate credit management know-how and consumer credit information. On the other hand, the credit card default rate is lower than in the United States, although it has been rising in recent years.

Credit cards should be distinguished from prepaid cards, in which no credit is involved and a certain amount of cash is already paid by the cardholders. Prepaid cares are a convenient way of obtaining some goods and services such as train tickets and telephone calls without using cash. Prepaid telephone cards, in particular, are widely used.

See also **consumer credit**.

Addresses

JCB Co.
6, Kanda Surugadai 1-chome, Chiyoda ku, Tokyo 101
Tel: (3) 3294-8111

Nippon Shinpan Co.
33-5, Hongo 3-chome, Bunkyo-ku, Tokyo 113
Tel: (3) 3811-3111   Fax: (3) 3815-6650

References

Alexander, Arthur. 1997. Consumer credit in Japan since the bubble economy's end. *JEI Report* 23A, June 20.

Ando, Kiyoshi. 1997. High-stakes dispute over cards pits JCB against U.S. giant. *Nikkei Weekly*, December 22: 8.

Credit cards. *Japan Economic Almanac*. Various years. Tokyo: Nihon Keizai Shimbun.

Hardy, Quintin. 1991. Credit-card users facing an unaccustomed crunch. *Asian Wall Street Journal Weekly*, September 16: 3.

Iwasaki, Kazuo. 1990. Burgeoning credit card industry maturing in wake of decade-long consumer binge. *Japan Economic Journal*, Winter suppl.: 12.

Rate of credit-card purchases falling steeply. *Nikkei Weekly*, April 20, 1998: 3.

credit cooperatives   Financial institutions in the form of cooperatives to serve **small and medium enterprises**. At the end of 1997, they had ¥21.8 trillion in deposits and ¥17 trillion in loans. Their number has declined from 414 in 1990 to 368 in March 1996.

See **banking system**.

cross-shareholding   The practice of many Japanese companies, banks, insurance companies, and so forth, to hold each other's shares, without the intention of selling them for gains, in order to provide mutual support and maintain friendly business relationships. It is an important part of the larger "stable shareholders" network cultivated by Japanese companies to provide a stable and supportive business environment.

Cross-shareholding was an important aspect of the organization of prewar *zaibatsu* in which members of a *zaibatsu* group held each other's shares. In the postwar period two types of cross-shareholding can be distinguished:

1. Although the *zaibatsu* were dissolved after the war, new postwar **keiretsu**, or business groups of various types, have been established around a **city bank**, a general **trading company**, or a large industrial corporation. These *keiretsu* practice cross-shareholding as a means to cement group ties; the core company of a group may also use it to exert influence over, and/or to provide support to, its affiliates. In 1988 the average percentage of a member firm's stock held by other group members ranged from 12.2% to 26.9% for the largest *keiretsu*. In FY 1989 the average percentage of cross shareholding in the six bank-centered *keiretsu* was 21.64%. In industrial *keiretsu* such as the Hitachi Group and the Toyota Group which are organized around a large industrial corporation, cross-shareholding is mainly one-sided. Hitachi Ltd., for example, is said to have a policy of holding 50% or more of the shares of every member of the Hitachi

Group, including Hitachi Cable Ltd., Hitachi Metals Ltd., Hitachi Chemical Co., and Hitachi Construction Machinery Co.

2. Cross-shareholding is widely practiced among companies that regularly do business with each other—such as suppliers, distributors, banks,
and insurers—even without specific group ties. It is practiced in these
cases primarily as a token of goodwill and mutual support, of their intention to continue and foster the business relationship. These friendly
shareholders also help to forestall hostile takeovers. For example, after the
Japanese **stock market** crash of 1965, many companies were fearful of
foreign takeovers because of their depressed share prices and increasingly
liberal foreign investment regulations. Consequently they increased their
mutual shareholding with friendly firms. In the case of large banks and
insurance companies that hold their customers' shares, cross-shareholding
is one-sided with the banks and insurers providing some needed capital
to client companies to maintain or expand business.

All cross-shareholders are valued as stable shareholders. Other stable
shareholders are institutional investors such as trust funds, pension funds,
and **insurance companies** that hold stock portfolios for long-term gains.
A 1989 survey by the *Nihon Keizai Shimbun*, a leading business newspaper, shows that more than 60% of publicly traded Japanese companies
regard it desirable to have 60% to 70% of outstanding shares held by stable
shareholders. The reason is that it gives executives more time to concentrate on business goals and not to worry about possible takeovers.
Some scholars agree. Nakatani (1984) describes cross-shareholding as a
shock-absorbing, "mutual insurance" arrangement that benefits both the
company and employees in the long run. Similarly McDonald (1989)
considers cross-shareholding as part of Japan's reciprocal corporate relationship that contributes to "collective risk reduction." In other words,
cross-shareholding is an institutional device to combine the best of the
two worlds—to have the benefits of the impersonal equity market without its impersonal nature, namely the instability and risks it entails. These
are the *mochiai* effect of "joint stockholding" (*kabushiki mochiai*). *Mochiai*
literally means to hold mutually; it also implies "shared interdependence"
and "helping one another" (Gerlach 1987: 132).

These benefits are not without their social costs. The stable shareholders reduce the competitiveness of the capital market at the expense of
outsiders, particularly the small individual investors. From the point of
view of the stable shareholders, cross-shareholding helps cement business
ties at low cost as long as share prices are rising. In fact their unrealized

capital gains from such shareholding are recognized in Japan as "latent capital" which can be used as collateral for loans and are calculated as part of banks' own capital. Cross-shareholding becomes a burden, however, when share prices decline, resulting in "latent losses." For example, share prices declined greatly in 1990, and corporate shareholders saw the value of their stocks decline by about 40%. The economy has remained depressed since then, and most banks have experienced mounting bad debts and have become reluctant to hold more shares at the request of clients. In fact in 1997 some banks sold some of their cross-shareholdings to avoid further losses.

Additionally in recent years cross-shareholding has generated friction with Washington. American critics of Japan's business practices charge that cross-shareholding keeps share prices high and promotes exclusive business ties, thereby making it virtually impossible for foreign companies to purchase complete control of a Japanese company. Consequently, in the U.S.–Japan **Structural Impediments Initiative** talks in 1989–90, Washington pressed Tokyo for changes in disclosure and other rules concerning cross-shareholding. The issue has become important to Washington, since Japanese companies have bought up American companies and real estate with relative ease while foreign investors face investment barriers in Japan.

In response to Washington's request for more openness, a number of changes have been made. In late 1990 the **Ministry of Finance** enacted a rule requiring members of giant corporate groups, *keiretsu*, to disclose more about transactions within the group. Another new rule requires investors to report holdings of 5% or more in a company.

It should be pointed out that cross-shareholding is not unique to Japanese firms. It also exists in Europe, particularly Germany where hostile corporate takeovers are rare. Dore (1989) argues that Japan's market "liberalization" is not necessarily "Americanization" and that there are competing models of capitalism other than that of the Anglo-Saxon countries. He implies that in the evolution of Japanese capitalism, the pros and cons of specific business practices should be assessed from a broader perspective other than that of Japan–U.S. trade relations.

See also *keiretsu* **and business groups.**

References

Choy, Jon. 1991. Patterns and implications of Japanese stockholdings. *JEI Report*, January 25.

Dore, Ronald P. 1989. "Liberalization" not necesarily "Americanization." *Japan Economic Journal*, November 4: 9.

Flath, David. 1993. Shareholding in the Keiretsu, Japan's financial groups. *Review of Economics and Statistics* 75: 249–257.

Flath, David. 1994. Keiretsu shareholding ties: Antitrust issues. *Contemporary Economic Policy* 12: 24–36.

Gerlach, Michael. 1987. Business alliances and the strategy of the Japanese firm. *California Management Review* 30, 1: 126–42.

Japan's stocks caught in vicious circle due to reliance on cross-shareholding. *Asian Wall Street Journal*, October 15, 1990: 32.

Kester, W. Carl. 1991. *Japanese Takeovers: The Global Contest for Corporate Control.* Boston: Harvard Business School Press. Chs. 3, 8.

McDonald, Jack. 1989. The *mochiai* effect: Japanese corporate cross-holding. *Journal of Portfolio Management* 16, 1: 90–95.

Mizuno, Yuko. 1989. Popularity of equity financing threatening *keiretsu* system. *Japan Economic Journal*, December 30: 35–36.

Nakao, Shigeo. 1995. *The Political Economy of Japan Money.* Tokyo: University of Tokyo Press.

Nakatani, Iwao. 1984. The economic role of financial corporate grouping. In *The Economic Analysis of the Japanese Firm*, ed. by Masahiko Aoki. Amsterdam: North-Holland.

Sheard, Paul. 1994. Interlocking shareholdings and corporate governance. In *The Japanese Firm: Sources of Competitive Strength*, ed. by Masahiko Aoki and Ronald Dore. Oxford: Oxford University Press.

customer sovereignty   It is sometimes said that postwar Japan has been producer oriented rather than consumer oriented, and that the Japanese government has promoted producers' interests at the expense of consumers' interests for the sake of pursuing rapid economic growth. As evidence for this proposition, proponents have pointed to the importance that the government has given to its **industrial policy**, the weak implementation of the **Antimonopoly Law**, the relative weakness of the **consumer groups**, the lack of a product liability system, the high prices of consumer goods and food in Japan, and so forth. The implication is that "consumer sovereignty"—a basic tenet of Western economics—does not exist in Japan.

It should be noted that the pursuit of rapid economic growth is not necessarily contrary to consumers' long-term interests. Consumers' income is increased as more jobs are created and labor productivity is raised. Product quality and variety are improved, and prices are likely to come down as industries grow and companies compete in the market, even to the extent of "excessive competition." New products are created as firms invest in R&D.

Nevertheless, in the context of postwar Japan, the concept of consumer sovereignty, whether it exists or not, is not adequate to capture the all-important relationship between buyers and sellers in the market and their respective power. It is more meaningful to talk about "customers sovereignty" at both the company and industry level to characterize the most important players of the Japanese market place. The term "consumers" as used in Western economics refers to a large, amorphous group of people who are theoretically merely interested in consuming as much final goods and services as possible at the lowest possible prices. It is further postulated in Western neoclassical economics that consumers can best attain their goal in an impersonal, "perfectly competitive" market without any personal ties. In contrast, the term "customers" (or the "honorable customers" in Japanese) is a relation-laden concept, reflecting not only the relationship between buyers and sellers but also the desire to maintain and cultivate that valued relationship, which is essential for long-term business growth. Furthermore "customers" include both individual customers who are consumers and corporate customers who are themselves producers. Viewed in this light, most seasoned observers of Japan would agree with the late Knosuke Matsushita, founder of Matsushita Electric Industrial, that "the customer is God" in Japan. Matsushita might have merely had the individual customers of his world-famous consumer electronic products in mind, and he gave it as an advice to business managers. But it can be taken as an accurate description of the important role and status of the "honorable customers"—both individual and corporate customers—in Japan.

At the retail level, individual customers exert great influence over the retailers. Japanese shoppers are said to be very "fussy" about quality, price, delivery, and services. On the other hand, retailers are said to spare no efforts to please and to retain their customers (Johansson and Nonaka 1996; Kang 1990). The merchants are very attentive to their customers' needs and whims, not only because it makes good business sense but also because culturally it is deeply ingrained since Japan's feudal period that it is the merchants' obligation to give their best to their customers, who were traditionally considered to be their social superiors (Kang 1990: 4). It is true that retail prices of many products are higher in Japan than elsewhere. However, retail costs are also higher in Japan because land and store space are more expensive. In addition retailing is more labor intensive in Japan because it usually includes personal attention, delivery and postsale services; careful and attractive wrapping is also customary for many consumer goods even if they are not intended as gifts.

Similarly corporate customers are assiduously catered to by their suppliers. Here the unequal bargaining power between the buyers and the sellers further enhances the customer sovereignty. The buyers are often large corporations and members of *keiretsu* or business groups. In some industries such as the automobile and electronics industries, the giant manufacturers have literally hundreds of small subcontractors to supply parts, who in turn may have numerous subcontractors of their own. In this hierarchy of large buyers and layers of small suppliers, it is the buyers who dictate, within the bounds of reason, the terms of the transactions. Sakai (1990) likens the power relationship of this hierarchical order of Japanese manufacturing to the feudal order of lords–samurai–common people of Japan before the late ninetieth century. Although the analogy exaggerates the permanence and lopsidedness of the business relationship and ignores the fact that such a relationship is voluntary and has to be mutually beneficial to be viable, it does highlight the sovereignty of the corporate customers.

For similar reasons Dore (1990: 371) characterizes Japanese firms' transactions as those of "customers' market" rather than of "auction markets" assumed in Western neoclassical economics. Furthermore he regards their behavior as justified in efficiency terms because such business relationship ensures quality, prompt delivery, collaboration in technical improvements, new product design, and so forth.

See also **consumer groups**, *keiretsu* **and business groups, pricing practices, subcontracting system**.

References

March, Robert M. 1990. *The Honourable Customer: Marketing and Selling to the Japanese in the 1990s*. Melbourne: Longman Professional.

Dore, Ronald. 1990. An outsider's view. In *Japan's Economic Structure: Should It Change?* ed. by Kozo Yamamura. Seattle: Society for Japanese Studies.

Johansson, John K. and Ikujiro Nonaka. 1996. *Relentless: The Japanese Way of Marketing*. New York: Harper Business.

Kang, T. W. 1990. *Gaishi: The Foreign Company in Japan*. New York: Basic Books. Chs. 1–2.

Saki, Kuniyasu. 1990. The feudal world of Japanese manufacturing. *Harvard Business Review* 68, 6 (November–December): 38–47.

D

daimyo bonds   Yen-denominated bonds issued in Japan by nonresidents but sold to investors on the Euromarket.
  See *samurai* bonds.

dango   Bid-rigging or the practice of prebidding collusion in the **construction industry**, resulting in overpricing and the exclusion of foreign firms from Japan's construction market.
  See **construction industry, pricing practices**.

decision making   Japanese companies and other organizations typically seek a broad-based consensus in their decision making. Consequently decision making often involves a lengthy process of discussions and the formation of consensus.
  Two phases of the traditional decision-making process can be distinguished. The first one, sometimes referred to as *nemawashi*, is the informal, pre-decision process of discussions and accommodations of views to prepare the ground for the formation of consensus. In its original usage as a nursery term, *nemawashi* refers to the practice of digging the ground around a large tree and cutting the roots, except for the tap root and large side roots, a year or two before it is to be transplanted, to allow feathery rootlets to grow in order to make it easier to transplant. This is also performed so that trees will bear large fruits. Thus figuratively, it means laying the groundwork to achieve the organization's objective. In consensus-based decision making, such careful preparations are needed.
  The second phase involves the formal drafting of a proposal for circulation among units of an organization for consultation, comments and approval. The procedure is referred to as the *ringi* system, where *rin* means submitting a proposal to one's superior for approval and *gi* means deliberations and decisions. In the procedure, a low-echelon management staff

member first drafts a formal document (*ringisho*), outlining a problem and his recommendation. The document is then reviewed and approved by the related units of the organization and finally evaluated and approved by the top-level management. After the approval the document is returned to the original drafter for implementation.

The consensus-based *ringi* system has been described by Western scholars as the "bottom-up" decision making. One implication of the system is that top executives lack the power of their Western counterparts to make quick "top-down" decisions. Even if the idea originally comes from a top executive, he would still entrust a lower staff member who would be involved in its implementation to draft the *ringi* document. In this way the final decision would have the cooperation of more people after the proposal has gone through the "due process."

The system provides a mechanism for consultation with various departments, helps to coordinate their activities, and ensures the smooth implementation of the proposal once it is adopted. However, it is a time-consuming process. In addition consensus-based decision making reduces accountability and shields individuals from direct responsibility if the proposal proves to be ill-advised. Increasingly therefore, in situations in which a quick decision is desirable, Western-style decision-making involving only top-level management has been adopted. This can take the form of issuing and circulating the *ringisho* at the upper management level, thereby shortening the decision-making process (author's interview with NEC management, June 16, 1993). It is also noteworthy that the Japanese decision-making system has not always worked well in Japanese subsidiaries in the United States for precisely the reasons mentioned above.

At the operational or shop-floor level of an enterprise, decision making tends to be decentralized and organized on the basis of small groups. The famous **quality control** circle is an example. Ozaki (1991: 30–34) argues that this type of decision making is superior to the more centralized type of the American firms because it promotes the sharing of technical know-how among workers and cultivates "a habit of thinking holistically" on the part of workers, thereby avoiding the demoralization and alienation of workers found in an American firm.

The **subcontracting system**, which is prevalent in Japanese manu-facturing industries, is tantamount to delegating decision making on the production of parts to the subcontractors (Ozaki 1991: 52–53). Compared with the alternative system of relying on in-house production of parts, the subcontracting system effectively decentralizes decision making at some stages of the manufacturing process, thereby giving both large manu-

facturing firms and their numerous subcontractors the benefits of specialization and flexibility in the organization of production.

How is decision made in the case of Japanese joint ventures with
American companies? Obviously there can be no general rule except that
some balance and compromise are necessary, if the experience of Toshiba
Corp. and IBM Corp. is any guide. In August 1995 the two giant com-
panies launched, on a 50–50 basis, a U.S.-based joint venture, Domimion
Semiconductor, located in Manassas, Virginia, to manufacture 64-megabit
DRAM chips. Because the two companies are equal partners but with
very different business cultures, some meshing of the two has been necessary. The top executives come from the two sides in equal number.
According to its American president, when it comes to decision making
the Japanese executive tend to take more time but sometimes defer to
American managers. On the other hand, the American managers recog-
nize that "on certain business issues it is counterproductive to push our
Japanese partners.... We simply have to give our Toshiba managers
more time so that they can caucas among themselves or communicate
with senior management in Tokyo." The main lesson learned is the "need
for balance between the two partners" (*JEI Report* 6A, February 13, 1998:
4–5).

Consensus decision making also characterizes the government bureaucracy at various levels. The process is typically time-consuming, particularly when more than one ministry or agency is involved because of
bureaucratic inflexibility and turf-fighting. The Kobe earthquake of January 1995 revealed the fatal flaws of such a decision making in a crisis.
Wanner (1995: 4) writes that not only was government response slow in
that crisis but also the initial response was typically tepid and inadequate.
She also criticizes the government for lacking in anticipatory decision
making by consensus.

References

An insider's views on U.S.–Japan production joint ventures: An interview with M.
Alexander Graham, president, Dominion Semiconductor. *JEI Reports* 6A, February 13, 1998.

Lincoln, James R. 1989. Employee work attitudes and management practice in the U.S. and
Japan: Evidence from a large comparative survey. *California Management Review* 32, 1: 89–
106.

Lincoln, James, and Arne L. Kalleberg. 1989. *Culture, Control, and Commitment: A Study of
Work Organizations and Work Attitudes in the U.S. and Japan.* Cambridge: Cambridge University Press.

Ozaki, Robert. 1991. *Human Capitalism*. New York: Penguin.

Takeuchi, Hiroshi. 1985. Motivation and productivity. In *The Management Challenge: Japanese Views*, ed. by Lester C. Thurow. Cambridge: MIT Press.

Taplin, Ruth. 1995. *Decision-Making and Japan: A Study of Corporate Japanese Decision-Making and Its Relevance to Western Companies*. Folkstone, Britain: Japan Library.

Wanner, Barbara. 1995. Tokyo confronts crisis management shortcomings in wake of Hansin earthquate disaster. *JEI Report* 4A, February 3, 1995.

Yoshino, M. Y. 1968. *Japan's Managerial System: Tradition and Innovation*. Cambridge: MIT Press. Ch. 9.

declining industries   Any growing economy has its declining industries, and Japan is no exception. In Japan, public policy has played an active role along with voluntary industry efforts in promoting the necessary structural adjustments in declining industries in response to shifting market demand.

Prior to 1978 only ad hoc government measures were taken to facilitate adjustments in declining industries such as textiles and shipbuilding. However, the first oil crisis (1973–75) adversely affected so many industries that a comprehensive legislation for assistance became necessary. Consequently the 1978 Law of Temporary Measures for Stabilization of Specific Depressed Industries was enacted. It provided for low-interest loans to "structurally depressed industries" for shifting production to a new line of business and for retiring redundant personnel. It also provided for guarantees for new private bank loans to pay off existing loans on plants and equipment.

The criteria for structurally depressed industries are (1) more than 50% of the industry's firms experiencing financial difficulties due to changes in domestic or international economic conditions, (2) severe overcapacity of the industry with poor prospects for improvement, (3) firms representing two-thirds of the industry's capacity seeking designation as structurally depressed, and (4) a consensus that some scrapping of facilities has become necessary. Fourteen industries met these criteria, including electric and open-hearth steel, aluminum smelting, nylon staple, polyester staple, polyesterfilament, ployacrylnitrate filament, ammonium, urea, phosphoric acid (by wet process), cotton and wool spinning, wool yarn, ferrosilicon, corrugated cupboard, and shipbuilding.

The law authorizes the **Ministry of International Trade and Industry** (MITI) or some other designated agency to formulate, after consultation with advisory committees, a "Basic Stabilization Plan" for the specific industries. The plan would establish the extent of overcapacity on the basis of supply and demand forecasts and determine the proper method of reducing excess capacity. The plan has to be approved by the Fair Trade Commission, after which it would be implemented by industrial **cartels**, formed under MITI's guidance and exempted from the **Antimonopoly Law**.

The following measures were taken to help implement the capacity-reduction plan: (1) A total of $148 million loans and loan guarantees was given between 1978 and 1983. (2) In the textile industry, a special "scrapping fund" was created to guarantee repayment of loans collateralized by equipment that was to be scrapped. (3) **Administrative guidance** was used by the Ministry of Transport to curtail output in the **shipbuilding industry**. (4) Administrative guidance was used to encourage or assist industries to shift to other product lines.

The implementation of the stabilization plan has had different successes in different industries. It was very successful in aluminum smelting—an industry that is extremely energy intensive—where actual reduction in capacity has exceeded the plan target by 70%. It was also successful in shipbuilding in which about 100% of the target was achieved. It was moderately successful in all other structurally depressed industries except cotton spinning where actual reduction in capacity fell short of targeted reduction by 22%. Analysts attribute the failure to reduce capacity in the textile industry to its fragmented structure, because of ease of entry, and to its political clout.

As the 1978 Law expired in 1983, the 1983 Law of Temporary Measures for the Structural Adjustment of Specific Industries was enacted. It has the same criteria and procedure as the 1978 Law for the designation of structurally depressed industries. As a result 11 of the previous 14 industries remain covered by the 1983 Law (excluding shipbuilding, cotton, and wool). In addition 11 new industries are covered, including fertilizer, ethyline, polyolefine, polyvinyl chloride, ethylene oxide, unpasticized polyvinyle chloride pipes, paper, viscose rayon staple, sugar refining, and cement.

The 1983 Law provides for a wider range of monetary and fiscal support measures, including low-interest loans, government subsidies for investment in energy-conserving equipment, and a special depreciation system for modernization and capacity-reduction investment. In addition it provides for various types of business tie-ups to cut cost—production tie-ups allow an underutilized company to produce for a competitor, transportation tie-ups allow a company nearest the customer to make delivery for sales made by other companies in order to reduce cross-hauling, and sales tie-ups utilize a common selling agent for several companies. All these tie-ups require prior approval by the Fair Trade Commission.

In 1988 the Adjustment Facilitation Law was enacted to replace the 1983 Law. The new law shifts the focus of assistance by specifying equipment (18 types) to be scrapped rather than designating industries or firms eligible for assistance as under previous laws. According to Sekiguchi (1994: 63) the reason for the change was Washington's criticism that adjustment assistance to specific industries might give some firms unfair advantage to compete in those industries.

The 1988 Law provides financial incentives to encourage (1) business conversion, (2) business partnerships for overcoming difficulties, and (3) new investments in specified depressed regions. The incentives include low-interest (5%) loans by the **Japan Development Bank**, loan guarantees, reduced taxes on land purchases, accelerated depreciation allowances, and increased carryover of past losses from capacity scrapping.

There is also the 1987 Law for Promotion of Regional Employment to be implemented by the Ministry of Labor. The Law was enacted, in part, because the unemployment created by the declining industries affected some regions more severely than others. Another reason is that when Japanese companies move their labor-intensive operations abroad to reduce costs, job losses will be more severe in some regions.

See also **industrial policy**.

References

Alexander, Authur J. 1994. Japan's policy toward declining industries: a blueprint for handling economic obsolescence? *JEI Report* 4A, January 28.

Anderson, Douglas D. 1986. Managing retreat: Disinvestment policy. In *American versus Japan*, ed. by Thomas K. McCraw. Boston: Harvard Business School Press.

Lawrence, Robert Z. 1989. A depressed view of policies for depressed industries. In *Trade and Investment Relations among the United States, Canada, and Japan*, ed. by Robert M. Stern. Chicago: University of Chicago Press.

Lesbirel, S. Hayden. 1991. Structural adjustment in Japan: Terminating "old King Coal." *Asian Survey* 31: 1079–94.

Peck, Merton J., Richard C. Levin, and Akira Goto. 1987. Picking losers: Public policy toward declining industries in Japan. *Journal of Japanese Studies* 13: 79–123.

Sekiguchi, Sueo. 1994. An overview of adjustment assistance policies in Japan. In *Troubled Industries in the United States and Japan*, ed. by Hong W. Tan and Haruo Shimada. New York: St. Martin's Press.

Sekiguchi, Sueo, and Toshihiro Horiuchi. 1988. Trade and adjustment assistance. In *Industrial Policy of Japan*, ed. by Ryutaro Komiya, Masahiro Okuno, and Lotaro Suzumura. Tokyo: Academic Press Japan.

Sheard, Paul. 1991. The role of firm organization in the adjustment of a declining industry in Japan: The case of aluminum. *Journal of the Japanese and International Economics* 5: 14–40.

Uekusa, Masu. 1987. Industrial organization. In *The Political Economy of Japan*, vol. 1: *The Domestic Transformation*, ed. by Kozo Yamamura and Yasukichi Yasuba. Stanford: Stanford University Press.

Uriu, Robert M. 1996. *Troubled Industries: Confronting Economic Change in Japan*. Ithaca: Cornell University Press.

defense expenditures   Japan's peace constitution, adopted under U.S. pressure, renounces "war as a sovereign right of the nation and the threat or use of force as a means of settling international disputes" (Article 9). Only a small Ground Self-defense Force is maintained, authorized in 1976 at 180,000 personnel. However, the Treaty of Mutual Cooperation and Security of 1960, through which the United States created a special relationship with Japan as part of its postwar strategy, has provided Japan with U.S. military protection, including the stationing of some 50,000 U.S. troops in Japan.

Consequently throughout most of the postwar period Japan's defense expenditures as a percentage of GDP was typically below 1% (see table D.1), although the percentage would be as high as 1.6% of GDP in 1995 if expenditures on coastguard, space program and officers' pension costs were included. By contrast, in 1995 the percentage of GDP spent on defense was 3.8% in the United States, 7.4% in Russia, 5.7% in China, and 3.1% in both France and Britain (*The Economist*, October 12, 1996: 38). Japan's average annual rate of increase in defense spending during 1980–90 was 6.4%, which was consistent with the 6%-plus spending increase that Pentagon officials had urged Tokyo to maintain. Also, in absolute dollar figures, Japan is now the third largest military spender in the world behind the United States and Russia.

Japan's relatively light defense burden during the postwar period is considered by many analysts to have contributed to its fast economic growth. As U.S.–Japan trade frictions mounted in the 1970s and 1980s, it has also prompted foreign criticism of Japan for enjoying a "free ride" on security from the United States and has led the U.S. Congress to demand greater Japanese defense burden sharing.

Partly as a response, since the early 1980s Japanese leaders have broadened their concept of defense to include foreign aid as part of Japan's "comprehensive security." They are willing to step up their aid to

Table D.1

Defense expenditures

Fiscal year	Expenditure[a] (in ¥ billions)	Percentage of GDP[b]
1955	136	1.78%
1965	307	1.07
1975	1,397	0.94
1980	2,272	0.95
1985	3,202	1.00
1990	4,277	0.99
1991	4,465	0.97
1992	4,613	0.98
1993	4,626	0.97
1994	4,662	0.97
1995	4,745	0.98
1996	4,874	0.97
1997	4,973	0.98

Source: Ministry of Finance.

a. Figures through FY 1995 are based on settled accounts, those for 1996 on supplemented budget, and those for 1997 on the initial budget.

b. Figures for FY 1955 and 1965 are percentages of GNP.

developing countries as Japan's contribution to world security. Japan was the largest aid donor in the world in 1989 and 1991–96.

Because of the ending of the cold war, Tokyo plans to have slower increases in defense spending since FY 1991. This is the lowest annual rate of growth in defense spending since 1960.

See also **foreign aid**.

References

Auer, James E. 1991. Defense Burdensharing and the U.S.–Japan Alliance. In *Japan and the United States: Troubled Partners in a Changing World*. Cambridge, MA: Institute for Foreign Policy Analysis.

Balassa, Belas, and Marcus Noland. 1988. *Japan in the World Economy*. Washington: Institute for International Economics. Pp. 158–66.

Japan Defense Agency. Annual. *Defense of Japan*.

Military budget in line for cuts. *Nikkei Weekly*, June 16, 1997: 3.

Military budget increase to be held at 2.1%. *Nikkei Weekly*, December 18, 1995: 3.

The real cost of Japanese defence. *The Economist*, October 12, 1996: 38.

Sharing the defense burden with Japan: How much is enough? *JEI Report* 19A, May 13, 1988.

defense industry   Reborn from the ashes of World War II, Japan's defense industry received a critical boost during the Korean War (1950–53) when military orders from the U.S. armed forces for repairs and supplies started to pour in. Subsequent rapid growth and technological development of the Japanese economy also greatly benefited the industry.

Japan's defense industry is dominated by a small group of firms. Mitsubishi Heavy Industries (MHI) is by far the largest defense contractor. Called the "Japanese Arsenal," MHI is the only comprehensive supplier of major weapons for all divisions of the Japanese Self-defense Force; it is also the dominant contractor of most of the licensed production of major weapons, and has developed many sophisticated weapons of its own (Ikegami-Andersson 1992: 79). MHI is trailed by Kawasaki Heavy Industries, Mitsubishi Electric, Ishikawajima-Harima Heavy Industries, and Toshiba (see table D.1). However, all these companies including MHI are generally diversified companies and are not engaged solely or mainly in defense production. For example, in FY 1991 Mitsubishi Heavy Industries and Kawasaki Heavy Industries derived only 17.7% and 15.7%, respectively, of their revenues from defense contracts. The figures for the other defense contractors are even lower.

The industry is constrained first and foremost by the relatively low level of **defense expenditures**—generally around 1% of GDP. The industry is also constrained by Japan's ban on the export of military hardware, although the line between military and nonmilitary equipment is often blurred because of the proliferation of dual-use technologies. Analysts believe that Tokyo is not likely to lift the ban in the foreseeable future, since the world's arms market is already oversupplied and any such exports from Japan will only aggravate the strained economic relations between Japan and the United States.

Most of Japan's advanced weapon systems are produced under license from U.S. manufacturers. For example, Mitsubishi Heavy Industries makes F-15 fighter and the surface-to-air Patriot missile, and Mitsubishi Electric Corp. makes the second-generation Hawk surface-to-air missile, all built with technology licensed from the United States.

However, Japanese companies have developed some weapons on their own, including anti-tank missiles, air-to-air missiles, and Mitsubishi Heavy Industries' ground-based anti-ship missiles (SSMI). According to some Western analysts, Japan's strength lies in dual-use technologies, which were originally developed for civilian uses but subsequently have military applications. For example, Toray Industries produces carbon-fiber composites, a tough, light material for tennis rackets and golf clubs. The product is also sold to the United States for use in jet-fighter airframes. NEC's telecommunication technologies and semiconductors are used in military telecommunication systems. Toshiba's electrooptics used in home-video cameras can be used in missile-guidance systems.

Given the relatively small size of Japan's defense industry, it makes economic sense for Japan to import advanced defense technology from the United States rather than developing it on its own, as some American officials and Japan's own critics of "buy Japanese" policy have argued. In some cases the cost differentials between Japanese-designed or produced weapons and foreign equivalents are said to be substantial (*Nikkei Weekly,* June 22, 1991: 3). However, until 1991 Tokyo was interested in promoting self-sufficiency in arms production, even at the cost of economic efficiency. This is shown in its initial decision in the late 1980s to develop a new fighter plane for the 1990s by Mitsubishi Heavy Industries. After much urging from Washington, the two governments agreed in 1988 to jointly develop an advanced version of F-16, code-named FSX, by Mitsubishi Heavy Industries and General Dynamic. However, because of the intractable U.S. trade deficits with Japan, some members of the U.S. Congress subsequently objected to the joint project, fearful that it would give Japan undue technological and commercial advantages. After complicated and contentious negotiations between the two governments and the two companies, Mitsubishi Heavy Industries was confirmed in a 1989 agreement as the project's lead contractor with General Dynamic as a secondary contractor similar to two other Japanese participants, Kawasaki Heavy Industries and Fuji Heavy Industries. However, there are provisions for the transfer of Japanese wing technology developed for FSX free of charge to General Dynamic, paid for by the Japanese government. There were also subsequent cost and other problems that plagued the "troubled partnership" (Lorell 1996).

There are indications since 1991 that because of increased pressure from Washington, Tokyo would relax its policy of nurturing Japan's armaments industry and increase imports of U.S.-made weapons. The Gulf War played a major role in this policy change because of the growing consensus to support U.S. military power.

See also **defense expenditures**.

References

Auer, James E. 1991. Defense Burdensharing and the U.S.–Japan Alliance. In *Japan and the United States: Troubled Partners in a Changing World.* Cambridge, MA: Institute for Foreign Policy Analysis.

"Buy Japanese" called inefficient, expensive in weaponry. *Nikkei Weekly*, June 22, 1991: 3.

Drifte, Reinhard. 1986. *Arms Production in Japan: The Military Applications of Civilian Technology*. Boulder, CO: Westview.

Ikegami-Anderson, Masako. 1992. *The Military-Industrial Complex: The Cases of Sweden and Japan*. Aldershot, Engalnd: Dartmouth Publishing Co.

Japan Defense Agency. Annual. *Defense of Japan*.

Japan's weapons makers: Ready and able. *The Economist*, February 2, 1991: 67.

Lorell, Mark. 1996. *Troubled Partnership: A History of U.S.–Japan Collaboration on the FS-X Fighter*. New Brunswick: Transaction Publishers.

Samuels, Richard J. 1994. *Rich Nation, Strong Army: National Security and the Technological Transformation of Japan*. Ithaca: Cornell University Press.

Samuels, Richard J., and Benjamin C. Whipple. 1989. The FSX and Japan's strategy for aerospace. *Technology Review*, October: 43–51.

Wanner, Barbara. 1993. Japanese defense industry grapples with post-cold war conversion. *JEI Report* 12A, April 12.

deferred pricing   The practice of finalizing prices after sales in some industires.
   See **pricing practices**.

demography
See **population**.

department stores   Sales of all department stores (total of 2,267), large and medium sized, amounted to ¥20 trillion in 1994, or about 17% of total retail sales in Japan. Large-scale department stores are defined as employing 50 or more employees and having 3,000 square meters or more of store space in the ten largest cities and 1,500 square meters or more in the rest of the country. These large department stores accounted for ¥11 trillion retail sales in 1996, down from their peak of ¥12.1 trillion in 1991.

   The market shares of Japan's department stores in the retail business are low compared with the situation in other industrial countries. The growth of the number of large-scale department stores in the postwar period has also been slower than the growth of total retail sales. The number was 325 in 1975, 360 in 1985, and 431 in 1996. The reason for this is that until 1990, the government had protected small retailers by restricting the establishment of large department stores and supermarkets through the Department Store Law of 1956 and the **Large Retail Store Law** of 1974 which superseded the 1956 law. It was not until Washington complained about the restriction and its impact on imports during the **Structural Impediments Initiative** talks between Washington and Tokyo in 1989– 90 that changes were made. In May 1990 the government relaxed the implementation of the Large Retail Store Law. In 1991 revisions were made in the law to shorten the period before large department stores can be opened. Thus analysts expect large department stores to grow in the future in terms of store numbers and retail market share. During the late 1980s the stock market boom and economic growth in Japan led to high levels of consumer spending. Department stores experienced rising sales and profits. Thus as soon as the implementation of the Large Retail Store Law was relaxed, large department stores were engaged in a competition to build new and ever-larger stores in the major cities during 1990 to 1992. However, just as the large investment and expansion scheme was taking place, the economy was hit with a recession that depressed sales and profits (see table D.2).

From their peak in 1991, department store sales declined continuously afterward except in 1996. This is due in part to the sluggish economy and consumer spending and in part to the steady growth of supermarket sales. In 1995 the sales of large supermarkets started to exceed those of large

Table D.2
Leading department stores (in ¥ billions)

	FY 1991[a]		FY 1997[a]	
	Sales	Profits[b]	Sales	Profits[b]
Takashimaya	843.0	13.4	1,097.5	11.7
Mitsukoshi	876.6	11.0	734.0	4.4
Seibu Department Stores	916.9	—	628.4	5.4
Daimaru	608.3	6.1	506.5	4.0
Marui	569.1	57.3	508.8	29.0
Matsuzakaya	502.0	10.0	422.0	2.3
Isetan	468.2	14.1	432.0	12.8[c]
Tokyu Department Stores	410.6	9.2	315.8	1.7
Hankyu Department Stores	355.2	15.1	315.0	4.0[c]
Sogo	310.6	7.3	168.4	0.3

Sources: *Japan Economic Almanac* (1993: 239), *The Nikkei Weekly* (April 26, July 5, 1993, and April 27, 1998), *Japan Company Book* (Summer 1998).
a. Business FY 1991 ended in 1992 at the end of January for Marui and Tokyu, end of March for Isetan and Hankyu, and end of February for the rest.
b. Pretax profits.
c. Estimates.

department stores. The increase in **consumption tax** in April 1997 from 3% to 5% further depressed department store sale and profits in 1997.

Of Japan's top department stores, Mitsukoshi is particularly prestigious. Originally founded as a dry goods store in 1673 by the merchant Mitsui family (founder of the Mitsui *zaibatsu*), it became Japan's first modern department store in 1904. In the postwar era it is a core member of the **Mitsui Group**, reputed for its wide variety of deluxe merchandise, both Japanese and foreign. It has 14 stores, including operations in Europe and the United States. Seibu Department Stores Ltd. is the core company of the Saison Group.

In addition to merchandise, Japanese department stores ordinarily offer various types of services, entertainment, and regular cultural exhibitions. The more prestigious department stores carry a wide variety of high-priced brand-name products, including imports. Because many Japanese consumers are brand-name conscious and are willing to pay substantially higher prices for the presumed quality and prestige, especially when shopping for the obligatory biannual gift giving, large department stores have long occupied a special niche in the Japanese retail market, particularly in the **gift market**.

See also **distribution system, gift market, Large Retail Store Law**.

Addresses

Japan Department Stores Association
2-1-10 Nihonbashi, Chuo-ku, Tokyo 103
Tel: (3) 3272-1666   Fax: (3) 3281-0381

Mitsukoshi
1-4-1 Nihonbashi-Muromachi, Chuo-ku, Tokyo 103
Tel: (3) 3241-3311

Seibu Department Stores
28-1, Minami Ikebukuro 1-chome, Toshima-ku, Tokyo 171
Tel: (3) 3462-0111

Takashimaya Department Store
4-1, Nihonbashi 2-chome, Chuo-ku, Tokyo 103
Tel: (3) 3211-4111

References

Japan Company Handbook. Quarterly. Tokyo: Toyo Keizai.

Japan Economic Almanac. Annual. Tokyo: Nihon Keizai Shimbun.

Japan Statistical Yearbook. Annual. Tokyo: Management and Coordination Agency.

deposit insurance system   Jointly established by the government and private financial institutions, the system protects depositors and covers their demand deposits, time deposits, money trusts, and loan trusts with principal compensation contracts. It will reimburse depositors up to ¥10 million per depositor in case of bank failure, although this has not been necessary to date. All banks and credit cooperatives are required by law to join the system. Annual insurance fee was set at 0.012% of the insured deposit until it was raised to 0.084% in 1996 because of the huge bad debts of most banks that resulted from excessive real estate loans of the late 1980s.

The Deposit Insurance Corporation was established in 1971 to administer the system. Its initial capital of ¥455 million was jointly contributed by the government, the **Bank of Japan**, and private financial institutions. Its director is the deputy governor of the Bank of Japan as stipulated by law. In 1973 a separate Savings Insurance Corporation was established to cover agricultural cooperatives and fishery cooperatives.

When a financial institution becomes, or is in danger of becoming insolvent, rescue attempts are encouraged. Since 1986 the insurance system has the authority to provide low-interest loans to help another institution take it over in a merger or other form of rescue. Each category of financial institutions also has mutual aid schemes for such emergencies, with the help of the deposit insurance system if necessary. The Resolution and Collection Bank was established in 1995 to take over the assets and liabilities of failed **credit cooperatives**. The Deposit Insurance Corp. borrowed ¥100 billion and turned it over to the Resolution and Collection Bank to write off bad loans.

Since 1995 a number of banks have failed because of real estate related bad debts and depreciated assets. Because it was feared that the Deposit Insurance Corporation would not have adequate funds to protect depositors in the case of more bank failures, the government was authorized by the Diet in early 1998 to provide ¥17 trillion (including ¥10 trillion government guarantee and ¥7 trillion cash equivalent bonds) from the **postal savings** system to a special account at the Insurance Deposit Corporation to strengthen the latter's insurance program. In addition a ¥30 trillion borrowing facility was created from public funds for the Deposit Insurance Corporation (author's interview, Bank of Japan, April 1, 1998).

References

Federation of Bankers Associations of Japan. 1994. *The Banking System in Japan.*

Suzuki, Yoshio, ed. 1987. *Japanese Financial System.* Oxford: Oxford University Press. Ch. 5.

Yokota, Kazunari. 1997a. Deposit insurer to seek private loans. *Nikkei Weekly*, May 12: 13.

Yokota, Kakunari. 1997b. Deposit safety net draws guarded praise. *Nikkei Weekly*, December 22: 1.

deposits system   Deposits are a major source of funds for many financial institutions and an important type of financial assets to households and business firms, which use them as a means of payment and a means of savings. Deposits are accepted by all commercial banks, ***shinkin* banks, credit cooperatives**, labor credit associations, **agricultural cooperatives**, and fishery cooperatives. The **postal savings** system also accepts deposits, although it is not a financial institution.

The major categories of deposits are as follows:

1. *Demand deposits.* These can be withdrawn on demand without prior notice. Interest rates on demand deposits were deregulated in October 1994. There are three types of demand deposits:

• Current deposits (current accounts). These are noninterest-bearing deposits used mainly by business firms for the payment of bills by checks drawn on the account. Other payments can also be made automatically through current deposits.

• Ordinary deposits. Held by individuals and business enterprises, these are payable on demand and have no restrictions on deposit or withdrawal amounts. They differ from current deposits in that withdrawals are made by presentation of a passbook and not by writing checks. Deposits and withdrawals may also be made at automatic teller machines (ATMs) or cash dispensers through the use of cash cards. They can be used to accept salary, pension, and fund transfer payments, and for automatic payments of public utility charges, taxes, insurance premiums, credit card payments, and so forth. Interest is paid semiannually.

• Notice deposits. These cannot be withdrawn until seven days after the day of deposits and require two days' notice. They are used mainly by companies for investing temporary surplus funds. The minimum deposit is ¥50,000, and the unit for calculating interest is ¥10,000. The interest is slightly higher than that paid on ordinary deposits.

2. *Fixed-term deposits*

• Time deposits. The term of the deposits is fixed, and the deposit cannot be withdrawn during the period. The bulk of deposits for savings are in the form of time deposits. The term ranges from one month to five years. Before 1988, as part of Japan's *maruyu* system (tax exemption for small savers), interest on time deposits up to certain limits could be tax exempt. In June 1993 the interest rate on bank time deposits was deregulated.

• Installment savings. A fixed amount of money is deposited regularly (usually monthly) during a certain period, and a specified amount is given back to the depositor on the date of maturity. Bank employees usually come to the depositor to collect the deposits. Individuals usually use this type of savings for a specific purpose such as for education or a wedding. Installment savings tend to be concentrated in **shinkin** banks, credit cooperatives, and agricultural cooperatives.

3. *Negotiable certificates of deposits (CDs).* First issued in 1979, CDs may be sold to third parties. Most CDs are issued by **city banks**, and most buyers are corporations and local government bodies because of the high minimum unit of issue (reduced from ¥100 million to ¥50 million since April 1988). The maturities are between two weeks and five years. The interest rate is freely determined in the money market.

At the end of March 1997, total demand deposits amounted to ¥138.4 trillion, of which ¥63.5 trillion were held by individuals and ¥61.1 trillion by private corporations. Total time and savings deposits were ¥280.9 trillion, of which ¥185.9 trillion were held by individuals and ¥75 trillion by private corporations. Other holders of deposits are government bodies and financial institutions.

Deposits are insured by the **deposit insurance system**. The **postal savings** service is discussed separately because it is not part of the private financial system.

See also **interest rate structure, money market, postal savings**.

References

Bank of Japan. Annual. *Economic Statistics Annual.*

Federation of Bankers Associations of Japan. 1994. *The Banking System in Japan.* Tokyo: Zenginkyo.

Federation of Bankers Associations of Japan. Annual. *Japanese Banks, '92.* Tokyo: Zenginkyo.

Suzuki, Yoshio, ed. 1987. *The Japanese Financial System.* Oxford: Oxford University Press. Ch. 5.

Tatewaki, Kazuo. 1991. *Banking and Finance in Japan.* London: Routledge.

Depressed Industries Law, 1978   A law enacted to reduce capacity and balance supply and demand in structurally depressed industries.

See **business-cycle indicators and forecasting, declining industries, industrial policy, steel industry**.

direct overseas investment In the global economy, multinational corporations and financial institutions commonly invest across national borders in pursuit of profits and/or some other objectives. There are two types of such cross-border investment, direct investment and portfolio investment. The former refers to investment that entails significant ownership and managerial control of production units or properties in foreign countries through the establishment of subsidiaries, **mergers and acquisitions**, joint ventures, and so forth. The latter involves the purchase of foreign securities for financial gains. Outward direct investment made by Japanese multinational corporations and financial institutions in foreign countries is discussed here as direct overseas investment (DOI), following the common usuage in Japan. Inward direct investment made by foreign firms and financial institutions in Japan is discussed separately in **foreign direct investment in Japan**.

Japan's DOI has increased rapidly since the early 1980s. From a modest $4.7 billion in FY 1980, it rose to $22.3 billion in 1986, and to a peak of $67.5 billion in 1989; it declined in 1990–92 because of declined corporate profits due to the recession. It has risen again since 1993 (see table D.3). The accumulated total as of March 31, 1996, was $514.3 billion, which makes Japan the third largest foreign investor in the world behind the United States and Britain. It dwarfs the amount of total accumulated **foreign direct investment** in Japan, which was only $37.9 billion as of March 31, 1996.

Table D.3
Direct overseas investment (in $ billions)

Fiscal year	Amount	Fiscal year	Amount
1951–1975	$15.9	1987	33.4
1976	3.5	1988	47.0
1978	4.6	1989	67.5
1980	4.7	1990	56.9
1981	8.9	1991	41.6
1982	7.7	1992	34.1
1983	8.1	1993	36.0
1984	10.2	1994	41.1
1985	12.2	1995	50.7
1986	22.3	1996	50.0

Source: Ministry of Finance.
Note: The figures are the value of approvals and notification.

The rapid increase of Japan's DOI is the result of various factors. Before the 1980s Japan's DOI was primarily for the purposes of securing the supply of raw materials and fuels and for taking advantage of cheaper skilled labor in developing Asian and South American countries. Thus countries such as Hong Kong, South Korea, Indonesia, Brazil, and Australia have been important recipients of Japanese DOI. In the 1980s, as Japan's trade surplus and excess domestic **savings** accumulated and its industrialized trading partners became more protectionist, it became desirable for Japanese companies to make defensive investment in the United States and Western Europe to protect their market share (see table D.4). For example, Japanese automakers and consumer electronics firms have set up plants in the United States and Western Europe. Defensive investment in Western Europe has been accelerated by the European integration in 1992, with a large share going to Britain. Since 1993 Japanese manufacturers have speeded up the relocation of production overseas because of yen's rise, and investment in China and Southeast Asia has increased sharply. Overall, North America, particularly the United States, has received the bulk (nearly 50% in FY 1996) of Japanese DOI, followed by Asia and Europe, as shown in table D.4. The Asian stock market and currency crises of 1997–98 may reduce Asia's share of Japanese DOI in the future.

This trend to invest in the industrialized countries in the 1980s was reinforced by other economic factors. As Japanese industries became more knowledge intensive after the oil crises, raw materials have become rela-

Table D.4
Direct overseas investment by area (FY 1996)

	Amount (in ¥ billions)	Percentage
North America	¥2,593 billion	47.9%
United States	2,479	45.8
Asia	1,308	24.2
Europe	831	15.3
Latin America	501	9.3
Oceania	101	1.9
Africa	49	0.9
Middle and Near East	27	0.5
Total	5,409	100.0

Source: Ministry of Finance.

tively less important. The appreciation of the yen since the mid-1980s has made it cheaper to acquire assets and to produce in the industrial countries. Finally, through acquisitions, Japanese banks and investment firms have also utilized their excess funds to expand their presence abroad, especially in the United States and Western Europe. Direct overseas investment thus became an attractive outlet for Japan's large trade surplus and excess **savings**. In the 1990s, however, Japanese banks and investment firms have reduced their DOI because of their weakened financial conditions.

In terms of sectoral distribution, manufacturing typically dominates Japanese DOI, followed by finance and insurance, and real estate. For example, in FY 1996 ¥2,282 billion (42.2% of the total) was invested in manufacturing, ¥876 billion (16.2%) in finance and insurance, ¥700 (12.9%) in real estate, ¥539 billion (10%) in commerce, and ¥456 billion (8.4%) in services. The relative importance of manufacturing has increased in recent years, whereas that of services and transportation has declined.

Dunning (1993) analyzes the activities of multinational corporations in terms of the ownership (O), location (L), and internalization (I) advantages they possess. Thus Japanese DOI in the early 1980s in the United States and Europe was to protect the competitive or "O" advantage of Japanese made products. Hence it was defensive in nature. The United States received more Japanese DOI because of its "L" advantage. In the late 1980s Japanese firms adopted offensive strategies in their DOI because they had to transform themselves from exporters to "insiders" in the United States and Europe. Two events were important in this change. First, the **Plaza Accord** of 1985 that revalued the yen against the dollar. This made Japanese exports expensive and American assets cheap to the Japanese. The second was the decision at the end of 1992 to create a single European market. This gave Europe substantial "L" advantages and boosted Japanese DOI (Dunning 1993: 148–49).

As Japanese corporations invested abroad, they have also brought with them Japanese business practices, which have been met with mixed responses. First, Japanese business managers are said to favor Japanese suppliers, especially those from the same *keiretsu*, in their business dealings to the chagrin of local companies and officials. Second, Japanese group-oriented management practices have been introduced with mixed success, but the job security of Japanese personnel practice has been welcomed by local workers. Third, the traditional male-chauvinist attitude of some Japanese managers (see **business ethics**) may have been transplanted abroad in some cases and may have created some sexual discrimination against women. In 1996 Mitsubishi Motor Manufacturing of

America, a U.S. subsidiary of the Mitsubishi Motor Corp., was sued by the U.S. Equal Employment Opportunity Commission for sexual harassment. Finally, DOI in the 1990s has raised concern in Japan about the "hollowing out" (*kudoka*) of Japanese industries. It is feared that the movement of labor-intensive operations abroad, particularly to low-wage Asian countries, will reduce job opportunities and raise unemployment ratio in Japan. Defenders of DOI contend that this will not happen because high-tech R&D and high-skilled jobs will still remain in Japan.

See also **mergers and acquisitions, trade pattern**.

References

Balassa, Bela, and Marcus Noland. 1988. *Japan in the World Economy*. Washington: Institute for International Economics. Ch. 5.

Drake, Tracey A., and Richard E. Caves. 1992. Changing determinants of Japanese foreign investment in the United States. *Journal of the Japanese and International Economies* 6, 3: 228–46.

Dunning, John H. 1993. *The Globalization of Business: The Challenge of the 1990s*. London: Routledge. Ch. 6.

Encarnation, Dennis J. 1986. Cross-investment: A second front of economic rivalry. In *America versus Japan*, ed. by Thomas K. McCraw. Boston: Harvard Business School Press.

Kester, W. Carl. 1991. *Japanese Takeovers: The Global Contest for Corporate Control*. Boston: Harvard Business School Press.

Lii, Sheng-Yann. 1994. Japanese direct foreign investment and trade flows in the Asia-Pacific region. *Asian Economic Journal* 8, 2: 181–203.

Tejima, Shigeki. 1992. Japanese foreign direct investment in the 1980s and its prospects for the 1990s. *EXIM Review* 11, 2: 25–51.

Tokunaga, Shojiro, ed. 1992. *Japan's Foreign Investment and Asian Economic Interdependence*. Tokyo: Tokyo University Press.

Wong, Kar-yiu, and Kozo Yamamura. 1996. Japan's direct investment in the United States: causes, patterns, and issues. In *The Effects of Japanese Investment on the World Economy: A Six-Country Study, 1970–1991*, ed. by Leon Hollerman and Ramon Myers. Stanford: Hoover Institution Press.

Yamamura, Kozo, ed. 1989. *Japanese Investment in the United States: Should We Be Concerned?* Seattle: Society for Japanese Studies.

Yoshida, Mamoru. 1987. *Japanese Direct Manufacturing Investment In the United States*. New York: Praeger.

Yoshihara, Hideki. 1991. Overseas transfer of the Japanese-style production system. *Japanese Economic Studies* 19, 3: 19–42.

distribution *keiretsu*   Sales networks established by or affiliated with some large manufacturers such as in the consumer electronics and automobile industries. Traditionally they carry only particular manufacturers' product lines and have therefore been criticized for engaging in exclusionary practice.

See **distribution system**, *keiretsu* **and business groups**

distribution system   Japan's system for distributing products, including imports, to the consumers and industrial users is characterized by the predominance of numerous small retailers, the existence of multi-layers of small- and medium-sized wholesalers, and the prevalence of the sole import agents. It is considered by foreign critics, and some Japanese as well, as inefficient and exclusionary but is defended by many Japanese as open and functionally efficient in the Japanese context.

At the retail level there were 1.5 million retail stores in 1994, or 120 retail stores per 10,000 people, which is high in comparison with other industrialized countries. Small food retail stores in particular proliferate in Japan. In 1994 there were 45 small food stores per 10,000 people in Japan, accounting for more than one-third of retail stores.

There are three categories of retail establishments in Japan:

1. *Small- and medium-sized retail stores that employ 1–49 persons.* As of 1994 there were 1.49 million such retail stores. They accounted for 99.3% of all retail establishments and 77% of total retail sales in 1994. About 75% of them are small "Mom-and-Pop" stores, employing only 1–4 persons. Since most Japanese housewives buy their groceries daily, the convenience and customer services provided by these small stores are extremely important to them. This type of store also provides employment to a large number of elderly people with inadequate pensions. However, their number and market share have been declining. On the other hand, medium-sized discount store chains and self-service stores have grown. They are usually located in populated suburban residential areas and carry foods, clothing, and many other consumer goods.

2. *Large* **department stores** *and self-service stores or supermarkets that employ more than 50 persons.* In 1996 they had total sales of ¥23 trillion, which accounted for only 15.7% of total retail sales, far below that of other industrialized countries. The government has restricted their growth and protected the small retailers through the Department Store Law of 1956, the **Large Retail Store Law** of 1974, and other restrictive regulations. The number of department stores has grown slowly, from 325 at the end of 1975 to 360 in 1985 and 431 at the end of 1996. The number of large supermarkets has also grown slowly, from 1,613 at the end of 1980 to 2,013 at the end of 1991 and 2,569 at the end of 1996.

3. *Nonstore retailers, which include businesses that sell through catalogs, tele-phones, vending machines, and door-to-door sales.* Their sales are relatively small but have expanded rapidly in recent years. There are six large listed mail-order companies; some **department stores** also have mail-order business. In 1996 total mail order sales amounted to ¥2.1 trillion; total vending machine sales were ¥6.6 trillion.

At the wholesale level there were about 429,300 wholesale establish-ments in 1994, or about 34 per 10,000 people. Most Japanese wholesalers are relatively small. In 1994 about 73% of them employed 1–9 employ-ees. Most goods go through two or more layers of wholesalers. As a re-sult the ratio between the total value of wholesalers and that of retails (W/R) is much higher in Japan (about 3.6 in 1994) than in other indus-trialized market economies (about 1.6 in the United States).

Wholesalers are very important in the distribution system because they provide a number of important functions to the retailers: (1) Since most retailers are small and have minimal floor space and stocking capacity, wholesalers usually make daily deliveries of small quantities. (2) Whole-salers provide financing to retailers by accepting long-term payments. (3) Since retailers usually buy on commission, wholesalers accept the return of unsold merchandise, thus bearing the burden of inventory risk.

In the consumer electronics industry, some large manufacturers circum-vent the traditional wholesalers by establishing their own distribution networks, referred to as distribution **keiretsu**. Matsushita Electric, for example, has a network of wholesalers and "National Shops." They are either wholly owned by, or affiliated with, the company. Toshiba Corp., Hitachi Ltd., and Sanyo Electric Co. also have thousands of keiretsu shops. In the automobile industry, automobiles are domestically sold through the manufacturers' sales networks that sell only their automaker's models.

In international trade, the traditional "general import agents" system gives exclusive contracts to some wholesalers, particularly the large **trad-ing companies**, to import brand-name products. This has given them the monopoly power to control the marketing channels and the prices of imported goods, even though the Japanese government authorized the "parallel import" system as early as 1972. Under this system any com-pany can import any foreign product in parallel with the general import agents. One problem with the system is post-sale services because general import agents have refused to service products imported under parallel import.

Japan's foreign competitors have long complained that Japan's com-plex distribution system has effectively kept them out of the Japanese market and is responsible for the high prices in Japan. Consequently, in the **Structural Impediments Initiative** talks between Washington and Tokyo in 1989–90, Washington made reforms in the distribution system one of its key demands. In particular, it wanted to see the removal of restrictions on the establishment of large retail stores, which are said to be more likely to carry imports. In early 1990 Tokyo decided to revise the Large Retail Store Law. Starting in May 1990, the implementation of the law was relaxed. Effective January 31, 1992, revisions were made to shorten government approval for a large store to a maximum of one year.

Defenders of the Japanese distribution system, including many ordinary citizens and authors, contend that the Japanese system is open to foreign companies and products, and oppose imposing changes on it on cultural and functional grounds. Culturally, it is contended that the system was formed over a long period of time, integrating aspects of the culture, economy, and society. Hence the government should let it evolve on its own, and should not force it to change under U.S. pressure (Shioya 1989). Functionally, it is argued that the existence of numerous neighborhood retail stores generates employment for a large number of people, provides quality services, and makes daily household shopping more convenient for urban households without the need to drive to suburban areas where larger supermarkets tend to be located. Daily grocery shopping is necessary in Japan to economize household storage space in small living quarters. For the small retailers to function efficiently with their limited resources and space, a large number of wholesalers are needed to provide the essential services to the retailers, as mentioned above. Thus Japan's distribution system has a logic of its own, given Japan's socioeconomic conditions, and the supposedly more efficient American system is not appropriate for Japan. Finally, Itoh (1991) argues that Japan's decentralized distribution system facilitates information sharing and coordination between manufacturers and wholesalers, and between wholesalers and retailers, which promotes product improvement/development and superior services far beyond what a simple market mechanism can ever provide.

Whatever the merit and demerit of the Japanese distribution system, there is evidence that it is changing with the time. From a peak of 1.72 million in 1982, the number of retail establishments has declined slowly to 1.5 million in 1994. The number of large- and medium-sized retail outlets and wholesalers has also grown. Furthermore the Japanese government is promoting the "parallel import system" in order to increase competition and reduce import prices. Japanese companies are also assembling inexpensive consumer electronics products in other Asian nations, using Japan-made components, and shipping them back to Japan. These products are known as "reimports."

In regard to market access for foreigners, there is growing evidence that foreign companies can successfully join or circumvent the Japanese distribution network. For example, in the 1980s the American Amway Corp. successfully organized a direct-distribution system in Japan to sell its products, thus bypassing the complex Japanese distribution system. An alternative strategy is to utilize Japan's own distributional network. In October 1989 the Swedish appliance giant AB Electrolux formed an alliance with Japan's Sharp Corp. to market household appliances in Japan; its products will be marketed through Sharp's retail stores. In late 1991 the American firm Toys R Us established its new branch store in Japan, directly retailing toys from the manufacturers at discounts. By early 1998 it has opened 64 stores. In recent years a number of large American retailers such as The Gap, Foot Locker, Nike, OfficeMax, Office Depot, Pier 1 Imports, The Sports Authority, Tower Records, and Warner Bros. Studio Stores have followed suit and opened stores in Japan. Preliminary evidence suggests that they are all doing well. Even in mail order business, L. L. Bean, an American outdoor-goods retailer, had $2 billion mail orders from Japanese customers in 1995, which amounted to 15–20% of the company's total world sales (*Nikkei Weekly*, April 7, 1997: 1).

See also **department stores, Large Retail Store Law, pricing practices, trading companies**.

Addresses

Japan Chain Stores Association
13-1, Toranomon 5-chome, Minato-ku, Tokyo 105
Tel: (3) 3433-1290

Japan Department Store Association
1-10, Nihonbashi 2-chome, Chuo-ku, Tokyo 103
Tel: (3) 3272-1666   Fax: (3) 3281-0381

References

Ariga, Kenn and Yasushi Ohkusa. 1996. Price formation and the structure of the distribution system. In *Japanese Firms, Finance and Markets*, ed. by Paul Sheard. Melbourne: Addison Wesley Longman.

Czinkota, Michael R., and Jon Woronoff. 1991. *Unlocking Japan's Markets*. Chicago: Probus.

Czinkota, Michael, and Masaki Kotabe, ed. 1993. *The Japanese Distribution System*. Chicago: Probus.

Ito, Takatoshi. 1992. *The Japanese Economy*. Cambridge: MIT Press. Ch. 3.

Itoh, Motoshige. 1991. The Japanese distribution system and access to the Japanese market. In *Trade with Japan*, ed. by Paul Krugman. Chicago: Chicago University Press.

Itoh, Motoshige, Seung-Jaei Lee, and Takatoshi Yajima. 1990. Creating a competitive commercial sector. *Japan Echo* 17, 3: 17–22.

Kikuchi, Takeshi, ed. 1994. *Japanese Distribution Channels*. Binghamton, NY: International Business Press.

Laumer, Helmut. 1986. The Distribution system: Its social function and import-impeding effects. In *Japan's Response to Crisis and Change in the World Economy*, ed. by Michele Schiegelow. New York: Sharpe.

Sakaiya, Taichi. 1990. Retailing on the eve of a revolution. *Japan Echo* 17, 3: 12–16.

Shioya, Takafusa. 1989. Japan's distribution system is a result of economy, society and culture—MITI. *Business Japan*, no. 8, August: 57–63.

Takahashi, Hideo. 1989. Structural changes in Japan's distribution system, *JEI Report* 43A, November 10.

Weigand, Robert E. 1989. The gray market comes to Japan. *Columbia Journal of World Business* 24, 3: 18–23.

Yosuke, Uehara. 1995. The distribution system in turbulence. *Journal of Japanese Trade and Industry*, no. 1: 22–24.

Dodge Plan   A stabilization plan introduced in 1949 by Joseph Dodge, an American banker and advisor to General MacArthur, the Supreme Commander for the Allied Powers, to end Japan's immediate postwar inflation and set up a single exchange rate. The plan relied on tightening government budget, and it succeeded in bringing inflation under control. The exchange rate was set at ¥360 to the dollar.
    See **postwar reforms and reconstruction.**

dollar-call market   An interbank money market in which financial institutions trade foreign currency funds among themselves for short periods.
    See **money markets.**

E

Economic Council A top advisory council to the prime minister on economic policies and economic planning. It is assisted by the Economic Planning Agency in the latter task.

See **economic planning, housing**.

economic planning Although Japan's postwar economy has never been a centrally planned economy, the Economic Planning Agency has made economic plans to provide economic projections and growth targets to the private sector and to help coordinate government economic policies and activities. A precursor to the first economic plan was the **Dodge Plan** of 1949, which brought early postwar inflation under control through tight monetary policy and thus provided favorable macroeconomic condition for economic planning. Economic planning started in 1948 with the Five-Year Economic Recovery Plan for 1948–52. Since then, 13 other plans have been made—most of them for a five-year period and a few for six to ten years. These include the Five-Year Plan for Economic Self-support (1956–60), the New Long-Range Economic Plan (1958–62), the National Income Doubling Plan (1961–70), various socioeconomic development plans throughout the 1970s and early 1980s, the 1992–96 Five-Year Plan, and the latest Social and Economic Plan (1996–2000). There are no formal annual plans derived out of the five-year plans. Instead the Economic Planning Agency publishes an annual "Economic Outlook" early in the year that outlines its projections for the year and the government's basic policy position on the economy.

The Economic Recovery Plan of 1948 mainly provided background information for the government in requesting U.S. aid. The National Income Doubling Plan for 1961–70 was well known because of its broad scope and long-term nature, and because Japan was then entering the period of high growth (more than 10% annually). It had a target GNP growth rate of 7.8% annually to double the national income within a decade. It attempted to develop social overhead capital, human resources, and science and technology, to accelerate industrialization and eliminate the dual industrial structure, and to promote export. Between the early 1970s and the early 1980s, changes in the domestic and world economy—higher Japanese standard of living, the oil crises and the stagflation it brought about in various industrial countries, the floating exchange rate system, and Japan's increased role in world trade and its surpluses in the balance of payments, and so on—have prompted planners to pay more attention to the improvement in the quality of life and to restoring equilibrium in the international balance of payments. Since the late 1980s, because of continuing changes in Japan and the world economy, planners are increasingly focusing on the development of new technology, market liberalization, overseas investment, and the aging of the population. The last Five-Year Plan (1992–96) emphasizes improvements in the quality of life—a 40-hour workweek, affordable housing, and improved social infrastructure—and Japan's contribution to global issues such as environmental issues and assistance to former communist countries. The current Five-Year Plan (1996–2000), coming in the midst of a prolonged post-bubble stagnation, emphasizes structural reforms. Specific policy measures to be carried out include deregulation, developing competition policy, restructuring existing industries and developing new ones, financial reforms, and so forth.

In terms of planning organization, the Economic Stabilization Board was established in 1946 on the recommendation of the Allied Occupation Forces to stabilize and reconstruct the economy.It was reorganized as the Economic Deliberation Board in 1952. In 1954 the present Economic Planning Agency was established as Japan's economic recovery was completed and government priority was shifted to economic growth.

Currently the Economic Planning Agency serves as the secretariat of the Economic Council, a top advisory committee to the prime minister appointed to deliberate on important economic policies and to formulate long-term economic planning. The Economic Planning Agency, comprising mainly of economists, assists the Council in the technical tasks of econometric estimates and projections. The planning procedure is as follows: First the prime minister conveys to the Economic Council the major goals of the plan. The Council deliberates on various policy aspects of the goals. The Economic Planning Agency works on various policy implications in consultation with other ministries and uses macroeconometric models to develop detailed estimates and projections. When the plan is completed, it is submitted by the Economic Council to the Cabinet for approval. When approved, it becomes the official National Economic Plan. Japan's national economic plan is broadly based in its making, and in turn it helps to form consensus in the government and to coordinate the policies of various ministries. Since any minister in the cabinet can veto it, the Economic Planning Agency has to consult with various ministries, particularly the **Ministry of Finance** and the **Ministry of International Trade and Industry** during the drafting of the plan to incorporate their views. In addition it has to communicate with other ministries to utilize their special expertise and to obtain statistics in their respective specialized fields. The Economic Council is composed of prominent and experienced persons from diverse backgrounds, including the academe, business, labor, the press, and retired officials. Its members therefore reflect the diverse interests and experiences of mainstream Japan. Once the plan is adopted by the Cabinet, various specialized plans and programs of the government such as the National Land Use Plan, plans for regional development, or public investment plans, as well as the policies of each ministry, are expected to be consistent with it. In addition, because all government ministries and agencies and public enterprises have to submit budget requests for deliberation and approval by the Ministry of Finance, the latter makes sure that the approved budget is consistent with the economic plan. In this manner the plan is integrated into the government budgeting process for implementation.

One weakness of the plan is that local governments do not participate in the planning process. Yet their collaboration is important to the success of the plan because more than half of government expenditures in a plan are those of local governments. There are two ways through which the central government can influence local governments. First, the central governments allocate subsidies to local governments, although this does not guarantee plan implementation at the local level. Second, and more important, the National Land Agency makes the National Development Plan for regional development, which is formulated to be consistent with the economic plan, and each local government is required to draw up a long-term plan that is consistent with the Land Agency's plan. Some analysts contend that local governments exert much influence on the National Land Agency in its planning, especially concerning the granting of subsidies to local governments (author's interview, Economic Planning Agency, April 10, 1998).

However, Japan's economic plan is indicative in nature as in many Western European countries, unlike the central planning of the former

Soviet Union. It provides desired targets and projections for various areas of the economy that are consistent with government policy priorities and the underlying capabilities of the economy, but it does not provide mandatory directives to the private sector to follow in order to reach the targets. Hence its ability to affect the overall allocation of resources in the economy is limited. Major plan target such as GNP growth rate, inflation rate, and balance of payments are often very different from the initial plan figures. Before the oil crises of the early 1970s, the planned annual real GNP growth rates were invariably below the actual rates by 2.5–3.5%, whereas after the early 1970s the planned growth rates tended to be above the actual rates. In the three plan periods between 1967 and 1977, projected annual inflation rates (3–4.4%) were much lower than the actual rates (5.7–12.8%). Projected balance-of-payments surpluses throughout 1961 to 1980 were far below the actual figures. When such discrepancy develops between the initial plan and the actual economic conditions, the Economic Planning Agency will revise its plan figures accordingly.

See also **business-cycle indicator and forecasting, economic/ business research and publications.**

Address

Economic Planning Agency
1-1, Kasumigaseki 3-chome, Chiyoda-ku, Tokyo 100
Tel: (3) 3581-0261

References

Economic Planning Agency. 1990. *Economic Planning in Japan.*

Economic Planning Agency. Annual. *Economic Survey of Japan.*

Economic Planning Agency. 1992. *The Five-Year Economic Plan—Sharing a Better Quality of Life around the Globe.*

Economic Planning Agency. Annual. *The Japanese Economy: Recent Trends and Outlook.*

Economic Planning Agency. 1995. *Social and Economic Plan for Structural Reforms towards a Vital Economy and Secure Life.*

Komine, Takao. 1993. The role of economic planning in Japan. In *The Japanese Experience of Economic Reforms,* ed. by Juro Teranishi and Yutaka Kosai. New York: St. Martin's Press.

Nakamura, Yoichi. Undated. *Economic Planning in Japan.*

Okita, Saburo. 1985. Economic planning in Japan. In *The Management Challenge,* ed. by Lester Thurow. Cambridge: MIT Press.

Economic Planning Agency   An important government agency, comprising mainly of economists, under the Prime Minister's Office. Its main functions include the following: (1) It drafts the national economic plan under the guidance of the Cabinet and the **Economic Council**. (2) It monitors and analyzes economic changes in the economy, particularly in relation to the different phases of **business cycles**, and makes short-term economic forecasts. (3) It compiles detailed national income accounts. (4) It publishes many publications on various aspects of the economy.

In the forthcoming **administrative reform**, the agency is to be absorbed by the cabinet office in the year 2001 (author's interview, Economic Planning Agency, April 10, 1998).

See **business cycles, business-cycle indicators and forecasting, economic planning, economic/business research and publications, price indexes and price levels.**

economic/business research and publications   Economic/business research and publishing are essential to an economy in the information age. In Japan such research is conducted at a variety of institutions— universities, government ministries and agencies, government-affiliated research institutes, private research institutes, and private business publishers.

1. *Universities.* Scholars at major universities conduct research on various economic issues. These universities include Tokyo University, Kyoto University, Hitotsubashi University, Keio University, Waseda University, Sophia (Jochi) University, Aoyama University, and Osaka University, among others. Distinguished economists from top universities often serve on government commissions or research panels or work with private research institutes. The University of Tokyo Press is a major publisher of scholarly books. However, compared with the government's program in economic research and publishing, that of Japanese universities is very limited. Also, compared with major research universities in the United States, Japanese universities are not considered to be active in their research and publishing.

2. *Government research departments and institutes.* Japan government research and publishing on the economy is well organized and very comprehensive. All government ministries and agencies have their research/ statistics departments to serve the needs of their respective policy makers and to author official publications of the organizations, including annual reports (usually in the form of White Papers) and statistical yearbooks. In

addition several ministries have separate in-house research institutes for research and publications on broader or longer-term policy issues in which academicians from Japanese universities may participate. Most notable in these endeavors are the following:

• The research and Statistics Department of the **Bank of Japan** publishes the *Economic Statistics Annual* and *Economic Statistics Monthly* (in both Japanese and English) and other research reports, including a closely watched quarterly industry survey, *Tankan* (Short-Term Economic Outlook). The Institute for Monetary and Economic Studies of the Bank publishes the *Bank of Japan Monetary and Economic Studies*.

• The **Economic Planning Agency** under the prime minister's office publishes the annual *Keizai Hakusho* (Economic White Paper; English version published as *The Economic Survey of Japan*), which surveys trends in the economy and gives in-depth analyses of selective aspects of the economy such as **income distribution**, household saving rates, energy supply and demand, and regional development. It also publishes annual reports on business cycle indicators, for example. The Economic Research Institute of the Agency compiles the national income accounts of Japan and publishes such statistics in great detail in its *Annual Report on National Accounts* (in Japanese).

• The Statistics Bureau of the Management and Coordination Agency under the prime minister's office conducts regularly 15 different surveys (including the quinquennial population census, monthly labor force survey, monthly retail price survey, and annual family savings survey) and publishes the survey results; it also publishes the voluminous *Japan Statistical Yearbook* (in both Japanese and English).

• The **Ministry of Finance** publishes various financial reports. Its Institute of Fiscal and Monetary Policy publishes the *Monthly Finance Review*.

• The **Ministry of International Trade and Industry** publishes the important *White Paper on International Trade*, which details Japan's trade performance and policy. The Ministry's Research Institute of International Trade and Industry publishes special monographs on various aspects of the economy and the Ministry's policies.

The research institutes at both the Ministry of International Trade and Industry and the Bank of Japan have special research programs that accept eminent scholars from abroad to conduct research at the institutes. Most government publications can be purchased at the Government Publications Service Center in Tokyo, which also has branches in all major cities.

3. *Government-affiliated research institutes.* These are semigovernmental, nonprofit research institutes, established in accordance with a legislation and subsidized by the government. They are affiliated with a ministry and/or other government agencies and sponsor research conducted by either in-house researchers or outside scholars. For example, the Japan Institute of Labor was founded in accordance with a 1958 law passed by the Diet and is affiliated with the Ministry of Labor. It published a series of monographs on aspects of the labor force authored by experts. The Japan Real Estate Institute is affiliated with the Ministry of Finance, the Land Planning Agency, the Ministry of Construction, and the Ministry of Home Affairs. The Institute of Developing Economies, founded in 1958, is affiliated with the Ministry of International Trade and Industry and conducts research on developing countries. It publishes *The Developing Economies* (quarterly, in English), *Ajia Keizai* (Asian Economies, monthly in Japanese), and several other periodicals in Japanese on Asia, Middle East, Latin America, and Africa.

4. *Private research institutes.* All large banks, securities companies, industrial corporations, and trading companies have their in-house research departments and experts. In addition a number of them have set up separate but affiliated research institutes or *shinku tanku* (think tanks) for research in their specific areas of interests. There are also a few nonprofit economic research institutes that are not affiliated with any financial institution or corporation and conduct research projects for clients. All of these institutes are members of the Japan Association of Independent Research Institutes ("Japan Association of Think Tanks"). Leading private research institutes include the following:
• Daiwa Institute of Research. Concerned with macro- and microeconomic trends, general financial and management studies. Affiliated with Daiwa Securities Co.
• Japan Center for Economic Research. A member-supported nonprofit research organization established in 1963. Engaged in short-term and longer-term economic projection of the economy. Also trains forecasting specialists for corporate clients and conducts contract research. Publishes series of special reports on domestic and international economic issues, including *JCER Report* and *Quarterly Forecast of Japan's Economy.*
• Japan Research Institute. Established in 1962 and serves as a research forum for big business in general. Sponsors general economic and industry studies. Publishes topical reports in its *Business Japan* series in English and various reports in Japanese.

• Mitsubishi Research Institute. Founded in 1932. Engaged in macro-economic forecasting, industry studies, corporate management, urban and regional economic studies, data processing and database services. Also strong in public policy studies, with more than 50% of its annual research revenues coming from government projects. Publishes the *MERI's Monthly Circular* in English and various other publications in Japanese. Affiliated with the **Mitsubishi Group**.

• Nikko Research Center. Specializes in macro- and microeconomic forecasting, international and domestic money markets, and capital asset management. Affiliated with Nikko Securities Co.

• Nomura Research Institute. The largest of the private research institutes. Conducts macro- and microeconomic surveys and projections, investment research, public policy analyses, and provides consulting services among other services. Affiliated with Nomura Securities Co. Publishes the *Quarterly Economic Review* and *NRI Quarterly* in English and a large number of reports in Japanese.

• The 21st Century Policy Research Institute. Established in April 1997 within the Japan Federation of Economic Organizations (*Keidanren*) to enhance the federation's ability to propose policies to the government. Research focus includes the Diet and **administrative reform**, foreign affairs and security, macroeconomy, and the problems of an industrial society.

These private research institutes are regarded by some observers as more closely resembling American-style management consulting firms rather than genuine think tanks, such as the Brookings Institution or the Rand Corporation in the United States. However, their access to information is considered excellent. In addition Nomura Research Institute has established collaboration with the Brookings Institution and a number of other well-known foreign research institutes in an effort to expand the scope of its research.

It should also be added that the Japan Economic Institute, based in Washington, DC, is a U.S. research organization funded in part by Japan's Ministry of Foreign Affairs. It publishes a weekly two-part *JEI Report*, which contains timely background information on current development in Japan and in Japan–U.S. relations. It is is authored by the Institute's in-house experts on Japan. It also publishes *Japan–U.S. Business Report* (monthly) and *Japan Economic Survey* (monthly).

5. *Private business publishers.* Japan's major business publishers not only report significant findings of government and private economic studies, they also conduct periodic industry surveys and opinion polls and under-

take industry and market analyses of their own. The two largest business publishers are the following:

• Nihon Keizai Shimbun, Inc. (Nikkei). This is the oldest (1876) and by far the largest business publisher in Japan. It publishes Japan's largest business daily, *Nihon Keizai Shimbun* (Japan Economic Daily, circulation more than 3 million), and its weekly English version, *Nikkei Weekly* (formerly *Japan Economic Journal*, before June 1, 1991). It also publishes three other Nikkei newspapers in Japanese—*Nikkei Kinyu Shimbun* (Nikkei Financial Daily), *Nikkei Sangyo Shimbun* (Nikkei Industrial Daily), and *Nikkei Ryutsu Shimbun* (Nikkei Marketing Journal)—and many other Japanese publications on business and corporations. On the basis of its database on the stock market, it calculates and publishes the Nikkei Stock Average (Nikkei 225) Index and other market indexes. Finally, it publishes the *Japan Economic Almanac* (in English), an annual survey of various sectors of the Japanese economy.

• Toyo Keizai, Inc. It publishes more than 20 periodicals, including the *Shukan Toyo Keizai* (Weekly Toyo Keizai, in Japanese) and the *Oriental Economist Report* (monthly, in English; formerly the *Tokyo Business Today* during 1986–96 and the *Oriental Economist* during 1934–85). On the basis of its database on Japanese companies, it publishes a quarterly report on Japanese companies—*Kaisha Shikiho* in Japanese and *Japan Company Handbook* (two volumes) in English. The quarterly report gives comprehensive information on all Japanese companies (2,314 as of Summer 1998) listed on the first and second sections of the **Tokyo Stock Exchange**. A 1991 English publication, the *Japan Company Datafile*, is an encyclopedia of Japanese companies. It covers all corporations listed on the first sections of the Tokyo, Osaka, and Nagoya Stock Exchanges.

See also **business-cycle indicators and forecasting, education system**.

Addresses

Government Publications Service Center
2-1, Kasumigaseki 1-chome, Chiyoda-ku, Tokyo 100
Tel: (3) 3504-3885

Institute of Developing Economies
42, Ichigaya Onmuracho, Shinjuku-ku, Tokyo 162
Tel: (3) 3353-4231

Japan Center for Economic Research
6-1, Nihonbashi Kayabacho, 2-chome, Chuo-ku, Tokyo 103
Tel: (3) 3639-2801   Fax: (03) 3639-2839

Mitsubishi Economic Research Institute
3-1 Marunouchi, 3-chome, Chiyoda-ku, Tokyo 100
Tel: (03) 3214-4416   Fax: (03) 3214-4415

Nihon Keizai Shimbun, Inc.
1-9-5 Otemachi, Chiyoda-ku, Tokyo 100
Tel: (3) 3270-0251

Nomura Research Institute
27-1, Shinkawa 2-chome, Chuo-ku, Tokyo 104
Tel: (3) 3297-8100   Fax: (3) 3297-8364

Toyo Keizai, Inc.
1-2- Nihonbashi Hongokucho, Chuo-ku, Tokyo 103
Tel: (3) 3246-5655   Fax: (3) 3241-5543

References

Institutes consulting more than "thinking." *Japan Economic Journal*, February 24, 1990: 27.

Matsuoka, Mikihiro and Brian Rose. 1994. *The DIR Guide to Japanese Economic Statistics.* Oxford: Oxford University Press.

Neilan, Edward. 1995. The problem of corporate think tanks: Why Japan can't think. *Tokyo Business Today*, July: 4–9.

Tomkin, Robert. 1990. Japanese "think tanks": An imperfect hybrid. *Japan Economic Journal*, February 24: 26.

Saito, Tadashi. 1994. Think tanks in Japan. *JEI Report* 18A, May 6.

Zielinski, Robert, and Nigel Holloway. 1991. *Unequal Equities.* Tokyo: Kodansha International. Pp. 83–95.

eigyo tokkin   Corporate investment accounts directly managed by brokerage houses on a discretionary basis.
   See **securities companies, *tokkin* funds**.

education system   Japan's formal education system consists of kindergartens, elementary schools, lower secondary schools, high schools, technical colleges, junior colleges, universities, special training schools, and miscellaneous schools (see table E.1). There are also special education schools for the blind, the deaf, and other handicapped people. Informal education consists of educational programs of the national public television, cram schools that prepare students for examinations, and various types of company in-house training for employees.

Japan's compulsory education includes six years of elementary school and three years of lower secondary school (*chugakko*). Students enter elementary school at age 6 and graduate from lower secondary school at 15.

Table E.1
Number of schools and students (May 1, 1996)

	Schools[a]	Students (1,000)	Student/ teacher ratio[b]
Kindergartens	14,790	1,798	17.3
Elementary schools	24,482	8,106	19.0
Lower secondary schools	11,269	4,527	16.7
High schools	5,496	4,547	16.3
Technical colleges	62	56	13.1
Junior colleges	598	473	23.3
Universities	576	2,597	18.6
Special training schools	3,512	800	21.7
Miscellaneous schools	2,714	307	19.4

Source: Ministry of Education.
a. Include branches.
b. Include full-time teachers only.

Virtually all elementary schools and about 94% of lower secondary schools are public schools, established and supervised by prefectural or municipal authorities. There is a very small number of national schools and private schools at the elementary and lower secondary levels.

Nearly all lower secondary schools graduates (96% in 1996) enter high schools or upper secondary schools (*koto gakko*) and technical colleges. The dropout rate for high school students is very low. Japanese secondary education is widely regarded as highly efficient in teaching fundamental skills, factual knowledge, and cooperative group behavior, which are the foundation of Japan's well-trained cooperative labor force. International comparative studies invariably rank Japanese secondary students among the top in math skills and scientific knowledge. However, because the main focus of Japanese high schools is to prepare students for passing rigorous university entrance examinations ("examination hell"), skills such as verbal expressions, critical and creative thinking, and cultural values that are not tested in written examinations tend to be neglected. Furthermore most high school students attend private cram schools (*juku*) that drill them for university entrance examinations. Many lower secondary school students also attend cram schools to prepare for high school entrance examinations; it is important to enter high schools with a good track record of sending students to the elite universities. About a quarter of the nation's high schools are private ones.

Technical colleges (*koto senmon gakko*) are five-year technical schools for lower secondary school graduates. Most of them are run by the national government, and 82% of their students in 1996 were male. Special training schools (*senshu gakko*) and miscellaneous schools (*kakushu gakko*) are private schools that offer vocational and practical training to graduates of lower secondary schools for 1–5 years. The special training school system was first established in 1976. The majority of students are enrolled in curriculums in medical science, technology, and home economics. Miscellaneous schools are those that cannot meet the requirements for special training schools. The most popular types in terms of enrollment are preparatory schools (*yobi-ko*), automobile driving schools, and schools for foreigners.

In 1996, 39% of Japan's high school graduates entered junior colleges (*tanki daigaku*, literally short-term universities) and universities. Junior colleges offer two-year education to predominantly female high school graduates (91% in 1996). Regular four-year universities are male dominated both in terms of students (67% in 1996) and faculty (86%). Of the 576 universities as of May 1, 1996, 98 are national universities run by the Ministry of Education, 53 are public universities founded and run by prefectural or municipal authorities, and 425 are private ones. Several of the nation's top universities, including Tokyo University, Kyoto University, and Hitotsubashi University, are national universities. Tokyo University, in particular, is the most prestigious university in the nation. Initially established in 1877 to train top government officials, its graduates still far outnumber those of other elite universities among top government officials and corporate executives. Top private universities such as Keio University and Waseda University are also prestigious, and their alumni are influential in business and political circles.

To foreign critics such as Cutts (1996), the fact that all Japanese leaders graduated from elite universities or "cartels of the mind" complicates U.S.–Japan communication because the homogeneous Japanese system teaches its students that Japanese values are unique and cannot be shared with other civilizations.

Because the status of the universities is very important to their graduates' careers, studying to enter an elite university by passing entrance examinations has been the abiding obsession of Japan's high school students. Once they enter universities, however, the intensity of their education is said to slacken off considerably. According to Rohlen (1992: 338), "undergraduate instruction is notoriously lax and uninspired. Elite universities are aspired to more for their status than their quality of instruction."

Japanese education at the graduate level is said to be weak by international standards and "very few Japanese universities today can be said to be oriented toward either world-class research or training" (Rohlen 1992: 337). In 1996, 14.0% of the nation's university graduates entered graduate schools (4.5% in 1970). This ratio is said to be lower than that in the United States, England, and France. In addition the areas of graduate training are very uneven; about half of the graduate students are enrolled in engineering. There are few MBA programs; those offered at Keio University, Waseda University, and Nihon University are the top ones, which cater heavily to foreign students.

The above discussion does not mean that practical postgraduate training and research are lacking in Japan. In Japan's corporate system, companies themselves provide their employees with continuous in-house business and technical training, much more than their Western counterparts. Large companies also train their own R&D personnel. The skills thus learned are much more company-specific and immediately applicable. These training activities are an integral part of the Japanese corporate culture that emphasizes long-term employment, continual skill improvement, and intrafirm labor mobility.

Finally, it should be mentioned that in Japan as elsewhere (some would say more than elsewhere), the education system teaches more than just knowledge and skills; it also inculcates cultural values. Rohlen and LeTendre (1996: 370) note that "across virtually the entire sequence of organized learning from school to company, one encounters an ideal of group living." This "socialization model" emphasizing learning as a shared, collective experience is also "utilized in the various clubs, activities, and social organizations in which Japanese participate as children, adolescents, and adults."

"Groupism" is a central value of the Japanese society. It is embedded in various business practices and institutions as a central part of Japanese **business ethics**. It is not surprising, therefore, that it is also the underlying value that unifies the different facets of the Japanese education system.

See also **business ethics, management practices**.

Addresses

Hitotsubashi University
1, Naka 2-chome, Kunitachi, Tokyo 186
Tel: (425) 72-1101

Keio University
15-45, Mita 2-chome, Minato-ku, Tokyo 108
Tel: (3) 3453-4511

Kyoto University
Yoshida Hon-machi, Sakyo-ku, Kyoto 606
Tel: (75) 753-7531

Ministry of Education
2-2, Kasumigaseki 2-chome, Chiyoda-ku, Tokyo 100
Tel: (3) 3581-4211

Tokyo University
3-1, Hongo 7-chome, Bunkyo-ku, Tokyo 113
Tel: (3) 3812-2111

Waseda University
6-1, Nishi Waseda 1-chome, Shinjuku-ku, Tokyo 113
Tel: (3) 3203-4141

References

Cutts, Robert L. 1996. *The Empire of Schools: Japan's Universities and the Molding of a National Power Elite.* Armonk, NY: M.E. Sharpe.

Ishikawa, Toshio. 1991. *Vocational training.* Tokyo: Japan Institute of Labor.

Lee, Shin-ying, Theresa Graham, and Harold W. Stevenson. 1996. Teachers and teaching: Elementary schools in Japan and the United States. In *Teaching and Learning in Japan,* ed. by Thomas P. Rohlen and Gerald K. LeTendre. Cambridge: Cambridge University Press.

Leestma, Robert, and Herbert Walberg, eds. 1992. *Japanese Educational Productivity.* Ann Arbor: Center for Japanese Studies.

Lewis, Catherine C. 1996. Fostering social and intellectual development: The roots of Japanese educational success. In *Teaching and Learning in Japan,* ed. by Thomas P. Rohlen and Gerald K. LeTendre. Cambridge: Cambridge University Press.

Rohlen, Thomas P. 1983. *Japan's High Schools.* Berkeley: University of California Press.

Rohlen, Thomas P. 1992. Learning: The mobilization of knowledge in the Japanese political economy. In *The Political Economy of Japan,* vol. 3: *Cultural and Social Dynamics,* ed. by Shumpei Kumon and Henry Rosovsky. Stanford: Stanford University Press.

Rohlen, Thomas P., and Gerald K. LeTendre, eds. 1996. *Teaching and Learning in Japan.* Cambridge: Cambridge University Press.

White, Merry I. 1989. *Japan's Educational Challenge: A Commitment to Education.* New York: Free Press.

electronics industry   The premier industry of the 1980s, the electronics industry, occupies a special place in Japan's manufacturing industries. It exemplifies excellence in manufacturing, quality product, and continual product development through R&D.

The industry produces a wide range of products. They can be classified into three categories: (1) consumer electronics (audiovisual equipment, etc.), (2) industrial electronic equipment (communication gear, computers, measuring devices and office automation equipment, etc.), and (3) electronic components and devices (semiconductor parts, liquid crystal display devices, etc.). In terms of production value, in 1996 electronic components and devices led with over ¥12 trillion followed by industrial electronic equipment (¥9 trillion) and consumer electronics (¥2 trillion). Industrial electronics (especially computers) and electronic parts (especially memory chips) are known to go through generational changes in technology and cyclical changes in demand ("silicon cycle"), affecting production and the market in a cyclical manner. The industry as a whole experienced rapid, double-digit annual growth rates during the 1980s through 1988. Growth slackened in 1989–90. The value of production started to decline in 1991 and did not recover until 1996, in part because of stagnant domestic demand and in part because of increased supply and competition in the world market. Semiconductors, in particular, have experienced cyclical changes in world demand and prices.

The industry has a sizable number of famous companies whose products are world renown. Most of the companies make a large variety of products, but they have different strengths in different products, as seen in their market shares (in %) of major products in 1996 (*Japan Economic Almanac 1998: 275–98, 303*):

1. Camcorders (domestic shipments): Sony, 40.7%, Sharp, 22.6%, Matshushita, 15.6%; Victor Co., 14.4%.

2. CD Players (domestic shipments): Sony, 39.0%; Matsushita, 38.0%; Kenwood, 12.0%; Aiwa, 5.0%; Nippon Columbia, 3.0%.

3. Color TVs (domestic shipments): Matsushita, 16.5%; Sharp, 12.1%; Toshiba, 12.0%; Sony, 11.9%; Sanyo Electric, 8.5%.

4. Personal computers (domestic shipments): NEC, 39.4%; Fujitsu, 21.7%; IBM Japan, 12.2%; Apple Computer, 10.0%; Toshiba, 7.5%.

5. Semiconductors (domestic sales): Intel, 12.0%; NEC, 7.5%; Motorola, 6.0%; Hitachi, 5.7%; Toshiba, 5.7%.

6. VCRs (domestic shipments): Matsushita, 20.2%; Sony, 13.6%; Victor Co., 11.9%; Toshiba, 11.8%; Sharp, 10.1%.

The leading companies of the industry in terms of overall sales and profits are given in table E.2. Matsushita Electric Industrial Co. is the

Table E.2
Leading electronics manufacturers (in ¥ billions)

Company	FY 1991		FY 1996	
	Sales	Profits[a]	Sales	Profits[a]
Matsushita Electric Industrial Co.	4,995	196	4,798	143
Hitachi Ltd.	3,925	129	4,311	84
NEC Corp.	3,049	62	4,029	108
Toshiba Corp.	3,185	71	3,822	97
Fujitsu Ltd.	2,434	40	3,124	96
Mitsubishi Electric	2,611	62	2,845	61
Sony Corp.	1,979	24	2,170	86

Sources: *Japan Company Handbook*, Autumn 1992 and Summer 1998.
Note: Some of these companies (particularly Hitachi, Toshiba, and Mitsubishi Electric) are diversified electrical machinery manufacturers that produce more than electronics products.
a. Pretax profits.

largest electronics manufacturer not only in Japan but also in the world. Other giants of the industry are more diversified manufacturers. For example, Hitachi derives about 18% of its sales revenue from electric power equipment, Toshiba has 23% of its sales in heavy electric equipment, and Mitsubishi Electric depends on heavy electric machinery and industrial machinery for 40% of its sales.

The industry owes much of its initial success to the "founder type of personality." Kinosuke Matsushita (1894–1991), founder of Matsushita Electric Industrial, did not finish grade school, and had a humble beginning as a mechanic in a bicycle-repair shop. Through personal ingenuity, perseverance, and emphasis on technology, he led the company he founded in 1935 through difficult periods of Japan to become the world's largest electronics firm. He created harmonious labor relations in his company, and his management philosophy is much revered in Japan. Kotter (1997) considers him the twentieth century's most remarkable entrepreneur. Another prominent personality of the industry is Akio Moria, cofounder and former chairman of Sony Corporation. Unlike Matsushita, Morita is a graduate of science and engineering at Osaka University, a globe-trotter, and very internationally oriented. His emphasis on research, product development, and product quality guided the company from its small postwar beginning into one of the world's leading electronic firms, and its products have become a symbol of quality in consumer electronics.

Although emphasis on R&D characterizes all firms in the electronics industry, computer-related companies have also benefited from active government promotion of high technology, including computer technology. Government support took various forms, including subsidies in R&D, infant industry protection, and technical assistance as part of the **industrial policy** of the **Ministry of International Trade and Industry** (MITI). Japan is not unique in this respect; it is well known that many American high-technology companies have benefited, perhaps to a greater extent, from government-supported research and from defense contracts. The extent of Japanese government subsidies to computer companies was modest and limited to the phase of technology research rather than the commercialization of the product development.

An example of government-assisted R&D project is the VLSI (very large-scale integrated circuit) Research Cooperative, set up by MITI to develop the technology required for the fourth generation computers. MITI took the initiative to set up and coordinate the joint R&D venture of five computer companies (Fujitsu, Hitachi, Mitsubishi Electric, NEC, and Toshiba) in 1976. The purpose of the cooperative was to integrate the research capacities of the five companies, to capture the large externalities associated with R&D. The cooperative was disbanded in April 1980 after it had accomplished its objective. The legal life of the cooperative was limited in order to prevent it from extending monopolistically into the joint production and marketing of the product that results from the new technology. MITI paid ¥29.1 billion, or 39.5%, of the project's costs. Its role of initiation and coordination, however, was more important. It consulted with potential corporate participants who helped select promising technologies to research and develop.

In consumer electronics, although the Japanese makers are well known for their excellent manufacturing, some analysts have criticized them as relatively lacking in innovative product development. They are said to have a "pack mentality," with many companies producing the same line of goods but reluctant to try something new unless it has been tried somewhere else first (Schlesinger 1992: 4). Sony is considered to be the outstanding exception, with its innovative products such as the Walkman, the Handycam, and the recordable compact disk player.

See also **industrial policy, Semiconductor Agreement**.

Addresses

Electronic Industries Association of Japan
3-2-2 Marunouchi, Chiyoda-ku, Tokyo 100
Tel: (3) 3213-1371

Fujitsu Ltd.
6-1, Marunouchi 1-chome, Chiyoda-ku, Tokyo 100
Tel: (3) 3216-3211   Fax: (3) 3216-9365

Hitachi, Ltd.
4-6, Kanda-Surugadai, Chiyoda-ku, Tokyo 101
Tel: (3)-3258-1111   Fax: (3) 3258-5480

Matsushita Electric Industrial Co.
1006, Kadoma, Kadoma City, Osaka Prefecture 571
Tel: (6) 908-1121   Fax: (6) 908-2351

NEC Corp.
7-1, Shiba 5-chome, Minato-ku, Tokyo 108
Tel: (3) 3454-1111   Fax: (3) 3457-7249

Sony Corp.
6-7-35 Kitashinagawa, Shinagawa-ku, Tokyo 141
Tel: (3) 5448-2111   Fax: (3) 3448-2183

Toshiba Corp.
1-1, Shibaura, 1-chome, Minato-ku, Tokyo 105-01
Tel: (3) 3457-4511   Fax: (3) 3456-4776

References

Anchordouguy, Marie. 1990. A challenge to free trade? Japanese industrial targeting in the computer and semiconductor industries. In *Japan's Economic Structure: Should It Change?* ed. by Kozo Yamamura. Seattle: Society for Japanese Studies.

Choy, Jon. 1996. Computer usage in Japan: Revolution or fashion? *JEI Report* 3A, January 26.

Choy, Jon. 1997. Advanced television in Japan: Getting the picture. *JEI Report* 27A, July 18.

Electronics. In *Japan Economic Almanac*. Various years. Tokyo: Nihon Keizai Shimbun.

Fransmain, Martin. 1990. *The Market and Beyond: Cooperation and Competition in Information Technology in the Japanese System*. Cambridge: Cambridge University Press. Ch. 3.

Imai, Ken'ichi. 1988. Industrial policy and technological innovation. In *Industrial Policy of Japan*, ed. by Ryutaro Komiya, Masahiro Okuno, and Kotaro Suzumura. Tokyo: Academic Press Japan.

Kobayashi, Koji. 1991. *The Rise of NEC*. Cambridge, MA: Blackwell.

Kotter John. 1997. *Matsushita Leadership: Lessons From the 20th Century's Most Remarkable Entrepreneur*. New York: Free Press.

Morita, Akio. 1986. *Made in Japan*. New York: Dutton.

Ouchi, William, and Michele Kremen Bolton. 1988. The logic of joint research and development. *California Management Review* 30, 3: 9–33.

Prestowitz, Clyde V., Jr. 1988. *Trading Places*. New York: Basic Books. Ch. 2.

Schlesinger, Jacob M. 1992. Japan's vaunted electronics industry hits rut as lack of innovation hinders growth. *Asian Wall Street Journal Weekly*, May 4: 4, 6.

Shinjo, Koji. 1988. The computer industry. In *Industrial Policy of Japan*, ed. by Ryutaro Komiya, Masahiro Okuno, and Kotaro Suzumura. Tokyo: Academic Press Japan.

Tan, Benjamin, and Ilan Vertinsky. 1995. Strategic advantages of Japanese electronics firms and the scale of their subsidiaries in the U.S. and Canada. *International·Business Review* 4, no. 3.

Yamashita, Toshihiko. 1987. *The Panasonic Way*. Tokyo: Kodansha International.

employment discrimination As in many other countries, discrimination in employment exists in Japan, reflecting the prejudices of society. Victims of discrimination include women, social outcasts, foreign residents, and the disabled.

1. *Women.* Japanese female workers generally do not receive the same treatment as male workers at major Japanese companies. Their earnings are lower, and they are not usually eligible for promotion to executive positions. The disparity is considered by many to be the worst among the industrialized nations. Although the **Equal Employment Opportunity Law** of 1986 was enacted to rectify this, progress has been slow. Various manifestations of the disparity are discussed in **labor force** and **women in the labor force**.

2. *Social outcasts.* More than one million Japanese are social outcasts called *burakumin* (literally the hamlet people) because their ancestors during the feudal period were *eta* (literally the dirty), people who worked as butchers and tanners; these occupations were and still are considered unclean by traditional Japanese standards. Although *burakumin* are ethnic Japanese, they face severe discrimination in employment, housing, and marriage. They are physically indistinguishable from the ordinary Japanese, but potential employers or marriage partners can find out their outcast background by checking their household registry record. As a result they tend to earn their living by engaging in their ancestors' occupation of leather working and other low-status jobs while living in traditional *burakumin* ghettos.

3. *Foreign residents, particularly Koreans.* There are 1.41 million foreigners living in Japan as of December 31, 1996, of which about 46% are Koreans and 17% Chinese. Although all foreign residents, particularly Asian and black residents, face various degrees of employment discrimination, Koreans are said to have fared worst. Reportedly, many Japanese are prejudiced against the Koreans. The bulk of the Koreans in Japan are descendents of the two million forced laborers conscripted from the former Japanese colony of the Korean peninsula before and during World War II to work in munition plants, coal mines, and construction projects.

Korean residents are discriminated against in employment, **housing**, and education. Because naturalization is extremely difficult in Japan for foreign residents—even if they are born in Japan and are the second- and third-generation holders of permanent residence—their "alien" legal status also disqualifies Korean residents for many government job and the legal profession. As a result Korean residents in Japan are forced to perform low-paying, unskilled labor or to operate their own businesses in areas in which barriers to entry are low such as construction, drinking establishments, *pachinko* (pinball) parlors, and services.

4. *The disabled.* Japanese companies are said to be reluctant to hire disabled workers, reportedly for the same reason that *burakumin* and Koreans are discriminated against: strong Japanese cultural bias against those who are different. As a result of Japan's more than 1.3 million disabled citizens of working age, only 20% have jobs. The government has adopted measures to help employing the disabled. A 1960 law, amended in 1976, requires that in private companies with more than 63 employees, 1.6% of employees be workers with physical or mental disability; that percentage is raised to 1.8% in July 1998. For public organizations and special corporations, the quota is 1.9%. Subsidies are given to companies that achieve the quota, while public disclosure and a fine are the penalty for noncompliance. Unfortunately, the implementation of the law has not been effective. Two-thirds of the companies covered by the law routinely pay the small fine rather than hire more disabled workers. A survey taken by the Ministry of Labor in June 1997 shows that nearly 50% of the companies surveyed failed to achieve the legal quota. Large companies with over 1,000 employees have attained a lower percentage than small companies.

In addition to employers' reluctance to hire them, the wheelchair-bound encounter extreme difficulties commuting in crowded trains and suffer from lack of special access facilities in train stations with steep stairs and in office buildings. As a result many disabled persons are discouraged from seeking employment.

See also **labor force, women in labor force.**

Address

Physically Handicapped Persons' Employment Council, Ministry of Labor
2-2, Kasumigaseki 1-chome, Chiyoda-ku, Tokyo 100
Tel: (3) 3593-1211

References

Fabre, Olivier. 1991. Physical, mental barriers hinder the disabled. *Japan Economic Journal*, February 16: 6.

Johnstone, Christopher B. 1996. "Virtual" citizens: Japan's foreign residents and the quest for expanded political rights. *JEI Report* 27A, July.

Itoh, Yoshiaki. 1991. Ministry gives firms 5 months to increase hiring of disabled. *Nikkei Weekly*, June 22: 4.

Ministry of Labor. 1997. *Labor Administration: Toward a Secure, Comfortable and Active Society*.

Murdo, Pat. 1992. Roles of government, industry in the life of disabled Japanese. *JEI Report* 41A, October 30.

Neary, Ian. 1996. Burakumin in comtemporary Japan. In *Japan's Minorities: The Illusion of Homogeneity*, ed. by Michael Weiner. London: Routledge.

New regulations create interest in hiring disabled. *Nikkei Weekly*, May 11, 1998: 17.

Park, Yonug Myung. 1990. Japan's Koreans live with prejudice, fear. *Tokyo Business Today*, February: 40–44.

Suh, Yong Dal. 1991. Many doors in Japan remain closed to minorities. *Asian Wall Street Journal Weekly*, July 29: 12.

employment insurance   Japan's employment insurance is broader than Western unemployment insurance; it includes unemployment benefits and employment promotion. It is based on the Employment Insurance Law enacted in 1974 and is administered by the Employment Security Bureau of the Ministry of Labor. It covers employees in the private sector and daily laborers. Seamen are covered by a separate Seamen's Insurance plan.

For unemployment benefits, both employees an employers contribute 0.55% of wages. However, older workers who are seeking employment after having retired from a company are exempt from paying the premiums. For services in employment promotion, workforce development and training, employees contribute 0.35% of their wages.

The amount and duration of unemployment benefits are determined as follows:

1. *Amount of benefits.* The daily amount of basic allowance depends on the level of wages and the nature of employment. For regular workers the benefits range from ¥2,550 to ¥10,660 in 1997, depending on their wage levels. For daily wages between ¥3,190 and ¥4,240 the allowance is 80% of the wages. The percentage declines to 60% when daily wages are between ¥10,250 and ¥17,770.

Table E.3
Duration of unemployment benefits, for regular insured workers, 1997 (unit: days)

| | Period of employment insured | | |
Age	1–4 years	5–9 years	10 and more years
Below 30	90	90	180
30–44	90	180	210
45–54	180	210	240
55–64	210	240	300
Disabled			
up to 45	240	240	240
46–64	300	300	300

Source: Ministry of Labor.
Note: For employment of less than one year, the duration of benefits is 90 days for regular workers, disabled workers, and part-time workers.

2. *Duration of benefits.* This is determined by the period of employment ensured, the age of the worker and the nature of employment. Table E.3 shows the duration of benefits for regular workers in 1997. For example, for regular workers younger than 30, they are eligible for 90 days of benefits if they are insured for 5–9 years, and for 180 days if insured for 10 years or more. For disabled persons who have difficulty in obtaining employment, the duration is increased selectively. The duration of benefits for part-time workers (who work 22–33 hours a week) is reduced somewhat, with the same minimum of 90 days but maximum of 210 days (with ten years or more of insured employment). For anyone ensured for less than one year, the duration of benefits is 90 days. Unemployed seasonal workers are entitled to a lump-sum equivalent to only 50 days of benefits.

Japan's unemployment benefits have been criticized for being lower than those of other OECD countries (OECD 1997). On the other hand, it can be argued that a relatively modest level and short duration of unemployment benefits would give the unemployed a stronger incentive to seek a new job quickly (Ostrom 1997). The high unemployment benefits of some European countries may have been responsible for their high unemployment levels.

The National Employment Adjustment Subsidy Program was established in 1975 as part of the employment insurance scheme to improve employment. Under the system eligible employers who need to reduce employment because of recessions can receive subsidies from the government up to one-half (for large firms) or two-thirds (for small- and medium-sized firms) of their payments to their temporarily laid-off workers for a maximum of 75 days. These temporarily laid-off workers are not counted as unemployed in the Japanese labor statistics. To be eligible for the program, the employer's sector as a whole must be listed on the program. To be listed, the sector must have experienced a quarterly production downturn of at least 5% year on year or within two years. Once a sector is listed, it stays on the list for at least one year. As of January 1998, 88 sectors were listed (*Nikkei Weekly*, May 4, 1998: 1).

A recent example is the manufacturers of home appliances. Because of low consumer demand in 1997–98, the Japan Electrical Manufacturers' Association applied to the Ministry of Labor to designate home-appliance makers as eligible for the program.

Address

Employment Security Bureau, Ministry of Labor
2-2, Kasumigaseki 1-chome, Chiyoda-ku, Tokyo 100
Tel: (3) 3593-1211

References

Employment and Employment Policy. 1988. Tokyo: Japan Institute of Labor.

Hiraishi, Nagahisa. 1987. *Social Security.* Tokyo: Japan Institute of Labor.

Ministry of Labor. 1997. *Labour Administration: Toward a Secure, Comfortable and Active Society.*

Organization for Economic Cooperation and Development (OECD). 1997. *Implementing the OECD's Job Strategies: Lessons from Member Country Experiences.* Paris: OECD.

Ostrom, Douglas. 1997. Prospects for economic reform in Japan: Where is the safety net? *JEI Report* 37A, October 3.

Yokota, Kazunari. 1998. More companies line up to use public funds for averting layoffs. *Nikkei Weekly,* May 4: 1, 3.

employment pattern   Of Japan's total employed labor force of 64.9 million in 1996, about 11.8% were self-employed/employers, 6.9% were family workers, and 82.1% were employees. By sector, only 5.1% of them were engaged in agriculture. Services are the largest sector—employing about a quarter of the labor force—followed by wholesale/retail trade and manufacturing, as shown in table E.4. Between 1980 and 1996, agriculture's share of employment has declined, while that of services has grown. The other industries' shares have remained relatively stable. Of these industries, mining, construction, transportation and communications,

Table E.4
Employment by sector (in million people and %)

	1980		1996	
Total	55.4	100%	64.9	100%
Agriculture and forestry	5.3	9.6	3.3	5.1
Fisheries	0.5	0.8	0.3	0.5
Mining	0.1	0.2	0.1	0.2
Construction	5.5	9.9	6.7	10.3
Manufacturing	13.7	24.7	14.5	22.3
Transportation, communications, and utilities	3.8	6.9	4.5	6.9
Wholesale/retail and food	12.5	22.5	14.6	22.5
Finance, insurance, and real estate	1.9	3.5	2.6	4.0
Services	10.0	18.1	16.0	24.7
Government	2.0	3.6	2.1	3.2

Source: Management and Coordination Agency.

and government employ much more male than female employees. In wholesale/retail trade, finance, and services, the numbers of male and female employees are close.

Of all employees, about 90% are regular employees and the rest nonregular employees. The latter consist of different groups of workers with various status such as temporary employees (1–4 month employment term), day laborers, part-timers (less than 35 hours a week), and *arubaito* workers (side-job holders, usually students). Table E.5 shows the number of regular and nonregular employees by sex.

As table E.5 shows, while more than 10% of all employees are nonregular employees in 1996, the percentage is much higher for women. In particular, temporary employees are predominantly (71%) female, constituting 15% of all female employees.

See also **labor force, women in the labor force.**

References

Japan Institute of Labour. Annual. *Japanese Working Life Profile.*

Management and Coordination Agency. Annual. *Labor Force Survey.*

Management and Coordination Agency. Annual. *Japan Statistical Yearbook.*

endaka   High yen or yen appreciation; often specifically used to refer to the yen's appreciation after the September 1985 **Plaza Accord.**
   See **yen–dollar exchange rates.**

Table E.5
Regular and nonregular employees (1996 average)

	Total	Regular employees	Nonregular employees		
			Total	Temporary employees	Daily employees
Number (in million)					
Total	53.2	47.5	5.7	4.5	1.2
Male	32.4	30.6	1.8	1.3	0.5
Female	20.8	17.0	3.8	3.2	0.7
Percentage[a]					
Total	100.0	89.3	10.7	8.5	2.3
Male	100.0	94.4	5.6	4.0	1.5
Female	100.0	81.7	18.3	15.3	3.3

Source: Management and Coordination Agency.
a. Because of rounding, the percentages do not always add up to 100.

enterprise tax   (or business tax) A prefectural tax levied on the net incomes of corporations and unincorporated businesses located in the prefectures. Also called the *business tax.*
See **tax system**.

Equal Employment Opportunity Law, 1986   Legislated in 1985 after heated debate in Japan, the law became effective in April 1986. It was inspired by and conformed with the United Nations Convention on the Elimination of All Forms of Discrimination against Women, which Japan signed in 1980. It was revised in 1997, to take effect April 1999.

The 1986 law forbids employers to discriminate on the grounds of sex in regard to employee training, retirement, and benefits and requires employers to "endeavor" to provide women the same opportunities as men in recruiting, hiring, job assignment, and promotion. It forbids employers to require female employees alone to be unmarried or below a certain age, or to require female employees to do work that would be detrimental to pregnancy, childbirth, and breast-feeding. It extends maternity leave from 12 weeks as provided for in the Labor Standards Law of 1947 to 14 weeks.

Thus the law combines protective provisions for women with promotion of equality between the sexes. Protective legislation for women in postwar Japan started as early as 1947 with the Labor Standards Law which restricted overtime and night work for women. However, such protection has been criticized as counterproductive because it raised the

price of female labor and thereby gave employers an excuse for their reluctance to hire and promote women. Although the overtime and night
work restrictions were relaxed in 1986, Saso (1990: 106) questions
whether equal opportunity can be implemented while a certain measure of
protective legislation remains in force. In the revised law, such protective
restrictions are removed.

The original law has no sanctions for violations, and complaints are to
be mediated or submitted to arbitration committees. The revised law provides for the publication of the names of companies that violate the rules
for equal hiring, placement and promotion of women. Whether this will
be effective remains to be seen. Some changes have already been brought
about. Flagrant discrimination against women in terms of recruitment and
starting wages for new entrants has been reduced. Some companies have
begun to ask female employees when they are hired whether they prefer a
career on the general management (sogo shoku) track with all its commit-
ments or just a job on the clerical (ippan shoku) track. The former provides
extensive training and advancement opportunities but may entail long
hours and transfers; the latter offers lower salaries, little promotion opportunity, and shorter working hours. Previously companies would automatically place women on the clerical track and men on the general
management track. Thus opportunities for women have increased. Also
the law has made it possible for some women to enter many professions
formerly open only to men. The revised law bans sexual harassment at
workplace and requires employers to take preventive measures under the
guidance of the Ministry of Labor.

On the other hand, the number of women actually selected for management track remains small. According to the International Labor Organization, in 1995 women occupied only 8.2% of managerial positions in
Japan, compared with 42.7% in the United States and 18.7% in Hong
Kong (Nikkei Weekly, February 23, 1998: 1). In addition, Lam (1993: 211)
charges that companies are moving toward more indirect, yet institutionalized, ways of segregating the majority of women into inferior career tracks.
And women still face discrimination in job assignment and promotion.

The Japanese national government has been at the forefront of promoting female employment, but overall it remains male dominated, especially
at the higher levels. The number of female career bureaucrats increased to
1,912 in FY 1995. However, this was only 5.3% of the total number of
career bureaucrats. The Ministry of Agriculture, Forestry, and Fisheries
had the largest number, 199, as of March 1996.

See also **employment discrimination, women in labor force.**

References

Edwards, Linda N. 1994. The status of women in Japan: Has the Equal Employment Opportunity Law made a difference? *Journal of Asian Economics* 5, 2: 217—40.·

Hasegawa, Michiko. 1984. Equal opportunity legislation is unnecessary. *Japan Echo* 11, 4: 55—58.

Lam, Alice. 1993. Equal employment opportunities for Japanese women: Changing company practice. In *Japanese Women Working*, ed. by Janet Hunter. London: Routledge.

Murdo, Pat. 1991. Women in Japan's work world see slow change from labor shortage, Equal Employment Law. *JEI Report* 33A, August 30.

Omori, Hiroko. 1990. Equality proves elusive for women in job market. *Japan Economic Journal*, December 15: 4.

Saso, Mary. 1990. *Women in the Japanese Workplace*. London: Hilary Shipman.

Suzuki, Kazue. 1996. Equal job opportunity for whom? *Japan Quarterly* 43, 3: 54—60.

Eurodollar warrants Warrant bonds denominated in dollar, issued by Japanese corporations, and traded on the Euromarket and in Japan.
See **warrant bonds**.

Euroyen bonds Yen-denominated bonds issued on the Euromarket. They are issued primarily by Japanese corporations, but since 1986 as part of Japan's **financial liberalization** foreign corporations, sovereign countries, and supranational organizations such as the World Bank, and foreign banks can also issue them. The volume of new Euroyen bonds issued was ¥2.9 trillion in FY 1987 and ¥10.7 trillion in FY 1994. It is several times larger than that of its major competing debt instrument, the *samurai* **bonds**, which are yen-denominated bonds issued in Japan by nonresidents.
See also *samurai* **bonds**.

Euroyen futures Contracts to trade three-month deposits at a given interest rate on a specific future date on the Euromarket.
See **financial futures market**.

Export-Import Bank of Japan (JEXIM) A government bank established in 1950 to facilitate Japan's economic interchange with foreign countries. It extends suppliers credit to Japanese exporters, buyers credit to foreign companies, and bank-to-bank loans to foreign governments or banks to facilitate Japanese exports. In addition it extends loans and loan guarantees to support Japanese overseas investment, and loans to foreign governments, corporations, and financial institutions to support their economic development, restructuring, and Japanese investment.

Although JEXIM is a government-owned bank, it enjoys independence in its decision making. Nevertheless, it strives to coordinate its policy with the **Ministry of Finance** and the **Ministry of International Trade and Industry**. In fact the history of JEXIM closely parallels the history of Japan's evolving trade/development strategy and international involvement. When the Bank was first established in 1950, it was initially named the Export Bank of Japan. This reflected the importance that the government attached to export promotion as a strategy of development. The Bank's mission was to provide long-term loans for the export of such capital goods as ships, rolling stock, and plant equipment. In 1952 the Bank was renamed the Export-Import Bank of Japan because it had begun to extend loans for the import of important raw materials. This aspect of the Bank's activities remained important throughout Japan's rapid growth in the 1950s and 1960s as Japan's imports of petroleum, iron ore, and other primary products soared. The Bank also helped finance Japanese companies' overseas investment in resource development. During the 1960s the rapid growth of world trade and world consumption of petroleum led to a growing world demand for large-scale tankers. The Bank played an important role in financing the Japanese **shipbuilding industry**.

Between 1958 and 1975 the Bank was active in providing government yen loans as part of Japan's **foreign aid** program through bilateral agreements. In 1975 another government agency, the **Overseas Economic Cooperation Fund**, was created to take over this function. After 1966 the Bank also began to directly extend its own loans to foreign governments and organizations in the form of buyer's credits and bank-to-bank loans. The Latin American countries and the Inter-American Development Bank were the major recipients.

The 1970s was a decade of worldwide instability because of the oil crises, stagflation, trade imbalances, and currency fluctuations. Japan began to experience growing trade surplus, and as a result of Washington's decision to devalue the dollar in 1971 (the **Nixon Shock**), the Japanese yen began to appreciate. As part of the Japanese government's response to these problems, the JEXIM introduced foreign-currency-denominated loans, raised interest rate on export loans, and expanded loans to aid Japanese **direct overseas investment**. It also introduced untied direct loans (which are not tied to the procurement of goods and services from Japan) to foreign governments and international development organizations.

During the 1980s the Bank's activities were influenced by the debt crisis of the developing countries, Japan's growing trade surplus, and the yen appreciation after the **Plaza Accord** of 1985. The Bank expanded its untied direct loans, which was not part of Japan's official development assistance, as a way for Japan to recycle its trade surplus to promote development and structural adjustment in the developing countries. Support of Japanese foreign investment also increased while export loans were restricted; the latter accounted for only 10% of the Bank's lending by the end of the decade. Because of yen appreciation, loans were denominated in foreign currencies.

As of March 1997, the Bank had more than ¥9 trillion in loans outstanding. During FY 1996, it extended more than ¥1.4 trillion in financing, including ¥55.2 billion in loan guarantees. Overseas investment loans constituted the largest share (47%) of total financing, followed by export loans (23%), untied loans (22%) and import loans (4%).

As of March 31, 1997, Asia has received the largest share of the Bank's financing (38%), followed by Latin America and the Caribbean (16%), North America (15%), Europe (12%) and the Middle East (5%). Within Asia, Indonesia is the largest recipient in terms of the cumulative amount received, followed by China, Thailand, and the Philippines.

In recent years JEXIM tends to focus on supporting Japanese participation in industrial and infrastructural projects in Asia such as power plants, telecommunications network, and natural gas liquefaction facilities. These projects lead to export of equipment from Japan, and may produce products imported by Japan.

The Bank's main source of funds is borrowings from the government's **Fiscal Investment and Loan Program** (Trust Fund Bureau and Post Office Life Insurance and Annuity Special Account). At the end of March 1997, it had total borrowings of ¥7.8 trillion and ¥986 billion of capital. Its capital is wholly subscribed by the Japanese government.

As part of the **administrative reform** of the Japanese government, JEXIM and the **Overseas Economic Cooperation Fund** are merged in the summer of 1998.

See also **foreign aid, government financial institutions**.

Address

Export-Import Bank of Japan
4-1, Otemachi 1-chome, Chiyoda-ku, Tokyo 100
Tel: (3) 3287-9101   Fax: (3) 3287-9539
Internet: www.japanexim.go.jp/

References

The Export-Import Bank of Japan. Annual. *Annual Report.*

The Export-Import Bank of Japan. 1992. *The Course: Forty Years of the Export-Import Bank of Japan.*

Johnstone, Christopher B. 1997. How much bang for the buck? Japan's commercial diplomacy in Asia. *JEI Report* 13A, April 4.

F

Fair Trade Commission   A government commission under the prime minister's office established to implement the **Antimonopoly Law** of 1947. Once considered a relatively ineffective agency, it has vigorously enforced the Antimonopoly Law since the early 1990s.
See **Antimonopoly Law, cartels**.

Federation of Economic Organizations   (Keidandren) Japan's most important business organization.
See **business organizations**.

financial debentures   Bonds issued by long-term credit banks, the Bank of Tokyo-Mitsubishi, the Norinchukin Bank, and the Shoko Chukin Bank.
See **bond market**.

financial futures market   Formally called the *Tokyo International Financial Futures Exchange* (TIFFE), this market was established in June 1989 by the Federation of Bankers' Associations of Japan. Membership includes banks, **securities companies**, and other financial companies, Japanese and foreign. Three financial instruments are traded: yen–dollar currency futures, three-month Euroyen, and Eurodollar interest-rate futures. Euroyen futures are the world's first and account for the bulk of its transactions.

Yen futures consist of contracts to buy or sell yen at a given exchange rate on a specific future date. Euroyen and Eurodollar interest-rate futures are contracts to buy or sell three-month deposits at a given interest rate on a specific future date on the Euromarket. These financial instruments are designed to protect investors, banks, and companies against unpredictable future fluctuations in exchange rate and interest rates. The volume of Euroyen futures transactions increased from 9 million contracts in 1989 to 28.8 million contracts in 1990 and 51 million contracts in 1997.

financial institutions
See **Bank of Japan, banking system, city banks, government financial institutions, insurance companies, postal savings, securities companies**.

financial liberalization   The gradual decontrol by the government, and hence the growing market orientation, of the Japanese financial system since the late 1970s. It consists of many changes in different areas of the financial system, including the introduction of new financial instruments and markets, the decontrol of foreign exchange, the gradual deregulation of deposit interest rates and of banking businesses.

From the immediate postwar period to the early 1970s, Japan's financial system was highly regulated by the authorities for the purpose of providing abundant and cheap funds for rapid industrialization in a stable environment. Bank deposit rates were regulated at low levels, bank activities were regulated by the **Ministry of Finance** and the **Bank of Japan**, banks were obliged to purchase and hold **government bonds** at low yields, opportunities for financial investment were very limited, and foreign exchange was controlled.

The oil crisis of the early 1970s led to stagnation and inflation. This made the low deposit rates untenable as the public could not hedge against inflation. The rapid increase in the issue of government bonds after 1975—more than what the banks were willing to hold at low yields —caused the Bank of Japan to rely increasingly on the purchase of bonds rather than lending as the main monetary instrument for controlling **money supply;** hence its open market operations became increasingly important.

In the late 1970s various short-term **money markets** and instruments —including the *gensaki* market, the negotiable certificate of deposit (CD) with a free market interest rate—as well as a secondary bond market developed. These developments made the financial system increasingly market oriented. The Foreign Exchange Law of 1980 eased foreign exchange controls and made it possible for both residents and nonresidents to invest in domestic and overseas markets. In April 1984 the acquisition of commercial papers (CPs) and CDs issued overseas was permitted for investors. In December 1984 the issuance of the Euroyen CD was allowed for overseas branches of Japanese banks. In July 1985 foreign-currency-denominated convertible bonds were issued by banks in overseas market. At the same time access to free overseas financial markets prompted Japanese investors and financial institutions to demand further domestic financial liberalization.

Throughout the 1980 new financial instruments and markets were introduced and the banking businesses were increasingly deregulated. For example, dealing in public bonds by banks was started in June 1984, yen-denominated bankers' acceptance market was opened in June 1985, short-term (six-month) treasury bills were first issued in February 1986, public issue of 20-year governments bonds began in October 1986, and the auction method for underwriting them was implemented in September 1987. **Stock-index futures trading** was started in September 1988. In June 1989 the stock index option was started, and the Tokyo **financial futures market** was established. The Japanese government bond futures option was started in May 1990.

The deregulation of deposit interest rates proceeded at a slow pace. It consists of the gradual lowering of the minimum amount required for four types of large deposits that have unregulated or deregulated interest rates so that the market-determined rate of return becomes increasingly within the reach of the average depositor. These types of deposits are (1) negotiable certificate of deposit (the minimum amount was ¥500 million in May 1979; it was lowered to ¥50 million in April 1988), (2) large time deposits (the minimum was ¥1 billion in October 1985; it was lowered in several steps to ¥100 million in April 1988 and to ¥10 million in October 1989), (3) money market certificate (MMC) (the minimum was initially ¥50 million in April 1985; it was lowered to ¥10 million in October 1987, and in October 1989, MMC was abolished), and (4) small MMC (the minimum was ¥3 million in June 1989; it was lowered to ¥1 million in April 1990 and ¥500,000 in April 1991. In June 1992 it was reduced to zero, and in June 1993 small MMC was abolished).

Effective June 22, 1992, interest rates on all bank deposits and **postal savings**, excluding three-year bank time deposits and ten-year term postal savings (*teigaku*), are liberalized. Interest rates on bank time deposits were deregulated in June 1993 and on saving deposits in June 1994. The barriers between banking and securities businesses was reduced in April 1993 when the Financial System Reform Act went into effect. It permits banks to set up subsidiaries to enter some securities business and securities houses to set up subsidiaries to enter some trust-banking businesses.

Analysts have criticized Japan's financial liberalization as too slow and incremental. In the mid-1990s the need for more drastic financial reforms became apparent as the economy was suffering from a long stagnation and the nation's financial institutions were greatly weakened by large bad debts that resulted from the decline in land and stock prices after the **bubble economy** of 1986–89. In November 1996 then Prime Minister Hashimoto called for comprehensive financial reforms to make Japan's financial markets "free, fair, and global" and Tokyo a major international financial center. The reform program, to be implemented by 2001 and popularly called the **Big Bang**, is in fact the continuation of financial liberalization in an accelerated and expanded form, with much more political support. The major reforms introduced in the late 1990s include the revision of the **Antimonopoly Law** to lift the ban on **holding companies**, including financial holding companies (March 1998), and the revision of the Foreign Exchange and Foreign Trade Control Law to permit free foreign exchange transactions (April 1998). Further deregulation of the **banking system, securities companies**, and **insurance companies** is scheduled for 1999–2001.

See also **banking regulation and deregulation, Big Bang, deposit system, foreign exchange control and decontrol,** *gensaki* **market, holding companies, interest rate structure, money markets.**

References

Federation of Bankers Association of Japan. Annual. *Japanese Banks*. Tokyo: Zenginkyo.

Kishi, Masumi. 1996. Regulation issues in the era of financial liberalization: Japan, Korea and Taiwan. *Journal of Asian Economics* 7, 3: 487–502.

Mabushi, Masaru. 1993. Deregulation and legalization of financial policy. In *Political Dynamics in Contemporary Japan*, ed. by Gary D. Allinson and Yasunori Sone. Ithaca: Cornell University Press.

Otsuka, Isao. 1994. The reform of the financial system in Japan. In *Japanese Commercial Law in an Era of Internationalization*, ed. by Hiroshi Oda. London: Graham and Trotman/Martinus Nihjoff.

Royama, Shoichi. 1985. The Japanese financial system: Past, present, and future. In *The Management Challenge: Japanese Views*, ed. by Lester C. Thurow. Cambridge: MIT Press.

Royama, Shoichi. 1990. Aspects of financial restructuring in contemporary Japan. *Japan Review of International Affairs* 4: 42–65.

Shigehara, Kumiharu. 1991. Japan's experience with use of monetary policy and the process of liberalization. *Bank of Japan Monetary and Economic Studies* 9, 1: 1–21.

Teranishi, Juro. 1994. Japan: Development and structural change of the financial system. In *The Financial Development of Japan, Korea, and Taiwan*, ed. by Hugh T. Patrick and Yung Chul Park. New York: Oxford University Press.

financial markets
See **bond markets, money markets, over-the-counter market, postal savings, stock index futures trading, stock index options trading, stock market, Tokyo Stock Exchange.**

Fiscal Investment and Loan Program (FILP) An important government credit program that uses funds from **postal savings**, public pension funds, postal insurance funds, and so forth, to make loans to, and to invest in, **government financial institutions, public corporations**, local government bodies in order to promote social and economic development or specific policy objectives. In addition it makes loans to selected categories of private business that are regarded as particularly important for the development of the economy or for social policy objectives. It may also fund projects that cannot find adequate financing in the private sector. Most government loans to private enterprises are administered through special banks or finance corporations.

Introduced in 1953, FILP has grown rapidly in size over the years. It is not part of the regular government budget, but because of its importance every year the proposed FILP has to be approved by the Diet along with the regular government budget. Throughout the 1970s, 1980s, and the early 1990s, the annual FILP amounted to about one-half the size of the general account of the central government. Since FY 1992, however, FILP has grown to about 65% of the size of the general account of the central government. In FY 1997, for example, the general account of the central government was ¥77.4 trillion, whereas the FILP was ¥51.4 trillion. The ordinary account of local governments totaled ¥87.1 trillion.

The major sources of funds for FILP are postal savings, public pensions (e.g., National Pension, Employees' Pension), and postal life insurance. Money from these sources is deposited in the following four funds:

1. Funds of the Trust Fund Bureau of the **Ministry of Finance**. Postal savings, employees' pensions, and national pensions are deposited in this fund.

2. Postal Life Insurance Fund.

3. Government-guaranteed bonds and borrowings. When government institutions, public corporations, or public bodies issue bonds or borrow funds from private financial institutions, the government may guarantee the payment of interest and principal.

4. Industrial Investment Special Account. The investments of the FILP are made through this special account. It provides funds as capitalizations,

which are free of debt-servicing requirements, to government banks, public finance corporations, public bodies, and so forth.

The funds from these sources are dispensed, primarily in the form of loans, by the FILP to the following organizations and special accounts for use:

1. Special accounts such as National Forest Service Special Account, National Schools Special Account, Postal Savings Special Account.

2. **Government financial institutions** such as Housing Loan Corporation, People's Finance Corporation, Small Business Finance Corporation, Japan Finance Corporation for Municipal Enterprises, **Japan Development Bank**, and **Export-Import Bank of Japan**.

3. **Public Corporations** such as Pension Welfare Service Corporation, Japan Highway Corporation, Japan National Railways Settlement Corporation, and **Overseas Economic Cooperation Fund**.

4. Local governments.

5. Others such as the Shoko Chukin Bank, Kansai International Airport Co., the East Japan Railway Co., Electric Power Resources Development Co.

The Housing Loan Corporation and the Pension Welfare Service Corporation have been the two top recipients of funds from the FILP. In FY 1997 they received ¥10.6 trillion and ¥4.5 trillion, respectively. In terms of final uses, the bulk of the funds in the past has gone to the following areas: **housing, small and medium enterprises**, living environment improvement, and roads.

The FILP has been criticized by Kihara (1997) as being bloated and encroaching on the territory of the private sector. The root of the problem is said to be the large and ever-growing **postal savings** which are the main source of funds for FILP. One way to reduce the FILP, therefore, is to reduce or to privatize the postal savings system. One might add that another cause of the problem is the large number of **government financial institutions** and **public corporations** in Japan that require public funds. In the proposed **administrative reform**, the number of these institutions and corporations will be reduced. Another possibility is to allow these government institutions to issue bonds individually so that they do not have to rely on postal savings (Kihara 1997).

See also **government budget, government financial institutions, public corporations and special corporations.**

References

Bank of Japan. Annual. *Economics Statistics Annual.*

Ministry of Finance. Annual. *Financial Statistics of Japan.*

Ishi, Hiromitsu. 1993. The Fiscal Investment and Loan Program and public enterprises. In *Japan's Public Sector: How the Government Is Financed,* ed. by Tokue Shibata. Tokyo: University of Tokyo Press.

Kihara, Shinichi. 1997, A first step towards reform of the Fiscal Investment and Loan System. *Japan Research Quarterly* 6, 2: 74–81.

Ogura, Seiritsu, and Naoyuki Yoshino. 1988. The tax system and the fiscal investment and loan program. In *Industrial Policy of Japan,* ed. by Ryutaro Komiya, Masahiro Okuno, and Kotaro Suzumura. Tokyo: Academic Press Japan.

Ostrom, Douglas. 1994. The flip side of FILP: Japan's public-sector institutions and economic policymaking. *JEI Report* 21A, May 7.

fiscal policy
See **Fiscal Investment and Loan Program, government bonds, government budget, tax reform, tax system.**

flexible manufacturing system (FMS) Order-based small-batch production with computer-aided design and manufacturing to increase product variety and to cut labor and inventory costs. A growing number of companies are introducing FMS because of the rising demand for product varieties in Japan as well the need to cut cost to be competitive. In the semiconductor industry, for example, the demand for mass-produced general-use chips has declined and that for application-specific integrated circuits (ICs) increased. In the auto market the demand for customized features has also increased.

FMS takes different forms in different industries and companies. At Yokogawa Electric Corp., Japan's largest maker of industrial measuring instruments, various machines and tools are used to change assembly line configurations quickly to enable workers to assemble different products. At Mitsubishi Electric Corporation's Kochi prefecture plant, computer-controlled assembly lines can process up to 2,000 different types of application-specific ICs. In the auto industry, it takes the form of engineering workstations and robots, which allow the same assembly line to produce different models. In all these cases FMS results in "soft automation."

Thus the FMS enables factories to easily switch from mass production of a small number of products or models to small-batch production of a broad range of products or models. In addition it reduces the need for new equipment investment, although R&D spending may increase. When factories change to the production of new items, it is not necessary to retool, as is necessary with traditional mass production. Technicians simply reprogram machines to handle different products.

While FMS yields these benefits, its successful implementation demands high exacting skills as well. Technologist Kodama (1991) estimates that the standards of an FMS require efficiency increases by a factor of one or two over traditional mass production in every aspect of processing precision, **quality control**, reliability, maintenance, and worker skills. Alexander (1994: 278–79) and Jaikumar (1986) argue that the higher skill requirement is the main reason why Japan leads the United States in the number of FMS installed and in the efficiency and flexibility of its use. In Jaikumar's (1986) comparative study of FMS use in Japan and the United States, more than 40% of the workforce in the Japanese companies studied were college-educated engineers, and all had been trained on computer-numerical-controlled (CNC) machines. In the U.S. companies, only 8% were engineers, and fewer than 25% had CNC training.

See also **computer-integrated manufacturing system**.

References

Alexander, Arthur J. 1994. Comparative innovation in Japan and the United States. In *Troubled Industries in the United States and Japan*, edited by Hong W. Tan and Haruo Shimada. New York: St. Martin's Press.

Athey, Susan, and Armin Schmutzler. 1995. Product and process flexibility in an innovative environment. *Rand Journal of Economics* 26: 557–75.

Eaton, B. Curtis, and Nicolas Schmitt. 1994. Flexible manufacturing and market structure. *American Economic Review* 84: 875–88.

Jaikumar, Ramachandran. 1986. Postindustrial manufacturing. *Harvard Business Review*, November–December.

Kagawa, Masato. 1990. Flexible plants allows customized production. *Japan Economic Journal*, February 24: 24.

Kodama, Fumio. 1991. Flexible manufacturing frees industry to concentrate on visions of the future. *Japan Economic Journal*, May 25: 8.

Kumar, K. R., A. Kusiak, and A. Vannelli. 1986. Grouping of parts and components in flexible manufacturing system. *European Journal of Operation Research* 24: 387–97.

Kusiak, A. 1985. The part families problem in flexible manufacturing systems. *Annals of Operations Research* 3: 279–300.

Oishi, Nobuyuki. 1990. Automakers boosting factory use of robots. *Japan Economic Journal*, May 5: 15.

Owa, Masataka. 1990. Flexible assembly eases inventory needs. *Japan Economic Journal*, March 3: 21.

Table F.1
Japan's aid to developing countries (in $ millions; multilateral aid excluded)

Region	1980	1990	1996
Asia	1,383 (70.5%)	4,117 (59.3%)	4,127 (49.4%)
Middle East	204 (10.4%)	705 (10.2%)	561 (6.7%)
Africa	223 (11.4%)	792 (11.4%)	1,067 (12.8%)
Latin America	118 (6.0%)	561 (8.1%)	986 (11.8%)
Oceania	12 (0.6%)	114 (1.6%)	198 (2.4%)
Eastern Europe		153 (2.2%)	200 (2.4%)

Source: Ministry of Foreign Affairs.

foreign aid Japan's foreign aid or official development assistance (ODA) program originated in its payments of war reparations to Asian nations from the mid-1950s through 1965. Since then the amount of aid has increased steadily. and became the world's largest in 1989 and 1991–96. In addition to ODA, there is a small private aid program run by nongovernmental organizations.

Before the first oil crisis of 1973, Japanese aid was extended primarily to Asian nations and was tied to the purchase of Japanese products. After the oil crises of the 1970s, Tokyo felt the need to strengthen its ties with other regions, particularly the Middle East. From 1980 to 1996, the share of Asia declined from 71% to 50% (see table F.1). Of all recipients of Japan's aid, China and Indonesia were the two top recipients in the 1990s, followed by the Philippines and Thailand. In the early 1990s Eastern Europe began to receive aid from Japan.

The Japanese government often has been criticized for lacking a consistent principle or philosophy besides self-economic interests in its giving of aid. In the 1980s aid was seen as a good way to use, and to deflect foreign criticism of, Japan's ever-growing trade surplus. The focus of its aid program was initially on large-scale infrastructural projects, which also promoted Japan's exports. Then as foreign criticism mounted that its aid program was export oriented, Tokyo increasingly shifted the focus of its aid during the 1980s from large-scale infrastructural projects to projects to meet "basic human needs" such as rural and agricultural development, human resource development, and small- and medium-sized businesses. In response to the criticism that its aid projects were destructive of the local environment, in 1990 Japanese aid officials first took into account the environmental impact of projects in screening aid projects. In 1991 the government attempted to use foreign aid for strategic purposes. It indicated

Table F.2
Composition of Japan's Foreign aid (in $ millions; disbursement basis)

Type of aid	1970	1980	1985	1990	1995	1996
Bilateral aid	372	1,961	2,557	6,940	10,557	8,356
Loans	250	1,308	1,372	3,920	4,170	2,780
Grants-in-aid	100	375	636	1,374	2,973	} 5,570
Technical assistance	22	278	549	1,645	3,462	
Multilateral aid	87	1,343	1,240	2,282	4,170	1,252
Total aid	458	3,304	3,797	9,222	14,728	9,608

Source: Ministry of Foreign Affairs.

that it would take into account, when offering aid, the potential recipients' military spending, weapon production and trade, and promotion of democracy, market orientation, and human rights. These new aid principles have been criticized as impractical, and for making Japan's aid program susceptible to political pressures.

In 1986 Japan surpassed France to become the second largest aid donor in the world—$5.6 billion as compared with $9.6 billion given by the United States. The figure increased to $9 billion in 1989, which made Japan the largest aid donor in the world compared with $7.7 billion given by the United States in 1989. It remained the largest donar in 1991–96 with a peak of $14.7 billion in 1995 (see table F.2). The dollar amount declined in 1996 and was cut further in 1997–98 because of domestic economic stagnation and decline in public support for aid. Hence Tokyo has been emphasizing the importance of quality rather than quantity of ODA in recent years.

Part of the increase in Japan's dollar-denominated aid reflects the yen appreciation since 1985. As a percentage of GNP, Japan gave annually about 0.28% of its GNP in 1994–95, about average among the developed donor countries, and 0.2% in 1996, which was below average.

ODA consists of two categories, bilateral aid given to another country and multilateral aid contributed to international organizations such as the World Bank. Bilateral aid consists of loans which have to be repaid at concessional terms (i.e., long grace period, long repayment period, and low interest rates) and grants which are not to be repaid. Grants take the form of either grants-in-aid (i.e., monetary disbursement to the recipient country) or technical assistance, in which the assistance providers in donar country receive the payments. Until 1992 Japan's ODA consisted of more loans than grants. The opposite is true since 1993 (see table F.2). This is part of the quality aspect of Japanese ODA touted by Japanese aid officials.

The Foreign Ministry has the greatest influence over aid policy. However, the **Ministry of Finance**, the **Ministry of International Trade and Industry**, and the **Economic Planning Agency** also share the responsibility. The Japan International Cooperation Agency coordinates grant giving and technical cooperation, and the **Overseas Economic Cooperation Fund** administers concessional loans. Thus there is no unified leadership in the administration of Japan's aid program.

Japan has a small private aid program run by nongovernmental organizations. These NGOs are said to be underfunded and understaffed. In FY 1994 they had total revenues of ¥18.5 billion or less than $150 million, mostly from individual donations; Japanese companies are lacking in their contributions. Most of NGOs have been established since 1980 to deal with the refugee problems in the late 1970s and early 1980s. Hence they are most active in Asia, followed by Africa and South America. The Foreign Ministry started in 1989 to subsidize NGO projects, with a total budget of ¥1.2 billion in 1997 for 252 projects. The Ministry of Posts and Telecommunications introduced in 1991 the Voluntary Postal Savings for International Aid program, which donates 20% of interest earned on individual accounts to NGO activities. In 1997 this program generated only ¥1.06 billion because of low interests rates in Japan.

See also **defense expenditures**.

Addresses

Japan International Cooperation Agency
1-1, Nishishinjuku 2-chome, Shinjuku-ku, Tokyo 163
Tel: (3) 3346-5311

Ministry of Foreign Affairs
2-1, Kasumigaseki 2-chome, Chiyoda-ku, Tokyo 100
Tel: (3) 3580-3311

Overseas Economic Cooperation Fund
4-1, Otemachi 1-chome, Chiyoda-ku, Tokyo 100
Tel: (3) 3215-1311

References

Altback, Eric. 1998. Japan's foreign aid program in transition: Leaner, greener—with more strings attached? *JEI Report* 5A, February 6.

Grimm, Margo. 1992. Japan's foreign aid program: Setting priorities, policies in 1992. *JEI Report* 46A, December 11.

Iida, Tsuneo. 1991. In defense of Japan's aid program. *Japan Echo* 18, 3: 41–44.

Ishibashi, Yasako. 1998. Public, private aid groups see icy relations beginning to melt. *Nikkei Weekly*, February 2: 1, 4.

Islam, Shafiqul, ed. 1991. *Yen for Development: Japanese Foregin Aid and the Politics of Burden Sharing*. New York: Council on Foreign Relations Press.

Islam, Shafiqul. 1993. Foreign aid and burdensharing: Is Japan free riding to a coprosperity sphere in Pacific Asia? In *Regionalism and Rivalry: Japan and the United States in Pacific Asia*, ed. by Jeffrey A. Frankel and Miles Kahler. Chicago: University of Chicago Press.

Japan's ODA: The blessing and the bane. *Tokyo Business Today*. September 1991: 10–17.

Klamann, Edmund. 1990. Aid machine struggles with ecology issue. *Japan Economic Journal*, June 30: 1, 5.

Kohama, Hirohisa. 1995. Japan's development cooperation and economic development in East Asia. In *Growth Theories in Light of the East Asian Experience*, ed. by Takatoshi Ito and Ann Ol Krueger. Chicago: University of Chicago Press.

Koppel, Bruce M., and Robert M. Orr, Jr., eds. 1992. *Japan's Foreign Aid: Power and Policy in a New Era*. Boulder CO: Westview Press.

Ministry of Foreign Affairs. Annual. *Japan's Official Development Assistance: Annual Report*. Tokyo.

Mori, Katsuhiko. 1995. *The Political Economy of Japanese Official Development Assistance*. Tokyo: International Development Journal.

Orr, Robert M., Jr. 1990. *The Emergence of Japan's Foreign Aid Power*. New York: Columbia University Press.

Yasutomo, Dennis T. 1986. *The Manner of Giving: Strategic Aid and Japanese Foreign Policy*. Lexington, MA: D.C. Heath.

foreign companies in Japan   There are more than 3,000 foreign companies operating in Japan. Commonly called *gaishi* (literally foreign-capital) companies or foreign-affiliated companies, these include Japanese subsidiaries of foreign companies, joint ventures with at least one foreign parent, and other companies of foreign origin or ownership.

IBM Japan is one of the largest and most profitable foreign-affiliated company in Japan. Established in 1937, it is 100% owned by the IBM World Trade Corp. It is now the third largest computer maker in Japan, closely behind Fujitsu and NEC, with more than 21,000 employees and sales of ¥1,491 billion in FY 1995. Other large *gaishi* companies include Ford Motor, Exxon Corp., Matsushita Electronics, Mitsubishi Petrochemical, Tonen Corp., Mazda Motor, Coca-Cola Japan, Esso Sekiyu, and Amway Japan.

Foreign-affiliated companies have had mixed performance in Japan. Some companies such as IBM Japan have done remarkably well. Other companies have not done so well and have complained about various difficulties of doing business in Japan such as market barriers and excessive government regulations.

In order to throw light on the difficulties that foreign-affiliated companies have experienced in Japan, a survey was conducted among some 2,300 such companies in early 1994 by LBS Co., a subsidiary of IBM Japan. A total of 308 companies responded; 53% of them had the parent company in North America and 33% in Europe. The main points from their responses are summarized below (*The Gaishi*, no. 1, 1994):

1. Difficulties of operating in Japan compared with other advanced countries: 58% say that it is more difficult; 32% say that there is little difference between countries; only 6% report that it is easier to do business in Japan.

2. Reasons why it is more difficult to do business in Japan than elsewhere: land and rents are high, 73%; consumer goods are expensive, 52%; government regulations are too many, 40%; it is difficult to secure qualified personnel, 38%; standards are more complicated than elsewhere, 37% (multiple answers allowed for this and the following questions).

3. Difficulties encountered on entry into the Japanese market: securing needed personnel, 59%; access to marketing and distribution channels, 47%; market surveys, 29%; finding and negotiating with potential partners, 27%.

4. Problems encountered after entering the Japanese market: difficult to employ qualified personnel, 45%; different standards in Japan than in other advanced countries, 43%; strong ties between *keiretsu* companies, 30%; tough, unreasonable regulations and guidelines, 29%; nebulous character of Japanese business practices, 27%.

The above survey results are generally consistent with those of a 1991 survey of 1,211 American companies conducted by the American Chamber of Commerce in Japan (1991). What is interesting about the 1991 survey is that it also identified significant restrictions on business emanating from the United States, including (1) a short-term management perspective driven by the need to report quarterly improvements in operating profits and a strict adherence to financial return-on-investment targets, (2) the inability or unwillingness of many companies to modify products to suit the Japanese markets, (3) the inability or unwillingness of many companies to investigate and/or strive for Japanese quality standards which often exceed norms outside of Japan. These include product quality, pre-sale service, packaging, and post-sale service standards.

In 1995 another survey of 127 American and European firms was made by the American Chamber of Commerce in Japan (1995). The results show that hiring qualified personnel is the greatest difficulty that these firms encountered.

Analysts suggest that one reason for the difficulty in hiring qualified personnel is that some Japanese do have misgivings about the the business practices of the *gaishi* companies—the fears that the *gaishi* are quick to lay off staff and do everything their way, that the parent company or the *gaishi* bosses can dictate everything, that the Japanese working for *gaishi* companies can become isolated, and so on (*The Gaishi*, no. 2, 1994). There are reasons to believe that these fears can be alleviated with better dissemination of actual *gaishi* practices. In a survey of 133 *gaishi* companies operating in Japan conducted by the Nihon Keizai Shimbun, Japan's leading business daily, in 1997, it was found that a high percentage of them have adopted Japanese personnel practices. For example, 44.4% of them said that seniority was their primary consideration in evaluating employee salaries and benefits, 92.4% had the Japanese bonus system, 98.5% offered retirement bonus based on years of service, 80% provided corporate housing facilities or housing subsidies, 37.6% practiced the Japanese bottom-up method of **decision making** (*Nikkei Weekly*, November 3, 1997: 8). In addition there is evidence that Japanese attitude toward working for *gaishi* companies is changing and that more people are willing to work for them.

Asian companies have somewhat different challenges in doing business in Japan, according to a survey conducted by Nikkei Research, Inc., in November and December 1996. Of 114 Asian companies with local operations in Japan, 60.8% cited "demanding Japanese clients" as the biggest problem. High wage and salary costs are the second problem. Of 62 companies with no base in Japan, 54.5% give high wage and salary costs as the biggest obstacle to establishing operations in Japan (*Nikkei Weekly*, March 17, 1997: 21).

A general social problem faced by all foreign companies operating in Japan is the extraordinary emphasis that the Japanese place on being insiders (see **business ethics**). Foreign companies are by definition outsiders, at least initially, but they can become insiders—or semi-insiders as Kang (1990: 67) calls IBM Japan—through persistent efforts in cross-cultural communications and relationships-building. This means that aside from the need to study the Japanese language and business culture, networking is extremely important and is indispensable to any foreign companies attempting to do business in Japan.

Keenly aware of this need, IBM Japan established a subsidiary, the LBS Co., in 1993 as a consulting company for foreign companies operating in Japan to provide information and corporate communications services. It publishes a magazine, *The Gaishi*, and operates a club for corporate members to facilitate business communications and networking (author's interview, IBM Japan and LBS Co., June 9, 1995). The American Chamber of Commerce in Japan also assists American businessmen in providing information and contact. It has a large number of product- and issue-specific working groups working on improving American access to the Japanese market in specific areas.

One quick way to become an insider or semi-insider is through partnership with a Japanese businessman. It should be realized, however, that a successful partnership requires the meshing of or balance between two different business cultures, especially in **decision making**. Kang (1990: 183–218) discusses the pros and cons of such an arrangement and considers it to be valuable. He offers some useful advises on picking the right partner and negotiating with him. He also provides some sensible guidelines that will promote the success of such a partnership. In the late 1990s the weak financial conditions of Japanese banks, securities firms, and insurance companies and the on-going financial reforms (**Big Bang**) have created new opportunities for foreign firms to increase their presence in the financial sector through alliances with their Japanese counterparts.

Acquisition of an existing Japanese company is another way to enter the Japanese market quickly. Abegglen and Stalk (1985: 232) consider such an option "especially attractive," because "through acquisition of a successful company, the most serious problems of entry to the Japanese market can be quickly resolved." It should be noted, however, that acquisitions in Japan are relatively rare and difficult, not because of government regulations or legal restrictions but because of unfavorable cultural attitude toward the sales of companies, although this attitude is changing in recent years (see **mergers and acquisitions**). Where **lifetime employment** prevails, company executives and employees, who have considerable control over company decision on such matters, tend to oppose the sales of their companies. This is particularly true with successful companies.

If a *gaishi* company chooses to operate in Japan without partnership or acquisition, it is essential that it penetrate the multilayered Japanese **distribution system**. Although this is considered a major difficulty in surveys, recent experience indicates that it is possible for foreign companies to surmount it in various ways. It is also essential that it recruit high-level Japanese personnel for its operations.

In recent years the Japanese government and some local business organizations have adopted measures to attract and assist foreign companies. At the national level, The **Japan Development Bank** has a preferential loan program to finance investment projects undertaken by foreign-affiliated firms that will increase the import of certain manufactured goods and processed foods into Japan (author's interview, June 9, 1995). For foreign companies interested in exporting to or investing in Japan, it will also provide practical information on available government assistance in Japan, and on locating, training, financing, business practices in Japan, and so forth.

At the local level, the Kansai Economic Federation, the **Osaka** prefectural government, the Osaka municipal government, and the **Yokohama** municipal government are all actively involved in their respective local economic development programs that include the promotion of foreign business and investment as one of their goals. **Nagoya and Central Japan** are also actively attracting foreign business in preparation for the World Exposition to be held in Seito city near Nagoya in 2005.

Finally, the costs of land and rents have declined significantly in recent years (see **land uses and policies**). The labor market has become less tight as Japanese companies have cut back on hiring. **Financial liberalization** and other deregulations have also reduced government rules and made them more transparent. All of these bode well for foreign companies in Japan.

See also **business ethics, distribution system, foreign direct investment, mergers and acquisitions, Nagoya and Central Japan, Osaka and Kansai, Yokohama**.

Addresses

American Chamber of Commerce in Japan
4-1-21, Toranomon, Minato-ku, Tokyo 105
Tel: (3) 3433-5381   Fax: (3) 3436-1446
Home page: http://www.accj.org.jp

IBM Japan
3-2-12, Roppongi, Minato-ku, Tokyo 106
Tel: (3) 5563-4297

Japan Development Bank
9-1, Otemachi 1-chome, Chiyoda-ku, Tokyo 100
Tel: (3) 3270-3211   Fax: (3) 3245-1938

Japan Development Bank, Washington Chief Representative
1101 17th Street, NW
Washington, DC 20036
Tel: (202) 331-8696   Fax: (202) 293-3932

LBS Co.
2-12, Roppongi 3-chome, Minato-ku, Tokyo 106
Tel: (3) 55563-4500   Fax: (3) 5563-4886

References

Abegglen, James C., and George Stalk, Jr. 1985. *Kaisha: The Japanese Corporation.* New York: Basic Books. Ch. 9.

American businesses in Japan. *JEI Report* 12A, March 31, 1995.

American Chamber of Commerce in Japan. 1991. *Trade and Investment in Japan: The Current Environment.* Tokyo: The American Chamber of Commerce in Japan.

American Chamber of Commerce in Japan. 1995. *Japan in (R)evolution.* Tokyo.

Foreign affiliated companies in Japan: a Comprehensive directory. Tokyo: Toyo Keizai, 1994.

Huddleston, Jackson N., Jr. 1990. *Gaijin Kaisha: Running a Foreign Business in Japan.* Armonk: Sharpe.

Japanese society as seen from the eyes of managers in 308 foreign-affiliated companies. *The Gaishi,* no. 1, 1994: 3–12.

Kang, T. W. 1990. *Gaishi: The foreign company in Japan.* New York: Basic Books.

Kishi, Nagami, and David Russell. 1996. *Successful Gaijin in Japan: How Foreign Companies Are Making It in Japan.* Lincolnwood, IL: NTC Business Books.

Results of our recruitment survey of foreign-affiliated companies. *The Gaishi,* no. 2, 1994: 3–18.

Tokuda, Kenji. 1994. Continuing growth of *gaishi* firms in Japan. *Tokyo Business Today,* December, 34–36.

Weinstein, David. 1996. Structural impediments to investment in Japan. In *Foreign Direct Investment in Japan,* ed. by Masaru Yoshitomi and Edward M. Graham. Cheltenham, England: Edward Elgar.

foreign direct investment in Japan   Foreign direct investment (FDI) in Japan or inward direct investment is defined by the Foreign Exchange and Foreign Trade Control Law to include the following activities by a foreign investor: (1) acquisition of more than 10% of shares in a domestically listed company, including businesses listed on the **over-the-counter market**; (2) acquisition of shares or ownership of a domestic unlisted company from a nonforeign investor; (3) establishment of a branch office or plant.

Compared with Japan's **direct overseas investment**, FDI in Japan is small relative to the large size of the Japanese economy. The reasons are the perceived difficulties for foreign companies to do business in Japan. Aside from the differences in business practices, government regulation of foreign investment was relatively restrictive until 1980.

Until the early 1970s the government restricted FDI on the ground that domestic industry was weak and needed protection. Liberalization reforms made during 1967–73 permitted foreign ownership with prior government approval in all but 17 industries. Further reform in 1980 reduced the restricted industries to four—petroleum, leather, mining and agriculture, and forestry and fishery. Instead of prior government approval, only prior notification to the **Ministry of Finance** was required. Nevertheless, the amount of annual FDI in Japan was only $432 million in FY 1981. It rose steadily to $940 million in 1986 and $3.2 billion in 1988. In 1991, with Washington's prodding for further liberalization, the requirement of prior notification was changed to ex post facto reports except for the four restricted industries. It is doubtful that this had much effect on FDI because the annual amount of FDI remained in the $3–4 billion range during the post-bubble years of 1991–95 (see table F.3).

As shown in table F.4, the United States is by far the largest foreign investing country in Japan in terms of the cumulative total. The Netherlands and Switzerland are, respectively, the second and third largest. The amount of FDI in Japan is dwarfed, however, by Japan's direct overseas investment, which amounted to $67.5 billion in FY 1989 and $50.0 billion

Table F.3
Foreign direct investment in Japan (in $ millions)

Fiscal year	Total amount	Manufacturing	Nonmanufacturing
1951–80	7,336		
1981–86	4,357		
1987	2,214	782	1,430
1988	3,243	818	2,425
1989	2,860	1,688	1,172
1990	2,778	1,208	1,570
1991	4,339	2,444	1,896
1992	4,084	2,476	1,609
1993	3,078	1,514	1,564
1994	4,155	2,189	1,965
1995	3,837	2,373	1,464

Source: Ministry of Finance.

in FY 1996. The cumulative total of Japan's direct overseas investment during FY 1951–95 is $514.3 billion, more than 13 times that of FDI in Japan during FY 1951–95.

Of the total FDI in Japan in FY 1950–95, the bulk was invested in manufacturing, particularly machinery and chemicals. Of nonmanufacturing investment, commerce and services are the most important.

Surveys taken in 1991–94 of American companies operating in Japan suggest the following as the major problems in investing in Japan: high rents and land prices, difficulties in hiring and keeping personnel, complicated business practices and **distribution system**, exclusionary *keiretsu* practices, and vague government regulations (see **foreign companies in Japan**). Related to these is the fact that corporate **mergers and acquisitions** are relatively rare in Japan and particularly difficult for foreign companies. Most of these difficulties were raised by Washington in the **Structural Impediments Initiative** talks with Tokyo in 1990. There is evidence that these difficulties have been alleviated since the early 1990s.

In addition to these "host country" factors, Mason (1992) points out that there are important "home country" factors. First, American companies have slipped in their competitiveness in some industries behind their Japanese counterparts. Second, as many observers have noted, American firms have not tried hard enough to invest in Japan. They are criticized for making three strategic errors—lack of patience, lack of knowledge, and lack of effort.

See also **direct overseas investment, foreign companies in Japan, mergers and acquisitions**.

Table F.4
Foreign direct investment in Japan by country (as of March 31, 1996; in $ million)

Country	FY 1951–95	Share
United States	15,613	41.2%
Netherlands	3,361	8.9
Switzerland	2,250	5.9
Germany	2,026	5.3
Canada	1,663	4.4
Britain	1,643	4.3
Hong Kong	747	2.0
Foreign companies in Japan	3,951	10.4
Total	37,925	100.0

Source: Ministry of Finance.

References

Brauchli, Marcus W. 1989. U.S. to prod Tokyo on easing investment. *Wall Street Journal,* November 2: A14.

Dunning, John D. 1996. Explaining foreign direct investment in Japan: Some theoretical insights. In *Foreign Direct Investment in Japan,* ed. by Masaru Yoshitomi and Edward M. Graham. Cheltenham, England: Edward Elgar.

Feldberg, Gregory H. 1990. Joint ventures in Japan suffering wedding bell blues. *Japan Economic Journal,* August 25: 1, 7.

Kester, W. Carl. 1991. *Japanese Takeovers.* Boston: Harvard Business School Press.

Lacktorin, Michael J. 1989. *Foreign Direct Investment in Japan: The Long-Term Strategy for the Japanese Market.* Tokyo: Sophia University.

Mason, Mark. 1992. United States direct investment in Japan: Trends and prospects. *California Management Review* 35, 1: 98–115.

Saito, Tadashi. 1991. Foreign direct investment in Japan. *JEI Report* 35A, September 20.

Special feature on direct investment in Japan. *Nikkei Weekly,* June 16, 1997: 10–11.

Weinstein, David. 1996. Structural impediments to investment in Japan. In *Foreign Direct Investment in Japan,* ed. by Masaru Yoshitomi and Edward M. Graham. Cheltenham, England: Edward Elgar.

foreign exchange control and decontrol   In the early postwar period, Japan's balance of payments was in chronic deficits and foreign exchange in great shortage; hence the Japanese government deemed it essential to control the small amount of foreign currency available for financing necessary imports. Thus the Foreign Exchange and Foreign Trade Control Law was enacted in 1949, which authorized government control of foreign capital flows into and out of Japan. Japanese companies that acquired foreign exchange through international trade had to turn it over to a government account. Importers had to apply to the government for foreign exchange allocation. Japanese investment abroad was prohibited. Foreigners were prohibited from purchasing most Japanese securities or equities.

In the 1970s economic changes were working for the relaxation of such restrictions. First, by the early 1970s Japan had overcome its chronic balance of payments problems. Second, the two oil crises of 1973 and 1979 reduced economic growth and investment opportunities in Japan. Corporate borrowing from banks was reduced. Japanese institutional investors such as **insurance companies** and securities **investment trusts**, therefore, had increasing incentives to invest abroad. At the same time, interest rate liberalization and relaxation of capital control in the United States in 1979 provided good investment opportunities for Japanese investors.

In 1974 some of the restrictions on capital outflow and inflow were partially relaxed. In December 1980 the Foreign Exchange and Foreign Trade Control Law was revised, which further liberalized international movement of financial capital. Japanese investors were given complete freedom in overseas investment. Except for four specifically prohibited industries, foreign investors were allowed to enter Japan. The law of 1980, therefore, is commonly regarded as a milestone in the growing globalization of Japanese capital and in the opening of its domestic capital market.

As part of the **financial liberalization** of the 1990s, an amendment to the law took effect in April 1998. It permits any company or individual to engage in foreign-exchange activities without prior permission. The provision of the 1980 law limiting foreign-exchange transactions to licensed banks is lifted.

Thus it has taken about 50 years (1949–98) for Japan to fully liberalize its postwar foreign exchange control. This slow pace of liberalization is incongruous with the rapid expansion of its exports and shows the uneven nature of its globalization.

See also **Big Bang, financial liberalization, foreign direct investment in Japan, Yen–Dollar Accord, 1984.**

References

Calder, Kent E. 1993. *Strategic Capitalism.* Princeton: Princeton University Press. Chs. 1–2.

Koo, Richard C. 1993. International capital flows and an open economy: The Japanese experience. In *Japanese Capital Markets*, ed. by Shinji Takagi. Oxford: Blackwell.

Rosenbluth, Frances McCall. 1989. *Financial Politics in Contemporary Japan.* Ithaca: Cornell University Press. Ch. 3.

foreign workers in Japan   There are three categories of foreign workers in Japan: (1) those who are permanent residents, (2) temporary residents who are admitted into Japan for temporary (6 months–3 years) employment, and (3) illegal workers who overstay their visas or who are in Japan legally but work illegally. Categories 1, 2, and those in 3 who are in Japan legally, coupled with other permanent residents not in the labor force, constitute the total foreign residents in Japan, which at the end of 1996 numbered 1.41 million or 1.1% of Japan's total population of 125.86 million.

Of the 631,554 total permanent foreign residents of Japan in 1994, 588,437 or 93% are Koreans. Most and them are ethnic Koreans who came or were forced to come to Japan during World War II and their descendents. There are 27,381 Taiwanese and Chinese, also mostly of the same origin. Because it is very difficult to become a naturalized citizen in Japan—being born in Japan or being married to a Japanese citizen does not automatically qualify one for citizenship—most of the second- and third-generation descendents of the Koreans and other East Asians who came to Japan during the War have remained noncitizens. As with temporary foreign residents, they are required to register with the Ministry of Justice as foreign residents. When they enter the labor force, they often face **employment discrimination.**

The Immigration Control Law restricts foreigners admitted to Japan for temporary legal employment to business managers, university-level instructors, entertainers, providers of advanced or specialized know-how, others with special skills not possessed by the Japanese (cooks in Chinese or French restaurants, Western-style confectioners, language teachers, etc.), and officially accepted trainees. In 1996, 45,536 people entered Japan as trainees. More than 30,000 of them came from Asia, with China, Indonesia, and the Philippines leading the list.

Illegal foreign workers tend to be tourists and students from Southeast Asia and other East Asian countries who overstay or who are in Japan legally but work illegally. There are no accurate statistics on the number of illegal foreign workers in Japan. According to the Immigration Bureau of the Ministry of Justice, as of November 1995, there were some 285,000 illegal foreigners in Japan, down from an estimated peak of about 300,000 in November 1993. The decline is attributed to the stagnation of the economy and the decrease in employment opportunities for illegal aliens. That total number, however, does not include many foreigners who are in Japan legally as tourists or students but are illegally employed. Illegal workers tend to work as construction workers, factory workers, restaurant workers, bar hostesses, and so on. In other words, they tend to fill the undesirable 3-K jobs (*kitanai, kiken, kitsui,* or dirty, dangerous, and demanding).

In the 1960s and 1970s Japanese employers and **labor unions** resisted foreign workers. Although a shortage of unskilled workers developed after years of economic growth, Japanese industries decided to automate to relieve the shortage rather than to hire foreign workers. As the labor shortage spread to many sectors of the economy in the 1980s, many small businesses began to hire illegal foreign workers willing to take low-paid undesirable jobs shunned by the Japanese. Thus illegal foreign workers have contributed to Japan's economic growth by performing useful functions at relatively low-wage costs.

Yet the presence of a growing number of foreign workers in a hitherto homogeneous society has created various problems and concerns for the Japanese. Foreign workers tend to concentrate in ghettos with poor living conditions. Their different cultural backgrounds have caused social frictions with the Japanese. They are said to have a higher crime rate and to ignore Japanese social customs. Critics also believe that if their numbers continue to increase, they will take jobs away from unskilled Japanese workers and will slow the modernization of labor-intensive industries. As a result growing incidents of Japanese discrimination against foreign workers have been reported. Reportedly foreign workers have encountered discrimination in housing and are not given as much job safety protection and benefits as the Japanese workers.

There is no consensus among Japanese employers on the issue of foreign workers. Owners of small businesses in the service sector, particular construction where the shortage of labor is most acute, tend to welcome foreign workers, whereas executives and union leaders at large corporations tend to have the opposite view. The latter favor hiring more women and retirees. To alleviate the problems of labor shortage and illegal foreign workers, the Japanese government decided in 1991 to set up a foreign trainee program. The Japan International Training Cooperation Organization (JITCO) was established under the government's auspice to train 100,000 foreigners a year for member companies, who pay membership fees to support such training and can request trainees through the organization. Trainees receive living expenses but not salaries, are allowed to stay as interns but must return home after completion of training (maximum of two years). In this way technology transfer to developing countries is also effected.

Currently trainees are allowed to stay a maximum of three years and are given a monthly allowance of ¥80,000–90,000, which is about 30% lower than Japanese workers' wages. After one year, if they can pass tests in work skills and Japanese language proficiency, they become senior trainees and are entitled to the same pay as Japanese workers.

Labor economist Shimada (1994) supports this training system but suggests that in the long run the status of foreign workers in Japan will depend on the kind of nation that the Japanese want. He feels that given the Japanese cultural values, the ideals of full integration and equal rights for foreign workers will not be attainable; foreign workers will continue to be discriminated against. But he does not want to completely ban foreign workers. He suggests a two-pronged strategy. On the one hand, he would promote industrial reform and rationalization so that Japanese industry will not be heavily dependent on unskilled foreign labor. On the other hand, he would accord whatever foreign workers admitted into Japan the same human rights and treatment as given to Japanese citizens. This is his vision of an "open, fair, and self-help nation" for Japan.

Note that Shimada's ideal of a "self-help nation" through industrial reform and rationalization is proposed in the context of the Japanese domestic economy. In the global context, Japan's industrial reform and rationalization involve moving labor-intensive operations to neighboring low-wage countries, as many Japanese companies have done to reduce wage costs. By relying on foreign workers abroad rather than in Japan, Japan's **direct overseas investment** may help alleviate the "problem" of foreign workers in Japan.

There is a group of foreign workers who have been given special treatment. They are the *nikkeijin*, foreigners of Japanese descent, usually from Brazil, Peru, and other South American countries. Revisions of Japan's immigration law in June 1990 gave *nikkeijin* the status of long-term residents that allows them to work legally in the country. Some companies are actively recruiting them because of the labor shortage and the fact that it is easier for *nikkeijin* to adjust to the Japanese society. As a result their number in Japan soared from 8,500 at the end of 1988 to 160,000 at the end of 1994.

See also **employment discrimination, labor force.**

Addresses

Immigration Bureau, Ministry of Justice
1-1, Kasumigaseki 1-chome, Chiyoda-ku, Tokyo 100
Tel: (3) 3580-4111

Ministry of Labor
2-2, Kasumigaseki 1-chome, Chiyoda-ku, Tokyo 100
Tel: (3) 3593-1211

References

Herbert, Wolfgant. 1996. *Foreign Workers and Law Enforcement in Japan.* London: Kegan Paul International.

Johnstone, Christopher B. 1996. "Virtual" citizens: Japan's foreign residents and the quest for expanded political rights. *JEI Report* 27A, July 19.

Labor ministry plans to ease restrictions on foreign workers. *Nikkei Weekly,* May 30, 1992: 11.

Low-cost, illegal workers boon for business, worry for society. *Nikkei Weekly*, August 1, 1992: 11.

Nishio, Kanji. 1990. The danger of an open-door policy. *Japan Echo* 17, 1: 51–56.

Sellek, Yoko. 1996. Nikkeijin from Latin America: The phenomenon of return migration. In *Japan's Minorities: The Illusion of Homogeneity*, ed. by Michael Weiner. London: Routledge.

Shimada, Haruo. 1990a. A possible solution to the problem of foreign labor. *Japan Review of International Affairs* 4, 1: 66–90.

Shimada, Haruo. 1990b. The labor shortage and workers from abroad. *Japan Echo* 17, 1: 57–62.

Shimada, Haruo. 1994. *Japan's "Guest Workers": Issues and Public Policies*, trans. by Roger Northridge. Tokyo: University of Tokyo Press.

Takahashi, Hideo. 1990. Illegal foreign workers in Japan. *JEI Report*, June 15, 1990.

Wada, Tsutomu. 1997. Government slow to open door to foreign laborers. *Nikkei Weekly*, September 8: 1, 19.

Watanabe, Toshio. 1990. A flawed approach to foreign labor. *Japan Echo* 17, 1: 45–50.

fukumi "Latent capital" or the unrealized value of assets when their market prices exceed their book value.

See **banking system, city banks**.

G

gaiatsu Foreign pressure (for policy changes). This concept is important in Japan because it is widely held that most major reforms in Japan were executed by pressure from abroad, particularly the United States. This is because **decision making** by the government is typically based on consensus among competing interests, which makes it extremely difficult to initiate and implement meaningful policy changes. Thus foreign pressure has played an important role in pushing for reforms. This is most clearly seen in **agricultural policy** and **trade policy**, although many other areas of the economy have also seen changes under foreign pressure.

See also **agricultural policy, Antimonopoly Law, distribution system, Structural Impediments Initiative, trade policy.**

gaijin A slightly derogatory term meaning outsiders for foreigners. It is used widely in place of *gaikokujin*, the proper term for foreigners.

See also **business ethics.**

gaishi **companies** Foreign-affiliated companies, including Japanese subsidiaries of foreign companies, joint ventures with a least one foreign parent, and other companies of foreign origin or ownership.

See **foreign companies in Japan.**

GDP, GNP, and GNP per capita These are important national income indicators that measure the overall performance of an economy. GDP (gross domestic product) is the sum of all final goods and services produced (i.e., income made) within the borders of a country by its residents in a year, including resident foreigners. GNP (gross national product) is the sum of income made by the citizens of the country in a year, including net income earned abroad. It equals GDP plus the income received from abroad by the citizens of the country minus the income paid to foreigners.

GNP divided by the country's total population equals GNP per capita, which is a measure of the standard of living of the country. GDP is the best indicator of the size of an economy, whereas GNP shows the total income of its citizens, which determines their standard of living. Japan's national income accounting nowadays emphasizes GDP over GNP, as is the practice in other countries and with international organizations.

Using these national income indicators, one can see that from the destruction of World War II, Japan has succeeded in building the second largest economy in the world after the United States. Table G.1 shows its nominal GDP (i.e., in current prices, which include inflation) and real GDP in 1990 prices. The annual growth rate of real GDP of the postwar period through 1990 was generally high, often the highest among the industrial-

Table G.1
GDP and growth rates (in ¥ trillions and %)

	Nominal GDP	Real GDP	Annual growth rate
1955	8.4		—
1960	16.0		9.0
1965	32.9		9.1
1970	73.3	188.3	10.9
1975	148.3	234.5	3.1
1980	240.2	290.6	2.8
1985	320.4	343.0	4.4
1986	335.5	352.9	2.9
1987	349.8	367.6	4.2
1988	374.0	390.3	6.2
1989	400.0	409.2	4.8
1990	430.0	430.0	5.1
1991	458.3	446.3	3.8
1992	471.1	450.9	1.0
1993	475.4	452.3	0.3
1994	479.3	455.2	0.6
1995	483.2	461.9	1.5
1996	499.9	480.0	3.9

Source: Economic Planning Agency.
Note: Average annual growth rate of real GDP:

1971–75: 5.0%   1976–80: 5.5%
1981–85: 3.4%   1986–90: 4.6%
1991–96: 2.2%

Nominal GNP is calculated in current prices. Real GNP is calculated in 1990 prices. Annual growth rate is that of real GDP over the previous year, except for 1960, 1965, and 1970 figures, which are five-year average growth rates.

ized countries. This was particularly the case in the 1950s and 1960s. It declined sharply since 1992 because of the bursting of the **bubble economy**.

The same growth pattern can be seen in Japan's GNP (not shown in table), the sum of incomes earned by citizens in the domestic economy and from abroad. Until 1982 Japan's GDP and GNP were virtually the same. Since 1983 its GNP began to exceed its GDP slightly, implying that its citizens were receiving more income from abroad than what they paid foreigners. This reflects the growing importance of Japanese investments overseas. The difference, however, was not large, especially when converted into per capita figures. In 1996, for example, Japan's GNP per capita was ¥4,020,000, whereas its GDP per capita was ¥3,976,000.

GNP devided by total population gives GNP per capita (see table G.2). Because Japan's GNP has been growing faster than its population, its GNP per capita has grown steadily over the years. For comparative purpose, GNP per capita in yen in each year is divided by the average **yen–dollar exchange rate** of that year to give GNP per capita in dollar. These are given in table G.2. According to these figures, in 1987 Japan's GNP

Table G.2
GNP per capita (in current ¥ and $ prices)

Year	In 1,000 yen	In dollar	PPP estimates[a]
1955	¥94	$261	
1970	707	1,964	
1980	2,056	9,694	73.4
1985	2,662	12,355	71.5
1986	2,772	17,558	
1987	2,883	21,254	74.7
1988	3,070	24,308	
1989	3,274	23,315	83.5
1990	3,508	25,510	79.4
1991	3,752	28,310	87.6
1992	3,825	30,747	87.2
1993	3,850	35,771	84.3
1994	3,869	38,889	81.7
1995	3,890	40,982	82.0
1996	4,020	35,978	

Sources: Economic Planning Agency and the World Bank.
a. Purchasing power parity estimates of GNP per capita, with U.S. figure as 100 each year. The figures for 1980, 1985, 1989, and 1991 are PPP estimates of GDP per capita.

per capita ($21,254) began to exceed that of the United States ($18,530), and by 1994 it was far larger than that of the United States ($38,889 vs. $25,860).

However, international comparison of GNP per capita based on simple annual exchange rates can be misleading because exchange rates can fluctuate wildly from year to year. Furthermore the differences in the prices of countries are not fully reflected by the exchange rates. In a Japan–U.S. comparison, the use of the yen–dollar exchange rate is particularly misleading because Japan's chronic trade surplus has led to a strong yen vis-à-vis the dollar since 1985 that exaggerates the purchasing power of the yen in Japan. The reason is that only the prices of internationally traded goods and services determine the market exchange rates between currencies. Although the Japanese prices of exported goods such as automobiles and consumer electronics are relatively cheap, the prices of many goods and services such as **housing** and personal services that are not internationally traded are very high (see **price indexes and price levels**), and these high prices play no role in determining the yen–dollar exchange rates. Consequently the yen–dollar exchange rate does not reflect the overall purchasing power of the yen and the dollar in the two countries in buying both internationally traded and nontraded goods and services. In fact a dollar typically can buy more in the United States than its yen equivalent can in Japan at the prevailing exchange rate.

To minimize such problems, the World Bank since the mid-1980s has re-estimated the GNP per capita of its member countries by using purchasing power parity (PPP). The PPP is a number indicating that so many units of a currency (e.g., yen) has the same purchasing power in Japan as one U.S. dollar has in the United States. It is derived by calculating the ratio between the cost of a given basket of goods and services (both internationally traded and nontraded) in yen in Japan and the cost to buy the same basket in dollar in the United States. The PPP is then used to calculate the so-called PPP estimates of GNP per capita, which give a more realistic picture of the purchasing power of each country's average citizen, given the price structure of that country. For ease of international comparison, these PPP estimates are further converted into index numbers, using the United States GNP or GDP per capita in each year as 100. Such index numbers for Japan are given in table G.2. For example, the numbers 79.4 in 1990 and 82.0 in 1996 mean that the real purchasing power of Japanese GNP per capita in those years was 79.4% and 82% of that of the United States in those years. In general, in the 1980s and first half of 1990s Japanese PPP GNP or GDP per capita ranged between 71.5%

(1980) and 87.2% (1992) of that of the United States. This is a far cry from the inflated GNP per capita figures in dollar that are based on simple yen–dollar exchange rates.

Nevertheless, starting from the abject poverty of the early postwar period, Japan has come a long way to have become the world's second largest economy and to have reached a high standard of living that is more than 80% that of the United States. Considering that Japan has a severe shortage of natural resources, this accomplishment is remarkable among nations.

See also **business cycles, price indexes and price levels, yen–dollar exchange rates.**

References

Economic Planning Agency. Annual. *Annual Report on National Accounts.*

Ostrom, Douglas. 1998. Limping toward the millennium: Japan's economy in the late 1990s. *JEI Report* 14A, April 10.

Saito, Tadashi. 1992. Quality of life in Japan: Is it affluent or not? *JEI Report* 22A, June 12.

The World Bank. Annual. *World Development Report.*

general import agents   Exclusive importers of brand-name products.
See **distribution system.**

general trading companies   (*sogo shosha*) The 16 largest of Japan's 1,700 trading companies that are responsible for the bulk of Japan's imports and exports. They are also engaged in domestic trade and other diverse businesses, including **direct overseas investment.**
See **trading companies.**

gensaki **market**   The market for the trading of bonds with a repurchase agreement.
See **bond market, money markets.**

gift market   For centuries gift giving has been a very important part of the social and business life in Japan, so much so that in premodern times there were formal guidelines prescribing various aspects of the practice, from the appropriate gift for various occasions to the wrapping materials. Although such formalities are no longer important, gift giving remains very important in social and business relations as an appropriate expression of appreciation and goodwill and an indispensable means to cement the existing relationship. Consequently the gift market constitutes an important segment of the consumer market.

The gift market is highly seasonal. Although gifts are given throughout the year, there are two major gift-giving seasons, midyear (*chugen*) in July and end of year (*seibo*) in December. The latter is the bigger of the two, in part because of the rising popularity of Christmas gifts. During these two seasons, gifts are given to those to whom the giver is indebted. Thus companies give presents to important clients; families give to friends, superiors, teachers, doctors, and so forth. Leaders of the major factions of the Liberal Democratic Party give year-end gifts to members of their groups.

Throughout the year, gifts are given for various reasons. Cash gifts are popular for weddings, funerals, births, and illnesses. Members of the Parliament give gifts throughout the year for weddings and funerals of their constituents. It is also customary to give parting gifts to someone leaving on a long trip, which obligates the receiver to bring back gifts for the givers. One gift-giving custom imported or adapted from the West is the so-called *giri* or obligatory chocolates given on St. Valentine's day by women to male associates at work, which is said to express a sense of group belonging. On "White Day" some weeks later, gifts go the other way from men to women.

For **department stores**, gift purchases account for as much as one-fifth of annual sales. Gift sales reached record levels in the late 1980s during the **bubble economy**. Popular gifts then included expensive imports as well as the higher-priced varieties of alcohol, seasoning, canned goods, and confectionery. The long stagnation of the 1990s has cut gift sales somewhat, and shoppers are said to have turned to less expensive and more practical items such as beer, juice, packaged foods, and so forth. Corporate gift giving, in particular, is said to have been cut back.

Japanese companies pay out their semiannual bonuses at midyear and year-end, coinciding with the gift-giving seasons. Thus the size of the bonuses, which varies with the company's profits and may amount to several months' salary, influences the amount of gift spending.

References

Craft, Lucille. 1986. Presents at *o-seibo* time. *Tokyo Business Today*, November: 60–63.

Gift certificates overcome tacky image. *Nikkei Weekly*, February 1, 1992: 18.

Gift rapt. *The Economist*, December 13, 1986: 78.

Oshima, Izumi. 1989. Summer gift certificate sales soar. *Japan Economic Journal*, July 29: 6.

Sato, Makoto. 1995. Major stores look to summer gifts to heat up sales. *Nikkei Weekly*, July 3: 9.

Sumiya, Fumio and Laureen Fredman. 1994. Sluggish Vlentine's Day sales making retailers heartsick. *Nikkei Weekly*, February 14: 10.

Takeuchi, Hiroshi. 1989. Gift-giving transends traditional role as urbanites seek sense of belonging. *Japan Economic Journal*, August 12: 10.

Weisman, Steven R. 1990. The days of wine and $115 mellons: It's gift time. *New York Times*, December 21: A4.

Yamamoto, Yuri. 1996. Stores bask as summer sales heat up. *Nikkei Weekly*, July 15: 10.

government bonds and public debts   Government bonds are the major type of public bonds issued by the national government (the other public bonds are local government bonds and public corporation bonds). On the basis of their authorized purposes, government bonds are classified into construction bonds, deficit-financing bonds, and refunding bonds. In terms of maturity, they consist of interest-bearing long-term government bonds (10 and 20 years), interest-bearing medium-term government bonds (2 to 4 years), discount government bonds (5 years), and short-term treasury bills (introduced in 1985 and included in bond statistics). Long-term bonds and treasury bills constitute more than two-thirds of the total.

Before the mid-1970s the amounts of government bonds were relatively small (see table G.3), and their yields very low. The sale of long-term bonds was negotiated between the **Bank of Japan** and an underwriting syndicate composed of all types of banks and other financial institutions. The bonds were simply allocated to the syndicate members according to negotiated fixed shares. Syndicate members were willing to hold the mandatory low-yield bonds in exchange for access to the Bank of Japan's discount window. On the other hand, the Bank of Japan used the monthly amount of of bond issue as an important monetary tool to adjust the liquidity of the banks and the economy.

The banks were not allowed to resell them to the public. After 1975 flotations of government bonds increased rapidly because of rising government deficits. It became too costly for banks to continue to hold them. Thus, starting in 1977, banks were allowed to resell the bonds to the public at free prices if they had held them for more than a year. In April 1981 the minimum holding period imposed on banks before resale was reduced to one hundred days. Since April 1983 banks were allowed to make over-the-counter sales of new issues of long-term government bonds.

Until April 1989 the coupon rate, as well as the issuing price of the 10-year bonds, the major long-term government bonds, was determined

Table G.3
Government bonds (in ¥ trillions)

End of FY	Issue	Redemption	Outstanding amount
1970	—	—	2.8
1975	—	—	15.0
1980	14.6	3.0	70.5
1985	23.0	10.3	133.4
1986	25.9	15.2	145.1
1987	27.3	20.6	151.8
1988	23.3	18.3	156.8
1989	27.0	22.9	160.9
1990	39.0	32.6	166.3
1991	37.3	32.0	171.6
1992	46.1	39.4	178.4
1993	54.8	40.6	192.5
1994	54.7	40.7	206.6
1995	68.4	49.9	225.2
1996	70.6	51.2	244.7

Source: Bank of Japan.
Note: Domestic flotation only, excluding financing bills.

through negotiations between the **Ministry of Finance** and the syndicate. In April 1989, 40% of new issues of 10-year bonds was put to auction instead of syndicate allocation. The ratio was raised to 60% in October 1990 and 100% in April 1991. Bonds of other maturities are offered to the public on the basis of competitive bidding.

Yields on Japanese government bonds have fluctuated from year to year and from month to month in tandem with changes in the economic conditions and Japanese monetary policy (see table G.4). In the late 1980s they were substantially lower than those on U.S. government bonds, prompting sizable Japanese investment in U.S. government bonds. For example, in early 1989, 10-year Japanese government bonds carried a yield of about 5% as compared with about 9% for the U.S. equivalent. In early 1990, however, Japanese 10-year bonds yield increased rapidly toward 7% because of the higher Bank of Japan discount rate. Since September 1991, however, it has declined steadily as the Bank of Japan continued to reduce its discount rate in an attempt to stimulate the stagnant economy. It fell below 2% at the end of 1997.

The outstanding amount of government bonds continued to rise as the amount of new issues far exceeded the amount of redemption every year

Table G.4
Yields on government bonds (10 years)

Year	Month	Coupon rate	Issue price	Yield
1989	3	4.8	98.75	4.987
	6	4.9	98.75	5.088
	9	4.9	100.04	4.894
	12	5.3	99.96	5.306
1990	3	6.4	99.99	6.401
	6	6.4	100.97	6.242
	9	7.3	98.66	7.534
	12	6.9	100.60	6.799
1997	3	2.6	100.45	2.543
	6	2.7	100.84	2.594
	9	2.3	100.41	2.249
	12	2.0	100.07	1.991

Source: Bank of Japan.

(see table G.3). This was particularly the case during 1993–96 when the need for government expenditures increased steadily while tax revenues lagged behind due to the stagnant economy, resulting in a record issuance of ¥70.6 trillion government bonds in FY 1996 and an outstanding amount of ¥244.7 trillion. These bonds constitute the national debt, or the debt of the national government, which is about 73% of Japan's total public debt. In addition to this, there are also the following forms of public debt: (1) short-term government financing bills, with ¥189 trillion issued in FY 1996, resulting in an outstanding balance of ¥30.6 trillion; (2) local governments issued ¥7.6 trillion local government bonds in FY 1996 with an outstanding amount of ¥38.7 trillion; (3) **public corporation** bonds, most of which are government-guaranteed bonds, for financing government corporations and other government agencies; there were ¥3.0 trillion in new issues and ¥23.1 trillion in outstanding balance in FY 1996.

Thus Japan's public finance depends heavily on public debts. Outstanding national government bonds alone amounted to 49% of GDP in 1996. The sum of national and local government bonds and government-guaranteed bonds, ¥337 trillion in FY 1996, amounted to about 67% of Japan's GDP in 1996. Some analysts see even more government borrowings "hidden" in the **government budget**, and predict an impending doomsday when the total public debts will reach 100% of GDP.

See also **bond market**.

References

Bank of Japan. Annual. *Economic Statistics Annual.*

Choy, Jon. Japanese debt markets: An overview. *JEI Report,* June 10, 1988.

Japan Securities Research Institute. 1998. *Securities Market in Japan, 1998.* Ch. 4.

Ohkawa, Masazo. 1986. Government bonds in *Public Finance in Japan,* ed. by Tokue Shibata. Tokyo: University of Tokyo Press.

Pettway, Richard H. 1990. Underwriting Japanese long-term national bonds. In *Japanese Capital Markets,* ed. by Edwin J. Elton and Martin J. Gruber. New York: Harper and Row.

Tatewaki, Kazuo. 1991. *Banking and Finance in Japan.* London: Routledge. Ch. 6.

government budget   The government budget (i.e., authorized revenue and expenditure) consists of the budget of the national government and of local (prefectural and municipal) governments during a fiscal year, which runs from April 1 of the calendar year to March 30 of the following year. The focus here is on the budget of the national government.

The national government has three types of budget:

1. *General account budget (ippan kaikei).* This is the government budget in a narrow sense. It provide funds for the regular operations of government ministries, agencies, and other offices. Its sources of revenue are taxes and **government bonds**.

2. *Special account budget (tokubetsu kaikei).* More than double the size of the general account budget (see table G.5), this consists of accounts for specific projects such as road improvement or specific social programs such as national pensions, worker's insurance, and so forth. Funds for these accounts include allocations from the general accounts as well as operating receipts or program premiums such as social security contributions.

3. *Budgets of government-affiliated agencies (seifu kankei kikan).* These agencies include two special banks—**Japan Development Bank**, and **Export-Import Bank of Japan**—and nine public finance corporations (see **government financial institutions**). Unlike the regular government ministries and agencies covered in the general accounts, these government-affiliated agencies have separate legal status from the state and have their independent operating revenues. They also receive loans from the **Fiscal Investment and Loans Program** of the government and budgetary allocations from the general accounts.

Table G.5
Budget of the national government (revenue in ¥ trillions)

Fiscal year	General accounts	Special accounts	Affiliated agencies	Net total[a]
1960	¥1.6	¥3.8	¥1.5	¥4.3
1970	8.0	18.4	6.1	19.5
1980	42.6	95.1	20.3	94.0
1985	52.5	125.7	13.2	108.5
1990	66.2	191.8	5.6	140.2
1993	72.4	230.7	7.1	166.3
1994	73.1	247.6	7.6	176.6
1995	71.0	267.0	8.0	184.7
1996	75.1	282.3	7.8	197.3
1997	77.4	285.6	7.6	207.2

Source: Ministry of Finance.
a. Net total is the sum of the three accounts less duplications or the amounts of transfers from the general account.

Because both special account budget and the budgets of government-affiliated agencies receive transfers from the general account budget, the net total of the national government budget is the sum of the three budgets less the amount of duplications. Table G.5 shows the amounts of the three budgets and their net total.

In FY 1997 the major expenditure categories of the general account budget and their shares are as follows:

1. **Social security:** ¥14.6 trillion (18.8%). This includes public assistance, social welfare, social insurance, public health service, and unemployment assistance.

2. Debt servicing: ¥16.8 trillion (21.7%).

3. Tax grants to local governments: ¥15.5 trillion (20.0%).

4. Education and science promotion: ¥6.3 trillion (8.1%).

5. Public works: ¥9.7 trillion (12.5%).

6. Defense: ¥4.9 trillion (6.3%).

7. Pensions for public officials: ¥1.6 trillion (2.1%).

8. **Foreign aid:** ¥1.1 trillion (1.4%).

The **Ministry of Finance** is responsible for the making of the budget. This, along with its regulatory power over banking, securities, and taxes gives it much influence in the Japanese economy. Various government ministries and agencies submit their budget requests to the Ministry of Finance and negotiate with it for their budgetary allocations. The final budget has to be approved by the cabinet and the Diet (parliament). However, the budget may be revised during the fiscal year if economic conditions warrant it. For example, a supplementary budget was adopted in 1993 to stimulate economic recovery from a prolonged recession of the early 1990s, and in 1995 to aid recovery from the Great Hanshin Earthquake of January 1995. The settlement of the budget is audited by the Board of Audit, an independent organization of the state.

The **Fiscal Investment and Loans Program** of the government is not part of the government budget, although it is sometimes referred to as the capital budget or the "second National Budget" of the government. It is best understood as a government-run credit program. It uses funds from **postal savings**, public pension funds, insurance funds, and so forth, to make loans to various **public corporations**.

Besides giving the Ministry of Finance enormous power, the Japanese budget-making process has been criticized as inflexible and irresponsive to the nation's changing social, political, and economic goals. In response to these criticisms, the budget process for FY 1998 introduced some changes: (1) The prime minister, Mr. Hashimoto, played a large role in setting budget goals. (2) The traditional use of budget ceiling as a planning tool was dropped in favor of setting limits for each major spending category. (3) Funds were set aside for special projects, to be allocated on a competitive basis (*JEI Report* 34B 1997: 5).

See also **Fiscal Investment and Loan Program, government bonds, government financial institutions, tax system.**

Address

Budget Bureau, Ministry of Finance
1-1, Kasumigaseki 3-chome, Chiyoda-ku, Tokyo 100
Tel: (3) 3581-4111

References

Furuta, Seiji, and Ichiro Kano. 1993. The general account budget. In *Japan's Public Sector: How the Government is Financed*, ed. by Tokue Shibata. Tokyo: University of Tokyo Press.

Ishi, Hiromitsu. 1993. *The Japanese Tax System*, 2nd ed. Oxford: Clarendon Press.

Ishi, Hiromitsu. 1996. Budgets and the budgetary process in Japan. *Hitotsubashi Journal of Economics* 37: 1–19.

Ito, Takatoshi. 1992. *The Japanese Economy*. Cambridge: MIT Press. Ch. 6.

Kato, Takashi. 1993. National finance administration. In *Japan's Public Sector: How the Government is Financed*, ed. by Tokue Shibata. Tokyo: University of Tokyo Press.

Noguchi, Yukio. 1987. Public finance. In *The Political Economy of Japan*, vol. 1: *The Domestic Transformation*, ed. by Kozo Yamamura and Yasuichi Yasuba. Stanford: Stanford University Press.

government financial institutions Aside from the central bank, the **Bank of Japan**, government financial institutions in Japan include two banks—the **Export-Import Bank of Japan** and **Japan Development Bank**—and nine finance corporations. As stipulated by law, the two government banks concentrate their loans in export-import and development finance. At the end of March 1997 the Export-Import Bank had capital of ¥986 billion, borrowed money of ¥7.8 trillion, and loans and discounts of ¥9.0 trillion. Japan Development Bank's capital was ¥332 billion. Its borrowings from the government were ¥14.8 trillion, while its loans outstanding were ¥15.8 trillion at the end of March 1997.

The names and outstanding loans of the nine government finance corporations are given in table G.6. It is clear that the Housing Loan Corporation is by far the most important of the government finance corporations. Its outstanding loans were larger than those of the others put together. All the finance corporations finance their loans with funds borrowed from the government (Trust Fund Bureau and **postal savings**) and with funds raised by issuing debentures. They cannot accept deposits because they are designed to supplement private-sector finances and are prohibited by law from competing with private financial institutions.

Table G.6
Government finance corporations (end of 1997; in ¥ trillions)

Name	Outstanding loans
Agriculture, Forestry, and Fisheries Finance Corp.	4.4
Environmental Sanitation Business Finance Corp.	1.1
Housing Loan Corp.	72.8
Hokkaido-Tohoku Development Corp.	1.5
Japan Finance Corp. for Municipal Enterprises	19.9
Okinawa Development Finance Corp.	1.7
People's Finance Corp.	9.1
Small Business Credit Insurance Corp.	0.6
Small Business Finance Corp.	7.1

Source: Bank of Japan.

In a broader sense, the post offices—with their life insurance and postal annuity accounts—and the Trust Fund Bureau of the **Ministry of Finance** can be regarded as government financial institutions as well. The government also has a small capital share in the Shoko Chukin Bank and the Norinchukin Bank, but these are not considered to be government financial institutions.

See also **Export-Import Bank of Japan, Japan Development Bank, postal savings**.

Addresses

Export-Import Bank of Japan
4-1, Otemachi 1-chome, Chiyoda-ku, Tokyo 100
Tel: (3) 3287-1221

Housing Loan Corporation
4-10, Horaku 1-chome, Bunkyo-ku, Tokyo 112
Tel: (3) 3812-1111

Japan Development Bank
9-1, Otemachi 1-chome, Chiyoda-ku, Tokyo 100
Tel: (3) 3270-3211

References

Bank of Japan. Annual. *Economic Statistics Annual.*

Suzuki, Yoshio, ed. 1987. *The Japanese Financial System.* Oxford: Clarendon. Ch. 5.

Tatewaki, Kazuo. 1991. *Banking and Finance in Japan.* London: Routledge. Ch. 9.

gyosei shido Administrative guidance, the guidance or suggestions given by bureaucrats to firms.
See **administrative guidance**.

H

health insurance   Japan has a number of health insurance plans to cover different groups of people—company employees, day laborers, seamen, government employees, teachers, the self-employed, and so forth. Most of these plans are based on employment or occupation, while one is based on the local community. Thus virtually everyone in the country is covered by one of the following insurance plans:

1. A health insurance (*kenko hoken*) plan for employees of large corporations (with more than 300 employees) managed by the company's health insurance society (or a joint society of several companies). As of March 31, 1995, this plan covered 32.1 million people, about 25% of the population, including the dependents of the insured. The premiums may vary from one society to another. The average was 8.2% of the employee's monthly wages, shared equally between the employee and the employer. The plan offers the following benefits as of March 31, 1997: 90% of medical costs for the insured, 70% of outpatient costs and 80% of hospital costs for the dependents. The insured pay the balance.

2. A health insurance plan, managed by the Social Insurance Agency of the government, for employees of small- and medium-sized companies. As of March 31, 1996, this plan covers 37.8 million people or about 30% of the population. The premiums are about 8.2% of the insured worker's monthly pay, shared equally by the insured and the employer. The benefits are the same as in the plan for employees of large companies.

3. Government-managed health insurance for day laborers, including construction workers and workers hired by the day (about 0.4% of the population). The employers pay 60% of the premiums and a special stamp fee, and the workers pay 40% of the premiums, which are based on the wages.

4. Seamen's insurance, organized by the government (0.4% of the population). The coverage is similar to that of other employer-based plans. Premiums are 8.5% of the insured's monthly pay.

5. Insurance managed by mutual aid associations for government employees and private school teachers and employees (9.7% of the population). Premiums are 8.1% of the insured's monthly pay. The coverage is the same as the other employer-based plans.

6. The community-based national health insurance (*kokumin kenko hoken*) covers the self-employed (farmers, doctors, etc.) and employees of small businesses not otherwise covered. Also, when members of employee-based insurance funds retire, they typically join this plan. The plan is managed by the municipalities (covering 43.2 million people or 34% of the population as of March 31, 1996) and the National Health Insurance Associations (covering 3% of the population). The benefits cover 70–80% of the medical costs for both the insured and dependents. Premiums are fixed locally on the basis of income, property, and the number of people to be covered. Maximum monthly payments by the insured is the same as in other schemes.

7. Health insurance for the aged. This program was established in 1983 because of the aging population. As of 1997, the elderly (those over age 70 and those between ages 65 and 70 with disability) pay a fixed charge of ¥710 per day for hospitalization and ¥1,020 per month for outpatient care. About 70% of the costs are covered by various group insurers (employees' insurance—e.g., government-managed health insurance or mutual aid association—and the national health insurance). The national government and local governments (municipalities and prefectures) contribute 20% and 10%, respectively, in subsidies.

Finally, when the patients are indigent, their costs are paid by the government's livelihood protection subsidies.

Rising medical costs due to the aging of the Japanese **population** have undermined the financial soundness of the health insurance system. In June 1997 a law was enacted to strengthen the system by reducing benefits and increasing the costs that the insured have to pay. In April 1998 many changes went into effect, including the following: (1) Company workers and government employees pay 20% instead of 10% of medical costs of hospitalization. (2) Premiums for workers of small and medium businesses increase from 8.2% of their monthly salaries to 8.5%. (3) Elderly outpatients pay ¥500 for each hospital/clinic visit, with a maximum of ¥2,000 per month. (4) The daily hospitalization charge for the elderly is raised to ¥1,100, and it will be raised to ¥1,200 in April 1999. (5) The costs of prescription drugs for outpatients are raised.

The comprehensiveness of Japan's health insurance is said to be an important factor in giving Japan the world's longest life expectancies (77.0 years for men and 83.6 years for women in 1996) and one of the world's lowest infant mortality rates (4 deaths per 1,000 births). Yet Japan spent only ¥27 trillion, or about 7.2% of its GDP, for total medical expenses in FY 1995, compared with about 13.1% in the United States.

See also **social security system.**

Addresses

Health Insurance Bureau, Ministry of Health and Welfare
2-2, Kasumigaseki 1-chome, Chiyoda-ku, Tokyo 100
Tel: (3) 3503-1711

References

Fujii, Mitsiru, and Michael Meich. 1988. Rising medical costs and the reform of Japan's health insurance system. *Health Policy* 9: 9–24.

Hoshino, Shinya. 1996. Paying for the health and social care of the elderly. *Journal of Aging and Social Policy* 8, 2–3: 37–55.

Inglehart, John K. 1988a. Health policy report: Japan's medical care system. *New England Journal of Medicine* 319, 12 (September 22): 807–12.

Inglehart, John K. 1988b. Health policy report: Japan's medical care system, part two. *New England Journal of Medicine* 319, 17 (October 27): 1166–72.

Ministry of Health and Welfare. Annual. *White Paper on Health and Welfare.*

Murdo, Pat. 1991. Japanese health-care system no panacea for ailing U.S. program. *JEI Report,* July 5.

Murdo, Pat. 1993. The health care debate: what America is considering, what Japan has done. *JEI Report* 8A, March 5.

Norbeck, Edward, and Margaret Lock, eds. 1987. *Health, Illness and Medical Care in Japan: Cultural and Social Dimensions.* Honolulu: University of Hawaii Press.

Okimoto, Daniel I., and Aki Yoshikawa. 1993. *Japan's Health System: Efficiency and Effectiveness in Universal Care.* New York: Faulkner & Gray.

Powell, Margaret, and Masahira Anesaki. 1990. *Health Care in Japan.* London: Routledge.

Suzuki, Yumiko. 1997. Higher fees first remedy for insurance. *Nikkei Weekly,* June 23: 3.

Heisei Boom   The economic expansion in Japan from November 1986 to April 1991, one of the longest in the postwar period. Much of the boom coincided with the **bubble economy** (1986–89) when rising land and stock prices spurred much speculative investments, which contributed to the expansion but aggravated the problems of the financial system after the bubble burst.

See **bubble economy, business cycles**.

Hitachi Group   Japan's largest industrial group, consisting of Hitachi, Ltd. and its more than 680 subsidiaries, including Hitachi Cable, Hitachi Metals, Hitachi Chemical, Hitachi Construction Machinery, and Hitachi Credit Corp. Hitachi, Ltd. holds a high percentage of the shares of the other companies.

See **cross shareholding,** *keiretsu* **and business groups**.

holding companies   (*mochikabu gaisha*) Companies that are set up to own enough stock in other companies to control their policies and management. Common in the United States and Europe, they were banned in Japan from 1947 to 1997.

Holding company were the instruments used in the prewar *zaibatsu* by wealthy families to control *zaibatsu* companies. The *zaibatsu* were powerful conglomerates with companies in diverse fields; they dominated the economy and were considered to have contributed to Japan's prewar industrial growth and military strength. Consequently, after the end of World War II, General MacArthur, the Supreme Commander for Allied Powers (SCAP) in Japan, dissolved the *zaibatsu*. The **Antimonopoly Law** was passed in order to ban holding companies and other anticompetitive business practices.

As the Japanese economy developed and became the second largest of the world, many of its large corporations have developed many divisions or set up subsidiaries in diversified operations, forming large corporate groups.

Since the early 1990s, a growing number of Japanese corporate leaders as well as economists have voiced support for revising the **Antimonopoly Law** in order to legalize holding companies. They argue that a holding company will facilitate the control of large operations in diverse business areas. Also, because the different divisions will operate as different companies under the holding company, it will be easier for the parent company to dump unprofitable operations and focus on profitable ones. Similarly it would be easier for unprofitable companies to lay off workers and pay lower wages than if they are divisions of a company. Finally, a holding company would allow firms under it to cooperate closely in research, marketing, and production activities without merging their staffs and corporate cultures.

On the other hand, the proposal to legalize holding companies has raised concern, especially abroad, that it might lead to greater economic concentration and the revival of prewar *zaibatsu*-type conglomerates (*JEI Report* 4B, February 2, 1996: 2). This suggests that a legal limit on the size of the company would be desirable.

In 1996 the Ministry of Posts and Telecommunications and Nippon Telegraph and Telephone, Japan's largest telecommunications company, reached an agreement to break up the latter into three companies—one long-distance telephone company and two local telephone companies—under a holding company which will hold their shares. The agreement made it certain that the ban on holding companies would be lifted because of the crucial importance of restructuring Japan's **telecommunications industry**.

In 1997 the **Antimonopoly Law** was revised to make holding companies legal, effective December 17, 1997. However, corporate groups with total assets of more than ¥300 billion will have to notify the Fair Trade Commission when they set up a holding company. In addition three types of holding companies are banned:

1. Business groups with assets exceeding ¥15 trillion or those that have assets of more than ¥300 billion in each of five or more business fields may not become holding companies. The purpose of this ban is to prevent the revival of the diversified *zaibatsu* groups.

2. A corporate group is prohibited to control both a financial company with assets of more than ¥15 trillion and a nonfinancial firm with more than ¥300 billion in assets. The purpose is to prevent the creation of powerful financial conglomerates.

3. A company is prohibited from controlling leading companies in more than five related areas (autos, tires, etc.). A leading company is defined as one that has more than a 10% share of its market or a sales ranking of third place or higher in a market. This ban is aimed at preventing one company from dominating an entire industry.

Prior to the lifting of the ban on holding companies, a "5% rule" of the Fair Trade Commission limited a bank's stock holding of other companies to 5% and that of an insurance company to 10%. The Commission would now wave the rule in the case of brokerage and financial institutions. This would permit the establishment of financial holding companies that own banks, brokerage or life insurers.

Daiei Inc., Japan's largest supermarket operator, is the first company to set up a holding company, Daiei Holding Co. in December 1997. In a press interview, Daiei president indicated that the purpose of setting up a stock holding company is "to divide capital and management" and to give more autonomy to subsidiaries (Nikkei Weekly, December 22, 1997: 7). Many other large companies including Toshiba Corp. have indicated their intention to set up holding companies. The Fuyo group, led by Fuji Bank, plans to establish a financial holding company, which will include Yasuda Trust & Banking Co., Yasuda Mutual Life Insurance Co., and Yasuda Fire & Marine Insurance Co.

See also **Antimonopoly Law**, *kaisha*, *zaibatsu*.

References

Lifting of holding-company ban set to take effect this week. 1997. *Nikkei Weekly*, December 15: 2.

Tax changes would clear way for wider use of holding companies. 1997. *Nikkei Weekly*, December 29: 20.

housing   Because of the shortage of land and a high population density, houses in Japan are typically smaller and less well equipped than their Western counterparts. The average floor space per dwelling was only 92 square meters (110 square yards) in 1993. The percentage of houses with flush toilets was 76% in 1993. Most houses have no central heating and use kerosene heaters for heating. In 1993, 6.5% of Japanese houses had no bathtub.

Housing services are not as bad as the figures given above would suggest, however. The Japanese have traditionally adopted various practices to compensate for their limited floor space and facilities. Many rooms can serve multiple purposes; people may sleep on a *tatami* floor (*tatami* is the traditional Japanese floor mat), and room furnishings are minimal to save space; some people go to a public bath. These practices are still preserved by many people as part of their way of life so that comparative statistics between Japan and other countries on housing have to be interpreted with caution. Some Europeans have mocked Japanese homes as "rabbit hutches." This is both unkind and unjustified.

The number of new housing starts has fluctuated cyclically with the conditions of the economy. As shown in table H.1, it was only 843,000

Table H.1
New housing starts (in 1,000 units and million square meters)

	Units	Total floor area
1955	257	15.0
1965	843	50.0
1970	1,566	104.7
1975	1,356	112.4
1980	1,269	119.1
1985	1,236	103.1
1987	1,674	132.5
1988	1,685	134.5
1989	1,663	135.0
1990	1,707	137.5
1991	1,370	117.2
1992	1,403	120.3
1993	1,486	131.7
1994	1,570	145.6
1995	1,470	136.5
1996	1,643	157.9

Source: Ministry of Construction.

units in 1965, with an average floor area of only 58.9 square meters. Housing starts rose rapidly and reached a postwar peak of 1.91 million units in 1973 with an average of 75.4 square meters and then plunged to 1.32 million units in 1974 because of the 1973 oil shock. The bottom was reached in 1983 at 1.14 million units. During the real estate and stock market boom years of 1986–89, housing starts were at a high level of more than 1.66 million units annually. The number reached 1.71 million in 1990, the highest since 1973. It then declined to 1.37 million in 1991 before it recovered gradually to 1.64 million in 1996.

The high price of housing is a serious problem. The ownership of a small suburban house, particularly in the Tokyo metropolitan area, is virtually beyond the reach of most middle-class families because of its very high price. In 1989 a small condominium in the Tokyo area with 75 square meters of floor space cost an average of ¥54,975,000, about 8.62 times the average annual wage of salaried workers (*Japan Economic Journal*, January 20, 1990: 11). In 1991, a new condo of the same size would cost an average of ¥65.6 million in tokyo, ¥54.4 million in Osaka, and ¥36.9 million in Nagoya (*Nikkei Weekly*, May 30, 1992: 4).

The major cause of high housing price is the high price of land, particularly in the major metropolitan areas, which was fueled by large bank loans for speculative real estate development in the late 1980s. Since the real estate bubble burst in 1990–91, land prices have come down substantially. The Economic Council, which advises the prime minister, has suggested that house prices should average five times the average family income. For many Japanese that goal is still unattainable. The Economic Council proposed that 2.6 million housing units be built within a 30-kilometer radius of Tokyo by the year 2000 to help achieve that goal.

See also **housing finance, investment**.

References

Ito, Takatoshi. 1993. The land/housing problem in Japan: A macroeconomic approach. *Journal of the Japanese and International Economies* 7, 1: 1–31.

Ito, Takatoshi. 1994. Public policy and housing in Japan. In *Housing Markets in the United States and Japan*, ed. by Yukio Noguchi and James M. Poterba. Chicago: University of Chicago Press.

Noguichi, Yukio. 1994. Land prices and house prices in Japan. In *Housing Markets in the United States and Japan*, ed. by Yukio Noguchi and James M. Poterba. Chicago: University of Chicago Press.

Okumura, Tsunao. 1997. Housing investment and residential land supply in Japan: An asset market approach. *Journal of the Japanese and International Economies* 11: 27–54.

Ostrom, Douglas. 1989. Japanese housing: The international dimension. *JEI Report* 30A, August 4.

Sanger, David. 1990. Tatami or colonial, a house is wishful thinking. *New York Times*, October 17: A4.

Takagi, Shintaro. 1991. Are land and house prices too high in Japan? *Japanese Economic Studies* 20, 1: 57–86.

housing finance   Housing in Japan is financed by a number of financial institutions. Table H.2 gives the shares of housing credit provided by various sources.

Some trends can be seen in table H.2: (1) The share of **city banks** in housing credit has increased significantly since 1985. At the end of 1997 their outstanding loans were ¥31.7 trillion. (2) The share of other banks such as regional banks and *shinkin* **banks** has declined steadily since 1975. (3) The shares of financial institutions set up for specific sectors such as labor, agriculture, forestry, and fisheries have declined steadily. (3) The role of specialized financial institutions for housing has increased. At the end of 1992, specialized institutions provided 46.5% of total housing

Table H.2
Main sources of housing finance (end of month/year; in % of total loans outstanding)

Institutions	March 1975	1985	1992	1997
City banks	16.9	13.6	21.8	22.8
Regional banks	14.3	10.3	8.6	11.5
Regional banks (II)[a]	7.6	5.6	4.7	6.0
Trust accounts, all banks	6.8	5.6	2.4	1.6
Shinkin banks	11.7	8.1	6.5	7.9
Labor credit associations	4.0	2.3	1.7	2.8
Agricultural cooperatives	7.9	3.4	2.6	4.1
Insurance companies	3.8	6.6	5.9	4.7
Housing loan companies[b]	3.9	8.3	10.3	0
Housing Loan Corporation	19.5	35.0	36.2	46.3

Source: Bank of Japan.
Note: The figures do not add up to 100% because some minor institutions are not included.
a. Second-tier regional banks, called *sogo* banks before 1989.
b. Liquidated in 1996 because of bad debts.

credit. **Housing loan companies** are subsidiaries set up by banks after 1971 specifically for housing finance. There were eight such companies. In 1996 they were liquidated because of huge unrecoverable loans made during the **bubble economy** (1986–89). The Housing Loan Corporation is a government financial institution. It is now the largest housing credit institution, extending more than 46% of the total. At the end of 1997 its outstanding loans were ¥64.5 trillion.

The total amount of outstanding housing credit has grown from ¥21.2 trillion at the end of 1985 to ¥139.2 trillion at the end of 1997. The interest rate on housing loans is based on the long-term prime lending rate.

See also **housing, housing loan companies**.

Address

Housing Loan Corporation
4-10, Koraku 1-chome, Bunyko-ku, Tokyo 112
Tel: (3) 3812-1111

References

Bank of Japan. Annual. *Economic Statistics Annual.*

Seko, Miki. 1994. Housing finance in Japan. In *Housing Markets in the United States and Japan,* ed. by Yukio Noguchi and James M. Poterba. Chicago: University of Chicago Press.

housing loan companies   Subsidiaries set up by commercial banks to specialize in housing loans. They are commonly called *jusen* (*jutaku kinyu senmon gaisha,* literally housing finance specialized companies). They provided more than 10% of the nation's outstanding housing credit in the early 1990s. They became insolvent in the mid-1990s and caused a panic in the financial and government circles. The *jusen* crisis proved to be the opening salvo of the nation's financial crisis in the wake of the bursting of the **bubble economy**.

Eight *jusen* companies were established in the 1970s by banks to provide housing loans. They obtained funds from the founding banks and other financial institutions and made loans at higher interest rates. The original objective of the *jusen* companies was to provide housing loans to individuals. At the end of FY 1980, loans to individuals amounted to 98% of *jusen* loans. In the bubble economy of the late 1980s *jusen* companies, along with other financial institutions, lent an increasing amount to real estate developers on the basis of the inflated collateral value of their assets. This trend was accelerated after April 1990 when the **Ministry of Finance** restricted other financial institutions to lend to realtors in an attempt to halt the land-property inflation. As a result *jusen* loans to realtors rose further, and the share of *jusen* loans to individuals declined to 20% at the end of FY 1994. Reportedly the Ministry of Finance was aware of the inherent risks of such a situation but did not act in time to avert a crisis.

With the bursting of the bubble economy in the early 1990s, property value began to plummet and much of the *jusen* loans became irrecoverable. In 1995 it was found that the total amount of nonperforming loans was ¥8.13 trillion. This meant huge losses not only for *jusen* themselves but also for their founding banks and other lenders to *jusen* such as the **agricultural cooperatives**. Because the agricultural cooperatives employ many people and are political powerful, the government deemed it necessary to minimize their losses. In 1996 the Ministry of Finance made a proposal to use public funds—about $685 billion in FY 1996 and possibly more in the future—to liquidate seven *jusen* and their nonperforming loans. Over much outcry from the public and objection from the opposition parties, the Diet approved the proposal lest the entire **banking system** become severely weakened. A new agency, the Jusen Resolution Corp., was created. The public money, along with the *jusen* loans of ¥6.5 trillion, was transferred to the agency, which will try to recover the loans over a period of 15 years.

See also **housing finance**.

References

Passage of bills on liquidation of the housing loan companies (jusen). *Zenginkyo Financial Review*, 1997, no. 27: 1–3.

Sato, Hiroshi. 1996. Passing the *jusen* buck. *The Japan Times Weekly International Edition*, March 4–10: 8.

Shimmura, Toshio. 1996. Audits underscore careless jusen lending. *Nikkei Weekly*, February 12: 1.

Housing Loan Corp. A government financial institution set up for the purpose of providing housing credit. It receives investments and loans from the government's **Fiscal Investment and Loan Program** and has extended more than one-third of the nation's outstanding housing credit.

See **Fiscal Investment and Loan Program, government financial institutions, housing finance.**

human resource development
See **corporate personnel practices, education system, labor-management relations, lifetime employment, population.**

I

impact loans   Bank loans in foreign currency by foreign exchange banks with no restrictions on the use of the funds. Until the early 1990s the amount of total impact loans extended grew very rapidly. It increased by 50% in FY 1989. The growth rate declined to 17% in FY 1990 as banks curtailed their overall loans to meet the new 8% capital adequacy requirement set by the Bank for International Settlements. In FY 1997, ¥42 trillion impact loans were made, which amounted to 8.1% of total loans made by financial institutions.

See also **city banks**.

income distribution   Japan's income distribution is quite equal by international standards. This is reflected in the fact that, in government surveys conducted annually since 1960, more than 85% of the respondents have consistently indicated that they belonged to the middle class except for 1960 with 76.2%. This predominance of middle-class consciousness has contributed greatly to the country's social stability and low crime rate.

Because the Japanese perception of middle-class status is cultural as well as economic—middle class is perceived as diligent and frugal, which are widely shared values—the above figures are not the best indicator of income distribution. A better indicator is the Gini coefficient, which is a widely used measure of income inequality (it ranges from 0, perfect equality, to 1, perfect inequality). Table I.1 gives estimates of the Gini coefficients of household income based on two sets of government family income and expenditure surveys. These estimates are all below 0.3; they are very low by international standards. Alternatively, Bronfenbrenner and Yasuda (1987: 110–111) and Choo (1991: 5) have cited higher Gini coefficients of Japan estimated by other scholars. They range from 0.313 for 1955, to 0.319 and 0.407 for the 1960s and 1970s, to 0.334 for 1980

Table I.1
Gini coefficients of household income

Year	NSFIE[a]	FIES[b]
1979	0.271	—
1980	—	0.272
1981	—	0.273
1982	—	0.279
1983	—	0.275
1984	0.280	0.272
1985	—	0.285
1986	—	0.290
1987	—	0.287
1988	—	0.280
1989	0.293	0.286
1990	—	0.292
1991	—	0.296
1992	—	0.293
1993	—	0.292
1994	0.297	0.292
1995	—	0.296

Sources: Economic Planning Agency (1996) and Mishizaki, Yamada, and Ando (1997).
Note: Excludes one-person households.
a. Based on Management and Coordination Agency, *National Survey of Family Income and Expenditure*.
b. Based on Management and Coordination Agency, *Family Income and Expenditure Survey*.

(no figures for other years in the 1980s). Even these higher estimates, however, are slightly lower than the Gini coefficients of the other industrialized countries in the same period. Choo (1991: 5) also cites estimates of Gini coefficients of Japanese farm households, which range from 0.229 to 0.327 for selective years in 1955–89. Thus one can conclude that income distribution in Japan has remained relatively equal throughout the postwar period.

One reason for this relative income equality is that Japan has no "permanent economic underclass" due to large-scale immigration of cheap labor (Brongenbrenner and Yasuda 1987: 110). Another reason is that among company employees, the income differentials between different groups with different education and employment status are relatively small. Table I.2 gives the annual earnings (wages plus bonuses) in 1995 of male employees with different educational background at different ages. Thus at age 22, a university graduate just starting work made less than a

Table I.2
Earnings of male standard employees by education (1995; in ¥1,000 per year)

Age	Lower secondary	Upper secondary	University
22	2,762	3,058	2,450
30	3,456	4,375	5,004
40	5,215	6,402	7,700
50	6,786	8,873	10,538
55	7,190	9,156	11,085

Source: Ministry of Labor.

Table I.3
Employee earnings by position (in ¥1,000 per year)

Position	1978	1980	1985	1990	1995
Director	6,201	6,966	8,420	9,958	10,660
Section chief	4,926	5,491	6,762	7,999	8,717
Chief clerk	3,979	4,448	5,451	6,393	6,825
Regular worker	2,482	2,795	3,498	4,138	4,623
Top/bottom ratio	2.50	2.49	2.41	2.41	2.31

Source: Ministry of Labor.

lower secondary-school graduate with several years of seniority or an upper secondary-school graduate with four years of seniority. At age 30 the university graduate's earnings slightly exceeded those of these other two groups. At age 55, near retirement, the earning ratio between university graduate and lower secondary-school graduate was 1.5 and between university graduate and upper secondary-school graduate was only 1.2.

Table I.3 gives the annual earnings (wages plus bonuses) of different groups of corporate employees. It is shown that the directors' incomes are less than double that of chief clerks, and no more than 2.5 times that of blue-collar workers. These numbers should not be taken as indicators of the distribution of real income, however. Corporate executives often enjoy huge fringe benefits such as a chauffeur-driven car, dining and drinking and golfing on expense accounts, and various other benefits that are said to be more than what their counterparts in other countries enjoy.

All employees' earnings constitute the labor income component of national income; other components are income from assets and business income. As shown in table I.4, the share of labor income in national income has increased from 54% in 1970 to 73% in 1995. This rising share of labor income has contributed to the overall income equality in Japan,

Table I.4
Distribution of national income (in %)

Income category	1970	1975	1980	1985	1990	1995
Employees' income	54.0	67.5	66.8	68.8	69.2	73.1
Income from assets	8.3	10.9	10.6	9.7	11.0	7.0
Business income[a]	37.7	21.6	22.6	21.4	19.7	19.9

Source: Economic Planning Agency.
a. Includes incomes of private corporations, public corporations and individual proprietorships, agriculture, forestry, and fishery, imputed service from owner-occupied dwellings, net of dividend receipts and payments.

given the fact that the distribution of labor income is relatively equal as discussed above.

See also **wage structure**.

References

Bronfenbrenner, Martin, and Yasukichi Yasuba. 1987. Economic welfare. In *The Political Economy of Japan*, vol. 1: *The Domestic Transformation*, ed. by Kozo Yamamura and Yasukichi Yasuba. Stanford: Stanford University Press.

Choo, Hakchung. 1991. A comparison of income distribution in Japan, Korea and Taiwan. In *Making Economies More Efficient and More Equitable*, ed. by Toshiyuki Mizoguchi. Tokyo: Kinokuniya.

Dore, Ronald. 1994. Equality-efficiency trade-offs: Japanese perceptions and choices. In *The Japanese Firm: the Sources of Competitive Strength*, ed. by Msahiko Aoki and Ronald Dore. Oxford: Oxford University Press.

Economic Planning Agency. Annual. *Economic White Paper*.

Jones, Randall S. 1987. Japanese income distribution. *JEI Report*, August 28.

Ministry of Labor. Annual. *Basic Survey on Wage Structure*.

Nishizaki, Fumihira, Yutaka Yamada and Eisuke Ando. 1997. Income Distribution and Poverty in Japan. *Discussion paper 80*. Tokyo: Economic Planning Agency.

Ostrom, Douglas. 1991. Economic Equality in Japan. *JEI Report*, February 1.

Tachibanaki, Toshiaki. 1996. *Public Policies and the Japanese Economy: Savings, Investments, Unemployment, Inequality*. New York: St. Martin's Press.

individual income taxes   For individual or personal income tax, the individual rather than the household is the unit of taxation. Two-wage earner couples are taxed separately. Individuals in Japan pay two types of income tax—national individual income tax (called *income tax* in Japan)

Table I.5
National income tax rates for individuals (in ¥ millions and %)

Taxable income	Tax rate
Under 3.3	10%
3.3–9.0	20
9.0–18.0	30
18.0–30.0	40
30.0 and over	50

Source: Gomi (1997: 116).

levied by the national government and local income tax (called inhabitant tax) levied by the 47 prefectures and over 3,000 municipalities.

National income tax is the largest source of tax revenue for the national government. In FY 1997, the national government collected ¥20.9 trillion, or 35.1% of its total tax revenue, from the tax. Prefectural inhabitant tax is the second largest tax for the prefectural governments. In FY 1997, it yielded ¥4.1 trillion, or 28.4% of total prefectural tax revenue. Municipal inhabitant tax has been since 1964 the most important municipal tax. In FY 1997, it yielded ¥8.5 trillion or 41.6% of the total municipal tax revenue.

Effective January 1, 1998, both national and local income taxes were reformed as part of the 1988 tax reform package to introduce the new **consumption tax**. The number of income brackets and the tax rates were reduced, and the level of exemptions was increased. As of 1997 the following figures apply:

1. *National income tax.* There are five brackets of taxable income, with the tax rate ranging from 10% to 50%, as shown in table I.5. Personal exemptions include: (a) A basic exemption of ¥380,000 each for spouse and dependents, up to two dependents; the exemption is ¥580,000 if the dependent is a parent or grandparent of the taxpayer, and is ¥680,000 if the dependent is severely handicapped. (b) A special exemption for the taxpayer: ¥270,000 for the handicapped (¥350,000 for severely handicapped), widows or widowers, and working students, and ¥500,000 for persons aged 65 and over (if their income is below ¥10 million).

2. *Local income (inhabitant) tax.* Both the prefectures and the municipalities levy inhabitant taxes on the same taxpayers. There are only three taxable income brackets: ¥2 million or less, between ¥2 and ¥7 million, and over ¥7 million. The combined prefectural and municipal tax rates are

5%, 10%, and 15%, respectively, for these brackets. Exemptions are similar to those of the national income tax but smaller in amount (¥330,000 for spouse and each dependent).

One problem with the income tax before reform was that different types of income were treated unequally. Wages and salaries were taxed by withholding at the source. Dividends and capital gains on stocks were almost tax free. Interest incomes from a variety of savings—*maruyu* savings, **postal savings**, national and local bonds, savings for the formation of employee's assets, and postal installment savings for housing— were tax exempt within certain limits. Since April 1988 tax exemption for interests from these privileged savings was eliminated except for the handicapped, people over 65, and working widows. A 20% withholding tax is imposed on nearly all interest income from deposit accounts. In April 1989 a flat tax rate of 26% (20% for national and 6% for local income tax) was imposed on capital gains earned by individuals. As of 1995 the rate was 32.5% (25% for national and 7.5% for local income taxes) for long-term capital gains up to ¥40 million from the sale of assets held for five years or more, and 39% (30% for national and 9% for local income taxes) for capital gains over ¥40 million. Short-term capital gains are subject to 40% national and 12% local taxes (Kuboi 1995: 119).

See also **corporate income tax, tax system.**

Addresses

National Tax Administration Agency
1-1, Kasumigaseki 3-chome, Chiyoda-ku, Tokyo 100
Tel: (3) 3581-4161

Local Tax Bureau, Ministry of Home Affairs
1-2, Kasumigaseki 2-chome, Chiyoda-ku, Tokyo 100
Tel: (3) 3581-5311

References

Gomi, Yuji. 1997. *Guide to Japanese Taxes, 1997–98.* Tokyo: Zaikei Shohosha.

Ishi, Hiromitsu. 1993. *The Japanese Tax System,* 2nd ed. Oxford: Oxford University Press.

Kuboi, Takashi. 1995. *Business Practices and Taxation in Japan.* Tokyo: The Japan Times.

Ministry of Finance. Annual. *An Outline of Japanese Taxes.*

Odden, Lee. Tax reform 1989. *Tokyo Business Today,* March 1989: 24–27.

industrial policy Once officially defined as the systematic selection of industries to be encouraged or discouraged by government action or deliberate inaction, industrial policy entails the use of various government policy measures to change the allocation of resources among industrial sectors and to influence the organization of specific industries in accordance with the economic objectives of the government and its selection of priority industries for development. The **Ministry of International Trade and Industry** (MITI), formed in 1949, is the principal designer and executor of industrial policy.

Industrial policy in Japan has gone through three major periods. During the first period from 1949 to 1965, the policy was to revive and expand basic manufacturing industries such as coal, steel, electric power, transport industries, automobile, petrochemicals, petroleum refining, and machinery industries. The second period, from 1965 to 1973, was a transitional one. Liberalization of trade policies took place as Japan joined GATT in 1963 and IMF and OECD in 1964. The industries promoted by MITI shifted from basic manufacturing to knowledge-intensive industries. In the third period, from 1973 to the present, trends of the second period continued. In addition, because the first oil crisis (1973–75) adversely affected many industries in Japan, MITI adopted additional policy measures to facilitate structural adjustment and capacity reduction in the **declining industries**. Overall, however, the role of industrial policy has declined in the third period because of the successful development of the economy.

Industrial policy is implemented mainly through **administrative guidance**, that is, suggestions given by MITI bureaucrats to companies for voluntary compliance. This is reinforced with other measures such as relaxing the **Antimonopoly Law** by permitting the formation of **cartels**, and the provision of financial incentives, trade protection, and so forth, to help promote priority industries or to reduce the capacity of declining industries. For example, in the early 1960s MITI encouraged the mergers of firms in steel and auto industries in order to attain economies of scale to compete with foreign producers; the **steel industry** followed the suggestion but not the **auto industry**. Trade protection in the forms of tariffs, quotas, restrictive standards, and regulations for imports have been used to protect some industries. Special tax exemptions have been granted by MITI to favored industries. Subsidies and technical assistance were given to various priority industries, particularly the **electronics industry**, to foster technical development. However, the amount of funds involved was relatively small. For example, in the VLSI (very large-scale integrated circuit) project of 1976–80 to develop VLSI circuits for the fourth-generation computers, only ¥29.1 billion or 39.5% of total R&D expenditures came from the government. MITI's important role lay in the coordination of the project of five major computer firms. In 1990 MITI launched a ¥50 billion 10-year program to promote the **computer-integrated manufacturing system**. MITI was also involved in the import of foreign technology. It provided information to Japanese firms and negotiated with foreign corporations on their behalf. Vestall (1993: 65) argues that this was justified because the international markets for technology are not perfectly competitive. Small Japanese firms could not have bargained intelligently with foreign technology suppliers, who were either monopolists or oligopolists.

For declining industries slated for capacity reduction such as textiles and shipbuilding in the 1970s, administrative guidance has been used to encourage shift into new product lines. **Cartels** have been permitted for industry rationalization. The Depressed Industries Law was passed in 1978 and extended in 1983 to provide financial incentives to declining industries to reduce capacity.

There is no consensus among scholars on the effectiveness and prospects of Japan's industrial policy. Among believers of its efficacy and success, Johnson (1982) attributes the "success" to the capability, dedication, and wide authority of the elite MITI bureaucracy and the "market-conforming" nature of their policy measures. Noboru Makino, former chairman of Mitsubishi Research Institute, attributes the strength of Japanese manufacturing to MITI's policy of weeding out the weak in industry in contrast to the **Ministry of Finance**'s "convoy system" policy of keeping weak financial institutions alive (*Japan Economic Journal*, April 13, 1991: 14). Vittas and Cho (1994) argue that the Japanese government's use of credit policy was effective in promoting growth industries and in phasing out declining industries because it was narrowly focused, limited in scale and duration, and was well monitored. Vestal (1993) contends that industrial policy was successful in most target industries such as steel and shipbuilding because they fitted the infant industry justification for assistance; it was not successful in coal and marine transport, which were not infant industry cases.

Critics of industrial policy question the wisdom and visions of MITI officials and the prospects of industrial policy in Japan. For example, Eads and Yamamura (1987) contend that industrial policy has often merely reflected the needs and demands of those being "guided," not the other way around. They predict that the role of industrial policy will decline in the future in Japan because of the reduced policy tools available to policy makers due to capital market liberalization, trade liberalization, diminished funds for subsidies, and so on. Another criticism of industrial policy is that the use of subsidies by MITI is susceptible to political influence. For example, Okimoto (1989) charges that the coal and textile industries have been given much more subsidies than are justified on economic grounds. A more fundamental criticism is that MITI is not omniscient, as shown in its failed plan in the mid-1960s to create a world-class petrochemical industry despite Japan's total dependency on oil imports, given that industry has encountered serious problems since the first oil crisis. Okimoto (1989) argues that given its fallibility, MITI's involvement in high-tech R&D in the future can send companies into the wrong directions with costly consequences.

One interesting assessment of industrial policy is offered by Prestowitz (1988: 150) from a broad comparative perspective. He feels that industrial policy has served Japan well, given Japan's own policy objective. "Japan's industrial policy response is essentially an expression of its age-old drive to preserve its exclusivity. It does violence to American economic thinking, but it is not necessarily wrong. It is difficult, after all, to criticize Japan's economic performance, and the policy is only wrong if one accepts Western economic theory, which Japan does not."

See also **administrative guidance, declining industries, Ministry of International Trade and Industry.**

References

Calder, Kent E. 1993. *Strategic Capitalism: Private Business and Public Purpose in Japanese Industrial Finance.* Princeton: Princeton University Press.

Dore, Ronald. 1987. *Taking Japan Seriously.* Stanford: Stanford University Press. Ch. 10.

Eads, George C., and Kozo Yamamura. 1987. The future of industria policy. In *The Political Economy of Japan,* vol. 1: *The Domestic Transformation,* ed. by Kozo Yamamura and Yasukichi Yasuba. Stanford: Stanford University Press.

Johnson, Chalmers. 1982. *MITI and the Japanese Miracle: The Growth of Industrial Policy, 1925–1975.* Stanford: Stanford University Press.

Komiya, Ryutaro, Masahiro Okuno, and Kotaro Suzumura, eds. 1988. *Industrial Policy of Japan.* Tokyo: Academic Press Japan.

Komiya, Ryutaro, and Keiichi Yokobori. 1991. *Japan's Industrial Policy in the 1980s.* Tokyo: Research Institute of International Trade and Industry, MITI.

Nester, William R. 1990. *The Foundation of Japanese Power: Continuities, Changes, Challenges.* London: Macmillan. Ch. 11.

Okimoto, Daniel I. 1989. *Between MITI and the Market: Japanese Industrial Policy for High Technology*. Stanford: Stanford University Press.

Okazaki, Tetsuji. 1996. The government-firm relationship in postwar Japanese economic recovery: Resolving the coordination failure by coordination in industrial rationalization. In *The Role of Government in East Asian Economic Development: Comparative Institutional Analysis*, ed. by Aoki, Masahiko, Hyung-ki Kim, and Masahiro Okuno-Fujiwara. Oxford: Clarendon Press.

Okuno-Fujiwara, Masahiro. 1991. Industrial policy in Japan: A political economy view. In *Trade with Japan*, ed. by Paul Krugman. Chicago: University of Chicago Press.

Prestowitz, Clyde, Jr. 1988. *Trading Places: How We Allowed Japan to Take the Lead*. New York: Basic Books. Ch. 5.

Vestal, James. 1993. *Planning for Change: Industrial Policy and Japanese Economic Development, 1945–1990*. Oxford: Clarendon Press.

Vittas, Dimitri, and Yoon Je Cho. 1994. The role of credit policies in Japan and Korea. *Finance and Development*, March: 10–12.

industrial regions   Japan has three major industrial regions. They are, in order of importance, the Kanto area with Tokyo–Yokohama as its center, Kansai area with Osaka as the center, and Central Japan with Nagoya as the center.

See **Nagoya and Central Japan, Osaka and Kansai, Tokyo and Kanto, Yokohama**.

inhabitant tax   A type of local income tax levied by prefectural and municipal governments on individuals and corporations.

See **corporate taxes, individual income taxes, tax system**.

inheritance tax   A national tax imposed on the statutory heirs of inherited assets.

See **tax reform, tax system**.

insurance companies   Japan's insurance industry consists of life insurance companies and nonlife or casualty-liability insurance companies. They are regulated by the banking bureau of the **Ministry of Finance** in terms of entry into the market, product type, industrywide premiums, and dividend rates on policies. Since the mid-1990s, however, deregulation is fast reducing the restrictions on the industry.

Life insurance in Japan is concentrated in relatively few companies. In late 1995 there were only 29 life insurance companies in Japan, The assets as of March 31, 1997, of the top eight are given in table I.6, along with

Table I.6
Leading life insurance companies (FY 1996; in ¥ trillions)

Company	Premium revenues	Profit[a]	Total assets
Nippon Life Insurance	5.9	492	40.0
Dai-Ichi Mutual Life Insurance	3.9	343	28.0
Sumitomo Life Insurance	3.4	304	23.4
Meiji Mutual Life Insurance	2.5	208	16.7
Asahi Mutual Life Insurance	1.7	78	12.0
Mitsui Mutual Life Insurance	1.6	36	10.2
Yasuda Mutual Life Insurance	1.5	182	9.2
Chiyoda Mutual Life Insurance	0.9	17	5.8

Source: *Japan Economic Almanac* (1998: 37).
a. Pretax profit in ¥ billions.

their premium income and profit. In FY 1996 these eight companies had a combined market share of about 73% in assets.

Japanese life insurance companies grew very rapidly in the 1980s. Their total assets grew from ¥22.7 trillion on March 31, 1980, to ¥116.2 trillion at the end of FY 1989 and ¥130.3 trillion at the end of FY 1991 (Ministry of Finance). Several factors may account for their rapid growth: (1) Since the disposable incomes of Japanese households continued to increase in the 1980s, most households (92% in 1989) had some type of life insurance, with increasingly larger or multiple policies. (2) Since the interest rates were low in the second half of the 1980s, life insurance companies were able to siphon much in deposits from banks with high-yielding policies such as the popular single-premium endowment insurance. (3) Companies made intensive door-to-door sales efforts, employing more than 400,000 saleswomen. Utilizing personal connections and persistent persuasion, these "Life Insurance Ladies" have greatly promoted sales. Reportedly some saleswomen even gave gifts on their own to promote sales (Yonetama 1994: 185). This type of sales technique also makes it difficult for foreign insurance companies to enter the Japanese insurance market. (4) The elimination in 1988 of tax-exemption for small savers at banks and the post office (*maruyu*) increased the tax advantages of life insurance. All of these created an industry boom that led Yoneyama (1994: 167) to remark that on per capita basis, "Japan is the most insurance-conscious country in the world."

The 1990s saw hard times and changes for the industry, especially the smaller companies. The depressed economy led to slow policy sales and stagnant premium revenues and profits; there were even policy cancellations. Low investment returns due to record low interest rates and low stock prices forced the life insurance companies, most of which are organized as mutual companies, to reduce dividends paid to policyholders. The bankruptcy of Nissan Mutual Life Co., a major life insurer, further eroded policyholders' confidence in the financial soundness of the industry and led to increases in policy cancellations. Deregulation also increased competition in the industry and spurred structural changes. The revision of the Insurance Business Law came into effect on April 1, 1996, permitting life and nonlife insurance companies to enter each other's business through the establishment of subsidiaries. The Japan–U.S. insurance talks accelerated the reform because of American companies' interest in entering the market.

In order to increase their investment incomes, life insurance companies have diversified their investment. Up to 1984 more than 50% of their funds were used as loans to corporations. Since then, that percentage has declined (36% in 1995); more funds (48% in 1995) have been invested in securities both in Japan and overseas. The companies have also invested in domestic and foreign real estate and in tie-ups with foreign (mainly European) financial institutions. With the depressed stock and property prices in the 1990s, the financial conditions of the companies have caused concern in Japan.

Casualty-liability insurance covers property insurance, automobile insurance, workers compensation, cargo insurance, and so forth. The industry is highly concentrated. In 1996 Japan had 26 companies. Their total assets amounted to ¥29.5 trillion in 1995. The largest five as of March 31, 1997, are Tokio Fire and Marine Insurance Co., Yasuda Fire and Marine Insurance Co., Mitsui Marine and Fire Insurance Co., Sumitomo Marine and Fire Insurance Co., and Nippon Fire and Marine Insurance Co. They have a combined market share of about 50%. Most nonlife insurers also experienced stagnant or declining investment yields and profits in the 1990s, as was the case with life insurers.

Most of the individual casualty-liability insurance policies have an attractive feature—premiums are invested and returned to policyholders when their policies mature. They combine, in effect, savings with insurance protection.

There is a "third sector" in the industry. It includes health insurance, medical insurance, casualty insurance, and care of the elderly. Because of strong U.S. interest in this sector, Tokyo and Washington reached an agreement in the Japan–U.S. insurance talks in late 1996 on the following

reform measures: permitting Japanese life insurers to enter the third sector through their nonlife subsidiaries starting January 1997, deregulation of nonlife premiums by July 1998, and the elimination of restrictions on entering the third sector by January 2001.
See also **Big Bang, financial liberalization.**

Addresses

Life Insurance Association of Japan
4-1, Marunouchi 3-chome, Chiyoda-ku, Tokyo 100
Tel: (3) 3286-2624   Fax: (3) 3286-2630

Marine and Fire Insurance Association of Japan
9, Kanda Awajicho 2-chome, Chiyoda-ku, Tokyo 101
Tel: (3) 3255-1211   Fax: (3) 3258-1211

Nippon Life Insurance Co.
1-1, Yuraku-cho 1-chome, Chiyoda-ku, Tokyo 100
Tel: (3) 3503-0311

References

Insurance. In *Japan Economic Almanac*. Various years. Tokyo: Nihon Keizai Shimbun.

Komiya, Ryutaro. 1990. *The Japanese Economy: Trade, Industry, and Government*. Tokyo: University of Tokyo Press. Ch. 6.

Ministry of Finance. Annual. *The Insurance Yearbook*.

Nakamura, Minoru, and Koj Yamada. 1996. Financial institutions of Japan. In *Japanese Financial Markets*, ed. by Shigenobu Hayakawa. Cambridge: Gresham Books.

Ostrom, Douglas. 1992. Japan's sleeping insurance giants: Roused and ready? *JEI Report* 17A, May 1.

Ostrom, Douglas. 1998. From colossus to casualty: The transformation of Japan's insurance industry. *JEI Report* 2A, January 16.

Yamamoto, Yuri. 1997. Insurer performance mixed in deregulation. *Nikkei Weekly*, June 16: 13.

Yamamoto, Yuri. 1998. Life insurers falling behind in money-management race. *Nikkei Weekly*, June 15: 1, 13.

Yoneyama, Takau. 1994. The industrial organization of Japanese life insurance: Historical aspects. In *Japanese Business Success: the Evolution of a Strategy*, ed. by Takeshi Yuzawa. London: Routledge.

interest rate structure   There are many types of interest rates in Japan. Both the **Bank of Japan** and the **Ministry of Finance** influence the interest rates in accordance with the conditions of the economy—the former through the official discount rate and guidelines and the latter through regulations on interest rate ceilings. Because of the **financial liberalization** since the late 1970s, most regulations of interest rates have been liberalized. The most important types of interest rates are discussed below.

1. *Official discount rate.* This is the basic interest rate that the **Bank of Japan** charges commercial banks for its loans. Determined by the Policy Board of the Bank, it is an important policy instrument, for it affects other interest rates and the conditions of the financial markets. The discount rate has changed over time in terms of categories and percentage levels. Before 1972 there were several discount rates for different types of loans. They were generally in the 4.25–5.75% range; the rates were lowest (4.25% in early 1972) on commercial bills, on loans secured by government securities, and on export bills.

Since 1972 there are two types of discount rates: the discount rate on commercial bills and on loans secured by government bonds or specially designated securities, and the discount rate on loans secured by other assets. The latter is invariably 0.25% higher than the former. The discount rate on commercial bills rose from 4.25% in October 1972 to 9.0% in December 1973, and it declined steadily thereafter, remaining in the 4–6% range throughout the 1970s. With the exception of the relatively high rate in 1980 (8.25–9%) and the low rate in early 1987 (2.5%), it fluctuated in the low-level range of 3–6% throughout most of the 1980s and during 1990–92. It was reduced to 2.5% in February 1993, and further reduced successively to a historic low of 0.5% in September 1995 in an effort to stimulate the stagnant economy. As of mid-1998 it remains at 0.5%.

2. *Deposit rates.* All categories of banks as well as the **postal savings** system accept deposits. Prior to 1979 interest rates on deposits were highly regulated. Since then they have been gradually deregulated. The deregulation of deposit interest rates consists of two parts. (1) The minimum amount required for four types of banks deposits that have unregulated interest rates were gradually lowered by June 1992 so that the market-determined rates of interest became increasing within the reach of the average depositor. These deposits include certificates of deposits (CDs), large time deposits, money market certificates (MMCs), and small MMCs. (2) The elimination of interest ceilings on time deposits in June 1993 and on savings deposits in October 1994.

Despite deposit rate deregulation, the Bank of Japan has issued guidelines on maximum deposit rates that are followed by banks voluntarily.

For example, current (demand) deposits are interest free per Bank of Japan guideline. The interest rates on **postal savings** are set by the Ministry of ·Posts and Telecommunications. They are traditionally higher than bank deposit rates.

Deposit rates vary with the type of deposits and maturity period. A few deposit rates, as of December 1997, are given below. Corresponding deposit rates in 1991, generally at record high levels, are given in parentheses for comparison.

	Certificates of deposits	3 months, 0.872% per annum (7.701%)
Commercial banks	Installment savings	3 years, 0.44% (3.93%)
	Ordinary deposits	0.10% (2.08%)
	Notice deposits	0.22% (2.33%)
Trust banks	Designated money in trust	1 year, 0.25% (6.08%) 5 year, 0.68% (7.1%)
Postal savings	Fixed-sum deposit certificate (*teigaku chokin*)	Rises from 0.25% for less than 1 year to 0.45% for more than 3 years (4.58% to 6.33%)
	Ordinary savings	0.25% (3.48%)

3. Lending rates. Since 1975 *short-term lending rates* on loans of less than one year in maturity are determined by negotiations between banks and their customers; the upper limits, however, have varied with the official discount rate at the request of the Bank of Japan. The average short-term lending rate of all banks at year-end was 4.71% in 1978, 5.796% in 1985, 8.022% in 1990, and 1.985% in 1997. The *short-term prime rate* is the interest rate that banks charge their most favored corporate clients on loans and discount of bills of high credit-worthiness. It serves as the lower limit for short-term lending rates. It was reformed in January 1989 to reflect market interest rate, that is, to be based on short-term money rates in the **money market** plus other fixed costs. However, changes in short-term prime rates tend to be announced by a price leader among the banks, invariably one of the large banks, and quickly followed by other banks, leading some analysts to suspect that the rates are really decided among bankers at behind-the-scene discussions.

Long-term lending rates are interest rates on loans of more than one year in maturity. They are said to be tied to *long-term prime rates*, which are the lending rates charged by **long-term credit banks** and **trust banks** on long-term loans to highly credit-worthy corporations such as electric power companies. However, as Suzuki (1987: 147) notes, long-term prime rates have not always been the basic rate for long-term lending; since the mid-1980s both **city banks** and long-term credit banks have used lower rates for long-term lending. The average long-term lending rate of all banks at year-end was 7.589% in 1978, 7.282% in 1985, 7.558% in 1990, and 2.702% in 1997. The long-term prime rate was between 7.0% and 7.7% in 1985, and between 6.8% and 8.9% in 1990. Since then it has declined steadily to 2.3% in October 1997. In April 1991 some city banks adopted a new formula for determining the long-term prime rate. It is calculated by adding to the short-term lending rate 0.3% for loans up to three years and 0.5% for loans of more than three years.

4. *Call rates.* These are the interest rates on call loans. The **call money market** is the central part of the short-term interbank **money markets** where banks with deficient funds borrow from banks with temporary surplus. The rate is determined by the market and has not been controlled by the Ministry of Finance or the Bank of Japan since 1979. However, it has had little influence on other interest rates. Since the 1950s different types of call rates have been introduced. The collateralized overnight call rate averaged 7.457% in 1991 and 0.43% in 1997. The noncollateralized overnight call rate averaged 3.669% in 1987, rose to 7.525% in 1991, and then declined steadily to 0.48% in 1997. The seven-day call rate, averaged 11.053% in 1980, 7.555% in 1991, and 0.57% in 1997.

For much of the postwar era, Japan's various interest rates are considered by most analysts to have been lower than their counterparts in the United States and Europe. This has led to the widespread belief that Japan has pursued a "low interest rate policy" in the postwar era and that this policy has greatly stimulated Japan's rapid economic growth. However, Horiuchi (1984) has argued that Japan's interest rates are not really low, and that they have been high enough to reflect the scarcity price of capital in Japan. In any case, as shown above, Japan's interest rates have fallen from record high levels in 1990–91 to record low levels in 1995–97. This unprecedented pace and magnitude of decline reflects the severity of the stagnation of the Japanese economy in the postbubble period. The low lending rates have squeezed the profit margins of banks, and reduced their ability to write off their huge bad debts due to the bursting of the bubble economy. Yet the low interest rate policy has not been effective in stimulating economic recovery and growth. Many analysts are convinced, therefore, that only a thorough and rapid reform of the entire Japanese financial system such as envisioned in the **Big Bang** can reinvigorate the economy.

See also **banking system, Big Bang, call money market, deposits system, financial liberalization, money markets, postal savings.**

References

Bank of Japan. Annual. *Economic Statistics Annual.*

Campbell, John Y., and Yasushi Hamao. 1993. The interest rate process and the term structure of interest rates in Japan. In *Japanese Monetary Policy,* ed. by Kenneth J. Singleton. Chicago: University of Chicago Press.

Federation of Bankers Associations of Japan. 1994. *The Banking System in Japan.* Ch. 4.

Horiuchi, Akiyoshi. 1984. The "low interest rate policy" and economic growth in postwar Japan. *Developing Economies* 22: 349–71.

Isono, Naoyuki. 1991a. Long-term prim rise tempers relief from debt. *Japan Economic Journal,* April 13: 31.

Isono, Naoyuki. 1991b. Yen jitters: World watches BOJ-MOF tussle. *Japan Economic Journal,* April 21: 1.

Kester, W. Carl, and Timothy A. Luehrman. 1992. The myth of Japan's low-cost capital. *Harvard Business Review* 30, 3: 130–38.

Suzuki, Yoshio, ed. 1987. *The Japanese Financial System.* Oxford: Oxford University Press. Ch. 4.

Tatewaki, Kazuo. 1991. *Banking and Finance in Japan.* London: Routledge. Ch. 3.

Yokota, Kazunari. 1997. Bank margins cut by low interest rates. *Nikkei Weekly,* March 3: 13.

investment   Aggregate investment or gross domestic capital formation in Japan is known for its persistent high level and is regarded by some analysts as the engine of Japan's economic growth. As a ratio of GDP, it was 32.8% in 1975, 32.6% in 1980, 28.2% in 1985, 32.3% in 1990, and 29.9% (¥149.5 trillion) in 1996 (see **savings** and table S.1). These are higher than those in the other industrial nations. Investment in the economy comprises **housing** investment, plant and equipment investment, inventory investment, and general government investment. They are affected by different factors, but all fluctuate over time.

1. *Housing investment* in the form of new housing starts has experienced two long-term cycles in the postwar period. From a low level in the 1950s, it rose steadily in the 1960s, reached a peak of 1,863,000 units in FY 1972, and then declined in the rest of the 1970s and the first half of the 1980s. After it bottomed at 1,135,000 units in 1983, it rose again. It peaked at 1,729,000 units in FY 1987 but remained at a high level of more

Table I.7
Gross domestic capital formation (in ¥ trillions in current prices)

	1980	1990	1995	1996
Total	84.2	138.9	138.2	149.5
Housing investment	17.8	25.5	24.1	27.6
Plant and equipment	38.5	83.1	72.1	77.0
Government investment	26.3	28.1	41.3	43.8
Inventory investment	1.6	2.4	0.5	1.2

Sources: Bank of Japan; Economic Planning Agency.

than 1,660,000 units yearly during 1988–90. It declined to 1,370,000 units in 1991, and then recovered gradually to 1,643,000 units in 1996. In terms of total value, a peak of ¥25.2 trillion was reached in 1990 and another peak of ¥27.6 trillion was reached in 1996 (see table I.7).

There are three categories of new housing construction, namely rental housing, owner-occupied housing, and houses for sale in order of importance. The latest upswing in new housing starts began with a boom in the construction of rental housing in greater **Tokyo** in 1986, which was followed by a boom in **Osaka** and **Nagoya**. According to the Economic Planning Agency (1991: 48–49), all types of housing starts are inversely related to the level of interest rate and the price of land. In addition the amount of **savings** is positively correlated with owner-occupied housing starts; the number of marriages affects housing starts for owner-occupied housing and houses for sale, while the number of people in the 15–24 age bracket affects rental housing starts. The demand for building replacements also plays a role. In 1993 the size of housing stock was 45.9 million units and the average replacement period was 34 years in 1990, down from more than 40 plants in the early 1980s.

2. *Plant and equipment investment* is made for various reasons—for replacement, to save energy, to save labor, for expanded production and increased sales, for R&D, new products, and so on. Because the Japanese economy is becoming more service oriented, the rate of equipment investment is increasing faster in nonmanufacturing industries than in manufacturing industries. The **Economic Planning Agency** (1997: 24) has found that rate of increase in real equipment investment is closely correlated with the rate of return on assets over and above the rate of interest on loans. The value of plant and equipment investment is positively correlated with the growth rate of real GD but negatively correlated with the real interest rate and the real capital stock. There are, of course, excep-

tions to such generalizations. The value of plant and equipment investment reached a record high of ¥89.7 trillion (19.6% of GDP) in 1991 when the interest rates were relatively high; it declined to ¥70.2 trillion in 1994, and increased little in 1995–96 when interest rates were reduced to record low levels.

Plant and equipment investment in Japan is high by international standards; it is invariably over 15% of GDP and was nearly 20% of GDP in 1989–91. Such high level of corporate fixed capital investment is criticized by Prestowits (1988: 325–26) as overinvestment which creates overcapacity, leading to variable cost pricing (i.e., pricing below average cost; see **pricing practices**) and the incentive to dump the output abroad. On the other hand, there are Japanese authors who argue that it is Japan's export success that gives Japanese corporations large profits to finance a high level of corporate investment. In other words, the causation is in the opposite direction. This is the "export-led" growth and investment thesis (Takenaka 1997).

3. *Inventory investment* refers to the increase in the stocks of finished and semi-finished goods in manufacturing and mining. It tends to fluctuate with **business cycles**. First, as the economy recovers from a recession, accumulated inventories will be reduced as shipments increase. Then, as production picks up during the economy's expansion, the decline in inventories will be halted, and inventories will be maintained at a suitable level. Finally, as the economy slows down in its expansion and eventually enters a recession, inventories will accumulate again. Overall, however, inventory investment is relatively small (¥1.2 trillion in 1996) and much less important than housing investment and equipment investment in influencing the economy.

4. *General government investment* or public sector capital formation primarily takes the form of infrastructural capital projects such as highways and airport construction; about 20% of it is in the form of equipment investment for the public sector. Hence it is determined by government policy objectives. Its importance in the economy has increased in recent years not only in absolute amount but also as a ratio of aggregate investment and of GDP. The amount of ¥43.8 trillion in 1996 is a record, about 55% more than the amount in 1990. It is 29.3% of the aggregate investment in the economy and 9.7% of GDP, compared with 20.3% and 6.6%, respectively, in 1990. The reason for the large increase is the sluggish private consumption and hence the need for the government to use public works to stimulate the stagnant economy.

The high level of investment in postwar Japan is regarded by Minami (1994: 142–48) as a major factor in Japan's rapid postwar economic growth. There are two reasons for this. First, investment and consumption are the main components of domestic demand; they are much larger than exports. Second, the high investment level has raised Japan's capital-labor ratio and hence its labor productivity; the average worker has more fixed capital to work with and therefore has become more productive. He concludes that capital formation is the engine of economic growth for Japan; in other words, Japanese economic growth in the postwar era has been "investment-led" rather than export-led.

See also **savings**.

References

Alexander, Arthur J. 1997. The role of investment in the Japanese economy: past, present and future. *JEI Report* 4A, January 31.

Bank of Japan. Annual. *Economic Statistics Annual*.

Dekle, Robert. 1995. Saving, investment, and capital mobility: lessons from Japanese interregional capital flows. In *The Structure of the Japanese Economy: Changes on the Domestic and International Fronts*, ed. by Mitsuaki Okabe. New York: St. Martin's Press.

Economic Planning Agency. Annual. *Economic Survey of Japan*.

Minami, Ryoshin. 1994. *The Economic Development of Japan: A Quantitative Study*, 2nd ed. New York: St. Martin's Press.

Prestowitz, Clyde V., Jr. 1988. *Trading Places*. New York: Basic Books.

Takenaka, Heizo. 1991. *Contemporary Japanese Economy and Economic Policy*. Ann Arbor: University of Michigan Press. Chs. 5–6.

Takenaka, Heizo. 1997. Investment belongs in driver's seat. *Nikkei Weekly*, August 25, 1997: 21.

Yoshikawa, Hiroshi. 1995. *Macroeconomics and the Japanese Economy*. Oxford: Clarendon Press. Ch. 7.

investment advisory companies   Japan has some 147 licensed investment advisory companies or asset management companies and 568 registered investment advisory companies as of October 31, 1996. The licensed companies are licensed to manage clients' financial assets, to provide investment information, and to give investment advice, and so forth, for fees. Also called *securities investment advisers*, they differ from the securities investment trust management companies because they are not involved in **investment trusts** business. The top companies are affiliates of leading **securities companies**.

See also **investment trusts, securities companies**.

investment trusts   Investment trusts are a special type of investment instrument whereby funds of the general investing public are channeled by investment management companies into trust funds for investment in securities. The system generally works as follows, although the details may vary with the type of trust: First, the "securities investment trust management company," or fund manager, who is the manager as well as owner of the trust, sells beneficiary certificates to the general public (the beneficiaries) who do not have large funds or knowledge to make their own investment. The funds thus collected are then entrusted through a trust contract to a trust bank (the trustee) as trust funds for investment in securities in accordance with the directions of the trust owner. They can be invested in stocks, **government bonds**, corporate bonds, and foreign securities. The trust owner will manage the payment of dividends and redemption of principal to the beneficiaries.

There are 37 securities investment trust management companies in Japan as of October 31, 1996—including Nomura Securities Investment Trust Management Co. and Nikko Securities Investment Trust and Management Co.—all of which are affiliates of securities houses. When the system of securities investment trusts was first established under the Securities Investment Trust Law of 1951, the management operations for investment trusts were carried out by **securities companies**. In 1960 the management of trusts was separated from securities companies and assigned to independent securities investment trust management companies. These companies are licensed by the **Ministry of Finance** to meet certain requirements.

Investment trusts have always been viewed as a conservative savings instrument. Investors are said to have valued stability over the rate of return. Although there are several types of investment trusts, the basic distinction is between the open-end trust fund and unit-type or closed-end trust fund. The latter was, until 1992, the more popular type, in which trust share is sold to investors at a fixed amount per share. Once the trust fund is established, no new principal can be added, and the funds can only be partially redeemed during the trust period, which can range from two to seven years. In the open-end trust the principal can be added whenever market conditions justify it, and the funds can be redeemed by investors at any time.

Trust management companies have traditionally preferred the closed-end trust funds because they provide a more stable fund to manage. However, with the **stock market** slump in 1990, investors saw the value

Table I.8
Investment trusts (in ¥ trillions)

Year	Stock investment trusts[a]		Bond investment trusts	
	Net increase[b]	Net assets[c]	Net increase[b]	Net assets[c]
1976	0.31	2.49	0.15	1.59
1980	−0.34	4.03	0.17	2.02
1985	2.18	10.38	−0.76	9.59
1986	7.09	19.12	3.27	12.96
1987	12.61	30.61	−0.45	12.30
1988	5.32	39.25	1.28	13.65
1989	2.21	45.55	−0.81	13.10
1990	0.24	35.07	−2.30	10.92
1991	−6.44	28.56	1.72	12.91
1992	−3.95	21.10	9.11	22.20
1993	−2.37	19.55	8.72	31.19
1994	−2.42	17.45	−5.15	25.96
1995	−2.64	14.68	7.21	33.28
1996	−1.19	12.78	2.61	35.89

Source: Tokyo Stock Exchange.
a. Convertible bonds investment trusts are included in stock investment trusts.
b. Net increase is the difference between new issues and redemptions.
c. Net assets are year-end figures.

of their shares plummet by nearly 30% in the closed-end funds. Since 1993 the open-end funds have been more popular than the closed-end ones. The Ministry of Finance allowed four foreign asset management firms to set up Japanese investment trust units. The purpose was to make the industry more competitive.

Table I.8 shows the size of stock investment trusts and bond investment trusts. The former were about three times as large as the latter in the late 1980s. However, because of the fall of the stock market in 1990–91 and the stagnant stock prices afterward, bond investment trusts became larger in 1992. The disparity has continued to grow in 1993–96.

See also **Tokyo Stock Exchange**.

Addresses

Japan Investment Trusts Association
5-8, Nihonbashi, Kayabacho 1-chome, Chuo-ku, Tokyo 103
Tel: (3) 3667-7471

References

Japan Securities Research Institute. 1998. *Securities Market in Japan, 1998*. Ch. 8.

Koyanagi, Takehiko. 1990. Market forces loom for investment trusts. *Japan Economic Journal*, July 14: 31–32.

Tanabe, Noboru. 1992. Japan's investment trust: The current evolution and issues toward the future. In *Capital Markets and Financial Services in Japan*. Tokyo: Japan Securities Research Institute.

Tomkin, Robert. 1990. Fund managers to assume limelight as investment trusts take center stage. *Japan Economic Journal*, Winter suppl.: 22.

Tokyo Stock Exchange. Annual. *Tokyo Stock Exchange Fact Book*.

Izanagi Boom   The 57-month economic expansion from October 1965 to July 1970 that set a postwar record.
   See **business cycles**.

J

Japan Association of Corporate Executives (Keizai Doyukai)   A leading business organization.
See **business organizations.**

Japan Chamber of Commerce and Industry (Nissho)   A leading business organization.
See **business organizations.**

Japan Development Bank   Created in 1951, Japan Development Bank (JDB) is a major government bank that extends government policy-based loans to the private sector. Its objective in the 1950s and 1960s was to provide long-term equipment loans to private enterprises for economic reconstruction and industrial development for which financing by private financial institutions was difficult or inadequate. Since the early 1970s its focus has shifted to economywide objectives such as environmental protection, energy, and technology development. Currently it does not emphasize any specific industries. It also has a program to assist **foreign direct investment in Japan** and to promote imports.

JDB is under the administrative supervision of the **Ministry of Finance.** Its initial capital of ¥10 billion came from the U.S. Aid Counterpart Fund—the yen proceeds from the sale in Japan of U.S. aid products— provided by the Supreme Command for the Allied Powers. Since then JDB's principal sources of funds are the capital subscription by the Industrial Investment Special Account—a special government account established to succeed the Counterpart Fund for capital subscriptions of and loans to government institutions—and borrowings from the government, especially from the Trust Fund Bureau of the **Ministry of Finance** as part of the government's **Fiscal Investment and Loan Program.** The total amount of money it borrowed from the government was ¥14.8 trillion, and its capital ¥332 billion at the end of March 1997.

Total loans outstanding at the end of fiscal year increased rapidly from ¥374 billion in 1955 to ¥3.3 trillion in 1975, ¥7.6 trillion in 1985, and ¥15.8 trillion in 1996. The loans are extended mostly in the form of joint financing with private financial institutions.

JDB is under the supervision of the Ministry of Finance but has much autonomy in its decision making. Naturally its activities supported the government's policies. In the 1950s and 1960s when **industrial policy** as implemented by the **Ministry of International Trade and Industry** (MITI) was important to Japan's development, JDB supported MITI's targeted industries. Thus the bulk of JDB's loans in the 1950s went to MITI's designated strategic industries—electric power, shipping, coal, and steel. In the 1960s JDB also extended large "structural credit" loans to large companies that merged. Mergers were promoted by MITI in the mid-1960s as a way to achieve economies of scale, thereby cutting the prices of Japanese products and promoting export. In the 1970s and 1980s the Japanese government increasingly emphasized social development, technology, environment, and the quality of life. As a result JDB's policy-based finance focused increasingly on projects in urban development, regional development, conservation of resources and energy, and development of new technology. Also as trade disputes with the United States reached new heights in the 1980s, JDB launched a program in 1983 for the "promotion of internationalization," that is, to promote foreign direct investment in Japan and to encourage imports.

The promotion of internationalization consists in extending long-term (15–25 years) loans at low interest rates (2.1–2.6% as of March 1998) to foreign-affiliated companies (with 50% or more overseas ownership) for investing in Japan and for enhancing their import facilities. It also provides information and other services such as market information, consultation for investment projects, introduction of research institutes for feasibility studies, and introduction of potential partners for foreign companies intending to invest in Japan. Eligible companies include importers, wholesalers, or retailers of manufactured goods and processed foods listed in sections 0, 1, 5, 6, 7, and 8 of the Standard International Trade Classification. Accumulated loans from April 1983 to March 1997 amounted to ¥518 billion. American companies have received the bulk of loans in 1993–94, but Asian companies became dominant in 1996. Interested companies should contact the bank's Center for the International Cooperation Department of JDB in Tokyo or any of its five overseas representative offices in Washington, DC, Los Angeles, New York, London, and Frankfurt.

See also **government financial institutions, industrial policy.**

Address

Japan Development Bank
9-1, Otemachi 1-chome, Chiyoda-ku, Tokyo 100
Tel: (3) 3270-3244   Fax: (3) 3245-1938

References

Japan Development Bank. *Annual Report*. Various years.

Japan Development Bank. Quarterly. *JDB Dispatch*.

Johnson, Chalmers. 1982. *MITI and the Japanese Miracle*. Stanford: Stanford University Press. Ch. 6.

Suzuki, Yoshio, ed. 1987. *The Japanese Financial System*. Oxford: Oxford University Press. Ch. 5.

Tatewaki, Kazuo. 1991. *Banking and Finance in Japan*. London: Routledge. Ch. 9.

Japan External Trade Organization (JETRO)   A public organization with branches abroad to promote trade with foreign countries.
See **business organizations.**

Japan National Railways (JNR)   Japan's former government-run railway system until it was privatized and broken up, in 1987, into six regional Japan Railway companies and one national freight company.
See **railway companies.**

Japan Railway Group (JR Group)   The group of six regional Japan Railway companies and a national freight company created through the privatization and breakup of the Japan National Railways in 1987.
See **railway companies.**

JCB card   Japan's most popular credit card, issued by JCB Co, Japan's largest bank-affiliated credit card company.
See **credit card industry.**

Japan–U.S. economic relations
See **airline industry, automobile industry, Beef-Citrus Quotas Agreement, direct overseas investment, foreign investment in Japan, Semiconductor Agreement, steel industry, Structural Impediments Initiative, trade pattern, trade policy, Yen–Dollar Accord, yen–dollar exchange rates.**

JTUC-Rengo   Japan Trade Union Confederation.
See **labor unions.**

jusen   Housing loan companies, which went bankrupt in the mid-1990s and caused a financial crisis and government intervention.
See **housing loan companies.**

just-in-time system   Also called the *Toyota production system*, or the *kanban* system, this is an inventory-control system developed by Toyota Motor Company in which materials and parts are produced and delivered just before they are needed. The objective is to minimize the level of inventories, especially when different models or parts are to be produced. Toyota Motor Company developed the system to coordinate in-plant activities between different processes of production and also to control the timing of deliveries made by subcontractors. The system is now widely used in Japan.

The system is commonly referred to as the *kanban* system in Japan because it relies on *kanban*, a type of production-ordering cards, in its implementation. Literally a "shop sign," a *kanban* card comes in the form of a small piece of paper in a square vinyl holder. It indicates the type and quantity of parts needed and the production process using them, and is attached to the container holding the parts. When the parts are assembled, the worker at the process returns the *kanban* to the preceding process to pick up a new batch of parts needed. The workers at the preceding process then produce and supply the amount of parts written on the just returned *kanban*. For the production-ordering *kanban* card to a subcontractor, delivery times, the store shelf to deliver, and the gate to receive, for example, are also specified. In this way the parts are produced or delivered "just in time" to eliminate or minimize inventories. The system has been characterized as a "pull" system because parts are pulled from parts fabrication into assembly just when they are needed in accordance with the latter's production schedule. By contrast, in the traditional "push" system, parts are produced according to a separate schedule and pushed into inventories regardless of subsequent processing needs.

Initially introduced by Toyota in the early 1950s, the system spread throughout Japan in the 1970s. When Toyota set up plants overseas, the system was also introduced. In addition a growing number of Western firms have also adopted it. Newly industrializing countries such as South Korea and Taiwan began adopting the system in the late 1980s.

Starting in 1982, some Japanese companies have tried to extend the kanban system to production and marketing. The idea of the so-called New Production System (NPS) is to link production directly to sales at market outlets without the need for inventory. The rationale for this is the belief that because of volatile consumer demand, companies need to produce more varieties of products in small quantities to meet current market demand, hence the need to base production on current sales data instead of market forecast. For the same reason mass production and distribution are inappropriate in many industries because they result in slow responses to changing market demand and expensive inventories.

To implement the new production system, Toyota Motor has completed an on-line computer system that links its production division to its nationwide dealership communications network in order to meet new orders quickly. Similarly Sekisui Chemical Co. and a growing number of other companies have set up a network to communicate directly with retail outlets in order to respond immediately to market changes.

One problem with the just-in-time system in the Japanese automobile industry in its relationship with subcontractors is that it requires frequent deliveries. This is said to have aggravated the labor shortage of some firms and to have contributed to air pollution and traffic jams. Another problem is that under the system, relying on a supplier for major parts can leave the firm short of parts, as happened to Toyota after the Great Hanshin Earthquake in January 1995 and after a fire at its largest parts supplier in February 1997. Accordingly the system is being reviewed by the industry.

In the United States where the JIT system has been adopted by many companies, it has not always worked smoothly. Zipkin (1991) states that it has strained some companies' supplier relations and that it has created stress among workers. The basic reason is that "JIT requires patient effort, persistence, and meticulous care on the factory floor," and such qualities are often in short supply.

See also **automobile industry, kanban system.**

References

Abegglen, James C., and George Stalk, Jr. 1985. *Kaisha: The Japanese Corporation*. New York: Basic Books. Ch. 5.

Alonso, Ramon L., and Cline W. Frasier. 1991. JIT hit home: A case study in reducing management delays. *Sloan Management Review* 32, 4: 59–67.

Black, J. T., ed. 1987. *JIT Factory Revolution*. Cambridge, MA: Productivity Press.

Cusumano, Michael A. 1985. *The Japanese Automobile Industry*. Cambridge: Harvard University Press. Pp. 275–305.

Karmarkar, Uday. 1989. Getting control of just-in-time. *Harvard Business Review* 67, 5: 122–31.

Monden, Ysuhiro. 1983. *Toyota Production System*. Atlanta: Industrial Engineering and Management Press.

NPS tries to improve on the just-in-time production system. *Tokyo Business Today*, September 1989: 28–30.

Taylor, Curtis R., and Steven N. Wiggins. 1997. Competition or compensation: Supplier incentives under the American and Japanese subcontracting systems. *American Economic Review* 87: 598–618.

Zipkin, Paul H. 1991. Does manufacturing need a JIT revolution? *Harvard Business Review* 69, 1: 40–50.

K

kabushiki   Stocks of a company.

kabushiki kaisha/gaisha   Joint stock companies, which include about half of all Japanese companies and most of the large companies.
　See *kaisha*.

kabushiki mochi-ai   Stock or share cross-holdings. Japanese companies with business ties or in a *keiretsu* or business group typically hold each other's shares to provide mutual support and to maintain friendly business relationships.
　See **cross-shareholding**.

kaisha   The (Japanese) company. As of December 1997 there were 2,884,497 companies in Japan (communications from the Ministry of Home Affairs). Under Japanese commercial law private enterprises are classified into the following categories of *kaisha*:

1. *Joint stock companies (kabushiki kaisha/gaisha, KK; 1,190,438 as of December 1997).* Their capital comes from shareholders, whose financial liability is limited to the amount of capital invested in the shares. The capital requirement for joint stock companies is ¥10 million, up from ¥350,000, effective April 1991.
　Of the joint stock companies, slightly more than two thousand are listed companies; that is, their stocks are listed on the stock exchanges for public trading. Of these, about 1,300 are listed in the first section of the Tokyo and/or Osaka Stock Exchanges. These are the largest and most prestigious companies, sought after by college graduates for employment. They constitute the typical Japanese "big business." There are strict criteria for listing in the first section. Those listed in the second section of the

stock exchanges are smaller and less prestigious but can be graduated into the first section if some criteria are met.

The rest of joint stock companies are unlisted companies, which tend to be family owned. Some of them may have their shares traded in the **over-the-counter market**. A small number of unlisted companies are large companies. They include (a) companies owned by a family or families such as Seibu Department Stores and Suntory, (b) subsidiaries of other listed companies or foreign companies such as Fuji-Xerox and IBM Japan, and (c) large newspapers, TV and radio broadcasting companies, publishing houses, and so on (Komiya 1990: 160).

Holding companies (*mochikabu gaisha*) are a special type of companies, banned by the **Antimonopoly Law** from 1949 until December 17, 1997, that are set up to hold enough shares of other companies in order to control them. For fear of excessive concentration of corporate power, there are certain restrictions on the establishment of holding companies (see **holding companies**).

2. *Limited liability companies (yugen gaisha; 1,595,940 as of December 1997).* These tend to be small- or medium-sized enterprises. Their capital comes only from members, whose liability is limited to their capital contribution, as with a joint stock company. However, unlike the joint stock companies, the ownership shares in a limited liability company may not be transferred to a nonmember without the approval of the general shareholders' meeting. Effective April 1996, the minimum capital requirement for a limited liability company is ¥3 million, up from ¥100,000.

3. *Partnership.* There are two types of partnership, unlimited and limited. As their names imply, the liability of the partners is unlimited in an unlimited partnership (*gomei gaisha;* 19,396 in 1997), but is limited to partners' capital contribution in a limited partnership (*goshi gaisha;* 78,723 in 1997). There is no minimum capital requirement for partnership.

A large company tends to have many related companies in terms of ownership and/or business ties. They are classified into three categories:

1. Subsidiaries (*ko gaisha*) are established by the parent company (*oya gaisha*), who owns at least 50% of their shares. Set up primarily for the purpose of corporate diversification, subsidiaries in Japan have a large degree of freedom in operations and can expand independently of their parent company.

2. Affiliated companies (*kanren gaisha*) differ from subsidiaries in that the large company owns only between 20% and 50% of their shares.

3. Subcontracting companies (*shitauke gaisha*) perform many tasks for a large manufacturing company at relatively low costs and are therefore very important in the Japanese industry, particularly in the **automobile industry**. They may or may not be the subcontractee's subsidiaries or affiliated companies, depending on the extent to which the subcontractee owns the shares of the subcontracting companies.

Companies in a **keiretsu** or other type of business group are related in the sense of group affiliation but are not necessarily related companies in terms of ownership as defined above. In a horizontal keiretsu which consists of many large companies in different businesses, a company typically owns only a few percentage of the other companies' shares. In a vertical *keiretsu* which consists of a large manufacturing company and its numerous suppliers and/or distributors, the former is likely to have many subsidiaries, affiliated companies and subcontractors among the latter.

Foreign-affiliated (*gaishi*) companies include Japanese subsidiaries of foreign companies, joint ventures with at least one foreign parent, and other companies of foreign origin or ownership. There are more than 3,000 *gaishi* companies in Japan; IBM Japan is one of the largest and most successful.

Some enterprises are organized as cooperatives (*kumiai*), a type of mutual aid organization established by persons engaged in specified occupations or by consumers such as agricultural cooperatives, consumers cooperatives, credit cooperatives, and the Central Cooperative Bank for Agriculture and Forestry (Norin Chukin Bank). These are set up under different legislative provisions, are subject to different regulations and enjoy certain tax advantages. Members of a cooperative have to meet certain qualifications; each member has one vote in the decision-making process, regardless of the amount of capital each has contributed. Thus cooperatives are not *kaisha*. For historical reasons, major life **insurance companies** are organized as mutual companies (*sogo gaisha*). All policy contractors are members of the company. They contribute capital in the form of contract premiums and receive dividends from company profits. They elect up to 50 persons among themselves as their representatives to oversee company operations.

Finally, **special corporations** (*tokushu hojin*) are a broad category of government-affiliated enterprises. They include **public corporations** that are government-owned and financed enterprises, set up under special legislation to perform specific economic or social functions. They also include mixed enterprises or the so-called special companies (*tokushu gaisha*), which have mixed private-government ownership and are organized in the form of joint-stock companies. For example Nippon Telegraph and Telephone (NTT), Japan Tobacco, and several railways companies became special companies after they were privatized in 1985–87, but the government still retain some shares.

See also **agricultural cooperatives, foreign companies in Japan, *keiretsu* and business groups, public corporations and special companies, subcontracting system.**

References

Abegglen, James C. and George Stock, Jr. 1985. *Kaisha: The Japanese Corporation.* New York: Basic Books.

Aoki, Masahiko, and Ronald Dore. 1994. *The Japanese Firm: Sources of Competitive Strength.* Oxford: Oxford University Press.

Ballon, Robert J., and Iwao Tomita. 1988. *The Financial Behavior of Japanese Corporations.* Tokyo: Kodansha International. Chs. 1–2.

Komiya, Ryutaro. 1990. *The Japanese Economy: Trade, Industry, and Government.* Tokyo: University of Tokyo Press. Chs. 4–6.

Odagiri, Hiroyuki. 1992. *Growth through Competition, Competition through Growth.* Oxford: Clarendon Press. Ch. 6.

***kanban* system**   One of the core techniques of the **just-in-time system**. The *kanban*, literally a "shop sign," is used here as an production order in the form of a small piece of paper in a square vinyl holder. The *kanban*, indicating the kind and quantity of parts, is attached to the container holding the parts. When the parts are assembled, the worker at the process returns the *kanban* to the preceding process to pick up the necessary number of parts. The workers at the preceding process then produce and supply the number of parts written on the just returned *kanban*. The idea of the system is that the parts are produced "just in time" to minimize the inventory level.

Toyota engineers have worked out the following *kanban* formula (Cusumano 1985: 292):

$$y = \frac{D(T_w + T_p)(1 + n)}{a},$$

where

y = number of *kanban*,

D = demand (units per period),

T_w = waiting time for *kanban*,

T_p = processing time,

a = container capacity (not more than 10% of daily requirement),

n = policy variable (not more than 10% of daily requirement).

The Toyota Motor Company introduced the system in its production in the late 1960s. It has also used the system with its subcontractors or parts suppliers in ordering parts.

See also **just-in-time system**.

Address

Toyota Motor Corporation
1, Toyota-cho, Toyota City, Aichi Prefecture 471
Tel: (565) 28-2121

References

Cusumano, Michael A. 1985. *The Japanese Automobile Industry*. Cambridge: Harvard University Press. Pp. 275–305.

Japan Management Association, ed. 1989. *Kanban: Just-in-Time at Toyota*, trans. by David J. Lu. Cambridge, MA: Productivity Press.

Shingo, Shigeo. 1989. *A Study of the Toyota Production System from an Engineering Viewpoint*, trans. by Andrew P. Dillon. Cambridge, MA: Productivity Press. Ch. 9.

Suzuki, Kioyoshi. 1987. *The New Manufacturing Challenge: Techniques for Continuous Improvement*. New York: Free Press. Pp. 146–68.

Kansai   The prosperous region in southwestern part of Honshu that encompasses six prefectures and that has Osaka as its principal city. It also includes the port of Kobe and the ancient capital of Kyoto.

See **Osaka and Kansai**.

Kanto   Japan's most industrialized region that includes Tokyo and six neighboring prefectures. It has the highest concentration of population, industries, government organizations, educational institutions, transportation networks, as well as the highest per capita income in Japan.

See **Tokyo and Kanto, Yokohama**.

karoshi   Death from overwork, said to be more common in Japan than in other countries because of long **working hours and stress**.

See **working hours and stress**.

Keidanren   Federation of Economic Organizations, Japan's most powerful business organization.
   See **business organizations**.

keiretsu **and business groups**   Variously translated as business groups,
corporate groups, enterprise groups, industrial groups, and supplier-
manufacturer-distributor networks, *keiretsu* are groups of affiliated companies in related or unrelated fields that were formed in Japan in the postwar
period. However, there is no consensus on the proper scope or exact
meaning of the term. Originally it referred to groups of large firms
organized around a bank, the so-called horizontal *keiretsu* or financial *keiretsu* (*kingyu keiretsu*). Subsequently it has been extended to hierarchical
or vertically related production groups (*sangyo keiretsu*), manufacturers-
distributor groups or distribution *keiretsu* (*ryutsu keiretsu*), and even
groups of parent company-subsidiaries that have capital ties but not business ties (*shihon keiretsu* or *konzern*; Gerlach 1992a: 68–69). Thus the term
has proliferated in common usage, but some scholars do not approve of
such expanded usage because it weakens the meaningfulness of the term
and insist that only the horizontal type or the vertical type of grouping is
the legitimate or meaningful category of *keiretsu*. There is no consensus
among scholars on this issue.
   Whatever the proper scope of *keiretsu*, the following categories of business groups can be distinguished in Japan:

1. Six horizontal *keiretsu* or financial *keiretsu*. These are groups of affiliated
companies loosely organized around a large city bank. These six can be
further classified into two subcategories.
• Three groups—Mitsubishi, Mitsui, and Sumitomo Groups—are based
on prewar **zaibatsu** (financial cliques) ties. These ex-*zaibatsu* groups consist of dozens of large corporations, along with a major **city bank** as the
main bank and a giant general **trading company**, most of them using
the same former *zaibatsu* name. The **Mitsubishi Group**, the largest and
most cohesive of the three, contains 29 core companies that are closely
associated as members of the Presidents' Club where company presidents
meet regularly. The **Mitsui Group** and **Sumitomo Group** have 24 and
20 core companies in their respective Presidents' Club. All three groups
have a much larger number of loosely affiliated companies.
• The other three groups are Fuyo, Sanwa, and Dai-Ichi Kangyo Groups.
They contain a somewhat smaller number of member companies, but they
also include a large city bank (Fuji, Sanwa, and Dai-Ichi Kangyo banks)

and a general trading company (Marubeni, Nissho-Iwai, and Itochu). However, members of these groups do not have the prewar *zaibatsu* ties as those of the first type. In addition analysts feel that they are less cohesive and that their group relations are largely limited to bank-client relations with little interactions among nonfinancial members.

In these financial *keiretsu*, members of the groups are linked primarily by finances—by **cross-shareholding** and bank loans from the group's main bank. Otherwise, they are independent companies operating in diverse areas of business. However, since the financial power of the large corporations grew in the 1980s, the role of the main bank is no longer that important. The extent of cross-shareholding has also declined. According to the Fair Trade Commission, the cross-shareholding ratio within a group averaged 21.64% in fiscal 1989, down from 25.5% in 1981 and 22.7% in 1987.

2. Vertical production *keiretsu* such as the Toyota Group and the NEC Group that consist of a core manufacturing company and its numerous subcontractors, subsidiaries, and affiliates, linked by manufacturer-supplier business relations, stockholdings, and personnel ties. For example, the Toyota Motor Co. is engaged primarily in automobile assembly and relies on numerous primary, secondary, and tertiary subcontractors for the supply of parts. Some 175 primary subcontractors are part of the Toyota Group, with substantial cross-ownership within the group. Some 4,000 secondary subcontractors have looser affiliation with the group. Often the core companies of these groups are themselves members of other horizontal *keiretsu*. For example, Toyota is a member of the Mitsui Group, NEC is a member of the Sumitomo Group, and Nissan Motor is a member of the Fuyo Group.

3. In the electronics industry, vertical distribution *keiretsu* with a large number of affiliated retail shops ("*keiretsu* stores") formed by giant manufacturers in order to boost sales and maintain high prices. However, these manufacturers also sell through other retailers such as consumer electronics stores, department stores, and chain stores. Some *keiretsu* stores have been dissolved because of low profitability.

4. Dozens of other groupings are based on the flow of capital from a parent company and not on manufacturer-supplier or distributor relationships. Some of these consist of a big industrial corporation (Hitachi, Bridgestone, Matsushita Electric, Toshiba, etc.) and its numerous subsidiaries. The core company of the group is usually the largest shareholder of the other group members. The Hitachi Group is the largest of

such groups, comprising some 680 subsidiaries of Hitachi Ltd., which is Japan's largest comprehensive electric machinery manufacturer and its second largest industrial corporation after Toyota Motor Co. Hitachi Ltd. is reputed to hold more than 50% of the shares of the group's member companies, but otherwise group members are independent and do not have much intragroup business. Other groups do not have a industrial corporation as the core company. For example, the Saison Group has the Seibu Department Store at the top, and includes a supermarket chain, a consumer credit company, an insurance company, and a hotel chain. The Seibu Railway Group, a brother group to Saison, consists of a railway company at its core and diverse leisure businesses. The Tokyu Group also consists of a railway company and many other business (see **railway companies**).

5. There are diverse small-business groups and strategic alliances. In the former, small firms in local communities form producer and purchaser cooperatives, industrial estates, neighborhood associations, and so on, to collaborate with each other and to better compete with the larger firms. Strategic alliances are ad hoc cooperative groupings formed between large firms and small high-technology firms to utilize new technology for specific purposes such as joint ventures, project consortia, and other forms of cooperation (Gerlach 1992a: 69).

Horizontal *keiretsu* have been of particular interest to scholars because they include many of Japan's largest and most prestigious corporations. In addition, unlike vertical *keiretsu*, they are not based on, or justified by, direct production or distribution relationships. Yet in a broad business context they are said to yield business benefits to group members. These may include information exchange, lower transaction costs, sharing the expertise of other member firms, and lower costs of funds from the group bank. Nakatani (1984) emphasizes the benefit of risk sharing in a group. Imai (1990, 1992) also argues that business groups, seen as "corporate networks," reduce risk and facilitate information exchange for innovation and investment, which the market alone cannot provide. Similarly Kester (1991: 13) contends that Japanese companies in *keiretsu* groups enjoy the "best of both worlds" because they have the incentives of the market and the benefits of selective market intervention by large banks, trading companies, and other stable shareholders. Kester's point is clearly supported by the experience of Mitsui Construction Co. in 1997. Burdened by huge debt and debt guarantees amounting to nearly ¥500 billion as of March

1997, the company was able to restructure its finance due to support from major members of the Mitsui Group. The support came in the forms of emergency loans, preferential orders, selling and utilizing properties, and so forth (Nikkei Weekly, August 8, 1997: 6).

However, the benefits of being a *keiretsu* member are by no means guaranteed. Caves and Uekusa (1976) suggest that the group bank might have exploited its privileged position as a stockholder. But this is unlikely to be the case any more because the financial power of big corporations has grown since the late 1970s. There is also evidence that *keiretsu* firms are not necessarily more profitable than non-*keiretsu* firms (Nakatani 1984). In recent years *keiretsu* stores in the electronics industry have not been doing very well because discount stores offer lower prices. Some observers suggest that electronics manufacturers have engaged in price fixing with their *keiretsu* stores, which is a violation of Japan's **Anti-monopoly Law**.

Washington believes that *keiretsu* are unfairly closed to foreign companies, thereby keeping Japanese industries and market impenetrable by foreign companies. U.S. trade negotiators therefore have made *keiretsu* a central issue in the U.S.–Japan **Structural Impediments Initiative** talks in 1989–90 and in their subsequent follow-up meetings. Washington's demand is that intra-*keiretsu* dealings should be made more "transparent" and less exclusionary. As part of the agreement resulting from the talks, the **Ministry of Finance** issued in late 1990 a ruling requiring *keiretsu* members to disclose more about transactions within the group. Also investors have to report holdings of 5% or more in a company.

Lending support to Washington's position, Lawrence (1991, 1993) contends that the level of manufactured imports tends to be lower in sectors of the Japanese economy in which *keiretsu*-related firms are dominant. He also argues that the horizontal *keiretsu* are more exclusionary; the vertical ones may be exclusionary, but they also enhance efficiency. However, the validity of his methodology is challenged by Saxonhouse (1991). Gerlach (1992b) concludes, after a comprehensive survey of the literature, that the criticism of *keiretsu* as a closed trading system underestimates its significance and viability in the Japanese economy.

Many Japanese scholars and officials, in responding to American criticisms of *keiretsu*, have reiterated the benefits of *keiretsu* in the Japanese economy, as mentioned above. In addition some of them have discussed the issue of the alleged *keiretsu* exclusivity. The discussions include three major points:

1. The horizontal *keiretsu* are only loosely organized and do not make decisions for their members. Their presidents' clubs are basically social gatherings (Economic Planning Agency 1996: 338–39). Furthermore the intragroup transactions of the horizontal *keiretsu* are not inordinately high and have been declining. For example, the Fair Trade Commission (1994) reports that horizontal *keiretsu* are no more prone to conduct intragroup business than to deal with outsiders. In FY 1992 only an average of 6.9% of the total sales of group members went to other group members, while group members made an average of 7.8% of their purchases from other group members. Both of these figures were over 10% in FY 1981.

2. It is recognized that vertical *keiretsu* involving subcontracting tend to be closed to outsiders, although such subcontracting relations are economically efficient. In this trade-off between efficiency and openness, Masu Uekusa of Tokyo University is willing to sacrifice some efficiency in order to have more openness and harmonious relations with foreigners. He has even suggested to the **Ministry of International Trade and Industry** that regional distribution centers be built in Japan for foreign parts-producers so that they can supply Japanese manufacturers expeditiously (author's interview, July 13, 1992).

3. It is admitted that distribution *keiretsu* would have violated the Antimonopoly Law if the manufacturers set and enforced high retail prices for the *keiretsu* stores. In any case, it is agreed that the distribution *keiretsu* should be made more open.

See also **corporate finance, cross-shareholding, Mitsubishi Group, Mitsui Group, Structural Impediments Initiatives, Sumitomo Group,** *zaibatsu*.

References

Caves, Richard, and Masu Uekusa. 1976. Industrial organization. In *Asia's New Giant,* ed. by Hugh Patrick and Henry Rosovsky. Washington: Brookings Institution.

Economic Planning Agency. 1996. *Economic Survey of Japan, 1995–1996.*

Fair Trade Commission. 1994. *Report on the Fifth Survey of Business Groups.*

Flath, David. 1996. The *keiretsu* puzzle. *Journal of the Japanese and International Economies* 10: 101–21.

Gerlach, Michael L. 1992a. *Alliance Capitalism: The Social Organization of Japanese Business.* Berkeley: University of California Press.

Gerlach, Michael L. 1992b. Twilight of the keiretsu? A critical assessment. Journal of Japanese Studies 18, 1:78–118.

Imai, Ken-ich. 1990. Japanese business groups and the structural impediments initiative. In *Japan's Economic Structure: Should It Change?* ed. by Kozo Yamamura. Seattle: Society for Japanese Studies.

Imai, Ken-ich. 1992. Japan's corporate networks. In *The Political Economy of Japan*, vol. 3: *Cultural and Social Dynamics*, ed. by Shumpei Kumon and Henry Rosovky. Stanford: Stanford University Press.

Kester, W. Carl. 1991. *Japanese Takeovers: The Global Contest for Corporate Control*. Boston: Harvard Business School Press. Chs. 3, 8..

Lawrence, Robert Z. 1991. Efficient or exclusionist: The import behavior of Japanese corporate groups. *Brookings Papers on Economic Activity*, no. 1: 311–30.

Lawrence, Robert Z. 1993. Japan's different trade regimes: an analysis with particular reference to *keiretsu*. *Journal of Economic Perspectives* 7, 3: 3–20.

Lincoln, James R., Michael L. Gerlach, and Christina L. Ahmadjian. 1996. *Keiretsu* networks and corporate performance in Japan. *American Sociological Review* 61: 67–89.

Nakatani, Iwao. 1984. The economic role of financial corporate grouping. In *The Economic Analysis of the Japanese Firm*, ed. by Masahiko Aoki. Amsterdam: North-Holland.

Odagiri, Hiroyuki. 1992. *Growth through Competition, Competition through Growth*. Oxford: Clarendon. Ch. 7.

Saxonhouse, Gary R. 1991. Efficient or exclusionist: The import behavior of Japanese corporate groups. Comments and discussion. *Brookings Papers on Economic Activity*, no. 1: 331–36.

Uekusa, Masu. 1990. Government regulations in Japan: Toward their international harmonization and integration. In *Japan's Economic Structure: Should It Change?* ed. by Kozo Yamamura. Seattle: Society for Japanese Studies.

Keizai Doyukai Japan Association of Corporate Executives, a leading business organization.
See **business organizations**.

kenko hoken Health insurance plans for company employees and day laborers.
See **health insurance**.

Kenshinren The prefectural-level credit federations of agricultural cooperatives.
See **agricultural cooperatives**.

Kintetsu Group A business group consisting of Kinki Nippon Railway Co., the largest private railway company in Japan, as its core company and its more than 160 subsidiaries, including the Kintetsu Department Store.
See **railway companies**.

kinyu keiretsu   Financial keiretsu, the six bank-centered business groups (Mitsubishi, Mitsui, Sumitomo, Fuyo, Sanwa, and Dai-Ichi Kangyo).
    See *keiretsu* and **business groups**.

kokumin kenko hoken   National health insurance.
    See **health insurance**.

kokumin nenkin   National pension that covers the self-employed and other people.
    See **pension system**.

kosei nenkin   Employees' pension insurance, which covers most salaried workers of private companies.
    See **pension system**.

kudoka   The "hollowing out" of the industrial base in Japan due to the shifting of manufacturing operations abroad, particularly to low-wage Asian countries.
    See **direct overseas investment**.

kyosai nenkin   Mutual aid associations pensions, which cover employees of the national government, local governments, private schools, and cooperative associations.
    See **pension system**.

kyosairen   The 47 prefectural insurance cooperatives.
    See **agricultural cooperatives**.

L

labor credit associations   Cooperative-type financial institutions to serve labor unions, consumer cooperatives, and so on.
See **banking system**.

labor force   Japan's labor force is a well trained and motivated workforce and arguably the mainspring of Japan's economic growth. Because of continuous economic and social development, particularly in the 1980s, it has also undergone significant changes.

Of Japan's total **population** of 125.9 million in 1996, 105.7 million were 15 years old and over. Of this number 67.1 million were in the labor force—employed or actively seeking employment—giving Japan a labor force participation rate of 63.5%. Of this labor force 64.9 million were employed and 2.3 million unemployed, giving an unemployment rate of 3.4% of the labor force (see table L.1). Employed workers are further classified into self-employed workers, family workers, and employees. Employees include regular employees and nonregular employees (part-timers and temporary workers).

Labor force participation rate has declined in the postwar period, reflecting mainly the longer schooling years of the young people. It was 69.2% in 1960 and is projected to reach 62.5% in 2000. Of Japan's labor force women constituted 31.8% in 1965, 34.1% in 1980, 39.9% in 1990, and 40.5% in 1996. However, female labor force participation rate has been much lower than that of men. The rate was 54.5% and 84.8% for women and men, respectively, in 1960. It declined to a postwar low in 1975 for both sexes before it gradually increased again for women. It was 50.0% and 77.7% for women and men, respectively, in 1996.

Partly because of the increasing number of **women in the labor force**, the number of part-time workers—nonagricultural workers who work less than 35 hours a week—in the labor force has increased, from 0.7

Table L.1
Population, labor force, and employment (in millions)

Year	Total population	Aged 15 and over	Labor force	Employed	Unemployment rate (%)
1965	98.3	72.9	47.9	47.3	1.2
1975	111.9	84.7	53.4	52.4	1.9
1980	117.1	89.6	56.7	55.5	1.7
1985	121.0	94.7	59.6	58.1	2.6
1986	121.7	95.9	60.2	58.5	2.8
1987	122.3	97.2	60.8	59.1	2.8
1988	122.8	98.5	61.7	60.1	2.5
1989	123.3	99.7	62.7	61.3	2.3
1990	123.6	100.9	63.8	62.5	2.1
1991	124.0	102.0	65.1	63.7	2.1
1992	124.5	102.8	65.8	64.4	2.2
1993	124.8	103.7	66.2	64.5	2.5
1994	125.0	104.4	66.5	64.5	2.9
1995	125.6	105.1	66.7	64.6	3.2
1996	125.9	105.7	67.1	64.9	3.4

Source: Ministry of Labor.

million in 1975 to 2.3 million in 1985 and 4.9 million in 1995. Although this represented only 7.3% of the total labor force in 1995, part-time workers constituted a sizable percentage of employees in specific industries, such as wholesale and retail trade (25.3% in 1995) and manufacturing (10.5% in 1995). As of 1994, 35.7% of women workers were part-timers, whereas the figure was only 11.4% for male workers.

The average educational background of the labor force is high and is becoming higher as more graduates of junior colleges and universities enter the labor market. As shown in table L.2, the number of labor market entrants with only lower secondary-school education decreased dramatically in the early 1970s, whereas the number of entrants with junior college and university education increased steadily until 1992.

Because of the relatively slow growth of the population and of the labor force in comparison with the rate of economic growth and job expansion, a labor shortage occurred in the 1980s, which was particularly acute in the late 1980s and in 1990. This can be seen in the job openings/applications ratio. The ratio was 1.6 in 1970, 0.8 in 1980, 1.2 in 1988, and 1.4 to 1.5 in 1989–91. The shortage eased in 1992 as the ratio declined to 1.0 because of the recession in the economy, and it became a labor surplus in 1993 as the recession continued and the job openings/applications ratio declined to 0.7 in 1993–94 and 0.6 in 1995.

. **Table L.2**
Educational level of labor market entrants (in 1,000 persons)

Year	Lower secondary	Upper secondary	Junior college	University
1965	549	690	35	135
1975	63	577	103	233
1980	44	581	129	285
1985	50	547	141	288
1986	48	622	140	292
1987	46	589	133	295
1988	45	578	161	298
1989	43	591	174	300
1990	40	608	181	324
1991	36	607	188	348
1992	31	584	194	350
1993	27	522	192	340
1994	23	447	173	325
1995	20	396	161	331

Source: Ministry of Education.

Partly as a result of the labor shortage in the late 1980s, the number of **foreign workers** has also grown. The number of legally employed foreigners remains very small—20,500 in 1984, 36,300 in 1987, and 49,400 in 1989—because of a strict immigration policy. However, the number of illegally employed foreign workers in Japan is estimated to be 285,000 as of November 1995, although no accurate statistics exist.

The percentage of the labor force that is unionized has declined from a postwar peak of 46.2% in 1950 to 30.8% in 1980 and 23.8% in 1995 (see table L.4, **labor unions**). This is the result of the relative decline of the traditional manufacturing sector and the rise of the nonunionized service and high-technology sectors, the increase of part-time workers in the labor force, and other factors.

See also **employment pattern, employment insurance, foreign workers in Japan, labor unions, unemployment, women in labor force.**

Addresses

Japan Institute of Labor
2-3-1 Nishishinjuku, Shinjiku-Ku, Tokyo 163
Tel: (3) 5321-3074   Fax: (3) 5321-3015

Ministry of Labor
2-2, Kasumigasek 1-chome, Chiyoda-ku, Tokyo 100
Tel: (3) 3593-1211

References

Hashimoto, Masanori. 1990. *The Japanese Labor Market in a Comparative Perspective with the United States.* Kalamazoo, MI: W. E. Upjohn Institute for Employment Research.

Japan institute of Labor. Annual. *Japanese Working Life Profile.*

Management and Coordination Agency. Annual. *Labor Force Survey.*

Ministry of Labor. Annual. *Labour Administration.* Tokyo: Japan Institute of Labor.

labor laws   A number of labor laws were enacted in 1945–48 by the Supreme Commander of the Allied Powers (SCAP) in an attempt to improve workers' welfare and to democratize the Japanese society. The most important of them were the Trade Union Law (1945), the Labor Relations Adjustment Law (1946), and the Labor Standards Law (1947). In 1985 the **Equal Employment Opportunity Law** was enacted to eliminate discrimination against women in employment, and in 1995 the Family-Leave Law was legislated to meet the needs of an aging society.

The Trade Union Law was modeled on the American Wagner Act. It gave workers, with the exception of certain classes of public servants, the right to organize, to bargain collectively, and to strike. It also provided, along with the Labor Relations Adjustment Law, for the establishment of the machinery for bargaining. A National Labor Relations Board and 46 prefectural boards, consisting of equal numbers of workers, employers, and public representatives, were set up with the power to mediate and arbitrate in industrial disputes.

The Labor Standards Law was based essentially on International Labor Organization conventions and was introduced to protect workers. It set up legal minimums for working conditions and terms of work. It laid down maximum hours (8 hours per day and 48 hours per week), minimum holidays, overtime provisions, and so on, and had protective provisions for women and children. It also dealt with such matters as unemployment insurance, workers' compensation, and old age social security programs. To implement these laws, the Ministry of Labor was set up in 1947. As a result of these laws, union membership increased rapidly from zero in 1945 to more than 6 million in 1948.

Employees in **public corporations** are governed by Public Corporation and National Enterprise Labor Relations Law enacted in 1948. They are allowed to bargain collectively but are prohibited from striking. Civil service trade unions are governed by the National Public Service Law.

In the 1980s, as the Japanese economy prospered and trade surplus developed and persisted, Japanese workers' long working hours and few vacation days were criticized by foreigners as having contributed to Japan's alleged "oversaving" and "underconsumption," including the underconsumption of imports. Partly as a response to foreign criticism, the Labor Standards Law was revised in 1988 to help introduce a shorter 40-hour work week and to ensure that employees take all the holidays that they are entitled to. Japanese employees customarily take fewer vacation days than they are entitled to in compliance with the social pressure that equates it with dedication to one's company. The new law also makes the normal working hours more flexible.

The **Equal Employment Opportunity Law** was legislated in 1985 and became effective in April 1986 to eliminate discrimination against women in employment. However, it had no sanctions for violations. It was revised in 1997, to take effect in April 1999. The revised law provides for the publications of the names of companies that discriminate against women. It also bans sexual harassment at the workplace and requires employers to take preventive measures. Because of its importance, the Equal Employment Opportunity Law is discussed in more details in a separate entry.

As the Japanese life expectancy rises and the **population** becomes more older, the need for caring for sick relatives becomes more important. Many workers have to give up their jobs in order to take care of their sick family members. As of May 1993, only 16.3% of Japanese companies and only 51.9% of the large companies permit employees to take leave of absense up to three months to care for sick family members. In 1995 the Family-Leave Law was legislated; it would require all companies as well as national and local governments to permit workers to take up to three months leave for each of employee's spouse, parents, children, and spouse's parents. Although the law will not be effective until April 1999, the legislation encourages employers to introduce the system before it takes effect.

See also **Equal Employment Opportunities Law**.

References

Family-Leave Law allows time to take care of sick relatives. *Nikkei Weekly*, June 12, 1995: 18.

Gould, William B. 1984. *Japanese Reshaping of American Labor Law*. Cambridge: MIT Press.

Kojima, Noriaki. 1997. Japanese employment and labor laws in transition. *Journal of Japanese Trade and Industry*, no. 4: 8–11.

Saso, Mary. 1990. *Women in the Japanese Workplace*. London: Hilary Shipman.

Sugeno, Kazuo. 1992. *Japanese Labor Law*, trans. by Leo Kanowitz. Tokyo: University of Tokyo Press.

Woodiwiss, Anthony. 1992. *Law, Labour, and Society in Japan*. London: Routledge.

labor-management relations   The right to organize, to bargain collectively, and to strike is provided by Japan's **labor laws** for private-sector
employees. Labor-management relations in Japan, however, are generally
characterized by cooperation, not confrontation, since the early 1970s.

Labor-management relations in postwar Japan have gone through two
period of changes. The 1950s and 1960s were a period of radical unionism, and there were some serious labor disputes. Disruptive strikes were
staged at a number of large enterprises such as Nissan Motor, Omi
Henshi, Amagasaki Seiko-sho, Japan Steel Works, Oji Paper Co., and
Mitsui Mining Co. Toward the end of the 1960s, however, both labor and
management realized the futility of confrontation, so the number of labor
disputes gradually decreased. In the second period since the first oil crisis,
the number of labor disputes decreased steadily, and labor-management
relations became generally cooperative and harmonious.

These cooperative relations can be seen in a number of ways. Annual
wage increases, for example, are determined in an institutionalized bargaining process called the **spring offensive** (*shunto*) with reasonable
outcomes and without serious work stoppage. Table L.3 compares labor
disputes in Japan, the United States, Germany, and Britain in terms of
workdays lost due to labor disputes. It is clear that Japan and Germany
have very low numbers compared with those of the United States and
Britain. The United States has a labor force nearly twice as large as that of
Japan, but the number of workdays lost in 1995 was 74 times as large.

Table L.3
Workdays lost due to labor disputes (in 1,000 days)

Year	Japan	United States	Germany, FR	Britain
1978	1,353	23,774	4,281	9,405
1980	1,001	20,844	128	11,964
1982	538	9,061	15	5,313
1984	354	8,499	5,618	27,135
1986	253	11,861	28	1,920
1988	174	4,364	42	3,702
1989	220	16,996	100	4,128
1990	145	5,926	364	1,890
1991	96	4,584	154	761
1992	231	3,984	1,545	528
1993	116	3,981	593	649
1994	85	5,022	219	—
1995	77	5,771	—	—

Source: International Labor Organization.

Britain has a labor force that is slightly less than half that of Japan, but its workdays lost in 1993 was 5.6 times that of Japan. In terms of the number of workers involved in labor disputes (not shown in the table), Japan and Germany again have considerably lower numbers, although the number for Germany has fluctuated much more every few years.

The rate of unionization among workers declined in Japan in the 1970s and 1980s due to the decline of traditional industries with heavy unionization and the increased use of nonunionized temporary and part-time workers in the economy. This may have contributed to the low incidences of labor dispute in Japan, but most analysts attribute Japan industrial peace to more fundamental reasons. A widely accepted concept is that of the "company community"—in the sense that the company employees form a community with which they can identify—so employees have an important stake in profit sharing (bonuses), job security, and **decision making** (Abegglen and Stalk 1985; Dore 1987; Ozaki 1991). Or as Shimada (1992) puts it, Japanese management and unions operate within the same "industrial culture." Workers are not treated as hired labor, bought and sold in the corporate labor market, and the company is not the property of the stockholders to be bought or sold as they wish. Thus the Japanese corporate model differs fundamentally from the Western neoclassical model of the firm (Aoki 1988), which originated in nineteenth-century Britain where it is still practiced and taught as well as in the United States. Interestingly Dore (1989), Thurow (1992: 32–39), and others have also pointed out that the German company approximates the community model but not the Anglo-Saxon neoclassical model.

In Japan the sense of corporate community on the part of workers is strengthened by the fact that there are no marked differences between blue-collar and white-collar workers within a company; both belong to the same enterprise union, and income differentials between top executives and the rank and file workers are relatively small (see **income distribution**). Workers are trained by the companies to acquire wide-ranging skills, which further blurs the distinction between blue-collar and white-collar workers. All these constitute what Koike (1988) calls the "white-collarization" of workers. Workers' sense of participation is enhanced by such widespread practices as workers' participation in **quality control** circles for product improvement, joint labor-management consultation system concerning various aspects of work, and complaint settlement system to adjudicate workers' grievances. In all of these practices the Japanese respect for consensus ensures that workers' views are taken seriously.

In the public sector, civil servants at the national and local levels do not have the right to bargain over pay or to strike. The National Personnel Authority and the local personnel commissions make recommendations to the government on pay adjustments for civil servants on the basis of wage conditions in the private sector; the government may revise it, depending on the budget conditions. Employees of **public corporations** and national enterprises have the right to bargain collectively but not to strike. The right to bargain collectively is considered by Shirai (1987) to be meaningless because public corporations and national enterprises are not in a position to negotiate pay increases with unions, since their budgets are controlled by the **Ministry of Finance**. Ultimately therefore it is up to the National Enterprise and Public Labor Relations Commission to mediate between the employees and the management and establish a compulsory arbitration for implementation, subject to legislative approval.

See also **corporate personnel practices, decision making, labor laws, labor unions, quality control, spring offensive.**

References

Abegglen, James C., and George Stalk, Jr. 1985. *Kaisha: The Japanese Corporation*. New York: Basic Books.

Araki, Tadashi. 1994. Flexibility in Japanese employment relations and the role of the judiciary. In *Japanese Commercial Law in an Era of Internationalization*, ed. by Hiroshi Oda. London: Graham and Trotman/Martinus Nijhoff.

Dore, Ronald. 1987. *Taking Japan Seriously*. Stanford: Stanford University Press.

Dore, Ronald. 1989. "Liberalization" not necessarily "Americanization." *Japan Economic Journal*, November 4: 9.

Hazama, Hiroshi. 1997. *The History of Labor Management in Japan*, trans. by Mari Sako and Eri Sako. London: MacMillan Press.

Inagami, Takeshi. 1988. *Japanese Workplace Industrial Relations*. Tokyo: Japan Institute of Labor.

International Labor Organization. Annual. *Yearbook of Labour Statistics*.

Kinzley, W. Dean. 1991. *Industrial Harmony in Modern Japan*. London: Routledge.

Koike, Kazuo. 1988. *Understanding Industrial Relations in Modern Japan*, trans. by Mary Saso. London: Macmillan.

Kuwahara, Yasuo. 1989. *Industrial Relations System in Japan*. Tokyo: Japan Institute of Labor.

Ozaki, Robert. 1991. *Human Capitalism*. New York: Penguin.

Shimada, Haruo. 1992. Japan's industrial culture and labor management relations. In *The Political Economy of Japan*, vol. 3: *Cultural and Social Dynamics*, ed. by Shumpei Kumon and Henry Rosovsky. Stanford: Stanford University Press.

Shirai, Taishiro. 1987. Recent trends in collective bargaining in Japan. In *Collective Bargaining in Industrialized Market Economies: A Reappraisal.* Geneva: International Labor Office.

Sugeno, Kazuo. 1994. The structure of industrial relations in Japan. In *Japanese Commercial Law in an Era of Internationalization,* ed. by Hiroshi Oda. London: Graham and Trotman/ Martinus Nijholl.

Sumiya, Mikio. 1990. *The Japanese Industrial Relations Reconsidered.* Tokyo: Japan Institute of Labor.

Thurow, Lester. 1992. *Head to Head.* New York: William Morrow.

labor unions   There were 31,601 labor unions (or 70,699 basic union units) in Japan in 1996, of which about 95% were enterprise unions, 2% crafts unions, and 1.6% industrial unions. An enterprise union is organized on the basis of an enterprise or workplace rather than a trade or an industry. It includes all regular employees in the enterprise, both blue- and white-collar workers, as its members. Thus line managers, supervisors, and junior management personnel are included. Gould (1984: 5) contends that this has affected the style and attitude of unions in Japan by "inhibiting militance, providing expertise, and creating more contact and perhaps some egalitarianism between blue-collar and white-collar employees." Temporary workers and subcontract workers, however, are not included.

Japanese unions play an active role in matters of direct concern to workers such as wage increases, employee benefits, and working conditions. In addition enterprise unionism is said to have various advantages over trade unionism, which is typical in the West. One advantage is that there are no jurisdictional disputes concerning union jobs in enterprise unions. This permits flexibility in in-company training and job assignment and is conducive to greater labor productivity. Under enterprise unions, **labor-management relations** have been remarkably cooperative except for the early postwar period. Labor disputes and union strikes have been more serious in the public sector.

Enterprise unions are usually members of a union federation that covers one or more industries. Until late 1987 labor unions were led by four major federations: Sohyo (the General Council of Trade Unions of Japan), the largest, which included government employees; Rengo, the association of private-sector unions; Domei (the Japanese Confederation of Labor), a right-wing splinter of Sohyo, and Churitsu Roren (the Federation of Independent Unions). In November 1987 a new labor federation, the Japan Trade Union Confederation (JTUC-Rengo), or the new Rengo, was founded by the private sector unions. It became the largest federation in Japan with 5.55 million members drawn from a number of other federations, and Domei and Churitsu Roren voluntarily disbanded. In 1989 Sohyo dissolved itself and merged with the new Rengo, boosting membership in the latter to over 8 million workers, or 65% of Japan's organized labor. For the first time in Japan, both public and private sector unions are under the same national leadership.

Neither the union federations before 1987 nor the new Rengo since 1987 took part in collective bargaining with employers. It is the enterprise unions themselves that negotiate with the management of their firms in the annual **spring offensive**. Rengo, however, serves as the voice for unions in general and publicizes unions' general demands concerning wages and other working conditions. It also represents labor's interests vis-à-vis government ministries and business organizations.

Union membership has increased only very slowly since the 1960s, from 10.1 million in 1965 to 12.6 million in 1975. Since then it has declined slightly to 12.5 million in 1996. As a percentage of the labor force, the unionization rate declined from 35.4% in 1970 to slightly less than 30% in 1983 and 23.2% in 1996 (see table L.4).

The major reason for the declining unionization rate is the sectoral shift of employment in the economy—from the more highly unionized manufacturing, transportation, and communication to the lowly unionized wholesale and retail trade and services. In particular, the decline in em-

Table L.4
Union membership and unionization rate

Year	Membership (in millions)	Unionization rate (in %)
1965	10.1	34.8
1970	11.6	35.4
1975	12.6	33.7
1980	12.4	30.8
1985	12.4	28.9
1988	12.2	26.8
1989	12.2	25.9
1990	12.3	25.2
1991	12.4	24.5
1992	12.5	24.4
1993	12.7	24.2
1994	12.7	24.1
1995	12.6	23.8
1996	12.5	23.2

Source: Ministry of Labor.

ployment in steel, shipbuilding, and electrical machinery industries has eroded the traditional center of union strength. Retail and service businesses tend to be small establishments that are difficult to organize, and they employ many part-time and temporary workers who do not see benefits in union membership.

The erosion of union strength, however, is evident in virtually all sectors of the economy. As shown in table L.5, with the exception of construction, the unionization rate has declined in all other sectors between 1980 and 1996. The decline was particularly large in the service sector, from 21.0% to 12.3%, as employment in the sector expanded rapidly in the 1980s to reach 25.2% of total employment in the economy in 1996. It is interesting to note that public service has become the most highly unionized sector of the economy just as **privatization** of some public companies took place in the 1980s.

In addition to the sectoral shift in employment, other factors have contributed to the decline of the unions. The slower growth of the economy in the 1970s and early 1980s and the yen appreciation after the mid-1980s have forced companies to eliminate excess workers, resist large wage increases and unionism, and move labor-intensive production to cheap-labor countries. These changes have reduced the unions' wage bargaining power for the workers and hence the benefits of union membership. The increase in the **labor force** of part-time workers who are not unionized also contributes to the lower unionization rate.

In response to these socioeconomic changes, union federations were consolidated into the new Rengo in 1987, as mentioned above. The JTUC-Rengo has announced a goal of restoring the union membership

Table L.5
Unionization rate by industry (in %)

Industry	1980	1996
Agriculture, forestry, fishery, and mining	30.3	8.0
Construction	16.5	19.7
Manufacturing	35.3	28.4
Electricity, gas, heat supply, and water	80.1	55.3
Transportation and communication	62.3	41.7
Wholesale and retail trade, eating and drinking places	9.4	8.7
Finance, insurance, real estate	56.1	44.6
Services	21.0	12.3
Public service	74.6	69.1

Source: Japan Institute of Labor.

rate to 30% of the labor force. In addition to improving wages and working conditions, it has included improvements in work rules and in the quality of life—such as **working hours**, child care, **housing** conditions, and **social security**—as its goals.

Although there is a growing number of **foreign workers in Japan**, they are rarely in the unions. Legal foreign workers are mostly specialists who do not see the need for union membership. Illegal foreign workers are not willing to be organized for fear of exposure.

In the literature on the union movement in Japan, enterprise unionism is generally credited with having contributed to postwar corporate growth and the improvement of the working conditions and living standards of company employees. Kawanishi (1992) surveys various Japanese authors' theories of enterprise unions and raises some questions about the validity of the theories by presenting his own case studies.

See also **labor-management relations, labor laws, spring offensive.**

Address

Japan Trade Union Confederation
3-2-11, Kanda-Surugadai, Chiyo da-ku, Tokyo 101
Tel: (3) 5295-0526

References

Freeman, R. B. and M. E. Rebick. 1989. Crumbling pillar? Declining union density in Japan. *Journal of Japanese and International Economics* 3: 578–605.

Gould, William B. 1984. *Japan's Reshaping of American Labor Law.* Cambridge: MIT Press.

Japan Trade Union Confederation. 1998. *The Spring Struggle for a Better Living; Rengo White Paper, 1998.* Tokyo: JTUC-Rengo.

Kawanishi, Hirosuke. 1992. *Enterprise Unionism in Japan,* trans. by Ross E. Mouer. London: Kegan Paul International.

Koike, Kazuo. 1987. Human resource development. In *The Political Economy of Japan,* vol. 1: *The Domestic Transformation,* ed. by Kozo Yamamura and Yasukichi Yasuba. Stanford: Stanford University Press.

Koike, Kazuo. 1988. *Understanding Industrial Relations in Modern Japan.* London: Macmillan. Ch. 7.

Ministry of Labor. Annual. *Basic Survey on Labor Unions.*

Mochizuki, Mike. 1993. Public sector labor and the privatization challenge: The railway and telecommunications unions. In *Political Dynamics in Contemporary Japan,* ed. by Gary D. Allinson and Yasunori Sone. Ithaca: Cornell University Press.

Shirai, Taishiro. 1984. A theory of enterprise union. In *Industrial Relations in Japan*, ed. by Tashiro Shirai. Madison: University of Wisconsin Press.

Sumiya, Mikio. 1990. *The Japanese Industrial Relations Reconsidered*. Tokyo: Japan Institute of Labor.

Tsujinaka, Yutaka. 1993. Rengo and its osmotic networks. In *Political Dynamics in Contemporary Japan*, ed. by Gary D. Allinson and Yasunaori Sone. Ithaca: Cornell University Press.

land uses and policies   Of Japan's total land area (377,829 square kilometers), 66.6% consists of woodlands, 13.4% is used as agricultural land, 4.5% is occupied by residential and industrial buildings, 3.5% is taken up by rivers and 3% by roads. The amount of land is so small—smaller than California—relative to its **population** that Japan has one of the highest population densities in the world. In 1996 Japan had 333 persons per square kilometer compared with 28 persons per square kilometer in the United States and 306 in India. Furthermore the population is heavily concentrated in the major metropolitan areas. Agricultural land is fragmented into small farms.

In Japan as in any other country, land uses are determined by geo-environmental factors, the stage of economic development, and government policies on land use. However, because of the severe shortage of land in Japan, government planning and control are particularly important. The National Land Agency under the Prime Minister's Office heads the nation's land planning and control. It works with prefectural and municipal government agencies to develop guidelines and programs for land use. All major land uses—residential, commercial, industrial, forest, recreational, and agricultural—are subject to national, prefectural, municipal, and neighborhood plans and controls. The instruments used in land policy implementation are land price approval and publication, building codes, zoning ordinances, building permits, designation of urban promotion and urban control areas, expropriation, preemptive rights, and environmental controls. Because of the wide ramifications of land use, policy coordination between the National Land Agency and other ministries and agencies —such as the Ministry of Agriculture, Forestry, and Fisheries, the Ministry of Construction, the Ministry of Transport, and the National Tax Administration Agency—are needed to effectively implement land use policies.

Agricultural land use and urban housing land supply have been two major policy concerns. In the immediate postwar period, a land reform was carried out in 1945–49 (in accordance with Owners-Farmer Establishment Law of 1946) as part of the Occupation's attempt to democratize and decentralize the economy. It limited landlord's holding to one *cho* or

2.45 acres (10 acres in Hokkaido); the excess was sold to the government. Tenant farmers acquired land from the government. As a result the proportion of total agricultural land area worked by tenant farmers was reduced from 46% in November 1946 to 10% in August 1950. In 1952 the Agricultural Land Act was enacted. It severely restricted land transfers, tenure, tenant rents, and so forth, in an attempt to prevent reconcentration of land and to protect the welfare of tenants.

The postwar land reform was successful in promoting widespread ownership of farmland. In addition subsequent inflation reduced the value of land compensation to the landlords and the cost of land to the farmers. On the other hand, farmland became fragmented, and many farms are too small to be efficient. The average farm—about 1.65 acres—became smaller than the prewar average. The policy of banning joint-stock companies from owning farmland and allowing **agricultural cooperatives** to own farmland only if they do actual farming also prevented the consolidation of land into large farms. Starting in 1970–75, the government adopted a new policy of promoting farmland consolidation in order to raise agricultural productivity. Restrictions on land transfers were relaxed; small farmers were encouraged to sell their land to farmers with higher productivity. Since 1995, after Japan agreed to lift the ban on rice import as part of the 1993 Uruguay Round agreement, subsidized loans are made available to eligible buyers to buy and consolidate farmland. Where the small owners are not willing to sell, the consignment of farm work to more efficient farmers is encouraged. Progress in farm consolidation to date is said to be slow (author's interview, Ministry of Agriculture, Forestry and Fisheries, March 26, 1998; see **agricultural policy**).

Because of the limited supply of urban land and the growing demand for land for **housing** and commercial uses, land prices in Japan's large cities have become very high by world standards. Several factors on the supply and demand sides are involved. On the supply side, one factor that has contributed to the shortage of land for urban housing and buildings is the government's rice policy. The high prices of rice due to government subsidies and the ban on the import of cheaper foreign rice prior to 1993 have given farmers the incentives to remain in farming, with many small plots of farms in metropolitan areas cultivated by part-time or "weekend" farmers, who derive the bulk of their incomes from nonfarm activities. Another supply-side factor is that because of low fixed property taxes, high transactions taxes, and a law that makes it extremely difficult for owners of buildings to evict tenants, landowners have little incentives to sell or redevelop their land. In addition, prior to 1992, farmland was subject to lower rate of taxation than nonfarmland, giving farmers in urban areas no incentive to convert their land to other uses.

On the demand side, steady economic growth in Japan and the continuing concentration of business activities in the large cities have led to a growing demand for urban land. There was also the speculative demand for land based on the popular belief that land prices in Japan can only go up, and hence landholding is a good investment. In the late 1980s the booming **stock market** and easy credit from financial institutions to developers and real estate firms helped to fuel a speculative investment boom in urban land and property. As a result residential land prices rose 2.5 times in **Tokyo** and 3 times in **Osaka** between 1983 and 1991, far greater than the rate of wage increases, making a house beyond the reach of the average salaried employee. This has led to a growing realization that changes in land use policies are needed to relieve the shortage of urban land for housing.

Other consequences of the high price of land are:

1. It increases the inequality of income distribution. In the late 1980s many of the top income earners were people who sold their land for profit.

2. Even landowners who did not sell their land for profit could borrow more money using their inflated land as collateral. In the early 1990s as urban land prices declined, much land-based loans could not be recovered. This led to the huge losses of the Japanese banks and other financial institutions, especially the **housing loan companies** (*jusen*) whose losses have touched off a financial crisis.

3. It made public works very costly where land has to be acquired. Other public facilities such as urban pedestrian roads, parks and playgrounds are similarly discouraged (Tsuru, 1993: 169–71).

The government has adopted some measures since 1990 to alleviate urban land problems. In April 1990 the **Ministry of Finance** imposed temporary restrictions on real estate lendings by **nonbank financial institutions**. In January 1991 the government urged local governments to use their authority to convert most farmland in city areas to sites for housing and public facilities. The National Tax Administration Agency sharply raised the assessed values of real estate for inheritance and gift taxes to prevent speculation and thus slow the rise in real estate prices. Finally, after much debate, a new landholding tax was introduced in January 1992 to make landholding less lucrative. However, because of opposition from businesses, the tax rate was only 0.2% in 1992 and 0.3% from 1993 onward of the official assessed value for calculating inheritance tax, which is only about 50–60% of the actual market value. In addition the basic deduction from the landholding tax is high: ¥1 billion or ¥30,000 times the square meter area of each plot, whichever is higher. Consequently analysts doubt that the new tax itself will be effective in inducing changes in land uses. They suggest that additional measures such as a new land use plan and the revision of the Land Lease and Rental House Law should be adopted to stabilize land prices and ensure the supply of land for housing. In the 1990s in the wake of the bursting of the economic bubble, land prices declined continually. While this has made **housing** more affordable, it has also increased the bad debts from land-based loans made by banks and other financial institutions during the late 1980s. In order to stabilize land prices, in FY 1996 the landholding tax was reduced from 0.3% to 0.15% of the assessed value.

A serious aspect of land use problems in Japan stems from the excess concentration of businesses and government offices in Tokyo. Unless this is changed, the demand for land in Tokyo will remain at a high level. Some steps have been taken to encourage the dispersion of corporate and government offices to other areas. More thorough measures, however, have to await the government's decision on whether the nation's capital will be moved from Tokyo, as recommended by a special government council.

In the 1980s land trusts were popular with urban landowners as a means of having their land developed and receiving income from it. Under the system a landowner would entrust his land to a **trust bank**, which would raise funds, build a commercial building, manage or sell the building (not including the land), and pay the trust owner earnings from the operation. After the contract expires (usually after 20 years), the owner would get the property back. However, the popularity of land trusts has declined because of the subsequent bursting in 1990–91 of the speculative stock market and the real estate market, the twin pillars of the **bubble economy** of the late 1980s.

See also **housing, rice production and distribution**.

Address

National Land Agency
2-2, Kasumigaseki 1-chome, Chiyoda-ku, Tokyo 100
Tel: (3) 3593-3311

References

Dore, R. P. 1959. *Land Reform in Japan*. London: Oxford University Press.

Economic Planning Agency. Annual. *Economic White Paper*.

Haley, John O., and Kozo Yamamura, ed. 1992. *Land Issues in Japan: A Policy Failure?* Seattle: Society for Japanese Studies.

Hasegawa, Tokunosuke. 1994. Land acquisiiton and property tax. In *Japanese Commercial Law in an Era of Internationalization*, ed. by Hiroshi Oda. London: Graham and Trotman/Martinus Nijhoff.

Ito, Takatoshi. 1993. The land/housing problem in Japan: A macroeconomic approach. *Journal of the Japanese and International Economies* 7, 1: 1–31.

National Land Agency. Annual. *White Paper on Land* (in Japanese).

National Land Agency. 1997. *Land and Property in Japan*.

Saito, Tadashi. 1991. Government unveil land reform package. *JEI Report* 5B, February 8: 5–6.

Stone, Douglas, and William T. Ziemba. 1993. Land and stock prices in Japan. *Journal of Economic Perspectives* 7, 3: 149–65.

Takagi, Keizo. 1989. The rise of land prices in Japan: The determination mechanism and the effect of taxation system. *Bank of Japan Monetary and Economic Studies* 7, 2: 83–139.

Takagi, Shintaro. 1991. Are land and house prices too high in Japan? *Japanese Economic Studies* 20, 1: 57–86.

Tsuru, Shigeto. 1993. *Japan's Capitalism: Creative Defeat and Beyond*. Cambridge: Cambridge University Press. Ch. 6.

Large Retail Store Law, 1974   Also translated as Large-Scale Retail Store Law (Daitenho), this law superseded the Department Store Law of 1956 to protect the small retailers by regulating the growth of large-scale stores, including department stores and chain supermarkets. It stipulates that the establishment of stores with store area of 3,000 square meters or more in the ten biggest cities and of 1,500 square meters or more in the rest of the country is to be supervised by the **Ministry of International Trade and Industry** (MITI). After consultations with local retailers and city officials, MITI could order the reduction of the planned floor space, postponement of the opening, earlier closing hours, or more days on which the store has to remain closed, if these are thought to be necessary to mitigate the effect of the store on the resident small shops.

As originally intended, any big store could open and any necessary adjustments made within a year or two after the application has been filed. In practice, however, it has taken seven to as long as ten years from the initial planning for a large store to open.

When **department stores** and supermarket chains began to open stores all over the country with a selling area below 1,500 square meters, local governments demanded regulations on medium-sized stores. Consequently in 1979 MITI extended the law to stores with a shopping area of 500 square meters. In 1982 MITI issued new guidelines governing the size of stores that could be opened in cities of various population and increased the role of localities in the opening of big retail operations. MITI also used **administrative guidance** to slow the spread of supermarket chains. Thus the establishment and expansion of supermarket chains were made more difficult, reflecting the political power of the smaller retailers and the government policy that favors them.

In the late 1980s the law was increasingly under attack. Some domestic business groups argue that it should be abolished. U.S. trade officials regard it as limiting American access to the Japanese **distribution system** and foreign imports into Japan (since large stores are more likely to carry imports) and would like to see it repealed. Japanese defenders of the law admit that small retail stores are inefficient but argue that they promote full employment and that their presence is important for elderly consumers who live in downtown areas and cannot drive to suburban areas where large retailers are usually located.

Members of the ruling **Liberal Democratic Party**, however, have been reluctant to abolish the law for fear of losing the political support of small retailers. In June 1989 a MITI advisory panel recommended that the law be applied more flexibly to implement its original intent. In 1990, as part of the basic agreement between Japan and the United States on the removal of "structural impediments" to trade, Tokyo agreed to revise the law in stages so that the power of small shopowners to block the construction of large stores in their districts could be curtailed. Starting in May 1990, the implementation of the law was relaxed. On January 31, 1992, revisions went into effect that would shorten the time needed for final government approval for a large store to a maximum of one year.

A large American toy retailer, Toys "R" Us, succeeded in opening its store in Japan in 1991. By 1998 it has opened 64 stores. Other large American stores such as The Gap, Foot Locker Inc., Nike Inc., OfficeMax Inc., Office Depot Inc., Pier 1 Imports, Inc., The Sports Authority, Inc., Tower Records, and Warner Bros. Studio Stores, Inc. have also opened their stores in recent years.

In late 1997 two MITI advisory councils reviewed the Law and recommended its repeal; it suggested that a new law be enacted to give local governments the right to approve the opening of large retail stores. Surprisingly MITI accepted the recommendations.

A new law, tentatively named Large Retail Store Location Law, will be enacted to provide guidelines to local authorities. It is expected to go into effect in the spring of the year 2000. At that time the Large Retail Store Law will be repealed. There is some fear in Washington that local bureaucrats may be more susceptible to pressure from small and midsize stores to restrict the establishment of large stores. Hence Washington has asked Tokyo to take measures to ensure that this will not happen (MacKnight 1998: 8).

See also **department stores, distribution system**.

References

Ito, Takatoshi. 1992. *The Japanese Economy*. Cambridge: MIT Press. Ch. 13.

Ito, Takatoshi, and Masayoshi Maruyama. 1991. Is the Japanese distribution system really inefficient? In *Trade with Japan*, ed. by Paul Krugman. Chicago: University of Chicago Press.

MacKnight, Susan. 1998. Japan to Replace Large Retail Store Law. *JEI Report* 11B, March 20: 7–8.

Sekiguchi, Waichi. 1990. Big-store law revision means small change for imports. *Japan Economic Journal*, April 14: 1, 5.

Smith, Charles. 1991. Reforms in store. *Far Eastern Economic Review*, January 17: 44–48.

Takahashi, Hideo. 1989. Structural changes in Japan's distribution system. *JEI Report*, November 10: 7–10.

Upham, Frank. 1993. Privatizing regulation: The implementation of the large-scale retail stores law. In *Political Dynamics in Contemporary Japan*, ed. by Gary D. Allinson and Yasunari Sone. Ithaca: Cornell University Press.

latent capital   Unrealized capital gains, namely the difference between book value and market value of a stock portfolio and property.

See **cross-shareholding**.

leading indicators   Some 15 business indicators selected by the **Economic Planning Agency** that are sensitive to, and tend to lead, changes in overall business conditions. They are useful for short-term forecasting purpose.

See **business-cycle indicators and forecasting**.

Liberal Democratic Party (LDP)   The dominant political party in Japan since its founding in 1955. It consists of several factions, led by senior politicians, contending for power. The leader of the dominant faction typically becomes the Prime Minister.

In close collaboration with Japan's bureaucrats, the LDP has implemented policies that have won the support of the middle class, businessmen, and farmers. Its economic policy is pro-business, particularly big business, which has traditionally supported it with political contributions. Its **agricultural policy** protected domestic farmers and banned rice imports until 1993, and its **trade policy** has promoted exports and restricted imports, thus creating frictions with the West. Its politicians have also used public works spending to favor their constituents.

Since 1988–89 LDP has been weakened by corruption scandals and unpopular measures such as the introduction of the new **consumption tax** in 1989. It lost majority control in the upper house of the parliament in 1989 and its majority in the lower house for the first time in 1993. In June 1994 it was forced to form a coalition with the Social Democratic Party of Japan (formerly the Socialist Party) and the New Sakigake Party. The Social Democratic leader, Tomiichi Murayama, became the Prime Minister. In January 1996 a new LDP president, Ryutaro Hashimoto, succeeded him to be the prime minister.

Coming into office in the midst of a prolonged stagnation of the economy and an unprecedented weakening of its financial system, Hashimoto has initiated a large comprehensive financial reform, dubbed the **Big Bang**, aimed at deregulating the financial system, and an **administrative reform** aimed at making the bureaucracy leaner and more efficient.

See also **administrative reform, agricultural policy, Big Bang, industrial policy, trade policy**.

lifetime employment   This refers to the commitment by both employers and employees to maintain the employment relationship throughout an employee's career. This practice was developed by large companies during the early postwar period to attract and retain scarce skilled labor, although the practice also existed in the 1910s and 1920s on a smaller scale. Currently it still prevails in many large corporations. Fresh college graduates are hired by large firms with the understanding that they will stay with the same company for the rest of their careers. For their part, the companies train the new employees and reward their loyalty with seniority-based salary increases and advancements. Employees therefore have the incentives to stay with the same company. Midcareer job changes were shunned as signs of disloyalty. However, smaller companies have not adopted the system.

There are various ways to avoid the high cost of being saddled with incompetent and highly paid senior employees. (1) An early mandatory retirement age of 55 to 60 is adopted, after which the retired employee may work at a subsidiary of the company at a reduced pay. (2) A large company may hire temporary workers for tasks that are not expected to last long. These workers are paid less than regular workers and do not enjoy job security, although they may be rehired year after year. (3) The company may rely on subcontractors for many tasks. The subcontracted work can be curtailed as needed. (4) The company may send some workers to subcontractors, distributors, or other affiliated firms for temporary employment if the latter need temporary workers. The temporary employer pays the wages, but the sending firm may pay a subsidy as well as fringe benefits such as insurance (Odagiri 1992: 57).

When permanent employees become old and redundant because they cannot adjust with new technology or because they can no longer take on real responsibilities, they are often given a job of no real importance. They then become members of the so-called *madogiwazoku*, literally the window-side tribe, people who are given a desk at the periphery of the office by the window. This is a signal for retirement before the mandatory retirement age.

Since the early 1980s the slower growth and restructuring of the economy have put strains on the system. The strong yen has forced companies to cut costs, including hiring part-time workers, resisting large wage increases, and moving labor-intensive production abroad. As a result lifetime employment is no longer as highly valued. In some cases companies are willing to assist employees in job changes, although they may be reluctant to fire them. Midcareer job changes are becoming more common as opportunities for advancement in the same company are becoming scarce or as new job openings at other companies become available. In 1996 a government survey showed that there were 7.4 million workers or 11.7% of all employed workers who wanted to change jobs, and that 2.4 million of them were actively seeking a new job. People's attitude toward the employment system itself has also changed. A 1995 government survey also showed that the number of respondents who regarded the lifetime employment system as "good" for both employers and employees had declined from a similar survey of eight years before, while the number of respondents who regarded it as "not good" had increased (Iwase 1997: 22–23).

See also **corporate personnel practices**.

References

Hasegawa, Mina. 1992. Slump strains lifetime employment. *Nikkei Weekly*, October 3: 1.

Inoue, Tatsuya. 1997. Recruiting changes shake up job market. *Nikkei Weekly*, August 25: 8.

Iwase, Takashi. 1997. Changing Japanese labor and employment system. *Journal of Japanese Trade and Industry*, no. 4: 22–24.

Kojima, Noriaki. 1997. Japanese employment and labor laws in transition. *Journal of Japanese Trade and Industry*, no. 4: 8–11.

Naruse, Takeo. 1997. Toward a new Japanese-style employment system. *Journal of Japanese Trade and Industry*, no. 4: 16–19.

Nishimura, Hiroyuki. 1993. System of lifetime jobs resisting change. *Nikkei Weekly*, February 1: 1.

Odagiri, Hiroyuki. 1992. *Growth through Competition, Competition through Growth*. Oxford: Clarendon Press. Ch. 3.

Oshima, Izumi. 1998. Career-hopping gaining popularity. *Nikkei Weekly*, April 6: 17.

list price system   The government-guided pricing system in the steel industry during 1958–91. Also called the "open sales system."
   See **steel industry**.

livelihood protection   Public assistance given to the indigent for medical care and living expenses.
   See **health insurance, social security system**.

local taxes   Taxes levied by the 47 prefectural governments and more than 3,000 municipal governments, including inhabitant tax, business tax, and property tax.
   See **tax system**.

long-term credit banks   Japan has three long-term credit banks, which were founded in accordance with the Long-Term Credit Bank Law of 1952 to specialize in extending long-term loans. They are the Industrial Bank of Japan, the Long-Term Credit Bank of Japan, and the Nippon Credit Bank.
   Before World War II long-term financing was provided by the semi-governmental "special banks." After the war the Occupation authority abolished the special banks in favor of the capital market for providing long-term funds. Because the capital market was too inadequate at that

time, the Long-Term Credit Bank Law was passed in 1952 to establish the system of long-term credit banks.

These banks have played an important role in Japan's postwar banking system and industrial growth by supplying long-term credit to industries, thereby relieving the ordinary banks of the pressure for long-term financing. This was particularly important during Japan's high-growth period before the early 1970s. As a means of raising funds for long-term lending, they are authorized to issue five-year interest-bearing debentures as well as one-year discount debentures up to 30 times their combined total of capital and reserves. However, they are restricted in deposit taking; they can only accept deposits from their borrowers. They also have fewer branches than ordinary banks.

With the slower growth of the economy after the first oil crisis in 1973, the growing trade surplus since the late 1970s, and the maturing and liberalization of the capital and money markets in Japan in the 1980s, the financial needs of the economy have changed as well. The long-term credit banks have responded to the changes by lending actively to wholesale and service trades, private housing finance companies, and consumer credit companies. They have also been active in lending to foreign operations of Japanese corporations as well as to foreign governments and corporations.

The Industrial Bank of Japan, the largest of the three long-term credit banks, was originally founded in 1902 as a "special bank," a quasi-public bank under government control to finance industrial development. During World War II it aided the war effort by providing loans to the military and the war industry. The Long-Term Credit Bank Act of 1952 eliminated the government's shares in the Bank. Since then it has played an important role in Japan's rapid industrial growth by providing long-term loans. The Long-Term Credit Bank of Japan and the Nippon Credit Bank were established in 1952 and 1957, respectively.

The three long-term credit banks collectively had ¥45.2 trillion loans outstanding at the end of 1997. Nearly half of the total was lent to **small and medium enterprises**. Like all other Japanese banks, the long-term credit banks incurred large bad debts because a large amount of loans made in the late 1980s could not be recovered as land and stocks used as collateral declined greatly in value in the 1990s. In FY 1997 some of the bad loans were written off against the banks' core business profit, resulting in large pretax loss for the Industrial Bank of Japan and Long-term Credit Bank of Japan (see table L.6). The Nippon Credit Bank had positive

Table L.6
Long-term credit banks (in ¥ billions, FY 1997)

Bank	Core-business profit	Pretax profit/loss
Industrial Bank of Japan	231	−357.7
Long-Term Credit Bank of Japan	164	−320.0
Nippon Credit Bank	130	16.3

Sources: *Nikkei Weekly* (June 1, 1998: 12).

pretax profit because it disposed of a smaller amount of bad loans in FY 1997. In order to restore its financial health, it started restructuring in 1997, including forming an alliance with Bankers Trust Corp. of the United States.

The Long-Term Credit Bank of Japan could not avoid insolvency due to its bad debts and the decline in the value of its stockholdings. In October 1998 it requested temporary government takeover. The request was immediately granted and the state's control is expected to last about one year until a receiver bank can be selected to take over its operations.

See also **banking system, city banks**.

Addresses

Industrial Bank of Japan
3-3, Marunouchi 1-chome, Chiyoda-ku, Tokyo
Tel: (3) 3214-1111   Fax: (3) 3214-0377

Long-Term Credit Bank of Japan
2-1-8, Uchi-Saiwaicho, Chiyoda-ku, Tokyo
Tel: (3) 5511-5111   Fax: (3) 5511-5505

Nippon Credit Bank
13-10, Kudan-kita 1-chome, Chiyoda-ku, Tokyo
Tel: (3) 3263-1111   Fax: (3) 3239-8065

References

Calder, Kent E. 1993. *Strategic Capitalism: Private Business and Public Purpose in Japanese Industrial Finance*. Princeton: Princeton University Press. Pp 158–73.

Federation of Bankers Association of Japan. 1994. *Banking System in Japan*. Tokyo: Zenginkyo. Ch. 1.

Hamada, Koichi, and Akiyoshi Horiuchi. 1987. The political economy of the financial market. In *The Political Economy of Japan*, vol. 1: *The Domestic Transformation*, ed. by Kozo Yamamura and Yasukichi Yasuba. Stanford: Stanford University Press.

Ishibashi, Asako. 1998. Top banks set record for loan disposal. *Nikkei Weekly*, April 6: 12.

Ishizawa, Masato. 1998. Nippon Credit draws rosy view but also doubts. *Nikkei Weekly*, June 1: 12.

Suzuki, Yoshio, ed. 1987. *The Japanese Financial System*. Oxford: Oxford University Press. Ch. 5.

Tatewaki, Kazuo. 1991. *Banking and Finance in Japan*. London: Routledge. Ch. 7.

long-term prime rates   The lending rates charged by **long-term credit banks** and **trust banks** on long-term loans to credit-worthy corporations. See **interest rate structure**.

M

madoguchi shido Window guidance given by the **Bank of Japan** to commercial banks concerning the amounts of their loans and the direction of their operations. It was abolished in mid-1991.
See **Bank of Japan.**

main bank The bank that provides the largest share of lending to a company is commonly (but not legally) called that company's main bank. Most Japanese companies, large and small, have a main bank because they typically rely on banks as a major source of external funds. This was particularly true in the high-growth period of the 1950s and the 1960s when the capital market was not well developed. The main bank to large companies is usually one of the **city banks** or the Industrial Bank of Japan.

The relationship between a company and its main bank is an important long-term business relationship. This relationship is cemented by institutional arrangements such as **cross-shareholding** between the bank and the firm; managers of the main bank often sit on the firm's board as directors or auditors. Managers of the client firms may come from the main bank. The business activities conducted on the basis of this relationship are described as "relationship banking."

The system provides a stable business environment that benefits both sides. The benefits to the firms include the following:

1. The main bank is a secure source of funds, even when credit is tight. The interest rate it charges is more stable than the interest rates in general.

2. The main bank is usually a top shareholder of the firm. Although its holding of a firm's shares is legally limited to 5%, it can mobilize the voting power of other related companies to protect a client firm from hostile takeover. This is particularly true when both the main bank and its client firm are members of a *keiretsu* or corporate group, with many group-affiliated companies.

3. Most important, when a firm experiences a financial distress, its main bank can come to its rescue in various ways. It may renegotiate debt claims, supply new capital, or arrange asset sales. It may take responsibility in the firm's restructuring or **merger and acquisition.** It may dispatch executives to the firm to assume senior managerial positions, and it may even remove the firm's top management (Sheard 1994b).

In exchange for assuming these special responsibilities, the main bank is given preferred access to the client firm's banking-related business such as corporate bank deposits, bond issues, foreign exchange transactions, and the banking businesses of client's business partners such as suppliers and dealers.

In addition the main bank is given access to the information of the client firm. This enables it to perform an effective monitoring role. Some of the information gathered can be passed on to other lenders, thereby minimizing the information cost of their lending. More broadly, the fact that a bank chooses to remain the main bank of a firm is in itself a testimony to the credit worthiness of the firm for the financial community. To Patrick (1994: 359), "strong information collecting, related monitoring capabilities, and management consulting" are the essence of the main bank system.

Since the 1980s, **financial liberalization** has made bank loans less important as a source of funds to large companies. Many companies have relied more on equity capital and equity-related bonds (warrant and convertible bonds). Campbell and Hamao (1994) show, however, that firms with one of the 19 large banks as their main bank did not reduce their reliance on bank debt during 1983–91 as much as other firms that do not have such affiliation. In addition, even in issuing bonds, companies with a main bank tend to issue more bonds with bank guarantees than those without a main bank. This shows that while main bank's traditional role of providing loans may have declined, that of fee-generating services has increased.

During the speculative **bubble economy** of the late 1980s, **city banks** lent large sums to real estate development companies, **nonbank financial institutions,** and other companies and individuals with land and stocks as collateral. The huge bad debts that emerged after the bursting of the bubble in the early 1990s indicates the weakened monitoring capacity of main banks in the new market environment (Aoki, Patrick, and Sheard 1994: 48). Thus the main bank system may be evolving, although it will remain important in the foreseeable future.

See also **city banks, corporate finance.**

References

Aoki, Masahiko, Hugh Patrick, and Paul Sheard. 1994. The Japanese main bank system: An introductory overview. An *The Japanese Main Bank System*, ed. by Masahiko Aoki and Hugh Patrick. New York: Oxford University Press.

Campbell, John T., and Yasushi Hamo. 1994. Changing patterns of corporate financing and the main bank system in Japan. In *The Japanese Main Bank System*, ed. by Masahiko Aoki and Hugh Patrick. New York: Oxford University Press.

Fukuda, Atsuo, and Shin'ichi Hirota. 1996. Main bank relationship and capital structure in Japan. *Journal of Japanese and International Economies* 10, 3: 250–261.

Kitagawa, Hiroshi, and Yoshitaka Kurosawa. 1994. Japan: Development and structural change of the banking system. In *The Financial Development of Japan, Korea, and Taiwan*, ed. by Hugh Patrick and Yung Chul Park. New York: Oxford University Press.

Patrick, Hugh. 1994. The relevance of Japanese finance and its main bank system. In *The Japanese Main Bank System*, ed. by Masahiko Aoki and Hugh Patrick. New York: Oxford University Press.

Sheard, Paul. 1989. The main bank system and corporate monitoring and control in Japan. *Journal of Economic Behavior and Organization* 3: 399–422.

Sheard, Paul. 1994a. Interlocking shareholdings and corporate governance. In *The Japanese Firm: Sources of Competitive Strength*, ed. by Masahiko Aoki and Ronald Dore. Oxford: Oxford University Press.

Sheard, Paul. 1994b. Main banks and the governance of financial distress. In *The Japanese Main Bank System*, ed. by Masahiko Aoki and Hugh Patrick. New York: Oxford University Press.

Sheard, Paul. 1994c. Delegated monitoring among delegated monitors: principal-agent aspects of the Japanese main bank system. *Journal of the Japanese and International Economies* 8: 1–21.

Management and Coordination Agency   (*Somu-cho*) A large government agency under the prime minister's office in charge of the central management and coordination of the national government. It is responsible for the following areas: (1) personnel management, (2) government administrative management, (3) administrative inspection, (4) traffic safety and youth affairs, (5) pension programs, and (6) government statistics.
See also **economic/business research and publications.**

management practices   The term "Japanese-style management" (*nihonteki keiei*) was used by many Japanese and Western authors, particularly before the 1990s, to refer to a host of "traditional" management practices outlined below that have been common until recently in large corporations in postwar Japan. Since the early 1990s the Japanese economy has been in a state of flux, and many changes have been introduced in the midst of tradition. "Continuity and change" best characterize Japanese management practices of the 1990s.

1. Market share or corporate growth, rather than short-term profits or share prices, was considered to be the dominant corporate goal. This is consistent with the Japanese management emphasis on long-term performance rather than short-term profits. As a result the Japanese company pursues high corporate **investment** rather than high dividend distribution. This does not mean that profits are not important. However, some analysts argue that profits are important to Japanese firms mainly because they are a means to investment and not because they are the primary corporate goal itself. Since the early 1990s, however, as the growth of the economy slowed down and as many companies experienced declining profits, an increasing number of Japanese companies and managers are emphasizing the primacy of profits.

2. **Corporate governance** is shared among management, employees and institutional shareholders. Kester (1991:79) characterizes Japanese managers as "agents of the entire coalition of stakeholders rather than of the shareholders or any other single group." Stakeholders include workers, management, and shareholders, among which are banks and other companies who are the "stable shareholders" in **cross-shareholding** relationships as well as individual shareholders. The company's **main bank,** in particular, is much more important than individual shareholders; the latter do not exercise much control and are likened by Agegglen and Stalk (1985) to preferred stockholders in a Western company. Employees participate in company **decision making** and share in profits in the form of semiannual bonuses.

3. **Corporate personnel practices** include **lifetime employment** and a seniority-based wage system and promotion, which are considered to be conducive to employee loyalty and work incentives. Companies also regularly undertake extensive employee training without fear of losing trained personnel. These personnel practices suggest to Ozaki (1991) and others that the Japanese management system values corporate human resources more than its Western counterpart. By the late 1990s, however, a growing number of companies are emphasizing merit over seniority in wage increases and promotion, and midcareer job changes are increasingly common.

4. Enterprise-based **labor unions** and extensive consultation between management and employees contribute to cooperative **labor-management**

relations and productivity growth in contrast to the adversarial labor-management relations commonly observed in the West.

5. **Decision making** emphasizes group consensus but tends to be time-consuming in its process and may not respond effectively to a rapidly changing situation. Group consensus, however, facilitates the implementation of the decision.

6. Management respect for workers' views helps to mobilize workers' initiatives, as reflected in their active participation in the **quality control** circles.

7. Innovative and cost-cutting production management methods, particularly the **just-in-time system**—a production system that minimizes the level of inventories—are characteristics of the Japanese style of management. Since the late 1980s the **computer-integrated manufacturing system** and **flexible manufacturing system** have been increasingly introduced.

8. Aspects of Japanese **corporate finance,** such as a relatively high debt–equity ratio and a low dividend–payout ratio, are considered by some authors to be an integral part of Japanese approach to management in order to have a high rate of investment and growth. However, during the **bubble economy** in the second half of the 1980s, the debt–equity ratio of the average company declined because of the increased importance of equity finance.

In general, Japanese managers have traditionally placed much more emphasis than their Western counterpart on human relationships, both between managers and employees within a company and between companies. Analysts have given conflicting assessments of such a management style. For example, Ozaki (1991) considers the Japanese management practices to be superior to American management practices in generating a high level of workers' incentives, productivity, and corporate growth. He characterizes the Japanese enterprise system as "human capitalism" for the high value it places on its human resources over capital resource. Kaku (1997), a former president and board chairman of the Canon Corp., uses the popular term *kyosei* (living and working together for the common good) to characterize the traditional Japanese emphasis on cooperation within a company and between companies. He contends that it is the practice of *kyosei* that is responsible for Canon's success. In a large comparative survey of workers in the United States and Japan, Lincoln (1989) finds that the Japanese management practices produced higher work motivation, although American workers have a high level of satisfaction.

On the negative side, Yoshimura and Anderson (1997: 101) question the nature of human relationships in a company. They regard the touted familylike cooperation as nothing more than employees yielding to "pressure to adhere to group norms and to get along with others whose approval they need in order to maintain group membership." Inoguchi (1998) criticizes Japanese corporate executives for being weak at risk management and poor in communication skills and in relating disparate parts to the whole. He considers Japan's corporate elite to be less competent than America's because managers who rely "solely on custom, personal connections and intuition are second- and third-rate managers."

Criticism of Japanese corporate elite is not new, and it has come from its established members as well. For example, Akio Morita (1992), then chairman of Sony Corp. and long an advocate of the Japanese style of management, questions the appropriateness of some Japanese management practices in the contemporary world in an article published in a Japanese magazine, *Bungei Shunju*. In particular, he criticizes Japanese companies for paying workers too little while demanding long **working hours**, and for paying small dividends to shareholders while operating on small profit margins to keep investment high and prices low. In addition he is concerned that these practices may have given Japanese manufacturers unfair competitive advantages in pricing in the world market (author's interview with Sony management, July 10, 1992). Although many top Japanese corporate leaders disagree with Morita, the ensuing discussions touched off by his criticisms can be seen as manifestations of a serious and timely self-examination by the Japanese corporate world about its own management practices.

The continuing slow growth of the Japanese economy in the 1990s has diminished considerably the attraction of the Japanese style of management. As Japanese companies become more globalized and intergrated into the world economy, and as they face more foreign competition at home due to domestic deregulation, their management practices are likely to undergo more changes in the future.

See also **business ethics, corporate finance, Structural Impediments Initiative.**

References

Abegglen, James C. 1992. Morita's argument misses bigger issues. *Tokyo Business Today,* April: 14–16.

Abegglen, James C., and George Stalk, Jr. 1985. *Kaisha: The Japanese Corporation.* New York: Basic Books. Chs. 7–8.

Aoki, Masahiko. 1990. Toward an economic model of the Japanese firm. *Journal of Economic Literature* 28: 1–27.

Aoki, Masahiko, and Ronald Dore, ed. 1994. *The Japanese Firm: The Sources of Competitive Strength.* Oxford: Oxford University Press.

Asian Productivity Organization. 1996. *Redesign of Japanese Management Systems and Practices: Innovation toward Creative Management.* Tokyo: Asian Productivity Organization.

Dore, Ronald. 1987. *Taking Japan Seriously.* Stanford: Stanford University Press. Chs. 6–8.

Inoguchi, Takashi. 1998. Japan's elite less competent than America's. *Nikkei Weekly,* April 6: 16.

Kaku, Ryuzaburo. 1997. The path of *kyosei. Harvard Business Review* 76, 4: 55–63.

Kester, W. Carl. 1991. *Japanese Takeovers: The Global Contest for Corporate Control.* Boston: Harvard Business School Press.

Lincoln, James R. 1989. Employee work attitudes and management practice in the U.S. and Japan: Evidence from a large comparative survey. *California Management Review* 32, 1: 89–106.

Morita, Akio. 1992. A critical moment for Japanese management. *Japan Echo* 19, 2: 8–14 (abridged trans. from *Bungei shunju,* February 1992: 94–103).

Morita shock: New paradigm needed for Japanese management. *Tokyo Business Today,* March 1992: 40–42.

Mroczkowski, Tomasz, and Masao Hanaoka. 1989. Continuity and change in Japanese management. *California Management Review* 31, 2: 39–53.

Ozaki, Robert. 1991. *Human Capitalism.* New York: Penguin.

Yoshimura, Noboru, and Philip Anderson. 1997. *Inside the Kaisha: Demystifying Japanese Business Behavior.* Boston: Harvard Business School Press.

maruyu A privileged saving system which, until 1988, exempted the interest earnings of small savers from income tax in order to encourage individual savings. As of the end of September 1987, about ¥300 trillion ($2.3 trillion) of Japan's ¥637 trillion of personal savings were in accounts benefiting from the tax exemption. In 1987 these savings constituted nearly all of Japanese **postal savings** and about two-thirds of personal deposits in commercial banks. However, the interest rate paid was controlled by the government at a low level—0.2% on a savings account at a commercial bank, 2.7% on a one-year time deposit, and 3.64% on the popular ten-year savings certificates at the post office.

Although there was a limit of ¥3 million per savings account that was eligible for the tax-exempt privilege, there were various abuses such as illegal multiple accounts, sometimes under assumed names, that circumvented the limit. As a result large savers benefited much more from it than small savers. Ishi (1989: 128) shows that in 1986, 78.9% of families used the *maruyu* system. For families with annual incomes of less than ¥2 million, only 56.4% used the system. The percentage increased as the income level rose. For families with annual incomes over ¥7 million, 93.0% benefited from it.

Starting in April 1988, as part of Japan's **tax reform,** eligibility for the tax exemption is restricted to disabled, elderly people over 65 and working widows. A 20% withholding tax is imposed on nearly all interest income from deposit accounts.

See also **postal savings, tax reform.**

References

Ishi, Hiromitsu. 1989. *The Japanese Tax System.* Oxford: Oxford University Press.

Viner, Aron. 1987. *Inside Japan's Financial Markets.* London: The Economist Publications. Ch. 7.

When $2.3 trillion looks for a new Japanese home. *The Economist,* February 20, 1988: 83–84.

mergers and acquisitions (M&A)   In the West a corporate merger or the acquisition of an existing firm is often a convenient way for a company to grow or to diversify, and for investors, particularly foreign investors, to enter a business; hence it is widely practiced. However, until the late 1980s the number of M&A in Japan is small. Wholesale and retail trade is the industry that has had the highest number of M&A, followed by manufacturing.

Mergers have to be reported to the Fair Trade Commission in accordance with the **Antimonopoly Law,** but not acquisitions. Hence reliable statistics on acquisitions are difficult to obtain, and different sources give different figures. Furthermore these statistics understate the real extent of acquisitions because the acquisitions of small companies are not recorded (author's interview with Kanji Ishizumi, attorney at Chiyoda Kokusai Law Offices, August 11, 1992). In any case analysts agree that M&A transactions are small in Japan and that it is rare for foreign firms to acquire Japanese firms.

Analysts have offered several reasons for the traditional paucity of M&A transactions in Japan. The first is the unfavorable sociocultural attitude. The company is regarded by Japanese managers and workers alike as a family or a community, and the idea of selling a company by its owner or CEO for financial considerations has the connotation of "flesh peddling" (Kester 1991a: 12) or as much a betrayal as "the captain of a ship deserting his crew in a storm" (Ishizumi 1988: 14). Even in a friendly merger between two Japanese companies, the firms reportedly often have difficulty integrating because of employees' continuing loyalties to the former firms (Choy 1990: 10). These are consistent with Ito's (1991) finding that M&A activities substantially increase the stock market valuation of target firms in the United States but lower that of both acquiring and target firm in Japan.

Furthermore Kester (1991b) argues that given Japan's economic institutions and business practices, the purposes that are served in the West by means of M&A are more readily served in Japan in the traditional ways that are more socially acceptable. For example, in the West M&A serve to extend corporate control over another company or business area (vertical integration). This is not necessary for Japanese companies that maintain long-term stable relationships with their suppliers, distributors, customers, and subcontractors. Alternatively, M&A might be pursued in the West as a means to correct abuses by stakeholders, including management. Such abuses are said to be fewer in Japan and more easily corrected without gaining majority control. Thus there has been much less incentive for Japanese companies to use M&A to achieve what it is used to achieve in the West.

It is difficult and rare for foreign companies to acquire Japanese companies. The reasons are that in addition to the traditional reluctance to sell, the idea of selling to a foreign firm is particularly alien and unsettling to the Japanese. It is feared that foreign companies will pursue short-term profits and disregard long-term relationships and time-honored practices, including job security for employees. The practice of **cross-shareholding** also facilitates the defense against any hostile takeover. Finally, the government did not ease its restrictions on **foreign direct investment** in Japan until 1980.

The situation started to change in the 1980s, particularly after the mid-1980s, as Japanese corporate relationships, economic structure, social attitude, and government policies were changing. Japanese corporations were acquiring a lot of cash, became less dependent on their banks in their business relations, and had more incentives to invest their funds for higher returns. As a result the practice of cross-shareholding is not as important as previously. Government **financial liberalization** is easing the restrictions on foreign ownership in Japan as well as increasing competition in the financial market. Socially M&A is said to be increasingly acceptable as making money becomes more important and business managers realize what can be accomplished with M&A in their global business plans (Choy 1990: 13).

Japanese M&A activity abroad increased rapidly between 1986 and 1990 (see table M.1). About half of the transactions took place in the United States (176, 194, and 229 cases in 1988, 1989, and 1990, respectively; about $15 to 18 billion annually during 1988–90). These increases reflect changes in the Japanese domestic economy itself. Between 1986 and 1990 a number of factors enabled Japanese companies to acquire firms in the United States. The yen's appreciation after the **Plaza Accord** of 1985 has reduced Japanese companies' competitiveness in some export markets and hence increased the need to diversify; it has also reduced the cost of acquiring foreign assets. The Japanese **stock market** boom facilitated the raising of equity capital, and the low interest rates and the rising real estate values enabled companies to borrow more money at low cost, using their inflated properties as collateral.

Since 1991 the number of Japanese acquisitions of foreign companies has declined because of diminished corporate funds due to the decline in the Japanese stock market and the real estate market. The number of acquisitions between Japanese firms declined only slightly between 1991 and 1995 and started to increase in 1996. On the other hand, the number of foreign acquisitions of Japanese firms, although still small, increased steadily since 1992. So did the number of mergers since 1991, although it fluctuated more (see table M.1). A common explanation offered by analysts for these increases is that many **small and medium enterprises,** which have been weakened by the long economic stagnation, are now more open to M&A for the purpose of restructuring. In other words, they are looking for stronger business partners in the face of declining profits and increased competition.

Proposed mergers in Japan have to be reported to the Fair Trade Commission (FTC). FTC will then select cases for closer examination, applying the so-called 25% rule. Under the rule, proposed mergers in which one party has 25% or more of the market or both parties will have a combined market share of 25% or more will be regarded as reducing market competition (Iyori and Uesugi 1994: 170–71). In those cases the proposed mergers are usually approved with conditions, such as the selling off of some assets to reduce the market share. There were exceptions in the past to the 25% rule such as the Nippon Steel Corp. case in 1970 in which two large steel companies were merged without conditions.

Analysts expect Japanese M&A activity in the domestic market and abroad and foreign participation in the Japanese market through M&A to

Table M.1
Number of mergers and acquisitions

	Japanese firms acquired		Foreign firms acquired	
	Japanese firms	Foreign firms	Japanese firms	Mergers
1981	122	48	6	1,044
1984	140	44	6	1,096
1985	163	100	26	1,113
1986	226	204	21	1,147
1987	219	228	22	1,215
1988	223	315	17	1,336
1989	240	405	15	1,450
1990	293	440	18	1,751
1991	302	294	18	2,091
1992	257	183	37	2,002
1993	259	172[a]		1,917
1994	286	175	43	2,000
1995	293	199	52	2,520
1996	323	240	48	2,271
1997	520	175	50	

Sources: Yamaichi Securities Co., Ltd. Figures for 1997 are from Nomura Research Institute. Figures on mergers are from the Fair Trade Commission on a fiscal year basis.
a. Includes foreign acquisitions of Japanese firms.

increase in the future. The primary reason is the on-going domestic deregulation including the **Big Bang,** which will further open up the market and increase competition. A secondary reason is the lifting of the ban on **holding companies** in late 1997, which might give impetus to M&A as a business strategy for large companies or corporate groups to expand.

See also **direct overseas investment, foreign direct investment in Japan.**

References

Choy, Jon. 1990. Japan and Mergers: Oil and Water? *JEI Report* 14A, April 6.

Daiwa Securities Co. 1992. M&A transactions by Japanese Companies. In *Capital Markets and Financial Services in Japan.* Tokyo: Japan Securities Research Institute.

Eide, Tord. 1991. *How to Establish Business in Japan.* Deventer, The Netherlands: Kluwer Law and Taxation Publishers.

Fair Trade Commission. Annual. *Antimonopoly White Paper.*

Henderson, Dan Fenno. 1994. Foreign takeover of Japanese corporations. In *Japanese Commercial Law in an Era of Internationalization*, ed. by Hiroshi Oda. London: Graham and Trotman/ Martinus Nijhoff.

Ito, Kunio. 1991. The effect of M&A activity on company value in Japan and the United States: A comparative study. *Hitotsubashi Journal of Commerce and Management* 26, 1: 1–14.

Iyori, H., and A. Uesugi. 1994. *The Antimonopoly Laws and Policies of Japan*. New York: Federal Legal Publications. Ch. 10.

Kester, W. Carl. 1991a. *Japanese Takeovers: The Global Contest for Corporate Control*. Boston: Harvard Business School Press.

Kester, W. Carl. 1991b. Global players, Western tactics, Japanese outcomes: The new Japanese market for corporate control. *California Management Review* 33, 2: 58–70.

Odagiri, Hiroyuki. 1992. *Growth through Competition, Competition through Growth*. Oxford: Oxford University Press. Ch. 5.

Pettway, Richard H., Neil W. Sicherman, and Takeshi Yamada. 1990. The market for corporate control, the level of agency costs, and corporate collectivism in Japanese mergers. In *Japanese Capital Markets*, ed. by Edwin J. Elton and Martin J. Gruber. New York: Harper and Row.

Saywell, Martin. 1994. The ultimate barrier revisited: mergers and acquisitions in Japan. In *Japanese Commercial Law in an Era of Internationalization*, ed. by Hiroshi Oda. London: Graham and Trotman/Martinus Nijhoff.

Shishido, Zenichi. 1992. Corporate takeovers in Japan. In *Capital Markets and Financial Services in Japan*. Tokyo: Japan Securities Research Institute.

minimum wages Japan does not have uniform national minimum wages; instead, it has different minimum wages for different prefectures and industries.

Under the minimum wage system set up on the basis of the Minimum Wage Law of 1959, each prefecture has a Minimum Wage Council consisting of public, labor, and management representatives. The Council makes recommendations concerning the prefectural minimum wage per day to the chief of the Prefectural Labor Standards Office, who acts on it with the approval of the Ministry of Labor. Thus there are 47 prefectural minimum wages in the economy. In FY 1991, for example, they ranged from ¥4,570 per day in Tokyo, Kanagawa, and Osaka, to ¥4,452 in Aichi, to ¥3,923 in Nagasaki, Miyazaki, and Okinawa. As of March 31, 1997 they ranged from ¥5,252 per day in Tokyo, Kanagawa, and Osaka to ¥4,521 in Miyagi and Okinawa.

In addition there are separate industrial minimum wages that apply to low-paid employees of different trades in different prefectures. The Minimum Wage Councils as well as Prefectural Labor Standards Offices and the Ministry of Labor are involved in the decisions. Within an industry

Table M.2
Average minimum wages by industry (in ¥ per day, as of March 31, 1996)

Industry	Minimum wages	Number of cases
Foodstuff	5,141	7
Textiles	5,160	11
Lumber, woodwork, interior equipment and furniture	5,421	4
Pulp, paper, and paper goods	5,560	3
Publishing and printing	5,625	4
Ceramic and related goods	5,329	5
Machinery and metal processing	5,543	157
Automobile repair	5,175	1
Wholesale and retail	5,429	52
Mining[a]	6,968	3
Others	6,013	7
All industries	5,521	

Source: Ministry of Labor.
a. Centrally determined.

there are dozens of minimum wages because they are determined locally. For example, as shown in table M.2, the foodstuff industry had 7 different cases of minimum wages determined as of March 31, 1996. The weighted average of the industry's minimum wages was ¥5,521.

Thus most low-paid workers have overlapping prefectural and industrial minimum wages applying to them. The higher of the two will be the effective one. The Ministry of Labor is in charge of the overall administration of the minimum wage system. It makes sure that the minimum wages are revised every year in accordance with changes in wages and prices.

The dilemma with minimum wages anywhere is that if they are set too high relative to the supply of and demand for workers, some employers will either try to evade them or hire fewer workers. On the other hand, if they are set relatively low, more workers will be hired but only at near-poverty wage level. Effective enforcement of the minimum wages is also difficult. All of these problems exist in Japan. First, as Tachibanaki (1996: 254) points out, "enforcement of the [minimum wage] law is not so strict, partly because punishment is weak, and monitoring is imperfect." In addition workers themselves are not always aware of the existence and the level of minimum wages. For this reason the Ministry of Labor conducts an annual ten-day campaign in November to distribute information on minimum wages. Finally, in age-conscious Japan, some employers may pay the legal minimum wages to adults but less to 18-year-old starting workers. Japan's **labor unions** would like to see this situation rectified (JTUC-RENGO, 1998: 88).

See also **wage structure.**

Address

Central Minimum Wages Council, Ministry of Labor
2-2, Kasumigaseki 1-chome, Chiyoda-ku, Tokyo 100
Tel: (3) 3593-1211

References

JTUC-RENGO (Japanese Trade Union Confederation). 1998. *The Spring Struggle for a Better Life, 1998.*

Ministry of Labor. Annual. *Handbook of Labor Statistics.*

Ministry of Labor. Annual. *Labour Administration.*
Tachibanaki, Toshiaki. 1996. *Public Policies and the Japanese Economy: Savings, Investments, Unemployment, Inequality.* New York: St. Martin's Press.

Ministry of Finance   Established in 1870, the Ministry of Finance (MOF) is the most elitist and powerful of all ministries in Japan. The post of the minister is invariably held by an influential person or faction leader of the ruling **Liberal Democratic Party** and a potential candidate for the position of the prime minister. The power of the Ministry over the economy is exercised by bureaucrats in its various bureaus which are responsible for diverse areas of the economy.

The Budget Bureau of the Ministry is responsible for the national government's budget. The Tax Bureau is concerned with the overall design of the tax structure. The National Tax Administration collects taxes. The Finance Bureau raises nontax revenues and is responsible for government bond issues and the **Fiscal Investment and Loan Program.** The Banking Bureau and the Securities Bureau oversee banking and securities businesses, respectively, and hence influence the nation's monetary policy along with the **Bank of Japan.** Other bureaus deal with customs and tariffs, international finance, local finance, and so on.

Given the Ministry's vast jurisdiction, it is inevitable that some of its bureaus have conflicting interests. For example, the National Tax Administration occasionally objects to the tax changes proposed by the Tax Bureau unless an alternative source of revenue is offered. Critics have also pointed out that the Ministry is seriously understaffed, given its tremendous responsibilities, which makes its **decision making** time-consuming and prevents it from responding to changing conditions efficiently.

As is common with all Japanese ministries, MOF officials rely heavily on **administrative guidance** to implement its policies. The private sector generally complies with this guidance. However, the power of the Ministry is not absolute, and it has shown signs of erosion in the last two decades. There are two reasons for this. First, other ministries and government institutions, which have different priorities, also exercise influence over financial policies. For example, the **Ministry of International Trade and Industry** (MITI) controls the **Export-Import Bank** and the **Japan Development Bank** and has some leverage over foreign exchange. MITI is known to be more concerned with economic expansion, whereas MOF is more concerned with budget balancing. The Bank of Japan shares with the MOF the responsibility for monetary policy. The Bank is known to be more cautious and more interested in macroeconomic stability and in fighting inflation, whereas the MOF tends to be more concerned with the orderly growth of the financial industries and the international impact of Japan's financial policies. Occasionally the minister of finance and the director of the Bank of Japan have openly expressed their policy differences, such as on the appropriate level of the Bank's official discount rate. Where such differences exist, the Bank rather than the MOF is more likely to make the accommodating changes.

Second, **financial liberalization** and the internationalization of Japanese banking and securities businesses have eroded somewhat the power of the MOF. Since 1970 the MOF has lost several of its policy instruments: exchange-rate controls, credit allocation through quotas on bank lending, and interest-rate ceilings on various types of deposits in the late 1980s and early 1990s.

With the revelation, in 1991, of illegal investment-loss compensation made by **securities companies** to their large clients, the MOF was severely criticized by the public for its failure to prevent such scandals. Its interactions with the financial industries were criticized as being more concerned with the interests of the industries rather than those of the public. In addition the **administrative guidance** which the MOF has used as a major means of exercising its regulatory power was criticized as too vague and lacking in "transparency."

Since the mid-1990s the Ministry has been under constant attack for a number of financial crises and scandals: the collapse of **housing loan companies** (*jusen*) in 1995 and the use of ¥685 billion public money to liquidate them and their debt in 1996, the closure of Hokkaido Takushoku Bank and Yamaichi Securities Co. in November 1997, and the arrests of several senior ministry officials for bribery charges. The MOF is denounced as the most "tyrannical and corrupt" of all ministries by economist Hirofumi Uzawa (*Economist*, January 6, 1996: 28), and there have been growing calls for the breakup of the Ministry.

In July 1992, following the securities companies scandals, the Securities and Exchange Surveillance Commission was created to supervise the securities industry despite MOF's resistence. In June 1998, as part of the **Big Bang**, the Financial Supervision Agency was established for the inspection and supervision of private financial institutions. These changes have eroded the power of MOF. In the forthcoming **administrative reform** to be implemented by 2001, the MOF will be restructured as the Ministry of Treasury and will retain its power to set fiscal policy and supervise the financial sector.

See also **administrative guidance, administrative reform, Bank of Japan, banking system, financial liberalization, securities companies.**

Address

Ministry of Finance
1-1, Kasumigaseki 3-chome, Chiyoda-ku, Tokyo 100
Tel: (3) 3581-4111

References

Chandler, Clay. 1991. Scandal raises questions about system of guidance by Japan's Finance Ministry. *Asian Wall Street Journal Weekly*, July 22: 22.

Hartcher, Peter. 1997. *The Ministry*. Boston: Harvard Business School Press.

Ishibashi, Asako. 1998. Clouds over Finance Ministry persist. *Nikkei Weekly*, May 4: 1, 3.

Ishizawa, Yasuharu. 1995. Unchallenged power without public support. *Tokyo Business Today*, July: 20–23.

Kawakita, Takao. 1991. The Ministry of Finance. *Japanese Economic Studies* 19, 4: 3–29.

Miyao, Takashiro. 1996. A proposal for dismantling the Ministry of Finance. *Japan Echo*, Spring 25–27.

Ministry of International Trade and Industry (MITI) Popularly called *MITI*, the Ministry was established in 1949 through the merger of the Ministry of Commerce and Industry and the Board of Trade. It is a relatively small ministry in terms of budget and staff, smaller than the

Ministry of Transport. Its prestige and influence, however, are far greater than its size would indicate. MITI is an important ministry that has been instrumental in guiding Japan's postwar industrialization and export expansion. From its beginning, ministry officials regarded the promotion of international trade as their primary objective. However, industrial expansion, the rationalization of enterprises, and technological improvement were considered to be the prerequisites for trade expansion. These are precisely what have taken place with the Ministry's help.

Through its **industrial policy,** MITI attempted to promote growth industries that would enjoy growing export demand in the world market. At the same time **declining industries** were encouraged to retrench and diversify. Economic incentives such as cheap credit and tax advantages, as well as **administrative guidance,** are used to elicit industry cooperation. In addition Ministry officials have at times deliberately circumvented the **Antimonopoly Law** to assist industries in their industry rationalization and in their development of new technologies.

Until the mid-1960s MITI had adopted restrictive tariff barriers to protect domestic infant industries. It also restricted **foreign direct investment in Japan** until the early 1980s. Since then, however, it has cooperated with Washington in easing the restrictions on foreign investment and in implementing the **voluntary export restraints** on automobile and steel exports, and so forth. Some **nontariff barriers to trade** have remained, however.

Since the late 1980s and early 1990s, with Japan's persistent trade surplus and mounting foreign pressure to reduce it, MITI has increasingly promoted foreign imports to reduce the trade surplus. In 1992 it started to emphasize the quality of life and consumer interests, in contrast to its past one-sided emphasis on producers' interests. However, with the growing deregulation of the Japanese economy and internationalization of Japanese corporations, MITI's influence over the economy and companies has also declined.

The wide scope of MITI's power is reflected organizationally in the diverse bureaus of which it consists—International Trade Policy Bureau, International Trade Administration Bureau, Industrial Policy Bureau, Industrial Location and Environmental Protection Bureau, Basic Industry Bureau, Machine and Information Industries Bureau, and Consumer Goods Industries Bureau.

MITI is advised by a large number (29 in 1997) of councils in its **decision making.** These councils consist of about 50 members who are prominent in their respective fields such as business, academe, government, **labor unions, consumer groups,** and the press. Councils are organized either along industry lines to deal with specific industries such as mining, petroleum, and aircraft, or along functional/structural lines to deal with an important aspect of the economy such as industrial structure, industrial technology, international trade insurance, and **small and medium enterprises.** The Industrial Structure Council, which advises MITI on its industrial policy, is considered one of the most important councils. Critics have argued, however, that council members are handpicked to be supportive of government policies and that they do not have real power to make decisions.

MITI also has the following specialized agencies in charge of specific aspects of the economy: Agency of Industrial Science and Technology, Agency of Natural Resources and Energy, Patent Office, and Small and Medium Enterprise Agency.

In the forthcoming **administrative reform** to be implemented by 2001, MITI is to be reorganized into the Ministry of Economy and Industry. Other than this change in name, it is believed that MITI will remain intact and no less powerful. In fact it could even become more powerful because it will absorb some telecommunications divisions from the Ministry of Posts and Telecommunications. However, the new ministry will be more concerned about the overall economy rather than the promotion of specific industries or foreign trade. Consequently **industrial policy** is likely to be less important in the future.

A long-standing complaint made by some Japanese businesspeople and economists as well as foreigners about MITI is this: Japan no longer needs such a powerful ministry to protect and guide its industry now that the industry is developed and should compete on its own in the market. Given the fact that the Japanese economy is increasingly deregulated, it is inevitable that the policy focus of MITI and the soon-to-be Ministry of Economy and Industry as well as the role of the Ministry in the economy will continue to change in the future.

See also **administrative guidance, Antimonopoloy Law, industrial policy, trade policy.**

Address

Ministry of International Trade and Industry
3-1, Kasumigaseki 1-chome, Chiyoda-ku, Tokyo 100
Tel: (3) 3501-1511

References

Johnson, Chalmers. 1982. *MITI and the Japanese Miracle.* Stanford: Stanford University Press.

MITI Handbook. Annual. Tokyo: Japan Trade and Industry Publicity.

MITI seeking new role for itself in mature economy. *Nikkei Weekly,* May 30, 1992: 1.

Nakamae, Hiroshi. 1994. MITI loosens grip on economy; seeks to unravel regulation web. *Nikkei Weekly,* June 6: 1, 2.

Oishi, Nobuyuki. 1994. MITI seeks overhaul beyond deregulation. *Nikkei Weekly,* November 21: 2.

Okimoto, Daniel I. 1989. *Between MITI and the Market.* Stanford: Stanford University Press.

Yokoyama, Kiho. 1997. MITI to change identity but expected to retain muscle. *Nikkei Weekly,* November 11: 1, 4.

Mitsubishi Group The largest and most cohesive bank-centered **keiretsu,** or business group, in Japan, with a "three-diamonds" (*mitsu bishi*) logo and a prewar *zaibatsu* origin. It consists of some 160 companies in virtually all sectors of the economy with half a million employees. The three most important companies are Mitsubishi Corporation, Mitsubishi Heavy Industries, and Bank of Tokyo-Mitsubishi (formerly Mitsubishi Bank). Mitsubishi Corp. is one of Japan's largest general **trading companies.** Mitsubishi Heavy Industries is a giant and diversified heavy machinery producer, Japan's top defense contractor, and largest shipbuilder. Bank of Tokyo-Mitsubishi is Japan's largest **city bank.**

The Mitsubishi Group had its origin in the prewar Mitsubishi *zaibatsu,* a large conglomerate that emerged in the 1870s and 1880s. It was founded by Y. Iwasaki and controlled by his family through a **holding company.** Initially the family business was in shipping, finance, currency exchange, mining, and ship repairs. It expanded into shipbuilding in 1887 with government subsidy as the state-owned Nagasaki shipbuilding yards were transferred to it. In 1917–19 many independent companies including a holding company, Mitsubishi Bank and Mitsubishi Trading Company were created. During the Second World War the group supported the government's war efforts.

After the war the Americans outlawed the holding company and dissolved the Mitsubishi *zaibatsu.* All the group companies became legally independent, but personal ties of company executives remained, which became the basis of the reconstituted postwar Mitsubishi Group. Group members maintain ties through various means. The Kinyokai (The Friday Club) is the monthly forum, held on the second Friday of each month, where the presidents of 30 core companies meet to exchange views. Reportedly they do not make important decisions there that affect the operations of the group companies, although some authors such as Eli (1990: 20) claim that the opposite is true. Through **cross-shareholding,** group members maintain financial ties with one another and prevent hostile takeovers. The group bank, Bank of Tokyo-Mitsubishi, serves as the **main bank** for members of the group in extending loans. Because group members are in diverse sectors of the economy, many group companies are often involved together in an industrial project, especially when selling or investing abroad. In this case the general **trading company** Mitsubishi Corporation would be the negotiator with foreigners and the coordinator for the Mitsubishi companies involved.

The business fields in which Mitsubishi companies are active include the following:

Banking: Bank of Tokyo-Mitsubishi, Mitsubishi Trust and Banking

Chemicals: Mitsubishi Chemical Corp., Mitsubishi Gas Chemical, Mitsubishi Plastics Industries

Construction: Mitsubishi Construction

Electrical/electronics: Mitsubishi Electric

Food and drink: Kirin Beer

Glass: Asahi Glass

Insurance: Meiji Life Insurance, Tokio Marine and Fire

Machinery: Mitsubishi Kakoki

Mining and metals: Mitsubishi Kinzoku, Mitsubishi Aluminum, Mitsubishi Densen Kogyo, Mitsubishi Materials

Oil: Mitsubishi Oil

Optics: Nihon

Paper: Mitsubishi Paper

Real estate: Mitsubishi Jisho

Shipbuilding and heavy machinery: Mitsubishi Heavy Industries

Steel: Mitsubishi Seiko

Synthetic fibers and plastics: Mitsubishi Rayon

Trading: Mitsubishi Corp.

Transportation and communication: Nihon Yusen, Mitsubishi Warehouse and Transportation

Vehicles: Mitsubishi Motors

In recent years the Mitsubishi Group, more than any other *keiretsu* groups, has used mergers to attain economies of scale and strengthen group members. The most recent and important one was the merger on April 1, 1996, between Mitsubishi Bank and Bank of Tokyo, both large **city banks**, to create Bank of Tokyo-Mitsubishi, currently the largest city bank. In 1994 Mitsubishi Kasei Corp. merged with Mitsubishi Petrochemical Co. to form Mitsubishi Chemical Corp., Japan's largest chemical manufacturer. In 1990 Mitsubishi Metal Corp. merged with Mitsubishi Mining and Cement Co. to become Mitsubishi Materials Corp., the largest nonferrous metals manufacturer in Japan.

The Mitsubishi Group is traditionally strong in heavy industries and chemicals and relatively weak in computers, communication equipment, and vehicles. With the structural shift of the economy from the former toward the latter, the Mitsubishi Group's challenge is to successfully adjust to the structural changes in order to maintain its leadership role in the economy. The evidence to date indicates that it has done so very well.

See also ***keiretsu* and business groups, Mitsui Group, Sumitomo Group.**

Addresses

Bank of Tokyo-Mitsubishi
7-1, Marunouchi 2-chome, Chiyoda-ku, Tokyo 100
Tel: (3) 3240-1111   Fax: (3) 3240-2820

Mitsubishi Corp.
6-3, Marunouchi 2-chome, Chiyoda-ku, Tokyo 100
Tel: (3) 3210-2121   Fax: (3) 3210-8051

Mitsubishi Heavy Industries
5-1, Marunouchi 2-chome, Chiyoda-ku, Tokyo 100
Tel: (3) 3212-3111   Fax: (3) 3212-9860

References

Mighty Mitsubishi is on the move. *Business Week*, September 24, 1990: 98–107.

Eli, Max. 1990. *Japan Inc.: Global Strategies of Japanese Trading Corporations.* New York: McGraw-Hill. Ch. 2.

Financial *keiretsu* strengthen solidarity. *Tokyo Business Today.* February, 1992: 26–30.

Gerlach, Michael L. 1992. *Alliance Capitalism.* Berkeley: University of California Press. Chs. 3–4.

Ito, Takatoshi. 1992. *The Japanese Economy.* Cambridge: MIT Press. Ch. 7.

Mitsusada, Hisayuki. 1995. Bank coup exemplifies Mitsubishi culture. *Nikkei Weekly*, April 3: 8.

Odagiri, Hiroyuki. 1992. *Growth through Competition, Competition through Growth*. Oxford: Clarendon. Ch. 7.

Mitsui Group   One of Japan's largest horizontal *keiretsu* or conglomerates with a prewar Mitusi *zaibatsu* origin. The group comprises 76 companies in diverse areas of businesses, of which 24 are core companies. The flagship of the group is Mitsui and Co., one of Japan's largest general **trading companies.** The group's bank, Sakura Bank, is a large **city bank.**

As in other postwar corporate groups and unlike the prewar *zaibatsu*, these group members are independent companies. However, various financial ties and business relations such as an interlocking directorate, **cross-shareholding,** joint ventures, and regular executive conferences promote information exchange and help coordinate business activities. The presidents of the 24 core companies meet on the second Thursday of each month in their Second-Thursday Club (Nimoku Kai), while senior executives of the 76 Mitsui companies meet twice a month on Mondays. These meetings serve as a forum for exchange of views and sometimes to mediate disputes and coordinate actions. Reportedly no major decisions affecting group companies are made at these meetings.

Mitsui and Co., the group's oldest and most important core company, has its origin in the merchant house of Mitsui in the early 1600s. The company was established in 1876 as a trading company, shortly after the Meiji Restoration of 1864 and the new government's decision to open the country to foreign trade. The former Mitsui Bank (now Sakura Bank), Japan's first modern commercial bank, was established in 1887 on the foundation of the money-lending business of the house of Mitsui. Other businesses in mining, textiles, shipping, and so forth, soon followed. In 1907 a **holding company** was organized, which controlled 15 major companies and strongly influenced many others (Roberts 1989: 186). This became the prototype of the prewar *zaibatsu*, which was controlled by a family through a holding company.

After World War II all *zaibatsu* in Japan were dissolved under the Allied Command. New postwar corporate groups emerged, however, in the 1950s, and the Mitsui Group was one of them. The postwar Mitsui and Co. was reestablished in 1947. It was fully reorganized in 1957 after a series of **mergers and acquisitions,** which consolidated a number of specialized trading companies established by employees of the prewar Mitsui and Co.

The group's bank, the former Mitsui Bank, was a large **city bank.** On April 1, 1990, it merged with the Taiyo Kobe Bank to become the Mitsui Taiyo Kobe Bank. The new bank was renamed Sakura Bank on April 1, 1992.

Important members of the Mitsui Group are prominent in the following fields:

Banking: Sakura Bank, Mitusi Trust and Banking

Cement: Onoda Cement

Commerce: Mitsukoshi (Japan's most prestigious department store group), Nihon Unisys (computer sale, service, and software)

Chemicals: Mitsui Petrochemical Industries, Mitsui Toatsu Chemicals

Construction: Mitsui Construction

Electrical/electronic equipment: Toshiba Corp.

Food and beverages: Sapporo Breweries, Suntory (beer, wine, etc.)

Insurance: Mitsui Mutual Life Insurance, Mitsui Marine and Fire Insurance (formerly Taisho Marine and Fire Insurance before April 1, 1991)

Machinery: Mitsui Engineering and Shipbuilding, Sanki Engineering

Mining and metals: Mitsui Mining, Mitsui Mining and Smelting

Oil: Mitsui Oil

Paper: Oji Paper

Real estate: Mitsui Real Estate Development

Steel: Japan Steel Works

Synthetic fibers and plastics: Toray Industries

Transportation: Mitsui O.S.K. Lines

Warehousing: Mitsui Warehouse

As is typical with other horizontal *keiretsu,* some core companies of the group have separate groupings of their own, based on financial ties such as cross-shareholding and/or business ties such as supplier-distributor relationship. For example, Mitsui and Co. has nearly 3,000 affiliates and subsidiaries in Japan and abroad. Toshiba Corp., Japan's second largest diversified electronics/electric machinery maker, has numerous business affiliates and subsidiaries.

The major rival of the Mitsui Group is the Mitsubishi Group. They compete in many fields, but they also have different strengths in different fields.

See also *keiretsu* **and business groups, Mitsubishi Group,** *zaibatsu.*

Address

Mitusi and Co.
2-1, Ohtemachi 1-chome, Chiyoda-ku, Tokyo 100
Tel: (3) 3285-1111   Fax: (3) 3285-9800

References

Eli, Max. 1990. *Japan Inc.: Global Strategies of Japanese Trading Corporations.* New York: McGraw-Hill. Ch. 2.

Ito, Takatoshi. 1992. *The Japanese Economy.* Cambridge: MIT Press. Ch. 7.

Gerlach, Michael L. *Alliance Capitalism.* Berkeley: University of California Press. Chs. 3–4.

Mitsui Public Relations Committee. Undated. *Mitsui Group.*

Odagiri, Hiroyuki. 1992. *Growth through Competition, Competition through Growth.* Oxford: Clarendon. Ch. 7.

Roberts, John G. 1989. *Mitsui: Three Centuries of Japanese Business,* 2nd ed. New York: Weatherhill.

mochiai   The cross-holding of stock among publicly traded companies and financial institutions.
   See **cross-shareholding.**

monetary policy
See **Bank of Japan, financial liberalization, Ministry of Finance, money supply, interest rate structure.**

money market dealers   These are companies that specialize in the intermediation of transactions in the short-term **money markets.** Because of their important role, they are directly under the supervision of the **Ministry of Finance.** The **Bank of Japan** also provides guidance for their business activities.
   Currently there are six money market dealers, or *tanshi* companies—Tokyo Tanshi, Yamane Tanshi, Ueda Tanshi, Nippon Discount Tanshi, Yagi Tanshi, and Nagoya Tanshi (*tanshi* literally means "short-term loans"). Their operations include (1) **call money market** transactions, (2) bill trading transactions, (3) transactions in government bills, (4) intermediation of foreign exchange trading, (5) intermediation of dollar-call market financing, (6) trading transactions in certificates of deposits, (7) transactions in yen-denominated bankers' acceptances, and (8) inter-

mediation of inter-bank deposit transactions. In some of these operations such as transactions in the call funds and CDs, the dealers can either serve as brokers by bringing lenders and borrowers together or trade on own accounts as dealers.

In their operations money market dealers interacts with the Bank of Japan in the following ways: (1) Each dealer maintains a current deposit account at the Bank of Japan for the settlement of call and bill transactions. (2) The dealers utilize exchange transactions between the head office and branches of the Bank of Japan to carry out transactions in call funds and bill trading with financial institutions throughout the country. (3) The Bank of Japan may lend to the dealers for transactions in the call money market and for the purchase of certificates of deposits, or it may lend to **securities finance companies** for their margin transactions through the money market dealers. (4) The Bank of Japan's market operations in private bills and government bills are carried out through the money market dealers. Thus the money market dealers help promote the smooth functioning of the money market, the implementation of the government's monetary policy, and the integration of the markets in various parts of the country.

As a reflection of the close relations between the six money market dealers and the Bank of Japan, the presidents of the six **tanshi** companies are often ex-Bank of Japan officials. Also nearly 30% of their board members are former Bank of Japan officials.

The money market dealers have been criticized by large Japanese banks, who are the main borrowers on the money market, for giving preferential treatment to the big lenders. Furthermore the lack of competition among the *tanshi* companies provides no incentives for them to offer discounts on commission fees.

Financial liberalization, when fully implemented, is expected to diminish the money market dealers' core business. However, it will also expand their business areas, such as dealing in securities by establishing securities subsidiaries. For example, in late 1997 both Tokyo Tanshi Co. and Nihon Tanshi Co. set up a subsidiary for securities brokerage business.

Because of foreign pressure, the Bank of Japan has permitted foreign banks operating in Japan to deal with large Japanese banks directly. In addition the U.S. Treasury Department has requested that the money brokering business be opened to foreign institutions.

See also **money markets.**

References

Inoue, Tatsuya. 1997. Call-money brokers eager to expand. *Nikkei Weekly*, October 6: 15.

Japan Securities Research Institute. 1998. *Securities Market in Japan, 1998.* Tokyo. Chs. 1, 11.

Mizuno, Yuko. 1989. Money market magnates draw criticisms at home and abroad. *Japan Economic Journal*, December 23: 31–32.

Suzuki, Yoshio, ed. 1987. *The Japanese Financial System.* Oxford: Oxford University Press. Pp. 269–73.

Viner, Aron. 1987. *Inside Japan's Financial Markets.* London: The Economist Publications. Ch. 8.

money markets   Money markets are short-term financial markets in which financial assets of maturity of less than one year are traded. They can be divided into two broad categories: the interbank money market and the open market. The former is larger than the latter. Each in turn is composed of a number of markets, as explained below:

1. *Interbank market.* Lending and borrowing take place among financial institutions. It includes the following:

• **Call-money market,** which is the traditional interbank money market for the transfer of funds from banks with temporary surplus to those with temporary deficit for very short terms (overnight to three weeks). The interest rate on call money has been rather free from direct government or **Bank of Japan** control. The call money market remains the largest interbank market. At the end of 1997, it had an outstanding balance of ¥22.9 trillion.

• Bill market, in which holders of bills that have not matured sell them to buyers at a discount to obtain funds. The bills may be high-grade commercial and industrial bills, trade bills, high-grade promissory notes, and yen-denominated export and import bills. The market is considered to be an extension of the call market. The interest rates on the bill market were controlled by the Bank of Japan until 1975. In 1985 the Bank of Japan also deregulated the bill market, lifting restrictions on the type of financial institutions that could participate in the market. The types of bills traded in the bill market include one-month bills, two-month bills, and over-three-month bills. At the end of 1997 the market had an outstanding balance of ¥10.3 trillion.

• Dollar-call market, or the Tokyo dollar-call market, in which financial institutions borrow and lend foreign currency funds among themselves for short periods. Started in 1972, it passed the trillion dollar level in

1985. The loan period ranges from overnight to over one month. The total value of transactions was $322 billion in 1997, down from record high of $2.4 trillion in 1989.

2. *Open market.* Nonfinancial institutions may participate in the open market. It includes the following:

• *Gensaki* market or the bond repo market, the market for the trading of bonds with a repurchase agreement whereby the seller agrees to repurchase the bonds at a specified time at a higher price. Although the transactions involve the buying and selling of securities, they are short-term borrowing and lending in substance because of the repurchase agreement. The repurchase period ranges from one month, two months, to three months. Initially developed in the 1970s to provide nonbank short-term financing for securities houses, it became popular with banks, other financial institutions, and business corporations because it was one of the few financial markets with a market-determined interest rate. However, **securities companies** remain the largest sellers of *gensaki* (i.e., borrowers in the market). In recent years the rates of the *gensaki* and the call markets have moved virtually in tandem. At the end of 1997, the transaction balance was ¥10.0 trillion.

• Certificate of deposit (CD) market. As an increasing number of corporations switched their liquid funds from bank deposits to the more attractive *gensaki* instruments, banks lobbied to issue alternative competing instruments. In May 1979 they were permitted to issue negotiable certificates of deposits. A secondary market for trading in these instruments was opened in May 1980. In 1997 the average CD balance was ¥36.1 trillion, a record level despite the economic stagnation.

• Bankers' acceptance (BA) market. Established in June 1985, this is the market for trading in yen-denominated fixed-term bills of exchange, which are issued by companies such as importers and exporters to settle contracts and are guaranteed by foreign exchange banks. The market had a late start because very little of Japanese trade has been in yen.

• Treasury bill market. This market was created in February 1986, following the 1984 recommendations by the Japan–U.S. Yen–Dollar committee that Japan foster a short-term government bond market. Although the market has grown steadily since its establishment, its size remains relatively small. The outstanding amount sold by the Bank of Japan was ¥12.8 trillion at the end of 1997. Japan's treasury bills are issued with low yield to minimize government interest burdens, and almost all are accepted by the Bank of Japan. The latter has sold its treasury bills at market prices. These prices, however, have not affected other money market rates. Thus treasury bill operations as a monetary tool of the Bank of Japan have not been effective.

• **Commercial paper market.** This market was established only in November 1987. Because a commercial paper (CP) is an unsecured promissory note, only corporations and banks with high credit ratings are eligible for issuing it. It is a way to raise low-cost funds. At the end of 1997 the outstanding amounts of commercial paper stood at ¥12.0 trillion, down from ¥15.76 trillion at the end of 1990.

• The **Tokyo offshore market,** established in December 1986, is a banking market where foreign exchange banks conduct business with nonresidents. It is relatively free from domestic regulations. The value of transactions in the market was $6.6 trillion in 1997.

Transactions in the money markets are dominated by six *tanshi* companies, Japan's **money market dealers.** Presidents of these companies are often ex-Bank of Japan officials. The Bank of Japan buys discount bills, commercial paper, and other financial instruments through the *tanshi* companies in order to adjust money in the market on a daily basis.

See also **call money market, commercial paper market, money market dealers, Tokyo offshore market.**

References

Bank of Japan. Annual. *Economic Statistics Annual.*

Federation of Bankers Associations of Japan. 1994. *The Banking System in Japan.* Tokyo: Zenginkyo. Ch. 4.

Japan Securities Research Institute. 1998. *Securities Market in Japan, 1998.* Ch. 1.

Suzuki, Yoshio, ed. 1987. *The Japanese Financial System:* Oxford: Oxford University Press. Ch. 4.

Tatewaki, Kazuo. 1991. *Banking and Finance in Japan.* London: Routledge. Ch. 4.

Viner, Aron. 1987. *Inside Japan's Financial Markets.* London: The Economist Publications. Ch. 8.

money supply   Of the various measures of money supply, the **Bank of Japan,** Japan's central bank, focuses on the broad measure of M2 + CD (and sometimes also M3 + CD) in contrast with the United States, which focuses on the narrow measure of M1. M1 is defined as currency in circulation plus demand deposits; M2 equals M1 plus time deposits, while CD stands for certificates of deposit; M3 is M2 plus trust accounts, loan trusts, and **postal savings.**

The Bank of Japan focuses on the broad measure for two reasons. First, it is found that in Japan M2 + CD has a closer relationship with future potential income and expenditure than M1. The latter is more closely correlated with current income and expenditure (Suzuki 1986: 187). Since the Bank of Japan is more concerned with future income and expenditure and their impact on prices, the broad measure is considered more appropriate. Second, it is easier for the Bank of Japan to control M2 + CD than M1. Strict limits exist on the Bank's ability to have short-term control of M1 (Suzuki 1987: 33; author's interview, Bank of Japan, July 16, 1992).

The Bank of Japan does not set a target for money supply, but it announces a quarterly "forecast," which is based on the planned policy actions of the Bank anyway. Thus a forecast differs little from a target except that it implies less policy commitment and can be more easily changed as circumstances change. In fact the actual growth rates of M2 + CD have been very close to the forecasts announced by the Bank of Japan.

Japan's outstanding M2 + CD at year-end was ¥125 trillion in 1975, ¥314.9 trillion in 1985, and ¥600.1 trillion in 1997. The figure for M1 was ¥49.9 trillion in 1975, ¥89.0 trillion in 1985, and ¥204.3 trillion in 1997 (see table M.3). The annual rate of growth of M2 + CD averaged 13.1%

Table M.3
Money supply and growth rates (in ¥ trillions and %)

End of year	M1	Growth rate	M2 + CD	Growth rate
1975	49.9	11.1	125.3	14.5
1980	69.6	−2.0	209.0	7.2
1985	89.0	3.0	314.9	8.7
1986	98.2	10.4	343.9	9.2
1987	103.0	4.8	380.9	10.8
1988	111.8	8.6	419.7	10.2
1989	114.5	2.4	470.0	12.0
1990	119.6	4.5	505.0	7.4
1991	131.0	9.5	516.3	2.3
1992	136.1	3.9	515.3	−0.2
1993	145.6	7.0	526.8	2.2
1994	151.7	4.2	541.4	2.8
1995	171.5	13.1	559.3	3.3
1996	188.1	9.7	577.0	3.2
1997	204.3	8.6	600.1	4.0

Source: Bank of Japan.

during 1975–78, declined to less than 10% between 1979 and 1986 (except in 1981), and then rose to an average of 11% during 1987–89. In the early 1990s it declined substantially. Overall, however, the annual growth rates of M2 + CD were relatively even compared with those of M1, which fluctuated greatly and somewhat erratically over the years. The reason for this is that households and corporations can easily shift in their holdings of monetary assets between currency and demand deposits (M1), on the one hand, and time deposits and CDs, on the other hand, all of which are components of M2 + CD. Thus it is easier for the Bank of Japan to control and forecast the growth of the latter. The relatively even growth of M2 + CD has, no doubt, contributed to Japan's low rate of inflation since the mid-1970s.

See also **Bank of Japan, interest-rate structure, money markets.**

References

Bank of Japan. Annual. *Economic Statistics Annual.*

Grivoyannis, Elias C. 1991. *Current Issues in Monetary Policy in the United States and Japan: The Predictability of Money Demand.* New York: Praeger.

Suzuki, Yoshio, 1986. *Money, Finance, and Macroeconomic Performance in Japan.* New Haven: Yale University Press. Chs. 3, 6, 8.

Suzuki, Yoshio, ed. 1987. *The Japanese Financial System.* Oxford: Oxford University Press. Ch. 6.

Yoshikawa, Hiroshi. 1993. Monetary policy and the real economy in Japan. In *Japanese Monetary Policy*, ed. by Kenneth J. Singleton. Chicago: University of Chicago Press.

N

Nagoya and Central Japan With a population of 2.14 million as of April 1997, Nagoya is the fourth largest city in Japan. It is located approximately at the center of the long Japanese archipelago. It is the capital city of Aichi prefecture and the hub of Japan's third largest industrial region. It is also the business center of Central Japan (*chubu*, which includes Aichi, Gifu, Mie, and Shizuoka prefectures) and one of Japan's largest foreign trade ports.

In FY 1989 Nagoya had a gross municipal product of ¥10.87 trillion, or 2.7% of Japan's gross domestic product, which was the third largest among the major cities of the nation. Transportation equipment is the leading industry, followed by general machinery. Aichi prefecture has other centers of industry and commerce, including Toyota city (automobiles), Ichinomiya (textiles), and Seto (ceramics). Central Japan manufactures approximately 56% of all Japanese vehicles and about 50% of the machine tools. Many automakers—including Toyota, Honda, Mitsubishi, Suzuki, and others—have their corporate headquarters and/or plants located in Central Japan. About 6,000 subcontractors are located in Aichi, Shizuoka, and Mie prefectures. Other industries of Central Japan include machine tools, aerospace, precision instruments, electronic/electric instruments, ceramics, textiles or apparel, steel, petrochemicals and musical instruments. The port of Nagoya handled ¥5.7 trillion exports and ¥2.1 trillion imports in 1995, making it the third largest port in Japan.

With the World Export 2005 scheduled to be held in the Aichi prefecture near Nagoya, various construction projects have been underway in the region. The largest is the Chubu International Airport, being built offshore on an artificial island 30 kilometers south of Nagoya. It will be opened in the year 2005 with two runways.

See also **Osaka and Kansai, Tokyo, Yokohama**.

Address

City of Nagoya
1-1 Sannomaru 3-chome, Naka-ku, Nagoya 460-08
Tel: (52) 961-111

References

Chukeiren. 1997. *Chubu: Central Japan, 1996*. Nagoya: Chubu Economic Federation.

City of Nagoya. Undated. *Nagoya*.

City of Nagoya. Annual. *Nagoya Statistical Yearbook* (in Japanese).

National Tax Administration   An agency of the **Ministry of Finance** in charge of tax collection.
See **Ministry of Finance, tax system**.

National taxes   Taxes levied by the national government, including individual income tax, corporation tax, consumption tax, and inheritance tax.
See **tax system**.

nemawashi   An informal, pre-decision-making process of discussions in a corporation or organization to facilitate the formation of concensus in subsequent formal decision making.
See **decision making**.

nenko   Seniority-based wage system.
See **corporate personnel practices, lifetime employment, wage structure**.

nihonteki keiei   Japanese-style management.
See **corporate finance, corporate personnel practices, management practices**.

Nikkei Stock Average   An index of the average price of 225 stocks listed on the first section of the **Tokyo Stock Exchange**, compiled by Nihon Keizai Shimbun, Inc.
See **stock price indexes, Tokyo Stock Exchange**.

nikkeijin   Foreigners of Japanese descent. Unlike other foreigners, they are given long-term resident status and can work legally in Japan.
See **foreign workers in Japan**.

Nikkeiren   Japan Federation of Employers' Associations, a leading business organization.
See **business organizations**.

Nissho   Japan Chamber of Commerce and Industry, a leading business organization.
See **business organizations**.

Nixon shock   A term coined by the Japanese to refer to the U.S. New Economic Program, announced on August 15, 1971, by U.S. President Richard Nixon, which took the Japanese by surprise and which adversely affected the Japanese economy.

In 1971 the United States experienced its first trade deficit since 1893, largely because of its trade deficit with Japan. In addition the U.S. economy was suffering from stagflation. To help cope with these problems, in August 1971 Nixon suspended convertibility of the dollar into gold, devalued the dollar, and introduced the floating exchange rate system to replace the fixed exchange rate system that had been in place since the Bretton Woods Agreement was signed in 1944. The U.S. government also imposed a temporary 10% surcharge on imports into the United States, which was aimed primarily at reducing imports from Japan.

The Japanese yen was revalued upward by 17% in January 1972, ending the fixed exchange rate of ¥360 to the dollar which had been maintained since 1949.

In Nakamura's (1981: 106–107) view, the Nixon shock symbolized the international economic friction of the 1970s. The underlying source of the friction lay in the "widening gap between the Japanese perception of their own economy as ever a small, backward latecomer, and its evaluation by the international economic community."
See also **yen–dollar exchange rates**.

References

Nakamura, Takafusa. 1981. *The Postwar Japanese Economy: Its Development and Structure.* Tokyo: Tokyo University Press. Translated by Jacqeline Kaminski. Ch. 6.

Nokyo   The nationwide network of **agricultural cooperatives** and their national federation.
See **agricultural cooperatives**.

nonbank financial institutions   Japan has some 19,000 nonbank financial institutions, or *nonbanks*, as they are commonly called. They include consumer finance companies, business loan companies, credit card companies, credit sales companies, and the seven former **housing loan companies** (*jusen*), which were liquidated in 1996.

Nonbanks provide individual and business credit in diverse areas such as **consumer credit**, business loans to **small and medium enterprise**, bank-affiliated credit card business, store credit sales, housing loans, and leasing. They traditionally obtain the bulk of their funds from bank loans. In turn, they lend at higher interest rates to medium and small businesses, real estate firms, and the like, which have higher risks. In June 1993 the **Ministry of Finance** decided to permit nonbanks to issue commercial papers (CPs) under strict conditions. Nonbanks are required to receive ratings of A-2 or better from at least two credit-rating agencies, and they are not allowed to use the money obtained from CPs to make loans. Beginning in 1998, they are allowed to raise funds by issuing straight bonds. Because of the long stagnation of the economy in the 1990s, the outstanding loans of 300 major nonbanks declined from ¥66.9 trillion at the end of September 1991 to ¥55.8 trillion at the end of March 1995.

In the 1980s nonbanks were heavily involved in making real estate loans against the collateral of shares and pieces of property. These contributed greatly to the speculative rises of land prices of the 1980s, making affordable **housing** beyond the reach of middle-class families in the major metropolitan areas. As stock prices declined since 1990, the portfolios of the nonbanks were put in a precarious situation. It is estimated that the total amount of unrecoverable loans held by nonbanks was as high as ¥40 trillion (Morishita 1996). The bad debt of the seven now-defunct housing loan companies alone was more than ¥8 trillion.

Since many nonbanks are the subsidiaries of banks and **securities companies**, their bad loans had come to aggravate the financial woes of their parent banks/companies, which had huge bad debt of their own as a legacy of the **bubble economy**. In 1996 some of the bad loans of the affiliated nonbanks were absorbed and written off by their parent banks/companies, resulting in large pre-tax losses for them. For independent nonbanks, many of them had gone bankrupt (56 in 1991, 83 in 1992, 64 in 1993, 50 in 1994, and 70 in 1995; *Japan Economic Almanac* 1997: 77). In 1996 the five largest bankruptcies in Japan involved independent nonbanks.

Nonbanks are mostly under the jurisdiction of the **Ministry of International Trade and Industry**, but they are also loosely regulated by the

Ministry of Finance, in contrast to the latter's tight control of the banking institutions. The Money-Lending Regulation Act required them to disclose only their total financial balances. The land price inflation of the late 1980s, however, prompted the Diet to revise the law in May 1991, which now requires nonbanks with financial balances above a certain level to itemize their loans portfolios and provide a description of their real estate loans. See also **consumer credit, credit card industry**.

References

Fujino, Keisuke. 1990. Non-bank finance firms suffering from ever-tightening bank credit. *Japan Economic Journal*, May 26: 36.

Inose, Hijiri. 1991a. Diet bill gives MOF power over non-banks. *Japan Economic Journal*, May 26: 36.

Inose, Hijiri. 1991b. Non-banks taking body blows. *Nikkei Weekly*, October 26: 1.

Japan's "non-bank" financing houses placed under government surveillance. *Japan Economic Review*, March 15, 1991: 5.

Morishita, Kaoru. 1996. Nonbank bad loans poised to overshadow jusen crisis. *Nikkei Weekly*, March 18: 1, 23.

Nonbanks. *Japan Economic Almanac*, various years.

Nonbanks come under fire. *Tokyo Business Today*, December 1991: 10.

Sawada, Masaru. 1990. Non-banks left with devastating portfolios as land-price magic proves to be myth. *Japan Economic Journal*, Winter suppl.: 17.

Yokota, Kazunari. 1996. Nonbank units siphon off broker profits. *Nikkei Weekly*, October 28: 18.

nontariff barriers to trade   Policy measures, economic institutions, and business practices that have the effect of discouraging or restricting imports from foreign countries, whether or not such an effect is intended. Thus they complement tariffs in reducing imports. Usually quotas are the most important form of nontariff barriers to trade.

Although Japan's tariffs are no higher than those of other industrialized countries, foreign critics have argued that various types of nontariffs barriers to trade have greatly reduced imports and contributed to the trade imbalance between Japan and its trading partners. The barriers most often cited are the following:

1. *Custom procedures.* The inspection procedure is said to be bureaucratic and time-consuming, and until recently it was very difficult to appeal unfavorable custom rulings.

2. *Restrictive standards and regulations.* For certification purpose, the technical standards adopted are very high, and government regulations are said to be restrictive according to foreign critics. Japanese standards are often written in terms of design criteria rather than performance specifications. This leaves discretionary power for officials to delay or even prohibit entry of foreign goods into the Japanese market even though the products may perform adequately. In addition Japanese officials do not accept foreign test data. This is particularly true with respect to pharmaceuticals. In response, Japanese officials and industry representatives contend that high technical standards have to be maintained because Japanese consumers insist on them and that the Japanese react differently to pharmaceuticals than the Westerners.

3. *Quota restrictions on imports of agricultural products.* Although Japan is a high-cost producer of most agricultural products due to lack of land, it restricts its imports through quotas. Rice was banned completely until 1993. Japanese officials cite the importance of self-sufficiency in food, the need for the rural **population** to supplement their incomes through farming, and the importance of preserving traditional values as embodied in farming as the reasons for such restrictions. Foreign observers have pointed out that it is the inordinate political power of the farmers—political districts were drawn on the basis of immediate postwar population distribution and they have not been revised—that make the restriction of cheaper agricultural imports possible and that the **Liberal Democratic Party**, Japan's ruling party since 1955, derives much of its support from the rural areas and is simply placing its political interests ahead of the economic interests of the economy and fairness in international trade. There is also the so-called "prior confirmation system," which acts, in effect, like a quota. Under the system imports of specific products such as Korean and Taiwanese silk products and tuna require prior approval by the **Ministry of International Trade and Industry** (Balassa and Noland 1988: 55).

4. *Differences in language, customs, the marketing system, and consumer preferences.* Japan's multilayered **distribution system** is complex and difficult to penetrate. Japanese consumers seem to believe strongly that Japanese products are superior in quality. Japanese language and customs are difficult for foreigners to master. All of these make the cost of doing business in Japan higher. Tokyo's response is that if foreigners are genuinely interested in doing business in Japan, they should make more effort to understand and to overcome these differences.

Komiya and Irie (1990: 84–87) dismiss the alleged nontariff barriers in Japan as "myths" on the ground that conceptually and statistically they are difficult to measure and compare internationally. Subsequently Komiya admits to the existence of nontariff barriers in Japan but argues that they are not unique to Japan as all other countries have them (author's interview, July 7, 1992). Japanese officials and authors generally do not deny that nontariff barriers to trade exist in Japan but regard them as either justified or unimportant. Japan's trading partners think otherwise and regard them as a source of trade imbalance.

Nanto (1997: 126) describes the role of Japan's nontariff barriers to trade picturesquely in the following way: "The official Japanese defense against imports consists first of a shallow moat of tariffs with occasional deep holes, second of sporadic barricades of import quotas and third of inner gates of rules and regulations . . . The regulatory gates usually are narrow and only slightly ajar and can connect to lengthy passageways which can lead the neophyte nowhere."

See also **rice production and distribution, trade pattern, trade policy**.

References

Balassa, Bela, and Marcus Noland. 1988. *Japan in the World Economy*. Washington: Institute for International Economics. Ch. 3.

Bergsten, C. Fred, and Marcus Noland. 1993. *Reconcilable Differences? United States–Japan Economic Conflict*. Washington: Institute for International Economics. Ch. 3.

Komiya, Ryutaro, and Kazutomo Irie. 1990. The U.S.–Japan trade problem: An economic analysis from a Japanese viewpoint. In *Japan's Economic Structure: Should It Change?* ed. by Kozo Yamamura. Seattle: Society for Japanese Studies.

Lincoln, Edward J. 1990. *Japan's Unequal Trade*. Washington: Brookings Institution. Ch. 2.

Nanto, Dick K. 1997. Japan's official import barriers. *Current Politics and Economics of Japan* 5, 2/3: 125–66.

Sazanami, Yokyo, Shujiro Urata, and Hiroki Kawai. 1995. *Measuring the Costs of Protection in Japan*. Washington: Institute for International Economics.

Vogel, David. 1992. Consumer protection and protectionism in Japan. *Journal of Japanese Studies* 18, 1: 119–54.

Norinchukin Bank   The Central Cooperative Bank for Agriculture and Forestry.

See **agricultural cooperatives, banking system**.

O

official discount rate   The interest rate that the **Bank of Japan** charges on loans to commercial banks. It is an important monetary policy instrument of the Bank of Japan because its level affects other interest rates and the conditions of the financial market. The Bank of Japan lowered the official discount rate to a record low of 0.5% in September 1995 in an effort to stimulate the sluggish economy.

See **Bank of Japan, interest-rate structure**.

Okura sho   The **Ministry of Finance**, the most powerful of Japan's government ministries and agencies. Plagued by a series of financial scandals and failures in Japan since the early 1990s, the ministry is to be reorganized by 2001 as the Ministry of Treasury with reduced power.

See **Ministry of Finance**.

Osaka and Kansai   Osaka City is Japan's third largest city in terms of population, and the hub of Kansai, Japan's second largest industrial region. As of April 1997 it has 2.6 million people. Its daytime population, however, rises by 46% because many workers commute from the surrounding areas to Osaka to work. Historically Osaka was the commercial center of Japan before the rise of **Tokyo** as the capital. Now it has Japan's second biggest stock exchange after Tokyo, is home to two of Japan's largest **city banks** (Sakura Bank, formerly Mitsui Bank, and Sumitomo Bank) and some of Japan's largest general **trading companies** (Itochu Corp., Marubeni Corp., Nissho Iwai Corp., and Sumitomo Corp.), and manufacturers (Matsushita Electric Industrial, Sanyo, Sharp, etc.), some of which are located in Osaka prefecture.

Osaka prefecture, which has Osaka city as its principal city, has Japan's second largest gross prefectural product, second only to that of metropolitan Tokyo. It accounted for 8% of Japan's gross domestic product (GDP) in FY 1994 (metropolitan Tokyo's share was 17.1%).

Kansai (literally "west of the pass") refers to the prosperous region in southwestern part of the Japanese archipelago that encompasses six prefectures (Hyogo, Kyota, Nara, Osaka, Shiga, Wakayama) with Osaka City as its hub. The region also includes the port of Kobe and the ancient capital of Kyoto. Kansai's gross regional product accounted for 18.9% of Japan's gross domestic product in FY 1994. Its population was 20.4 million at the end of March, 1996, which was 16.3% of Japan's total population.

The Kansai region has become increasingly important since the late 1980s for two reasons. (1) Because the Tokyo area is already saturated and overcrowded, Kansai provides the major alternative, particularly to overseas companies, for expansion in Japan. (2) Hundreds of development projects have been launched in Kansai in recent years, providing many business opportunities.

Three large infrastructural projects were introduced to help stimulate the regional economy. (1) The new Kansai International Airport, built on an artificial island in the Osaka Bay at the cost of about ¥1.5 trillion, was opened to passenger and cargo service in September 1994 but construction of two additional runways is still underway. (2) The Kansai Science City is a satellite city being built within reach of the cities of Osaka, Kyoto, and Nara for high-tech research institutes, costing over ¥4 trillion; it will not be completed until the beginning of the twenty-first century. (3) The new train station of Kyoto City, massive (Japan's largest) as well as controversial because of its sharp contrast with the rest of Kyoto, was completed in 1997. It is expected to attract more tourists to one of the most popular tourist spots of Japan.

With the Kansai International Airport in operation, Osaka is actively soliciting overseas trade and investment, particularly from the neighboring Asian countries. It has built various facilities in the Osaka Bay area for such purpose.

See also **Tokyo and Kanto**.

Addresses

Kansai Economic Federation
2-27, Nakanoshima 6-chome, Kita-ku, Osaka 530
Tel: (6) 441-0104

Osaka Municipal Government
1-3-20, Nakanoshima, Kita-ku, Osaka 530
Tel: (6) 208-8962. Fax: (6) 232-2749

References

Kansai Economic Federation. 1997. *An Introduction to the Kansai Economy*. Osaka: Kankeiren.

Osaka Municipal Government. 1995. *Economic Profile of Osaka City*.

over-the-counter market   The market in which shares of medium-sized companies are traded. Japan's over-the-counter (OTC) market is relatively small but has grown rapidly since the late 1980s. It is supervised by the Japan Securities Dealers Association but is less organized than the stock exchange. Transactions are executed over the counter of securities' dealers. Prices are determined through negotiations between a buyer and a seller. Thus prices can vary from one firm to another.

The number of companies listed on the Tokyo OTC market was only 121 in 1980. After the relaxation of standards for the listing in 1983, the number grew steadily to 159 in December 1987, 446 at the end of 1991, surpassing the number of medium-sized companies listed on the second section of the **Tokyo Stock Exchange**, and to 779 at the end of 1996. The volume of transactions grew from 464.2 million shares in 1988, which was only 11.5% of the volume of the second section of the Tokyo Stock Exchange. It grew to 1,263.1 million shares in 1990, and 2,547 million shares in 1996, which was 82.9% of the volume of the second section of the Tokyo Stock Exchange.

The OTC market, however, is not as robust as the growth in the number of OTC companies and the volume of transactions would indicate. The Nikkei OTC Average, an index of the OTC stock average calculated by the Nihon Keizai Shimbun, Inc., has declined steadily in the mid-1990s—from nearly 2,000 in July 1994 to 1,078 in early August 1997 and 780 in early July 1998. A major reason for the decline is the stagnation of the economy and the uncertain profit prospects of the OTC companies. Although some leading OTC companies have grown rapidly despite the slump in the economy, the market average declined as more companies offered their shares in a market where demand is rather limited. Individual investors constitute the largest group of investors in the OTC market, unlike the stock exchanges where large institutional investors dominate. Overall, the OTC market is still considered a risky market shunned by major investors.

See also **stock market, Tokyo Stock Exchange**.

Address

Japan Securities Dealers Association
5-8 Nihonbashi Kayabacho 1-chome, Chuo-ku, Tokyo 103
Tel: (3) 3667-8451   Fax (3) 3666-8009

References

Isaacs, Jonathan. 1992. *Japanese Equities Markets*. London: Euromoney Publications. Ch. 6.

Ishibashi, Asako. 1995. Deregulation bolsters market, profits. *Nikkei Weekly*, October 30: 13.

Japan Securities Research Institute. 1998. *Securities Market in Japan, 1998*. Ch. 3.

Matsuoka, Minoru. 1992. Outline of the Japanese OTC stock market. In *Capital Markets and Financial Services in Japan*. Tokyo: Japan Securities Research Institute.

Mizuno, Yuko. 1991. High-flying start-ups keep trading lively on OTC. *Japan Economic Journal*, May 4: 31.

OTC listings likely to pass TSE 2nd section. *Nikkei Weekly*, November 2, 1991: 14.

Weak investor confidence debases OTC shares. *Nikkei Weekly*, April 14, 1997: 15.

Yokyoyama, Kiho. 1998. MITI calls for wide-open OTC trading. *Nikkei Weekly*, March 9: 2.

Overseas Economic Cooperation Fund (OECF)   A major development finance institution of the Japanese government, providing long-term, low-interest loans to developing countries. Established in 1961, it has become the principal executing agency of Japan's official development assistance (ODA). OECF loans are *not* tied to Japan's exports and account for about 40% of Japan's ODA, which make it one of the world's major development finance institutions. In FY 1996 its loans had a long repayment period of 30 years with a grace period of 10 years; interest rate was 2.5%.

OECF is scheduled to be merged with Japan's **Export-Import Bank** in 1999 as part of Japan's administrative reform (author's interview, OECF, April 13, 1998). Its current functions will be carried out by the new expanded institution.

See also **foreign aid**.

Address

Overseas Economic Cooperation Fund
Takebashi Godo Building
4-1, Otemachi 1-chome, Chiyoda-ku, Tokyo 100
Telephone: (3) 3215-1419

References

Overseas Economic Cooperation Fund. Annual. *Annual Report*. Tokyo.

Overseas Economic Cooperation Fund. Monthly. *OECF News Letter*. Tokyo.

Overseas Economic Cooperation Fund. *Operational Guidance on OECD Loans*. Tokyo.

P

parallel import system   A new import practice that permits competing importers of foreign products to break the monopoly of the exclusive general import agents.
  See **distribution system**.

patent system   First established in 1885, way behind England (1623) and the United States (1790), Japan's patent system has grown rapidly. In 1990 it introduced the world's first "paperless" application system, but it is still plagued by long delays in its processing of applications.
  Japanese companies typically file a large number of patent applications. In 1994 Japan's Patent Office processed 370,652 applications, of which 50,477 were filed by foreigners. Normally only 30% or less of the applications prove to be successful, although the ratio rose to 57% of 376,615 applications in 1996. Japanese companies also send a large number of patent applications abroad, and have received a large number of patent awards. According to the Patent and Trademark Office of the U.S. Department of Commerce, of the 109,646 patents granted in 1996, 23,053 (21%) were granted to Japanese individuals and companies. Of the ten companies receiving the most U.S. patents in 1996, the second, and the fourth through the tenth are Japanese.
  Aside from the growing inventiveness of the Japanese, the nature of Japan's patent system and the attempts to thwart patent applications by rivals also help explain such large numbers of patent applications. In Japan, as in most European countries, a patent goes to the first person to file an application, not to the first inventor, as in the United States. In addition, as in Europe, the Patent Office automatically makes patent applications public 18 months after they have been filed regardless of whether a patent is ultimately granted. Therefore an inventor cannot exploit his invention as a trade secret in Japan if he fails to receive a patent. If he is granted the

patent, however, he can ask for compensation from those who imitated his invention.

From the Japanese perspective, the first-to-file system is less prone to result in litigations. In addition it fosters the growth of large industry, whereas the first-to-invent system stresses the protection of small entrepreneurial inventors.

The application process consists of two steps. As of 1997 inventors can apply and pay the initial fee (¥21,000) and then decide within seven years whether to complete the application and pay the remaining fee of at least ¥858,000 for the 15-year-term of patent (note: this comes from the escalating annual fees, which are ¥40,600 in the 7–9th year, ¥81,200 in the 10–12th year, and ¥164,200 in the 13–15th year. In some cases the term of patent may be extended to 25 years, with higher annual fees). Although only about 30% of patent applications result in patents, this two-step application process permits and even encourages potential inventors to file patent applications in a defensive move to preempt the first claim from rivals.

Because of the large number of patent applications filed, it usually takes a long time—an average of 33 months in 1996 as compared with 19 months in the United States—for patents to be awarded. In a notorious and, no doubt, exceptional case, it took the Patent Office 29 years (February 1960 to October 1989) to give Texas Instruments its patent on the integrated circuit (New York Times, November 22 and 24, 1989). U.S. companies and trade officials have long complained that the usual delays are deliberately made to allow Japanese companies to create a competing product while preventing U.S. products from ever reaching Japan. The Japanese authority's response was that the Patent Office was understaffed. From 1980 to 1989, while the number of patent applications nearly doubled, the size of the Patent Office staff declined from 2,367 in 1980 to 2,336 in 1989 as a result of the general government staff reduction. By 1996 it had risen to 2,529 but the long delays have remained.

Japan also awards hundreds of narrowly defined patents that would be covered in a few broad generic patents in the United States. This practice invites countless challenges, many intended to force the applicant to surrender his technology. To make it worse, until recently opposition challenges from rivals could be filed even before patents were granted. In the United States, challenges can be filed only after the patent rights are granted. Small U.S. firms have complained that they can't afford to defend a barrage of opposition filings from Japanese competitors. In August 1994 in the continuing trade talks with Washington, Tokyo agreed to change the opposition filing system and allow only postgrant opposition, effective 1996.

Thus the Japanese patent system became an issue in the **Structural Impediments Initiative** (SII) talks between the United States and Japan in 1989–90. U.S. trade officials urged Tokyo to reform these practices that have hurt the U.S. interests. Private-sector advisers to the **Ministry of International Trade and Industry**, which supervises Japan's Patent Office, have also recommended that measures be taken to discourage "patent flooding"—the filing of numerous applications in an attempt to foil rivals—and promote the U.S. practice of awarding broader-coverage patents.

To reduce the delays in screening patent applications, the Japanese Patent Office started outside contracting for some patent inspection work in April 1989. A "paperless" electronic patent application system, the first in the world, was introduced in December 1990. These measures have reduced the average examination period—that is, the processing time between the filing of an application and the start of examining the case—from 38 months in 1988 to 25 months in 1994 and 22 months in 1996. One reason for this customary long delay is said to be the extremely detailed and burdensome documentation that is required.

Top patent applications in Japan include Canon Corp., Fujitsu Ltd., Hitachi Ltd, Matsushita Electric Industrial Co., Mitsubishi Electric Corp., NEC Corp., Sony Corp., and Toshiba Corp. It is reported that because of the long patent application process in Japan and of their global operations, these companies in the future will make relatively fewer patent applications in Japan and more abroad, especially in the United States.

Patent protection is only one aspect of intellectual property protection. The others are trademarks registration and protection of trade secrets. The Patent Office is in charge of trademarks registration. Trademarks registration in Japan is a slow process; it usually takes 30 months, as compared with one year in the United States. In addition Balassa and Noland (1988: 61) charge that in Japan foreign trademarks may be registered by domestic firms to preempt their subsequent registration by foreign firms that have already used them abroad. In response, the Japanese Patent Office explains that this practice is limited to foreign trademarks that are not well known in Japan.

See also **science and technology policy and research and development, Structural Impediments Initiative**.

Addresses

Japan Patent Information Organization
Sato Dia Bldg, 4-1-7, Toyo, Koto-ku, Tokyo 135
Tel: (3) 5690-5555   Fax: (3) 5690-5566

Patent Office, Ministry of International Trade and Industry
4-3, Kasumigaseki 3-chome, Chiyoda-ku, Tokyo 100
Tel: (3) 3581-1898   Fax: (3) 3581-0762

References

Akashi, Yoshihiko. 1990. Japan's patenting activity. *Osaka City University Economic Review*, 25: 13–26.

Balassa, Bela, and Marcus Noland. 1988. *Japan in the World Economy*. Washington: Institute for International Economics.

Choy, Jon. 1994. Framework talks yield patent agreement. *JEI Report* 33B, August 26: 3–4.

Japanese Patent Office. *Annual Report*.

Japanese Patent Office. 1988. *Guide to Industrial Property in Japan*.

Johnson, Chalmers. 1990. Revisionism, and the future of Japanese–American relations. In *Japan's Economic Structure: Should It Change?* ed. by Kozo Yamamura. Seattle: Society for Japanese Studies.

Maruko, Maya. 1994. Intellectual property rights accord with U.S. said necessary. *Japan Times Weekly*, May 9–15: 15.

Matsushita, Mitsuo. 1990. Protection of technology and the liberal trade order: A Japanese view. In *Japan's Economic Structure: Should It Change?*, ed. by Kozo Yamamura. Seattle: Society for Japanese Studies.

Patent plans follow production overseas. 1997. *Nikkei Weekly*, July 21: 6.

Patent war heating up. *Tokyo Business Today*, May 1992: 26–31.

Shioya, Yoshio. 1989. Intellectual property rights. In *Japan Economic Almanac, 1989*. Tokyo: Nihon Keizai Shimbun.

Spero, Donald M. 1990. Patent protection or piracy—A CEO views Japan. *Harvard Business Review* 68, 5: 58–67.

Tsuchiya, Hideo. 1989. Mother of invention too prolific for patent office. *Japan Economic Journal*, May 13: 20.

Yoder, Stephen. 1987. Rush to exploit new superconductors makes Japan even more patent-crazy. *Wall Street Journal*, August 27: 18.

pension fund market   The market where pension fund assets are managed and invested by fund managers to earn a rate of return and to meet pension payment obligations. Japan's total pension fund assets were about

¥220 trillion in 1996, the second largest in the world. Thus there has been competition for finanicial institutions, domestic and foreign, to become fund managers. However, because of low investment returns in the 1990s and expected rising pension payments due to the aging of the **population**, the possibility of the underfunding of pension plans has become an urgent social issue.

Japan's **pension system** consists of public pensions and private/ corporate pensions. Public pension funds are managed by the Pension Welfre Service Public Corporation. Private pension funds managers are restricted by government regulations to **trust banks**, life **insurance companies**, and **investment advisory companies**. Traditionally the government regulated the investment of pension funds, including the "5 : 3 : 3 : 2" rule whereby fund managers couldn't exceed these specified proportionate ceilings on investment in government bonds, loans, foreign investment, and equities. The rationale was to spread the risks and ensure the security of the funds. As a result pension funds were heavily dependent on government bonds and loans. However, because interest rates have been very low in Japan in the 1990s due to the long stagnation of the economy, the rule was changed in 1996 to allow fund managers to invest more in equities. Because Japanese fund managers have performed poorly, foreign trust banks and investment advisory companies have been permitted to compete to manage pension funds. They are said to have performed favorably, although they only manage a small portion of the total assets.

With the aging of the population, the rapidly rising pension payments, and the slow growth of contributions, the low investment yields portend an impending pension crisis. There are numerous proposal to reform various aspects of the system. Currently both public and private pension plans include defined pension benefits. One reform proposal for corporate pension plans is to change to defined employers' contributions only. Other proposals would lower the total (combined public and private) benefit level from the current 60% of previous wages. For public pensions, one proposal would increase the role of taxes in funding and reduce the reliance on pension contributions.

See also **pension system**.

References

Bronte, Stephen. 1996. Japan fund managers search for yield. *Asian Wall Street Journal Weekly*, December 2: 17.

Nakamura, Shuichi. 1996. Public pensions for an aging population. *Japan Echo*, Special issue: 48–53.

Suzuki, Yumiko. 1996. Corporate pension plans reeling as potential costs outstrip assets. *Nikkei Weekly*, October 7: 1, 4.

Yokoyama, Kiho. 1996. Funds banking on foreign managers. *Nikkei Weekly*, August 19: 12.

pension system   Extensively revised in 1986, Japan's pension system consists of the following major plans:

1. *National pension (kokumin nenkin).* This is the nonmedical portion of the **social security system.** All people living in Japan between the ages of 20 and 60 are required to join the plan. There were about 70 million participants as of 1996. Its benefits, called the *Basic Pensions*, include (a) the old age pension, payable at age 65, which is based on the period of coverage and is automatically adjusted in accordance with the Consumer Price Indexes, (b) the disability pension, and (c) survivor's pension for dependent spouse and children. The plan is financed by (a) premiums from insured persons who are not affiliated with any other pension plan (self-employed persons, farmers, and nonemployed persons), (b) contributions from pension insurance plans covering employees (see below), and (c) public revenue.

The benefits offered by the National Pension Fund are relatively low—only ¥55,000 a month in 1990 for those aged 65 or over, and ¥785,000 per year as of April 1996. Consequently, in April 1991, a second-tier National Pension Fund was introduced by the Ministry of Health and Welfare. The plan is designed for those who are not employed by firms or government offices with other pension plans. There are two types of supplementary National Pension Fund—a regional-type fund in each prefecture with more than 1,000 subscribers and a professional-type fund nationally for a group of more than 3,000 subscribers engaged in the same kind of industry or service. By May 1991 the regional type had been established in all 47 prefectures, and as of March 1995 there were 25 professional type National Pension Funds.

2. *Employees' pension insurance (kosei nenkin).* This provides the second tier of benefits to employees earning wages or salaries. Participation is mandatory for incorporated firms, which establish their own independent Employees' Pension Funds. In 1996 there were 33 million participants. The funds are managed by **trust banks,** life **insurance companies,** and **investment advisory companies** under the supervision of the Ministry of Health and Welfare. The benefits, including old age pension payable at

age 65, disability pension, and survivors' pension, are payable in addition to the Basic Program under the National Pension. The plan is funded by payroll deductions (total of 17.35% of wages as of October 1996) shared equally by employees and employers. The benefit level varies with the retiree's average wage level during the period of coverage and the length of the period. As of March 1996 the Fund was valued at ¥41.6 trillion.

3. *Mutual aid associations pensions (kyosai nenkin)*. Institutions such as the central government, local governments, private schools, and cooperative associations have organized their mutual aid pensions to cover their employees in addition to the National Pension.

As the Japanese **population** ages, the ratio of pension payments to national income will rise. It is estimated that in the year 2010, premiums will have to be as high as 31% of the average annual wage (or 16.9% of national income) to maintain the current levels of pensions. The task of investing the pension-fund assets in order to earn a satisfactory rate of return has also become a problem in the 1990s because of the slump of the economy.

See also **pension fund market, social security system**.

Address

Pension Bureau, Ministry of Health and Welfare
2-2, Kasumigaseki 1-chome, Chiyoda-ku, Tokyo 100
Tel: (3) 3503-1711

References

Bass, Scott A. 1996. An overview of work, retirement, and pensions in Japan. *Journal of Aging and Social Policy* 8, 2/3: 57–77.

Bronfenbrenner, Martin, and Yasukichi Yasuda. 1987. Economic Welfare. In *The Political Economy of Japan*, vol. 1: *The Domestic Transformation*, ed. by Kozo Yamamura and Yasukichi Yasuba. Stanford: Stanford University Press.

Hiraishi, Nagahisa. 1987. *Social Security*. Tokyo: Japan Institute of Labor.

Hoshino, Shinya. 1996. Paying for the health and social care of the elderly. *Journal of Aging and Social Policy* 8, 2/3: 37–55.

Isono, Naoyuki. 1990. Insurers lobby for lion's share of new fund. *Japan Economic Journal*, October 13: 30.

Kihara, Shin-ichi. 1997–1998. How should Japan's public pension system be revised? *Japan Research Quarterly* 7, 1: 64–113.

Murdo, Pat. 1990. Japan's social security and pension systems face need for new reforms. *JEI Report*, May 25.

Nakamura, Shuichi. 1996. Public pensions for an aging population. *Japan Echo*, Special issue: 48–53.

Shida, Tomio. 1990. Pension fund growth mirrors aging nation. *Japan Economic Journal*, May 12: 24.

Social Insurance Agency. 1996. *Outline of Social Insurance in Japan*.

Yamazak, Hiroaki. 1990. The employees' pension system in Japan: Past and present. *Annals of the Institute of Social Science* 32: 67–113.

Plaza Accord, 1985   An agreement reached by finance ministers of five major industrialized nations at New York's Plaza Hotel in September 1985 to cooperate by market intervention to bring about a gradual decline in the exchange rate of the U.S. dollar. As a result the yen appreciated rapidly.

See **yen shock, yen–dollar exchange rates.**

population   Japan's population in the postwar period has grown from 84 million in 1950 to 104.7 million in 1970 and 126 million in 1996. Because of a declining birth rate, the annual natural rate of increase—the difference between birth rate and death rate—has declined steadily from 17.2 per thousand population in 1950 to 11.8 in 1970 and 2.1 per thousand in 1995 (see table P.1). At the same time life expectancy at birth has risen steadily from 59.6 years for males and 63 years for females in 1950 to 77 years for males and 82.6 years for females (or average of 79.1) in 1996, which are the highest in the world. As a result of this slow growth of population and longer life expectancy, the average age of the population has become older.

Table P.2 gives official population projections made by the Ministry of Health and Welfare. The total population is projected to peak around 130 million around the year 2010. It will then start to decline around 2015 and reach 126 million or less after 2025. The percentage of people aged 65 and over in the population will increase steadily from 12.1% in 1990 to 21.3% in 2010 and 25.8% in 2025.

Table P.2 also gives the projected dependency index of the population. It shows the number of dependents (those aged 0–14 and 65 and above) that each 100 working adults aged 15–64 have to support in the economy. From a dependency index of 43.5 in 1990, the index is projected to rise steadily until it reaches a peak of about 70 in 2020. Then it is projected to decline to the high 60s in 2025 to 2030 before it peaks again at

Table P.1
Population size, birth rate, and death rate (in millions; births/deaths per thousand population)

Year	Total	Male	Female	Birth rate	Death rate
1950	84.1	41.2	42.9	28.1	10.9
1960	94.3	46.3	48.0	17.2	7.6
1970	104.7	51.4	53.3	18.8	6.9
1980	117.1	57.6	59.5	13.6	6.2
1985	121.0	59.5	61.6	11.9	6.3
1988	122.7	60.3	62.4	10.8	6.5
1989	123.2	60.6	62.7	10.2	6.4
1990	123.6	60.7	62.9	10.0	6.7
1991	124.0	60.9	63.2	9.9	6.7
1992	124.5	61.1	63.4	9.8	6.9
1993	124.8	61.2	63.5	9.6	7.1
1994	125.0	61.3	63.7	10.0	7.1
1995	125.6	61.6	64.0	9.5	7.4
1996	125.9	61.7	64.2	—	—

Source: Ministry of Health and Welfare.

Table P.2
Population projections

Year	Total (in millions)	Age 0–14 (in %)	Age 15–64 (in %)	Age 65 and above (in %)	Dependency index[a]
1990	123.6	18.2	69.7	12.1	43.5
2000	127.4	15.2	67.8	17.0	47.5
2005	129.3	15.6	65.2	19.1	53.4
2010	130.4	16.4	62.4	21.3	60.3
2015	130.0	16.3	59.5	24.1	68.1
2020	128.3	15.5	59.0	25.5	69.5
2025	125.8	14.4	59.7	25.8	67.5
2030	123.0	14.2	59.8	26.0	67.2
2040	117.3	15.3	56.7	28.0	76.4
2050	111.5	15.7	56.1	28.2	78.3
2070	101.0	16.6	58.2	25.2	71.8

Sources: Ministry of Health and Welfare.
a. Dependency index in calculated as (number of people aged 0 to 14 + number of people aged 65 and over)/(number of people aged 15 to 64) × 100.

78 in 2050. Such high dependency indexes, due primarily to the growing percentage of senior citizens in the population, will imply a heavy burden on the economy in two ways. First, there will be an increasingly tight labor market, since a smaller percentage of the population will be in the working age group. In 1990, 69.7% of the population (86.1 million) was between 15 and 64 in age. It will decline steadily to 67.8% (86.4 million) in 2000, 62.4% (81.3 million) in 2010, and 59.0% (75.8 million) in 2020. Second, there will be a growing demand for all sorts of social services, particularly pension, health care, and nursing care. The financing of these services will be a heavy burden on the economy and has become an important issue in policy discussions.

Thus Japan's demographic changes in the future will have a profound impact on the economy and serious policy implications for the government.

See also **social security system**.

Address

Council on Population Problems, Ministry of Health and Welfare
2-2. Kasumigaseki 1-chome, Chiyoda-ku, Tokyo 100
Tel: (3) 3503-1711

References

Coleman, Samuel. 1983. *Family Planning in Japanese Society*. Princeton: Princeton University Press.

Hodge, Robert William, and Naohiro Ogawa. 1991. *Fertility Change in Contemporary Japan*. Chicago: University of Chicago Press.

Hurd, Michael D., and Naohiro Yashiro, ed. 1996. *The Economic Effects of Aging in the United States and Japan*. Chicago: University of Chicago Press.

Noguchi, Yukio, and David A. Wise, ed. 1994. *Aging in the United States and Japan: Economic Trends*. Chicago: University of Chicago Press.

Ostrom, Douglas. 1996. Babies grow up: The changing demographics of the Japanese labor force. *JEI Report* 32A, August 23.

Takayama, Noriyuki. 1992. *The Greying of Japan: An Economic Perspective on Public Pensions*. Tokyo: Kinokuniya.

United Nations Development Program. Annual. *Human Development Report*. New York: World Bank/Oxford University Press.

postal savings Ever since 1875 the Ministry of Posts and Telecommunications has been operating the Postal Banking Service, which includes Postal Money Order and Postal Savings Services. The objective

Table P.3
Postal savings and personal savings deposits (outstanding balance in ¥ trillion)

End of FY	Postal savings	Banks	Total[a]
1977	37.7	60.4	143.0
1980	62.0	83.3	207.9
1983	86.3	106.6	272.2
1985	103.0	123.6	318.0
1988	125.9	156.3	393.8
1990	136.3	197.5	468.8
1991	155.6	205.6	505.0
1992	170.1	208.4	528.1
1993	183.5	215.9	555.0
1994	197.6	227.1	587.2
1995	213.4	237.0	613.3
1996	224.9	252.0	642.2

Source: Bank of Japan.
a. Sum of personal savings deposits at post offices, banks, shinkin banks, credit cooperatives, agricultural and fishery cooperatives, and labor credit association.

of the Postal Savings Service is to mobilize funds from small savers for social infrastructural **investment**.

The amounts of **savings** that have been deposited with the Postal Savings Service have been very large, almost as large as the amounts of personal savings deposited with commercial banks. At the end of FY 1985, the Postal Savings had an outstanding balance of ¥103 trillion (32.4% of total personal savings deposits), whereas bank personal savings amounted to ¥123.6 trillion. At the end of FY 1996, the Postal Savings had an outstanding balance of ¥224.9 trillion (34.7% of total personal savings), whereas commercial banks had ¥252 trillion savings deposits (see table P.3).

There are several types of postal savings deposits, including ordinary deposits, fixed-sum deposit certificates, time deposits, and installment deposits. The fixed-sum savings (*teigaku chokin*), a ten-year savings account in which depositors deposit a fixed sum at one time, is by far the most popular type. Depositors can withdraw the money at any post office without penalty after the first six months. However, the longer the money stays in the account (up to ten years), the higher the interest rate becomes, which is compounded semiannually.

Postal savings used to offer higher interest rates than commercial banks. However, since 1990 its interest rates have declined steadily in unison with the decline in bank interest rates, especially after June 1993 when all savings interest rates were dereguated as part of the **financial liberalization**. All types of interest rates have been at record low levels in Japan since the mid-1990s because of the long stagnation of the economy. As of June 1997, the interest rate of fixed-sum savings was only 0.85% a year for three-year deposits compared with 0.891% for three-year time deposits at banks. The rate is based in a complicated formula on that of three-year time deposits at commercial banks or on the nominal interest rate of ten-year government bonds, depending on specified market conditions. Similarly the interest rate on ordinary postal savings is tied to the interest rate of ordinary savings at commercial banks and to the three-month CD rate according to a specific formula, and it tends to be slightly higher than the bank rate. In June 1997 the postal rate was 0.25% on ordinary savings, whereas the bank rate was 0.1%.

Although postal savings system does not always offer higher interest rates than commercial banks, it still offers other advantages to savers:

1. *Accessibility.* The post office has more than 24,000 branches located throughout Japan, and most of them offer savings service. Forty percent of all post offices are in the rural areas, some of which do not even have bank branches. Thus the system facilitates household savings, and is traditionally a deposit-taker for small savers, especially in the rural areas.

2. *Absolute safety.* This is particularly important in the late 1990s because of the weakened financial conditions of Japanese banks due to real estate-related bad debts. In late 1997 several financial institutions went bankrupt, prompting shift of funds out of weaker banks to postal savings and stronger banks.

3. *Tax exemption for some.* Formerly the system also offered tax advantage, but this is no longer the case. Before 1988, interest earnings on postal savings up to ¥3 million were tax exempt. Since 1988, as part of the **tax reform**, tax exemption is restricted to the disabled, the elderly over 65, and widows.

4. *Financial services.* The system offers a variety of financial services, providing "one-stop shopping" convenience for depositors. There are postal pension plans (*teigaku* annuity savings) and *teigaku* housing savings for wage earners. The installment payments are deducted from monthly salaries and the interest earnings are tax exempt up to ¥3.85 and ¥5.5 million, respectively. Small depositor loans are available of up to ¥3,000,000, collateralized with postal savings accounts. Other postal services include postal life insurance plan, money orders, foreign currencies and traveler's checks, sale of public bonds, and so forth.

For these reasons, plus the fact that the Postal Savings Service does not have to pay heavy **corporate taxes**, commercial banks have long viewed postal savings as a competitor for deposits with unfair advantages. However, commercial banks have traditionally concentrated on servicing industries and urban customers, and they had little interest in providing deposit-taking offices in small towns and rural areas.

Postal savings are traditionally allocated by the Trust Fund Bureau of the **Ministry of Finance** to the government's **Fiscal Investment and Loans Program**, which makes loans to **public corporations** at a low interest rate. With the reform of tax exemption for small savers (*maruyu*), the postal system is permitted to invest a small percentage of its total deposits in securities, thus providing new competition for commercial banks. This is the *yucho* fund, officially translated as the "special account to deal with financial deregulation," established in June 1987. At the end of FY 1996, the fund reached ¥40 trillion. About 46% of it was invested in government bonds; the rest in corporate and bank debentures, municipal bonds, and designated money trusts.

Finally the postal savings system has introduced an innovative feature that links postal savings to Japan's **foreign aid** program. In January 1991 the Postal Savings for International Voluntary Aid (POSIVA) was inaugurated. It allows anyone in Japan with a postal savings account to support Japan's private aid projects by donating 20% of aftertax interest on ordinary deposits. The Ministry of Posts and Telecommunications collects the funds and allocates them to Japanese nongovernmental organizations (NGOs), which operates overseas aid projects. As of December 1996, 20.8 million depositors have participated in the program. The total amount of funds contributed, however, was only ¥2.8 billion in FY 1995 and ¥1.6 billion in FY 1996 because of the low level of interest rates. Nevertheless, it has provided much needed funds for Japanese NGOs.

According to government plan for **administrative reform**, postal savings as well as postal life insurance and mail delivery will be transferred to a new Postal Services Agency between 2001 and 2003, and to a new Postal **Public Corporation** after 2003.

See also **Administrative Reform, Fiscal Investment and Loan Program, interest rate structure, *maruyu*, tax reform.**

Address

Postal Savings Bureau, Ministry of Posts and Telecommunications
3-2, Kasumigaseki 1-chome, Chiyoda-ku, Tokyo 100
Tel: (3) 3504-4475   Fax: (3) 3507-8738

References

Bank of Japan. Annual. *Economic Statistics Annual.*

Iida, Masami. 1990. Banks hoping to lure postal savings deposits. *Japan Economic Journal,* February 24: 5.

Ishi, Hiromitsu. 1993. The fiscal investment and loan program and public enterprises. In *Japan's Public Sector: How the Government Is Financed,* ed. by Tokue Shibata. Tokyo: University of Tokyo Press.

Ministry of Posts and Telecommunications. 1997. *Postal Savings in Japan, 1996.*

Ministry of Posts and Telecommunications. 1997. *Japan's Postal Savings' Fund: Yucho, 1996.*

Ministry of Posts and Telecommunications. 1997. *The Postal Savings for Internatioal Voluntary Aid in Japan.*

Postal Savings Bureau. 1991. *Postal Banking in Japan, 1991.* Tokyo: Ministry of Posts and Telecommunications.

Suzuki, Yoshio, ed. 1987. *The Japanese Financial System.* Oxford: Oxford University Press. Chs. 3–4.

Tatewaki, Kazu. 1991. *Banking and Finance in Japan.* London: Routledge. Ch. 9.

Viner, James. 1987. *Inside Japan's Financial Markets.* London: The Economist Publications. Ch. 7.

Yokota, Hayato. 1991. Massive money shift alarms banks. *Nikkei Weekly,* November 9: 1.

prepaid cards   A popular way of paying for some goods and services. Prepaid vouchers in the form of magnetic cards can be purchased for set amounts to make telephone calls, buy train tickets, and so forth. Prepaid telephone cards are commonly used. Prepaid cards should be distinguished from credit cards.

See also **credit card industry**.

postwar reforms and reconstruction   At the end of the World War II in 1945, the Japanes economy faced serious problems. Air bombings since 1944 had decimated factories, residential houses, commercial ships, and the infrastructure of the economy. Disruption of production caused severe shortage of food and energy, and an inflation was raging out of control. The cessation of military production led to the **unemployment** of 4 million people; the demobilization of 7.6 million troops and the repatriation of 1.5 million civilians from abroad futher aggravated the unemployment problem.

From 1945 to 1952 Japan was occupied by the allied forces under the command of General Douglas MacArthur, the Supreme Commander for the Allied Powers (SCAP). MacArthur's primary objectives for Japan were demilitarization and democratization. Demilitarization was achieved through the suspension of military production, a ban on fleet and aircraft facilities, and restrictions on heavy industries and merchant vessels. Democratization consisted of five basic reforms: (1) recognition of the right of women to participate in politics; (2) establishment of the right of workers to organize; (3) democratization of the educational system; (4) abolition of absolutist politics, including the abolition of all laws and state organs that restricted human rights; (5) promotion of economic democratization (Uchino 1983: 19). A new Constitution was adopted in 1947 as the basis to implement demilitarization and democratization.

Economic democratization consisted mainly of three reforms: land reform, labor democratization, and the dissolution of *zaibatsu*:

1. *Land reform*. The objective of land reform was to broaden the democratic base of rural areas by limiting the landownership and hence the political power of rural elite and by enabling tenants to own the land they cultivated. The Revised Agricultural Lands Adjustment Law and the Owner-Cultivators Establishment Law of 1946 were adopted to implement the reform. A limit of one *cho* or 2.45 acres was placed on landlords' land ownership; the excess was bought by the government and redistributed to tenant farmers. By 1949, 1.87 million hectares were transferred to former tenants, which resulted in the proliferation of small farms (see **land uses and policies**).

2. *Labor democratization*. Three **labor laws**—the Trade Union Law (1945), the Labor Relations Adjustment Law (1946), and the Labor Standards Law (1947)—were adopted. They gave workers the right to organize **labor unions**, established methods for settling labor disputes, protected workers from forced labor, introduced the eight-hour work day and holiday systems, set limits on the employment of women and minors, and established work-related injury compensation. However, with the intensification of the Cold War in 1947–48, the growing militancy of Japanese labor uions, and the outbreak of the Korean War in 1950, the SCAP's zeal for labor reform had declined by 1950.

3. *The dissolution of* **zaibatsu**. Zaibatsu were the prewar business conglomerates, each controlled by a wealthy family through a **holding company**. They dominated the Japanese economy up to 1945, and were believed to have facilitated Japan's war effort. The purpose of this reform was to eliminate their monopoly power and thus to decentralize and democratize the postwar economy. The **Antimonopoly Law** (1947) was

enacted, which dissolved the holding companies. Former *zaibatsu* families and senior executives were purged from the companies. The individual companies became independent in terms of ownership and control. Subsequently, however, companies of three former *zaibatsu*—Mitsubishi, Mitsui and Sumitomo—regrouped as *keiretsu*, which are bank-centered interlocking corporate groups. They have remained powerful in the Japanese economy.

With the intensification of the Cold War in the late 1940s, the American policy shifted from democratization and reform to rebuilding Japan as a strong ally. The Economic Recovery Plan (1948) was drafted by the Economic Stabilization Board for 1948–52 to help reconstruct the economy with U.S. aid. To combat inflation, the Dodge Plan, a broad program of restrictive fiscal and monetary policies developed under the guidance of Joseph Dodge, was adopted. Dodge was an American banker brought to Japan in 1949 as a financial advisor to SCAP. He deemed it essential for Japan to have a balanced budget and a tight monetary policy to control Japan's inflation. In addition, to expose the Japanese economy to international competition, Dodge set a single exchange rate in 1949 at 360 yen to the dollar. Although Japan's postwar inflation abated by 1950, some scholars have criticized the Dodge Plan as being too restrictive and deflationary for the economy (Nakamura 1981: 39).

The Korean War broke out in 1950. The U.S. and U.N. procurement from Japan for the war created a boom for Japanese industries. The general increase in world trade since the 1950s also provided a growing market for Japan's exports. The Japanese economy was able to take advantage of these opportunities and entered the period of rapid growth during the 1950s and 1960s; the phase of postwar reconstruction was over. With the signing of the Peace Treaty of San Francisco in 1951 and the Japanese–American Security Pact in 1952, the occupation of Japan by the Allied Powers was officially ended in 1952.

Japan subsequently implemented many more reforms as its economy further developed and reached maturity, and its early postwar institutions became increasingly appropriate. These reforms have taken place in many areas of the economy and are discussed in **banking regulations and deregulation, Big Bang, Equal Employment Opportunity Law, financial liberalization, foreign exchange control and decontrol, tax reform**, and **trade policy**.

See also **Antimonopoly Law, economic planning**, *keiretsu* **and business groups, labor laws, land uses and policies**.

References

Kawagoe, Toshikiko. 1993. Land reform in postwar Japan. In *The Japanese Experience of Economic Reforms*, ed. by Juro Teranishi and Jutaka Kosai. New York: St. Martin's Press.

Miwa, Yoshiro. 1993. Economic effects of the antimonopoly and other deconcentration policies in postwar Japan. In *The Japanese Experience of Economic Reforms*, ed. by Juro Teranishi and Yutaka Kosai. New York: St. Martin's Press.

Nakamura, Takafusa. 1981. *The Postwar Japanese Economy: Its Development and Structure*, trans. by Jacquiline Kaminski. Tokyo: University of Tokyo Press. Ch. 2.

Tsuru, Shigeto. 1993. *Japanese Capitalism: Creative Defeat and Beyond*. Cambridge: Cambridge University Press. Chs. 1–2.

Uchino, Tatsuro. 1983. *Japan's Postwar Economy*, trans. by Mark A. Harbison. Tokyo: Kondansha International. Ch. 1.

Yoshikawa, Hiroshi and Tetsuji Okazaki. 1993. Postwar hyperinflation and the Dodge Plan, 1945–50: An overview. In *The Japanese Experience of Economic Reforms*, ed. by Juro Teranishi and Yutaka Kosai. New York: St. Martin's Press.

price fixing   There are two types of price fixing. (1) Resale-price maintenance, in which manufacturers set the retail prices of their products for retailers. This was once prevalent in some industries but has become much less so since the early 1990s. (2) Price fixing as part of an agreement among firms of an industry to form a **cartel**. There are different types of cartels for different purposes, but they invariably aim at restricting market competition and hence often entail price fixing.

Both types of price fixing violate the **Antimonopoly Law** unless approved by the Fair Trade Commission as exceptions to the law. Since the early 1990s the Commission has reduced the number of approved exceptions and cracked down on illegal ones.

See **Antimonopoly Law, cartels, pricing practices**.

price indexes and price levels   Japan publishes a number of price indexes, including the consumer price index, wholesale price index, corporate service price index, urban land price indexes, rural price indexes, and deflators for various national income accounts. The first two are the most important indicators of price levels and inflationary pressure.

The consumer price index (CPI) is published monthly by the **Management and Coordination Agency** under the Prime Minister's Office, currently with 1995 as the base period. It is based on survey data of 580 items of consumer goods and services, divided into ten basic categories, each given appropriate weight to reflect its relative importance in the consumer budget. These categories and their weights are foods (28.5%), housing (19.8%), transportation and communications (12.2%), cultural and recreation (10.9%), clothing and footwear (6.8%), fuel, light, and water (5.9%), furniture and household utensils (4.1%), education (4.6%), medical care (3.3%), and others (4.0%). Among these, services constitute 48.4% and commodities 51.6%.

There are regional variations in the CPI. For the **Tokyo** area the **Bank of Japan** publishes a separate series of the CPI in which the weights of the components are different, reflecting the different cost of living in Tokyo. Greater weight are given to housing (25.4%) and education (5.1%); foods, transportation and communication, furniture and household utensils, are given less weight. Overall, services constitute 55.9% and goods 44.1%.

The wholesale price index (WPI) is published monthly by the Bank of Japan, currently with 1995 as the base period. It is based on survey data of 1,427 commodities, of which 971 are domestic products for domestic market, 209 are for exports, and 247 are imported products. The industry origin of the products and their weights in the index are manufacturing industry products (90.8%), agricultural, forestry and aquatic products (3.4%), mining products (3.2%), electric power, gas, and water (3.5%), and others. These products can also be classified according to the stage of demand and use as follows: raw materials (4.2%), intermediate materials (43.6%), capital goods (14.0%), consumer goods (including consumer durables and nondurables, 25.3%), and exports (11.9%).

The CPI and WPI do not move in synchronization. In general, when exchange rate and oil price changes are the main causes of price changes, as was often the case, the WPI tends to lead the CPI in changes. Furthermore the WPI tends to be more sensitive to business fluctuations. Given Japan's complex distribution system, changes in the WPI tend to filter down to the CPI with a lag. However, in the late 1980s with a growing labor shortage, increases in consumer service prices led those in wholesale prices.

The growing labor shortage and the speculative land and real estate investment boom in the late 1980s led to rapid increases in the prices of some services in excess of increases in CPI. Land-use–related charges such as rents rose sharply in the large cities, particularly Tokyo. In order to measure and monitor this inflationary pressure, the Bank of Japan introduced a quarterly "corporate service price index" on January 1, 1991. Currently the index includes 89 items, including real estate rent (10.7%), other leasing and renting (13.4%), transportation charges (24.4%), information services (7.5%), communications (5.9%), advertising fees (6.1%), finance and insurance (5.2%), building maintenance and construction services (10.9%), and other services.

Rural price indexes are published by the Ministry of Agriculture, Forestry, and Fisheries. They include the rural consumer price index, the index of selling prices of agricultural products, and the price index of goods used in farm operation and rural livelihood. Thus they are of particular importance to the rural population.

The indexes of urban land prices are compiled by the Japan Real Estate Institute with 1990 as the base period. The indexes consist of two major categories: those of 223 cities and those of six major cities. Each is further classified into three subcategories according to the use of the land (commercial, residential, and industrial). As shown in table P.4, the indexes for the six major cities fluctuate much more than those for 223 cities. Furthermore both fluctuate much more than CPI and WPI. The dramatic and

Table P.4
Major price indexes (annual average)

Year	CPI	WPI	ULPI (1)	ULPI (2)	GDP deflators
1970	32.3		22.8	10.1	38.9
1980	76.3	120.3	52.8	24.5	82.7
1981	80.0	122.0	57.4	26.6	86.1
1982	82.3	124.2	61.5	28.4	87.6
1983	83.8	121.4	64.4	29.7	89.1
1984	85.7	121.1	66.5	31.3	91.5
1985	87.4	119.7	68.3	33.6	93.4
1986	88.0	108.8	70.2	38.4	95.1
1987	88.0	104.7	74.1	48.3	95.2
1988	88.6	103.6	81.5	61.8	95.8
1989	90.7	106.3	87.6	76.9	97.8
1990	93.5	108.5	**100.0**	**100.0**	**100.0**
1991	96.5	107.8	110.4	103.0	102.7
1992	98.1	106.1	108.4	87.0	104.5
1993	99.4	103.0	102.4	71.4	105.1
1994	100.1	101.0	97.7	63.2	105.3
1995	**100.0**	**100.0**	94.1	54.7	104.6
1996	100.1	100.1	90.0	48.6	104.1
1997	101.9	101.6	86.3	44.9	—

Sources: Bank of Japan, Economic Planning Agency, Management and Coordination Agency.
Note: CPI = consumer price index, WPI = wholesale price index, ULPI (1) = urban land price index (average of 223 cities), ULPI (2) = urban land price index (average of 6 major cities)

speculative rise of urban land prices in the major cities before 1991 and their rapid decline afterward were an important cause of the **bubble economy** of the late 1980s and its severe aftermath after the bubble burst in 1990–91.

Finally the deflators for gross domestic products, gross domestic expenditure, gross national expenditure, and so forth, are composite price indexes used to deflate nominal rational income and expenditure figures in current prices into real figures in constant base-period prices. They are compiled by the **Economic Planning Agency.**

From table P.4 it is clear that Japan's annual increases in CPI in the 1980s and early 1990s were very small by international standards. This was not the case in the early to mid-1970s when, in the aftermath of the first oil crisis in 1973, CPI rose 11.7% in 1973, 23.2% in 1974, 11.7% in 1975, and 9.4% in 1976.

The slow CPI increases in the 1980s would have made Japanese prices relatively low by international standards if exchange rates between yen and dollar had remained the same. Unfortunately, the yen rapidly appreciated against the dollar after 1985, making Japanese prices considerably higher than those in other major industrial countries in the late 1980s and early 1990s (when converted at the prevailing exchange rates). For example, the Economic Planning Agency conducted in November 1990 surveys of about 400 consumer goods and services in Tokyo, New York, Hamburg, and London. Against Tokyo's base prices of 100, New York's prices stood at 76, Hamburg's 80, and London's 96. Japan's prices were particularly high for beef, rice, and gas for cooking and heating.

Since then the price differentials between Tokyo and other large foreign cities have narrowed for two reasons. (1) Increasing domestic deregulation, including cheaper imports, and the slow growth of the economy have caused CPI to be virtually stationary since 1994 and WPI to decline steadily since 1990 (see table P.4). (2) Because of the weak economy and a series of failures of Japanese financial institutions, the yen has depreciated since late 1997. Thus the same Japanese prices in yen would translate into lower dollar prices.

See also **pricing practices, yen–dollar exchange rates.**

References

Bank of Japan. Annual. *Economic Statistics Annual.*

Corporate service price index: Movements and characteristics since 1985. *Bank of Japan Quarterly Bulletin* 1, 2, 1993: 51–70.

Economic Planning Agency. Annual. *Annual Report on National Accounts*.

Fukuda, Shin-ichi, Hiroshi Teruyama, and Hiro Y. Toda. 1991. Inflation and price-wage dispersions in Japan. *Journal of the Japanese and International Economies* 5: 160–88.

Leisure prices get own index. *Nikkei Weekly*, September 7, 1991: 3.

Management and Coordination Agency. Annual. *Japan Statistical Yearbook*.

Prices still too high in Japan: EPA. *Nikkei Weekly*, October 19, 1991: 4.

Tokyo most expensive, though less so. *Nikkei Weekly*, June 6, 1992: 3.

pricing practices   Pricing is at the very core of a firm's market behavior. Unfortunately, it is impossible to have a complete picture of pricing practices of diverse private businesses, since these relate to competitive business strategy which business managers are reluctant to talk about. Nor are textbook price theories very helpful, for no single theory—not even the "cost-plus" principle—can explain the pricing behaviors of Japanese firms (Komiya 1990: 204–205). From various reports, however, one can piece together a mosaic of pricing practices in some major sectors of the economy:

1. Many analysts suggest that a common pricing rule in manufacturing is reverse cost-plus pricing—that is, firms may first set a competitive selling price that is necessary to secure a certain market share and then strive to cut costs and profit margin to fit that price (Hasegawa 1986). In other words, cost and profit margin are the variables (obviously within some limits), the exact opposite of Western cost-plus pricing. Morita (1992), former chairman of Sony Corporation, affirms that this is indeed the case in the consumer **electronics industry**. So does the management of NEC Corp. (author's interview, June 16, 1993). Thus the cost-cutting efforts may be relentless, and large-volume production and sales are needed to help cut costs. Overseas sourcing is increasingly necessary in the face of rising domestic labor cost and yen appreciation. Profit margin may be sacrificed in the short run for the sake of market share.

The **automobile industry** seems to have increasingly adopted the same strategy since the mid-1990s. For example, plagued by the rising yen and the growing competitiveness of the American auto producers, Toyota Motor Corp. announced in August 1995 that it would make a low-priced compact "Asian car" for the Southeast Asian market starting in 1997. It is estimated that to be price competitive and to raise Toyota's market share, the model has to be priced at 360,000 Thai baht ($14,400). From this, the costs of auto parts are calculated and then the sources of supply are determined. Toyota's subsidiaries and joint ventures in various Southeast Asian countries will supply these parts. Honda Motor Co. also plans its production of its Asian car by sourcing major parts from its plants in Southeast Asia (Sumiya 1995).

On the other hand, Langlois (1997) finds that the pricing strategy of Japanese automakers in the U.S. market is to maximize the short-run profits per car rather than market shares. This may be because the U.S. market is highly competitive and well developed, whereas the emerging markets of Southeast Asia have much potentials for growth.

2. Alternatively, variable cost or marginal cost pricing may be used by some large manufacturing firms for exports. In his discussion of the competitive edge of Japanese business practices over those of the United States, Prestowitz (1988: 180–81) suggests that large Japanese manufacturers regard large interest payments on debt (bank loans being more important than equity capital to Japanese companies) and wages of lifetime employees as fixed costs, costs that have to be paid regardless of the output level. Thus Japanese firms' variable costs are lower than those of American firms, and hence they are willing to accept lower export prices as long as the prices are adequate to cover the firms' variable costs. The semiconductors industry is given as an example. Other analysts contend that the **steel industry** has also practiced variable-cost pricing in its exports while keeping domestic prices at a higher level to cover the fixed costs, thus giving rise to charges of export dumping (Ostrom 1996: 10).

3. In the retail trade it is often observed that Japanese retail prices are usually higher than their counterparts in Western countries. This can be due to a higher markup, higher retail cost, or retail price fixing. Kang (1990) argues that a higher retail markup is reasonable in Japan because of higher rent and more post-sale services such as delivery and repair. In other words, retailing is extremely labor intensive in Japan, and labor is costly in Japan.

In investigating the differentials between domestic and overseas prices, Baba (1995) finds that many manufacturing sectors also practice markup pricing. However, the markup ratios are generally higher in non-manufacturing sectors than in manufacturing sectors; they are particularly high in agriculture, forestry, fisheries, finance, and insurance which have been highly protected or regulated by the government until recently.

The fixing of retail prices of some products such as books and magazines, low-priced cosmetics, records and CDs, and some pharmaceuticals by manufacturers (*saihan*, resale price contract) has been accepted by the

Fair Trade Commission as exceptions to the **Antimonopoly Law** as long as free competition and other conditions exist. One reason is to keep numerous small retailers, particularly drug stores, in business. Critics have long argued, however, that illegal **price fixing** by manufacturers has existed in other industries such as consumer electronics and automobiles. None of them has been prosecuted, however, by the Fair Trade Commission for violating the Antimonopoly Law. It was only in early 1992, after the United States demanded a more rigorous implementation of the Anti-monopoly Law following the U.S.–Japan **Structural Impediments Initiative** talks that the Fair Trade Commission announced that fixed prices on 10 medicines and 13 cosmetic products will be abolished as of April 1993. The Commission has also warned *keiretsu* stores in consumer electronics against price fixing. In June 1995 Shiseido, the leading cosmetics manufacturer, was ordered by the Fair Trade Commission to allow retailers to discount its products. Shiseido has traditionally required retailers to have face-to-face contact with buyers. Such a contract tends to discourage discounting because of built-in labor costs.

4. A unique pricing practice—the so-called deferred pricing or postpricing system (*atogime*)—has existed in the petrochemical and paper industries. The practice allows makers of raw materials or semifinished products to negotiate or finalize their selling prices after the sales contract or delivery is made, or after the prices of the buyers' finished products are established. For example, in the petrochemical industry, producers of raw materials such as ethyline and polypropyline get their "fair" share of profits by finalizing their prices after their buyers such as the makers of vinyl chloride have fixed the prices of their own products. In the paper industry the practice was introduced in 1977–78 in the aftermath of the 1973 oil crisis. Small producers had difficulties setting prices in the midst of price declines during the recession in 1977 and the subsequent price increases during the economic recovery in 1978. They adopted the practice of "tentative" pricing that gave them the flexibility of renegotiating prices later with industry buyers.

Deferred pricing has brought buyers a mixed blessing. On the one hand, buyers have the right to demand rebates if the prices of their own products subsequently decline. On the other hand, it makes production costs uncertain and account settlements, budgeting, and planning more difficult.

Deferred pricing came under criticism during the U.S.–Japan Structural Impediments Initiative talks because it compounds the difficulties of foreign access to the Japanese market. In the petrochemical industry several ethylene producers have indicated their willingness to abandon it. One reason is the expected competition from South Korean exporters. Large Korean business groups such as Samsung and Hyundai are setting up plants to produce and export ethylene, with Japan as the targeted market. Given this impending competition, Japanese industry would benefit from a faster pricing mechanism that conforms to world standards. Thus analysts in Japan believe that the practice has outlived its usefulness and that it is a matter of time before it is abandoned.

5. In the **construction industry** the practice of *dango* (prebidding consultation) or bid-rigging in public works projects has been uncovered from time to time. It is a way to distribute public works projects among the contractors in which the designated contractor submits the lowest winning bid. *Dango* was brought up by Washington during the U.S.– Japan Structural Impediments Initiative talks as a barrier to entry that has prevented foreign construction firms from entering the Japanese construction market. Because it eliminated price competition, including that from foreign firms, it increased the cost of public works at taxpayers' expense. One estimate puts excess profits from *dango* at 16–33% of the industry's revenues (cited in Johnson 1990: 115).

6. In the **steel industry**, the **Ministry of International Trade and Industry** (MITI) has actively intervened in the pricing process because of the industry's importance. Between 1958 and 1991 MITI attempted to stabilize steel prices through the so-called list price system (*kokai hanbai sei*, literally, "open sales system"). Under the system the steel company sells a steel product to a designated wholesaler at the "list price" that it had previously reported to MITI. Price stability was considered essential to provide profitability and investment incentives. Because of the practice of list price "discounting" during recessions, analysts disagree on the effectiveness of the system in stabilizing actual market prices.

The practice of "price leadership" is said to have been important in the steel industry because of its concentrated structure. Nippon Steel, the largest firm that produces about 30% of the industry's output, is considered to be the price leader.

7. Pricing practices for exports and imports are subjects of much foreign criticism. It has long been observed that Japanese products are often cheaper abroad and do not usually increase proportionally, if at all, when the yen appreciates. On the other hand, imported foreign products are much more expensive in Japan at the prevailing exchange rate. As to high

import prices, the higher rent and labor costs mentioned above may explain part of the difference. Another cause has to do with the **distribution system**. The traditional "general import agents" system gives exclusive contracts to some wholesalers or **trading companies** to import brand name products. This has given them the monopoly power to control the distribution and prices of imported goods.

As to the relatively low export prices, which do not rise as much as the appreciation of yen, part of the explanation is that the prices of energy and other raw materials used to produce exports tend to decline as the yen appreciates. Over and above that, however, Johnson (1990: 110) and others have charged that Japanese manufacturers have deliberately set their export prices at lower levels than domestic prices in order to expand their foreign market shares and that they have used their high domestic prices to subsidize exports. Proponents of this view often cite the experience between 1985 and 1988 during which Japanese export prices (calculated in yen) fell relative to domestic wholesale prices.

In an empirical study Marston (1991) estimates that about one-half of the yen's real appreciation between February 1985 and December 1988 was neutralized by Japanese manufacturers by lowering their export prices relative to domestic prices. This type of price discrimination or "pricing-to-market" behavior is possible because the export and domestic markets are separated and have different demand characteristics. Also traditionally cheaper Japanese exports cannot reenter the Japanese market to undercut domestic prices due to government policy and various structural factors, although this has been changing since the late 1980s. However, Knetter (1993) finds that the extent of Japanese pricing-to-market is similar to that of the British and German exporters. Marston (1991: 139) expects Japanese pricing-to-market behavior in export to diminish in the future as they diversify their production facilities abroad and can respond to yen appreciation by shifting export production to plants abroad.

8. In the agricultural sector, the price of rice is the most important agricultural price in Japan because of the importance of rice in the Japanese diet and the government's long-standing policy (until 1993) to ban rice imports by subsidizing domestic rice production. The government purchases part of the annual rice output at a price (producer's rice price) set by the government. Since 1960 the price is set annually by the "production cost and income compensation" method, which takes into account the production costs, family labor cost and hired labor cost, and so forth. The precise formula for calculation has been revised from time to time to

reflect the supply-demand situation. For the 1990 crop the following factors were taken into account in calculating the price (Nakagawa 1991):
• Family labor cost (28% of price). This is evaluated according to the wages of manufacturing firms with 5 to 999 employees.
• Fertilizer, pesticide, and hired labor cost (50%).
• Interest on capital (4%). Both borrowed and owned capital are included in the calculation at a certain interest rate.
• Rent (21%). Rent on owned land is considered as interest on land asset, evaluated at a certain interest rate.
• Deduction of the price of by-product (−3%).

The government purchase price for a 60-kilogram-bag of brown rice was lowered from ¥16,500 for the 1990 crop to ¥16,392 for 1991–96, and ¥16,217 for 1997 because of changing supply-demand conditions. It was further lowered to ¥15,805 for 1998. In arriving at the latest purchase price, the government used a forumla that takes into account both the change in the free market price of rice and the change in the costs of production. In algebraic form,

$$\text{price(1998)} = \text{price(1997)} \times (0.5 \times A + 0.5 \times B),$$

where $A =$ the ratio between the average free market price of rice in 1995–97 and that in 1994–96; $B =$ the ratio between the average costs of production in 1996 and those in 1995 (author's interview, Ministry of Agriculture, Forestry, and Fisheries, April 15, 1998). The significance of this new formula is that changes in market prices are explicitly taken into account in setting the government price.

In conclusion, many Japanese prices are administered prices or monopolistic prices for various reasons—corporate marketing strategies, market power, government regulations and protection, and ineffective implementation of the Antimonopoly Law. In other words, domestic prices tend to be higher than what would have been competitive market prices, but the opposite may be true for export prices due to strategic business considerations.

See also **construction industry, distribution system, rice production and distribution, steel industry**.

References

Baba, Naohiko. 1995. On the cause of price differentials between domestic and overseas markets: Approach through empirical analysis of markup pricing. *Bank Of Japan Monetary and Economic Studies* 13, 2: 45–74.

Deferred pricing, another practice that outlives its initial usefulness. *Japan Economic Journal*, April 28, 1990: 29.

Hasegawa, Keitaro. 1986. *Japanese-Style Management: An Insider's Analysis*. Tokyo: Kodansha International.

Johnson, Chalmers. 1990. Trade, revisionism, and the future of Japanese–American relations. In *Japan's Economic Structure: Should It Change?* ed. by Kozo Yamamura. Seattle: Society for Japanese Studies.

Kang, T. W. 1990. *Gaishi: The Foreign Company in Japan*. New York: Basic Books. Ch. 1.

Knetter, Michael M. 1993. International comparisons of pricing-to-market behavior. *American Economic Review* 83 (June): 473–86.

Komiya, Ryutaro. 1990. *The Japanese Economy: Trade, Industry, and Government*. Tokyo: University of Tokyo Press. Ch. 5.

Langlois, Catherine. 1997. For profit or for market share? The pricing strategy of Japanese automakers on the U.S. market. *Journal of the Japanese and International Economies*. 11: 55–81.

Marston, Richard C. 1990. Pricing to market in Japanese manufacturing. *Journal of International Economics* 29 (November): 217–36.

Marston, Richard C. 1991. Price behavior in Japanese and U.S. manufacturing. In *Trade with Japan*, ed. by Paul Krugman. Chicago: University of Chicago Press.

Morita, Akio. 1992. A critical moment for Japanese management? *Japan Echo*, 19, 2: 8–14.

Nakagawa, Hiroshi. 1991. Rice price policy in Japan. Ministry of Agriculture, Forestry, and Fisheries. Mimeographed.

Ohno, Kenichi. 1989. Export pricing behavior of manufacturing: A U.S.–Japan Comparison. *International Monetary Fund Staff Papers* 36, 1 (March): 550–79.

Ostrom, Douglas. 1996. Japanese steel companies gird for new challenges. *JEI Report* 39A, October 13.

Petrochemical "post-pricing" is headed for the scrapheap. *Japan Economic Journal*, May 26, 1990: 29.

Prestowitz, Clyde V. 1988. *Trading Places*. New York: Basic Books.

Saxonhouse, Gary R. 1993. Pricing strategies and trading blocs in East Asia. In *Regionalism and Rivalry: Japan and the United States in Pacific Asia*, ed. by Jeffrey A. Frankel and Miles Kahler. Chicago: University of Chicago Press.

Sumiya, Fumiya. 1995. Toyota rolls out strategy to snare Asian market. *Nikkei Weekly*, August 28: 1, 27.

Yamawaki, Hideki. 1988. The steel industry. In *Industrial Policy of Japan*, ed. by Ryutaro Komiya, Masahiro Okuno, and Kotaro Suzumura. Tokyo: Academic Press Japan.

prime rates   Interest rates that commercial banks charge on loans and discounts of bills of exceptionally high credit standards. There are short-term prime rate for loans of less than one year in maturity and long-term prime rate for loans of longer maturity. The former is particularly important because banks use it as the lower limit to set other short-term lending rates.

See **interest rate structure.**

privatization   In 1985 and 1987 three major **public corporations**—Nippon Telegraph and Telephone, Japan National Railways, and Japan Tobacco—were privatized. The privatization was undertaken to reduce the deficit, provide management flexibility, and improve efficiency. The results to date are mostly favorable, although the process has not been easy and some difficulties remain.

Nippon Telegraph and Telephone (NTT), founded in 1952 as a government company, was privatized in April 1985. It is the world's second largest telecommunications company after American Telephone and Telegraph Co. The government had raised some ¥10 trillion by selling 1.95 million shares each in fiscal 1986 and 1987, and 1.5 million shares in 1988. Additional sales have been delayed repeatedly since fiscal 1989. As of 1997 the government still held the majority of shares. NTT is the largest private employer in Japan.

NTT's fares for telephone service have been reduced since privatization. Its customer service is said to have been improved. It remains the dominant firm in the telecommunications industry. The Ministry of Posts and Telecommunications, which regulates the industry, has long sought to break up the company to stimulate more competition and efficiency. In December 1996 an agreement was reached between the Ministry and NTT on the restructuring of the company. It would be broken up in 1999 into one long-distance company and two regional phone companies under a **holding company.** The **Antimonopoly Law** was revised in 1997 to lift its ban on holding companies.

Japan National Railways (JNR), founded in 1949 through the reorganization of a branch of the Ministry of Transportation, ran the state sector of Japan's railway system until it was privatized in April 1987. It excelled in train speed, safety, and punctuality but was plagued by deficit, interference from politicians, and labor strife. In April 1987 it was broken up into six regional Japan Railway companies and one freight company. Its old debt was assumed by a new JNR Accounts Settlement Corp., which also holds all shares of the new companies. Sales of shares to pay for the JNR debt has been delayed because of the stock market's decline.

The former Japan National Railways incurred deficits despite frequent fare increases, whereas the new Japan Railway companies are profitable and have rarely raised fares. Because of new managerial flexibility, the companies are diversifying into profitable travel-related services.

The former Japan Tobacco and Salt, a government monopoly, was founded in 1949 through the merger of two government monopolies in tobacco and salt. It was privatized in April 1985 and renamed Japan Tobacco. At the same time the government liberalized the tobacco import and wholesale businesses and opened them to both domestic and foreign firms. However, Japan Tobacco retains a monopoly on domestic production of tobacco products and is required to buy all domestically grown tobacco leaf regardless of quality. Thus privatization has not freed it of government control. Most shares are still held by the government. Nevertheless, because of greater management flexibility and competition from imports, the company is said to be more attentive to customer demand. For example, its product brands have been greatly increased.

Thus the three major cases of privatization in Japan—involving NTT, Japan National Railways, and Japan Tobacco and Salt—are not full privatization in the usual sense. The companies were changed into special companies with mixed private and public ownership. However, there have been four cases of full privatization that are less publicized: Japan Automobile Terminal Co. (1985), Tohoku Development Co. (1985), Japan Airlines (1987), and Okinawa Electric Power Co. (1988) (Uekusa 1994: 317). In the case of Japan Airlines, the government sold its 34.5% share following the liberalization of Japan's international cargo business and domestic passenger and cargo businesses in 1985.

As to future privatization, the government's housing loan business, the national hospital system, and the **postal savings** system have been suggested as candidates. However, most of the remaining **public corporations** are either **government financial institutions** or special-purpose corporations. Both were set up to assist specific sectors of the economy. For this reason they are either unprofitable to operate under private ownership (e.g., Japan Small Business Corporation) or require close contact with various government agencies during the course of their operations (e.g., **Japan Development Bank**). Such public corporations are not likely to be privatized.

See also **public corporations and special corporations, railway companies, telecommunications industry**.

References

Choy, Jon. 1990. Former Japanese public corporations: post-privaization update. *JEI Report* 32A, August 17.

Fukui, Koichiro. 1992. *Japanese National Railways Privatization Study: The Experience of Japan and Lessons for Developing Countries*. Washington: World Bank.

Ishibashi, Asako. 1995. State-owned shares staring at red light. *Nikkei Weekly*, July 10: 12.

NTT no longer acts like a graceful giant. *Tokyo Business Today*, June 1991: 46–48.

Ogawa, Joshua. 1996. Restructuring would put NTT into hot global arena. *Nikkei Weekly*, December 9: 1, 8.

Privatization keeps customers satisfied. *Nikkei Weekly*, March 28, 1992: 11.

Privatized rails make headway. *Nikkei Weekly*, April 18, 1992: 1.

Steiner, Robert. 1995. Japan's plunging market hurts privatization plans. *Asian Wall Street Journal Weekly*, July 3: 19.

Uekusa, Masu. 1994. The privatization of public enterprises: background and results. In *Business Enterprises in Japan: Views of Leading Japanese Economists*, ed. by Kenichi Imai and Rytaro Komiya. Cambridge: MIT Press.

property tax   The second largest tax for municipal governments, levied on owners of land, buildings, and other tangible assets.
   See **tax system**.

public assistance   A component of Japan's **social security system** designed to assist the indigent in medical care and living expenses.
   See **social security system**.

public bonds   A broad category of bonds that includes government bonds issues by the national government, local bonds, and **public corporation** bonds.
   See **bond market, government bonds**.

public corporations and special corporations   Special corporations (*tokushu hojin*)—also called public enterprises by scholars such as Ishi (1993) and Uekusa (1994)—are a broad category of heterogeneous government-affiliated enterprises. There are 85 of them as of January 1, 1998, including 42 government-owned public corporations of various types, 12 special companies (*tokushu gaisha*) or mixed enterprises with both private and public ownership, and 31 other smaller public enterprises receiving government subsidies (communications to the author, Ministry of Home Affairs, April 1998). Legally a special corporation is established by a special law enacted by the Diet (parliament), which specifies its functions, structure, financing, and governance including the national ministry or agency that will supervise its operations. Thus it has the legal status of a "special juridical person."
   Although all special corporations are subject to government regulation, the extent of regulations varies greatly. Large public corporations are

subject to stricter regulations than smaller ones, while mixed enterprises function virtually like regular private corporations. In principle, public corporations are based on the separation between management and ownership so that they enjoy more independence than government departmental undertakings. Their employees are nominally government employees, but they are not national civil servants.

All but three public corporations were created in the postwar period. The Japanese government has chosen the public corporations as a way of performing a certain task such as aiding a certain private sector without enlarging its ministries and agencies. Thus as the economy developed and became more complex, the number of public corporations increased from 53 in 1958 to 113 in 1976. The oil crises of 1973 and 1979 led to cut in public expenditures and decrease in the activities of public corporations. In addition, since 1985 privatization has decreased their numbers. Privatized former public corporations with some shares still owned by the government became mixed enterprises.

Because of the varied purposes and large number of public corporations, they are officially classified into several categories. The most important of them are the following (with their numbers as of January 1, 1998, given in parentheses):

1. Pre-1987 *kosha* were major public corporations that provided major public services in regulated sectors of the economy. Originally they were government departmental undertakings in the pre–World War II period, but during the Occupation they were reorganized into public corporations, fully owned and financed by the national government. This category includes Japan National Railways Corp., Japan Monopoly Corp., and Japan Telegraph and Telephone Corp. In 1985–87 they were privatized and organized into joint-stock companies, although the government still retains a majority of shares because of the depressed stock market.

2. *Kodan* (12) are public corporations or "public foundations" that carry out large-scale public works projects such as roads, highways, bridges, and airports financed in whole or in part by the national government. Most of their funds come from the Trust Fund Bureau of the **Ministry of Finance** and from local governments. They include Japan Housing Corp., Japan Highway Corp., Japan National Oil Corp., Japan Regional Development Corp., Agricultural Land Development Corp., Hansin Expressway Corp., and so forth.

3. *Jigyodan* (17) are public corporations or "enterprise foundations" that implement economic and social policy program but are smaller in scale

than *kodan*. They are generally government owned and financed. Examples include Small Business Promotion Corporation and **Japan International Cooperation Fund.**

4. *Koko* (9) are public financial corporations to finance socially important projects in special areas such as regional development, assistance to small business and publicly provided housing. They are financed by the national government. They include People's Finance Corp., Housing Loan Corp., Small Business Finance Corp., and Finance Corporation for Local Public Enterprises.

5. *Kinko* (1) and *ginko* (2) are, respectively, public financial depositories to assist cooperative societies, and state-owned banks. The former consists of the Bank of Commercial and Industrial Cooperatives. The latter includes **Japan Development Bank**, and the **Export-Import Bank of Japan.**

6. *Tokushu gaisha* (12) are special companies that used to be public corporations before privatization. After privatization they were reorganized into joint-stock companies or the so-called mixed enterprises with some government ownership of shares. The one important exception is the KDD (Kokusai Densin Denwa Co.), Japan's major international telecommunications carrier, which became completely privately owned in 1997 but remains a special company because the special law that governs it allows for strong government control (author's interview, Masu Uekusa, University of Tokyo, April 3, 1998).

7. Other special corporations (31) include research institutes, promotional organizations, mutual benefit associations for certain occupations, and so forth. Examples include Small Business Promotion Corp., Japan Broadcasting Corp., Japan External Trade Corp., and Electric Power Development Company.

There are five "national enterprises": Mint Bureau, Printing Bureau, National Forest Service, Postal Services, Alcohol Monopoly. They are included in the Business Special Account of the government budget and are directly managed by the national government. Hence they are not public corporations (Ishi 1993: 99–100).

At the local level, there are more than 6,600 local public enterprises (*chiho kosha*). They are engaged in land development, roads, public housing maintenance, and so forth, and are often called "third-sector companies" (Shibata 1993: 34). There are also various voluntary organizations such as neighborhood associations, fire brigades, parents and teachers associations, and so forth, which may receive subsidies from local public bodies because they render public services. They complement the public sector, although they are not public corporations.

Japan's wide use of special corporations as an alternative to expanded undertakings by the regular departments of the national or local governments is said to be "imaginative" (Skinner 1983: 52). It introduces some organizational decentralization and operational autonomy in the public sector. However, these numerous special corporations do obscure the boundary between the public sector and the private one and are aptly called the "hidden aspects" of the public sector by Shibata (1993: 32).

As in other countries, public enterprises in Japan tend to suffer from overstaffing and inefficiency. Consequently **privatization** was started in 1985–87. Likely candidates for future privatization include the Pension Welfare Service Public Corp., the Employment Promotion Corp., and the Housing and Urban Development Corp.

See also **Fiscal Investment and Loan Program, government-affiliated financial institutions, privatization.**

References

Ishi, Hiromitsu. 1993. The Fiscal Investment and Loan Program and public enterprises. In *Japan's Public Sector: How the Government Is Financed*, ed. by Tokue Shibata. Tokyo: University of Tokyo Press.

Management and Coordination Agency. 1997. *Survey of Special Corporations* (in Japanese).

Ministry of Home Affairs. 1998. *The Current Situation of Local Public Corporations* (in Japanese).

Shibata, Tokue. 1993. The economy and the public sector. In *Japan's Public Sector: How the Government Is Financed*, ed. by Toku Shibata. Tokyo: University of Tokyo Press.

Skinner, Kenneth A. 1983. Aborted careers in a public corporation. In *Work and Lifecourse in Japan*, ed. by David W. Plath. Albany: State University of New York Press.

Suzuki, Yumiko. 1997. Several public corporations to be singled out for reform. *Nikkei Weekly*, March 10: 1, 4.

Uekusa, Masu. 1994. The privatization of public enterprises: background and results. In *Business Enterprises in Japan: Views of Leading Japanese Economists*, ed. by Kenichi Imai and Ryutaro Komiya. Cambridge: MIT Press.

public finance
See **consumption tax, corporate taxes, Fiscal Investment and Loan Program, government bonds, individual income taxes, taxation system.**

Q

quality control Japanese quality control is characterized by company-wide total quality control and the participation of workers in a large number of quality control circles. Initially taught by American experts, Japanese companies have made quality control an integral part of their production management.

Quality control was first developed by W. A. Shewhart of Bell Laboratories in the United States in the 1930s. It was applied by the U.S. Army for weapons production during World War II. At that time quality control meant *statistical quality control*, which entailed the inspection of product samples and the rejection of the product if the rate of defect exceeds a certain statistical level. In the early 1950s the Japanese learned statistical quality control from visiting American experts. However, that approach was not effective in upgrading the quality of Japanese products because managers felt that quality control was an engineer's job and were indifferent to it.

Feigenbaum (1951) first emphasized companywide participation in total quality control (TQC) instead of statistical quality control by specialists. Visiting American experts as well as Japanese study groups to the United States introduced the new approach to Japan in the late 1950s. But it was Kaoru Ishikawa, Japan's foremost authority on TQC, who was instrumental in popularizing the concept and perfecting the techniques in Japan. He emphasized three main aspects of TQC: (1) Quality control should be extended from the inspection of product to the stages of manufacturing and new product development. In other words, it should start from the early stages of market research and product development and continue through production to final sales. (2) All company units, including top management and all divisions, should be involved in planning and coordinating quality control activities. (3) All workers should participate in quality control through their participation in quality control circles

(Ishikawa 1981, 1982, 1985, 1990). Ishikawa emphasized that with TQC, 100% defect-free production can be achieved. His famous slogan, "the next process is your customer," has been used effectively since the 1950s to combat sectionalism in Japanese companies (Ishikawa 1985: 107). The slogan embodies the idea that a defect-free final product comes only from defect-free materials and components, and hence all workers should participate in quality control. Because customers are much venerated in Japan (see **customer sovereignty**), Ishikawa astutely urges workers to think of their fellow workers at the next work process as their valued customers who want to "purchase" defect-free materials and components to produce quality product.

A quality control circle is a small group of workers in the same workshop organized to perform quality control activities, including the improvement of the workplace. It is based on one work unit, such as a section, and consists of a leader and several (average of seven) workers. Members of the group make suggestions for improvement, and they often have the discretion to implement the suggestions themselves. It also serves to promote communication between workers and management.

The first quality control circle was established by Nippon Telegraph and Telephone in 1962 to train foremen on statistical quality control. The idea rapidly spread to other companies for foremen and rank-and-file workers alike in total quality control. In 1965 there were 4,930 quality control circles. In 1985 there were 223,762 (Onglatco 1988: 15–17). According to surveys, quality control circles are more active and effective in large companies than in small ones. This is due to the fact that workers in large companies have a higher level of technical knowledge and skills, since most suggestions arising from quality control circles are highly technical.

See also **management practices.**

References

Feigenbaum, Armand V. [1951] 1983. *Quality Control.* New York: McGraw-Hill.

Lu, David. 1987. *Inside Corporate Japan: The Art of Fumble-Free Management.* Cambridge, MA: Productivity Press.

Ishikawa, Kaoru. 1981. *Quality Control, the Japanese Style* (in Japanese). Tokyo: Japanese Union of Scientists and Engineers.

Ishikawa, Kaoru. 1982. *Guide to Quality Control.* Tokyo: Asian Productivity Organization.

Ishikawa, Kaoru. 1985. *What Is Total Quality Control: The Japanese Way,* trans. by David J. Lu. Englewood Cliffs, NJ: Prentice Hall.

Ishikawa, Kaoru. 1990. *Introduction to Quality Control.* Tokyo: 3A Corporation.

Onglatco, Mary Lou Uy. 1988. *Japanese Quality Control Circles: Features, Effects and Problems.* Tokyo: Asian Productivity Organization.

Sako, Mari. 1994. Training, productivity, and quality control in Japanese multinational companies. In *The Japanese Firm: Sources of Competitive Strength,* ed. by Masahiko Aoki and Ronald Dore. Oxford: Clarendon Press.

Shea, Gregory P. 1986. Quality circles: The danger of battled change. *Sloan Management Review 27,* 3: 33–46.

quality control circle   A small group of workers in the same workshop organized as the basic unit to perform quality control activities and to improve the workplace in general.

See **quality control.**

quality of life
See **GDP, GNP, and GNP per capita, health insurance, housing, labor-management relations, population, price indexes and price levels, social security, working hours and stress.**

R

railway companies   Since trains are the main mode of transportation in Japan, the railway network is an integral part of the Japanese society and economy. In the postwar period it has exhibited technical virtuosity, operational punctuality (so much so as to set one's watch by), and some financial problems. Organizationally it has also become complex.

Before its breakup on April 1, 1987, the Japan National Railways (JNR) was Japan's state-run railway system, the mainstay of Japan's railway network that dated back to 1872. It operated 21,000 kilometers of track lines—including the world-famous *shinkansen* ("bullet train") which has been one of the world's fastest and safest trains—and employed 275,000 people. However, because of poor management and interference by politicians, deficits started to appear in 1964, which accumulated to ¥37.5 trillion ($250 billion at ¥150 = $1) by October 1986. The system was also plagued by union unrest. The privatization of JNR became an important part of Prime Minister Yasuhiro Nakasone's domestic program. Other public enterprises privatized by the Nakasone administration included Japan Monopoly Corporation and Nippon Telegraph and Telephone (NTT).

On April 1, 1987, JNR was divided into 11 organizations, including six regional passenger railway companies, one national freight company (Japan Freight Railway Co.), the JNR Accounts Settlement Corp. to settle the ¥25.5 trillion debt, the Railway Technical Research Institute, and a special public company (Shinkansen Holding Corp.) to own and lease the bullet trains to the passenger companies and to support new bullet train construction, with three new subsidiaries—the Railway Technical Research Institute, the Railway Telecommunication Co., and the Railway Information System Co.

The six regional passenger railway companies, making up the so-called JR Group along with the freight company, are East Japan Railway Co. (JR

East), Central Japan Railway Co. (JR Central), West Japan Railway Co. (JR West), Tokai Japan Railway Co. (JR Tokai), Shikoku Japan Railway Co. (JR Shikoku), and Hokkaido Japan Railway Co. (JR Hokkaido). The first three are the largest. The JR Group is shielded from the debt of JNR by the JNR Accounts Settlement Corp. and exempted from the costs of running the loss-making *shinkansen* service. Thus starting from a clean slate, they began to make profits in 1988.

The debt of JNR was to be repaid by selling JNR land and by selling shares of the new Japan Railway companies. The JNR Accounts Settlement Corp. is responsible for selling the shares and thus to oversee the railway's sale to the private sector. After repeated delays because of the sluggish stock market, there was public sale of shares in JR East Railway Co. (1993), JR West Railway Co. (1996), and JR Central Railway Co. (1997) as well as some real estate assets. However, because of the decline in stock and real estate prices during the 1990s, the debt of JNR Accounts Settlement Corp. has increased from ¥25.5 trillion to ¥27.8 trillion. An alternative solution is being sought to settle the debt. Taxpayers may eventually have to bear a large portion of the debt burden.

The breakup of JNR has created competition among the six regional JR companies and stimulated them to improve performance, including raising the speed of their "bullet trains" toward 300 kilometers per hour, and thereby competing with airlines for long-distance travel. They have also diversified their operations into new businesses such as marketing their own line of travel products and offering travel-related services. The Railway Technical Research Institute has developed the magnetically levitated (Maglev) train, with commercial development under experiment.

In the private sector proper of the railway network, there are 14 non–JR Group companies, including the Kinki Nippon Railway Co., the Tokyu Corp., and the Hankyu Co. They are all profitable companies and are members of conglomerates. Kinki Nippon Railway is the largest private railway company in Japan. It forms the Kintetsu Group with more than 160 subsidiaries, including Kintetsu Department Store. It is also engaged in large-scale urban redevelopment in **Osaka** and in resort development. The Tokyu Group is a large family-controlled conglomerate that was first established in 1922. It has some 350 companies engaged in diverse businesses among which are railways (Tokyu Corp. and Izukyu Corp.), an airline (Japan Air System Co.) railway rolling stock (Tokyu Car Corp.), a department store (Tokyu Department Stores Co.), supermarket chains (Tokyu Store Chain Co.), real estate (Tokyu Land Corp.), and construction

(Tokyu Construction Co.). All railway companies are regulated by the Ministry of Transport in fares and timetables.

See also **privatization.**

Addresses

East Japan Railway Co.
6-5, Marunouchi 1-chome, Chiyoda-ku, Tokyo 100
Tel: (3) 3212-4441

Japan Nongovernment Railways Association
6-4, Marunouchi 1-chome, Chiyoda-ku, Tokyo 100
Tel: (3) 3211-1401

Kinki Nippon Railway Co.
1-55, Uehon-machi 6-chome, Tennoji-ku, Osaka 540
Tel: (6) 771-3331   Fax: (06) 775-3468

References

Choy, Jon. 1996. Tokyo concerned with runaway railroad debt. *JEI Report* 33B, August 30: 8–10.

Fukui, Noichiro. 1992. *Japanese National Railways Privatization Study: The Experience of Japan and Lessons for Developing Countries.* Washington: World Bank.

Suzuki, Yumiko. 1996. Railway debt could cost taxpayers trillions of yen. *Nikkei Weekly,* April 1: 1, 19.

Suzuki, Yumiko. 1997. Railway spinoffs chug ahead with improvements. *Nikkei Weekly,* April 7: 1, 21.

recession cartel   (or depression cartel) An arrangement or agreement among firms of an industry facing a severe recession to reduce output by an agreed-upon percentage. The purpose is to restrict competition and avoid the bankruptcy of the weaker firms. It was relatively common in the 1950s and 1960s, but its number has declined steadily since then.

See **cartels, shipbuilding industry.**

regional banks   Some 130 commercial banks that operate within a specific prefecture.

See **banking system.**

retail trade
See **department stores, distribution system, pricing practices.**

rice production and distribution   Rice occupies a special place in the
Japanese society and political economy. It is the major staple food in the
Japanese diet, and its cultivation symbolizes the traditional rural way of
life. Also, because of the disproportionate political power wielded by
farmers, rice production is subsidized by the government and rice import
was banned until 1993. This had aggravated the trade frictions between
Japan and the United States.

Rice consumption has declined as household income increases and the
consumption of wheat, meat, and dairy products increases. Total annual
consumption of rice declined from 13 million metric tons in 1965 to 10
million metric tons in 1994 despite population growth from 98.3 million
to 125 million in the same period.

Rice production has declined slightly over the same period, as shown in
table R.1. The decline came about because, since 1969, the Ministry of
Agriculture, Forestry, and Fisheries has asked farmers to reduce rice acreage; under the **Staple Food Control Act** of 1942 the Japanese government was until 1995 formally in charge of all rice production, distribution,
and sales. Total area planted to rice declined from 3.3 million hectares in
1965 to 2.9 million hectares in 1970 and 2.1 million hectares in 1995.

Table R.1
Rice production and government purchase (unmilled, in million metric tons)

Year	Production	Government purchase
1965	12.4	7.2
1970	12.7	6.8
1975	13.2	6.4
1980	9.8	3.7
1983	10.4	3.4
1985	11.7	4.3
1988	9.9	2.1
1990	10.5	1.8
1991	9.6	1.1
1992	10.6	1.6
1993[a]	7.8	0.02
1994	12.0	2.1
1995	10.7	1.7

Source: Ministry of Agriculture, Forestry, and Fisheries.
a. 1993 was an anomaly. There was a crop failure due to bad weather. The government
authorized import of 1.05 million tons of rice to supplement domestic supply.

In the early 1960s the government introduced price support of rice after the Agricultural Basic Law was enacted in 1961 to support agriculture and farm income. A production-cost–parity formula was adopted to determine annual rice purchase prices in order to maintain farm and nonfarm incomes at comparable levels (see **pricing practices**). This resulted in a government purchase price that was as high as four times the world level. The high price induced farmers to maintain a high yield (about 5 tons per hectare) by using a high level of chemical fertilizers. This had led to surplus of rice supply over demand in some years. To avoid or reduce the surplus, the government introduced rice acreage control in 1969. It entailed subsidy payments to farmers for withdrawing paddy fields from production or diverting their use to nonrice crops.

Through its Food Agency, the government purchased substantial amounts of rice annually in the 1960s and 1970s, amounting to about half of the annual rice production (see table R.1). Although the amount of government purchase declined in the 1980s, it was still as large as one-third of rice production. This enabled the government to influence the market supply and price of rice in accordance with the Staple Food Control Law. Government-controlled rice was resold to licensed wholesalers and processors at government-determined prices. The rest of the rice output was collected from farmers by licensed collectors and sold to licensed wholesalers and processors at negotiated prices or auctioned off by the collectors to wholesalers at the rice exchanges. A small portion was sold by farmers in the black market. Thus with the decline in government purchase, the role of the free market in the distribution of rice has grown inexorably since the late 1980s. In recognition of this development, a new law was enacted in 1994 and came into effect in November 1995—the Law for Stabilization of Supply-Demand and Price of Staple Food. The new law formally changed the role of the government in rice distribution from "food control" to "supply-demand adjustments and stockpile management from a midterm perspective" (author's interview, Ministry of Agriculture, Forestry and Fisheries, March 26, 1998). Since then the free market in the private sector has been the predominant channel for rice distribution.

The government's purchase price for the producer (producer's price) is set every year. It is a multiple of the world price. Sometimes it is also higher than the government's selling price, resulting in an additional government deficit. The separation of producer and consumer prices means that there was no "countervailing power" to hold producer prices down. Thus even **labor unions** support high producer prices while they demand low consumer prices (Donnelly 1977: 151). In 1987 government purchase price was cut slightly for the first time in 31 years from ¥18,668 per 60 kilogram (nonglutinous unpolished rice) to ¥17,557. Since then, it has been cut further to ¥16,392 in 1991 and ¥16,217 in 1997. Both international pressures to end agricultural subsidies and government fiscal retrenchment have contributed to the price cuts. The producer's price for government-controlled rice is lower than that of nongovernment-controlled rice, which is of higher quality. For example, the former was ¥16,530 per 60 kilograms of 1991; the latter fluctuated around ¥20,000 in the same year.

As part of the government's control of rice, rice import was banned until 1993 except in processed forms. Tokyo's rationale for the ban was that self-sufficiency in rice is important for food security purposes. In addition domestic farm groups have long maintained that rice cultivation is part of Japanese culture that should not be given up in favor of imports. Surprisingly, **consumer groups** have not actively supported the lifting of the ban in order to reduce the rice price. The main reason is reportedly the Japanese consumers' demand for "high-quality" rice. Surveys indicate that consumers believe that foreign rice tastes bad because it is dry and not sticky. Hayami (1988) argues that Japanese consumers have become more tolerant of high rice prices because their food expenditure as a ratio of total expenditure has declined as their incomes rise (also author's interview, July 9, 1992).

Japan's policy on rice import was fundamentally changed in 1993. Because of a crop failure that year due to bad weather, the government authorized the import of 1.05 million metric tons of foreign rice in 1993 and 1.8 million tons in 1994, the largest since 1965. Although the imports did not sell well because of their "bad ordor and taste," there was important educational effect that came from the large-scale imports—cooking classes were conducted to show housewives how to cook foreign rice; foreign rice was mixed with domestic rice by retailers to stretch supply— with the realization by consumers that they could somehow live with imported rice. In December 1993 the Uruguay Round of GATT negotiations was concluded with an agricultural agreement in which Japan is committed to provide "minimum access" opportunities for foreign rice each year, beginning in 1995. The quantities of minimum access rice are 379,000 tons of milled rice in 1995, equivalent to 4% of domestic consumption, increasing to 758,000 tons in 2000, equivalent to 8% of domestic consumption. The rice imported under minimum access terms is managed by the Food Agency for market distribution and stockpiling for poor harvest. This is consistent with the government's new role in supply-demand adjustments and stockpile management.

See also **agricultural cooperatives, agricultural policy, pricing practices, Staple Food Control Act.**

Addresses

Central Union of Agricultural Cooperatives (Zenchu)
8-3, Otemachi 1-chome, Chiyoda-ku, Tokyo 100
Tel: (3) 3245-7500   Fax: (3) 5255-7356

Food Agency, Ministry of Agriculture, Forestry, and Fisheries
2-1, Kasumigaseki 1-chome, Chiyoda-ku, Tokyo 100
Tel: (3) 3502-8111

References

Donnelly, Michael W. 1977. Setting the price of rice: A study in political decisionmaking. In *Policymaking in Contemporary Japan,* ed. by T. J. Pempel. Ithaca: Cornell University Press.

Food Agency. 1996. *An Outline of New Food Systems.*

Food Agency. 1997. *An Outline of Japan's Stable Rice Supply in Accorance with the Staple Food Law.*

Fujiyasu, Minako. 1990. The power politics of rice. *Tokyo Business Today* (October): 26–35.

Hayami, Yujiro. 1988. *Japanese Agriculture under Siege: The Political Economy of Agricultural Policies.* London: Macmillan.

Kuroda, Yoshimi. 1992. Price-support programs and land movement in Japanese rice production. In *Land Issues in Japan: A Policy Failure?* ed. by John Haley and Kozo Yamamura. Seattle: Society for Japanese Studies.

Ministry of Agriculture, Forestry, and Fisheries. Annual. *Annual Report on Japanese Agriculture.*

Ministry of Agriculture, Forestry, and Fisheries. Monthly. *Monthly Statistics of Agriculture, Forestry and Fisheries.*

Moore, Richard M. 1990. *Japanese Agriculture: Patterns of Rural Development.* Boulder, CO: Westview.

Mori, Hiroshi. 1990. Agricultural price policies in Japan. In *Agricultural Output and Input Pricing.* Tokyo: Asian Productivity Organization.

ringi **system**   A formal procedure in decision-making process, widely used in large Japanese corporations, in which a drafted proposal is circulated among units of the organization for consultation and to seek consensus.

See **decision making.**

S

saihan   Resale price maintenance or the practice of fixing minimum retail prices by manufacturers. Once relatively common in the retail of some products, it has been increasingly banned by the **Fair Trade Commission** as a violation of the **Antimonopoly Law** since the early 1990s.

See **pricing practices.**

Saison Group A large conglomerate of some 200 firms with the Seibu Department stores as its core company.

See *keiretsu* **and business groups.**

samurai **bonds**   Yen-denominated bonds issued in Japan by non-residents. They were first issued by the Asian Development Bank in 1970 and the World Bank in 1971. In the 1970s the *samurai* bond market was open only to foreign governments, government agencies, and international organizations such as the World Bank and the Asian Development Bank. In the early 1980s it was open to foreign corporations and other nongovernment institutions with a single-A credit rating. Since August 1992, when the Japanese government eased the access to the market for foreigners, foreign government-affiliated bodies with a BB+ or a BBB rating are allowed to issue *samurai* bonds.

The volume of new issues was ¥1.1 trillion in FY 1984 and ¥1.2 trillion in 1985. In 1986–88 the annual volume of new issues declined rapidly to about half the 1985 level; it rose again to ¥1.0 trillion in 1989 and ¥1.4 trillion in 1990. The amount outstanding was ¥6.0 trillion in 1990. New issues declined to only ¥711 billion in FY 1991, then rose steadily to ¥2.1 trillion in 1995 and ¥3.8 trillion in 1996. The amount outstanding was ¥12.3 trillion in 1996.

The main reason for the rapid decline in new issues of *samurai* bonds in 1986–88 was the appreciation of the yen after 1985, as continuous appreciation of the yen vis-à-vis the dollar increased the cost of repaying the yen-denominated debt. By 1989 the **yen–dollar exchange rate** had stabilized considerably. In an effort to stimulate the market, the **Ministry of Finance** simplified the issuing process on the *samurai* bond market in October 1987. In addition interest rates in Japan remained relatively low, and the yen continued to play an important role in world trade. Consequently in 1989 the volume of new issues started to increase. The dollar's rise in 1989 also contributed to the new surge. U.S. borrowers, including state governments and financial institutions, have become the major issuers of *samurai* bonds. In late 1992 European nations moved to Japan to raise funds because of the European currency crisis and the lower interest rate in Japan. This was also facilitated by the easing, in August 1992, of the rating requirement. As a result the volume of new issuances rose rapidly in late 1992 and early 1993. European government entities such as the National Bank of Hungary and the Turkish government are among the issuers. In the mid-1990s Asian emerging-market issuers became the major borrowers. Individual Japanese investors, discouraged by the record low interest rates, became the major purchasers of *samurai* bonds, which offer relatively high yields.

The major competing debt instrument of *samurai* bonds is the **Euroyen bonds**, which are yen-denominated bonds issued in the Euromarket. In FY 1994 the volume of Euroyen bond issues was ¥10.7 trillion, about eight times that of *samurai* bonds. *Samurai* bonds should also be distinguished from the so-called *daimyo* bonds and *shogun* bonds. *Daimyo* bonds are yen-denominated bonds issued in Japan by nonresidents but sold to investors on the Euromarket. *Shogun* bonds are foreign currency-based bonds issued by nonresidents and sold in Japan. The market for the latter is limited.

See also **Euroyen bonds.**

References

Idei, Yas. 1993. *Samurai* market draws riskier issuers. *Nikkei Weekly*, March 15: 16.

Ishibashi, Asako. 1995. Samurai jousting spawns bond mispricings. *Nikkei Weekly*, October 30: 14.

Japan Securities Research Institute. 1998. *Securities Market in Japan 1998*. Ch. 4.

Tokyo Stock Exchange. 1998. *Tokyo Stock Exchange 1998 Fact Book.*

sarakin Consumer finance companies or consumer financing for salaried employees; abbreviation of "salaryman *kinyu*" (salaried-men's loans).
See **consumer credit.**

Table S.1
Saving and investment rates, Japan and the United States (in % of GDP)

Year	Saving/GDP		Investment/GDP	
	Japan	United States	Japan	United States
1967	35.6	23.1	35.4	17.3
1970	40.3	18.0	39.0	17.3
1975	32.8	17.8	32.8	16.8
1980	31.3	18.4	32.2	19.3
1985	31.5	16.7	28.2	19.4
1986	31.7	15.8	27.7	18.8
1987	31.7	15.2	28.5	18.3
1988	32.6	15.4	30.4	17.5
1989	32.7	16.0	31.3	17.5
1990	33.0	15.1	32.3	16.3
1991	33.8	14.5	32.2	14.8
1992	33.0	14.7	30.8	15.2
1993	32.0	15.3	29.7	16.2
1994	30.7	16.1	28.7	17.5
1995	30.0	16.2	28.5	17.5
1996	30.4	16.2	29.8	17.5

Source: International Monetary Fund.

savings Postwar Japan has maintained a very high saving rate that is unprecedented in Japan and unmatched in the rest of the world. Gross national saving rate in Japan as a percentage of GDP (gross domestic product) was 32.8% in 1975, 31.5% in 1985, and 30.4% in 1996 (see table S.1). In comparison, in the United States it generally ranged from 15% to 18% in the same period, which is below the average of industrial countries. Japan's high saving rate, coupled with the trade surplus throughout the 1980s, has led to criticisms by foreign countries, particularly the United States, that the Japanese save too much and do not consume and import enough. In response, many Japanese commentators and trade officials have argued that Americans save too little and consume too much.

Japan's high saving rate was necessary for its postwar reconstruction and industrial growth. It has financed a high rate of **investment** (gross domestic capital formation) that has been near or over 30% of GDP and GNP. It was only after 1976 (with the exception of 1979 and 1980) that the investment rate fell slightly below the saving rate. The excess savings led to large outflows of Japanese capital, which helped to finance the trade deficits of Japan's trading partners, particularly the United States.

While not denying that Japan's saving rate is higher than that of the United States, some economists have pointed out that methodological differences in measuring savings in the two countries have exaggerated the differences. For example, the United States inappropriately counts many durable goods such as furniture as consumer spending, whereas Japan does not. Furthermore, in deducting depreciation from gross savings to calculate net savings, the United States estimates depreciation at replacement cost, whereas Japan uses historical cost. During a period of inflation, replacement cost exceeds historical cost; therefore Japan's method of depreciation overstates its savings by U.S. standards (Horioka 1990: 51–54). Most experts agree, however, that after allowances are made for these differences, Japan's saving rate has consistently exceeded that of the United States by a substantial margin.

National savings are the sum of savings by households, nonfinancial corporations, the government, financial institutions, and private nonprofit organizations. The first three sectors are the most important. As shown in table S.2, households (including unincorporated businesses) had been the largest source of savings in Japan until 1987. Household savings as a ratio

Table S.2
Saving rates by sector (in %)

FY	HS/DT	HS/GNP	CS/GNP	GS/GNP
1975	22.8	20.3	7.7	2.3
1980	17.9	16.5	10.9	3.1
1985	15.6	14.4	11.3	4.8
1986	15.6	13.6	12.7	5.3
1987	13.8	12.6	13.3	6.8
1988	13.0	11.8	12.9	8.1
1989	12.9	11.2	13.1	8.5
1990	12.1	10.8	11.9	9.5
1991	13.2	11.7	11.4	9.6
1992	13.1	11.9	12.8	7.3
1993	13.4	12.1	13.0	6.4
1994	13.3	13.2	12.3	4.5
1995	13.7	12.7	14.0	3.9
1996	13.8	12.7	15.8	3.1

Source: Economic Planning Agency.
Note: HS/DI = household savings/disposable income (calendar year basis); HS/GNP = household savings/GNP (fiscal year). Private unincorporated nonfinancial enterprises are included. CS/GNP = nonfinancial corporations' savings/GNP; GS/GNP = general government savings/GNP.

of household disposable income declined gradually from nearly 23% in 1975 to 12.1% in 1990. It then rose to more than 13% in the early and mid-1990s.

Corporate savings were relatively low in the 1970s. They have been rising as a ratio of GNP since the late 1970s and have become the largest source of savings since 1987. They amount to 10.9% of GNP in 1980, 11.9% in 1985, and 15.8% in 1996. General government savings (including those of the central and local governments) used to be very low but had been rising as a percentage of GNP since the late 1970s. Compared with their respective investment, however, both the corporate and the government sectors have had excess investment over their savings in all years (except 1996 for the corporate sector and 1987–92 for the government); the opposite is true with the households. Thus excess household savings served to finance the excess investment of corporations and the government through the financial institutions. Finally financial institutions (not shown in table S.2) had little savings before 1984 and have had negative savings in most years since 1985.

The literature on Japanese savings has concentrated on household savings. Analysts have different explanations for the high household savings. Ishikawa and Ueda (1984) regard the semiannual bonuses paid by companies as buffer incomes that are easily saved because they are lumpy and uncertain, being tied to company performance. Horioka (1984) postulates that households maintain a high saving rate over their life cycle to pay for children's education, **housing**, and bequests. Balassa and Noland (1988) and Tachibanaki (1994) support the "bequest motive" hypothesis. According to this hypothesis, individuals have to maintain a high saving rate for many years for the purchase of houses, which are very expensive in Japan by international standards. After retirement they continue to save and maintain the value of their houses rather than dissave because they intend to bequest the houses to their heirs in exchange for financial and other assistance while living with them in the same household, as is still common in Japan. The quantitative importance of the bequest motive in increasing the saving rate, however, is disputed by Hayashi, Ito, and Slemrod (1988).

Still other analysts have argued that because of the underdeveloped **social security system**, households have to save for old age support, and that because the Japanese work more hours than workers in other industrial countries, they have less time to shop and consume. Finally Hayashi, Ito, and Slemrod (1988) and Ito and Kitamura (1994) contend that government efforts in the postwar period to encourage saving for postwar reconstruction and development have been successful. In particular, until it was reformed in 1988, the *maruyu* system, which exempted interest income from principal of up to ¥9 million per person, is considered to have been effective in promoting household savings. This tax exemption included interest from **postal savings.**

The saving rate as a percentage of GDP or GNP is expected to decline in the future because of the aging of the Japanese **population.** The percentage of the population aged 65 and over was only 12.1% in 1990, but it is expected to rise to 21.3% in 2010 and 26% in 2025 to 2030 (see table P.2, population). Since the elderly save less than the rest of the population, the overall saving rate will decline.

See also **consumption, *maruyu*, postal savings.**

References

Balassa, Bela, and Marcus Noland. 1988. *Japan in the World Economy.* Washington: Institute for International Economics. Ch. 4.

Economic Planning Agency. Annual. *Annual Report on National Accounts.*

Hayashi, Fumio. 1997. *Understanding Saving: Evidence from the United States and Japan.* Cambridge: MIT Press.

Hayashi, F., T. Ito, and J. Slemrod. 1988. Housing finance imperfections, taxation, and private saving: a comparative simulation analysis of the United States and Japan. *Journal of the Japanese and International Economies* 2, 3: 215–38.

Horioka, Charles Yuji. 1990. Why is Japan's household saving rate so high? A literature survey. *Journal of the Japanese and International Economies* 4: 49–92.

Horioka, Charles Yuji. 1994. Japan's consumption and saving in international perspective. *Economic Development and Cultural Change* 42, 2: 293–316.

Ishikawa, Tsuneo, and Kazuo Ueda. 1984. The bonus payment system and Japanese personal savings. In *The Economic Analysis of the Japanese Firm,* ed. by A. Aoki. Amsterdam: Elsevier Science.

Ito, Takatoshi, and Yukinobu Kitamura. 1994. Public policies and household saving in Japan. In *Public Policies and Household Saving,* ed. by James M. Poterba. Chicago: University of Chicago Press.

Management and Coordination Agency. Annual. *Family Saving Survey.*

Tachibanaki, Toshiaki. 1994. Housing and saving in Japan. In *Housing Markets in the United States and Japan,* ed. by Yukio Noguchi and James M. Poterba. Chicago: University of Chicago Press.

Tachibanaki, Toshiaki, and Seiji Takata. 1994. Bequest and asset distribution: Human capital investemnt and intergenerational wealth transfers. In *Savings and Bequest,* ed. by Toshiaki Tachibanaki. Ann Arbor: University of Michigan Press.

Takayama, Moriyuki, and Yukinobu Kitamura. 1994. Household savings behavior in Japan. In *International Comparisons of Household Saving,* ed. by James M. Poterba. Chicago: University of Chicago Press.

science and technology policy, and research and development
Through its science and technology (S&T) policy and its various organizations and financial provisions, the Japanese government actively promotes research and development (R&D) in Japan. However, its budget for public-sector R&D is relatively small. On the other hand, Japan's corporate sector spends a relatively high percentage of its sales revenues on R&D. Total national expenditures on R&D amount to about 3% of GNP, making Japan one of the most R&D-oriented countries in the world.

There is a hierarchy of government organizations and research institutes that coordinate and implement the nation's S&T policy and carry out R&D in the public sector. The highest government body responsible for S&T policy is the Prime Minister's Council for Science and Technology. The Council advises the prime minister on basic and general S&T policies, which set national goals and provide guidelines for the R&D and training activities of various government ministries and agencies. Council members include several ministers and several experts from the academic and business communities, thus providing the basis for broad consensus. Critics have charged, however, that the nation has no effective government strategy on S&T because the Council for Science and Technology, in practice, has little authority and cannot coordinate among the agencies and ministries which have different interests and policies (*Nikkei Weekly*, November 25, 1996, editorial).

The Agency of Science and Technology under the prime minister's office serves as the administrative secretariat of the Council and coordinates overall S&T policy and monitors policy implementation in various ministries and agencies of the government. Under the supervision of the Agency, there are seven special **public corporations** that are set up to promote public-sector R&D in specific areas. They are the Research Development Corporation of Japan, Japan Atomic Energy Research Institute, Power Reactor and Nuclear Fuel Development Corporation, National Space Development Agency of Japan, National Marine Science and Technology Center, Japan Information Center of Science and Technology, and Institute of Physical and Chemical Research.

Through their respective budget allocations, government ministries and agencies finance and direct the R&D activities in their respective areas. A few ministries and agencies typically predominate in their shares of government S&T expenditures because of the nature of their responsibilities. For example, of the total R&D budget of ¥3,003 billion in FY 1997, the Ministry of Education received ¥1,289 billion or 43% of the total. Much of this was used to finance university research-related expenditures and specific research contracts. The Science and Technology Agency received the second largest budget allocation (¥734 billion or 24%), followed by the **Ministry of International Trade and Industry** (MITI, ¥472 billion or 16%) and the Defense Agency (¥175 billion or 6%). MITI is in charge of Japan's **industrial policy** and has under its supervision the Agency for Industrial Science and Technology (AIST), which is in charge of the promotion of industrial technology. Under MITI and AIST there are some 17 industrial technology research institutes and laboratories, including the Electrotechnical Laboratory, National Institute of Bioscience and Human Technology, National Institute of Materials and Chemical Research, seven Government Industrial Research Institutes, Mechanical Engineering Laboratory, and National Institute for Resource and Environment. The Ministry of Agriculture, Forestry and Fisheries also has some 14 national research institutes under its jurisdiction.

In addition to the R&D activities carried out by government research institutes and universities, government S&T budget also provides a small amount of subsidies to private-sector R&D in important technology such as energy and funds some research contracts on R&D in selected advanced technology fields in the private sector. There is also a regional development dimension to the government's S&T policy. Because of the heavy concentration of industries in a few congested urban areas (**Tokyo-Yokohama, Osaka-Kobe**, and **Nagoya**), the national government since the 1960s has attempted to encourage the relocation and development of industries in less industrialized regions. Best known was the Technopolis Project of 1981 which was aimed at constructing 26 model towns throughout Japan with government subsidies to develop high-tech complexes. The "Brain Program" (Research-Core Program) of 1985–90 was aimed at halting the move of Japanese industries abroad due to the yen appreciation since 1985 by providing government "seed money" in collaboration with local governments and the private sector to set up 23 R&D centers in order to attract industries to less industrialized areas. The government also provides subsidized loans for the relocation of companies. The Japan Regional Development Corporation under the Ministry of International Trade and Industry was entrusted with its implementation. As of 1997 only 15 such centers have been completed. Initial assessment of the program is inconclusive (Bakos 1997).

Overall, the flow of research funds from the public sector to the private sector is small, especially when compared with that of other industrialized countries. The main reason for this is the low level of government **defense expenditures** in Japan (only about 1% of GNP), which leads to low levels of defense-related R&D contracts. The percentage of R&D expenditures financed by public funds in FY 1995 was only 23% in Japan compared with 35.5% in the United States, 33.3% in Germany, and 44.6% in France. When defense-related R&D expenditures are excluded, the percentage of total non-defense-related R&D expenditures financed by the government was 21% in Japan in FY 1995, 35% in France in 1995, and 17.3% in the United States in 1996 (Science and Technology Agency 1997: 6).

Similarly the Japanese national government's R&D budget has been relatively modest among the industrialized countries. In the late 1980s and early 1990s, it was slightly less than 3% of the government's general budget. It increased to 3.2% in FY 1994 and 3.9% in FY 1997. Recognizing this relatively low level of budget for R&D, the Council for Science and Technology recommended in 1996 that the government increases by 50% its R&D spending during FY 1996–2000 over the level of the previous five years. The recommendation was accepted by the government.

Direct R&D expenditures are not the only way used by the government to implement its S&T policy. The government also promotes R&D through preferential taxation and other financial provisions as explained below:

1. Tax deduction on experimental and research expense increments. This allows corporations to deduct from their tax assessment 20% of the increase over their previous highest expenditure for research.

2. Tax program for promoting R&D of basic technologies. This exempts businesses from 7% of the acquisition cost of assets, such as equipment and facilities, purchased for the purpose of conducting R&D in the basic technology areas.

3. Tax deduction for strengthening the technological foundation of **small and medium enterprises.** This allows these enterprises to deduct from their tax assessment a maximum of 6% of their overall research expenditures every tax year.

4. A number of organizations such as the **Japan Development Bank**, Japan Key Technology Center, and Technology Research Advancement Institution have low interest-loan programs for the promotion of technology. The Japan Finance Corporation for Small Business has special loans for technological advancement at small and medium enterprises.

5. The **patent system**, as in other countries, provides financial incentives to the private sector to engage in R&D for commercially profitable innovations.

In terms of the purpose of research expenditures, three categories of research are commonly distinguished: basic research, applied research and developmental research. During 1987–1992, Japan spent 13–14% of its total R&D funds on basic research, about 25% on applied research and 62–63% on developmental research. In FY 1995, the figures were 15% for basic research, 24.6% for applied research, and 60.5% for developmental research. Such heavy focus on applied and developmental research and the relative neglect of basic research are the result of the research spending patterns of Japan's corporation, research institutions and universities:

1. Corporate R&D is financed almost exclusively (more than 98%) by corporations themselves. Total corporate R&D expenditures far exceed those financed by the government, amounting to more than 80% of total national R&D expenditures since FY 1985. In FY 1995, only 6.6% of corporate research expenditures was devoted to basic research, 22% of it to applied research and 71.3% to developmental research.

2. Even government research institutions spent only about 16–20% of their research funds on basic research, and about 54–58% on developmental research in FY 1990–95.

3. Only universities and colleges spent more than 50% of the research funds on basic research. However, their research funds are relatively limited. In FY 1995 their R&D expenditures were ¥1,771 billion or 13.5% of total R&D funds; 64% of their R&D funds came from the national and local governments and 36% from private sources. This level of government support for the universities is much lower than that of other industrialized countries. It is considered by Herbig (1995: 92–93) to be the result of the universities' institutional history because "their mission is primarily knowledge dissemination rather than knowledge generation." The latter task is undertaken by companies themselves by training company personnel for company-specific R&D.

Japan's traditional weakness in basic research and strength in developmental research can also be seen in its relative lack of breakthrough ideas and innovations and in its strong adaptive innovations that refine ideas and technologies initially developed in the United States such as the transistor and the VCR. Many analysts have suggested that these weaknesses and strengths in creativity are imbedded in cultural and social factors. For example, Herbig (1995: 11–12) argues that Japanese Zen Buddhist emphasis on intuitive understanding and spiritual enlightenment and social emphasis on group harmony and respect for seniority discourage the development of radical new ideas and innovations but promote adaptive, cooperative, and integrated improvements in products and technology. In contrast, the United States emphasizes Cartesian·logic and individualism which fosters individual brilliance and creative breakthroughs but is relatively weak in steady improvements in process engineering and manufacturing which require group cooperation and integration.

Corporate R&D in Japan has fluctuated over time with the conditions of the economy. It rose rapidly in the late 1960s during the period of rapid economic growth, and then stagnated in the early 1970s. Since the late 1970s it had increased continuously through FY 1991, but the annual increase slowed in FY 1986, 1987, and 1991. In FY 1992–94 the total amount declined slightly due to the recession of the economy before it rose again in FY 1995 (see table S.3). The average industry ratio of R&D expenditures to gross sales increased from 1.48% in FY 1980 to 2.83% in FY 1992, and then declined to 2.73% in FY 1995. Some industries such as agriculture, construction, petroleum and coal products have a low ratio of less than 1%. Other industries are highly R&D intensive; pharmaceuticals had 8%, communications and electronics equipment 5.8%, precision machinery 5.2% in FY 1995.

Table S.3
Research and development expenditures by financing sector (in ¥ trillion)

FY	Government[a]	private[b]
1975	0.72	1.90
1980	1.21	3.47
1985	1.57	6.53
1986	1.65	6.76
1987	1.80	7.21
1988	1.80	7.97
1989	1.87	9.03
1990	1.99	10.09
1991	2.14	10.57
1992	2.31	10.47
1993	2.56	9.96
1994	2.50	9.90
1995	2.87	10.31
1996	3.16[c]	11.73[c]

Source: Science and Technology Agency (1997).
a. Includes national and local governments. The former's spending is much larger.
b. More than 90% are corporate expenditures.
c. Management and Coordination Agency (1997) figures.

The efficacy of a country's S&T policy and R&D expenditures can be assessed in a number of ways. Some indicators are discussed below:

1. The number of persons awarded the Nobel Prize in the natural sciences. The number for Japan lags far behind that of most other industrialized countries (5 for Japan through 1996 as compared with 180 for the United States, 67 for United Kingdom, 61 for Germany, 25 for France). This may reflect, to a large extent, Japan's continuing relative weakness in basic research. However, it can be argued that the number of prize winners is not solely determined by S&T policy and R&D expenditures. A country's **education system** and social values are also important. Japan's weakness in this area may reflect its rigid education or examination system and its emphasis on social conformity that do not encourage the development of creative talents. An alternative indicator is Japan's share of scientific papers published in major scientific journals around the world. In 1981, of the world total of 369,000 papers, Japan's share was 6.8% as compared with 35.9% for the United States, 8.3% for United Kingdom, and 7.3% for Germany. Japan's share increased steadily to 9.6% in 1994 as compared with 36.2% for the United States, 9.1% for United Kingdom, and 8.1% for Germany. However, Japan's share of total world R&D citations in scientific papers is lower than the average for other developed countries, indicating that "the world has less than average interest in what Japanese researcher write about R&D" (Björn, 1993:125).

2. The number of patent applications and patents granted. Japan has the largest number of patent applications in the world (320,175 in Japan in 1994 vs. 109,981 in the United States). This number, however, is not necessarily the best indicator of a country's technological progress because Japan's **patent system** awards patents to the first applicant and not the first inventor, as is in the United States, and thus encourages preemptive patent applications to prevent competitors from receiving patents. An alternative indicator is the number of patents granted in the United States that originated in different countries. Of this number, the percentage that come from Japan has steadily grown from 8.8% of the total in 1975 to 22.5% in 1992, and 21% in 1996, higher than that coming from any other foreign countries. The percentage of the total that originated within the United States was 54.7% in 1975 and 57.8% in 1996. Of the top ten corporations receiving the most U.S. patents in 1996, the second, the fourth through the tenth are Japanese corporations (Canon, NEC, Hitachi, Mitsubishi Electric, Toshiba, Fujitsu, Sony, and Matsushita Electric).

3. The balance of payments in technology trade. Japan has historically relied heavily on the imports of foreign technology for its industrial development. Such imports far exceeded Japan's technology exports, resulting in large deficits in its technology or royalty balance of payments. This pattern of technology import deficits continued during most of the 1980s, although the gap between payments and receipts had narrowed. In FY 1989–91 technology payments and receipts in dollars approximately balanced, and starting in FY 1993 there was a small but growing receipts surplus. In FY 1995 technology payments totaled $4.16 billion, whereas technology receipts were $5.97 billion (Science and Technology Agency 1997: 87).

From these statistics it can be concluded that overall Japan's S&T policy and R&D activities have been reasonably successful in raising the technological level of the economy, thereby contributing to Japan's industrial competitiveness and economic growth.

See also **education system, industrial policy, patent system.**

Addresses

Agency of Industrial Science and Technology
3-1, Kasumigaseki 1-chome, Chiyoda-ku, Tokyo 100
Tel: (3) 3501-1511

Science and Technology Agency
2-1, Kasumigaseki 2-chome, Chiyoda-ku, Tokyo 100
Tel: (3) 3581-5271

References

Alexander, Authur. 1997. Basic research and science in the Japanese Economy. *JEI Report* 11A, March 21.

Bakos, Gabor. 1997. Japanese R&D centers to help regional industries (the Brain Program). *Current Politics and Economics of Japan* 5: 1–23.

Björn, Michael. 1993. Japanese articles on research & development published in international journals. In *R&D Strategies in Japan: The National, Regional and Corporate Approach*, ed. by Jajime Eto. Amsterdam: Elsevier.

Choy, Jon. 1997. Research and development spending in Japan: Happy days are here again. *JEI Report* 39A, October 17.

Choy, Jon. 1998. Research and development in Japan: squeezing more from every yen. *JEI Report* 29A, July 31, 1998.

Goto, Akira, and Ryuhei Wakasugi. 1988. Technology policy. In *Industrial Policy of Japan*, ed. by Ryutaro Komiya, Masahiro Okuno, and Kotaro Suzumura. Tokyo: Academic Press Japan.

Harryson, Sigvald. 1998. *Japanese Technology and Innovation Management: From Know-How to Know-Who*. Northampton, MA: Edqard Elgar Publishing.

Herbig, Paul. 1995. *Innovation Japanese Style: A Cultural and Historical Perspective*. Westport: Quorun Books.

Ito, Minoru. 1995. The R$D system behind Japan's high technology products—Technology, human resources and work organization. In *Technology Management and Corporate Strategies: A Tricontinental Perspective*, ed. by Jose Allouche and Gerard Pogorel. Amsterdam: Elsevier.

Manaagement and Coordination Agency. 1997. *Report on the Survey of Research and Development*.

Motoyoshi, Kenya. 1993. The paradigm shift in U.S. and Japanese science and technology policy. *Japan Research Quarterly* 2: 51–87.

Noland, Marcus. 1996. Research and development activities and trade specialization in Japan. *Journal of Japanese and International Economies* 10: 150–168.

Okimoto, Daniel I., and Yoshio Nishi. 1994. R&D organization in Japanese and American semiconductor firms. In *The Japanese Firm: Sources of Competitive Strength*, ed. by Masahiko Aoki and Ronald Dore. Oxford: Oxford University Press.

Science and Technology Agency. Annual. *White Paper on Science and Technology*. Tokyo: Japan Information Center of Science and Technology.

Science and Technology Agency. 1997. *Indicators of Science and Technology*.

Wakasugi, Ryuhei. 1994. Organizational structure and behavior in research and development. In *Business Enterprise in Japan*, ed. by Kenichi Imai and Ryutaro Komiya. Cambridge: MIT Press.

Westney, D. Eleanor. 1994. The evolution of Japan's industrial research and development. In *The Japanese Firm: Sources of Competitive Strength*, ed. by Masahiko Aoki and Ronald Dore. Oxford: Oxford University Press.

Second Association of Regional Banks   National organization of the 65 second-tier regional banks, which were formerly *sogo* banks but converted themselves into regular commercial banks in 1989.

See **banking system,** *sogo* **banks.**

securities companies   Securities companies were established in accordance with the Securities and Exchange Law of 1948 for the underwriting and trading of securities, which banks are not permitted to enter except through subsidiaries. In addition they play a role in the **investment trust** and the **money market.** At the end of March 1997, there were 232 licensed securities companies in Japan, regulated by the **Ministry of Finance.**

Although many securities companies existed in the early postwar period (1,152 in 1949), most of them were small and financially weak and subsequently merged or went out of business. Total paid-in capital of all securities companies was only ¥3 billion in 1949, giving an average capitalization per company of ¥2.6 million. The total increased to ¥1,688 billion at the end of March 1997, which gives an average capitalization per company of ¥7.3 billion. This increase reflects the greatly increased volume of business of the securities industry during the 1980s as Japanese investors with surplus funds sought alternative forms of investment and as corporate borrowers increasingly raised funds in the equity and debt markets.

Securities companies are engaged in the following lines of business:

1. *The stock business.* This is the largest source of revenues. About 66% of the stock business is in the form of brokerage business to effect stock transactions on behalf of customers. The balance involves dealing in stocks for their own accounts.

2. *The bond business.* Securities companies are engaged in underwriting and distributing new issues of bonds as well as in trading outstanding issues. The bulk of the bond transactions they handle is for their own accounts (self-dealing). However, about 60% of the bond trading is in the form of *gensaki* trading, namely the sale of bonds with a repurchase agreement. With the massive offering of **government bonds** in 1975, the volume of bond transactions has increased rapidly. The internationalization of the securities market also increased the underwriting by securities companies of Japanese corporate bonds issued on foreign markets.

3. *Other lines of business.* Securities companies may be involved in aspects of **investment trust** business. They may also be engaged in the transaction of domestic certificates of deposit (CDs), yen-denominated banker's acceptance, commercial papers (CPs) issued on the domestic market, mortgage-backed securities, and CDs and CPs issues on foreign markets.

Until the closure of the Yamaichi Securities Co. in November 1997, the securities industry was dominated by the Big Four—Nomura Securities Co., Daiwa, Nikko, and Yamaichi Securities Co. Their share of the market, however, had declined over time. In 1980 they had nearly 60% of the market; in 1997 the four had a 30% market share in stock brokerage in the **Tokyo Stock Exchange.** The Big Four were followed by ten "second-tier" companies—Kokusai, Wako, Okasan, New Japan, Kankaku, Cosmo, Sanyo, Tokyo, Yamatane, and Dai-Ichi. In November 1997, Sanyo Securities Co. went bankrupt and Yamaichi Securities Co. voluntarily liquidated itself due to previously concealed huge losses, sending shock waves throughout the whole industry and economy. Between December

Table S.4
Leading securities companies (FY, in ¥ billions)

Company	Operating revenues			Pretax profits		
	1989	1992	1997	1989	1992	1997
Nomura	986.2	344.7	342.6	488.9	2.4	40.7
Daiwa	660.1	247.1	255.9	313.2	−7.3	5.1
Nikko	601.0	230.7	197.5	260.5	2.5	−38.2
Yamaichi[a]	573.5	188.7	—	233.7	−37.4	—
Kokusai	215.5	78.4	91.0	76.5	−17.4	10.8
Wako	150.5	52.2	52.5	47.8	−22.5	−6.0
Okasan	121.3	36.1	39.0	31.7	−18.5	−2.4
New Japan	207.2	69.1	76.3	50.1	−36.5	−4.9
Kankaku	180.3	46.2	46.0	44.1	−51.0	−51.0
Cosmo	97.1	24.5	23.6	24.2	−17.5	−2.4

Source: *The Nikkei Weekly*, April 27, 1998 and *Japan Company Handbook* (Summer 1998).
a. Went out of business in November 1997.

1997 and May 1998, a few other smaller securities companies also went out of business. This pace of business failures was unprecedented in the industry. It resulted not only from the depressed securities business and economy in the 1990s but also from years of unsound and unethical business practices (see below) and inadequate supervision given to the industry by the **Ministry of Finance.**

Table S.4 shows the revenues and profits of some leading securities companies. It is clear that the fall of stock prices that started in 1990 became a disaster for the industry in the 1990s. Some midsized and smaller securities companies were affected even more severely than the big ones.

Although the securities companies are regulated by the Ministry of Finance, the regulation is not as strict as in the United States, and new rules are introduced only when flagrant unethical practices have caused a public outcry and international criticisms. Stock price manipulation is one of those practices. Before 1988 the Big Four periodically promoted selected stock issues or sectors to customers, which made those prices to rise precipitously. The Brady Commission, a U.S. government special body on stock trading, criticized the Big Four's oligopolistic control of the Japanese **stock market** in its 1988 report. As a result the Ministry of Finance imposed in early 1988 an unwritten "30% rule," restricting each securities house to hold its percentage of trading volume in any stock to less than 30% of the stock's total volume each month.

Another unethical practice is the clandestine arrangement made by the big securities firms with their major clients to compensate them for trading losses. This helps to attract big businesses at the expense of small investors and is in violation of Japan's Securities and Exchange Law. They have done so through the device of shadowy discretionary *eigyo tokkin* accounts set up by securities firms for clients; these accounts are directly managed by the securities houses on a discretionary basis so that funds can be easily moved in and out of them (see **tokkin funds**). It was revealed in mid-1991 that the Big Four paid an estimated ¥120 billion to compensate major clients for stock trading losses from October 1987 to March 1991. Thirty smaller securities firms also paid top clients about ¥20 billion for loss compensation. Such scandals forced the resignation or demotion of senior executives of the Big Four, and various penalties were imposed by the government. In addition it was revealed that Nomura and Nikko had business dealings with an organized crime syndicate.

Rules against insider trading exist, but it was not until 1990 that the first prosecution of insider trading was filed. Government officials emphasize that the purpose of the rules is to prevent insider trading rather than to punish violators.

In Japan, banking business and securities business are separated by law. The separation was eased in April 1993 when, as part of the **financial liberalization**, the Financial Reform Act was instituted to permit banks and securities companies to enter each other's business through the establishment of subsidiaries.

Another policy issue concerns the participation of foreign securities firms in the industry. The slow opening of Japan's securities industry to foreign firms has been one of Washington's complaints about Japan's financial markets. However, with the implementation of the **Big Bang** aiming at accelerated financial reforms, the financial markets have become, and will continue to become, more open and foreign securities firms have begun to play a larger role in Japan. For example, in December 1997 Merrill Lynch Capital International Management Co. was given permission by the Ministry of Finance to begin full-scale investment management services. In February 1998 Merrill Lynch and Co. announced that it will hire up to 2,000 former employees of the failed Yamaichi Securities Co. and will buy 30 of its locations. In June 1998 Travelers Group Inc. agreed to acquire a 25% stake in Nikko Securities Co., Japan's third largest securities company.

See also **stock market**, *tokkin* **funds, Tokyo Stock Exchange.**

Addresses

Daiwa Securities Co.
6-4, Ohtemachi 2-chome, Chiyoda-ku, Tokyo 100
Tel: (3) 3243-2111

Japan Securities Dealers Association
5-8, Nihonbashi Kayabacho 1-chome, Chuo-ku, Tokyo 103
Tel: (3) 3667-8451   Fax: (3) 3666-8009

Nikko Securities Co.
3-1, Marunouchi 3-chome, Chiyoda-ku, Tokyo 100
Tel: (3) 3283-2211

Nomura Securities Co.
9-1, Nohonbashi 1-chome, Chuo-ku, Tokyo 103
Tel: (3) 3211-1811

References

Alletzhauser. 1990. *The House of Nomura.* London: Bloomsbury.

Elton, Edwin J., and Martin J. Gruber. 1990. *Japanese Capital Markets.* New York: Harper and Row.

Isaacs, Jonathan. 1990. *Japanese Equities Markets.* London: Euromoney Pulications. Ch. 7.

Japan Company Handbook. Quarterly. Tokyo: Toyo Keizai Inc.

Japan Securities Research Institute. 1998. *Securities Market in Japan, 1998.* Ch. 7.

Securities companies. *Japan Economic Almanac,* various issues.

Shimizu, Yasumasa. 1997. Payoff scandal threatens reign of Big Four. *Nikkei Weekly,* September 22: 1, 11.

Tatewaki, Kazuo. 1991. *Banking and Finance in Japan.* London: Routledge. Ch. 8.

Yamamoto, Yuri. 1998. Big Bang rattles securities hierarchy. *Nikkei Weekly,* April 27, 1998: 14.

Zielinski, Robert, and Nigel Holloway. 1991. *Unequal Equities: Power and Risk in Japan's Stock Market.* Tokyo: Kodansha International. Ch. 4.

securities finance companies   These are companies that specialize in the financing of securities. Nine such companies were established in 1950, one in each of the cities with securities exchanges, because of the depressed stock market following the dissolution of the *zaibatsu* and the dumping of their stocks on the market. In 1956 they were consolidated into the current three: Japan Securities Finance Company, Osaka Securities Finance Company, and the Chubu Securities Company (located in **Nagoya**). The last one is by far the smallest of the three. They are supervised by the **Ministry of Finance.**

Their business was initially limited to lending to **securities companies** for margin transactions. In 1960 they began lending to bond dealers for transactions in bonds. Because of the rapid growth of the primary and secondary markets in **government bonds** in the 1980s, the volume of bond dealer financing has grown rapidly to match that of stock margin transactions. At the end of 1997, their total outstanding loans were ¥1.2 trillion, down from the peak of ¥3.0 trillion at the end of 1989. Loans for margin transactions were ¥276 billion, whereas loans on bonds were ¥612 billion. There were also ¥315 billion loans on notes and bills.

Securities finance companies obtain their funds by borrowing from the **Bank of Japan**, the **city banks**, and the **call money market.** In 1988 they were allowed to raise money by issuing **commercial papers.**

See also **securities companies.**

securities investment trust management companies   Fund managers of **investment trusts.**

See **investment trusts.**

seibo   The year-end gift-giving season.

See **gift market.**

Seibu Railway Group   A large conglomerate with the Seibu Railway as its core company.

See *keiretsu* **and business groups.**

seikyo   Consumer cooperatives.

See **consumer groups.**

Semiconductor Agreement, 1991 and 1996   An agreement between Tokyo and Washington, singed on June 4, 1991, and effective from August 1, 1991, for five years, in which Tokyo pledges to promote the share of foreign firms in Japan's chip market to more than 20% by the end of 1992, although the Japanese government does not guarantee that market share. It replaces an earlier five-year accord, which expired on August 1, 1991.

To deter possible dumping, Japanese semiconductor companies will collect cost and price data and turn them over to Washington in the event of an antidumping investigation. Also, to prevent chip dumping in third countries, Tokyo and Washington will cooperate with third countries in any GATT action to investigate dumping.

Although Japanese electronics makers pledged to cooperate with the government in implementing the agreement, many have expressed misgivings about the 20% goal. Some questioned the ability of foreign companies to supply such a large amount. Others indicated that a longer period of joint development was needed to install chips in their products. Still others complained that delivery of foreign chips is often unreliable or expressed doubt about the quality of foreign-made chips. In general, Japanese executives do not think that the agreement would do much to restore the U.S. industry's competitiveness.

European Community officials feel that the agreement is discriminatory because it would pressure the Japanese to import more U.S. chips but not the European ones. In the last quarter of 1992 foreign chips attained 20.2% of Japan's semiconductor market, slightly exceeding the target. Since 1994 the market share of foreign chips continued to exceed the target: 22.4% in 1994, 25.4% in 1995, and 27.5% in 1996.

Because of these rising numbers, Tokyo insisted that numerical targets and share monitoring are not necessary in any new agreement to replace the 1991 agreement which expired in 1996. The new 1996 Semiconductor Agreement is a two-tier accord. At the government level, a Global Government Forum will be established, to which governments of other countries with semiconductor industries will be invited to join. It will address problems in the global semiconductor market, including market access and protection of intellectual property rights. At the industry level, a Semiconductor Council will be established which will serve as a multilateral industry forum. Semiconductor industries of other countries will be invited to participate if their governments agree to abolish tariffs on semiconductors.

See also **electronic industry.**

semiconductor industry
See **electronics industry.**

service price index
See **price indexes and price levels.**

shareownership   Financial institutions and business corporations are the largest categories of shareholders in Japan. Before 1972, however, individuals were the largest shareholders.

Table S.5 shows the changes in the patterns of shareownership in the postwar period. It includes only shares of companies listed on any one of

Table S.5
Shareownership of all listed companies (in %)

	1951	1972	1990	1997
Government and local government	3.1	0.2	0.7	0.5
Financial institutions	12.6	33.9	46.0	41.3
All banks	—	—	22.1	21.6
Investment trusts	—	—	3.7	2.0
Annuity trusts	—	—	0.9	2.3
Life insurance company	—	—	13.1	10.9
Non-life insurance company	—	—	4.1	3.4
Others	—	—	2.1	1.0
Business corporations	13.8	23.6	24.8	23.8
Securities companies	9.2	1.5	2.0	1.1
Individuals and others	61.3	37.2	22.6	23.6
Foreigners	—	3.6	3.9	9.8
Total	100.0	100.0	100.0	100.0

Source: Tokyo Stock Exchange.
Note: (1) On the basis of business years ending on March 31 of each year. (2) "Individuals and others" include unincorporated organizations.

the eight stock exchanges in Japan and excludes those traded in the over-the-counter stock market. Important changes include the following: (1) Financial institutions, including all banks and **insurance companies** but excluding **securities companies**, have become the largest shareholders since 1973. (2) Business corporations have more than doubled their share of ownership in the postwar period to become the second largest category. (3) From the largest group of shareowners before 1972, individuals and unincorporated organizations have declined in importance and account for only about 23% of shareownership in 1990–97. (4) Government shareownership has been less than 1% since 1954 (not shown in the table). Shareownership by foreigners has increased from 1.2% in 1953 to 9.8% in 1997. It fluctuated in the 4–6% range in the 1980s.

The steady decline of individuals' shareownership is unhealthy for market stability and the diffusion of economic power. In Japan large institutional investors tend to act together in the same direction in the market, thereby causing greater fluctuations than individual investors would (**Tokyo Stock Exchange** briefing, August 7, 1992). Developments in the 1990s have made it easier to attract individual investors for three reasons. (1) The ministock system, introduced in October 1995 by Daiwa Securities Co., permits small investors to buy stocks at a minimum unit of 100 shares, although they will not have voting rights. Normally the minimum is 1,000 shares, which is high by international standards. (2) The average dividend/payout ratio of domestic listed companies has been raised from 27.64 in 1990 to 58.18 in 1993 and 60.84 in 1997 (Tokyo Stock Exchange 1998: 35). It was less than 30% in the 1980s, which was lower than that of other industrial nations. (3) The record low levels of interest rates in Japan, especially after the mid-1990s, leaves small investors few alternatives for investment.

As of March 1997 Nippon Telegraph and Telephone (NTT) has by far the largest number of individual shareholders (1,486,000), followed by Tokyo Electric Power (728,000) and Nippon Steel (450,000). The revelation in 1991 that securities companies have compensated large companies for investment losses has alienated many individual investors.

Beneath the overall patterns of institutional shareownership are various underlying factors of the economy, including the following business relationships and practices that affect shareownership:

1. Companies that are members of a *keiretsu* or corporate group own each other's shares. In the financial *keiretsu*, the extent of **cross-shareholding** declined from 25.5% in 1981 to 21.64% in 1989. It has reportedly declined further in the 1990s because of the long stagnation of the economy, low stock prices, and the declined profits of many companies. In some industrial *keiretsu*, such as the Hitachi Group, the core industrial company of the group typically owns a significant percentage (50% or more in the case of Hitachi) of the shares of other group members.

2. Companies that do business with each other without *keiretsu* ties customarily hold a small amount of each other's stock as a token of goodwill and mutual support. Traditionally these shares will not be sold as long as the business relationship is maintained. The economic recession and the sluggish **stock market** of the 1990s, however, have prompted many companies to sell some of their shareholdings.

3. Institutional investors such as trust funds, pension funds, and **insurance companies** tend to hold shares for a long period of time for long-term capital gains. These are considered to be "stable shareholders."

4. Companies' **main banks** and insurance companies hold shares of their customers in order to promote business with them. They are also valued by the issuing companies as stable shareholders.

5. Between the mid-1980s and 1990, because of the appreciation of the yen and the rising **stock market**, many Japanese manufactures were heavily engaged in *zaiteku*, or active investment of funds, in the stock

market to increase their profits. The fall of the stock market and the recession of the economy since 1991 have dampened such activities.

In December 1997 the **Antimonopoly Law** was revised to permit the establishment of **holding companies**, including financial holding companies, that own enough stock in other companies and financial institutions to control their policies and management. This will facilitate the growth of corporate groups through ownership ties, although there are legal limits on the size and nature of holding companies. If this form of corporate organization and ownership proves to be popular, it will increase the concentration of institutional shareownership in favor of large corporations and financial institutions.

See also **cross-shareholding, holding companies,** *keiretsu* and business groups, Tokyo Stock Exchange.

References

Choy, Jon. 1991. Patterns and implications of Japanese stockholding. *JEI Report*, January 25.

Flath, David. 1993. Shareholding in the keiretsu, Japan's financial groups. *Review of Economics and Statistics* 75: 249–58.

Lincoln, James R., Michael L. Gerlach, and Christina L. Ahmadjian. 1996. Keiretsu networks and corporate performance in Japan. *American Sociological Review* 61: 67–89.

MacKnight, Susan. 1995. Ties that exclude: Manufacturer-distributor relationships in Japan. *JEI Report* 29A. August 4.

Tokyo Stock Exchange. 1998. *Tokyo Stock Exchange Fact Book, 1998.*

Zielinski, Robert, and Nigel Holloway. 1991. *Unequal Equities: Power and Risk in Japan's Stock Market.* Tokyo: Kodansha Interest. Chs. 2–3.

shinkin **banks**   Established on the basis of the 1951 *Shinkin* Bank Law, *shinkin* banks, or credit associations, are a special type of financial institution for small- and medium-sized businesses, roughly comparable to savings and loan institutions in the United States. They have their origins in the traditional credit cooperatives and are organized as nonprofit cooperatives or credit associations. Their members are **small and medium enterprises** (with no more than 300 employees and capitalization of no more than ¥900 million) and local residents. The number of *shinkin* banks has been declining steadily in the postwar period. There were 405 *shinkin* banks as of December 1997, down from 538 at the end of 1960.

Shinkin banks conduct their business primarily with their members, accepting deposits and installment savings, lending and discounting bills for them. The law permits them to lend to nonmembers up to 20% of their total lending. The maximum loan to a single borrower is set at 20% of the bank's capital or ¥1.5 billion, whichever is smaller. In exchange for these restrictions they are permitted to pay 0.1% more than ordinary banks for fixed-term deposits and 0.25% more for despots for tax payments and other deposits. Their total assets at year-end were ¥3.7 trillion in 1965, ¥40.9 trillion in 1980, and ¥113.6 trillion in 1997. At the end of 1997 their savings and deposits totaled ¥100.6 trillion, and their loans and discounts totaled ¥70.2 trillion.

As competition in the banking business intensified and interest rate liberalization drove up the cost of funds, some smaller *shinkin* banks have merged to increase their scale of operation. Some large ones are expected to join with **city banks** or to transform themselves into ordinary banks.

All *shinkin* banks are members of the Zenshinren Bank, the National Federation of *Shinkin* Banks. Zenshinren is engaged in deposit taking, lending, and funds transfer for members and for government and non-profit organizations. At the end of 1997 it had ¥12.2 trillion in deposits and ¥6.8 trillion in loans. In November 1990 the Federation expressed for the first time its support for mergers among *shinkin* banks.

See also **banking system.**

Address

The National Federation of Shinkin Banks
8-1, Kyobashi 3-chome, Chuo-ku, Tokyo 104
Tel: (3) 3563-4821

References

Bank of Japan. Annual. *Economics Statistics Annual.*

Federation of Bankers Association of Japan. 1994. *The Banking System in Japan.* Ch. 1.

Interest rate liberalization worries credit associations. *Nikkei Weekly,* October 19, 1991: 16.

Okamoto, Fumio. 1990. *Shinkin* banks offer service in fight against city giants. *Japan Economic Journal,* March 3: 31–32.

Suzuki, Yoshio, ed. 1987. *The Japanese Financial System.* Oxford: Oxford University Press. Ch. 5.

Takagi, Hisao. 1990. Co-ops brace for battle to survive. *Japan Economic Journal,* November 24: 1.

Tatewaki, Kazuo. 1991. *Banking and Finance in Japan.* London: Routledge. Ch. 7.

***shinpan* companies**   Sales finance companies, which provide credit for consumers' installment purchases.
    See **consumer credit.**

shipbuilding industry   From a very low level after World War II, Japan's shipbuilding industry developed so rapidly that Japan surpassed Britain in 1956 to become the world's largest shipbuilder. It has remained in that position ever since. However, because the world's demand for new ships slumped after the oil crisis of 1973, the industry went through a long depression in 1974 through 1988. During that period the industry had to adopt measures to restrict industry capacity. In the 1990s the industry has enjoyed a revival of world demand for new ships.
    Shipbuilding in Japan is regulated by the Ministry of Transport (MOT). The industry developed very rapidly from the early 1950s through 1973 when world seaborn trade tripled and bulk carriers and crude tankers were needed to transport major commodities such as crude oil, iron ore, coal, and grain. The industry was also assisted with long-term, low-interest loans from the **Japan Development Bank** and the **Export-Import Bank of Japan.** In 1973 the industry had about one-half (48.6%) of the world's orders for new ships.
    In the aftermath of the 1973 oil crisis, new orders fell sharply from a peak of 38 million gross tons in 1973 to 13.3 million tons in 1974 and 3.2 million tons in 1978. Under the MOT's **administrative guidance** the industry began, in 1976, to implement an industrywide reduction in output (28% reduction from peak year output). The Depressed Industries Law of 1978, designed to reduce capacity and balance supply and demand in "structurally depressed industries" or **declining industries**, facilitated further reduction in subsequent years. In 1979 production was limited to 39% of peak-year output. A recession **cartel** was also established in 1979 to oversee the reduction. The MOT also assisted qualified smaller shipbuilders to leave the industry with a buyout program.
    The orders for new ships recovered in 1980–81 to 9.8 million gross tons and to 10.7 million gross tons in 1983. It declined rapidly thereafter. A recession cartel was organized in 1987 to reduce industry output. In 1989 new orders rose to 9.7 million gross tons. During the 1980–89 period the MOT continued to regulate production, to prevent price declines, by setting construction goals for individual companies. Nevertheless, competition among companies and from the low-cost Korean shipbuilders led to declining prices of new ships throughout most of the 1980s.

Mirroring the long-term decline in the industry, the shipbuilding work-force declined from a peak of 361,000 persons (including subcontracted shipbuilders and related industries) at the end of 1974 to 209,000 at the end of 1984 and 126,000 at the end of 1990.

New orders climbed to 11.1 million gross tons in 1990, but declined in 1991–93 before recovering to 11.7 million tons in 1994. They have remained at a high annual level of 9 million tons or more since 1995 because of a worldwide high demand. Several factors have played a role in this development:

1. Many of the world's large tankers or VLCCs (very large crude carriers of more than 200,000 tons) built in the early 1970s are being scrapped for replacement, thus increasing the demand for new tankers.

2. A major change in tanker design and construction is playing a role in the latest demand for new ships. In the wake of the Exxon Valdez oil spill in March 1989, the International Maritime Organization adopted a new ruling in March 1992 to reduce the risk of oil spills. It requires that new tankers larger than 5,000 tons commissioned from July 1993 to be fitted with double hulls and that existing tankers larger than 20,000 tons to be retrofitted when they turn 25 years old. Since double-hull tankers cost about 20% more than the conventional tankers, the new ruling has impor-tant financial implications for the industry.

3. Japan's major international competitor, South Korea, is experiencing financial problems in the late 1990s. Many international shipping com-panies have therefore avoided placing orders with South Korean ship-builders. On the other hand, Japan's major shipbuilders have improved their productivity with cost cuts, rationalization, and computer-controlled production system. A weaker yen in 1997–98 also helped their price competitiveness.

Japanese shipbuilders are divided into seven groups. In each group shipbuilders often jointly design and produce their orders. The top shipbuilders are the so-called Big Seven: Mitsubishi Heavy Industries, Ishikawajima-Harima Heavy Industries, Mitsui Engineering and Ship-building, Hitachi Zosen, Kawasaki Heavy Industries, Nippon Kokan, and Sumitomo Heavy Industries (see table S.6). All of them are capable of building VLCCs. In addition they are all integrated heavy machinery com-panies that make many other products such as steel structures, "turnkey" plants, and aircraft engines. The diversified nature of their businesses helped to cushion the impact of recession in shipbuilding and enabled them to transfer idled workers from shipbuilding to other lines of busi-

Table S.6
Leading shipbuilders (FY 1996)

Company	Total sales (in ¥ billion)	Shipbuilding (in %)[a]
Mitsubishi Heavy Industries	2,733.8	16[b]
Kawasaki Heavy Industries	1,043.0	12
Ishikawajima-Harima Heavy Industries	845.0	16[b]
Hitachi Zosen	502.6	20[b]
Mitsui Engineering and Shipbuilding	369.1	30
Sumitomo Heavy Industries	327.3	30[b]

Source: *Japan Company Handbook, First Section* (Summer 1998).
a. Share of shipbuilding in total sales.
b. Includes steel structures or steel frames for shipbuilding.

ness. The "second-tier" shipbuilders are the medium- and small-sized companies that focus more narrowly on shipbuilding and depend on the big ones for technical and financial assistance.

Japanese shipbuilders have also developed high-tech ships to maintain their competitive edge. For example, Kawasaki Heavy Industries has developed high-speed vessels that can travel at about 80 kilometers per hour. Mitsui Engineering and Shipbuilding has introduced hovercraft for cargo use that may compete with overland truck transportation. Mitsubishi Heavy Industries is constructing luxury passenger liners.

See also **declining industries.**

Addresses

Ishikawajima-Harima Heavy Industries
2-1, Ohtemachi 2-chome, Chiyoda-ku, Tokyo 100
Tel: (3) 3244-5111   Fax: (3) 3244-5139

Kawasaki Heavy Industries
1-18, Nakamachidori 2-chome, Chuo-ku, Kobe 650
Tel: (78) 371-9530   Fax: (78) 371-9568

Mitsubishi Heavy Industries
5-1, Marunouchi 2-chome, Chiyoda-ku, Tokyo 100
Tel: (3) 3212-3111   Fax: (3) 3201-4517

Mitsui Engineering and Shipbuilding
6-4, Tsukiji 5-chome, Chuo-ku, Tokyo 104
Tel: (3) 3544-3147   Fax: (3) 3544-3050

Shipbuilders' Association of Japan
15-16 Toranomon 1-chome, Minato-ku, Tokyo 105
Tel: (3) 3502-2010   Fax: (3) 3502-2816

References

Japan Company Handbook, First Section. Quarterly. Tokyo: Toyo Keizai.

Reitman, Valerie. 1996. Japan shipbuilders buoyed by new wave of interest. *Asian Wall Street Journal Weekly*, April 8: 22.

Shipbuilding in Japan. Annual. Tokyo: Shipbuilders' Association of Japan.

Shipbuilding. In *Japan Economic Almanac*, various years. Tokyo: Nihon Keizai Shimbun.

Uriu, Robert M. 1996. *Troubled Industries: Confronting Economic Change in Japan.* Ithaca: Cornell University Press. Ch. 7.

Yonezawa, Yoshie. 1988. The shipbuilding industry. In *Industrial Policy of Japan*, ed. by Ryutaro Komiya, Masahiro Okuno, and Kotaro Suzumura. Tokyo: Academic Press Japan.

shitauke   Subcontract or subcontracting, which is widespread in Japan's manufacturing. It is particularly important in the **automobile industry** because of its cost advantage and flexibility in production, which fits into the industry's **just-in-time system.**
     See **automobile industry, subcontracting system.**

shogun **bonds**   Bonds issued in Japan in foreign currency, usually the dollar, by nonresidents.
     See **bond market,** *samurai* **bonds.**

shohizei   Consumption tax, an important national tax introduced in 1989 and currently set at 5% of consumer purchases.
     See **consumption tax, tax reform, tax system.**

shukko   The practice of transferring employees by large companies to related enterprises for a limited period of time.
     See **corporate personnel practices.**

shunto   Spring offensive, Japanese **labor unions'** annual wage bargaining campaign launched every spring.
     See **spring offensive.**

small and medium enterprises   The concept of small and medium enterprises (*chu-sho kigyo*) has its prewar origin in Japan, but its definition has changed over time. Currently, in manufacturing and construction, they are defined by law as incorporated or unincorporated enterprises with fewer than 300 employees and less than ¥100 million in capital; in wholesale trade, as those with fewer than 100 employees and less than ¥30 million in capital; and in retail trade and in services, as those with fewer than 50 employees and less than ¥10 million in capital. Small enterprises are defined as those with 20 or fewer employees in manufacturing and with 5 or fewer employees in commerce and services.

This definition is so broad that it covers more than 99% of all enterprises and 78% of employees in the 1980s and 1990s. These enterprises include nearly 100% of construction firms, wholesalers and retailers, real estate businesses, and many manufacturing enterprises. Most of these enterprises are relatively small subcontractors for large companies or family-owned businesses in service or trade sectors. It is primarily the small enterprises of this broad category that often face economic difficulties.

The problems of small enterprises include the following: It is difficult for them to compete with big companies to attract talented managers and skilled workers partly because they pay less. They have more difficulties in obtaining bank loans, they lack the resources for technology and innovation, and they are also the most vulnerable to recessions. The Small and Medium Enterprises Stabilization Law of 1952 was legislated to make it easier for them to form depression **cartels**.

The economic difficulties and the large voting power of the small businesses—Japan's Communist Party tried hard in the 1960s to win their votes—have prompted the ruling **Liberal Democratic Party** to enact the Small and Medium Enterprise Basic Law in 1963, which provided various measures to assist them: prevention of **bankruptcies** and aid to disaster victims; promotion of modernization through special subsidized loans and tax provisions; promotion of subcontracting; provision of consultation and guidance, and management training programs; and government procurement from small and medium enterprises.

In retail trade, the **Large Retail Store Law** of 1974 protects small retailers by regulating the growth of department stores and supermarkets. After 1990, however, the implementation of the law has been relaxed because of the Japan–U.S. **Structural Impediments Initiative** agreement in which Tokyo agrees to promote imports by permitting the establishment of more large stores, which are more likely than small retailers to carry imports.

In manufacturing, small and medium enterprises often serve as subcontractors for large firms. The Subcontractors' Protection Law of 1956 protects them from unfair practices by large firms such as late payments. The shift by many Japanese firms of their operations abroad ("hollowing out") has adversely affected the subcontractors' work.

The Small and Medium Enterprise Agency of the **Ministry of International Trade and Industry** is responsible for coordinating government assistance to small and medium enterprises; it also provides consultation, guidance, and technical assistance to them. Two **government financial institutions** are set up to provide financial assistance to small and medium enterprises—the Small Business Finance Corp. and the Small Business Credit Insurance Corp. The former had outstanding loans of ¥7,051 billion at the end of 1997, while the latter had outstanding loans of ¥597 billion at the end of 1997. Funds from the government's **Fiscal Investment and Loan Program** allocated to purposes related to small and medium enterprises increased from ¥552 billion in fiscal 1970 to ¥3,400 billion in 1980 and ¥4,495 billion in 1991, but then declined to ¥1,690 billion or 3.3% of the total FILP funds in FY 1997. Expenditures for small business assistance from the regular **government budget** are typically less than 1% of the government's budget (0.2% or ¥186.5 billion in FY 1997). These low figures suggest that small and medium enterprises are currently not a priority of government policy.

The number of bankruptcies among small and medium enterprises declined during the second half of the 1980s. Since 1991, however, the number has risen because of the long stagnation of the economy and tight bank credit. According to the Small and Medium Enterprise Agency (1997), of the 14,834 business failures in Japan in 1996, 14,731 were small and medium enterprises. The failure rate was the highest in construction (0.75%), followed by retail and wholesale trade (0.61%).

See also **Fiscal Investment and Loan Program.**

Addresses

Small and Medium Enterprise Agency, MITI
3-1, Kasumigaseki 1-chome, Chiyoda-ku, Tokyo 100
Tel: (3) 3501-1511   Fax: (3) 3501-7805

Small Business Corporation
5-1, Toranomon, 3-chome, Minato-ku, Tokyo 105
Tel: (3) 3433-8811

Small Business Finance Corporation
9-3. Otemachi 1-chome, Chiyoda-ku, Tokyo 100
Tel: (3) 3270-1261

References

Altbach, Eric. 1998. Crushed by the crunch: Small- and medium-sized businesses suffer from stagnant eeconomy, loan freeze. *JEI Report* 30A, August 7.

Koseki, Tomohiro. 1997. The resilience of tiny factories. *Japan Echo*, Spring: 50–53.

Matsushita, Mitsuo. 1993. *International Trade and Competition Law in Japan.* Oxford: Oxford University Press. Ch. 4.

Patrick, H., and T. Rohlen. 1987. Small-scale family enterprises. In *The Political Economy of Japan*, vol. 1: *The Domestic Transformation*, ed. by K. Yamamura and Y. Yasuba. Stanford: Stanford University Press.

Small and Medium Enterprise Agency. Annual. *White Paper on Small and Medium Enterprises in Japan.* Tokyo: MITI.

Whittacker, D. H. 1997. *Small Firms in the Japanese Economy.* Cambridge: Cambridge University Press.

Yokokura, Takashi. 1988. Small and medium enterprises. In *Industrial Policy of Japan*, ed. by R. Komiya, M. Okuno, and K. Suzumura. Tokyo: Academic Press Japan.

social insurance   The most important part of Japan's **social security system** consisting of **health insurance**, national pension, and **employment insurance.**

See **employment insurance, health insurance, pension system, social security system.**

social security system   Japan's social security system consists of social insurance, public assistance, social welfare services, children's allowances, public health, aid for war victims, and so forth. Social insurance is the most important component of the system. It consists of **health insurance**, national pensions, **employment insurance**, and employment accident compensation insurance. It provides for unforeseen circumstances with funds collected through payments by individuals and employers as well as with public subsidies. In both health insurance and **pension systems**, there are different programs for people of different employment statuses (employees of private firms, government employees, and the self-employed). These are discussed separately in **health insurance** and **pension system.**

Public assistance ("livelihood protection" subsidies) is given to the indigent who cannot support themselves. A minimum amount of livelihood expenses is calculated, which includes basic living expenses, **housing**, schooling, and medical expenses. Childbirth and funeral expenses are also included where relevant. The difference between this minimum amount and the household's actual income is the amount of assistance to be given. The system is implemented by welfare offices at the city, township, and village levels that ascertain the need and provide counseling and assistance. Thus there is no uniform national standard in implementation. Reportedly there is a feeling of stigma in accepting assistance.

The minimum amount of living expenses used to calculate the amount of assistance to be given to a household varies with the size and composition of the household and its location. Three examples are given below for FY 1996:

1. Basic household of three members (33-year-old man with disease and/ or injury, 29 year-old woman, and 4-year old child):
1st class (highest cost-of-living) region: ¥171,375 per month.
2nd class region: ¥157,121
3rd class region: ¥137,868

2. Household of two elderly (72-year-old man, 67-year-old woman):
1st class region: ¥145,809
2nd class region: ¥134,293
3rd class region: ¥117,748

3. Fatherless household of three: 30-year-old woman, 0- and 4-year-old children:
1st class region: ¥194,716
2nd class region: ¥179,151
3rd class region: ¥158,556

In FY 1995 an average of 880,693 people per month, or 0.7% of the **population**, received public assistance, down from the postwar peak of 1,469,000 people in 1984 (Health and Welfare Statistics Association 1997: 146–48).

Other welfare programs are designed for the elderly, the handicapped, and children with special needs. Among still other programs are a family rehabilitation loan program, a program for the rehabilitation and protection of women (prostitutes), and disaster relief.

The Ministry of Health and Welfare and its Social Insurance Agency are in charge of health insurance, pension, and social insurance, whereas the Ministry of Labor is responsible for employment insurance and employment accident compensation insurance.

See also **employment insurance, health insurance, pension system.**

Address

Ministry of Health and Welfare
2-2, Kasumigaseki 1-chome, Chiyoda-ku, Tokyo 100
Tel: (3) 3503-1711

References

Health and Welfare Statistics Association. 1997. *Health and Welfare Statistics in Japan.*

Ministry of Health and Welfare. Annual. *White Paper on Health and Welfare* (in Japanese).

Murdo, Pat. 1993. Japan's social security reforms target equity, solvency issues. *JEI Report* 32A, August 27.

Nishida, Yoshiaki. 1990. Reassessment of welfare services and the trend of welfare policy for the disabled. *Annals of the Institute of Social Science* (University of Tokyo) 32: 115–54.

Social Insurance Agency. 1996. *Outline of Social Insurance in Japan.*

Soeda, Yoshiya. 1990. The development of the public assistance system in Japan, 1966–83. *Annals of the Institute of Social Science* 32: 31–65.

Tabata, Hirokuni. 1990. The Japanese welfare state: Its structure and transformation. *Annals of the Institute of Social Science* 32: 1–29.

***sogo* banks**   Developed from the traditional mutual loan (*mujin*) companies in accordance with the *Sogo* Bank Law of 1951, *sogo* banks were mutual banks that specialized in financing small- and medium-sized companies until they converted themselves into ordinary banks, or the "new regional banks," in 1989 and became members of the Second Association of Regional Banks.

Sogo banks differed from ordinary banks in that their loans were in principle restricted to small- and medium-sized firms with employees up to 300 persons and a maximum capitalization of ¥100 million and that they were permitted to continue their traditional mutual installment savings and loans business. However, because of the changing needs of their clients, their mutual installment operations had declined since the late 1960s, and they became more similar to ordinary banks, particularly the regional banks. Their banking activities included taking deposits, lending, discounting bills, and transferring funds.

Over the years *sogo* banks had grown about as rapidly as *shinkin* banks, another type of specialized financial institutions for small- and medium-sized firms. Their total assets were ¥3.6 trillion in 1965, ¥7.6 trillion in 1970, and ¥55.5 trillion in 1988. As of 1988 there were 68 *sogo* banks. Their total deposits, including installment savings, were ¥46.2 trillion, and total loans, including mutual installment loans, were ¥38.3 trillion.

In 1989 all 68 *sogo* banks converted themselves into ordinary banks, as was permitted under the Law Concerning Merger and Conversion of Financial Institutions, and the National Association of *Sogo* Banks was changed to the Second Association of Regional Banks.

See also **banking system, *shinkin* banks.**

Address

Second Association of Regional Banks
5, Sanbancho, Chiyoda-ku, Tokyo 102
Tel: (3) 3262-2181

References

Bank of Japan. Annual. *Economic Statistics Annual.*

The Banking System in Japan. 1994. Tokyo: Federation of Bankers Associations of Japan.

Suzuki, Yoshio, ed. 1987. *The Banking System in Japan.* Oxford: Oxford University Press. Pp. 215–218.

Tatewaki, Kazuo. *Banking and Finance in Japan.* London: Routledge. Ch. 7.

sogo **shosha**   General **trading companies**, the giant trading companies that are responsible for the bulk of Japan's exporting and importing. They provide diverse trade-related services (financing, shipping, insurance, etc.) to clients and are heavily involved in Japan's **direct overseas investment.**
   See **trading companies.**

Sohyo   The General Council of Trade Unions of Japan, Japan's largest federation of unions before 1987. It merged with the Japan Trade Union Confederation (JTUC-Rengo) in 1989.
   See **labor unions.**

sokaiya   Shareholder-extortionist who extort money from companies by threatening to disrupt company's annual shareholders' meetings by revealing company's internal scandals.
   See **underworld "businesses."**

spring (labor) offensive   This is the common and literal translation of the Japanese term *shunto.* It refers to the unique institutionalized process each spring in which Japanese **labor unions** bargain for annual wage increases. The first *shunto* was organized in 1956. Since then *shunto* has been launched every spring, and it has played an important part in Japan's labor movement and wage determination.
   Spring is an appropriate time for wage bargaining because April 1 is the beginning of the fiscal year in Japan. April is also the time many companies recruit new workers, following the end of the school year in March, and set up entry-level wages and make adjustments in the wage

scales. As early as late fall of the previous year, however, the unions' joint *shunto* coordinating committee would meet and begin to put out tentative demands in the media. Representing employers is the Japan Federation of Employers' Association, or Nikkeiren. It counterbalances unions' initial demand by publicizing the reasons for any wage restraint. It tends to stress the need for Japan to reduce consumer prices rather than to raise wages and insists that wage increases should be based on productivity increases. This type of public airing of positions by the two sides will intensify, invariably with the help of the media and occasionally with the participation of officials. Unions may draw up strike plans, although actual strikes have been relatively few.

By February individual enterprise unions will have put forward their own demands to their management, occasionally with some advice given at the industry or national level. The actual bargaining also takes place at the enterprise level. Historically settlements in a few strategic industries have served as the pattern setters. These were private railway workers (1958–59, 1965, 1968), iron and steel workers (1969–70), autoworkers and shipbuilders (1977), and metal industries' workers (1982–84). In recent years, because of their relative decline, these industries have been replaced by computers, consumer electronics, telecommunications, and transportation industries as the pace setters. The pattern of settlements reached in the private unionized sectors are closely followed by settlements in the public sector. Small nonunionized firms also try to follow the same pattern, with some variations because of the varied conditions of the small firms.

Before the oil crisis of the early 1970s, the rate of wage increases ranged between 9% and 16%. Since then Japanese unions' wage demands have been relatively modest, especially in the 1990s, and generally in line with the conditions of the economy. The pay increases unions accepted usually amounted to only 60–70% of their initial demands. For example, in its annual sample survey of 288 large firms, the Ministry of Labor found that the unions demanded an average monthly wage increase of ¥15,157 but settled for ¥11,679 in FY 1980; in 1987, they demanded ¥12,861 but settled for ¥8,275. The average rate of actual wage increase for the sample firms was 6.74% in FY 1980, 5.03% in 1985, and 2.86% in 1996 (see table S.7). Unions' wage demands have been restrained by fear of inflation, increased Japanese investments in lower-wage countries which have eliminated jobs at home, and by the long stagnation of the economy in the 1990s. Note that the figures in table S.7 are based on a sample of major companies. **Small and medium enterprises** invariably

Table S.7
Shunto wage increases (in ¥ per month)

FY	Amount	Percentage
1956	1,063	6.3
1965	3,150	10.6
1975	15,279	13.1
1980	11,679	6.74
1985	10,871	5.03
1988	10,573	4.43
1989	12,747	5.17
1990	15,026	5.94
1991	14,911	5.65
1992	13,662	4.95
1993	11,077	3.89
1994	9,118	3.13
1995	8,376	2.83
1996	8,712	2.86

Source: Ministry of Labor.
Note: Figures before 1980 are simple averages of 288 major firms surveyed (160 firms for 1956). After 1980 the figures are weighted by the number of union members.

offer smaller wage increases in amounts and in percentage rates. For example, the average wage increase of 8,000 small and medium enterprises was ¥8,246 (4.8%) in 1985, ¥11,050 (5.5%) in 1990, and ¥6,148 (2.6%) in 1996.

Dore (1987: 70) attributes the continuing influence and viability of *shunto* to its "containment of the bargaining within a *predictable* procedure, and the heavy involvement of the media in the process." Japan's employers federation, however, has criticized unions' past *shunto* practice of concentrating on nominal wages. It regards Japan's nominal wages, already among the highest in the world, as excessive and has suggested multiyear wage bargaining coupled with greater wage differentials for different firms and industries on the basis of productivity. Japan's unions, on the other hand, emphasize the point that Japan's real wage levels and standards of living are still behind those of America and Europe and see *shunto* as the means to raise them. Analysts such as Takanashi et al. (1989) have concluded that multiyear wage bargaining is not likely in the foreseeable future and that *shunto* in its present form will remain intact as long as unions' right to bargain collectively is guaranteed by the law. Seike (1995) notes that the role of *shunto* in determining average wage levels has diminished because of growing variations of wages between industries and within the same industry, and because of a growing corporate preference for annual wage contracts with individual employees. Nevertheless, he contends that *shunto* can continue to play a meaningful role as a forum where labor and management can share labor-market information, which is needed even for individual wage contracts, and where acceptable macroeconomic policies can be explored and proposed.

Government civil servants do not have the right to bargain over their pay. Employees of **public corporations** and national enterprises have the right to bargain collectively and participate in the spring offensive. Their pay increases, however, are set by the National Enterprise and Public Corporations Labor Relations Commission in a process of mediation and compulsory arbitration because the managements of public corporations and national enterprises have no powers to negotiate pay increases with unions.

See also **labor-management relations, labor unions, working hours and stress.**

References

Dore, Ronald. 1987. *Taking Japan Seriously.* Stanford: Stanford University Press. Pp. 70–73.

Japan's labor unions work to meet new challenges. *JEI Report* 2A, January 15, 1988.

Koike, Kazuo. 1985. *Understanding Industrial Relations in Modern Japan,* trans. by Mary Saso. London: Macmillan.

Ministry of Labor. 1997. *Handbook of Labor Statistics.*

Seike, Atsushi. 1995. Annual wage talks still have a meaningful role to play. *Nikkei Weekly,* May 15: 7.

Shirai, Taishiro. 1987. Recent trends in collective bargaining in Japan. In *Collective Bargaining in Industrialized Market Economics: A Reappraisal.* Geneva: International Labor Office.

Suzuki, Yumiko. 1997. Ritualistic wage talks leave both sides cold. *Nikkei Weekly,* February 24: 1, 4.

Takanashi, Arikra, et al. 1989. *Shunto Wage Offensive: Historical Overview and Prospects.* Tokyo: Japan Institute of Labor.

stable shareholders   Companies, banks, insurance companies, and so forth, that hold other companies' shares on a long-term basis to maintain business ties or to realize long-term capital gains.

See **corporate finance, cross-shareholding, shareownership.**

Staple Food Control Act, 1942   An important legislation passed in 1942 that became the basis of **agricultural policy** in Japan until 1995.

Aiming to combine self-sufficiency in rice with stable consumer prices, the law authorized the government to buy certain major crops, particularly rice, from the producers at certain prices and sell them to consumers at different prices for different purposes. Government purchase prices of rice paid to producers are to be determined, for the purpose of securing reproduction of rice, by taking into consideration the cost of production, prices, and other economic conditions. Consumer prices of rice are to be determined, for the purpose of stabilizing the consumer's budget, by taking into consideration the cost of living, prices, and other economic conditions. The law also provides for government regulation on the distribution, exports and imports of major food crops.

Because of new domestic and international circumstances—growing domestic deregulation, **government budget** constraint, and the 1993 agricultural agreement of the Uruguay Round of GATT negotiations—the law was abolished in 1995. It is replaced by the Law for Stabiliation of Supply-Demand and Price of Staple Food. The new law changes the role of the government from "food control" to "supply-demand adjustments and stockpile management."

See also **agricultural policy, rice production and distribution.**

References

Food Agency. 1996. *An Outline of New Food Systems.*

Hayami, Yujiro. 1988. *Japanese Agriculture under Siege: The Political Economy of Agricultural Policies.* London: Macmillan.

Ministry of Agriculture, Forestry, and Fisheries. Annual. *Annual Report on Japanese Agriculture.*

Moore, Richard M. 1990. *Japanese Agriculture: Patterns of Rural Development.* Boulder, CO: Westview.

Sato, Hideo, and Gunther Schmitt. 1993. The political management of agriculture in Japan and Germany. In *The Politics of Economic Change in Postwar Japan and West Germany,* ed. by Haruhiro Fukui, Peter H. Merkl, Hubertus Müller-Groeling, and Akio Watanabe. New York: St. Martin's Press.

steel industry   The steel industry has been important to Japan's industrialization because steel is an essential industrial material for many other industries such as shipbuilding, automobiles, and machinery. It is also an industry where modern technology and large-scale production are extremely important to cost reduction. In the postwar period the Japanese government has played an important role in fostering the steel industry's growth.

In 1945 the industry had a capacity of only 2 million tons. In 1975 it had a capacity of 150 million tons. This unprecedented rapid rate of expansion was brought about by the government's nurturing and the industry's cooperation. The **Ministry of International Trade and Industry** (MITI), which is responsible for Japan's **industrial policy**, selected steel industry as a priority industry for support because of its intrinsic importance and export potential. In the 1950s it protected the industry from foreign competition but permitted the import of strategic technologies. It also helped to secure strategic supply of loans from **Japan Development Bank** and tax reductions for approved **investment.** Through its **administrative guidance**, it helped the industry to implement orderly expansion so that overcapacity and competitive price cutting would not result from unrestrained expansion and market competition. With the industry's cooperation, MITI throughout the 1960s and 1970s implemented a system of new capacity allocation by which the right to expand capacity was allocated on the basis of a firm's demonstrated efficiency. McCraw and O'Brien (1986: 94) consider this to be the key to the industry's modernization because it led to intense competition among the steelmakers to raise productivity in order to earn the right to expand.

Between 1958 and 1991 MITI also actively attempted to influence the industry's output levels and to stabilize steel prices. Price stability is important because investment might otherwise be discouraged for fear of competitive price cutting and declining profits. During the 1958 recession MITI sought to stabilize steel prices by introducing the "list price system" (*kokai hanbai sei*, literally, "open sales system") in which the steelmaker would sell a product to a designated wholesaler at a "list price" that it had previously reported to MITI. The purpose was to ensure that the price met MITI guidelines for price stability. Although the system has been revised subsequently, it was not officially abolished until 1991. Yamawaki (1988: 295–98) considers the system to be ineffective because of competitive price discounting during recessions. Other industry observers contend, however, that during the 1958–91 period, MITI was generally able to influence production and capacity levels of the industry and thus to maintain price stability.

Such blending of government guidance and competition paid off in growth and efficiency. By the mid-1970s Japanese steel companies had become the world's most modern and lowest-cost producers. Crude steel production peaked at 119.3 million metric tons in 1973, while exports of steel products peaked at 37 million tons in 1976 (see table S.8).

Table S.8
Steel production, exports, and imports (in million metric tons)

Year	Production	Exports	Imports
1960	22.1	2.5	1.2
1965	41.2	9.9	2.7
1970	93.3	18.0	3.2
1973	119.3	25.6	1.9
1976	107.4	37.0	0.9
1980	111.4	30.3	2.4
1985	105.3	33.3	4.5
1988	105.7	23.7	11.1
1989	107.9	20.2	10.9
1990	110.3	17.0	11.7
1991	109.7	18.0	13.8
1992	98.1	19.0	8.9
1993	99.6	23.5	9.2
1994	98.3	24.0	9.0
1995	101.6	23.0	11.7
1996	98.8	20.6	8.6
1997	104.6	23.5	9.6

Source: Japan Iron and Steel Federation.
Note: Figures refer to the production of crude steel and the exports and imports of all steel products.

Between 1973 and 1990 Japan's annual production of crude steel fluctuated between 100 and 110 million tons, depending on the level of domestic demand. The steep yen appreciation after 1985 reduced production considerably not only because of reduced export but also because of reduced domestic demand from other export industries. Unprecedented layoff of workers occurred in the industry. It also prompted the industry to seek diversification. Although production recovered in 1989–90, it declined substantially in 1992 and remained around or below 100 million tons annually in 1992–96 because of the prolonged stagnation of the economy. **Construction** and **automobile industries** are the two largest customers of the steel industry, and both industries have reduced output in the 1990s because of sluggish domestic demand. As automakers attempt to cut costs by pressing for lower steel prices and by using more aluminum, steel makers' profits have declined (see table S.9). Increased competition from new producers abroad has also constrained the industry's export growth.

Table S.9
Leading steel companies (FY 1990 and 1996; in ¥ billions)

Company	Sales		Pretax profits	
	1990	1996	1990	1996
Nippon Steel	2,608.3	2,184.8	160.9	84.7
NKK	1,326.8	1,185.0	50.4	34.3
Kobe Steel	1,321.4	1,142.0	56.5	26.7
Kawasaki Steel	1,185.4	944.7	80.5	23.6
Sumitomo Metal	1,156.9	1,016.3	73.6	22.4

Source: *Japan Company Handbook*, Autumn 1992 and Summer 1998.

Annual exports of all steel products was over 30 million tons in most of the years between 1974 and 1986. The major export markets have been the United States, China, Taiwan, and South Korea. Since 1987, however, exports have declined, in part because of new competition from South Korea, the yen appreciation, and the U.S. trade restrictions. The United States has negotiated a voluntary restraint agreement with Japan, which limited Japan's export to the United States to a certain percentage share of the U.S. market. Initially for the period from October 1984 to September 1989, the agreement was extended to March 1992. In January 1993 the U.S. Commerce Department imposed new tariffs on most steel imports from Japan for alleged dumping. The Commerce Department's action was partially upheld when the U.S. International Trade Commission ruled in July 1993 that Japanese exports of corrosion-resistant steel sheet to the United States damaged the U.S. steel industry. Consequently the Commerce Department imposed punitive tariffs of 40.19% on such imports from Japan. As a result, the importance of the U.S. market declined. By 1996, Southeast Asia has become the largest export market for Japanese steel, followed by South Korea, the United States, and China.

Imports of iron and steel into Japan have increased rapidly since the mid-1980s, from 4.5 million metric tons in 1985 to 13.8 million tons in 1991. They declined substantially in 1992 to 8.9 million tons and have grown only slightly ever since because of the stagnant domestic economy. South Korea is by far the largest source of imports, supplying 51% of the imports in 1997, followed by Taiwan (18%) and China (10%).

In making steel, the industry depends completely on imports for iron ore and coking coal. In 1996 Japan imported 119.2 million tons of iron ore. The major sources of imports are Australia, Brazil, and India. In the same year 61.7 million tons of coking coal were imported, which amounted to 99% of the total consumed. The major sources of imports are Australia, Canada, and the United States.

The industry is dominated by the "Big Five"—Nippon Steel, NKK (Nippon Kaikan), Kawasaki Steel, Sumitomo Metal Industries, and Kobe Steel. Nippon Steel, the largest steelmaker in Japan and in the world, has about 30% of the domestic market. It is also considered to be the price leader of the industry. It was formed through a merger of two leading steelmakers in 1970. NKK, the second largest, is among the top five steelmakers in the world. Table S.9 gives the sales and pretax profits of the top five steel producers in FY 1990 and 1996. Although sales of these companies declined only slightly from 1990 to 1996, profits of all five companies were down substantially from the 1990 levels because of the economy's stagnation in the 1990s.

Since the mid-1980s the steel industry has faced changes in world and domestic market conditions, and consequently structural changes in the industry have taken place, as outlined below:

1. Because of rising material and labor costs and competition from the newly industrializing countries, particularly South Korea, all major Japanese steel companies have diversified into new business lines such as machinery, engineering, electronics, communications, new basic materials, and even amusement parks.

2. Since the mid-1980s, all five largest steel companies have established tie-ups with U.S. companies, either through joint ventures or by acquiring stock shares. The most important partnerships are those between NKK Corp. and National Steel Corp., Nippon Steel and Inland Steel Industries, and Kobe Steel and U.S. Steel. This strategy enabled Japanese steel companies to increase production in the United States in the wake of the punitive tariffs imposed in 1993 on exports of corrosion-resistant steel to the United States.

3. The so-called "minimills" have become more important in the industry since the early 1980s. These are small steelmakers that use electric furnaces to process scrap or specially processed iron at lower labor cost than large integrated steel mills, which use blast furnace and coke to process iron ore. Of the 98.8 million tons of steel produced in 1996, 33 million tons were produced by minimills. The large integrated steel mills are being forced to restructure their operations and adopt new technology in order to cut cost.

Addresses

Kobe Steel
3-18, Wakinohama-cho, 1-chome, Chuo-ku, Kobe 651
Tel: (78) 261-5111   Fax: (3) 5252-7961

Japan Iron and Steel Federation
9-4, Otemachi 1-chome, Chiyoda-ku, Tokyo 100
Tel: (3) 3279-3613   Fax: (3) 3245-3216

Kawasaki Steel
2-3, Uchi-Saiwaicho 2-chome, Chiyoda-ku, Tokyo 100
Tel: (3) 3597-3111   Fax: (3) 3597-4911

Nippon Steel
6-3, Otemachi 2-chome, Chiyoda-ku, Tokyo 100
Tel: (3) 3242-4111   Fax: (3) 3275-5611

NKK
1-2, Marunouchi 1-chome, Chiyoda-ku, Tokyo 100
Tel: (3) 3212-7111   Fax: (3) 3214-8436

Sumitomo Metal Industries
5-33, Kaitahama 4-chome, Chuo-ku, Osaka 541
Tel: (6) 220-5111   Fax: (6) 223-0563

References

Hasegawa, Harukiyo. 1996. *The Steel Industry in Japan: A Comparison with Britain.* London: Routledge.

Higurashi, Ryoichi. 1994. Nerves of steel: aggressive little guy shakes up industry. *Tokyo Business Today*, September: 16–18.

Japan Iron and Steel Federation. Annual. *The Steel Industry of Japan.* Tokyo.

Klamann, Edmund. 1991. MITI steel cartel fades, yet stable order intact. *Nikkei Weekly*, August 3: 10.

Komatsu, Naoki. 1989. Japan's steel industry is restructuring its way back to profitability. *Tokyo Business Today*, November 1989: 40–45.

McCraw, Thomas K., and Patricia A. O'Brien. 1986. Production and distribution: Competition policy and industry. In *American versus Japan*, ed. by Thomas K. McCraw. Boston: Harvard Business School Press.

Milbank, Dana. 1993. Japan's big steelmakers feel pinch of minimills, promping a rethinking of the traditional approach. *Asian Wall Street Journal Weekly*, February 8: 24.

Ostrom, Douglas. 1996. Japanese steel companies gird for new challenges. *JEI Report* 39A, October 18.

Uriu, Robert M. 1996. *Troubled Industries: Confronting Economic Change in Japan.* Ithaca: Cornell University Press. Chs. 5, 7.

Vestal, James. 1993. *Planning for Change: Industrial Policy and Japanese Economic Development, 1945–1990.* Oxford: Clarendon Press.

Yamawaki, Hideki. 1988. The steel industry. In *Industrial Policy of Japan,* ed. by Ryutaro Komiya, Masahiro Okuno, and Kotaro Suzumura. Tokyo: Academic Press Japan.

Yokota, Kazunari. 1998. Sluggish markets take edge off of steel's profits. *Nikkei Weekly,* March 16: 1, 10.

Yonekura, Seiichiro. 1994. *The Japanese Iron and Steel Industry, 1850–1990: Continuity and Discontinuity.* New York: St. Martin's Press.

stock index futures trading   Introduced in September 1988, stock index futures trading is a form of contract trading in which the buyer and seller agree on the delivery of the money based on the difference between a certain numerical value of a stock index contracted between them in advance and that of the actual stock index on a certain future date. The primary purpose of the trading is to hedge against stock price fluctuations.

The two primary stock index futures markets are the **Tokyo Stock Exchange** and the Osaka Securities Exchange. The former trades futures contracts based on the Tokyo Stock Price Index (TOPIX), whereas the latter trades contracts based on the Nikkei Stock Index of 225 stocks. The trading unit of the Tokyo Stock Exchange is ¥10,000 times the TOPIX index, whereas in the Osaka Stock Exchange it is ¥1,000 times the Nikkei index. The method of settlement takes the form of cash payment. In February 1994 the Osaka Securities Exhange also began futures trading based on the Nikkei 300-Stock Index.

In terms of trading volume and value, the Nikkei 225-Stock Index futures trading is by far the largest, with a daily average of 29,000 shares and ¥600 billion in 1996, as compared with 12,000 shares and ¥186 billion for TOPIX futures trading. The Nikkei 300-Stock Index futures trading trailed with a daily average of 8,000 shares and ¥22.6 billion in 1996.

The **Ministry of Finance** regulates the stock futures market. In their attempt to avoid the possible amplification of stock price fluctuations due to futures trading, the stock exchanges limit price swings in futures trading to about 5% up or down from the last contract price of the preceding day (Japan Securities Research Institute, 1998: 134–35).

See also **stock index options market, stock market, stock price indexes, Tokyo Stock Exchange.**

References

Arai, Tomio, T. Akamatsu and A. Yoshioka. 1993. Stock index futures in Japan: Problems and prospects. *NRI Quarterly* 2, 1: 28–57.

Brenner, Menachem, Marti Subrahmanyam, and Jun Uno. 1990. The Japanese stock index futures markets: The early experience. In *Japanese Capital Market*, ed. by Edwin J. Elton and Martin J. Gruber. New York: Harper and Row.

Isaacs, Jonathan. 1990. *Japanese Equities Markets*. London: Euromoney Publications. Ch. 12.

Japan Securities Research Institute. 1998. *Securities Market in Japan, 1998*. Ch. 5.

Tokyo Stock Exchange. Annual. *Tokyo Stock Exchange Fact Book*.

stock index options trading   Stock index options trading is a form of trading in which the buyer pays a certain amount of money to obtain the right or option, not the obligation, to buy a certain amount of stocks on a specific date at a specific price. The trading unit is based on the stock price indexes, such as 1,000 times the Nikkei 225-Stock Average for the Nikkei Stock Average options traded at the Osaka Stock Exchange or 10,000 times the Tokyo Stock Price Index (TOPIX) points traded at the **Tokyo Stock Exchange**. If the right is not exercised after a specified time, the option expires. If the option is exercised, either **stock index futures trading** takes effect or cash settlement is made on the basis of the predetermined stock price.

The stock index options trading started in 1989 at the stock exchanges in **Tokyo, Osaka**, and **Nagoya**. The options offer investors not only a new investment instrument but also a hedge against the risk of an unfavorable stock price change. Thus they contribute to the stability and expansion of the **stock market** and the stock futures market. One problem, however, is that the minimum trading unit is relatively high, higher than that in the United States, so it is difficult for individual investors to participate in the trading.

The volume and value of stock index options trading have been small and declining since the early 1990s. The daily average trading volume and value based on Nikkei 225-Stock Index at Osaka Stock Exchange were 16,000 shares and ¥3.8 billion in 1996, whereas at both **Tokyo Stock Exchange** and Nagoya Stock Exchange they were merely 100 shares and ¥10 million.

See also **stock index futures trading, stock market, stock price indexes, Tokyo Stock Exchange**.

References

Isacs, Jonathan. 1990. *Japanese Equities Markets*. London: Euromoney Publications. Ch. 12.

Koshinaka, Hidefumi. 1989. Investors eager for stock index options debut. *Japan Economic Journal*, June 3.

Japan Securities Research Institute. 1998. *Securities Market in Japan, 1998*. Ch. 5.

Tokyo Stock Exchange. Annual. *Tokyo Stock Exchange Fact Book*.

stock market   A stock market consists of a primary market for new issues and a secondary market for stock trading. The latter in turn consists of trading on the stock exchanges and over-the-counter trading in the offices of **securities companies.** All these components of the market have evolved in Japan with various degrees of maturity.

In the primary market corporate funds are raised through the issuing of new shares or equities of the company. The issues are classified into compensated capital increases and noncompensated capital increases. The former requires subscribers to pay cash for the new shares. In the latter the company issues new shares in an amount equivalent to the legal reserves of its capital or the amount of cash payment that was in excess of its par value during its previous capital increase. In terms of the ownership of the new shares, they can be allocated to current stockholders or sold to general investors in a public offering. In the latter case the company can sell the shares by itself, or through underwriting by a securities company. The price to be paid can be based on the par value of the new shares, the market value, or a level between the two as set by the issuer. Currently the predominant method of issuing new shares is the compensated method in which new shares are sold to the public at market prices. This method is popular because the difference between the market price and the par value may be used as capital reserve to strengthen the capital base of the company.

Secondary stock transactions are divided into trading on the stock exchanges and over-the-counter trading in the offices of securities companies. There are eight stock exchanges in Japan—**Tokyo, Osaka, Nagoya,** Kyoto, Hiroshima, Fukuoka, Niigata, and Sapporo—and the **Tokyo Stock Exchange** is by far the largest of them. Stock exchange trading is limited to members who are securities companies with certain qualifications and to listed stocks that have met certain standards. All securities companies and stock exchanges are given **administrative guidance** by the **Ministry of Finance**, and the Securities Dealers' Association of Japan provides voluntary industry self-regulation. However, Japan does not have an independent regulatory agency comparable to the United States Securities and Exchange Commission to oversee its securities companies and transactions on the stock exchanges. A new Securities and Exchange Surveillance Commission was set up only in July 1992 to watch for stock market manipulation. Its effectiveness and independence remain to be seen.

The stock market was only a minor source of funds for companies in the high-growth era of the 1950s and 1960s. Bank loans at low interest rates were much more important. After the first oil crisis of 1973, as growth slowed down and interest rates were raised to control inflation, equity financing became cheaper than bank loans and the stock market became increasingly important. Stock exchange trading in Japan grew rapidly between 1985 and late 1989. One major reason is Japan's huge current account surplus which provided financial institutions and corporations with a large amount of capital for financial investment. Other contributing factors are the stronger yen since the **Plaza Accord** of September 1985, which increased the foreign-exchange risk in investing in overseas securities, and the falling oil prices and declining interest rates in Japan. Finally, some analysts have regarded Japan's stock market as highly speculative, at least during the late 1980s, and open to manipulation by brokers because of lax disclosure requirements (Zielinski and Holloway 1991).

The average price earnings ratio (PER, the price of a share divided by the aftertax earnings per share) of Japanese shares is much higher than in other industrialized economies. For example, in the first section of the Tokyo Stock Exchange, the average year-end PER was 47.3 in 1986, 58.4 in 1988, 70.6 in 1989, 39.8 in 1990, and 79.3 in 1996. Stockholders are often the company's own banks, insurers, suppliers, and customers. Foreign analysts have regarded such **cross-shareholding** as a major cause of the high PER. However, Ueda (1990) attributes the high PER to the declines in risk premium which investors require on stocks and to expectations of land price inflation. Zielinski and Holloway (1991: 137) point out that Japanese earnings figures are understated relative to U.S. companies because Japan's accounting rules allow companies to manipulate their earnings by putting profits into reserves, through sales to subsidiaries, and by treating extraordinary gains as recurring income. However, the PER of companies is not as important in Japan as in many other countries. Investors also look at the value of corporate assets, particularly land.

After years of rapid rises in share prices—with a peak of 2,884.8 in TOPIX (Tokyo Stock Price Index) on December 18, 1989, or 38,915.87 in Nikkei Stock Average Index on December 19, 1989—the Tokyo Stock Exchange started to experience a serious decline in early 1990. This was in part a belated correction of the excessively high share prices of the previous years. Tighter credit due largely to the higher official discount rate of the **Bank of Japan** since May 1989 also contributed to the fall in share prices. In addition banks reduced their lending in an effort to meet the 8% capital adequacy ratio which the Bank for International Settlements required by spring 1993. The decline continued through 1990 because of the Iraqi invasion of Kuwait. The total decline in 1990 amounted to an unprecedented 39% in Nikkei Index. Thus the "bubble economy" of the late 1980s—the speculative and inflated wealth in financial assets and land as epitomized by the stock market—is said to have burst in 1990.

To ease the pressure on individual investors to sell stocks bought on credit as stock prices continued to fall, the Ministry of Finance reduced, in February 1990, the purchase margin requirement (the percentage of cash required) from 60% to 50% of a stock's value. By late 1990 it was reduced to 30%. This is the easiest margin term in 25 years, and it has remained at that level through 1997. The interest rate that customers pay on the borrowed money to buy securities has been lowered steadily. When securities are used in lieu of cash for the margin requirement, their values are calculated by multiplying their market values by a given loan value rate or "haircut rate." The rate was raised to 80% in October 1990 to support the market and has remained at that level through 1997.

The fine-tuning of these policy tools to stimulate the market has proved to be inadequate. Japan's stock market has suffered severely from too many problems over the years—most of which are revealed only since the early 1990s—that it requires a radical surgery rather than a shaving of the margin requirement and interest rate and the raising of the "haircut rate" to recover. One problem is lax supervision. For example, insider-trading standards are vague in Japan, and their implementation not rigorous. Until its amendment in 1988 the Securities and Exchange Law of Japan did not even contain provisions that specifically made it unlawful to engage in insider trading (Kanzaki 1992: 20). The first prosecution of insider trading was filed only in 1990, although such practice is believed to be prevalent. Thus Japan's stock market is potentially open to abuses.

Another problem is the abuse of market power through collusion. It was revealed in mid-1991 that large securities companies had compensated major clients for trading losses at the expense of small investors and that affiliates of two such companies were involved in the speculative stock purchases of an organized crime syndicate. It was also revealed after the closure of the Yamaichi Securities Co., Japan's fourth largest, in November 1997, that the company had practiced *tobashi* to protect its corporate customers. *Tobashi* is a practice in which brokerages shift securities incurring losses from one account to another with a different book-closing time to protect corporate customers from having losses on their equity portfolios. Although *tobashi* is not illegal, it is unlawful for brokerages to buy back losses caused by *tobashi* trading (*Nikkei Weekly*, April 20, 1998: 16). This and other deceptive practices were used by Yamaichi

Securities Co. to conceal its accumulated off-the-book losses totaling more than ¥200 billion. Worse still, the company's own investigation team subsequently revealed that a bureau chief of the Ministry of Finance had urged the company to hide its losses stemming from off-the-hook *tobashi* deals. If true, it simply confirms what many critics have long complained —that the regulator itself is part and parcel of the problems plaguing the Japanese market and economy.

These scandals have severely shaken investors' confidence in the stock market. With the Japanese economy in a long stagnation due in part to other problems, the stock market has remained sluggish from 1991 through 1997; there have been only small increases in trading volume and value at all stock exchanges (see **Tokyo Stock Exchange**). Stock prices have seen the usual short-term ups and downs, but there has been no basic trend of recovery despite all the stimulative measures of the government. Analysts believe that its recovery and future growth will require a thorough reform of the entire market, including its relationship with the Ministry of Finance.

Aside from the stock exchanges, shares of some medium-sized companies are traded in the **over-the-counter market.**

See also **bond market, corporate finance, cross-shareholding, over-the-counter market, securities companies, shareownership, stock price indexes, Tokyo Stock Exchange.**

Addresses

Securities Dealers Association of Japan
5-8 Nihonbashi Kayabacho 1-chome, Chuo-ku, Tokyo 103
Tel: (3) 3667-8451   Fax: (3) 3666-8009

Osaka Securities Exchange
8-16, Kitahama 1-chome, Chuo-ku, Osaka, Osaka 541
Tel: (6) 226-0058   Fax: (6) 231-2639

Tokyo Stock Exchange
1, Nihonbashi Kabuto-cho 2-chome, Chuo-ku, Tokyo 103
Tel: (3) 3666-0141   Fax: (3) 3663-0625

References

Elton, Edwin J,. and Martin J. Gruber, eds. 1990. *Japanese Capital Markets.* New York: Harper and Row.

Isaacs, Jonathan. 1990. *Japanese Equities Markets.* London: Euromoney Publications.

Japan Securities Research Institute. 1998. *Securities Market in Japan, 1998.* Ch. 3.

Kanzaki, Katsuro. 1992. Regulation of insider trading. In *Capital Markets and Financial Services in Japan.* Tokyo: Japan Securities Research Institute.

McDonald, Jack. 1989. The *mochiai* effect: Japanese corporate cross-holdings. *Journal of Portfolio Management* 16, 1: 90–94.

Oda, Hiroshi. 1994. Latest developments of the Securities and Exchange Law. In *Japanese Commercial Law in an Era of Internationalization*, ed. by Hiroshi Oda. London: Graham and Trotman/Martinus Nijhoff.

Sakakibara, Shigeki, et al. 1988. *The Japanese Stock Market: Pricing Systems and Accounting Information.* New York: Praeger.

Schaede, Ulrike. 1991. Black Monday in New York, blue Tuesday in Tokyo: The October 1987 crash in Japan. *California Management Review* 33: 39–57.

Shiller, Robert J., Fumiko Kon-ya, and Yoshiro Tsutui. 1996. Why did the Nikkei crash? Expanding the scope of expectations data collection. *Review of Economics and Statistics* 78: 156–64.

Tokyo Stock Exchange. Annual. *Tokyo Stock Exchange Fact Book.*

Ueda, Kazuo. 1990. Are Japanese stock prices too high? *Journal of the Japanese and International Economies* 4: 351–70.

Viner, Aron. 1989. Inside Japan's Financial Markets. London: The Economist Publications. Ch. 4.

Yamaichi faults ministry for collapse. *Nikkei Weekly*, April 20, 1998: 16.

Yamashita, Takeji. 1989. *Japan's Securities Markets: A Practitioner's Guide.* Singapore: Butterworths. Chs. 2–5.

Zielinski, Robert, and Nigel Hoolway. 1991. *Unequal Equities: Power and Risk in Japan's Stock Market.* Tokyo: Kodansha International.

Ziemba, William T., and Sandra I. Schwartz. 1992. *Invest Japan.* Chicago: Probus. Chs. 1, 7, 8.

stock price indexes There are two major price indexes of stock prices of the **Tokyo Stock Exchange:** the Nikkei Stock Average and TOPIX, the Tokyo Stock Price Index.

First introduced in 1950, the Nikkei Stock Average, or the Nikkei index, is calculated by Nihon Keizai Shimbun, Inc., publisher of Japan's leading business newspaper. It gives the daily unweighted average of 225 issues selected from some 1,200 stocks listed on the first section of the Tokyo Stock Exchange. When one of the 225 issues included in the calculations suffers an exrights drop from capital increase, an adjustment is made in a coefficient so that continuity between past and present stock price levels can be maintained. However, the index can be misleading and open to manipulation. Trading blocks of shares in just a few small firms in the Nikkei sample can affect the index disproportionately. In addition, because the index was introduced in 1950, it is biased toward the heavy industry.

The 225 stocks included in the Nikkei index are reviewed and revised every year. Stocks with relatively low "market liquidity" (i.e., low trading volume and high price fluctuation) are replaced by those with high.market liquidity in order to reflect market changes. Changes in the listings of companies in the first section of the Tokyo Stock Exchange may also immediately affect the 225 stocks.

The TOPIX, introduced in 1969, is a composite index of all stocks listed on the first section of the Tokyo Stock Exchange. It gives the weighted average of all stocks, the weight being the number of listed shares of each stock. It is computed by dividing the current day's total market value by the base day's (January 4, 1968) total market value and multiplying the ratio by 100. To maintain the continuity of the indexes, the base market value is recalculated when there are new listings, delistings, and new share issues. In this way only price movements are reflected by the indexes. TOPIX is computed and published every other minute.

TOPIX is supplemented by subindexes for each of 28 industry groups and for each of 3 groups (large, medium, and small in terms of the number of listed shares) by which companies listed on the first section are classified. These subindexes are calculated in the same way and published six times a day.

The Nihon Keizai Shimbun, Inc. has also introduced some other stock price indexes. The broader Nikkei Stock Average (500) or Nikkei 500 was introduced in 1982. It includes 500 stocks from the first section of the Tokyo Stock Exchange and hence gives a broader picture of the market. The Nikkei Stock Index 300 (Nikkei 300), introduced in 1994, is designed to represent the overall market with 300 stocks. The Nikkei Over-the-counter Stock Average (Nikkei OTC Average), available since 1985, computes the stock price average of all registered over-the-counter stocks.

Stock prices rose rapidly during the second half of the 1980s during the **bubble economy.** The Nikkei Stock Average Index reached a peak of 38,915.87 on December 29, 1989, and TOPIX peaked at 2,884.8 on December 18, 1989. They declined precipitously thereafter through mid-1990 and less rapidly in 1991–92. The trend since 1992 is basically flat, with partial recovery but subsequent declines in 1994 and 1996. TOPIX subindexes show much greater fluctuations for small companies than for large and medium companies. As of late December 1997, TOPIX stood at about 1,200, whereas NIkkei Index was about 16,500. These are only 42% of their respective peak levels in late 1989.

Stock prices are determined by supply and demand, as are other prices. However the factors behind the supply of and demand for specific stocks are complex and difficult to predict. They can be classified into three categories:

1. *Microeconomic factors.* Dividends or yield (dividend divided by the stock price) shows the profit that a stock will yield. Hence expected future dividends are of primary importance to investors. Alternatively investors may attach greater importance to the price earning ratio (PER, i.e., the stock price divided by the earnings per share after tax). Dividends are closely correlated with a company's earnings, which in turn are affected by a host of other factors, including interest rate, the company's competitive position, technology, and market trends.

2. *National and international economic factors.* Changes in inflation rate, interest rate, tax rates, or announcement of changes in government policy, and so forth, affect the market environment, investors' confidence, and a company's earning power. Trade relations with the United States and the **yen–dollar exchange rate** affect the export prospects and profitability of export-oriented companies. Changes in oil prices affect the costs of production of some firms more than others. Trade and investment deals with China increase the profits of giant general **trading companies.**

3. *Noneconomic factors.* Domestic political changes affect government policies, the market environment, and investors' confidence. A Gulf War affects oil prices and export markets. Antipollution legislation may affect some companies' profits.

While it is easy to list the relevant factors that affect stock prices, it is virtually impossible to predict their quantitative effects on individual stocks. Some big Japanese **securities companies** in the past selectively promoted specific stocks to their clients, not on the basis of their ability to predict future changes and their effects on individual stocks but on the basis of their general knowledge of the stock market and their power to influence the prices of specific stocks.

See also **securities companies, shareownership, stock market, Tokyo Stock Exchange.**

References

Elton, Edwin J., and Martin J. Gruber, eds. 1990. *Japanese Capital Markets.* New York: Harper and Row.

Isaacs, Jonathan. 1990. *Japanese Equities Market.* London: Euromoney Publications. Ch. 3.

Japan Securities Research Institute. 1998. *Securities Market in Japan, 1998.* Ch 3.

Shiller, Robert J., Fumiko Kon-Ya, and Yoshiro Tsutsui. 1996. Why did the Nikkei crash? Expanding the scope of expectations data collection. *Review of Economics and Statistics*, 78: 156–64.

Stone, Douglas and William T. Ziemba. 1993. Land and stock prices in Japan. *Journal of Economic Perspectives* 7, 3: 149–65.

Stock Market Indices Databook. Tokyo: Nihon Keizai Shimbun. Undated.

Takeuchi, Satoshi. 1990. Accuracy of Nikkei average in tracking market questioned. *Japan Economic Journal*, January 20: 32.

Tokyo Stock Exchange. Annual. *Tokyo Stock Exchange Fact Book.*

Ueda, Kazuo. 1990. Are Japanese stock prices too high? *Journal of Japanese and International Economies* 4: 351–70.

Ziemba, William T., and Sandra L. Schwartz. 1992. *Invest Japan.* Chicago: Probus. Ch. 2.

Structural Impediments Initiative (SII)   Negotiations between Washington and Tokyo in 1989–90 on ways to remove Japanese barriers to free trade in order to improve American access to the Japanese market and to reduce the trade imbalance between the two countries.

The impediments to free trade in Japan were perceived by Washington in late 1980s to be embedded in the structure of the Japanese economy. The initiative was made by the Bush administration to ask Tokyo to remove the impediments to head off protectionist legislation being contemplated by Congress. The initiative was proposed in mid-1989, and SII talks with Japanese trade officials were conducted from June 1989 through spring 1990. A joint final report was issued in June 1990, with recommendations for both governments. It also provides for follow-up meetings to review the progress made in implementing the recommendations.

The six categories of Japanese structural impediments criticized by American negotiators are as follows:

1. *Japanese **saving** and **investment** patterns.* Excessive savings limit consumption and imports. Public investment is too low relative to savings.

2. *Land use pattern.* Inefficient land use and high land prices restrict the supply of **housing** and land for buildings in metropolitan areas.

3. ***Distribution system.*** The **Large Retail Store Law** restricts the establishment of large stores in favor of existing small retailers who are less likely to carry imports. The existing complicated distribution system discourages foreign firms to sell in Japan.

4. *Exclusionary business practices.* Practices such as price **cartels**, supply restraint cartels, market allocations, and bid-rigging violate the **Anti-**

monopoly Law and restrict fair and free competition and imports. Government delays in patent examinations hurt foreign firms.

5. *Keiretsu relationships.* Certain aspects of *keiretsu* relationships, including **cross-shareholding** and exclusive supplier-manufacturer-distributor relationships, promote preferential intragroup business, inhibit **foreign direct investment** in Japan, and give rise to anticompetitive business practices.

6. *Price mechanisms.* Price differentials between domestic and overseas markets are large and unreasonable due to government regulation of the domestic market and weak enforcement of the Antimonopoly Law.

These six areas do not exhaust all issues of trade disputes between the two countries. For example, the issue of Japan's ban on rice import is not included because it was turned over to the **Uruguay Round** of GATT negotiations.

The following structural impediments in the United States were brought up in the SII talks and in the final report. However, since they are not the real focus of SII, observers consider them to be a mere "face-saving" device for Japanese officials to agree to reductions in Japan's own structural impediments.

1. Excessive government deficits and deficient saving rates.

2. Low corporate investment activities and supply capacity.

3. Shortsighted corporate behavior that is not conducive to the productivity of U.S. workers and the competitiveness of U.S. corporations.

4. Government regulations on both exports and imports that discourage international trade and competition.

5. Insufficient research and development.

6. Ineffective export promotion.

7. Inadequate workforce education and training.

Both governments pledge to carry out a number of recommendations to reduce their respective structural impediments. For example, the Japanese government has agreed, in principle, to adopt measures to achieve the following: to increase public investment, especially in social overhead capital; to rationalize land prices and to promote further supply of housing and land for buildings in metropolitan areas; to relax the implementation of the Large Retail Store Law; to accelerate measures to facilitate imports; to enhance the Antimonopoly Law and its enforcement; to ensure greater transparency and fairness in **administrative guidance;** to strengthen monitoring by the Fair Trade Commission of transactions among *keiretsu* firms; to speed up patent examinations; to conduct joint price surveys with the U.S. government to promote a competitive market, and so on.

The SII talks and the final accord have elicited varied responses in both Japan and the United States. First, Japanese **consumer groups** have not particularly welcomed the proposed liberalization of Japan's market, even though it would benefit consumers in the form of lower prices. Many government officials and scholars have criticized the U.S. demands on Japan. They have two major arguments: (1) Many of the structural issues such as *keiretsu* and pricing mechanisms cannot be controlled or managed by the Japanese government. (2) Japan—U.S. trade imbalance is primarily the result of macroeconomic policy such as large U.S. government deficit and low savings, and not of Japan's structural factors. Changing the latter therefore would not necessarily help the trade balance (Komiya and Irie 1990).

Keiretsu or business groups are clearly the worst of Japan's structural impediments in Washington's view. In response, Imai (1990a, b) has reiterated that Japan's *keiretsu* are rational, evolving organizations that have engaged in market competition and that there is no clear evidence that they impede entry into business or discriminate against foreign firms in their transactions. Nakatani (1990) contends that the *keiretsu* system has been effective and resilient as the pillar of Japanese-style capitalism, but he agrees that it has been exclusionary and is therefore not accepted by the international community. He suggests that the government offer *keiretsu* groups incentives to welcome foreign companies to join them so that the international community will accept them without attempting to weaken them.

In the United States, MIT economist Dornbusch (1989) criticizes U.S. efforts to open Japan's market via SII as misguided. He distinguishes two issues—U.S. external imbalance and market access in Japan—and argues that the U.S. external imbalance requires macroeconomic adjustment at home, while access to Japan's market is best attained through a result-oriented **trade policy.** This trade policy would set multiyear targets for import growth, with an automatic, across-the-board tariff surcharge if performance is inadequate. Feldstein, a former chairman of the President's Council of Economic Advisers, criticizes the U.S. efforts to push up Japanese public works in order to reduce trade imbalance as ill-advised.

He argues that Japan should neither raise nor lower its domestic infra-structural investment artificially in order to manipulate its trade surplus and that any country's decision on such investment should be based on the value of such investment to its people and not on its impact on the current account balance (interview in *Japan Economic Journal*, August 11. 1990).

Johnson (1990) contends that the structural impediments have been indeed unique and important aspects of Japan in its rise as a state-fostered mercantile power, not a market-oriented free trader, but he doubts that the SII accord will be implemented at all because the opposition parties in Japan control the Upper House of the Diet and can block implementing legislation. He argues that postwar Japan has a history of agreeing to U.S. demands when the political pressure is great but failing to deliver its promises afterward.

Tyson (1991) argues that unfair trading practices and structural impedi-ments to Japan's market do exist in Japan, but these are not the only cause of Japan's trade surplus. She suggests managed trade through negotiations at detailed sectoral levels as the short-term answer and harmonization of policy practices and rules, while recognizing some differences in policy practices as the long-term solution.

See also *keiretsu* **and business groups, cross-shareholding, distri-bution system, patent system.**

References

Dornbusch, Rudiger. Misguided efforts won't open Japan's market. *Japan Economic Journal,* December 16, 1989: 9.

Imai, Ken'ichi. 1990a. The legitimacy of Japan's corporate groups. *Japan Echo* 17, 3: 23–28.

Imai, Ken'ichi. 1990b. Japanese business groups and the structural impediments Initiative. In *Japan's Economic Structure: Should It Change?* ed. by Kozo Yamamura. Seattle: Society for Japanese Studies.

Johnson, Chalmers. 1990. Trade, revisionism, and the future of Japanese–American relations. In *Japan's Economic Structure: Should It Change?* ed. by Kozo Yamamura. Seattle: Society for Japanese Studies.

Komiya, Ryutaro, and Kazutomo Irie. 1990. The U.S.–Japan trade problem: An economic analysis from a Japanese viewpoint. In *Japan's Economic Structure: Should It Change?* ed. by Kozo Yamamura. Seattle: Society for Japanese Studies.

Matsushita, Mitsuo. 1991. The structural impediments initiative: an example of bilateral trade negotiation. *Michigan Journal of International Law* 12: 436–49.

Nakatani, Iwao. 1990. Opening up fortress Japan. *Japan Echo* 17, 3: 8–11.

Sheard, Paul. 1991. The economics of Japanese corporate organization and the "Structural Impediments" debate: A critical review. *Japanese Economic Studies* 19, 4: 30–78.

Tyson, Laura D'Andrea. 1991. Managing trade by rules and outcomes. *California Management Review* 34, 1: 115–43.

Utagawa, Reizo. 1991. The U.S. structural impediments initiative (SII): Implications for Japan. In *Japan and the United States: Troubled Partners in a Changing World.* Cambridge, MA: Institute for Foreign Policy Analysis.

Yamamura, Kozo. 1990. Will Japan's economic structure change? Confessions of a former optimist. In *Japan's Economic Structure: Should It Change?* ed. by Kozo Yamamura. Seattle: Society for Japanese Studies.

subcontracting system Subcontracting (*shitauke*) is widespread and very important in Japanese manufacturing industries. The subcontractees are typically large manufacturers. The subcontractors are typically small- or medium-sized enterprises; a large majority of them have fewer than 20 employees. They produce parts or undertake a particular processing for a number of "parent" companies. By contrast, large U.S. manufacturing companies tend to make more "in-house" parts themselves.

The **automobile industry** in particular is highly dependent on subcontractors. Miwa (1994) considers the subcontracting relationships to be one of the most important reasons for the success of the Japanese automobile industry. Toyota Motor Corp., for example, is said to procure more than 20,000 parts per car from subcontractors. Furthermore, from the carmakers to their subsidiaries and independent parts makers, each has its own subcontractors, with the result that there is a hierarchy of primary, secondary, and tertiary subcontractors. The relationship between subcontractee and subcontractor is close and cooperative. They often share facilities and technical know-know. Japanese automakers are said to purchase about 70% of their parts from subcontractors, whereas the "buy ratio" for American automakers is said to be about 30%.

Because of the disparity in economic power between the large corporations and their subcontractors, abuses by the former such as late payments have occurred. To minimize them, the Subcontractors' Protection Law was enacted in 1956. It prohibits unfair practices such as late payments (over 60 days) for subcontracted work, refusal to accept subcontracted products, and compulsory purchase of materials from subcontractees. The Fair Trade Commission and the Small and Medium Enterprise Agency of the **Ministry of International Trade and Industry** (MITI) are empowered to implement the law.

From the perspective of large corporations, subcontracting offers them various advantages: (1) Since the small- and medium-sized enterprises have lower wages, it is economical to have simple labor-intensive parts produced by them. (2) It frees the large companies from numerous peripheral tasks and permits them to concentrate on the major production processes and the final assembly, thereby reaping the benefit of greater division of labor. (3) Japanese subcontractors are reputed to be reliable and produce high-quality parts. (4) In times of recession large corporations can cut back on their subcontracted work. This gives them flexibility in production while retaining their permanent employees. In other words, the subcontractors serve as buffers during recession for the large corporations. On the other hand, reliance on a subcontractor for major parts under the **just-in-time system**, which is commonly used in Japanese industry in which parts are delivered before they are needed, can entail risks. For example, Toyota experienced severe shortage of parts during the Great Hanshin Earthquate in January 1995 and also after a fire at its largest parts supplier in February 1997. Although Toyota decided to diversify its sources of supply—at least two suppliers for all critical parts—there are possible higher procurement costs, uneven quality, and greater monitoring costs of suppliers.

From the point of view of subcontractors, the system enables them to concentrate on their specialized lines of business while enjoying stable business relations with large corporations during normal times. However, in a business downturn, they are likely to have reduced orders and have to bear the brunt of business adjustment. Consequently, in order to protect themselves, subcontractors have begun to diversify and to have a number of subcontractees. Traditionally it was not rare for small parts makers to rely on a single customer for 80–90% of their sales. By the late 1980s it was felt that a single customer's share should not exceedd 30%. Furthermore, since 1982–83 when the economy experienced slower growth, a growing number of them have grouped together to form cooperatives for mutual help. In a cooperative, members can acquire orders for other member companies as well as for themselves. If an order is too large for a subcontractor, it can be shared by other members. Some cooperatives also help members to branch out into new business lines.

According to surveys conducted by MITI, the number of small manufacturing subcontractors declined from 465,369 at the end of 1981 to 378,046 at the end of 1987 (*Nikkei Weekly*, April 4, 1992; 1). The labor shortage of the 1980s and the soaring cost of starting up manufacturing units are said to be the reasons for the decline. If the trend continues, large corporations have to either rely more on overseas suppliers or increase in-house production of parts, as some companies have already started doing.

As the government agency in charge of assisting **small and medium enterprises**, the Small and Medium Enterprise Agency of MITI has been providing assistance to qualified subcontractors in setting up new businesses or acquiring new skills.

See also **customer sovereignty, just-in-time system, small and medium enterprises.**

Address

Small and Medium Enterprise Agency
3-1, Kasumigaseki 1-chome, Chiyoda-ku, Tokyo 100
Tel: (3) 3501-1511

References

Asanuma, Banri, and Tatsuya Kikutani. 1992. Risk absorption in Japanese subcontracting: A microeconometric study of the automobile industry. *Journal of the Japanese and International Economics* 6, 1: 1–29.

Klaman, Edmund. 1991. Lowly subcontractors begin to assert technological might. *Japan Economic Journal*, March 30: 1.

McMillan, John. 1990. Managing suppliers: Incentive systems in Japanese and U.S. industry. *California Management Review* 32, 4: 38–55.

Miwa, Yoshiro. 1994. Subcontracting relationships: The automobile industry. In *Business Enterprises in Japan: Views of Leading Japanese Economists*, ed. by Kenichi Iwai and Ryutaro Komiya. Cambridge: MIT Press.

Oishi, Nobuyuki. 1992. Subcontractor attrition eroding economic base. *Nikkei Weekly*, April 4: 1, 23.

Okamuro, Hiroyuki. 1995. Changing subcontracting relations and risk-sharing in Japan: An econometric analysis of the automobile industry. *Hitotsubashi Journal of Economics* 36: 207–18.

Patchell, Gerald. 1992. Shinchintaisha: Japanese small business revitalization. *Business and the Contemporary World* 4, 2: 50–61.

Sakai, Kuniyasu. 1990. The feudal world of Japanese manufacturing. *Harvard Business Review* 68, 6: 38–49.

Subcontractors join up to win order. *Japan Economic Journal*, January 30, 1988: 5.

Uekusa, Masu. 1987. Industrial organization. In *The Political Economy of Japan*, vol. 1: *The Domestic Transformation*, ed. by Kozo Yamamura and Yasukichi Yasuba. Stanford: Stanford University Press. Pp. 499–506.

Sumitomo Group   Along with the **Mitsubishi Group** and the **Mitsui Group**, the **Sumitomo Group** has a prewar *zaibatsu* origin. Smaller than the other two, the Sumitomo Group is considered to be more tightly organized than the Mitsui Group. It consists of more than 130 companies, with 20 core companies whose presidents meet regularly in the White Water Club (Hakusui Kai). The three most important companies are traditionally Sumitomo Bank, Sumitomo Metal Industries, and Sumitomo Chemical Co. Since the 1970s, Sumitomo Corp., NEC Corp., and Sumitomo Electric have also gained prominence.

The origin of the group goes back to the early seventeenth century when the Sumitomo family went into retail business and copper refining. During the Meiji period many more companies were founded, but copper, heavy industry, and chemicals were its strong fields. Before the Second World War, 239 companies belonged to the Sumitomo *zaibatsu*. An Osaka-based **holding company** controlled the group.

Although the *zaibatsu* was dissolved after the war, the group reemerged without a holding company and the Sumitomo family ties. Member companies are active in the following fields:

Banking: Sumitomo Bank, Sumitomo Trust and Banking

Cement: Sumitomo Cement

Chemicals: Sumitomo Chemical, Sumitomo Bakelite

Construction: Sumitomo Construction

Electrical/Electronics: Sumitomo Electric Industries, NEC Corp.

Food and Beverages: Asahi Breweries

Glass: Nippon Sheet Glass

Insurance: Sumitomo Life Insurance, Sumitomo Marine and Fire Insurance

Machinery: Sumitomo Heavy Industries

Metals: Sumitomo Metal Industries, Nippon Stainless Steel, Sumitomo Light Metal Industries

Mining: Sumitomo Coal Mining, Sumitomo Metal Mining

Real Estate: Sumitomo Realty and Development

Rubber: Sumitomo Rubber Industries

Trading: Sumitomo Corp.

See also *keiretsu* **and business groups, Mitsubishi Group, Mitsui Group.**

Addresses

Sumitomo Bank
4-6-5, Kitahama, Chuo-ku, Osaka 541
Tel: (6) 227-2111   Fax: (3) 3282-8480

Sumitomo Chemical Co.
4-5-33, Kitahoma, Chuo-ku, Osaka 541
Tel: (6) 220-3891   Fax: (3) 5543-5901

Sumitomo Corp.
5-15, Kitahama, Chuo-ku, Osaka 541
Tel: (6) 220-6000

Sumitomo Metal Industries
5-33, Kitahama 4-chome, Chuo-ku, Osaka 541
Tel: (6) 220-5111   Fax: (6) 223-0563

References

Eli, Max. 1990. *Japan Inc.: Global Strategies of Japanese Trading Corporations.* New York: McGraw-Hill. Ch. 2.

Gerlach, Michael L. 1992. *Alliance Capitalism.* Berkeley: University of California Press. Chs. 3–4.

Ito, Takatoshi. 1992. *The Japanese Economy.* Cambridge: MIT Press. Ch. 7.

Sumitomo Corporation. *The Sumitomo Group.* (No date).

Odagiri, Hiroyuki. 1992. *Growth through Competition, Competition through Growth.* Oxford: Clarendon. Ch. 7.

T

tankan   **Bank of Japan**'s quarterly business survey. It measures business executives' sentiments about the economy in the near future and is taken seriously by the business community, the media, and government officials as a predictor of economy in the near future.

See **business-cycle indicators and forecasting, economic/business research and publications**.

tanshi **companies**   Japan's six short-term credit brokers or money market dealers.

See **money markets, money market dealers**.

Tax (Advisory) Commission   A major advisory committee under the Prime Minister's office responsible for reviewing the tax system and recommending annual tax revisions for budget compilation and long-term tax policy changes. Established in 1953, its members are appointed by the prime minister and drawn from diverse people including academics, tax experts, tax lawyers, former government officials, business representatives, union leaders, and so on.

The Commission is assisted in its tasks by staff of the tax bureau of the **Ministry of Finance** and the Ministry of Home Affairs as its secretariat. In this way any tax recommendations made by the Commission would have taken into account the vested interests of various groups and the consensus of the Ministry of Finance and other ministries. This is important in facilitating legislation and implementation once the proposals are adopted by the government.

Critics have complained that Japan's government advisory committees in general lack independent power and genuine debates because their members are selected by top bureaucrats to ensure cooperation with

government positions and their deliberations are perfunctory and manip-
ulated by the bureaucrats.

See also **tax system**.

References

Aoki, Torao. 1993. The National Taxation System. In *Japan's Public Sector: How the Government Is Financed*, ed. by Tokue Shibata. Tokyo: Tokyo University Press.

Fukunaga, Hiroshi. 1995. Policy puppet show: how councils of inquiry "debate" key issues.
Tokyo Business Today, October, pp. 18–21.

Ishi, Hiromitsu. 1993. *The Japanese Tax System*, 2nd ed. Oxford: Clarendon Press. Ch. 1.

Kato, Takashi. 1993. National Finance Administration. In *Japan's Public Sector: How the Government Is Financed*, ed. by Toku Shibata. Tokyo: Tokyo University Press.

tax reform   Japan's postwar tax system was initially designed by American economist Carl Shoup in 1949 during the occupation. It was a system
based on comprehensive income tax in which all categories of income are
added together and are subject to the same tax rate. Shoup had also called
for the elimination of preferential tax treatment given to special interests
or strategic industries. However, Japanese officials preferred tax benefits
to subsidies to promote strategic industries; they felt that tax preferences
would be more effective because they are given only after an enterprise
has followed government suggestions, whereas subsidies are paid in advance. Consequently preferential tax provisions proliferated in the Japanese **tax system**, making the system highly inequitable.

The greatest inequity of the tax system was that virtually all of the
wage earner's income was subject to taxation, whereas many expenses
could be deducted from business or agricultural income. Dividends and
capital gains on stocks were almost tax free. To encourage **savings**, interest earnings from various types of savings within certain limits were tax
exempt.

Attempts at tax reform were made repeatedly over the years. They culminated in the 1988 tax reform with the following major changes: (1) A
new 3% **consumption tax** was introduced in 1989 to broaden the tax
base. Eight excise taxes were eliminated. (2) **Individual income tax** and
corporate income tax were simplified, and the tax rates reduced. (3) To
plug the old loopholes in the income tax, a flat 26% (20% national and 6%
local) capital gains tax was introduced. Tax exemption for interest income
from various types of privileged savings—small-saver *maruyu* savings,
postal savings, national and local bonds, savings for the formation of

employee's assets, and postal installment savings for **housing**—was eliminated and replaced by a flat rate of 20% withheld at the source. (4) The burden of the inheritance tax was reduced. The minimum taxable inheritance was raised to a basic minimum of ¥40 million plus ¥8 million per statutory heir. The top rate was reduced from 75% to 70%.

Hatta (1992) considers the 1988 tax reform to be regressive. According to his calculation, it benefits the higher-income groups more than the lower ones.

In 1997–98 there was a mini-tax reform, designed to broaden the government's tax base while cutting income taxes. First, the **consumption tax** was raised from 3% to 5% in FY 1997. This was accompanied by a one-time personal income tax cut of ¥2 trillion. The net result, however, was that consumers reduced their **consumption**, which aggravated the sluggish domestic market. Second, effective FY 1998, the top rate for national corporate income tax was reduced from 37.5% to 34.5%. Combining this with local income tax (called inhabitant tax) and prefectural enterprise tax, the top effective corporate tax rate was reduced from 49.98% to 46.36%. (Note: In calculating effective tax rate, prefectural enterprise tax is deducted from the taxable income for national and local income taxes. See **corporate taxes**.) Nevertheless, this effective corporate tax rate is still very high by international standards. Given the prolonged stagnation of the economy since the early 1990s, there are growing calls for a more thorough tax reform to reduce corporate tax burden. It is contended that such a tax reform is preferable to increased government spendings on public works to stimulate the economy. The reason is that tax cuts will stimulate new businesses, investment and entrepreneurial activities, whereas increased government spending will benefit mainly the established companies (Nakatani 1998).

See also **consumption tax, corporate taxes, individual income tax, maruyu, postal savings system, tax system**.

References

Hashimoto, Kyoji, et al. 1990. Japan's tax reform: Its effects on the tax burden. *Japanese Economic Studies* 19, 1: 31–60.

Hatta, Tatsuo. 1992. The Nakasone-Takeshita tax reform: A critical evaluation. *American Economic Review* 82, 2: 231–36.

Ishi, Hiromitsu. 1993. *The Japanese Tax System*. Oxford: Oxford University Press.

Kaizuka, Keimei. 1992. The Shoup tax system and the postwar development of the Japanese economy. *American Economic Review* 82, 2: 221–25.

Nakatani, Iwao. 1998. Right remedy is tax cuts, not public works. *Nikkei Weekly*, April 13: 16.

Noguchi, Yukio. 1987. Public finance. In *The Political Economy of Japan*, vol. 1: *The Domestic Transformation*, ed. by Kozo Yamamura and Yasukichi Yasuba. Stanford: Stanford University Press.

Noguchi, Yukio. 1992. The changing Japanese economy and the need for a fundamental shift in the tax system. *American Economic Review* 82, 2: 226–30.

Takahashi, Hiroyuki. 1997. Corporate income tax reform in Japan. *JEI Report* 46A, December 12.

tax system Japan's taxes can be divided into national taxes levied by the national government and local taxes levied by the prefectural and municipal governments. In total the former is nearly twice as large as the latter. For example, in FY 1996 total national tax revenue (including stamp revenue) was ¥54.9 trillion, whereas total local tax revenue was ¥33.1 trillion. However, part of the tax revenue collected by the national government is allocated to local governments.

Taxes can also be divided into direct and indirect taxes. The former are levied directly on individuals and corporations, while the latter are levied indirectly as consumption tax, excise tax, or charged as fees. For both national and local taxes, direct taxes are much more important as sources of revenues.

The structure of national taxes is given in table T.1. **Individual income tax** (called "income tax" in Japan) is the largest national tax, accounting

Table T.1
National taxes (FY; in ¥ trillions)

	1980	1985	1991	1997[b]
Total	28.37	39.15	65.22	59.48
Income tax	10.80	15.44	25.74	20.88
Corporate tax	8.92	12.02	19.27	14.43
Inheritance tax	0.44	1.06	2.05	2.46
Consumption tax[a]	1.04	1.53	4.94	9.81
Liquor tax	1.42	1.93	2.00	2.06
Tobacco tax	—	0.88	0.99	1.06
Gasoline tax	1.55	1.56	1.50	1.96
Custom duties	0.65	0.64	0.85	1.09
Stamp revenue	0.84	1.41	2.15	2.02

Source: Ministry of Finance.
a. Introduced in FY 1989. Figures for 1980 and 1985 are for the commodity tax.
b. Initial budget.

for 35.1% of total national tax revenue in FY 1997. Corporate income tax (called "corporate tax" or "corporation tax" in Japan) is the second largest national tax, accountant for 24.3% of total national revenue in FY 1997. Other national taxes are inheritance tax, liquor tax, gasoline tax, **consumption tax** (or commodity tax before April 1, 1989), and stamp revenue. In the 1988 **tax reform**, the rates for individual and corporate income taxes and the inheritance tax were cut; eight excise taxes (commodity tax, sugar tax, travel tax, electricity tax, gas tax, etc.) were eliminated, while the consumption tax was introduced. The latter has become the third largest national tax.

Total revenue from national taxes reached its peak in FY 1991 (¥65.22 trillion). It declined afterward through 1994 (¥54.0 trillion) because of the recession, and then increased slightly to ¥59.48 trillion in FY 1997. Consumption tax revenue increased from ¥6.05 trillion in FY 1996 to ¥9.81 trillion in FY 1997 because of an increase in tax rate from 3% to 5% in 1997.

Local taxes are the major source of revenue for local governments. They consist of prefectural taxes levied by the 47 prefectures (which include **Tokyo** Metropolis) and municipal taxes levied by 3,233 municipalities (665 cities, 1,992 towns, and 576 villages as of FY 1995). Other sources of revenue are taxes collected by the national government and transferred to local governments (called "local transfer tax"), national government grants (called "local grant tax"), and subsidies for specific uses (education, social welfare, public works, transportation, and regional development, etc.) and public bonds. The sizes of these sources of local revenues in FY 1990 and 1994 are given in table T.2.

The structure of local taxes is given in table T.3. The tax base and rates of major local taxes are legislated by the Diet and are the same in all

Table T.2
Sources of local revenues (in ¥ trillions)

	FY 1990	FY 1994
Local taxes	33.45	32.54
Local transfer tax	1.66	1.91
Local grant tax	14.33	15.53
National subsidy	10.63	13.71
Local government debt	6.26	12.30
Others	14.08	20.10
Total	80.41	96.00

Source: Ministry of Finance.

Table T.3
Local taxes (FY; in ¥ trillions)

	1985	1991	1996
Prefectural taxes: total	10.20	16.18	14.59
Prefectural inhabitant tax	2.95	5.31	4.14
Enterprise tax	3.94	6.75	5.34
Prefectural Tobacco tax	0.31	0.37	0.38
Automobile tax	1.04	1.34	1.65
Special local consumption tax	0.48	0.17	0.13
Municipal taxes: total	13.11	18.89	18.49
Municipal inhabitant tax	6.65	10.09	8.52
Property tax	4.17	6.56	7.70
Municipal tobacco tax	0.55	0.65	0.67
Total local taxes	23.32	35.07	33.08

Source: Ministry of Home Affairs.

prefectures and municipalities. The most important local taxes are explained below:

1. Inhabitant taxes are a form of local income tax levied on individuals and corporations. The prefectural inhabitant tax has two rates (2% and 3%) on the income of individuals, and one rate for corporations (5% of their national corporate taxes). The municipal inhabitant tax is the most important municipal tax. It has progressive rates on individual income.

2. The enterprise tax, also called a "business tax," is the most important prefectural tax. It is collected from both individuals (unincorporated businesses) and corporations on the basis of net income, not on sales or turnover. Its tax rates are progressive.

3. Municipal property tax is the second largest tax for municipal governments. It is levied on owners of land, buildings, and other tangible assets. According to Ishi (1993: 262), the assessed value of property for tax purpose tends to be only a fraction of its market value, and great disparity exists among property assessments of equal value. This has created sentiments of unfairness among taxpayers and among different communities.

4. Special-purpose taxes (not given in the table) include a number of minor taxes such as the automobile acquisition tax, the gas oil delivery tax, and the hunting tax at the prefectural level and the bathing tax, the establishment tax, and the city planning tax at the municipal level. Unlike "regular taxes," these are earmarked for specific uses.

The Tax Bureau of the **Ministry of Finance** is responsible for tax policy on the basis of recommendations made by the Tax Commission. The National Tax Administration Agency is in charge of tax administration. The Ministry of Home Affairs oversees local taxation.

See also **consumption tax, corporate taxes, individual income taxes, tax reform**.

Addresses

Local Tax Bureau, Ministry of Home Affairs
1-2, Kasumigaseki 2-chome, Chiyoda-ku, Tokyo 100
Tel: (3) 3581-5311

National Tax Administration Agency
1-1, Kasumigaseki 3-chome, Chiyoda-ku, Tokyo 100
Tel: (3) 3581-4161

Tax Bureau, Ministry of Finance
1-1, Kasumigaseki 3-chome, Chiyoda-ku, Tokyo 100
Tel: (3) 3581-4111

References

Aoki, Torao. 1986. The national taxation system. In *Public Finance in Japan*, ed. by Tokue Shibata. Tokyo: Tokyo University Press.

Aoki, Torao. 1993. The national taxation system. In *Japan's Public Sector: How the Government is Financed*, edited by Tokue Shibata. Tokyo: Tokyo University Press.

Gomi, Yuji. 1997. *Guide to Japanese Taxes, 1997–98*. Tokyo: Zaikei shohosha.

Ishi, Hiromitsu. 1993. *The Japanese Tax System*. Oxford: Oxford University Press.

Ishihara, Nobuo. 1993. The local public finance system. In *Public Finance in Japan*, ed. by Tokue Shibata. Tokyo: Tokyo University Press.

Kuboi, Takashi. 1995. *Business Practices and Taxation in Japan*, 6th ed. Tokyo: Japan Times.

Ministry of Finance. Annual. *An Outline of Japanese Taxes*.

Ministry of Finance. Annual. *Financial Statistics of Japan*.

Noguchi, Yukio. 1992. The changing Japanese economy and the need for a fundamental shift in the tax system. *American Economic Review* 82, 2: 226–30.

Ogura, Seiritsu, and Naoyuki Yoshino. 1988. The tax system and the fiscal investment and loan program. In *Industrial Policy of* Japan, ed. by Ryutaro Komiya, Masahiro Okuno, and Kotaro Suzumura. Tokyo: Academic Press Japan.

Ostrom, Douglas. 1997. Japanese taxes in international perspective. *JEI Report* 24A, June 27.

Saito, Tadashi. 1991. Local governments in Japan: National and international aspects. *JEI Report* 41A, November 1: 1–12.

Yonehara, Junshichiro. 1993. Financial relations between national and local governments. In *Japan's Public Sector: How the Government is Financed*, ed. by Tokue Shibata. Tokyo: Tokyo University Press.

teigaku chokin   Fixed-sum postal savings deposits with a ten-year term, popular with small savers because of its traditional high interest rate.
   See **postal savings**.

telecommunications industry   Japan's telecommunications industry is highly concentrated and is undergoing major restructuring. Until 1985, the industry was dominated by a government monopoly, Nippon Telegraph and Telephone (NTT). Although NTT was privatized in April 1985, the government still holds 65% of its shares, and it remains the largest company in the industry. Its operations as of 1998 have been limited to the domestic market. It had sales of ¥6,371 billion in FY 1996 and estimated sales of ¥6,413 billion in FY 1997, which make it the largest company in Japan.

   The domestic long-distance market is served by NTT and its small competitors, Daini Den Den (DDI) Corp. and Japan Telecom Co., which had sales of ¥555 billion and ¥378, respectively, in FY 1996. Domestic local services are provided by NTT and a number of small firms, including Tokyo Telecommunication Network Co. (TTNet). The smaller international market is dominated by Kokusai Denshin Denwa Co. (KDD), with two small competitors, International Digital Communications (IDC), and International Telecom Japan, Inc. (ITJ). In October 1997 International Telecom Japan and Japan Telecom Co. merged under the latter's name.

   As early as 1982 the Ministry of Posts and Telecommunications (MPT) proposed the break up of NTT to spur competition. In the ensuing prolonged debates, supporters of the proposal cited NTT's monopolistic practices, high charges for services, and slow pace in introducing new technologies. The proposal was resisted by NTT until late 1996 when it became clear that domestic deregulation and growing international competition would make such restructuring inevitable. In December 1996 an agreement was reached between MPT and NTT on the restructuring of the company. NTT would be broken up in 1999 into one long-distance company and two local phone companies. The former would provide both domestic and international services. The two local phone companies would serve Eastern Japan and Western Japan respectively. The three companies would be the wholly owned subsidiaries of a new **holding company** that will hold all of their shares. Because Japan's **Anti-**

monopoly Law banned holding companies, the Law was revised in 1997 to lift the ban.

The planned breakup will make both domestic and international telecommunications markets more competitive. Analysts believe that this is much needed in light of the global deregulation in the telecommunications market. NTT's ability to combine both domestic and international services is particularly significant. Traditionally the Ministry of Posts and Telecommunications has divided the industry into local, long-distance, and international services to regulate company operations, leading to operational inefficiency, lack of integrated services, and high prices. With growing international competition, both the government and NTT realized that deregulation and restructuring were essential. Japan was a participant in an agreement reached in 1997 in the World Trade Organization negotiations on telecommunications, which would open the telecommunications markets of Japan and other participant countries to foreign capital and competition.

In anticipation of this new global competition, other Japanese telecommunications companies have announced their restructurings. These include the following: (1) Kokusai Densin Denwa Co. (KDD), the nation's largest international carrier, and Tokyo Telecommunication Network Co., a regional phone company, will combine some sales operations and offer package services. (2) Japan Telecom, a domestic long distance company, and International Telecom, an international carrier, will have a merger. (3) KDD has formed an alliance with AT&T of the United States to provide global telecommunications services at low cost. (4) In early 1998, DII agreed to have an alliance with the Teleglobe Inc., a major Canadian telecommunications company.

Analysts expect consolidation of operations between more companies as well as more partnership with overseas international telephone carriers to take place in the near future.

Because of its sheer size, NTT's procurement of equipment and services has become an issue in Japan–U.S. trade talks. Washington has long charged that NTT discriminates against foreign suppliers in its procurement. An agreement was reached in 1980 to increase sales opportunities for American equipment producers. The agreement has been extended five times, the latest in October 1997. It will remain in effect until NTT is broken up into three companies as outlined above. The latest accord will improve access of American firms to technical information on network equipment requirements so that they can compete more equally with

Japanese manufacturers. NTT will also work with foreign companies to replace some of its network equipment standards with international standards.

See also **public corporations, privatization**.

Addresses

Kokusai Denshin Denwa Co.
2-3-2, Nishi-Shinjuku, Shinkuku-ku, Tokyo 163
Tel: (3) 3347-7111   Fax: (3) 3347-7000

Nippon Telegraph and Telephone
1-1-6, Uchi-Saiwaicho, Chiyoda-ku, Tokyo 100
Tel: (3) 3509-5111   Fax: (3) 3727-3424

References

Japan Company Handbook. Quarterly. Tokyo: Toyo Keizai.

Ogawa, Joshua. 1996. Restructuring would put NTT into hot global arena. *Nikkei Weekly*, December 9: 1, 8.

Sasaki, Sei. 1997. Telecom merger heeds competitive call. *Nikkei Weekly*, March 17.

Telecommunications. In *Japan Economic Almanac*. Various years. Tokyo: Nihon Keizai Shimbun.

Telecommunications: Survey. *The Economist*, September 30, 1995: 5–28.

The real cost of cheaper calls. 1996. *The Economist*, December 14: 62–3.

tenzoku   Long-term transfer of employees to a subsidiary.
   See **corporate personnel practices**.

***tokkin* funds**   a special type of **investment trust** funds with tax advantages for investors. *Tokkin* is the abbreviation of *tokutei kinsen shintaku*, which is translated literally as "specified money trust." It is a type of trust fund held at **trust banks** in which institutional investors give specific instruction for management. *Tokkin* funds are, in theory, managed by both investors and **investment advisory companies** for investment in stocks. They were popular in the 1980s with companies, commercial banks, and **insurance companies** because they are anonymous and pay out dividends that are tax free or taxed at relatively low rates. These funds grew rapidly in the 1980s. Partly as a result of the investment of these funds, trading volume on the **Tokyo Stock Exchange** increased very rapidly in the late 1980s.

Tokkin funds were an important source of profits for insurance companies in the late 1980s. The **Ministry of Finance** limited their investment in *tokkin* funds to 5% of their total assets until September 1990, when it was raised to 7%. The bad fall in the Tokyo Stock Exchange in 1990 prompted the increase in order to induce the insurance companies to keep their huge funds in the **stock market**. In the wake of the **securities companies'** scandals in 1991 and the depressed stock market, many trust fund investors have redeemed their monies because of the worsened prospects for returns. At the end of March 1993, the outstanding value of *tokkin* at trust banks was estimated at ¥18.92 trillion.

Eigyo tokkin funds are a shadowy version of *tokkin* funds. In pursuit of higher return, investors have the funds managed directly by the institutional sales departments of securities companies on a discretionary basis. Since these departments are not authorized to act as investment advisers, such accounts are surreptitious in nature. They charge no fees and are not registered with the Ministry of Finance. Such discretionary accounts enabled securities companies to easily move money in and out of clients' accounts. Some of these funds were used as an investment trust, and some to finance illegal activities such as supporting the share prices of companies who put up money in these *eigyo tokkin* funds. It is estimated that a total of ¥5 trillion was invested in *eigyo tokkin* accounts in 1989, with ¥2 trillion of them managed by the four leading securities companies (Nomura, Daiwa, Nikko, and Yamaichi).

To attract funds to these *eigyo tokkin* accounts, it was common, prior to 1991, for securities companies to promise investors guaranteed returns, although such a practice is illegal. In 1991 it was revealed that securities companies have widely used these accounts as a vehicle for compensating clients for investment losses, often without the latter's knowledge. Because these scandals have outraged the public and intensified foreign criticisms of Japanese business practices, the Ministry of Finance and the Japan Securities Dealers' Association have acted to tighten rules on the management of *tokkin* funds.

See also **securities companies**.

References

Isaacs, Jonathan. 1990. *Japanese Equities Markets*. London: Euromoney Publications. Ch. 8.

Nagano, Kenji. 1991. Push seen for new rules of integrity. *Nikkei Weekly*, July 6: 4.

Tightened *tokkin* fund rules to curb abuses. *Japan Economic Journal*, February 17, 1990: 31.

Tatewaki, Kazuo. 1991. *Banking and Finance in Japan*. London: Routledge. Ch. 8.

Tomomatsu, Hidetaka. 1991. Exposure of coziness chills securities industry. *Nikkei Weekly*, July 6: 1, 4.

Viner, Aron. 1987. *Inside Japan's Financial Markets*. The Economist Publications. Ch. 9.

Tokyo and Kanto   Tokyo is Japan's capital, its largest city, and the hub of its largest industrial region, Kanto. The Metropolis of Tokyo is a vast self-governing unit consisting of 23 special wards, 27 cities, 5 towns, and 8 villages, with a **population** of 11.78 million people (7.96 million for the 23 wards) as of October 1, 1996. It is the nation's political, business, and financial center and has the greatest concentration of corporate headquarters, financial institutions, government ministries and agencies, and cultural and educational institutions. It is also the center of the nation's transportation networks.

In FY 1994 Tokyo produced ¥82.67 trillion of gross municipal product, which was by far the largest among the nation's large cities. Tokyo' gross municipal product as a share of Japan's gross domestic product (GDP) grew from 16.7% in FY 1975 to 17.7% in FY 1985 and 19.2% in FY 1990, but then declined to 17.1% in FY 1994 because of the recession. Its major economic activities are finance, insurance, real estate, wholesale and retail trade, and corporate headquarters, but it also leads other major cities in some manufacturing activities. The **Tokyo Stock Exchange** is by far the largest in the nation, having 82% of the total stock trading volume on all eight stock exchanges in the nation in 1997. Tokyo also has some of Japan's most prestigious universities. These include the University of Tokyo, considered to be the top university of the nation, Hitotsubashi University, Keio University, and Waseda University.

The great concentration of population, corporate headquarters, and government ministries and agencies has produced overcrowding, traffic congestion, and high prices of land, **housing**, and many goods and services. Nevertheless, Tokyo's well-developed urban subway network along with the connecting suburban railways make it possible for a large number of people to commute to work from the outlying areas into Tokyo. It is estimated that the commuters increase Tokyo's day population by as much as 30%.

To relieve the concentration of population, business, and government activities in Tokyo, the National Land Agency proposed in 1992 relocating capital functions, such as the Diet, the Supreme Court, and the central-government ministries to somewhere within 60 to 300 kilometers outside Tokyo. In December 1995 a government panel proposed the construction of a new capital starting in 2000 and that the Diet should be moved to the new city in 2010. Aside from easing the concentration of political, administrative, judicial, and economic functions in Tokyo, the relocation reportedly will make the nation better able to endure natural disasters such as the Great Hanshin Earthquake which hit the Kobe area in January 1995. Because of opposition from local politicians and the tremendous costs of constructing a new capital—land purchases, office buildings, an airport, roads, and railways, estimated to cost ¥20 trillion—little to date has been undertaken toward such a move.

Tokyo is the hub of the Kanto region which also includes six other prefectures: Ibaraki, Tochigi, Gumma, Saitama, Chiba, and Kanagawa (where **Yokohama** is located). Literally "east of the pass," Kanto is Japan's largest industrial region. In FY 1994 it produced more than 36% of Japan's GDP. It has a population of 39.7 million in 1996, which amounted to 31.5% of Japan's total population. Many large corporations that are headquartered in Tokyo have factories, subsidiaries, and suppliers located in the greater Kanto area. Yokohama, 30 kilometers south of Tokyo, is Japan's largest port and second largest city in terms of population (3.28 million in 1996). Adjacent to it to the north is Kawasaki, Japan's ninth largest city with a population of 1.18 million in 1996. Both Yokohama and Kawasaki are heavily industrialized with electrical machinery, equipment and supplies, and general machinery as their major industries.

See also **housing, Osaka and Kansai, land uses and policies, Nagoya and Central Japan, Yokohama**.

Address

Tokyo Metropolitan Government
8-1 Nishi-Shinjuku 2-chome, Shinjuku-ku, Tokyo 163
Tel: (3) 5321-1111   Fax: (3) 5388-1329

References

Economic Planning Agency. Annual. *Annual Report on Prefectural Accounts* (in Japanese).

Management and Coordination Agency. Annual. *Japan Statistical Yearbook*.

Tokyo Metropolitan Government. 1997. *Tokyo*.

Tokyo Metropolitan Government. Annual. *Tokyo Statistical Yearbook*.

Tokyo-to Bunka Shinkokai. 1991. *Living in Tokyo: Guide to Foreign Students*. Tokyo: Tokyo Metropolitan Culture Foundation.

Waley, Paul. 1991. *Tokyo: City of Streets*. New York: Weatherhill.

Tokyo Commodity Exchange for Industry (TOCOM)   Japan's largest commodity exchange and the world's leading platinum exchange.
See **commodity markets**.

Tokyo offshore market   Officially called the Japan offshore market, this is the banking market, established in December 1986, in which banks conduct banking business with nonresidents (foreign corporations, foreign governments, international institutions, and overseas branches of foreign exchange banks). The market is free from government regulation of interest rates, reserve requirements on deposits, and deposit insurance. It is exempt from withholding tax; that is, interest repatriated by nonresidents is not taxed at the source. Nor are the transactions restricted to any currency. However, residents are prohibited from the market, and there are limits on the inflow of funds from the offshore accounts into domestic accounts.

The Tokyo offshore market was set up to serve as a center for the world's transactions in yen and thus promote the international business of Japan's banking institutions and the internationalization of yen. From $1.38 trillion in 1986, the transaction level increased to a peak of $7.89 trillion in 1995 before it declined to $6.59 trillion in 1997. Market participants have complained about the rigid separation of offshore accounts from domestic accounts, calling for deregulation.
See also **money markets**.

Tokyo Stock Exchange (TSE)   Japan has eight stock exchanges and the Tokyo Stock Exchange is by far the largest of them. As shown in table T.4, it had 87% and 86%, respectively, of total stock trading volume and value on all stock exchanges in 1989, which declined to 82.3% and 71.7%, respectively, in 1997. During the **stock market** boom of the late 1980s, TSE surpassed the New York Stock Exchange in stock market value and trading value to become the world's largest ($4.26 trillion in market value versus $2.9 trillion for New York Stock Exchange at the end of 1989). By the end of 1991, however, its market value had declined to $3.02 trillion, compared with $3.71 trillion for the New York Stock Exchange.

The Tokyo Stock Exchange was founded in 1878 as part of the Meiji government's modernization program. From 1943 to 1947 all of Japan's stock exchanges were merged into a single Japan Securities Exchange. The TSE in its present form was established in 1949.

Stock trading on the TSE reached its peak volume in 1989 with 283 billion shares and peak value in 1989 with ¥333 trillion. Following the

Table T.4
Stock exchanges and stock trading

Stock exchange	1989 Volume[a]	Value[b]	1997 Volume[a]	Value[b]
Tokyo	222,599	332,617	107,566	108,500
Osaka	25,096	41,679	15,407	27,024
Nagoya	7,263	10,395	6,098	12,758
Kyoto	331	443	668	2,114
Hiroshima	189	235	182	200
Fukuoka	267	330	244	204
Niigata	397	475	240	396
Sapporo	151	221	248	246
Total	256,296	386,395	130,657	151,445

Source: Tokyo Stock Exchange.
Note: Trading in foreign stocks is not included.
a. In millions of shares.
b. In ¥ billions.

stock market crash in 1990, stock trading on the TSE reached its nadir 1992 with 66 billion shares and ¥60 trillion in trading value. There has been feeble recovery since then, but as can be seen from table T.4, trading volume in 1997 was less than one-half and trading value was less than one-third of the 1989 level.

Trading is limited to listed securities. The Exchange is divided into two sections for domestic stocks—the first section for large companies and the second section for medium-sized companies and newly listed companies. There is a foreign section for foreign stocks. At the end of 1996 stocks of 1,327 companies are assigned to the first section, and those of 478 companies to the second section. Stocks of 60 foreign companies are listed in the foreign section in 1997, down from the peak of 125 companies in 1990–91.

A company applying for listing on the TSE is screened by both the Exchange and the **Ministry of Finance**. The securities traded are divided broadly into stocks and bonds. The Exchange was not open to foreign stocks until 1973, and it was only in December 1985 that six foreign securities companies, including Merrill Lynch, Morgan Stanley and Co., and Goldman, Sacks and Co., were approved as traders on the Exchange. At the end of 1997, there were 125 members in the Exchange, including 23 foreign security firms.

Two **stock prices indexes** are commonly used for the TSE—the Nikkei Stock Average and TOPIX, the Tokyo Stock Price Index. The former gives an unweighted average of 225 selected issues listed on the first section of the Exchange. The TOPIX is based on the weighted average of all stocks listed on the first section of the Exchange.

Japan does not have an independent regulatory agency comparable to the U.S. Securities and Exchange Commission to oversee its **securities companies** and activities on the securities exchanges. Instead, the Ministry of Finance gives securities companies and stock exchanges **administrative guidance** and the Securities Dealers' Association of Japan provides voluntary industry restraints. In July 1922 a new Securities and Exchange Surveillance Commission was established to watch for stock market manipulation.

See also **shareownership, stock market, stock price index.**

Addresses

Tokyo Stock Exchange
1, Nihonbashi Kabuto 2-chome, Chuo-ku, Tokyo 103
Tel: (3) 3666-0141   Fax: (3) 3663-0625

Tokyo Stock Exchange New York Representative Office
45 Broadway, New York, NY 1006
Tel: (212) 363-2350   Fax: (212) 363-2354

References

Japan Securities Research Institute. 1998. *Securities Market in Japan, 1998.* Ch. 6.

Maruko, Maya. 1997, TSE shores up sagging foreign listings. *Japan Times Weekly* (international edition), February 17–23: 13.

Sato, Kazuo. 1995. Bubbles in Japan's stock market: A macroeconomic analysis. *Japan Economic Studies* 23, 4: 32–58.

Tatewaki, Kazuo. 1991. *Banking and Finance in Japan.* London: Routledge. Ch. 6.

Tokyo Stock Exchange. Annual. *Tokyo Stock Exchange Fact Book.*

Viner, Aron. 1987. *Inside Japan's Financial Markets.* London: The Economist Publications. Ch. 3.

Yamamoto, Yuri. 1997. Stock prices slipping into danger zone. *Nikkei Weekly,* October 6: 1, 14.

Zielinski, Robert, and Nogel Holloway. 1991. *Unequal Equities.* Tokyo: Kodansha International.

Tokyu Group   A large family-controlled conglomerate of some 300 companies, including Tokyu Corp., a railway company, Tokyu Department Store, and Tokyu Store Chain Co.
   See **railway companies**.

TOPIX   Tokyo Stock Price Index.
   See **stock price indexes**.

toshi gingo (togin)   City banks, Japan's large commercial banks with headquarters in major metropolitan areas.
   See **banking system, city banks**.

total quality control   Quality control in product design and manufacturing in which all employees and management participate.
   See **quality control**.

Toyota Group   An industrial group comprising Toyota Motor Co. and its major suppliers, including Nippondenso, Toyoda Machine Works, Aisin Seiki Co., Toyoda Auto Body Co., Toyoda Automatic Loom Works Ltd., and Kanto Auto Works Ltd.
   See **automobile industry, keiretsu and business groups, subcontracting**.

trade pattern   Japan's international trade pattern can be discussed in terms of its products composition, trading partners, and export-import imbalance.
   Japan's exports are dominated by manufactured products, particularly machinery and equipment, although the most important product groups in terms of competitiveness and world market shares have changed significantly over time. In the 1950s unskilled labor-intensive products such as textiles, apparel, rubber and plastic products, leather and leather products, were important. The major export products were textiles, steel, and vessels in the 1960s, automobiles, steel, and chemicals in the 1970s and 1980s. Since the late 1980s high-tech equipment and electronics have become increasingly important, although automobiles, chemicals, and steel remain dominant. Automobiles are the largest category of export products, amounting to more than 14.4% of total exports in 1996 (see table T.5).
   Japan's imports are dominated by fuels, foodstuffs, metal ores, and other raw materials. Because of its lack of natural resources, Japan depends

Table T.5
Japan's exports by commodity (in $ billion, custom clearance basis)

	1973	1983	1990	1993	1996
Foodstuffs	0.8	1.4	1.6	2.0	2.0
Textiles	3.3	6.6	7.2	8.2	8.4
Chemicals	2.1	6.9	15.9	20.2	23.7
Metals	6.8	18.4	19.5	23.0	24.2
Iron-steel products	5.3	12.8	12.5	14.5	14.8
Machinery and equipment	20.4	99.6	215.1	274.4	300.8
Motor vehicles	3.6	26.1	51.0	58.4	56.9
ICs	—	—	7.6	13.1	18.3
Vessels	3.8	6.0	5.6	10.2	11.5
Precision instruments	1.0	5.4	11.6	14.3	18.1
Others	3.5	14.0	27.6	29.1	35.9
Total	36.9	146.9	286.9	360.9	395.6

Source: Japan Tariff Association.

heavily on imports for some primary products essential for consumption and industrial production. It imports about half of its caloric intake of food and about 30% of its total food value. It imports about all of its crude petroleum, iron ore, lead ore, bauxite, wool and cotton, and about 75% of its coal and zinc ore. On the other hand, the imports of machinery and equipment used to be relatively low (about 17% of total in 1990) but have increased significantly to 27.6% of total imports in 1996.

Because of the need to import fuels, foodstuffs, and raw materials, Japan has to export manufactured products to earn the necessary foreign exchanges. However, there is one complication. The developing countries and the Middle East, from which Japan imports raw materials and energy, do not have the population or income levels to buy sufficient manufactured goods from Japan to balance the bilateral trade. The oil export countries, in particular, run a large trade surplus with Japan. To offset these import deficits, Japan must run export surpluses with other countries. However, the export surpluses with other industrial countries in the 1980s have become excessive, far more than necessary to pay for imports, thereby becoming a source of friction with the West.

Japan's trade surplus was only $2.1 billion in 1980, but it rapidly increased to $20 billion in 1981, $56 billion in 1985, and to a peak of $96.4 billion in 1987 before it declined because of yen appreciation to $63.6 billion in 1990. However, recession and sluggish domestic demand of the early 1990s caused exports to rise more rapidly than imports, and

Table T.6
Japan's imports by commodity (in $ billions)

	1973	1983	1990	1993	1996
Foodstuffs	6.0	14.9	31.6	39.4	50.7
Textile materials	2.2	2.1	2.6	1.5	1.7
Textiles	1.7	3.0	12.8	16.6	25.6
Metal ores and scrap	4.0	6.5	9.1	7.0	8.3
Other raw materials	6.0	9.6	16.7	18.7	20.2
Mineral fuels	8.3	58.9	56.7	48.8	60.5
Coal	1.4	4.9	6.2	5.9	6.9
Petroleum	6.0	40.1	31.6	28.0	33.4
Chemicals	1.9	7.2	16.0	18.0	23.4
Machinery and equipment	3.5	10.4	40.9	46.6	96.2
Others	4.7	13.8	48.3	44.0	62.2
Total	38.3	126.4	234.8	240.7	349.1

Source: Japan Tariff Association.

trade surplus surged to $103.1 billion in 1991 and $144.4 billion in 1994. It then declined to $83.6 billion in 1996.

The large imbalance between Japan's exports and imports has been attributed by Western analysts to various factors that limit imports into Japan such as governmental **nontariff barriers to trade, keiretsu** (business groups), the exclusionary business practices that make Japanese firms favor doing business with other related Japanese firms, the trading practices of the **trading companies**, the high **savings** by Japanese households, and the **distribution system** with its numerous small retail stores. The attitude of the consumers is also considered to have played a role. For example, Lincoln (1990: 80) criticizes the "gullible public" who has limited exposure to foreign products in Japan, and who had accepted the "need" to protect small, weak Japanese firms from international competition, and the "myth" of overall Japanese superiority in the 1980s.

In response, Ryutaro Komiya of the Research Institute of the **Ministry of International Trade and Industry** disputes Lincoln's point and argues that on the contrary, Japanese consumers tend to regard imported foreign consumer goods as prestigious luxuries (author's interview, July 7, 1992). Various Japanese authors and officials have also criticized the inability or unwillingness of Western firms to learn and adapt to the Japanese market and institutions and to strive to satisfy the demand of the Japanese consumers. American automakers' failure, until recently, to change the driver's seat to the right in their cars exported to Japan is often given as an example.

In terms of trading partners, the United States has remained Japan's largest trading partner throughout the postwar period, although its importance has declined somewhat in the 1980s because of the growing importance of other countries. In addition the United States is more important as a market for Japan's exports (27.2% in 1996) than as a source of its imports (22.7% in 1996). Consequently there is substantial export surplus in Japan's trade with the United States ($31.2 billion in 1996; see table T.7). Japan's trade surplus vis-à-vis the United States was only $7 billion in 1979 but increased steadily to a peak of $52.1 billion in 1987 before it started to decline. This pattern of export surplus is true with vir-

Table T.7
Japan's trading partners (1996; in US$ billions)

Exports			Imports		
Rank	Country	Value	Rank	Country	Value
1	United States	107.0	1	United States	75.8
2	South Korea	28.0	2	China	38.7
3	Taiwan	24.8	3	South Korea	15.2
4	Hong Kong	24.3	4	Indonesia	14.5
5	China	20.9	5	Taiwan	14.3
6	Singapore	19.9	6	Australia	13.6
7	Thailand	17.5	7	Germany	13.5
8	Germany	17.4	8	Malaysia	11.2
9	Malaysia	14.7	9	United Arab Emirates	11.0
10	United Kingdom	11.9	10	Saudi Arabia	10.2
11	Netherlands	8.8	11	Thailand	9.8
12	Indonesia	8.7	12	Canada	9.7
13	Philippines	8.0	13	Singapore	7.0
14	Australia	7.1	14	United Kingdom	6.9
15	Panama	5.6	15	Italy	6.5
16	France	5.1	16	France	6.0
17	Canada	4.9	17	Philippines	4.3
18	Belgium, Luxemburg	4.1	18	Russia	3.8
19	Mexico	3.5	19	Brazil	3.6
20	Italy	3.2	20	Switzerland	3.4
Total exports		393.0	Total imports		333.8

Source: Ministry of International Trade and Industry.

tually all other industrial countries except Canada and Australia, which supply foodstuffs and raw materials to Japan. Japan also has export surplus with the newly industrializing economies of South Korea, Taiwan, Hong Kong, and Singapore and the developing countries in Southeast Asia, Latin America, and Africa.

Among the developing countries, China is Japan's largest trading partner, followed by Indonesia. Japan had trade surplus with China until 1988 when import deficit started to emerge. Japan has import deficit with Indonesia, Malaysia, Saudi Arabia, and United Arab Emirates because of the imports of raw materials and fuels.

In the analytical literature on Japan's trade pattern, an issue of particular interest to American economists has been the apparent low level of manufactured goods imported by Japan. For example, in 1990 Japan imported $117.5 billion of manufactured goods, slightly less than what Italy imported ($123.2 billion) in the same year despite the much larger size of the Japanese market and national income. These imports amounted to 50.9% of Japan's total imports in 1990, which was the lowest manufactured import ratio among the industrial countries (in the United States, it was 78.6%; Germany, 76.9%; Italy, 71.0%). The ratio in Japan was 22.8% in 1980, 31% in 1985, 50.4% in 1989, and 59.4% in 1996, all much lower than the corresponding ratios in the other industrial countries. The question is: Are these low levels of manufactured goods the result of market forces at work, or are they the result of government trade policy and/or other structural barriers to imports?

Balassa and Noland (1988: 239–54), Lawrence (1987, 1991) and Lincoln (1990: 18–25) have argued that Japan's imports of manufactured goods are lower than what one would expect, given its high income and industrial structure. Saxonhouse (1989) disagrees and maintains that Japan's specific factor endowments can adequately explain Japan's composition of imports. Grossman (1990) also argues that factor endowment explains Japan's trade pattern but does so in a dynamic setting of R&D and innovation. Lawrence (1991, 1993) further argues that the low level of manufactured imports is more pronounced in industries in which *keiretsu*-related firms are dominant. However, the validity of his methodology is challenged by Saxonhouse (1991, 1993). Adding to the debate, several Japanese economists have contended that American criticism of Japan's trade policy is unjustified because the U.S.–Japan trade imbalance is either due to the loss of international competitiveness of American firms or due to the strength of Japanese firms at home ("natural market barriers") and abroad, and not due to Japan's import barriers (cited in

Lincoln, 1990: 25–29). Komiya and Irie (1990) express the view widely held by Japanese officials that the U.S. trade deficits are macro problems stemming from government deficits and low domestic savings, and that Japan is one of the most open countries among OECD members. Thus there is no consensus among economists on the issue.

See also **trade policies**.

Addresses

Japan External Trade Organization (JETRO)
2-5, Toranomon 2-chome, Minato-ku, Tokyo 105
Tel: (3) 3582-5511

Ministry of International Trade and Industry
3-1, Kasumigaseki 1-chome, Chiyoda-ku, Tokyo 100
Tel: (3) 3501-1511

References

Balassa, Bela, and Marcus Noland. 1988. *Japan in the World Economy*. Washington: Institute for International Economics. Chs. 2–3.

Grossman, Gene M. 1990. Explaining Japan's innovation and trade: A model of quality competition and dynamic comparative advantage. *Bank of Japan Monetary and Economic Studies 8*, 2: 75–99.

Komiya, Ryutaro. 1990. *The Japanese Economy: Trade, Industry, and Government*. Tokyo: University of Tokyo Press. Ch. 1.

Komiya, Ryutaro, and Kazutomo Irie. 1990. The U.S.–Japan trade problem: An economic analysis from a Japanese viewpoint. In *Japan Economic Structure: Should It Change?* ed. by Kozo Yamamura. Seattle: Society for Japanese Studies.

Lawrence, Robert Z. 1987. Imports in Japan: Closed markets or minds? *Brookings Papers on Economic Activity*, no. 2: 517–48.

Lawrence, Robert Z. 1991. Efficient or exclusionist? The import behavior of Japanese corporate groups. *Brookings Papers on Economic Activity*, no. 1: 311–30.

Lawrence, Robert Z. 1993. Japan's different trade regime: an analysis with particular reference to keiretsu. *Journal of Economic Perspectives 7*, 3: 3–19.

Lincoln, Edward. 1990. *Japan's Unequal Trade*. Washington: Brookings Institution.

Ministry of International Trade and Industry. Annual. *White Paper on International Trade*.

Sato, Ryuzo, and Julianne Nelson, eds. 1989. *Beyond Trade Friction: Japan–U.S. Economic Relations*. Cambridge: Cambridge University Press.

Saxonhouse, Gary R. 1989. Differentiated products, economies of scale and access to the Japanese market. In *Trade Policies for International competitiveness*, ed. by Robert C. Feenstra. Chicago: University of Chicago Press.

Saxonhouse, Gary R. 1991. Efficient or exclusionist? The import behavior of Japanese corporate groups. Comments and discussion. *Brookings Papers on Economic Activity*, no. 1: 331–36.

Saxonhouse, Gary R. 1993. What does Japanese trade structure tell us about Japanese trade policy. *Journal of Economic Perspectives* 7, 3: 21–43.

trade policy   Japanese government policy on international trade has changed over time in its focus. In the 1950s–60s the infant-industry policy of protection was practiced to restrict imports and to nuture domestic industries with export potentials. In the 1970s–80s, as trade surplus mounted due to the success of its protective policy, policy makers were preoccupied with bilateral negotiations with Washington to minimize the concessions that Japan had to give to protect its largest export market. There are signs of further policy changes in the 1990s.

The underlying premises of Japan's trade policy in the early postwar period were (1) Japan is a resource-poor country that has to import most of its natural resources, (2) it has to pay for these imports by the export of manufactured goods, and (3) it can best do so by protecting and promoting its manufacturing industries. On the basis of these premises, an import-restricting and an industry- and export-promoting trade strategy was adopted in the 1950s. The ministry that is in charge of trade policy is the **Ministry of International Trade and Industry** (MITI). In fact the name of the Ministry itself is indicative of the close link between industry and trade to policy makers. In the separate area of agricultural products, import restriction, including total ban of rice import, has been adopted for domestic political reasons.

The protection and promotion of domestic industries was accomplished by keeping the domestic market from cheaper imports and **foreign direct investment in Japan**, and by giving incentives to domestic industries to raise productivity in order to be internationally competitive. Import restrictions were achieved by means of tariffs and **nontariff barriers to trade**. Tariffs were high in the early postwar period but had been successively reduced since the mid-1960s as Japan joined GATT and OECD. Currently tariff rates on nonagricultural products are generally no higher than their counterparts in the United States and the European Community. However, tariff rates remain high on fresh and processed agricultural products, alcoholic beverages, and wood products, for example. Nontariff barriers to trade remain numerous and restrictive. These include quotas on agricultural and fishery products, and stringent testing and certification requirements, and custom procedures. Restrictions on foreign direct investment in Japan have been gradually liberalized due to U.S. pressure.

To give domestic industries incentives to raise productivity and become internationally competitive, MITI has used **industrial policy** and **administrative guidance**. The purpose is to promote industries that are considered to have good growth prospects in the world market. MITI's policy measures are carefully crafted to raise productivity through industry rationalization, R&D, **investment**, and so forth, without fostering complacency and high costs. The **steel industry** in the 1960s and 1970s is the best example in which MITI's trade and industrial policies led to intense competition among domestic producers to raise productivity in order to qualify for capacity expansion. As a result Japan's steel industry became the world's largest and a major export industry in the 1970s. However, MITI's industrial policy has not always been effective, especially since the 1970s, and the protected and promoted industries have not always become efficient. The petrochemical industry is an example.

Until the mid-1960s when Japan joined the OECD and GATT, the government provided tax and monetary incentives to industries to expand exports. By the late 1970s Japan had become a major trading power and exporter of manufactured goods. However, throughout the 1970s and 1980s Japan's rapid expansion in some export products such as textiles, steel, electronics, and automobiles had caused growing protectionism in the West, and Tokyo's policy concern became increasingly the protection of its export markets. To ensure Japan's foreign market access and to forestall unilateral trade restrictions on its exports, MITI has been pragmatic in negotiating agreements on managed trade. These include the following: voluntary export restraints (VERs) on textile exports to the United States in the 1970s; VERs on the exports of steel, automobiles, color televisions, and semiconductors to the United States since 1981; VERs on automobile exports to the European Community from 1991 until the end of 1999. There was also the 1985 **Plaza Accord** to let the yen appreciate against the dollar in order to help reduce the U.S. trade deficit with Japan.

Since the mid-1980s, as Japan's trade surplus reached new heights (peak of $96.4 billion in 1987), Tokyo has, after some hard bargaining, increasingly accepted the U.S. demand to help increase the imports of certain products. These include the 1980 agreement to increase sales opportunities for American telecommunications equipment producers, the **Beef-Citrus Quota Agreement** (1988) with the United States to replace quotas with tariffs on beef and citrus imports, and the **Semiconductor Agreement** (1991) with the United States to increase foreign firms' semiconductor market share in Japan to over 20% by the end of 1992. There was also the broad-ranging **Structural Impediments Initiative** agreement (1990) with the United States, concluded despite much domestic opposition, to reduce business practices that are said to impede imports. As part of the new policy concern to reduce trade friction with the West, MITI has also encouraged Japanese companies, particularly automakers, to increase **direct overseas investment** and production, on the one hand, and to increase imports of foreign parts, on the other hand.

From voluntary export restraints to market-opening measures, all these trade agreements were negotiated in the framework of bilateral negotiations with the United States, Japan's largest trading partner with which Japan has had large trade surplus. Invariably Japan would first firmly reject Washington's demand in a protracted process, with negotiations seemingly reaching an impasse, and finally yielding to most of Washington's demands when severe trade sanctions were threatened by U.S. officials if no agreement was reached. Thus Japan's trade policy from the 1970s to the early 1990s can be characterized as mainly "reactive bilateralism" in nature, reacting to the growing U.S. tendency toward managed trade with quantitative targets. Washington's trade policy toward Japan has been criticized by Ostry (1997) as "unilateralism" in a multilateral world trade system. and by many other eminent economists including Bhagwati (1994) as counterproductive. Japan's policy orientation is also criticized by Bhagwati as a mistake for "encouraging too much bilateralism" because, "if people find that they can push Japan like this, they will do it to even weaker countries." He argues that Japan is not as closed as is often portrayed and that it should have taken its trade disputes with the United States to GATT for impartial adjudication. In 1996 when the Semiconductor Agreement came up for renewal, Tokyo did resist successfully Washington's demand for numerical targets. In the new agreement, international forms would be set up for producing countries to participate.

Japan was also involved in the Uruguay Round of multilateral GATT negotiations, and accepted its compromise agricultural agreement in 1993 that obligates Japan to provide "minimum access" opportunities for foreign exporters of rice. Japan banned the import of rice until 1993 because of political pressure from organized farmers, and is justly criticized by the United States and other rice exporting countries for that. Tokyo's rationalization of the ban in terms of domestic food security was neither convincing nor internationally acceptable. Instead of replacing the ban with tariffs, as was widely expected, the 1993 GATT agreement provides for specific annual minimum access quantities of rice imports for 1995–2000, after which renegotiation will take place. With the establishment of the

Wolrd Trade Organization (WTO) in 1995—which is itself the legacy of the Uruguay Round of GATT negotiations—trade dispute settlement mechanism is in place for adjudicating international trade disputes. Both Tokyo and Washington, as well as other countries, have begun to use it for dispute settlement. Japan was also a participant in a WTO telecommunications agreement reached in 1997. The agreement would open the telecommunications markets of participant countries to foreign capital and competition. This came at a time when Japan is increasingly deregulating its domestic market to spur competition and revive its sluggish economy. Thus the 1990s may be the beginning of genuine multilateralism for Japan's trade policy.

See also **trade pattern, yen–dollar exchange rate**.

Address

Ministry of International Trade and Industry
3-1, Kasumigaseki 1-chome, Chiyoda-ku, Tokyo 100
Tel: (3) 3501-1511

References

Balassa, Bela, and Narcus Noland. 1988. *Japan in the World Economy*. Washington: Institute for International Economics. Ch. 3.

Bhagwati, Jagdish. 1994. Both U.S. and Japanese trade policy off course. *Tokyo Business Today*, January: 34–36.

Katz, Richard. 1997. Japan's self-defeating trade policy: mainframe economics in a PC world. *Washington Quarterly* 20, 2: 153–81.

Komiya, Ryutaro. 1990. *The Japanese Economy: Trade, Industry, and Government*. Tokyo: University of Tokyo Press. Ch. 1.

Komiya, Ryutaro, and Kazutomo Irie. 1990. The U.S.–Japan trade problem: An economic analysis from a Japanese viewpoint. In *Japan's Economic Structure: Should It Change?* ed. by Kozo Yamamura. Seattle: Society for Japanese Studies.

Lincoln, Edward. 1990. *Japan's Unequal Trade*. Washington: Brookings Institution.

Prestowitz, Clyde V., Jr. 1987. U.S.–Japan trade friction: creating a new relationship. *California Management Review* 24, 2: 9–19.

Sato, Ryuzo, and John A. Rizzo. 1988. *Unkept Promises, Unclear Consequences: U.S. Economic Policy and the Japanese Response*. Cambridge: Cambridge University Press.

Sato, Ryuzo, and Julianne Nelson, eds. 1989. *Beyond Trade Friction: Japan–U.S. Economic Relations*. Cambridge: Cambridge University Press.

Shiraishi, Takashi. 1989. *Japan's Trade Policies: 1945 to the Present Day*. London: Athlone.

Yamakoshi, Atsushi. 1996. Taking the world trade organization to the next stage: Will Japan help move multilateralism forward? *JEI Report* 31A, August 16.

Table T.8
Leading trading companies (in ¥ billions)

	FY 1990		FY 1996	
Company	Sales	Profits[a]	Sales	Profits[a]
Mitsubishi Corp.	17,421.4	94.3	11.899.5	71.3
Sumitomo Corp.	19,212.6	77.2	12,710.7	107.7
Mitsui and Co.	18,234.1	66.1	13,339.8	64.1
Itochu Corp.[b]	20,596.0	54.4	14,176.4	51.7
Marubeni Corp.	19,015.6	54.8	13,498.9	15.9
Nissho Iwai Corp.	13,343.2	24.5	7,775.4	22.3

Sources: *Nikkei Weekly*, May 30, 1992 and May 26, 1997; *Japan Company Handbook*, various issues.
a. Pretax profits.
b. Better known in the West as C. Itoh and Co. before that name was dropped in October 1992.

trading companies   Unique to Japan, these companies are engaged in the marketing of products and other related services both in and outside of Japan. There are over 1,700 trading companies in Japan. Traditionally they are the main exporters and importers of the economy, although their shares of these businesses have declined since the early 1970s because of the structural changes in the economy.

About 16 of these companies are called *sogo shosha* (i.e., general trading companies). They deal with a wide range of products from raw materials to finished products and operate in many foreign countries. The industry is dominated by the six or nine largest general trading companies— Mitsubishi Corp., Sumitomo Corp., Mitsui and Co., Itochu Corp. (C. Itoh and Co.), Marubeni Corp., Nissho-Iwai Corp., Toyo Menka (Tomen), Nichimen Corp., and Kanematsu-Gosho. Of these, Itochu Corp. has had the largest sales in recent years, whereas Mitsubishi and Sumitomo Corp. have been the most profitable ones (see table T.8). Each of the top six is a core member of Japan's six financial **keiretsu**. In FY 1990 the top six alone had combined sales of ¥107.8 trillion, which declined to ¥99.8 trillion in FY 1991 and ¥73.2 trillion in FY 1996 because of recession in the economy. The financial problems of Southeast Asian countries in 1997–98 have also reduced their sales and profits, as all general trading companies have sizable business interests in those countries, particularly Indonesia.

Sogo shosha's traditional businesses have been in the low margin handling of bulk commodities such as crude oil, chemicals, metals, and machinery. The Big Nine alone typically handle more than half of Japan's imports (67% in 1987, 56% in 1990, and 38.5% in 1996). For the products they imported, they serve as the wholesalers in domestic distribution. They have also performed the exporting function for small manufacturers who are too small to engage in the export business themselves, and they have provided credit to small- and medium-sized companies. They serve as "quasi banks," since they borrow from banks and lend to their corporate clients. The large trading companies are also the first Japanese firms in the postwar period to make **direct overseas investments**. Often they assisted small Japanese firms to establish manufacturing facilities abroad by forming joint ventures with them and with local interests. They serve as general contractors for overseas development construction projects. They are also engaged in third-country trade where both the buyer and seller are non-Japanese. With the opening of the markets in Eastern Europe and the former Soviet Union, large trading companies are among the first to set up joint ventures there.

The strength of the general trading companies lies in their worldwide network of communications and business ties, their marketing expertise, financial resources, and their economies of scale. They are particularly adept in arranging complex package deals that involve simultaneously exporting, importing, and financing, such as counterpurchase trade with the (former) communist countries and the Third World countries. The largest six trading companies are members of the six financial *keiretsu* groups and can draw on the expertise of other companies of their respective groups in their business dealings. Yoshino and Lifson (1986) stress that *sogo shosha* perform a unique function of combining the flexibility of the market with the advantage of integrated planning for their clients, while the latter retain their freedom of choice and independence.

In the 1980s, as capital shortage became capital surplus in Japan, the financing function of the trading companies became less important. Most Japanese companies have also become more internationalized, selling their products through their own marketing departments. These have resulted in losses in the 1980s for many trading companies, especially the medium-sized ones. The telecommunications revolution has also produced many products that are new to them. The trading companies thus see diversification into new products or activities as crucial to their future vitality. For example, most of the leading trading companies are said to have set up special departments in recent years to advise clients on **mergers and acquisitions**. But the initial investment costs of starting new business lines are high for medium-sized trading companies. Consequently mergers may be a practical solution for them, as some have already opted to do.

In the late 1990s **financial liberalization** and the general corporate financial stringency have given large trading companies another business area for diversification, namely the securities business. Nissho Iwai Corp. was the first trading company to do so by establishing a securities subsidiary in 1998. The subsidiary is designed to expedite financing within the Nissho Iwai Group and to expand financial services for customers. It is not engaged in stock brokering for the general public.

See also *keiretsu* **and business groups, Mitsui Group, Mitsubishi Group, Sumitomo Group**.

Addresses

Itochu Corp.
1-3, Kyutaro-machi 4-chome, Chuo-ku, Osaka
Tel: (6) 241-2121   Fax: (3) 3497-7915

Marubeni Corp.
1-4-2, Ohtemachi, Chiyoda-ku, Tokyo
Tel: (3) 3282-2111   Fax: (3) 3282-2331

Mitsubishi Corp.
6-3, Marunouchi 2-chome, Chiyoda-ku, Tokyo 100
Tel: (3) 3210-2121   Fax: (3) 3210-8051

Mitsui and Co.
2-1, Ohtemachi 1-chome, Chiyoda-ku, Tokyo 100
Tel: (3) 3285-1111   Fax: (3) 3285-9819

Nissho Iwai Corp.
5-8, Imabashi 2-chome, Chuo-ku, Osaka 541
Tel: (6) 209-2111   Fax: (3) 3588-4919

Sumitomo Corp.
4-5-33, Kitahama, Chuo-ku, Osaka 541
Tel: (6) 220-6000   Fax: (3) 3217-6842

References

Choy, Jon. 1996. Japan's sogo shosha: Old dogs and new tricks. *JEI Report* 30A, August 9.

Eli, Max. 1990. *Global Strategies of Japanese Trading Corporations*. New York: McGraw-Hill.

Iwao, Ichiishi. 1995. Sogo shosha: Meeting new challenges. *Journal of Japanese Trade and Industry*, no. 1: 16–18.

Kim, W. Chan. 1986. Global diffusion of the general trading company concept. *Sloan Management Review* 27, 4: 35–43.

Market evolution saps trading house power. *Japan Economic Journal*, March 16, 1991: 14.

Sasaki, Sei. 1998. Traders hit by Asian woes, slump at home. *Nikkei Weekly*, May 25: 1, 3.

Sogo shosha: Sales department of Japan, Inc. *Tokyo Business Today*. April 1986: 50–55.

Sumiya, Fumio. 1993. Trading titans: Agile enough to thrive? *Nikkei Weekly*, July 26: 1.

Yonekawa, Shin'ichi, and Hideki Yoshihara, eds. 1987. *Business History of General Trading Companies*. Tokyo: University of Tokyo Press. Chs. 1–3.

Yoshino, M. Y., and Thomas Lifson. 1986. *The Invisible Link: Japan's Sogo Shosha and the Organization of Trade*. Cambridge: MIT Press.

treasury bill market   One of the short-term money markets open to both financial and nonfinancial institutions, in which short-term government treasury bills are traded to lend and borrow money.

See **money markets**.

trust banks   Trust banks are financial institutions that are engaged in both a trust business and banking operations and are required by law to maintain separate trust and banking accounts. In the trust business, they manage various types of assets (money, pension, securities, real estate, etc.) as trustees for their clients. In the banking business, they accept deposits, mainly demand deposits from large corporations and lend for working capital. Lending in the trust accounts is primarily long-term loans for plant and equipment.

There are seven traditional trust banks in Japan—Mitsubishi, Sumitomo, Mitsui, Yasuda, Toyo, Chuo, and Nippon—with a total of 426 branches as of June 1996. Six of them were converted from prewar trust companies in 1948. All seven concentrate on trust business. One **city bank** (Daiwa Bank) and two regional banks (Bank of Ryukyu and Bank of Okinawa) also operate a trust business, but banking operations are their major business area. Several foreign banks are also engaged in the trust business. Beginning in April 1993, **financial liberalization** permits **securities companies** to set up subsidiaries to enter some trust-banking business, but these subsidiaries are not full-fledged trust banks and their business volume has been small.

In the trust business, arrangements are made under which assets belonging to an individual or a company are placed in the custody of the trustee who, depending on the type of trust, manages them for the benefits of the owner or a third party. There are many types of trusts in Japan, including money trusts, pension trusts, loan trusts, securities investment trusts, employees' property formation benefit trusts, and land trusts. In a land trust the landowner entrusts the land to the trust bank, which raises funds, builds an income-producing structure such as an office building or a shopping mall, finds tenants and manages the building or sells it, and pays

Table T.9
Deposits and profits of trust banks

	Deposits (in ¥ trillions)		Pretax profits (in ¥ billions)
Bank	9/30/1990	3/31/1996	FY 1997
Mitsubishi Trust and Banking	30.40	31.85	5.6
Sumitomo Trust and Banking	28.13	29.32	−93.4
Mitsui Trust and Banking	26.13	27.84	4.4
Yasuda Trust and Banking	22.15	22.34	−151.3
Toyo Trust and Banking	17.01	19.10	16.0
Chuo Trust and Banking	10.66	11.92	9.1
Nippon Trust and Banking	3.46	3.58	−200.7

Sources: Federation of Bankers' Association of Japan for deposits and *Nikkei Weekly*, June 1, 1998, for profits.
Note: Excludes subsidiaries of securities companies that entered trust-banking business since 1993.

the trust owner the earnings from the operation. The trust bank usually receives between 5% and 10% of the rental income. After the contract period—usually 20 years—expires, the property owners get back full property rights and rental revenue or trust dividends. Land trusts were popular in the late 1980s because of the real estate inflation.

Table T.9 gives the total deposits (combining banking and trust accounts) of the seven banks. It shows that the deposits of trust banks had little growth between September 1990 and June 1996 while their pretax profits plummeted in FY 1997. Pretax profits were much smaller than core-business profits (not shown in table) in FY 1997 because large bad debts incurred during the **bubble economy** in the late 1980s were written off against core-business profits.

See also **banking system, city banks**.

Addresses

Mitsubishi Trust and Banking
4-5, Marunouchi 1-chome, Chiyoda-ku, Tokyo
Tel: (3) 3212-1211

Mitsui Trust and Banking
1-1, Nihonbashi-muromachi 2-chome, Chuo-ku, Tokyo
Tel: (3) 3270-9511

Sumitomo Trust and Banking
5-33, Kitahama 4-chome, Osaka-shi, Osaka
Tel: (6) 220-2121

Yasuda Trust and Banking
2-1, Yaesu 1-chome, Chuo-ku, Tokyo
Tel: (3) 3278-8111

References

Bank of Japan. Annual. *Economic Statistics Annual.*

Federation of Bankers Associations of Japan. 1994. *The Banking Systme in Japan.* Tokyo: Zenginkyo. Chs. 1, 4.

Ishibashi, Asako. 1998. Trust banks' core business hollowing out. *Nikkei Weekly*, June 1; 12.

Suzuki, Yoshio, ed. 1987. *The Japanese Financial System.* Oxford: Oxford University Press. Ch. 5.

Tatewaki, Kazuo. 1991. *Banking and Finance in Japan.* London: Routledge. Ch. 7.

Trust Fund Bureau   A bureau of the **Ministry of Finance**. Postal savings and public pensions are deposited with the bureau and used in the **Fiscal Investment and Loan Program**.
    See **Fiscal Investment and Loan Program**.

tsusansho (tsusan sangyo sho)   The **Ministry of International Trade and Industry** (MITI), the powerful ministry that has been responsible for formulating and implementing Japan's postwar **industrial policy** and **trade policy**. Various industries including the **small and medium enterprises** and various stores in the **distribution system** are under its jurisdiction.
    See **Ministry of International Trade and Industry**.

U

underworld "businesses" Japan has low crime rates by international standards. However, organized crime and its associated underworld "businesses" are present in some sectors of the economy.

Japan's National Police Agency estimates that the nation has a total of 3,490 mobster organizations and 90,600 gang members or *yakuza* at the end of 1992 and 79,900 members at the end of 1996. Of this number, 33,600 belonged to the Yamaguchi-gumi, the largest and most powerful crime syndicate. Other crime syndicates are Sumiyoshi-kai (10,900 members) and Inagawa-kai (8,800 members). Thus the Japanese penchant for big groups is seen even in underworld "businesses." Their largest source of income was dealing in drugs, followed by gambling and bookmaking, business-protection, mediation of disputes, credit collection, violence against companies, prostitution, and so on.

Gangsters are also involved in legitimate businesses such as money lending, construction, and real estate. However, even in these legitimate businesses, the gangsters resort to shady practices and profit from the power of their gangs. For example, indirectly through their ties with many finance companies, their loan sharking exacts high interest rates from the desperate borrowers, and late payments or defaults are dealt with harshly. The gangsters also control the day-labor market in construction.

Some gangsters have been involved in **stock market** manipulation with funding from securities firms. In 1991 it was revealed that affiliates of Japan's two leading securities firms, Nomura Securities Co. and Nikko Securities Co., were involved in gangster's speculative stock purchases. The crime syndicates were also compensated by the securities houses for investment losses.

Gangsters have also penetrated the real estate business. The *jisageya* are those who intimidate owners of land into selling their properties to developers. *Jisageya* are those who act to prevent the sale of collateral properties unless they are paid off by those trying to sell them.

There is a "traditionalist" side to *yakuza* that is said to appeal to some nostalgic Japanese. Japanese gangs are highly organized, and the gangsters are said to have a moral code of their own with extraordinary emphasis on seniority and loyalty, which evokes the ancient *samurai* (warrior) tradition.

Another type of unethical "business," uniquely Japanese, is practiced by extortionists who are usually tied to the gangsters. Called *sokaiya*, these extortionists are self-styled shareholders' rights advocates who exhort money from companies by threatening to disrupt shareholders' meetings by revealing company's internal scandals. They buy a minimum amount of a company's shares to get into shareholders' meetings. Once paid off by the companies, however, they intimidate other shareholders instead. In their peak in the 1970s, *sokaiya* were paid more than ¥10 billion annually. The revision of the Commercial Law in 1982 made such payments illegal and drove *sokaiya* underground. Their number is estimated to have declined from a peak of 6,800 in 1982 to about 1,000 in 1996 (*Japan Times*, July 7, 1996: 4). They have remained nevertheless powerful. In 1997 alone nearly two dozen senior executives from ten companies including Nomura Securities Co. and Dai-Ichi-Kangyo Bank were arrested for paying off such extortionists.

In their efforts to minimize possible disruption by these extortionists, many companies hold their annual shareholder meetings on the same day and try to speed up meeting proceedings. Some companies reportedly finish their meetings in less than 30 minutes! Such practice sacrifices shareholders rights for management expediency and raises serious questions about the nature of Japanese **business ethics** and **corporate governance**. Furthermore, the fact that such racketeers can still intimidate high corporate executives or the so-called "corporate *samurai*" despite the law banning their activities raises questions about the society itself.

A new law became effective in March 1992 that will enable Japanese police to deal with the crime syndicates more effectively. The syndicates may face prosecution if they are found to have engaged in any of 11 types of racketeering.

See also **business ethics, corporate governance**.

Address

National Police Agency
1-2, Kasumigaseki 2-chome, Chiyoda-ku, Tokyo 100
Tel: (3) 3581-0141

References

Corporate courage needed to fight "Mafia capitalism." *Nikkei Weekly*, July 13, 1991: 6.

Hirao, Sachiko. 1991. Despite new laws, *yakuza* groups find way into firms, capital. *Japan Times*, May 20–26: 8.

Idei, Yas. 1991. Corporate chiefs ready to face strong-arm *sokaiya*. *Japan Economic Journal*, May 4: 6.

Itoh, Yoshiaki. 1993. Anti-gang law wracks mob ranks. *Nikkei Weekly*. March 22: 1, 23.

Japan's gangsters: Honourable mob. *The Economist*, January 27, 1990: 19–22.

Kanabayashi, Masayoshi, and Marcus W. Brauchli. 1991. Japanese gangsters' expanding role in the economy worries law enforcement, government officials. *Asian Wall Street Journal Weekly*, June 10: 11.

Kaplan, David E., and Alec Dubro. 1986. *Yakuza*. Reading, MA: Addison-Wesley.

Lincoln, Edward. 1997. Crackdown won't open Japan's corporate closets. *Asian Wall Street Journal Weekly*, November 24: 21.

Morishita, Kaoru. 1997. Scandals put corporate culture on trial. *Nikkei Weekly*, June 23: 4.

Sokaiya playing new game, but message is same. *Japan Times*, July 24: 3.

Wanner, Barbara. 1998. *Sokaiya* scandals, economic woes spotlight Japanese corporate governance. *JEI Report* 3A, January 23.

unemployment   Unemployed persons in Japan are defined as those who have no jobs, do not do any work, but are able and willing to work and have made efforts to find a job. Unemployment as a ratio of the labor force in postwar Japan has been consistently much lower than that in other industrialized countries. Table U.1 shows the unemployment rate in Japan, the United States, Germany, and Britain in selective years.

The official unemployment statistics require some qualification, however. The figures for Japan understate the real extent of unemployment because workers temporarily released from work by companies with partial pay during a recession are not included in the statistics; yet these workers are not really working, although they are not laid off in the Western sense. In addition many "discouraged," disabled persons are not actively seeking work because of the discrimination against them and the great difficulties they encounter in getting to the workplace. Similarly unemployment figures for the United States do not include many "discouraged" workers who do not bother to look for work because of the futility of such attempts. Nevertheless, it is clear that real Japanese unemployment has been lower than that of other countries.

Table U.1
International comparison of unemployment rates (in %)

Year	Japan	United States	Germany, FR	Britain
1975	1.9	8.3	4.7	4.1
1980	2.0	7.0	3.8	3.8
1985	2.6	7.1	9.3	11.9
1988	2.5	5.4	8.7	5.4
1989	2.3	5.2	7.9	6.3
1990	2.1	5.5	7.2	5.9
1991	2.1	6.7	6.3	8.1
1992	2.2	7.4	6.6	9.9
1993	2.5	6.9	8.2	10.4
1994	2.9	6.1	9.6	9.2
1995	3.1	5.6	9.4	8.1
1996	3.3 (2.3)[a]	5.4 (7.2)	10.3 (4.0)	7.4 (2.1)
1997 (December)	3.45			
1998 (April)	4.13			

Source: Bank of Japan.
a. The number in parentheses indicates the number of unemployed in millions.

Table U.2 gives the unemployment rate by age and sex in 1990 and 1996. For both males and females in all age groups, the unemployment rates were significantly higher in 1996 than in 1990 when the **bubble economy** just ended. Also the unemployment rate of both males and females aged 15–19 is about triple that of the national rate. These teens are particularly hard hit by the long stagnation of the economy. Except for the groups aged 15–19, 55–64, and 65 and over, the female unemployment rate is higher than that of males. It can be seen that the unemployment rate of males aged 15–24 is double that of the national rate; it is also high for females of that age group. The rate for males aged 55 and over is also relatively high but is surprisingly low for their female counterparts. Presumably older women who have to work are willing to do low-paying menial work such as cleaning and vending that are shunned by younger workers.

Unemployed persons receive unemployment benefits if they have been covered by **employment insurance**. The amount and duration of benefits depend on the wage level while employed, age (longer for older unemployed), the period of employment insurance, and the nature of employment status (regular, part-time, or seasonal).

See also **employment discrimination, employment insurance**.

Table U.2
Unemployment rate by age and sex (in %)

Age	1990		1996	
	Male	Female	Male	Female
All ages	2.0	2.2	3.4	3.3
15–19	7.4	5.7	10.3	9.1
20–24	3.7	3.7	6.1	6.2
25–34	1.8	3.1	3.3	5.2
35–44	1.2	1.8	2.1	2.6
45–54	1.1	1.5	2.0	2.0
55–64	3.4	1.4	5.1	2.6
65+	1.4	0.0	2.1	0.6

Source: Management and Coordination Agency.

References

Bank of Japan. Annual. *Comparative Economic and Financial Statistics.*

Bank of Japan. Monthly. *Monthly Report of Recent Economic and Financial Developments.*

Institute of Labor. Annual. *Japanese Working Life Profile.*

Management and Coordination Agency. Annual. *Japan Statistical Yearbook.*

Uruguay Round   Started in September 1986, this is the eighth and last round of multilateral trade negotiations conducted under the auspices of the General Agreement on Tariffs and Trade (GATT). World agricultural trade liberalization was one of the main issues. It concluded in December 1993 with an agricultural agreement in which Japan is committed to importing specific "minimum access" quantities of rice annually between 1995 and 2000. This marked the end of the government ban on rice imports in Japan.

The Uruguay Round also established the World Trade Organization in 1995 to replace GATT as the institutional framework for international trade negotiations. Dispute settlement mechanism was set up to adjudicate trade disputes. It is expected that this will help steer the **trade policy** of Japan and the United States away from the bilateral negotiations of the 1970s and 1980s toward multilateral negotiations.

See also **rice production and distribution, trade policy**.

V

venture companies and venture capital Japan's venture companies or start-up companies face a number of obstacles to growth. One of them is the small size of the venture capital. The others, which stem from the structure of the economy, are the dominance of large established corporations in R&D spending and in manufacturing expertise; the complicated distribution network that favors brand names and personal contacts; the prestige, higher wages, and traditional **lifetime employment** system of large companies, which make it difficult for small businesses to recruit experienced managers and workers. These structural factors increase the risks of start-up venture companies and hence reduce the willingness of venture capitalists to invest in them.

There are two sources of venture capital, that is, funds to finance new business ventures independent of affiliation with an established large company. The first and relatively minor source is the three semipublic small business development companies jointly established by the government (the Small Business Finance Corporation) and the private sector. These companies are Tokyo Small Business Development Co., Osaka Small Business Development Co., and Nagoya Small Business Development Co. They provide **investment** consultation and may subscribe to the newly issued stocks of qualified small businesses. However, their funds are very limited.

Private venture capital companies constitute the second and a larger source of funds. There were 130 such companies in 1996, established and funded by banks, **securities companies**, and **insurance companies**. The largest by far of these is Japan Associated Finance Co., founded by Nomura Securities Co. in 1973. The second largest is Nippon Investment Finance Co., founded by Daiwa Securities Co. in 1982. In 1982–85, following the computerization of Japanese businesses and homes and the development of new high-technology industries, these venture capital companies were active in financing innovative start-up firms. However, many of the new high-tech firms failed in 1985–87, causing losses to the venture capitalists. Consequently venture capital companies have scaled down their investments and shifted their loans to the service sector, since the Japanese economy itself is becoming more service oriented. In addition some of the venture capital companies have invested in the newly industrializing economies of East Asia, particularly Hong Kong and Taiwan with their numerous small and innovative companies.

In the late 1980s and early 1990s Japan's venture capital companies underwent a period of new growth. Their number increased from 80 at the end of 1985 to 100 in mid-1990. One favorable factor was the development of the **over-the-counter** (OTC) **market**. Following the liberalization of the OTC market rules such as the public offering of shares, more medium-sized companies became interested in listing their shares on the market. Japanese investors saw growth potential in some of these companies. As a result the OTC market grew rapidly in the late 1980s and early 1990s, and its trading volume was not affected by the fall in the **Tokyo Stock Exchange** in 1990. Since venture capital companies assist unlisted firms for public offering of their shares in the OTC market, they have stepped up their business operations. Since 1993 when the separation between the securities business and the banking business was reduced by **financial liberalization**, both securities companies and banks are safeguarding their future businesses by various means, including the promotion of the venture capital business of their subsidiaries.

The mid-1990s (1994–96) saw increased flow of venture capital to venture businesses. There are three reasons for this. (1) Because of the prolonged stagnation of the economy and the lackluster performance of the large companies, investors as well as governments officials saw new innovative enterprises as the new area of growth to stimulate the economy. (2) Because of record low interest rates in the mid-1990s, returns on investment in the financial markets were also low. Financial institutions therefore were willing to provide more funds for investment in venture companies through their subsidiaries. In FY 1996 venture capital companies invested a record ¥231.8 billion in business ventures, up 51% from the previous year's level. (3) The government saw the importance of innovative small firms and took measures to promote them. In 1995 the Ministry of Finance approved the establishment of the Frontier Market, a second OTC market for fast-growing small companies with easier listing requirements. Some 100 firms went public on the OTC market in 1996.

The flow of venture capital quickly subsided in 1997–98 for three reasons. (1) The main reason was tightened credit because banks had to meet a higher capital/asset ratio as part of the banking reform, which led them to reduce loans (which count as asset). Amid such fund stringency, loans to venture companies were the first to cut. (2) To make matters worse, the expected high growth of venture firms did not materialize, thus hurting investors' confidence. (3) The rapid increase in 1996 in the initial public offerings of stocks by newly listed firms on the OTC market led to over-supply of stocks in the market. As a result the Nikkei OTC Average declined to a record low in April 1997. Bankruptcies of venture companies rose to 72 in FY 1997, up 80% from the previous year's level.

Because Japan's venture capital companies are set up by securities companies and banks, they have been criticized by analysts for favoring low-risk, established mid-sized businesses over developing firms, and for striving to develop new clients for their parent company's main business rather than to promote innovative venture businesses. There is a consensus that venture capitalism is weak in Japan. This has important implications for the future growth of the economy.

See also **over-the-counter market**.

References

Adventures in venture business. *Tokyo Business Today*, February 1995: 12–15.

Beresford, Martin D. 1996. Japan must take steps to spur venture capitalism. *Asian Wall Stree Journal*, December 9: 14.

Borton, James W. 1991. *Venture Japan: How Growing companies Worldwide Can Tap into the Japanese Venture Capital Markets*. Chicago: Probus.

Choy, Jon. 1995. Venture capital in Japan: If at first you don't succeed.... *JEI Report* 7A, February 24.

Clark, Rodney. 1987. *Venture Capital in Britain, America and Japan*. London: Croom Helm. Ch. 3.

Inoue, Tatsuya. 1998. Venture-capital stream slows to trickle. *Nikkei Weekly*, October 20: 10.

Morishita, Kaoru. 1997. Credit squeeze pinches venture firms. *Nikkei Weekly*, December 29: 6.

Niimi, Kazumasa, and Yuri Okina. 1995. What is stopping the growth of venture business in Japan? *Japan Research Quarterly* 4, 3: 3–60.

Takita, Makoto. 1995. Techno-ventures are thriving. *Tokyo Business Today*, December: 4–8.

VLSI Research Cooperative Very Large-Scale Integrated Circuit Research Cooperative, a government-guided research cooperative of five major computer companies between 1976 and 1980.

See **electronics industry, industry policy**.

voluntary export restraint (VER)   Requests made by Washington since
the 1970s to Tokyo, and also to some newly industrializing economies, to
"voluntarily" restrict exports of certain products (textiles, automobiles,
machine tools, steel, etc.) to the United States for a certain period of time
to prevent sharp increases in these imports. Tokyo invariably complied
with such requests in order to protect Japan's exports to the United
States, for the alternative would have been a more severe trade sanction
imposed by Washington. Because the United States had a large and
growing trade deficit with Japan, the U.S. Congress became increasingly
protectionist regarding Japanese exports and demanded such measures to
protect domesitc industries.

See **automobile industry, steel industry, trade pattern, trade policy**.

W

wage structure The wages an employee received in Japan depend on several factors—age, sex, education, job status, nature of industry, size of establishment, and so on. These factors affect both the starting wage level and subsequent annual wage increases; they affect both the regular monthly contractual wages and the biannual bonuses.

Most Japanese employees are recruited right after graduation from high school, junior college, or university, and work continually for one company until retirement or for a substantial number of years. These are the standard or regular employees who are the concern of most government statistics and who receive much more wages and benefits than nonregular employees.

Standard employees' starting wages are determined by the educational level and sex. High school graduates are usually the production workers; university graduates are the candidates for managerial positions. Female graduates are recruited for clerical-track positions, whereas male graduates are recruited for career-track positions. In subsequent years wages will increase every year with age or seniority. This is the *nenko*, or seniority-based, wage system which still prevails in most companies, although in some companies it is modified or outweighed by merit or performance. However, the annual increase will be different for different workers, depending on sex, education, job status, and so forth. The **spring offensive** is the ritualized procedure through which unions launch their demand for annual wage increases for negotiation with employers.

Employees' wage earnings include the monthly contractual wages and biannual bonuses, given in June–July and December, which are based on company profits. Individual employee's bonuses also vary with seniority, education, and job status.

Table W.1 shows the average contractual earnings of standard employees by age and sex. It shows that at age 50–54, female employee's wages

Table W.1
Contractual earnings of standard employees by age and sex

Age	Female	Male	Female/male ratio
18–19	163	191	85.3%
20–24	193	229	84.3
25–29	223	282	79.1
30–34	240	340	70.6
35–39	247	383	64.5
40–44	241	417	57.8
45–49	237	445	53.3
50–54	235	460	51.8

Source: Management and Coordination Agency.
Note: Average of all industries, in ¥1,000 per month; June 1996.

Table W.2
Earnings of standard employees by age and education (male, 1995 in ¥1,000)

Age	Senior high school graduates		University graduates	
	Wages/month	Bonuses/year	Wages/month	Bonuses/year
18	162.6	10.5	—	—
22	192.2	751.1	202.5	19.7
30	268.4	1,154.2	299.4	1,410.9
40	380.4	1,842.4	449.6	2,304.9
50	515.9	2,681.7	605.2	3,275.7
54[a]	549.0	2,795.1	664.7	3,707.0
60	438.8	2,416.1	597.0	3,083.7

Source: Ministry of Labor.
a. The age of peak earnings for both categories of employees.

in 1996 were 1.4 times those of 18- to 19-year-old females. for males the ratio was 2.4 times. It also shows that at the same age and with the same seniority, a man always makes more than a woman. Furthermore the differentials between male and female earnings increase with age due to limited opportunities for promotion for most women in their clerical-track positions.

The role of education as well as age can be seen in table W.2. In 1995 an average male high school graduate starting work at age 18 made ¥162,600 a month with small bonuses. A university graduate starting work at age 22 earned about the same wage as a high school graduate with four years of seniority, but with less bonuses. Two years later (not

Table W.3
Wage indexes of standard employees by sector (1995 = 100)

	1980	1990	1996
All industries	64.2	91.1	101.6
Mining	62.0	86.0	103.2
Construction	54.8	86.8	101.1
Manufacturing	62.0	90.6	102.5
Transport and communication	63.7	92.9	92.9
Wholesale and retail trade	69.1	91.7	91.7
Finance and insurance	60.9	90.6	90.6
Real estate	65.5	104.3	104.3
Services	69.7	93.3	93.3

Source: Ministry of Labor.

shown in table W.2), the university graduate would earn more salary and bonuses as well. Since the high school graduate is likely to be a production worker and the university graduate a management-track candidate, the differences in regular wages and bonuses continued to widen with the increase in ages. At age 54 the earnings of both reach their peak. At age 60 both persons are likely to have retired from the original company and are working at a subsidiary at reduced pay. The university-educated executive continued to draw high pay but reduced bonuses. It should be added that graduates of two-year junior colleges are likely to earn significantly less than university graduates because the former are predominantly women in clerical positions.

An employee's earnings are affected by his (her) position or job status, although this is correlated with age and education. For example, in 1995 a company director made an average of ¥629,200 in monthly regular salary and ¥3,109,700 in annual bonuses, a section chief made ¥515,600 and ¥2,529,500, and a chief clerk ¥420,200 and ¥1,809,800 for monthly regular wages and annual bonuses, respectively.

Finally employee wages vary from industry to industry. The ranking of industries in their employee wages also changes over time, reflecting structural changes of the economy and of the labor market. Table W.3 shows the wage indexes of standard or regular employees in various sectors. It can be seen that wholesale and retail trade and services were high-paying sectors in 1981 but were no longer so in 1996. On the other hand, construction was low paying in 1980 but had become a high-paying sector by 1996. Real estate was only slightly above average in wages in

1980 but became the highest-wage sector in 1990 and 1996. It should be added that the earnings of nonregular employees are much lower and are not included in the statistics.

Analytically some economists have debated the nature of bonuses of Japanese companies. Freeman and Weitzman (1987) regard them as profit sharing and hence a source of wage flexibility for companies. Others regard them as relatively rigid or as deferred wage payment (cited in Aoki, 1988: 176–78). The debate is inconclusive. In a different vein, Hart and Kawasaki (1995) regard bonus payments as returns to specific human capital investments, while Jones and Kato (1995) have found that increases in bonus stimulate employee incentives and productivity.

See also **minimum wages**.

References

Aoki, Masahiko. 1988. *Information, Incentives, and Bargaining in the Japanese Economy*. Cambridge: Cambridge University Press.

Freedman, R., and M. Weitzman. 1987. Bonuses and employment in Japan. *Journal of the Japanese and International Economies*, 1: 168–94.

Hart, Robert A., and Seiichi Kawasaki. 1995. The Japanese bonus system and human capital. *Journal of the Japanese and International Economies* 9: 225–44.

Jones, Derek C., and Takao Kato. 1995. The productivity effects of employee stock-ownership plans and bonuses: evidence from Japanese panel data. *American Economic Review* 85: 391–414.

Management and Coordination Agency. Annual. *Japan Statistical Yearbook*.

Ministry of Labor. Annual. *Basic Survey on Wage Structure*.

Tachibanaki, Toshiaki. 1996. *Wage Determination and Distribution in Japan*. Oxford: Clarendon Press.

warrant bonds   Also referred to as *equity-warrant bonds*, these are a special type of corporate bond with equity warrants attached to them to lower the interest cost of corporate borrowing. The warrants are certificates that give investors the right to buy a fixed amount of new shares of the issuing company at a predetermined price (called *exercise price*) for a relatively long period such as four years. If the stock price goes up during that period, investors can buy the shares at the lower exercise price, thereby making a profit. In return for this option, investors accept a lower interest rate on the bond. Warrants can also be detached from the bonds by the securities firm that underwrite them and traded on the secondary market. In 1990 their value was said to be about 20% of the face value of the warrant bond issued by Japanese corporations on the Euromarket. Thus, if the equity-purchase warrants are not exercised because of falling stock prices, investors stand to lose this amount.

Warrant bonds can be denominated in yen or in a foreign currency, mostly the dollar or Swiss franc. The Eurodollar warrant bond is traded in the Euromarket, primarily London. First introduced in 1981, the volume of Eurodollar bonds issues by Japanese corporations on the Euromarket grew rapidly in the late 1980s. Most of them were bought by Japanese investors, mainly institutions. However, with the slump in Japan's stock prices since 1990, the market dwindled; many warrants expired unexercised and became worthless. Some major **securities companies** reportedly have repurchased equity warrants near expiration to cover the losses of their major clients.

Domestic offerings of warrant bonds have been small. The largest total amount issued was ¥915 billion in FY 1989, after which it declined to ¥382 billion in FY 1990 and to zero in FY 1992 through 1996. Total outstanding amount stood at ¥277 billion at the end of FY 1996.

See also **bond market**.

References

Bank of Japan. Annual. *Economic Statistics Annual*. Japan

Securities Research Institute. 1998. *Securities Market in Japan, 1998*. Ch. 4.

welfare programs
See **social security system**.

wholesale trade
See **distribution system**.

wholesale price index
See **price indexes, and price levels**.

window guidance   Guidelines or **administrative guidance** given by the **Bank of Japan** to commercial banks concerning the appropriate levels of their loans. Once an important policy instrument of the Bank, it was officially discontinued in June 1991 as part of the **financial liberalization**.

See **Bank of Japan**.

women in the labor force Despite the constitutional guarantee of sexual equality (Article 14), the equal pay provisions of the Labor Standards Law, and the ratification of the **Equal Employment Opportunity Law** in 1986, Japanese women still lag behind their male counterparts in employment, wages, and promotion opportunities. Nevertheless, women's participation in the **labor force** has increased, and the number of management positions held by women has increased over the years, although the rate of increase is relatively slow.

Of Japan's labor force, women constituted 31.8% in 1965, 34.1% in 1980, and 40.5% in 1996. These steady increases can be attributed to three factors:

1. Expansion of the service sectors in the economy, such as retail, finance, and banking since the mid-1970s; these are traditionally female-intensive sectors.

2. Labor shortage in the economy in the 1980s.

3. Growing importance of women in the consumer market. This has led more companies to hire women for product development, marketing, and sales (Lam 1993: 199).

Yet the bulk of the female workers are concentrated in low-paying clerical jobs that require little training. For example, in 1995, 34.4% of female employees were clerical and related workers, 17.8% were craftswomen and production workers, and 12.6% were sales workers; only 14.8% were professional and technical workers. In addition a large percentage of female workers are part-time employees who work 35 hours or less a week with low pay and few benefits. These part-timers as a percentage of total female employees have increased from 12.2% in 1970 to 19.3% in 1980, and 34.9% in 1995. They tend to work in the wholesale and retail trade and other services in predominantly small-scale establishments with 1–29 employees.

Traditional family values, still strong in Japan, give women the primary responsibility for childcare and housework. In addition, day-care facilities are far from adequate for working women with young children. As a result women tend to interrupt their careers for marriage and child rearing after five to ten years of working. This reduces the average female employee's seniority as well as the employer's willingness to invest money in training female workers. After 10–15 years of absence from the labor market, a woman may return to work, but usually she has to restart at a low pay and often as a part-time worker. The part-time employment status gives her the flexibility needed to continue her role as the homemaker.

Given all these cultural, social, and economic factors, it is not surprising that few Japanese women hold management positions. According to the International Labor Organization, in 1995 only 8.2% of managerial positions in Japan were filled by women, compared with 42.7% in the United States and 18.7% in Hong Kong (*Nikkei Weekly*, February 23, 1998: 1). Most of the women who hold management positions are either section chiefs or deputy section chiefs, the lowest of managerial positions.

Women's earnings lag behind those of men with the same seniority, not only because they start up with a lower base pay but also because their salary increases are slower—they have less opportunities for promotion in their predominantly female clerical track as compared with the male-dominated general track from which management candidates are selected. As a result women's earnings as a percentage of those men of the same age decline with age. For example, according to the Ministry of Labor's survey statistics for June 1996, the average contractual earnings of standard female employees aged 18–19 were 85.3% of those male employees of the same age. The ratio declined to 70.6% at age 30–34, and 53.3% at age 45–49 (see table W.1, **wage structure**). Similarly, as of June 1996, a 20-year-old regular female production worker with senior high school education received 84% of the contractual wages of her male counterpart. The ratio declined to 71% at age 30 and 57% at age 40. Note that the figures are for regular employees who were hired immediately after graduation and who have worked continually for the same enterprise. For women who interrupted their career to raise children before returning to work, their earnings would be much less than those given for their ages.

Interestingly, an increasing number of Western companies with offices in Japan, unencumbered by the heavy weight of tradition, are hiring more educated Japanese women, especially those who have studied in the West, for managerial positions. Reflecting on this trend, Lansing and Ready (1988) have argued that this makes good business sense for foreign employers while contributing to worthy social changes in Japan.

In the future the role of women in the labor force is likely to increase further, partly because of the aging of the labor force and the labor shortage. The continuing diversification of the Japanese economy, including the growing importance of the service sector, will also provide new job opportunities for women.

Finally no discussion of discrimination against women in employment can be complete without mentioning the issue of sexual harassment.

Despite its modernization Japan remains a male-dominated society. As a microcosm of the society, the Japanese office, in businesses and government alike, invariably expects women to be in a subservient role. Although this is consistent with the Japanese culture, it can be argued that where institutionalized female subservience prevails, male transgressions may not be far behind. Instances of sexual harassment by superiors against female subordinates are increasingly reported in the press, but the society has yet to take them seriously. In a survey of 2,000 women conducted by the Ministry of Labor in June–July 1997, it was found that 62.1% of them had been victims of sexual harassment at least once. Only 5.5% of the companies surveyed had adopted any preventive measures, even though the revised **Equal Employment Opportunity Law** requires them to do so under Ministry of Labor guidelines (*Nikkei Weekly*, January 12, 1998: 17). However, when such a male-chauvinist attitude is transplanted to Japanese subsidiaries abroad, serious consequences can result, as shown by the law suit against the Mitsubishi Motor Co. in the United States in 1996 for alleged widespread sexual harassment. As Japanese executives begin to learn from their overseas experiences and realize that this aspect of Japanese culture has no place in the global economy, the situation in Japan in turn may be improved.

See also **employment pattern, Equal Employment Opportunity Law, labor force, labor laws, wage structure.**

Address

Women's Bureau, Ministry of Labor
2-2, Kasumigaseki 1-chome, Chiyoda-ku, Tokyo 100
Tel: (3) 3593-1211

References

Hill, M. Ann. 1990. Women in the Japanese labor force. In *Japan's Economic Challenge*. Washington: Government Printing Office.

Hunter, Janet, ed. 1993. *Japanese Women Working*. London: Routledge.

Lam, Alice. 1993. Equal employment opportunities for Japanese women: Changing company practice. In *Japanese Women Working*, ed. by Janet Hunter. London: Routledge.

Lansing, Paul, and Kathryn Ready. 1988. Hiring women managers in Japan: An alternative for foreign employers. *California Management Review* 30, 3: 112–27.

Lo, Jeannie. 1990. *Office Ladies, Factory Women: Life and Work at a Japanese Company*. Armonk, NY: M.E. Sharpe.

Maki, Omori. 1993. Gender and the labor market. *Journal of Japanese Studies* 19, 1: 79–102.

Murdo, Pat. 1991. Women in Japan's work world see slow change from labor shortage, Equal Employment Law. *JEI Report* 33A, August 30.

Ogawa, Naohiro and Robert L. Clark. 1995. Earnings patterns of Japanese women: 1976–1988. *Economic Development and Cultural Change* 43, 2: 293–313.

Ogawa, Naohiro, and John Ermisch. 1996. Family structure, home time demands, and the employment patterns of Japanese married women. *Journal of Labor Economics* 14, 1: 677–702.

Roberts, Glenda S. 1994. *Staying on the Line: Blue-Collar Women in Contemporary Japan.* Honolulu: University of Hawaii Press.

Saso, Mary. 1990. *Women in the Japanese Workplace.* London: Hilary Shipman.

working hours and stress   Japanese workers traditionally work more hours per year than their counterparts in other industrial countries. The number has declined only very slightly through 1991 despite repeated government urgings to reduce them. During the 1980s it was difficult to reduce working hours because of the **bubble economy** amid a labor shortage. The economic stagnation of the 1990s may finally be accomplishing what government exhortations have failed to achieve.

According to the Ministry of Labor surveys, the average *monthly* working hours for regular Japanese workers was 186.6 in 1970, 175.7 in 1978, 175.8 in 1985, 171.0 in 1990, 159.1 in 1995, and 159.9 in 1996. In manufacturing, which has longer hours than the average industry, the *annual* total working hours put in by Japanese workers were 1,975 per person in 1995, compared with 1,986 in the United States, 1,943 in Britain, 1,680 in France, and 1,550 in Germany. The Japanese regular *workweek* was 48 hours over 6 days until April 1989 when the Labor Standard Law was revised to cut statutory working hours from 48 to 44 hours. It was not until April 1997 that the Law was further revised to set 40 hours as the standard workweek.

Long working hours in Japan have led to the Western criticism that the Japanese overwork and underconsume, thereby contributing to Japan's export surplus. The Japanese bureaucrats have taken the criticism seriously, and since 1984 they have exhorted the private industries to cut their working hours despite the growing labor shortage in the economy in the late 1980s. In June 1992 the Miyazawa Cabinet adopted a five-year program to make Japan a "lifestyle superpower" in which the government set a new target of reducing working hours per person to 1,800 hours a year by the end of FY 1996. Clearly the nation failed to live up to the standard that the government had chosen for it.

There are wide variations among industries. In 1996 wholesale and retail trade, and restaurants, have the shortest working hours (150.1) per month, followed by finance and insurance (150.4) and services (152.3). Industries with the longest working hours are mining (182.1), fabricated metal products (181.0), lumber and wood products (180.0). These variations have changed over the years in accordance with labor market conditions.

Official survey statistics, however, should be taken with some qualifications. First, some numbers may be underestimates; respondents may have under-reported their working hours because working long hours is by now "politically incorrect," almost a social stigma. Second, the data do not include the unpaid overtime worked by employees at many companies, particularly the banks. Finally in many cases "there is no clear and formal distinction between working hours and leisure" in Japan (Deutschman 1991: 189). Male employees, in particular, are engaged in many "grey" activities which are neither work nor nonwork, such as socializing with colleagues after work or on weekends, unpaid overtime, and small-group activities. These activities may not be work in the technical sense, but they go with the job, are socially expected, but may not be welcomed by the individuals.

Official statistics on working hours cannot reflect the stress that come from such (traditionally long) working and nonworking hours and other corporate demands that many employees are obliged to comply with as part of the socially expected "salaryman loyalty." There is a special term, *karoshi*, that means literally death from overwork. The word has become part of the Japanese common vocabulary since the early 1980s, suggesting a widespread awareness of the phenomenon. Although the phenomenon is not unique to the Japanese, it is believed to be more prevalent among Japanese employees than among their counterparts elsewhere. Reliable statistics are lacking, however, because companies invariably deny its existence in order to avoid bad publicity and the legal and financial implications.

One particularly stressful demand of corporate life is related to job transfers to other cities for male office workers, often without the family accompanying them, lest the children's schooling for competitive examinations be disrupted. Because of all of these, many male office workers are said to suffer from alienation from their own families. Okifuji's (1990) portrayal of "men who can't go home" is a poignant reminder of the high human toll of the exacting corporate life in Japan, of which long working hours until recently are merely one manifestation.

See also **wage structure**.

References

Daimon, Sayuri. 1991. "Karoshi" phenonmenon spreading to female work force. *Japan Times* (weekly international ed.), September 3–October 6: 7.

Deutschmann, Christoph. 1991. The worker-bee syndrome in Japan: An analysis of working-time practices. In *Working Time in Transition: the Political Economy of Working Hours in Industrial Nations*, ed. by Karl Hinrichs, William Roche, and Carmen Sirianni. Philadelphia: Temple University Press.

Jorgenson, Dale W., and Masahiro Kuroda. 1990. Productivity and international competitiveness in Japan and the United States, 1960–1985. In *Productivity in the U.S. and Japan*, ed. by C. R. Hulten. Chicago: University of Chicago Press.

Kato, Tetsuro. 1994. The political economy of Japanese *karoshi* (death from overwork). *Hitotsubashi Jouranl of Social Studies* 26: 41–54.

Ministry of Labor. Annual. *Yearbook of Labor Statistics.*

National Defense Counsel for Victims of Karoshi. 1990. *Karoshi: When the "Corporate Warrior" Dies.* Tokyo: Madosha.

Okifuji, Noriko. 1990. Men who can't go home. *Japan Echo* 17, special issue: 48–52.

Saito, Tadashi. 1992. Quality of life in Japan: Is it affluent or not? *JEI Report* 22A, June 12.

Sakumoto, Tamokasu. 1997. Karoshi candidates and their working situation in Japan business. *Current Politics and Economics of Japan* 5, no. 1: 47–61.

Seward, Jack, and Howard Van Zandt. 1985. *Japan: The Hungary Guest—Japanese Business Ethics vs. Those of the U.S.* Tokyo: Lotus Press. Ch. 5.

Takahashi, Hideo. 1990. The long workweek in Japan: Difficult to reduce. *JEI Report*, March 16.

Y

yakuza   Japan's gangsters or members of organized-crime syndicate. See **underworld "businesses."**

yen bloc   A concept popular in the media and academic circles until recently that refers to the perceived East Asian economic bloc, centered on Japan, that is fast rising to rival the Western Hemisphere, centered on the United States, and Europe, centered on the European Community. Japan is seen as the center of the bloc in terms of trade, finance, and foreign direct investment, with the yen playing a pivotal role in all these areas.

Frankel (1993) finds that although East Asia has a preference for intraregional trade, Japan is not concentrating its trade with other Asian countries. However, there is evidence of Japanese influence in East Asia's financial markets. Part of the influence comes from the growing role of the yen in East Asia's trade and finance.

The concept implies that there is a conscious policy attempt, especially by Japan, to promote such a regional economic grouping. Frankel and Wei (1994: 312) contend, however, that "Japan is unusual among major countries in *not* having preferential trading arrangements with smaller neighboring countries." They conclude that there is no regional trading bloc centered on Japan.

See also **yen in international transactions.**

References

Brown, Drusilla K., Alan V. Deardorff, and Robert M. Stern. 1996. Computational analysis of the economic effects of an East Asian preferential trading bloc. *Journal of the Japanese and International Economies* 10: 37–70.

Frankel, Jeffrey. 1993. Is Japan creating a yen bloc in East Asia and the Pacific? In *Regionalism and Rivalry: Japan and the United States in Pacific Asia*, ed. by Jeffrey A. Frankel and Miles Kahler. Chicago: University of Chicago Press.

Frankel, Jeffrey, and Shang-Jin Wei. 1994. Yen bloc or dollar bloc: Exchange rate policies of the East Asian economies. In *Macroeconomic Linkage: Savings, Exchange Rates, and Capital Flows*, ed. by Takatoshi Ito and Anne O. Krueger. Chicago: University of Chicago Press.

Petri, Peter A. 1993. The East Asian trading bloc: An analytical history. In *Regionalism and Rivalry: Japan and the United States in Pacific Asia*, ed. by Jeffrey A. Frankel and Miles Kahler. Chicago: University of Chicago Press.

yen-denominated foreign bonds   Bonds issued in Japan in yen by nonresident institutions such as international agencies, foreign governments, and foreign private corporations. Popularly called *samurai* bonds. See *samurai* bonds.

Yen–Dollar Accord, 1984   An agreement reached in May 1984 between Tokyo and Washington in which Tokyo committed itself to substantial reforms of the Japanese financial markets.

Washington became involved in pressuring Tokyo for financial market reforms because of the large and growing trade deficits of the United States since the late 1970s. A large part of the deficits was with Japan. It was believed that one way to reduce the deficits was to increase the value of the yen vis-à-vis the dollar, thus making U.S. exports cheaper. The yen was considered by Washington to be undervalued in the early 1980s. Hence the initial negotiations were undertaken for the purpose of raising the yen value.

Because of the influence of the free market ideology during the Reagan administration in the early 1980s, Washington sought to raise the value of the yen, not through government intervention in the currency markets but through the reform of the Japanese financial markets (Brown 1994: 85). Such reform would help U.S. banks in Japan as well as U.S. exporters in general, many of whom had clamored for government assistance.

Tokyo yielded to Washington's pressure in order to avoid more protectionist measures that the U.S. Congress might otherwise undertake. It committed itself to the internationalization of the yen and the reform of the domestic **banking system.** The internationalization of the yen would end restriction on yen transactions in the Euromarket so that non-Japanese companies could issue unsecured yen-denominated bonds in the Euromarket. Washington hoped that this would increase the demand for the yen and hence its market value. The banking reform stipulated in the Accord involved deregulation of interest rates, access by foreign securities firms to the **Tokyo Stock Exchange**, liberalization of the government bond syndicate, the right for foreign banks to operate trust bank subsidiaries, and so forth. Washington hoped that interest rate deregulation would enable foreign banks in Japan to compete for deposits, and that it would also eliminate Japanese banks' low-cost advantage when operating abroad (Brown 1994: 110).

Tokyo has eventually implemented the provisions of the Accord, but at a deliberate pace as deemed appropriate by the **Ministry of Finance.** The scope of Japan's **financial liberalization** has subsequently exceeded what was envisioned in the Accord because of growing domestic pressure for deregulation. Nevertheless, the Accord constituted the first comprehensive commitment made by the Japanese government to financial reforms.

The rise of the yen, sought by Washington, proceeded rapidly in the late 1980s. It was brought about, not by the Yen–Dollar Accord itself but by the **Plaza Accord** of 1985 in which finance ministers from other major developed countries also took part. The positive impact of the rise of the yen on the U.S. trade balance, however, was not as great as expected. This is because Japanese firms adjusted to the high yen in various ways to reduce its adverse impact on exports.

See also **financial liberalization, Plaza Accord, yen-dollar exchange rate, yen shock.**

References

Brown, J. Robert, Jr. 1994. *Opening Japan's Financial Markets.* London: Routledge.

Frankel, Jeffrey A. 1984. *The Yen/Dollar Agreement: Liberalizing Japanese Capital Markets.* Washington: Institute of International Economics.

Rosenbluth, Frances McCall. 1989. *Financial Politics in Contemporary Japan.* Ithaca: Cornell University Press. Ch. 3.

yen–dollar currency futures   Contracts to trade yen and dollars at a given exchange rate on a specific future date.

See **financial futures market**

yen–dollar exchange rates   The yen–dollar exchange rate, the most important of the yen's exchange rates against major foreign currencies, has changed substantially in the postwar era. Government intervention in the value of the yen against the dollar has generally been passive since the end of the fixed exchange rate system in 1973. It is neither a policy of free floating exchange rate nor that of complete manipulation.

The exchange rate was first fixed by the American Occupation authorities in 1949 at 360 yen to the dollar. It remained unchanged until 1971 when it was changed to 308 yen. However, these rates are the "basic

rates" set by the **Ministry of Finance.** In the Tokyo foreign exchange
market there are other types of yen–dollar exchange rates that better
reflect the supply and demand conditions for the dollar and that can differ
substantially from the basic rates. The first is the interbank rate, the rate at
which dollar is traded between banks for spot exchanges (spot rate) or for
forward exchanges (forward rate). It accounts for the bulk of the foreign
exchange transactions. The second is the customer's rate, which includes
selling and buying rates for spot and forward exchange transactions between banks and customers.

Because interbank spot rate changes daily and even within a day, the
Bank of Japan calculates and publishes the annual spot rate in the Tokyo
foreign exchange market in two versions: the year-end closing rate and
the annual average of "central rate," which is the rate on transaction with
the largest volume (published since 1986). Table Y.1 gives both versions

Table Y.1
Yen–dollar exchange rates in Tokyo (interbank spot rate in ¥ per $)

	Year-end closing rate	Central rate average[a]
1971	314.75	350.68
1975	305.15	296.79
1980	203.60	226.74
1981	220.25	220.54
1982	235.30	240.08
1983	232.00	237.51
1984	251.58	237.52
1985	200.60	238.54
1986	160.10	168.03
1987	122.00	144.52
1988	125.90	128.20
1989	143.40	138.11
1990	135.40	144.88
1991	125.25	134.59
1992	124.65	126.62
1993	111.89	111.05
1994	99.83	102.18
1995	102.91	93.97
1996	115.98	108.81
1997	129.92	120.92

Source: Bank of Japan; International Monetary Fund.
a. Annual average of rates on transaction with the largest volume. Figures from 1986 are
from Bank of Japan, whereas those before 1986 are from the International Monetary Fund.

of Tokyo interbank spot rate. The differences between the two reflect the wide fluctuations that the yen–dollar exchange rate underwent in the Tokyo foreign exchange market in a year. The International Monetary Fund also publishes two versions of the yen–dollar exchange rates, the year-end closing market rate and the annual average of market rates. However, the scope of the "market" is not defined. The IMF annual averages of market exchange rates are nearly identical to the central rate averages. Because the central rate averages before 1986 are not published by the Bank of Japan, IMF market rate averages are used in the table for those years.

In early 1973, with the "dollar crisis," Japan abandoned the system of fixed exchange rates and allowed the yen to float. The yen appreciated in 1970–73 as it first emerged as a major international currency. In 1974–75 it fell to around 300 against the dollar because of the first oil crisis. It appreciated again in 1975–78 as the Japanese economy recovered from the oil crisis. However, Japan's trade deficit in 1979 because of the second oil crisis caused the yen to decline in 1979 and early 1980.

Between 1981 and 1984 the yen generally fell because of the increase in Japanese capital outflow due to high interest rates in the United States and the liberalization of foreign exchange laws in Japan in December 1980. Then it rose rapidly in value from about 250 yen to the dollar in 1984 to slightly above 200 yen in 1985 and 122 yen per dollar in 1987. The rise was precipitated by the **Plaza Accord** of September 1985 in which the finance ministers of five major industrial countries agreed to cooperate by market intervention to ensure a gradual depreciation of the dollar. The yen reached a high of 120.45 yen to the dollar on January 4, 1988. It then fell and fluctuated between the 125–150 range during 1989–92 before it rose to a historical high of nearly 80 yen to the dollar in mid-April 1995. Since then the trend was reversed, and the yen fell steadily to fluctuate around 130 in late 1997 and early 1998. The latest weakening of the yen is attributed by Alexander (1998) to two major factors: (1) capital flight because of low rates of return in Japan and loss of confidence in the Japanese economy, and (2) weak aggregate demand in Japan. He recommends raising domestic rates of return on capital by writing down the value of weakly performing assets in order to boost both **consumption** and **investment.**

Yen appreciation is called *endaka* in Japan. The *endaka* after 1985 created one of the most severe recessions in Japan, commonly referred to as the **yen shock.** The **steel industry** was among the most severely affected industries.

The strong yen has also affected Japan's trade with the United States and other countries. The nature and extent of the effect, however, is a matter of debate by analysts. Some believe that *endaka* has made Japan more open to the other Asian economies and has promoted division of labor and integration in Asia, creating an emerging "yen block" (*The Economist*, July 15, 1989). Corker (1989) estimates that, by late 1987, Japan had exported 19% less and imported 10% more than what it would have done without the yen appreciation since 1985. Corker (1991: 9) further concludes that Japanese trade flows have responded "in a remarkably flexible way to the economic environment of the late 1980s."

Because a substantial trade imbalance between Japan and the United States remained in the late 1980s, other analysts have either criticized the inappropriateness of using exchange rate adjustment to solve the imbalance or criticized Japan's economic structure and corporate behavior in limiting the improvement in the Japan–U.S. imbalance. In the first approach, some Japanese commentators have suggested that the yen–dollar exchange rate may have to go as low as 100 yen to the dollar before the Japan–U.S. trade imbalance can be eliminated, and that rate would have grave consequences for the Japanese economy. Even at the rate of about 128 yen to the dollar in 1987, McKinnon (1987) considered the yen to be grossly overvalued, thereby imposing undue deflationary pressure on Japan and leading to growing demand for protection to insulate domestic markets from the unpredictable fluctuations in the international economy. An exchange rate below that would drive the two currencies farther away from purchasing-power parity (i.e., the rate at which a dollar could buy the same basket of goods and service in the United States as a dollar's equivalent in yen would buy in Japan). McKinnon argues that what is needed is not yen appreciation but macroeconomic adjustment in the United States such as reducing the fiscal deficit. Similarly Komiya and Irie (1990) prescribe macroeconomic adjustments in the United States to solve the trade imbalance because they regard U.S. budget deficits and the low saving rate to be the root cause of U.S. trade deficit.

The second approach concentrates on Japan's structural factors and corporate behavior in explaining the presumed limited efficacy of yen appreciation in reducing trade imbalance. For example, some analysts have argued that yen appreciation has not raised Japanese export prices proportionally for the following reasons: (1) It has spurred cost cutting in export industries. (2) The cost of material imports declines with a stronger yen or a cheaper dollar. (3) Some manufacturers have reduced export prices relative to domestic prices (Marston 1991). (4) It has stimulated Japanese manufacturers' **direct overseas investment** and production.

On the effect of yen appreciation on Japanese imports, Petri (1991) contends that the effect has been dampened by the structural factors of the Japanese market such as the high distribution margins and the preference of Japanese businesses and government to buy from other Japanese suppliers. The same focus on the structural factors of the Japanese economy as the cause of trade imbalance underlied the U.S.–Japan **Structural Impediments Initiative** talks in which Washington requested Japanese reforms in many structural aspects of the economy such as the **distribution system,** *keiretsu* groups and "excessive" saving because they are believed to have impeded imports into Japan.

Japan's monetary authorities intervene occasionally in the foreign exchange market when the yen–dollar exchange rate changes are considered excessive or destabilizing. For example, the Bank of Japan bought yen in December 1997 and April 1998 to halt the decline of yen. The policy decision to intervene is formally made by the Ministry of Finance while the actual transactions are carried out by the Bank of Japan. Analysts do not have a consensus on the effectiveness of such interventions. Kawamura (1996: 103) does not think the effect is in proportion to the large sum involved, when compared with the cases of the United States and Germany. He concludes that intervention should not simply aim at suppressing market movements but should be flexible and reflective of market conditions.

See also **Structural Impediments Initiative, trade policy, yen in international transactions, yen shock.**

References

Alexander, Arthur J. 1998. Causes and consequences of the weak yen. *JEI Report* 26A, July 10.

Bank of Japan. Annual. *Economic Statistics Annual.*

Corker, Robert. 1989. External adjustment and the strong yen: Recent Japanese experience. *International Monetary Fund Staff Papers* 36, 2: 464–93.

Corker, Robert. 1991. The changing nature of Japanese trade. *Finance and Development,* June: 6–9.

Green, David Jay. 1990. Exchange rate policy and intervention in Japan. *Journal of Asian Economics* 1: 249–71.

International Monetary Fund. Annual and monthly. *International Financial Statistics.*

Kawamura, Sayuri. 1996. Problems in Japanese policy on foreign exchange market intervention and foreign currency reserves. *Japan Research Quarterly* 5, 3: 72–118.

Komiya, Ryutaro, and Kazutomoto Irie. 1990. The U.S.–Japan trade problem: An economic
analysis from a Japanese viewpoint. In *Japan's Economic Structure: Should It Change?* ed. by
Kozo Yamamura. Seattle: Society for Japanese Studies.

Komiya, Ryutaro, and Miyako Suda. 1991. *Japan's Foreign Exchange Policy: 1971–1982.* North
Sydney: Allen and Unwin.

Marston, Richard C. 1991. Price behavior in Japanese and U.S. Manufacturing. In *Trade with
Japan*, ed. by Paul Krugman. Chicago: University of Chicago Press.

McKinnon, Ronald I. 1987. Currency protectionism: Parity lost. *Wall Street Journal*, February
2.

McKinnon, Ronald I. 1996. *The Rules of the Game: International Money and Exchange Rates.*
Cambridge: MIT Press. Ch. 14.

Nishikawa, Hirochika. 1990. Influence of exchange rate fluctuation on Japann's manufacturing
industry—Empirical analysis, 1980–88. *BOJ Monetary and Economic Studies* 8, 1: 79–134.

Petri, Peter A. 1991. Market structure, comparative advantage, and Japanese trade under the
strong yen. In *Trade with Japan*, ed. by Paul Krugman. Chicago: University of Chicago Press.

yen in international transactions   The role of the yen in international
trade and finance is relatively small compared with that of the U.S. dollar
and German mark. It was used in only 35.8% of Japan's exports and 18.9%
of its imports in March 1997. Only 6% of the official holdings of foreign
exchange of all countries was in the yen in 1996, compared with 58.9%
for the dollar and 13.6% for the German mark.

The factors that would promote the international use of the yen are
(1) Japan's sizable share of world exports, (2) Japan's role as the world's
largest net creditor nation since 1985, and (3) Japan's low rate of inflation,
which is among the lowest in the developed countries.

However, in order for foreigners to hold financial instruments denominated in the yen for liquidity and investment and to pay for imports, the
access to such instruments must be relatively free from controls, and much
import must be denominated in the yen. This is not the case. Japan lacks
well-developed short-term financial markets that would satisfy foreigners'
need for liquid and safe financial instruments. Its treasury bill and **commercial paper markets** are not well developed, and restrictions exist on
some Euroyen investments. These factors reduced the yen's ability to
serve as a medium of exchange in international financial markets and as a
reserve currency for official holdings of foreign exchange.

The bulk of Japan's foreign trade is denominated in foreign currencies,
not in the yen, thus reducing the yen's use as an international unit of

account and medium of exchange. In particular, less than 10% of Japan's trade with North American is denominated in the yen. One reason for this is that the bankers' acceptance market in Japan is not well developed, which makes it difficult for Japanese firms to obtain trade financing in yen. Japanese banks not only lend abroad in foreign currencies to take advantage of higher yields abroad, they also borrow overseas in foreign currencies to make foreign currency loans to domestic firms (**impact loans**) to take advantage of the less stringent regulations on such loans. In addition Japanese exporters reportedly have sought to denominate their exports in foreign currencies in order to maintain their export market shares. Imports are denominated mainly in the currencies of other developed countries.

Nevertheless, since 1987 the share of Japan's foreign trade denominated in the yen has grown. The percentage of Japan's exports denominated in the yen was 29.4% in 1980, 33.4% in 1987, 39.4% in 1991, and 42.8% in March 1993. The percentage of imports denominated in the yen was 2.4% in 1980, 10.6% in 1987, and 15.6% in 1991. Japanese officials worry that this growing trend for Japanese companies to settle their foreign trade in yen instead of dollars will make it more difficult to cut the nation's trade surplus through exchange-rate manipulation.

See also **financial liberalization, yen–dollar exchange rates.**

References

Garber, Peter M. 1996. The use of the yen as a reserve currency. *Bank of Japan Monetary and Economic Studies* 14, 2: 1–21.

Inose, Hijiri. 1992. In trade, yen gains on dollar. *Nikkei Weekly*, February 15: 1, 10.

International Monetary Fund. Annual. *IMF Annual Report.*

Ito, Takatoshi. 1993. The yen and the international monetary system. In *Pacific Dynamism and the International Economic System*, ed. by C. Fred Bergsten and Marcus Noland. Washington: Institute for International Economics.

Maehara, Yasuhiro. 1993. The internationalization of the yen and its role as a key currency. *Journal of Asian Economics* 4: 153–70.

Taguchi, Hiroo. 1994. On the Internationalization of the Japanese yen. In *Macroeconomic Linkage, Savings, Exchange Rates, and Capital Flows*, ed. by Takotoshi Ito and Anne O. Krueger. Chicago: University of Chicago Press.

Tavlas, George S. and Yuzuru Ozeki. 1991a. The internationalization of the yen. *Finance and Development*, June: 2–5.

Tavlas, George S., and Yuzuru Ozeki. 1991b. The Japanese yen as an international currency. *IMF working paper* 91/2.

yen shock   The severe recession that stemmed from the large appreciation of the yen vis-à-vis the U.S. dollar since September 1985.

In 1978 there was a small yen shock (*yen shoku*) due to the rise in the
value of the yen. **Bankruptcies** among the small- and medium-sized businesses increased. By and large, however, the Japanese economy withstood
the shock and was not appreciably damaged by it.

Since the **Plaza Accord** of September 1985 when the world's leading
central banks agreed to further the dollar's decline, the value of the yen in
relation to the dollar increased by more than 60% by April 1987. The
short-term adverse impact on Japanese exports was severe. Bankruptcies
more than doubled in 1986. The industries hardest hit are the export-
oriented electronics, steel, and automobile. The **steel industry** had to
resort to unprecedented massive layoffs as well as production cutbacks.
While the Japanese industries were going through the difficulties, their
competitors in South Korea, Taiwan, Hong Kong, benefited from the
shock as their exports became relatively cheaper.

The shock has prompted Japanese industries and government officials
to reexamine their production and trade strategies. Some firms, such as
the electronics giant Matsushita Industrial, have decided to increase their
production of lower-value labor-intensive products or components in
Southeast Asian countries where labor cost is much cheaper. Still other
firms have decided to increase automation and concentrate on higher-
value models. Other firms have decided to diversify to reduce the impact
of high yen. Government officials have stressed the desirability of re-
orienting Japanese industries from the export market to the domestic
market. The yen shock illustrates vividly the vulnerability of Japanese industries because of their export dependence.

See also **yen–dollar exchange rates.**

References

Kanabayashi, Masayoshi, and Bernard Wysochki, Jr. 1986. Yen's rapid rise against the U.S.
dollar shakes Japan's export-oriented industry. *Wall Street Journal*, February 5.

McKinnon, Ronald I. 1987. Currency protectionism: Parity lost. *Wall Street Journal*, February
2.

Nishikawa, Hiroshika. 1990. Influence of exchange rate fluctuations on Japan's manufacturing
industry—Empirical analysis 1980–88. *Bank of Japan Monetary and Economic Studies* 8, 1: 79–
134.

Wysocki, Bernard Jr. 1987. Battling a high yen, many Japanese firms shift work overseas.
Wall Street Journal, February 27: 1, 10.

Yokohama Located on the western shore of Tokyo Bay in Kanagawa prefecture just 30 kilometers south of **Tokyo**, Yokohama is Japan's largest port and second largest city in terms of population (3.32 million as of April 1997). Yokohama also has much manufacturing industry, and is one of the industrial centers of Kanto, Japan's most industrialized region.

Yokohama was opened to world trade in 1859, after the Friendship and Commercial Treaty between Japan and the United States was signed in 1858. It has been Japan's leading foreign trade port since the mid-1960s. In 1996 it handled 15.8% of Japan's exports and 8.6% of its imports. Since the early 1990s there is a massive urban development project (*Minato Mirai* 21) under way to develop its waterfront area into an international business center. As of December 1997, about 30% of the project has been completed (communications to the author, Yokohama City Hall). A showcase of urban development in Japan, the waterfront development project is expected to attract more foreign as well as domestic businesses.

In FY 1994 Yokohama had a gross municipal product of ¥11.49 trillion, or 2.4% of Japan's gross domestic product, the fourth among the major cities behind Tokyo, **Osaka**, and **Nagoya**. Many of its residents commute to work in Tokyo, thereby producing more of Japan's GDP. Yokohama's major industries are electrical machinery and general machinery, but the service sector has been growing more rapidly. In FY 1993 services constituted 20.8% of gross production, whereas manufacturing contributed 20.6%.

See also **Nagoya and Central Japan, Osaka and Kansai, Tokyo and Kanto.**

Address

City of Yokohama
1-1, Minato-cho, Naka-ku, Yokohama 231
Tel: (45) 671-2655 Fax: (45) 663-3415

Reference

City of Yokohama. 1997. *Yokohama: Facts and Figures, 1997.*

yubin chokin (*yucho*) **Postal savings**, which are an important part of Japan's personal savings deposits. They are channeled through the government's **Fiscal Investment and Loan Program** as loans to **public corporations** and **government financial institutions.**

See **Fiscal Investment and Loan Program, postal savings.**

Z

zaibatsu Literally a "financial clique," *zaibatsu* refers to the prewar pyramid-type business conglomerates that dominated the Japanese economy up to 1945. In a *zaibatsu* a **holding company** owned by a wealthy family controlled various affiliated companies in diverse fields. Typically there were a bank, a **trading company**, and various companies in a number of manufacturing and mining industries. These companies maintained close cooperation with each other under the leadership of the holding company.

The older *zaibatsu* had their origins in the 1880s when the Meiji government sold many state-owned enterprises at low prices to a few wealthy families. Under private ownership and management and with government patronage, these enterprises soon became profitable and grew rapidly. Four *zaibatsu*—Mitsui, Mitsubishi, Sumitomo, and Yasuda—were the largest. At the end of World War II they accounted for a quarter of the nation's total paid-in capital. At that time there were also seven newly established *zaibatsu* and sixteen smaller localized ones. The new *zaibatsu* such as Nissan were developed in the 1930s and specialized in military and heavy chemical industries. Economically they were much weaker than the older *zaibatsu*.

Because *zaibatsu* enjoyed monopoly or oligopoly power, the postwar Occupation authorities believed that they contributed greatly to Japan's industrial might and war effort during World War II. *Zaibatsu* organization also ran counter to the American belief in competition and antitrust. Consequently the Occupation authorities took a number of measures in 1945–46 to dissolve them. *Zaibatsu* families and senior officials were purged from the companies. The holding companies were dissolved. The **Antimonopoly Law** of 1947, modeled on the American antitrust laws, was enacted to prohibit holding companies, monopolies, **cartel** agreements, and so forth, that would reduce market competition.

In the postwar era new types of corporate groups called **keiretsu** have emerged. Three of these groups—**Mitsui, Mitsubishi,** and **Sumitomo groups**—were based on prewar *zaibatsu*. They differ from the latter, however, in various ways, including the absence of holding companies and family control. Each company in a group is legally autonomous and independent, although the companies cooperate in various ways.

See also **Antimonopoly Law,** *keiretsu,* **Mitsui Group, Mitsubishi Group, Sumitomo Group.**

References

Bisson, T. A. 1954. *Zaibatsu Dissolution in Japan.* Berkeley: University of California Press.

Lockwood, William W. 1954. *The Economic Development of Japan: Growth and Structural Change, 1868–1938.* Princeton: Princeton University Press.

Yamamura, K. 1964. *Zaibatsu* prewar and *zaibatsu* postwar. *Journal of Asian Studies* 23, 4: 539–54.

zaikai Japan's big business circles, or specifically the major **business organizations**, composed of business leaders, that wield influence on the government and the economy.

See **business organizations.**

zaiteku Literally the know-how (*teku* from technology) in the management of financial assets (*zai*). It refers to corporate investment of surplus funds in securities and bonds for profits.

See **corporate finance.**

Zaito Abbreviation for *Zaisei Toyushi Keikaku,* the **Fiscal Investment and Loan Program** (FILP) of the government. Under the system, **postal savings** and other publicly pooled savings are lent, through the Trust Fund Bureau of the **Ministry of Finance,** to **public corporations** and **government financial institutions.**

See **Fiscal Investment and Loan Program, government budget.**

Zenchu Central Union of Agricultural Cooperatives, Japan's largest farmers' organization and a powerful farm lobby.

See **agricultural cooperatives.**

Zenginkyo Federation of Bankers Associations of Japan, the national organization of 72 regional bankers associations.

See **banking system.**

Zenkyoren National Mutual Insurance Federation of Agricultural Cooperatives, which is the national organization of the 47 prefectural insurance cooperatives.
   See **agricultural cooperatives.**

Zennoh National Federation of Agricultural Cooperative Associations.
   See **agricultural cooperatives.**

Zenshinren Bank National Federation of *shinkin* banks or credit associations, a special type of financial institutions for **small and medium enterprises.**
   See **banking system,** *shinkin* **banks.**

Index

522   Index